To all of the students
who have participated in one
version or another of our
Investigating Culture classes.

Carol Delaney

with Deborah Kaspin

Second Edition

An Experiential Introduction to Anthropology

WILEY-BLACKWELL

A John Wiley & Sons, Ltd., Publication

This edition first published 2011
© 2011 Carol Delaney

Wiley-Blackwell is an imprint of John Wiley & Sons, formed by the merger of Wiley's global
Scientific, Technical and Medical business with Blackwell Publishing.

Registered Office
John Wiley & Sons Ltd, The Atrium, Southern Gate, Chichester, West Sussex, PO19 8SQ, UK

Editorial Offices
350 Main Street, Malden, MA 02148-5020, USA
9600 Garsington Road, Oxford, OX4 2DQ, UK
The Atrium, Southern Gate, Chichester, West Sussex, PO19 8SQ, UK

For details of our global editorial offices, for customer services, and for information about how to
apply for permission to reuse the copyright material in this book please see our website at www.
wiley.com/wiley-blackwell.

The right of Carol Delaney to be identified as the author of this work has been asserted in
accordance with the UK Copyright, Designs and Patents Act 1988.

Library of Congress Cataloging-in-Publication Data

Delaney, Carol Lowery, 1940-
    Investigating culture / Carol Delaney. – 2nd ed.
        p. cm.
    ISBN 978-1-4051-5424-6 (pbk.)
    1. Anthropology.   I. Title.
    GN25.D45 2011
    301–dc22
                                        2010051049

A catalogue record for this book is available from the British Library.

This book is published in the following electronic formats: ePDFs 978-1-4443-9690-4;
ePub 978-1-4443-9691-1

Set in 10 on 13 pt Minion by Toppan Best-set Premedia Limited
Printed in the USA

4   2013

Contents

of the Western calendar and its rootedness in a sacred worldview, and birthdays and other markers of time.

4   Language: We Are What We Speak   113

Is language quintessentially human or do some other animals possess it? Communication versus language. Writing. The symbolic function and metaphor: different languages, different worlds? The social function: what information do you obtain from a person's speech? How are race, class, and gender inflected in language?

5   Relatives and Relations   153

Notions of kinship and kinship theory: to whom are we related and how? Is there any truth to the idea that "blood is thicker than water"? What constitutes a family? This chapter also discusses different meanings of friendship, romantic relationships, and parent–child relationships.

6   Our Bodies, Our Selves   205

***Are** we our bodies or do we **have** bodies? Different concepts of the body, the gendered body, the physical body, the social body. Techniques and modifications of the body. Tattoos. Body parts and organ transplants. Traffic in body parts. Body image, advertisements, and eating disorders. Bodies before and after death.*

7   Food for Thought   245

What constitutes food? What makes a meal? What does it mean to say that "food is love"? Relation of food to the environment. Fast food, slow food, genetically modified food ("Frankenfood"). Food and sex. Food and civility. Food and religion. Cooking.

Preface to Second Edition

Because the response from students and professors to *Investigating Culture* has been very positive, the publisher asked me to prepare a new edition. I procrastinated for several years due to other projects and commitments. After retiring from Stanford, I taught for two years at Brown University, where I used the first edition in a course of the same title. The students helped to pinpoint areas that needed updating. In particular, I wish to acknowledge Sarah Cocuzzo, Lydia Magyar, and Andrew Mathis, who met with me on a regular basis. As we went over each chapter, they made suggestions for revision and brought in material from their experience and independent research.

However, this new edition would not have happened without the gentle persistence of Rosalie Robertson at Blackwell Publishers. When she suggested that I find a collaborator, I thought, immediately, of Deborah Kaspin, who had been a fellow graduate student at the University of Chicago, and has taught at University of Virginia, Yale University, Wheaton College, and Rhode Island College. Working with her has been a great pleasure; not only has she corrected some of my grammar and awkward sentence structure, but also she has contributed in a major way by updating existing material, adding new material from her own research, making subtle but important elaborations and clarifications in the text, and, from her teaching experience, suggesting ways to make the material more accessible to a broader student population.

This book, unlike most introductory anthropology textbooks, is not so much intended to teach facts *about* other cultures as it is to help students learn how to go about studying any culture, including their own. Additionally, this book is not constructed according to traditional categories such as the family, religion, economy, and politics because we feel these domains cannot be so easily separated. Instead, the book is organized in terms of space, time, language, social relations, body, food, clothing, and culture icons – important people, places, and performances – in order to show how the system of cultural symbols and meanings spans a range of domains. Material gleaned from a variety of cultures is used primarily as illustration. The goal of the text and the ethnographic exercises is to enable students to think like anthropologists.

Carol Delaney
Deborah Kaspin

Acknowledgments

The course on which this book is based emerged as a result of "trial by fire" when I had to offer a course – to start in two weeks' time – in cultural anthropology and comparative religion to a small group of freshmen in the University Professors' Program at Boston University. I had very little time to prepare and decided to use the class as an experiment, that is, to use the experience of entering the university as an analogy to think about what it was like for anthropologists to go elsewhere. It worked. It was exciting. We had a great time and learned a lot. However, the book, with its accompanying course, is not just for freshmen: it can be, and has been, used at any time and place during the typical four-year college education and has also been used at campuses in Europe. (It could also be used productively for people posted to positions in foreign countries – military, diplomats, journalists, etc.) I continue to hear from the students who took that first course long ago (1986) who feel it set them on a path of discovery, which is what an undergraduate education ought to be. Over the years the course changed considerably; the insights and critiques of the students helped to shape the content into what became this book.

At Stanford, I was fortunate to get research funds to hire some of my students as research assistants. Not only did they make trips to the library while I was writing and look up material on the Internet, with which they were far more proficient than I, but also they served as "guinea pigs," telling me when the tone was all wrong or that a particular example was passé. They also suggested topics and then found material to address them. Here, then, I acknowledge the help of Alisha Niehaus (my first student research assistant), who was indefatigable in locating interesting material and telling me when I was "off." Sam Gellman and Andrea Christensen helped during the summer of 2001, and Andrea, along with Katie Cueva, helped during the final phases in the summer of 2002. They had a tough job: they had to do a lot of research on new topics and trace all the things I had neglected to record, and they served as editors, reading and rereading the chapters. To all of them I extend heartfelt thanks; the book is a better product because of their input, and I am deeply grateful for their help.

But I must also acknowledge the initial interest and enthusiasm of Jane Huber, my editor at Blackwell Publishers. Without her ongoing support, my energy might have flagged; in addition, she suggested material and broadened my perspective when my focus had narrowed. My daughter, Elizabeth Quarartiello, and colleagues Miyako Inoue (Stanford) and Don Brenneis (University of California, Santa Cruz) read and made suggestions for the language chapter. Steve Piker, a professor at Swarthmore, was brave enough to try out the penultimate draft on his students at the same time I used it with mine, and the response was gratifying. I hope the future users of this book find inspiration, new perspectives, and ways of making connections between things they never thought were related.

The author and publishers gratefully acknowledge the following for permission to reproduce copyright material in the respective chapters:

Chapter 1

Bohannan, Laura. "Shakespeare in the Bush." *Natural History* (August–September 1966): 28–33.

Chapter 2

Beckham, Sue Bridwell. "The American Front Porch: Women's Liminal Space." In *Making the American Home: Middle-Class Women and Material Culture, 1840–1940*, ed. Marilyn Ferris Motz and Pat Browne. Bowling Green, OH: Bowling Green State University Press, 1988, pp. 69–78, 82–9. © 1988 by the Board of Regents of the University of Wisconsin System. Reprinted by permission of The University of Wisconsin Press
(Poem in reading) Easter, Mary. Poem: "Sitting on the Porch." In *Absorb the Colors: Poems by Northfield Women Poets*, ed. Beverly Voldseth and Karen Herseth Wee. Northfield, MN: privately published, 1986. © Mary Moore Easter. Reprinted with the kind permission of the author.

Chapter 3

Fabian, Johannes. "Premodern Time/Space: Incorporation" and "Modern Time/Space: Distancing." In *Time and the Other: How Anthropology Makes Its Object*, new ed. New York: Columbia University Press, 2002, p. 27. Reprinted with permission of Columbia University Press and the author
Goodman, Ellen. "Time Is for Savoring." *Boston Globe*, October 1977. © 1977 by Globe Newspaper Co (MA). Reprinted with permission of PARS International.

Chapter 4

Dundes, Alan. "Seeing Is Believing." *Natural History Magazine* (May 1972): 8–12, 86–7. Reprinted by permission of *Natural History Magazine*.
LeGuin, Ursula. "She Unnames Them." In *Buffalo Gals and Other Animal Presences*. New York: Plume Books, 1987, pp. 194–6. © 1985 by Ursula LeGuin. First appeared in the

New Yorker. Reprinted with permission of the author and the author's agent, the Virginia Kidd Agency.

Chapter 5

Atwood, Margaret. "An Encyclopedia of Lost Practices: The Saturday Night Date." *New York Times Magazine*, Late Edition – Final, December 5, 1999, sec. 6, p. 148, col. 1. © O. W. Toad Ltd. First appeared in *The New York Times Magazine*, December 5, 1999. Reprinted with permission of the author c/o Curtis Brown UK and Larmore Literary Agency.

Eckert, Penelope. "Symbols of Category Membership." In *Jocks and Burnouts: Social Categories and Identity in the High School*. New York: Teachers College Press, 1989, pp. 49–72, 185–8. Copyright © 1999 by Teachers College Press. Reproduced with permission of Teachers College Press via CCC.

Hocart, A. M. "Kinship Systems." In *The Life-Giving Myth*. London: Tavistock/Royal Anthropological Society, 1973, pp. 173–84.

Chapter 6

Jong, Erica. "Is Life the Incurable Disease?" In *At the Edge of the Body*. New York: Holt, Rinehart and Winston, p. 17. © 1979, 1991 Erica Mann Jong. Used by permission of Erica Jong.

Miner, Horace. "Body Ritual among the Nacirema." *American Anthropologist* 58 (1956): 503–7.

Pope, Harrison, G., Katharine Phillips, and R. Olivardia. *The Adonis Complex: The Secret Crisis of Male Body Obsession*. New York: Free Press, 2000, p. 41. Courtesy Simon & Schuster/Zachary Shuster Harmsworth.

Chapter 7

Dubisch, Jill. "You Are What You Eat: Religious Aspects of the Health Food Movement." From *The American Dimension: Culture Myths and Social Realities*, 2nd ed., ed. Susan P. Montague and W. Arens. Palo Alto, CA: Mayfield, 1981, pp. 115–27 (The McGraw-Hill Companies Inc.). © Jill Dubisch. Reprinted with kind permission of the author.

Shell, Ellen Ruppel. "An International School Lunch Tour" (op-ed). *New York Times*, Late Edition – Final, February 1, 2003, sec. A, p. 19, col. 1. © Ellen Ruppel Shell 2003. Reprinted with the kind permission of the author.

Chapter 8

Ribeyro, Julio Ramon. "Alienation (An Instructive Story with a Footnote)." In *Marginal Voices: Selected Stories*, trans. Dianne Douglas. Austin: University of Texas Press, pp. 57–67. Copyright © 1993. Reprinted with permission of University of Texas Press.

Rosen, Ruth. Short extract from "A Statement about More Than Fashion." *San Francisco Chronicle*, May 13, 2001. Reprinted with permission.

Chapter 9

Delaney, Carol. "Let's Send All Our Missiles to the Sun" (letter to the editor). *New York Times*, December 30, 1991. © 1991 Carol Delaney.

Geertz, Clifford. "The Impact of the Concept of Culture on the Concept of Man." In *The Interpretation of Cultures: Selected Essays by Clifford Geertz*. New York: Basic Books, 1973, pp. 33–54. With permission from Dr. Karen I. Blu, executrix, Estate of Clifford Geertz.

CHAPTER 1

Disorientation and Orientation

Introduction; how culture provides orientation in the world; what is culture and how do anthropologists investigate it? Learning to think anthropologically.

Disorientation and Orientation

Introduction

A number of years ago, I was asked to teach a course on anthropology and comparative religion to incoming freshmen at Boston University. I was intrigued because freshmen do not usually enroll in anthropology courses and often do not know what it is. Furthermore, the course was to begin in two weeks, leaving me very little time to prepare a syllabus and order books. Consequently, I decided to take a bold approach. Rather than trying to do a typical survey course, beginning with human origins and moving on to hunters and gatherers, and then peasants, to modern urban society, I decided to treat the course as an anthropological experience. I wanted students to imagine themselves as anthropologists coming to study another culture, for, although they wouldn't think of it that way, that was a part of what they were doing when they entered college. I wanted them to learn not only *about* anthropology, but also about *being* an anthropologist.

That original course was an adventure for all of us, and it was a great success. However, when I first went to Stanford, I was not able to teach it as a freshman course because freshmen were tracked into a number of prescribed large lecture courses. Instead, I taught somewhat revised forms for upperclassmen, for students planning to go abroad for a time, and at the Stanford campus in Berlin. Other professors borrowed it, modified it, and taught it at Stanford campuses in Spain and Italy. When the university instituted a "freshman seminar" program, I was able, once again, to teach this course to entering freshmen. While the course can, obviously, be taught in a number of contexts, I still think it works best for freshmen as they enter college or university, not because the material is simplified, but because their experience is fresh.

Investigating Culture: An Experiential Introduction to Anthropology, Second Edition.
Carol Delaney with Deborah Kaspin.
© 2011 Carol Delaney. Published by Blackwell Publishing Ltd.

The course is an innovative way to introduce students to anthropology, and because it has been a success, I was asked by the publisher to write a textbook based on it so that it might become available to students elsewhere. Although each chapter is devoted to one of the topics I discuss in class, such as space or time or food, it is not meant to be an exhaustive analysis of any one of them. Otherwise, each chapter could easily have become a book on its own. Even less is this book meant to be an in-depth analysis of American, British, or any other culture, although it is intended for use in the United States and United Kingdom. I juxtapose a range of material – classical anthropological material about a variety of cultures; contemporary items drawn from the newspaper, the Web, Stanford, and Brown; and ethnographic material from my own fieldwork in Turkey – for the purpose of generating ideas and indicating the range of areas for further exploration.

While this book is a general introduction to anthropology, it also reflects my own journey as an anthropologist. This includes my graduate training at the Harvard Divinity School and the Department of Anthropology at the University of Chicago, my academic concentrations on gender issues and the Abrahamic religions, and my personal life as a teenager of the 1950s, a young wife of the 1960s, a divorcee, a welfare mother, and so on. All of this led me into and informed my academic career. This is how anthropology (and any life path) unfolds: the personal intertwines with the professional. So too, another anthropologist could write a similar book (or design a similar course) using the same canon of classic and current anthropology, but would read that canon into his or her own areas of specialization and personal biography. I think the subjective experience reveals the relevance of anthropology to everyday life, although this necessarily means that other worthwhile issues – including those of particular interest to the readers – are overlooked in the process. Such omissions are not meant as dismissals, but as invitations to take an anthropological approach to your own topics of interest.

I wrote the first edition of this book as my own enterprise, but the second edition is a collaborative effort with Deborah Kaspin. She was a graduate student in anthropology at the University of Chicago while I was, conducted fieldwork among Chewa in Malawi for her dissertation project, and more recently pursued fieldwork among modern orthodox Jews in New England. She has taught at several places of various types – private and public, universities and colleges – which are listed in the preface. Kaspin's contributions to the second edition include material from her own research, updates on topics in the first edition, and occasionally slightly different interpretations of issues developed in the first edition. She also pushed to make the subject matter more accessible to a wider range of students and educational settings. It is our hope that the new edition accomplishes this.

The goal of the second edition, like the first, is not to teach *about* other cultures. That is the normal pedagogical approach adopted in schools, but it is passive and distanced learning. I believe that people learn best when they are actively involved in the process. You will learn about anthropology and about culture by learning how to think like an anthropologist, that is, by becoming amateur anthropologists. Not everyone is able to go to another society to gain this experience, but it is possible to simulate it. As I illustrate below, you will learn to draw analogies between your own experience of entering and becoming acclimated to college life and the experience of anthropologists who go to study another culture. Both can be quite disorienting, at least initially. Hold on to the disorientation for a while, because it provides some mental space from which you can grasp, as they occur, aspects of the new culture you have entered and how these aspects relate to each other. Even while the focus must be on your own environment, the aim is not to illuminate merely the "culture" of your particular school, but also to explore the way those particular aspects connect to and represent concepts, values, and structures of the wider culture. Indeed, I think the use of the word *culture* in that restricted sense is inappropriate.

Clifford Geertz, probably the most influential American anthropologist of the last 40 years, made the point very clear: "[T]he locus of study is not the object of study. Anthropologists don't study villages (tribes, towns, neighborhoods …); they study *in* villages" (1973: 22). Substitute *college* for *village*, and you will see what I mean. Although I conducted my fieldwork in a village in central Turkey, my aim was to try to understand something about Turkish culture and how it was inflected in that one place. Analogously, the object of your study is the culture of your country even as you investigate it in your particular locale. My goal is to get you to learn *experientially*, to get you to adopt an anthropological approach that you can use to investigate any social or cultural phenomenon in any culture. Prerequisite is a mind open to new ways of thinking about things and willing to take nothing for granted. Anything is available for inspection, including the most ordinary, mundane items and events such as a McDonald's hamburger, a pair of blue jeans, a cell phone, a birthday or New Year's Eve, and so forth. These items and events are *clues* you can use to investigate your sociocultural system. Each of them provides a window into a much larger set of beliefs, power relations, and values. For example, what would you make of a community that celebrates death days rather than birthdays? How might that fact relate to other facets of that society? What other kinds of questions would you need to ask to begin to understand not just that practice but also the culture in which it occurs?

Disorientation

The experience of beginning college can be exhilarating, anxiety producing, and disorienting. This is magnified for those who come from other parts of the country or from foreign countries. Even when the language is familiar and you have not moved from your home town or city, college life is different from high school. You are entering a new world. You don't know where anything is or how to find it; you don't understand the time schedule or how to manage your time; you don't know the lingo – the insider abbreviations and acronyms; and you don't know the code of dress or behavior. For those who go away to college, it might be the first time you are away from home alone. It might be the first time you share a room with someone or have a room of your own. It might be the first time you have to schedule your own time.

Listen to the echoes of your experience in one of the most famous and oft-quoted sentences in anthropology. It was written by Bronislaw Malinowski, who is credited with inventing the anthropological method of intensive fieldwork. At the beginning of his work in the Trobriand Islands in the South Pacific, where he was interned during World War I, he wrote,

> Imagine yourself suddenly set down surrounded by all your gear, alone on a tropical beach close to a native village, while the launch or dinghy which has brought you sails away out of sight. ([1922] 1961: 4)

An analogous translation might be something like:

> Imagine yourself suddenly set down surrounded by all your gear, alone in your room but with unfamiliar people nearby, while the car that brought you drives away out of sight.

Many students, just like many anthropologists, get a feeling of panic at that moment: "What am I doing here?" "Why didn't I go to X?" "I want to go home." Anthropologists call this feeling of panic *culture shock*. The term is credited to Ruth Benedict, but Cora Du Bois defines it as a "syndrome precipitated by the anxiety that results from losing all your familiar cues" (cited in Golde [1970] 1986: 11); in short, you become disoriented. Culture shock is not confined to that initial moment but can resurface at various times at the beginning of any new adventure. Nor is it confined only to anthropologists or to students, for it can occur at other life-changing moments, for example when you take a new job or move to a new city. Anthropologists who have studied the phenomenon of culture shock have noted the following telltale signs: "frustration, repressed or expressed aggression against the source of discomfort, an irrational fervor for the familiar and comforting, and disproportionate anger at trivial interferences" (Golde [1970] 1986: 11).[1] It is useful to keep this in mind during the first few weeks of college life.

As an example, let me tell you about something that happened to me when I began my fieldwork in Turkey. I was excited to be there and ready to begin my fieldwork, but I didn't know how I was supposed to go about it or where to start. I recall that I got a craving for vanilla yogurt. This was a very trivial thing, and I was never even that fond of yogurt at home, but in Turkey I had to have vanilla yogurt. Now you have to realize that Turkey is full of yogurt; it is one of their basic foods. Yogurt, yogurt everywhere, but no vanilla to be found anywhere. I was frustrated and angry: how could they not have vanilla? What kind of people are they anyway? I began a frantic search, feeling that I would not be happy until I found it; vanilla yogurt would be my comfort food, my little piece of home. I eventually found a few desiccated pods of vanilla in a spice shop and ground my own. After that, I was prepared for anything.

In order to avoid severe culture shock and to overcome students' initial disorientation, it is no wonder colleges set aside some time, often several days, for "orientation."

Orientation

An orientation program is, obviously, intended to help you get oriented in the new environment. Often you are told something about the history, the resources, and the rules of the school; you are shown where to go for class, for books, for food, for exercise, and for help if you get sick. Such a program helps you to get your bearings, literally and figuratively.

The purpose of orientation programs is to help you feel at home and become acclimated to your new environment. It can also be viewed quite productively as an *initiation* ritual, for it does initiate you into your new status – that of undergraduate. Initiation rituals are one type of *rites de passage* first analyzed by a Flemish anthropologist Arnold Van Gennep in 1909 ([1909] 1960). Although there are a number of rites of passage, rites that mark transitions from one life stage to another, such as at birth, puberty, marriage, and death, Van Gennep focused primarily on initiation rites that occur around the time of puberty in a number of small-scale, kinship-based, hunter–gatherer societies, namely, those societies we have so condescendingly called "primitive."[2] Initiation rites are the rituals that transform youths or adolescents into adults; during the rituals, they are initiated by tribal elders into the lore of the tribe and into adult responsibilities. In some places, the rites occur over a number of weeks or months, but in others they have been known to last several years. Among Australian aborigines, for example, the initiation rites traditionally took about four years, exactly equivalent to a typical American college education.

According to Van Gennep's schema, most *rites de passage* have three stages. The first is rites of separation, when the person is detached from his or her group or family; the second is made up of rites that characterize the *liminal* period, which is *the* transitional stage. Victor Turner, a famous British anthropologist who developed Van Gennep's schema in his own studies of ritual, characterized this stage as "betwixt and between" fixed statuses when a boy, for example, is no longer a child but not yet a man with adult responsibilities (1967: 93–111). The third stage includes the rites of reaggregation, when the transformed person is inserted back into society.

You will have to analyze your own orientation programs for some of these features. The example that follows, from Stanford University, is meant to be used for comparative purposes and is not held up as the norm or as an ideal. I use it only because it was my locale. While some of the particulars vary from year to year, the orientation program follows quite closely the pattern laid down by Van Gennep. It is primarily for freshmen and takes place over a three-day weekend, *before* the other students arrive. Students leave their homes, familiar surroundings, and friends. This is the beginning of the "separation" phase. On Friday the freshmen arrive, often with their parents, siblings, and sometimes friends in tow. Some come by car; others arrive by plane, train, or bus. They are taken to their living quarters and introduced to their roommates and the resident heads. After a few activities that include parents, there is an announced time when parents (and friends) are supposed to leave. This truly marks the "separation" phase, though at this point the separation is often more traumatic for the parents. Students then have their first dinner with their assembled dorm mates.

Saturday resembles the "liminal" phase of the rite, when initiates are expected to undergo a number of *ordeals*. At Stanford, these can vary from being led around campus in the dead of night, not knowing where you are or where you are going, to being awakened at dawn and dragged out of bed to participate in a scavenger hunt. Later in the day students sit for hours and take placement exams that will determine the level of the classes in which they will enroll. They must also consider the other classes they will take and the extracurricular activities they will join. At least for a while, their choices will have an impact on their academic and social direction (or orientation). Other parts of the *ordeal* can include being quizzed on the names of other students and of residence heads, the local jargon that they should have memorized, and so forth. In the evening, they are sometimes required to participate in a race and gender sensitivity-training program, which can be unsettling for a number of students who must confront their prejudices. Then they are taught some of the new rules for academic and personal behavior – what is acceptable and what is not.

The culmination of orientation weekend is a football game, where the freshmen go *en masse* and sit in a special area reserved for them. Many alumni attend this game, and faculty are given free passes. The freshmen are being made into Stanfordites: they are shown the school symbols, they hear the school songs and cheers for the first time, and they are caught up in the school spirit, rooting for *their* team against the opponents. This could be imagined as the *reaggregation* ritual, for symbolically they are being incorporated into the Stanford community.

You could also easily see all four years of college as a prolonged initiation ritual, since you are separated from the rest of society for the entire period. You are no longer a child, but are not yet a fully functioning adult. You have a special, liminal, "student" status that is socially recognized; you receive certain benefits – discounts on buses, airplanes, movies, and so on, as well as a wide berth for some types of disruptive behavior. During the college years, students are freer than they ever will be again to "discover who they are," to try on various identities, and to prepare themselves for their adult roles in society. In this latter task, they are aided by the wisdom of the elders – professors and counselors – just as in initiation rites among traditional societies.

For some students, the liminal phase is more interesting or even comforting than what awaits them "outside" in the "real world," and they want to stay on as long as possible. Eventually, however, most of them pass through the initiation and come out ready to be reinserted, as adults, into society. This achievement is marked by the graduation ceremony, which, with ironic connotations, is called *commencement*, no doubt to indicate that this is the *beginning* of the rest of your life, as a newly fledged person.

Anthropology

The foregoing may not be *at all* your image of what anthropology is. Most people think it has to do with "stones and bones" and with *elsewhere* but not here. This is a very common assumption that I hear in the responses of people when I tell them that I am an anthropologist. They often launch into an account of some program they saw on television about an ancient site or a recent bone find. They are thinking of archaeology (the "stones") and physical anthropology (the "bones"). Yet, these are only two of the traditional four subfields of anthropology, while linguistics is a third. Other people sometimes think of Margaret Mead and realize that anthropology can also be about psychology and human behavior; the kinds of studies she conducted fall in the major "subfield" of the discipline – social and cultural anthropology. Many anthropologists today, myself included, no longer subscribe to the fourfield division of the discipline but feel, instead, that the defining element is not so much what one studies but the *theoretical* stance one takes toward the material one studies. The difference has to do with the way people define, or at least imagine, human nature and culture (see Segal and Yanagisako 2004).

Nature and Culture

To give you some sense of what this means in practice, think about some of the ways we often identify differences between *peoples*: environment, race, genetics, religion, economy, technology, and development. Often these differences are collapsed into broader categories of *nature* versus *culture*, with race and genetics put in the nature box and religion, economy, and technology in the culture box. Many people then conflate the nature and culture categories by assuming that peoples with the best natural gifts (genes, intelligence, and strength) produce the most advanced cultures.

But who makes these judgments about "advanced" and "primitive" cultures, and whose scale is used as the standard? And what exactly does *advanced* mean? If advanced means *complex*, then the Australian aborigines are among the most advanced peoples, judging by the extraordinary complexity of their kinship system and their religious concepts. Or perhaps some of the Western nations are the most advanced, as evidenced by the mechanical complexity of their locomotive technologies. Or perhaps Hindus and Buddhists are the most advanced, given the complexity and sophistication of their meditative and mental practices. In the nineteenth century, British and American social theorists ranked peoples of the world on an evolutionary, progressive, unilinear, and universal scale of culture that ended, not coincidentally, with themselves at the top. They simply assumed that all peoples necessarily tread the same path to civilization, for there was only one scale and one orientation – up and West.

A very popular notion about anthropology is that it is the search for human universals with the corollary that whatever is universal must, *ipso facto*, be natural. People want to know what is natural to the human species and often try to make analogies from animal behavior to human behavior, believing that the overlap indicates what is natural about human nature. For a long time, it was believed that *Homo sapiens* first developed their modern form (two-legged stance, opposable thumbs, and large brain), and *then* invented culture. Instead, it is now generally accepted not only that *Homo sapiens* developed from their ape-ical ancestors to their modern form, but also that culture was part of their development. Clifford Geertz wrote that "the greater part of human cortical expansion has *followed*, not preceded, the 'beginning' of culture" (1973: 64, emphasis mine). In other words, "cultural resources are ingredient, not accessory, to human thought" (Geertz 1973: 83).

And yet some scientists continue to see in animal behavior (not so) faint echoes of our own. They persist in drawing analogies *from* animal *to* human, all too often by drawing concepts and beliefs from human society, imposing them on animals, and then reading them back again to human society. Curiously, Marx was the first to notice this sleight-of-hand movement: "It is remarkable how Darwin recognizes among beasts and plants his English society with its division of labour, competition, opening of new markets, 'inventions,' and the Malthusian 'struggle for existence'" (cited in Sahlins 1976: 53). Engels continued,

> The whole Darwinian teaching of the struggle for existence is simply a transference from society to living nature of Hobbes's doctrine of *bellum omnium contra omnes* and of the bourgeois-economic doctrine of competition together with Malthus's theory of population. When this conjurer's trick has been performed ... the same theories are transferred back again from organic nature into history and it is now claimed that their validity as eternal laws of human society has been proved. (Cited in Sahlins 1976: 54)[3]

This in no way detracts from the general notion of human physical evolution that Darwin outlined, but it does call into question some of his assumptions about the motives and drivers of evolution. Even he found it too easy to project human behaviors on to animals and back again.[4]

A BBC film series, *A Planet for the Taking*, demonstrates how our expectations inform our "reading" of animal behavior. One film shows identical sequences of animal behavior but with different voice-over narrations, one describing male dominance and aggression, and the other grooming behavior and bonding. It was easy to *see* both accounts in the behavior on film – further evidence that we see what we are prepared to see.

According to Franz Boas, the founder of American anthropology, perception is molded not simply by extraneous suggestions, as the previous example implies, but also by long-term cultural training. This, according to his student, Ruth Benedict, was his insight during his fieldwork in Baffinland, where the local people could see different colors of seawater that were wholly unapparent to him. He concluded that the seeing eye is "not a mere physical organ but a means of perception conditioned by the tradition in which its possessor has been reared" (cited in Stocking, 1968: 146).

Alan Dundes develops this point further in "Seeing Is Believing," which "shows how American culture affects the way Americans experience their world" (1972: 14; see chapter 4). He also illuminates how we privilege sight in our value system by using it metaphorically to describe the acquisition of knowledge (see my examples in this and the preceding paragraphs).[5] A blind student in my Fall 2001 class made us all aware of the extent to which Americans depend on sight, and not just the metaphor of it, as the primary means of cultural knowledge. For instance, think how quickly we make judgments about people based solely on how they look or the clothes they wear. The *judgments* are made not because of sight but because of the meanings and values supplied by the culture.

While the capacity for culture is a human universal, this doesn't explain why cultures are so different. The facts that "everywhere people mate and produce children, have some sense of mine and thine and protect themselves in one fashion or another from rain and sun are neither false nor, from some points of view, unimportant" (Geertz 1973: 40), but they are questionable; Geertz says that "whether a lowest-common-denominator view of humanity is what we want anyway ... it may be in the cultural particularities of people – in their oddities – that some of the most instructive revelations of what it is to be generically human are to be found" (p. 43).

It is not only that humans developed along with culture in the generic sense, but also we are always within culture in the particular sense. Humans cannot exist outside of culture, the tales of "wolf boys" – children reared by wolves or other animals – notwithstanding. Stylites and their ilk – people who deliberately isolate themselves from society – are the exceptions that prove the rule. Stylites were hermit-like monks of the fifth to seventh centuries in what is now Syria and Turkey, who sat on top of pillars to separate themselves from society and devote themselves to prayer. The most famous Stylite was St. Simon. Despite their self-imposed and celebrated isolation, they had been reared in the society they rejected, and, even when totally alone, carried on a silent dialogue with it.

As Geertz explains, people "unmodified by the customs of particular places do not in fact exist, have never existed, and most important, could not in the very nature of the case exist" (1973: 35). Thus there is no backstage, no place outside of culture in both the generic and particular senses, where you can go to study the so-called naked ape stripped of his or her culture. People are molded by culture from the moment of birth, and probably even before that due to the cultural prescriptions for pregnancy and birth and the expectations that people have about the child.

For a very long time, however, the humanities have assumed that there *is* a constant human nature and that the differences among people are superficial. Thus a Shakespeare play, for example, should be meaningful to all people (once it is translated) because people everywhere should have the same concepts, emotions, and motivations. Indeed, Shakespeare's genius, like that of any great artist, supposedly rested on his ability to appeal to universal emotions and circumstances. Others, however, have asked if a people's emotions and responses are conditioned by the particularities of their culture. Anthropologist Laura Bohannan (1966) put this question to the test when she told the story of *Hamlet* to a group of Africans with whom she was living and conducting anthropological fieldwork. She encountered many problems with the translation not of the words, but of the concepts. Was it possible to translate Shakespeare's world into an African language and context and render the story understandable to them, or did the translation fundamentally alter it? Her famous article is included with this chapter.

To understand people and cultures, you have to get into the particulars, for this is where you pick up the clues. This is anthropology in a new key;[6] it does not dismiss human universals, but discovering them is not its primary goal since they do not help us understand why different peoples do things differently. In short, although universals give us the common human denominator, they do not tell us very much about specific cultures. What, then, is this "culture" that we should be mindful of it?

Because I think it is important for you to come to your own understanding of culture, I do not intend to give it a specific definition, although, in the next section, I will briefly discuss some general ideas that have been put forth by a variety of theorists who have dealt with the concept. Before reading this section, it would be useful to stop here and define *culture* for yourself and then see how your understanding of it changes as you read further in the book.

Culture

Culture is, admittedly, a slippery concept that is difficult to grasp. According to British social theorist Raymond Williams:

> Culture is one of the two or three most complicated words in the English language. This is so partly because of its intricate historical development, in several European languages, but mainly because it has now come to be used for important concepts in several distinct intellectual disciplines and in several distinct and *incompatible* systems of thought. (Williams [1976] 1983: 87, emphasis mine)

Culture has become such a contested word that some anthropologists think we should drop it. Since I have used the word in the title of this book, it is clear that I do not agree. To get some sense of the approach taken in this book, it is helpful, I think, to examine some of the meanings of the word. I begin with the historical etymology worked out by Williams in his helpful book, *Keywords: A Vocabulary of Culture and Society* ([1976] 1983).

According to Williams, "Culture in all its early uses was a noun of process: the tending *of* something, basically crops or animals." This is the sense behind such words as horti*culture*, vini-/viti*culture*, and agri*culture*. Beginning in the eighteenth century, the idea of *cultivation* was transferred to humans and with it was born the notion of a *cultivated* person. This had distinct class overtones and was closely related to the idea of *civilization*. That idea has not completely died out, for culture is still often associated with "great works" that are housed in libraries and museums or performed on stage. Poetry and literature, painting and sculpture, symphony and opera, theater and dance – these were, and still are to a large extent, what most people imagine when they think of culture. Not so long ago, these were the things you went to college to study, for to be a cultured person you had to know about and appreciate them. In addition, it was essential that upper-class youth complete their education with a European tour to absorb the great works of Western culture, presumed to be the epitome of civilization. When combined with a belief that culture is an evolutionary, unidirectional, and progressive phenomenon that all peoples are striving for, one can sense how assumptions about class, race, and gender hierarchy were reinforced by such a tour.

In the twentieth century, many anthropologists dropped this framework with the realization that different cultures are just different. And while cultures are conditioned by the global network of power and resources in which they are embedded, they nevertheless spring from different premises about life and from different goals and values. This idea stems from Johann Gottfried von Herder, an eighteenth-century German historian, who thought that every people (*Volk*) had their own values, language, and spirit (*Geist*). He also argued against the presumptions of European superiority:

> Men of all the quarters of the globe, who have perished over the ages, you have not lived solely to manure the earth with your ashes, so that at the end of time your posterity should be made happy by European culture. The very thought of a superior European culture is a blatant insult to the majesty of Nature. (Cited in Williams [1976] 1983: 89)

It is from Herder that the notion of culture in the plural derives, and it is in this sense that the concept entered anthropology, notably through Franz Boas. Boas is considered the founder of American anthropology, even though he was German and trained in the German intellectual tradition. In New York at Columbia University, he established the first department of anthropology in the United States. Boas was also a major player in championing *nurture* over *nature*, a debate that had then and has today racial underpinnings and implications. Thus, if your nature (now read *genes*) is responsible for your lowly position, nothing can be done. But if your (lack of) nurture – not only food and nutriments but also cultural and social resources – is responsible, then social measures can be instituted to ameliorate it.

Raymond Williams claims that "in archaeology and in *cultural anthropology* the reference to culture or a culture is primarily to *material* production, while in history and *cultural studies* the reference is primarily to *signifying* or *symbolic* systems" (p. 91). While that may be true in the British context, it is not so in the American. Culture, among American anthropologists, generally refers to signifying or symbolic systems, as we shall see. (More proof of George Bernard Shaw's dictum that England and the United States are two countries divided by a common language.) No wonder some anthropologists wish to abandon the term *culture* altogether. But Williams's take on this issue is, I believe, related to another important difference between British and American anthropology. As he notes, the adjective *cultural* came into prominence at the end of the nineteenth and early twentieth centuries with the emergence of anthropology. This usage develops in relation, and often in contrast, to the adjective *social*.

Social and Cultural Anthropology

Within the major subfield of social and cultural anthropology (see "Anthropology," above), contentious debates once revolved around the distinction between the social and the cultural, and left their mark on the vocabulary and methodologies of the discipline. For our purposes, *culture* refers to signifying, symbolic, or meaning systems, while *social* refers to institutions and arrangements of people and their activities in the realm of the concrete. Thus the alphabet, Euclidian geometry, and the story of creation in the Old Testament are systems of meaning, while the Stop and Shop, Stanford University, and the Vatican are social institutions. To some extent – some would argue a very large extent – the distinction is arbitrary, since one can't explain cultural systems except through the social institutions that use them, or explain social institutions without the systems of meaning that guide their invention and operation. Think of it this way: can (or should) a contractor build a house without a blueprint, or understand a blueprint without seeing a good many houses?

The debates between social and cultural anthropologists concern not the differences between the concepts but the analytical priority: which should come first, the social chicken or the cultural egg? British anthropology emphasizes the social. It assumes that social institutions determine culture and that universal domains of society (such as kinship, economy, politics, and religion) are represented by specific institutions (such as the family, subsistence farming, the British Parliament and the Church of England) which can be compared cross-culturally. American anthropology emphasizes the cultural. It assumes that culture shapes social institutions by providing the shared beliefs, the core values, the communicative tools, and so on that make social life possible. It does not assume that there are universal social domains, preferring instead to discover domains empirically as aspects of each society's own classificatory schemes – in other words, its culture. And it rejects the notion that any social institution can be understood in isolation from its own context. To some extent, this characterization of British and American anthropologies is an overstatement, since most anthropologists on both sides of the Atlantic try to account for and integrate both the social and the cultural. But it does capture important differences in orientation and emphasis.

Cultural and social anthropologies stem from somewhat different intellectual lineages. The American lineage draws, to a large extent, on the German tradition that began with Herder and was adopted by Boas, as noted above. Herder's preoccupations with a people's "spirit" (Geist) and Boas's with intellectual traditions led to concentrations in American anthropology on folklore, material arts, linguistics, and personality – all expressions of symbolic or meaning systems. The British lineage draws instead on utilitarianism, a socioeconomic theory developed by the philosophers Hobbes and Locke, and by the economists Malthus and Smith. Utilitarianism claims that everyone (or every British man) is a rational, self-interested actor pursuing universal wants. The British lineage also drew on French theorist Emile Durkheim, who gave social anthropology and sociology their distinctive framework.[7] Durkheim's principal contribution was his belief that society is *sui generis*, a thing of its own kind. This means that society cannot be reduced to or explained in terms of psychology or biology or economics, because it is a totality that operates according to its own principles. Just as physicists must discover the laws of the physical universe, so too sociologists and social anthropologists must discover the laws of society.

We can illustrate what is at stake in prioritizing social or cultural approaches by examining the institution of marriage and attempting to explain its meaning and purpose. If we take as our example a conventional American marriage – monogamous, heterosexual, and purportedly permanent – we discover numerous attributes that it can or should have. It should be based in love, maintain sexual exclusivity, and provide companionship for the husband and wife. It legitimates – and, for some, mandates – the bearing and raising of children. It is the foundation of a household and the division of labor required to sustain that household. It is a legal contract that turns two people into one legal person for establishing custodial duties, property rights, and inheritance. It is a sacrament created within a church or temple. And it is the actualization of God's plan for man and woman which he established with Adam and Eve in the Garden of Eden.

From this list, it is clear that marriage is not one thing, since it has numerous meanings, purposes, and implications. A social anthropologist would look at this list and determine that marriage means primarily one thing, while everything else is tangential. Perhaps the primary purpose of marriage is to legitimate childrearing and thereby establish rights of inheritance; this means that everything else – from romantic love to religious sacrament – are ideological grace notes dressing up what is fundamentally a legal-economic contract. A cultural anthropologist, in contrast, would say that the numerous meanings, purposes, and implications of marriage are of a piece and indivisible and must be treated as such.

She would then ask where else in this society we find similar constellations of emotional attachment, sexual discipline, property rights, and religious motifs, and perhaps decide to compare secular marriages to the lives of nuns and priests who are married to Christ and/ or the Church.

I have written this book with the premises and postures of cultural – and not social – anthropology in mind. This means, first, that the book is *not* organized around prescribed social domains, as introductory textbooks typically are, with a chapter on economy, a chapter on kinship, a chapter on politics, a chapter on religion, and so on. It is organized instead around interpretive problems which I will lay out at the end of this chapter. This also means that I prioritize culture – as symbolism, signification, and meaning – both in the selection of topics and in the directions of their investigation. Here I quote David Schneider, who spent much of his career defining and elaborating the centrality of culture as a system of symbols and meanings. He wrote,

> By symbols and meanings I mean the basic premises which a culture posits for life; what its units consist in; how those units are defined and differentiated; how they form an integrated order or classification; how the world is structured; in what parts it consists and on what premises it is conceived to exist, the categories and classifications of the various domains of the world of man and how they relate one with another, and the world that man sees himself living in. (Schneider 1972: 38)

I also quote Clifford Geertz, who saw the purpose of cultural anthropology as follows:

> The concept of culture I espouse is essentially a semiotic one. Believing with Max Weber, that man is an animal suspended in webs of significance he himself has spun, I take culture to be those webs, and the analysis of it to be therefore not an experimental science in search of law but an interpretive one in search of meaning. (1973: 5)

This, then, is our task: to learn to investigate culture in the exercise of an interpretive social science.

Culture and Power

When anthropology emerged as a discipline and developed its distinct form – including the split between social and cultural approaches – its arenas of study were primarily non-Western peoples on the frontiers of Western, colonial expansion. This began to change in the 1980s as social scientists and historians became increasingly preoccupied with internationalism and globalization. This included problems of state building and economic stagnation in Europe's former colonies, and the movement of capital, labor, and ideologies across nations and continents. These problems accelerated with the disintegration of the Soviet Union, which created new sites of political instability, economic hardship, and crumbling international borders.

In fact, internationalism was already embedded in the practice of anthropology, since European colonialism had brought anthropologists to their sites of study. But peculiarly, this was outside the purview of their discipline which seldom included the colonial project – the conditions of its own existence – as part of its subject matter. This changed in the 1980s, when anthropologists, like others throughout the social sciences and humanities, widened their gaze from the former colonies to the former colonizers, and from discrete societies to the relations between centers and margins of capital, politics, and influence. This meant, too, that anthropologists became increasingly preoccupied with problems of power.

To address new questions, anthropology needed new (or different) analytical models and found them in theories of political economy as conceived by Karl Marx and Friedrich Engels. Marx and Engels saw modes of production as the drivers of social processes and inequities, and anticipated revolutionary movements among the laboring classes who would seize control of the means of production and overturn the power elites. Beginning in the 1960s, Andre Gunder Frank[8] and Immanuel Wallerstein[9] used Marxist concepts to explain structural inequities emerging on the world stage, as capitalism expanded beyond the territorial borders of the first world through colonialism and industrial expansion. By the 1980s, cultural anthropologists and social historians were writing detailed accounts of the global character and local manifestations of Western capitalist expansion.[10]

Political economy theory opened up the field of study in important ways, but it also conflicted conceptually with aspects of culture theory. According to political economy theory, the mode of production is primary, while ideation – religion, philosophy, and the arts – are at best incidental and at worst "opiates" that conceal from the masses the real sources of their collective suffering. Ideation, or what Marxists called *super-structure*, was in some respects equivalent to the anthropologists' culture, but it was clearly demoted as tangential to the real engine of social life and conflict. In fact, political economy was more readily accommodated by social anthropology than by cultural anthropology, since social anthropology already treated symbolic systems as mere by-products of politics, economics, and the rest of the sociologically concrete.[11]

But cultural anthropologists soon found ways to incorporate and transform Marxist concepts by reading symbolic practice into political economy, and power into culture. Marshall Sahlins and other cultural anthropologists were already analyzing capitalism and its antithesis, the gift economy, as cultural systems, an interpretative project that continues to this day.[12] Others focused increasingly on the internalization and experience of capitalist culture at the centers and peripheries of the global economy. Here an important influence was Antonio Gramsci, an Italian intellectual of the early twentieth century, who wrote about the ability of small social groups to dominate society not through coercion, but by disseminating and naturalizing a consensus worldview through mass media and other practices. He called this *cultural hegemony*.[13] Cultural anthropologists adopted this notion to investigate the naturalization of power through media, state ritual, schooling, religious conversion, and other forms of symbolic practice.[14] This led in turn to the study of the *limits* of cultural hegemony, both in developed countries where the disadvantaged create forms of cultural resistance through parody, reinvention, and retreat, and in developing countries where Western cultural repertoires are but a few of the symbol systems available to shape, understand, and express local experiences.

In these developing arenas of culture and power analysis, an additional influence was the French philosopher and social theorist Michel Foucault. Inspired by Gramsci and other Marxist intellectuals, Foucault wrote about institutional locations of power – notably the prison, the church, and the clinic – whose social mandate is to impose cultural conformity on essentially captive subjects. He then investigated their means of domination through surveillance, confession, and therapy, and their impact on their principal field of operation, namely, the human body.[15] Although many criticize him for seeing *only* fields of power, his work inspired an explosion of new studies on sexuality, mental illness, militarism, and so on by cultural anthropologists, historians, and others.[16]

As cultural anthropologists explored and refined the interplay of culture and power, they remained committed to the methodologies for which the discipline was already known: empiricism, fieldwork, and contextualization. Most importantly, they insisted on examining not only the global, the grand, and the spectacular, but also the local, the commonplace, and the inconsequential. As Sherry Ortner writes, cultural analysis serves us best when it focuses on practice, that is,

> the little routines people enact, again and again, in working, eating, sleeping, and relaxing, as well as the little scenarios of etiquette they play out again and again in social interaction. All of these routines and scenarios are predicated upon, and embody within themselves, the fundamental notions of temporal, spatial, and social ordering that underlie and organize the system as a whole. In enacting these routines, actors not only continue to be shaped by the underlying organizational principles involved, but continually re-endorse those principles in the world of public observation and discourse. (1984: 154)

Subculture and Boundless Culture

In recent years, in the United States anyway, the idea of an "American" culture has been challenged; in a country with so many different ethnic groups, how can there be an overarching national culture? Instead, the word *culture* is usually associated with ethnicity, as in *Latino culture* or *African American culture*, part of the contested arena of identity politics in a multi*cultural* society. I am not yet ready to throw out the idea of a mainstream or hegemonic culture, for it seems to me that the various subcultures define themselves against it or in relation to it while simultaneously incorporating many of its concepts and values. But I do feel that the use of the term *culture* in phrases such as *corporate culture*, *university culture*, or the *culture of the Boy Scouts* is much too narrow and urge that it be dropped in those senses. What these uses seem to be alluding to is the ambience or spirit of a place or group. Generally, discussions of culture in these restricted uses fail to relate the particular cases to the prevailing system of beliefs and values. So, for example, when you conduct ethnographic research at your own school, you will, no doubt, reveal some unique features of that place, but you should not stop your analysis there. Instead, pick up the thread and follow it as it weaves into the concepts, values, and constraints of the broader cultural environment.

Since the United States *is* multicultural, is there any sense in which we can speak of an "American" culture? Is there anything we share? Actually, I think there is quite a lot we share – television, movies, news, politics and voting, laws, rights, notions of freedom, independence, opportunity, and a host of other things – albeit in different degrees and from very different standpoints.[17] For example, the notion and value of freedom will be very differently inflected in the life of a billionaire like Bill Gates and in the life of a welfare mother. Even the arch-intellectualist Claude Lévi-Strauss noted that "one has to be very naive or dishonest to imagine that men choose their beliefs independently of their situation" ([1955] 1975: 148). A cultural analysis should make explicit the social positions of the person doing the analyzing and the people being analyzed, as well as the differences of power and status among the individuals and the groups being studied. This is not always easy, however, for, as my colleague Sylvia Yanagisako and I argued in our coedited volume, *Naturalizing Power*, "differentials of power (often) come already embedded in culture ... [so that] power appears natural, inevitable, even god-given" (Yanagisako and Delaney 1995: 1). Thus, many people have come to America because to them it symbolizes freedom, opportunity, and equality, notwithstanding the entrenched structural characteristics that constrain their fulfillment. Investigating exactly what "America" means to its diverse citizens would make an excellent and important research project.

The notion of *a* national culture that is bounded and discrete has also recently been challenged. The challengers argue that the concept of culture is too often equated with nation-states with territorial boundaries. When scholars realized that nation-states were relatively recent constructions, national cultures were also called into question as artificial constructs. *Nation*, however, did not always mean *country*, but once referred to a *people* bound by language, religion, and birth (from the Latin word *natio*, which comes from the verb meaning "to be born") and not by territorial boundaries or government. The Ottoman Empire, for example, was composed of many nations – in addition to the Turkish-speaking Muslim majority, there were the Arab Muslim nation, the Jewish nation, the (Greek) Orthodox nation, and the Armenian nation – cultural groups defined by commonalities of language, ethnicity, and religion. Furthermore, the borders of the empire were not clearly demarcated. Although Mustafa Kemal Atatürk, the founder of the Republic of Turkey, wanted to create a nation-state on the model of European nations, he also wanted to create a national identity different from the ethnic identities of the Ottoman Empire. Turkish identity would be based on language and civilization, and different groups would be assimilated by means of education. This marked a significant departure from the Ottoman period, when *Turk* meant a country bumpkin and referred to the peasantry, rather than an ethnic identity. Unfortunately, the choice of Turkey rather than Anatolia (the traditional name for the Asian part of the land mass) as the name of the new nation intensified ethnic identities and divisions, rather than erasing them.

In my view, the concept of culture need not be coextensive with that of nation-state. Thus Turks living in Europe bring along many of the concepts, beliefs, values, feelings, foods, modes of social interaction, dress, and aesthetics that were inculcated in Turkey. Surely this is diluted in the second and third generations born outside of Turkey, but it is not entirely wiped out. Turkish culture exceeds the boundaries of the nation of Turkey. And if one thinks of culture not only as material items but also as a system of symbols and meanings, then there is nothing that confines it to a specific place. At the same time, it is extremely important to investigate the ways in which power, aggression, repression, and exploitation have had an important influence on the development and expression of culture. Turks in Europe have many restrictions placed on their cultural expression and are often the targets of state repression and private aggression. Their example helps to expose the processes of cultural production – who gets to make culture and how is it transmitted – as well as the creative ways that cultural expressions and productions persist and flourish in an often hostile environment. For example, by modifying their traditional *döner kebab* to suit German tastes, Turks have been extremely successful in creating a very popular fast-food snack in Germany. You can now find them sold on almost every street corner and at every train station, and Germans have taken to them with gusto.

The Personal Is Political

This discussion about culture and its many senses has been theoretical, but how you think about it affects your personal life. When you enter college or university, most of you will encounter some people very different from yourselves, people who come from different places, have different values, have different styles of interacting and of clothing, and have different tastes in food and music. How do you interpret these differences?

Do you simply dismiss them with the thought "They are just different" and then seek out those similar to yourself? Do you attribute the differences to their race or ethnicity, religious background, home region, socioeconomic class, or upbringing and family values? Or do you assume that they have different natural talents and endowments – intellectual, physical, and artistic?

At a small conference in 1993, Sylvia Yanagisako made an eloquent argument for retaining the concept of culture. "[W]e need to explore and refine explanations of difference other than what I call the three R's: Race, Religion, and Reason or Rationality. These three R's were the forms of explanation of social difference … in the 19th century" (1993: 9). They incorporated hierarchical and unidirectional notions of progress and advancement, but they end by putting the beliefs and values of white, Christian, Euro-American males at the top.

The concept of culture should be retained, she said, because it

> is the conceptual and discursive space we reserve to struggle to refine our understandings of social differences and similarities. It is that elusive abstraction we find it impossible to agree upon but one that we find it equally impossible to live without. (Yanagisako 1993: 10)

The main features of this elusive concept, Yanagisako noted, have been with us since the 1920s. Perhaps we understand what this concept *isn't* better than we understand what it is. Culture is "learned not inherited [i.e., it is not biological]; it is shared and not idiosyncratic [i.e., it is not psychological]; and it is particular and not universal [i.e., it is not a matter of philosophy]" (1993: 10).

The social differences noted above are important and need to be taken into our anthropological accounts. Rather than avoiding them, we need to become more aware of the ways these social differences and their *meanings* emerge in a particular cultural context. They are *culturally constituted*; that means they emerge in relation to interlocking patterns of meaning that are constructed by and struggled over by people who occupy different social positions that incorporate differentials of power. Some of these meanings we inherit (in the sense of being *socially,* not genetically, transmitted) from previous generations, some we can affect and change, and some we can even invent – but only in relation to what went before.

Investigating

So, how does one go about investigating such an elusive thing as culture? Where is it, and how do you find it? I find it helpful to think of culture as a mystery and the anthropologist as a detective. To me, the primary anthropological questions are as follows: Why are things the way they are and not some other way? Do you think the way things are is natural, inevitable, and maybe even necessary? How do you feel when you realize that people elsewhere do things differently – that your way is just one among a number of possibilities? Do you assume your way is best, or does the realization create doubt about your way? If the specter of doubt does not become too unsettling, it can be the goad to anthropological investigation. However, it does make some students nervous. That is how it should be. It is an indication of why anthropology is a very different enterprise from other disciplines. It is a critical discipline, one that calls into question conventional knowledge and taken-for-granted truths.

Claude Lévi-Strauss, the French anthropologist known for his structuralist theories, felt that anthropological fieldwork was the nursemaid of doubt:

> This anthropological doubt consists not merely in knowing that one knows nothing, but in resolutely exposing what one knows, even one's own ignorance, to the insults and denials inflicted on one's dearest ideas and habits by those ideas and habits which may contradict them to the highest degree. (Cited in Sontag 1966: 188–9)

While it is hard to imagine this most cerebral of anthropologists exposing his ignorance, that *is* what happens in fieldwork, and it can induce a kind of psychological vertigo.

As an example, I will relate one of my more humiliating experiences during fieldwork in the Turkish village. Most of the time, except for breakfast, I ate at other people's houses because there was no store in the village and, without fields and animals of my own, it was difficult to procure food. One day a fish vendor came to the village and I bought some to cook on my own. I was in the midst of steaming them with herbs and spices when several of my neighbors walked in. "That is no way to cook fish," they said. "The only way is to fry them in oil." I became defensive; not only did they think my way was barbaric, but they were also insulting my intelligence. I testily replied, "Well, I've been cooking for over 20 years, and this is one of the ways I prepare fish" (so there!). They left without trying any, shaking their heads at my strange ways and scoffing at my lack of expertise. I was unnerved. Through this and other such trials, I learned much about the rules and beliefs in that culture. These experiences also made me question the way "we" do things. I began to live teetering between two worlds – that is where the vertigo comes in – and my old world no longer seemed so stable, so resolutely obvious.

When anthropologists conduct "fieldwork," what they are really doing is collecting clues to help solve the mystery of culture: why do these people do things the way they do? What are their motivations and goals? How are they constrained by the cultural definitions of their race, gender, age, class, and so on? Where do you find the clues? I believe you can begin anywhere; there is no privileged place to begin the investigation. When a detective is investigating a murder, she may find obvious clues such as a gun tossed in a trash bin and then test it for fingerprints and identify its type and registration. But other clues are less obvious, may seem irrelevant at first, and yet end up more significant. The analogy, of course, goes only so far – culture, after all, is not a crime! However, it is mysterious. Becoming a perspicacious observer means training yourself to look at things anew, to take nothing for granted, and to prevent your preconceptions (or theory) from dictating what you will see and include as evidence. Pick any aspect or item of culture, and begin to ask questions about it. Who uses it? Where does it fit in the system of classifications? What resources are needed to make it, and how are these socially mobilized?

Take your classroom, for example. When I asked my graduate students to do a cultural analysis of our classroom, they were stumped. The freshmen got it much faster. You might begin by considering just who is sitting there. Only a certain segment of the population, a relatively privileged segment, is there. In order to be there, you must have completed high school or its equivalent and passed the rigorous entrance exams, and you or your parents must be able to pay for it whether in full or by a combination of scholarship and loans. Because you (or your parents) are willing to sacrifice a lot of money for a college education, you must think it is a worthwhile endeavor. Then you would need to contrast those who are sitting in the classroom with segments of the population who are not. How would you account for that? That should lead you to consider issues of class, race, gender, and social inequality. You could also begin by observing how the classroom is arranged spatially. Is the teacher in front, and are the desks set in rows facing him or her? Or do you sit around a big table? What different ideas and values are expressed just by this arrangement of space? One setup implies a lecture format with the teacher talking and conveying knowledge, while the other implies a discussion group where the ideas are tossed back and forth and argued over. Both types are in use in most colleges, but they are constructed from different theories of education and perhaps are intended for different types of students – freshmen versus upper-class or graduate students. Different theories of education relate to different theories of child development and other cultural values.[18] How quickly one gets from such an ordinary thing as a classroom to much deeper theories and values in a culture. By following the threads where they lead, you are pulling on the fabric of culture. You begin to understand that nothing in culture stands alone; each item is woven into a vast, interconnected web that no one person can ever really grasp in its entirety. That is the mystery and the challenge.

Fieldwork and Ethnography

Fieldwork is one of the things that sets anthropology apart from other academic disciplines – anthropologists must leave the library, the classroom, and their offices and go out and live for extended periods of time among the people they study. An ethnography is what anthropologists write up after completing their fieldwork. However, it is not just a *description* of a particular society and culture (e.g., "The X do it like this"), but also an *analysis* that tries to explain why. In writing ethnographies, anthropologists utilize the theories and jargon of the discipline at the time of writing and hope to contribute new theoretical insights and knowledge. The practice of fieldwork has been discussed theoretically, and there exist a number of descriptions *about* the experience of fieldwork,[19] but nothing captures the experience itself as much as the ethnographic novel *Return to Laughter* by Elenore Smith Bowen ([1954] 1964), the pseudonym for Laura Bohannan. Novels take us into the world they portray and immerse us in that world for the period of reading.

Her novel is set in Africa, where Bohannan actually conducted fieldwork. It was written in 1954, yet despite the outdated style and the problematics of doing fieldwork in an African nation under British colonial rule, it takes you into her *experience* of going to another culture and of how she gradually became oriented in it. She vividly describes the feeling of panic when she first arrived in the village where she was to live for a year; she lets us in on how and when she learned things, the ethical problems she encountered, and the humiliating but illuminating incidents she endured, and she confesses her feelings and prejudices about some of their ways and her rising doubts about some of her own society's ways.

As David Riesman, a former Harvard sociologist, notes in his foreword to the 1964 edition of the book, it "focusses less on the West African tribe … and more on her own emotional hegira as a neophyte anthropologist" ([1954] 1964: x). I generally assign the book in the first week of my class; it forms a common experience we use as we begin to conduct our own fieldwork and we refer back to it throughout the course.

Riesman was curious about why Bohannan decided to use a pseudonym for this book. Although she claimed it was to protect the tribe, he felt that she might also be afraid "that the book might hurt her reputation as a competent and objective ethnographer" (Riesman [1954] 1964: xvi). That was probably an accurate assessment of the times, but he went on to say that "as a work of ethnography, and as a primer of anthropological method, *Return to Laughter* can stand on its own feet" (p. xvi). Fieldwork is messy, and it contradicts the image most people have of scientific research; one cannot perform experiments on a living group, nor can one submit them to detached observation as a slide under a microscope. But that, too, was the image of science at the time. Today there is more awareness that even the "hard" physical sciences are not as objective as they were assumed to be, because the frameworks and theories of science are themselves human constructions that depend on all kinds of "subjective" features. These include the personal concerns of the scientists and the particular social and political milieux that determine, through networks of support, what to study and how to study it.[20]

For several decades now, anthropologists have been discussing the craft of ethnographic writing. It is a *construction* made from their experience in the field. What, then, is the difference between an ethnographic novel and a scholarly ethnography? If fieldwork is *one and the same* experience for the anthropologist, what provides the "facts" of a standard monograph and the "fictions" of an ethnographic novel? What is the difference between creating composite characters or events, and writing up marriage rules or kinship structures? These questions ask us to contemplate the nature of truth: how many kinds of truth are there, and what purposes do they serve?

Orientation to the Book

As I noted earlier, this book is not intended to be a compendium of knowledge about anthropology or about any particular culture. Nor does it make pronouncements about universals of human behavior or human nature because, as should be clear by now, I feel these are strongly inflected by particular cultures and the ways in which power is encoded and enacted. The purpose of the book and the course is, first, to sensitize you to the *culturally specific* ways that humans orient themselves – in space and time; by means of language and social relations; with the body, food, and clothes; by the structures of everyday life; and in terms of the symbols and frameworks provided by public myth, religion, and ritual. The book is not organized to focus on specific institutions or domains such as kinship, economy, or religion. Instead, these are discussed as they relate to the topics dealt with in each chapter.

Second, the goal is to get you to dig deeper and analyze both the particular meanings embodied in these phenomena and the ways they are interconnected. Aspects of power and economy are integrated into the discussion of each topic, and attention is paid to the way all of these are experienced differently depending on race, class, and gender. Examples are drawn from a number of different cultures, and throughout I will insert material from my own fieldwork in Turkey.[21]

It is expected that this book will be used in conjunction with other readings; a bibliography is appended at the end of each chapter from which you or your teacher can select additional material. Drawing on the readings, class discussions are meant to compare and contrast classic anthropological works with contemporary articles whether these are academic papers, newspaper articles, or material on the Web. At the end of each chapter, you will find ethnographic exercises for conducting your own research and applying what you have learned. (Sometimes I find that it is more exciting to conduct the research *before* the reading assignment.) With this textbook, the supplementary readings, the ethnographic exercises, and the class discussions, my expectation is that you will become aware that (each) culture is neither inevitable nor natural, but constructed by humans struggling to make meaning of their lives. As a constructed phenomenon, culture is available to the investigation of its explicit forms and implicit premises.

The next chapter takes up the topic of space in order to give you some metaphorical grounding, since space is the widest cosmological framework within which humans live. From there we move to time, another extremely important coordinate of human life, and ask if people perceive and categorize time the same way everywhere. If not, what are the consequences? Language is, of course, the major way we communicate with each other, but as you will see in chapter 4, it is also instrumental in constructing the world conceptually. Humans are social animals, so the fifth chapter is devoted to social relations. We are also physical beings, and chapter 6 takes up notions of the body, while chapters 7 and 8 discuss what we put into and onto our bodies, that is, food and clothes. Finally, the last substantive chapter looks at significant cultural icons – places, people, and events – that both grasp the imaginations of the majority of the population and symbolize important cultural values.

Most people believe that anthropologists have to work in faraway places, whether to study ancient archaeological sites or exotic "primitive" peoples. While that was true, to a large extent, when anthropology was emerging as a distinctive discipline, it is only partially true today. While some anthropologists still go off to cultures very different from their own, many others have turned their focus to modern, industrial societies, including their own. In either case, it is an adventure in which you learn as much about yourself as about the culture you are studying.

Notes

1. See also the introduction to Lewis and Jungman (1986).
2. Because of the pejorative connotations that have become attached to the word *primitive*, some anthropologists refuse to use it. For a defense of the term and the virtues of primitive society, see Stanley Diamond's *In Search of the Primitive* (1974), which is also a scathing critique of so-called modern, industrial society.
3. Hobbes is known for the phrase "the war of all against all," meaning that everyone is out for himself. He believed that in a state of nature, humans would be at each other's throats. This assumption, at the heart of his philosophy, is behind much of economic rationality.
4. For those who wish to explore this issue further, you might begin with Haraway (1989, 1991) and Marks (1995).
5. The words are *insight*, *illuminates*, and *see*.
6. This is an allusion to Suzanne Langer's book *Philosophy in a New Key* (1942), which Geertz acknowledges as being influential in bringing to scholarly attention the role and importance of the symbolic function in human life (1973: 3).
7. To get a more complete definition of utilitarianism, consult the *International Encyclopedia of the Social Sciences* (Darity, 2007). It is an excellent reference work that also includes articles on major theorists such as Durkheim, Spencer, and Hobbes.
8. See Andre Gunder Frank's *The Development of Underdevelopment* (1966) and *Latin America: Underdevelopment or Revolution* (1969).
9. Immanuel Wallerstein, (1974, 1979, 1980, 1984, 1986, 1989).
10. See, for example, Wolf (1982), Mintz (1985), and Hobsbawm (1975, 1987).
11. See the work of Meillassoux (1991), Althusser (1969, 1972), and Godelier (1977, 1986) for a school of thought called structural Marxism. For some problems with these theories, see Ortner (1984).
12. See Sahlins (1976) and Graeber (2001).
13. See Gramsci (1971).
14. See, for example, Herman and Chomsky (1988); Comaroff and Comaroff (1991, 1997); and Yanagisako and Delaney (1995).
15. See Foucault (1963, 1970, 1975, 1990, 2006).
16. See, for example, Bayer (1987), Weeks ([1981] 1989), and Brownell (1995).
17. I intended to include public schooling until one of my students reminded me that she was home-schooled, and that a lot of people in the United States are engaged in alternative forms of education. Then, too, there is no nationwide curriculum as in France or the United Kingdom; instead, each county in each state determines what will be taught and what books will be ordered. Nevertheless, for a time there was considerable overlap.

18. In Turkey, for example, children have to memorize vast quantities of knowledge. Education was not a "drawing out," as the etymology of the English word means, but was a "putting in." (See also Eickelman 1978.) This was the mode of teaching in the secular schools, yet the pedagogical precedent can be found in the religious schools, where memorization is very important. There are even illiterate villagers who can recite the entire Qur'an from memory in Arabic, a language totally unrelated to Turkish. They memorize in Arabic because it is held to be God's literal word communicated through the angel Gabriel. A translation is not the same, merely an interpretation.

19. For example, see Beteille and Madan (1974); Briggs (1970); Cesara (1982); Golde ([1970] 1986); Malinowski (1967); Maybury-Lewis (1965); Rabinow (1977); Srinivas, Shah, and Ramaswamy (1979); and Stoller and Olkes (1987), to name just a few.

20. One early and accessible presentation of this idea can be found in the first section of Suzanne Langer's *Philosophy in a New Key* (1942). See also Haraway (1978, 1989, 2002).

21. For a fuller account of that work, see Delaney (1991).

E X E R C I S E S

1.1. A Trip to a Foreign Land

You are about to leave for another culture (you may specify the one you are going to or would like to go to) for a stay of at least six months.

- What do you think you will need to take?
- What do you think will sustain you while you are there? Here you may think of favorite books or other items as well as certain psychological capacities.

1.2. Leaving Home for College (or Elsewhere)

When you were planning to leave home for college or university, what did you think you would need to bring? If going to college was not the first time you left home, describe where you did go that first time and answer the same questions.

- What did you bring? Why?
- What do you think will prove to be important? Unnecessary?
- What do you wish you *had* brought?
- What has been the most difficult thing to get used to since you arrived? How is it different from your former life?

Bibliography

Althusser, Louis (1969) *For Marx*, trans. Ben Brewster. New York: Pantheon.

Althusser, Louis (1972) *Lenin and Philosophy, and Other Essays*, trans. Ben Brewster. New York: Monthly Review Press.

Bayer, Ronald. (1987) *Homosexuality and American Psychiatry: The Politics of a Diagnosis*, new ed. Princeton, NJ: Princeton University Press.

Beteille, Andre, and Madan, T. N. (1974) *Encounter and Experience: Personal Accounts of Fieldwork*. Delhi: Vikas.

Bohannan, Laura (1966) "Shakespeare in the Bush." *Natural History* (August–September): 28–33.

Bourdieu, Pierre ([1972] 1977) *Outline of a Theory of Practice*, trans. Richard Nice. Cambridge: Cambridge University Press.

Bowen, Elenore Smith ([1954] 1964) *Return to Laughter: An Anthropological Novel*. New York: Doubleday.

Briggs, Jean (1970) *Never in Anger: Portrait of an Eskimo Family*. Cambridge, MA: Harvard University Press.

Brownell, Susan (1995) *Training the Body for China*. Chicago: University of Chicago Press.

Cesara, Manda (1982) *Reflections of a Woman Anthropologist: No Hiding Place*. New York: Academic.

Comaroff, John, and Comaroff, Jean (1991) *Of Revelation and Revolution*, vol. 1. Chicago: University of Chicago Press.

Comaroff, John, and Comaroff, Jean (1997) *Of Revelation and Revolution*, vol. 2. Chicago: University of Chicago Press.

Darity, William A. (2007) *International Encyclopedia of the Social Sciences*, 9 vols. New York: Macmillan.

Delaney, Carol (1991) *The Seed and the Soil: Gender and Cosmology in Turkish Village Society*. Berkeley: University of California Press.

Diamond, Stanley (1974) *In Search of the Primitive: A Critique of Civilization*. New Brunswick, NJ: Transaction.

Dundes, Alan (1972) "Seeing Is Believing." *Natural History* (May 1972): 8–12, 86–7.

Durkheim, Emile ([1915] 1965) *The Elementary Forms of Religious Life*, trans. Joseph Ward Swain. New York: Free Press.

Eickelman, Dale (1978) "The Art of Memory, Islamic Education and Its Social Reproduction." *Comparative Studies in Society and History* 20(4): 485–516.

Foucault, Michel (1963) *The Birth of the Clinic: An Archaeology of Medical Perception*. London: Tavistock.

Foucault, Michel (1970) *The Order of Things*. New York: Random House.

Foucault, Michel (1975) *Discipline and Punish: The Birth of the Prison*. New York: Vintage.

Foucault, Michel (1990) *The History of Sexuality*, vol. 1. New York: Random House.

Foucault, Michel (2006) *The History of Madness*. New York: Routledge.

Frank, Andre Gunder (1966) *The Development of Underdevelopment*. New York: Monthly Review Press.

Frank, Andre Gunder (1969) *Latin America: Underdevelopment or Revolution*. New York: Monthly Review Press.

Geertz, Clifford (1973) *Interpretation of Cultures*. New York: Basic.

Godelier, Maurice (1977) *Perspectives in Marxist Anthropology*, trans. Robert Brain. Cambridge: Cambridge University Press.

Godelier, Maurice (1986) *The Making of Great Men: Male Domination and Power among the New Guinea Baruya*, trans. Rupert Swyer. Cambridge: Cambridge University Press.

Golde, Peggy, ed. ([1970] 1986) *Women in the Field: Anthropological Experiences*. Berkeley: University of California Press.

Graeber, David (2001) *Toward an Anthropological Theory of Value: The False Coin of Our Own Dreams*. New York: Palgrave.

Gramsci, Antonio (1971) *Selections from the Prison Notebooks*, trans. and ed. Quintin Hoare and Geoffrey Nowell-Smith. New York: International.

Haraway, Donna (1978) "Animal Sociology and a Natural Economy of the Body, Parts 1 and 2," *Signs* 4: 21–36, 37–60.

Haraway, Donna (1989) *Primate Visions: Gender, Race, and Nature in the World of Modern Science*. New York: Routledge.

Haraway, Donna (1991) *Simians, Cyborgs, and Women: The Reinvention of Nature*. New York: Routledge.

Haraway, Donna (2002) "Situated Knowledges: The Science Question in Feminisim and the Privilege of Partial Perspective." In *The Gender of Science*, ed. J.A. Kourany. Upper Saddle River, NJ: Prentice Hall.

Harding, Sandra (1986) *The Science Question in Feminism*. Milton Keynes, UK: Open University Press.

Helmreich, Stefan (1998) *Silicon Second Nature: Culturing Artificial Life in a Digital World*. Berkeley: University of California Press.

Herman, Edward S., and Chomsky, Noam. (1988) *Manufacturing Consent*. New York: Pantheon.

Hobsbawm, Eric (1975) *The Age of Capital: 1848–1875*. New York: Scribner.

Hobsbawm, Eric (1987) *The Age of Empire: 1875–1914*. London: Weidenfeld and Nicolson.

Langer, Suzanne ([1942] 1979) *Philosophy in a New Key: A Study in the Symbolism of Reason, Rite, and Art*. Cambridge, MA: Harvard University Press.

Lévi-Strauss, Claude ([1955] 1975) *Tristes Tropiques*, trans. John and Doreen Weightman. New York: Atheneum.

Lewis, Tom J., and Jungman, Robert E., eds. (1986) *On Being Foreign: Culture Shock in Short Fiction: An International Anthology*. Yarmouth, ME: Intercultural Press.

Malinowski, Bronislaw ([1922] 1961) *Argonauts of the Western Pacific*. New York: Dutton.

Malinowski, Bronislaw (1967) *A Diary in the Strict Sense of the Term*. London: Routledge.

Marks, Jonathan (1995) *Human Biodiversity: Genes, Race, and History*. New York: Aldine de Gruyter.

Maybury-Lewis, David (1965) *The Savage and the Innocent*. London: Evans.

Meillassoux, Claude (1991) *The Anthropology of Slavery: The Womb of Iron and Gold*, trans. Alide Dasnois. Chicago: University of Chicago Press.

Mintz, Sidney (1985) *Sweetness and Power*. New York: Penguin.

Ortner, Sherry (1984) "Theory in Anthropology since the Sixties." *Comparative Studies in Society and History* 26(1): 126–65.

Rabinow, Paul (1977) *Reflections on Fieldwork in Morocco*. Berkeley: University of California Press.

Riesman, David ([1954] 1964) Foreword. In Elenore Smith Bowen, *Return to Laughter: An Anthropological Novel*. New York: Doubleday.

Sahlins, Marshall (1976) *Culture and Practical Reason*. Chicago: University of Chicago Press.

Schneider, David (1972) "What Is Kinship All About?" In *Kinship Studies in the Morgan Centennial Year*, ed. P. Reining. Washington, DC: Anthropological Society, pp. 32–63.

Segal, Dan, and Yanagisako, Sylvia, eds. (2004) *Unwrapping the Sacred Bundle: Reflections on the Disciplining of Anthropology*. Durham, NC: Duke University Press.

Sontag, Susan (1966) "The Anthropologist as Hero." In *Against Interpretation*. New York: Farrar, Straus & Giroux.

Srinivas, M. N., Shah, A. M., and Ramaswamy, E. A., eds. (1979) *The Fieldworker and the Field: Problems and Challenges in Sociological Investigation*. Bombay: Oxford University Press.

Stocking, George W., Jr. (1968) *Race, Culture, and Evolution: Essays in the History of Anthropology*. New York: Free Press.

Stoller, Paul, and Olkes, Cheryl (1987) *In Sorcery's Shadow: A Memoir of Apprenticeship among the Songhay of Niger*. Chicago: University of Chicago Press.

Turner, Victor (1967) "Betwixt and Between: The Liminal Period in *Rites de Passage*." In *The Forest of Symbols: Aspects of Ndembu Ritual*. Ithaca, NY: Cornell University Press, pp. 93–111.

Van Gennep, Arnold ([1909] 1960) *Rites de Passage*, trans. Monika B. Vizedom and Gabrielle L. Caffee. Chicago: University of Chicago Press.

Wallerstein, Immanuel (1974) *The Modern World-System*, vol. 1. New York: Academic Press.

Wallerstein, Immanuel (1979) *The Capitalist World-Economy*. Cambridge: Cambridge University Press.

Wallerstein, Immanuel (1980) *The Modern World-System*, vol. 2. New York: Academic Press.

Wallerstein, Immanuel (1984) *The Politics of the World-Economy: The States, the Movements and the Civilizations*. Cambridge: Cambridge University Press.

Wallerstein, Immanuel (1986) *Africa and the Modern World*. Trenton, NJ: Africa World Press.

Wallerstein, Immanuel (1989) *The Modern World-System*, vol. 3. New York: Academic Press.

Weeks, Jeffrey ([1981] 1989) *Sex, Politics and Society: The Regulation of Sexuality since 1800*. Trenton, NJ: Africa World Press.

Williams, Raymond ([1976] 1983) *Keywords: A Vocabulary of Culture and Society*. New York: Oxford University Press.

Wolf, Eric (1982) *Europe and the Peoples without History*. Berkeley: University of California Press.

Yanagisako, Sylvia (1993) "Defining Culture." Paper presented at a mini-conference held at Stanford University, Stanford, CA.

Yanagisako, Sylvia, and Delaney, Carol (1995) *Naturalizing Power: Essays in Feminist Cultural Analysis*. New York: Routledge.

Shakespeare in the Bush

Laura Bohannan

Just before I left Oxford for the Tiv in West Africa, conversation turned to the season at Stratford. "You Americans," said a friend, "often have difficulty with Shakespeare. He was, after all, a very English poet, and one can easily misinterpret the universal by misunderstanding the particular."

I protested that human nature is pretty much the same the whole world over; at least the general plot and motivation of the greater tragedies would always be clear – everywhere – although some details of custom might have to be explained and difficulties of translation might produce other slight changes. To end an argument we could not conclude, my friend gave me a copy of *Hamlet* to study in the African bush: it would, he hoped, lift my mind above its primitive surroundings, and possibly I might, by prolonged meditation, achieve the grace of correct interpretation.

It was my second field trip to that African tribe, and I thought myself ready to live in one of its remote sections – an area difficult to cross even on foot. I eventually settled on the hillock of a very knowledgeable old man, the head of a homestead of some hundred and forty people, all of whom were either his close relatives or their wives and children. Like the other elders of the vicinity, the old man spent most of his time performing ceremonies seldom seen these days in the more accessible parts of the tribe. I was delighted. Soon there would be three months of enforced isolation and leisure, between the harvest that takes place just before the rising of the swamps and the clearing of new farms when the water goes down. Then, I thought, they would have even more time to perform ceremonies and explain them to me.

I was quite mistaken. Most of the ceremonies demanded the presence of elders from several homesteads. As the swamps rose, the old men found it too difficult to walk from one homestead to the next, and the ceremonies gradually ceased. As the swamps rose even higher, all activities but one came to an end. The women brewed beer from maize and millet. Men, women, and children sat on their hillocks and drank it.

People began to drink at dawn. By midmorning the whole homestead was singing, dancing, and drumming. When it rained, people had to sit inside their huts: there they drank and sang or they drank and told stories. In any case, by noon or before, I either had to join the party or retire to my own hut and my books. "One does not discuss serious matters when there is beer. Come, drink with us." Since I lacked their capacity for the thick native beer, I spent more and more time with *Hamlet*. Before the end of the second month, grace descended on me. I was quite sure that *Hamlet* had only one possible interpretation, and that one universally obvious.

Early every morning, in the hope of having some serious talk before the beer party, I used to call on the old man at his reception hut – a circle of posts supporting a thatched roof above a low mud wall to keep out wind and rain. One day I crawled through the low doorway and found most of the men of the homestead sitting huddled in their ragged cloths on stools, low plank beds, and reclining chairs, warming themselves against the chill of the rain around a smoky fire. In the center were three pots of beer. The party had started.

The old man greeted me cordially. "Sit down and drink." I accepted a large calabash full of beer, poured some into a small drinking gourd, and tossed it down. Then I poured some more into the same gourd for the man second in seniority to my host before I handed my calabash over to a young man for further distribution. Important people shouldn't ladle beer themselves.

"It is better like this," the old man said, looking at me approvingly and plucking at the thatch that had caught in my hair. "You should sit and drink with us more often. Your servants tell me that when you are not with us, you sit inside your hut looking at a paper."

The old man was acquainted with four kinds of "papers": tax receipts, bride price receipts, court fee receipts, and letters. The messenger who brought him letters from the chief used them mainly as a badge of office, for he always knew what was in them and told the old man. Personal letters for the few who had relatives in the government or mission stations were kept until someone went to a large market where there was a letter writer and reader. Since my arrival, letters were brought to me to be read. A few men also brought me bride price receipts, privately, with requests to change the figures to a higher sum. I found moral arguments were of no avail, since in-laws are fair game, and the technical hazards of forgery difficult to explain to an illiterate people. I did not wish them to think me silly enough to look at any such papers for days on end, and I hastily explained that my "paper" was one of the "things of long ago" of my country.

"Ah," said the old man. "Tell us."

I protested that I was not a storyteller. Storytelling is a skilled art among them; their standards are high, and the audiences critical – and vocal in their criticism. I protested in vain. This morning they wanted to hear a story while they drank. They threatened to tell me no more stories until I told them one of mine. Finally, the old man promised that no one would criticize my style "for we know you are struggling with our language."

"But," put in one of the elders, "you must explain what we do not understand, as we do when we tell you our stories." Realizing that here was my chance to prove *Hamlet* universally intelligible, I agreed.

The old man handed me some more beer to help me on with my storytelling. Men filled their long wooden pipes and knocked coals from the fire to place in the pipe bowels; then, puffing contentedly, they sat back to listen. I began in the proper style, "Not yesterday, not yesterday, but long ago, a thing occurred. One night three men were keeping watch outside the homestead of the great chief, when suddenly they saw the former chief approach them."

"Why was he no longer their chief?"

"He was dead," I explained. "That is why they were troubled and afraid when they saw him."

"Impossible," began one of the elders, handing his pipe on to his neighbor, who interrupted, "Of course it wasn't the dead chief. It was an omen sent by a witch. Go on."

Slightly shaken, I continued. "One of these three was a man who knew things" – the closest translation for scholar, but unfortunately it also meant witch. The second elder looked triumphantly at the first. "So he spoke to the dead chief saying, 'Tell us what we must do so you may rest in your grave,' but the dead chief did not answer. He vanished, and they could see him no more. Then the man who knew things – his name was Horatio – said this event was the affair of the dead chief's son, Hamlet."

There was a general shaking of heads round the circle. "Had the dead chief no living brothers? Or was this son the chief?"

"No," I replied. "That is, he had one living brother who became the chief when the elder brother died."

The old men muttered: such omens were matters for chiefs and elders, not for youngsters; no good could come of going behind a chief's back; clearly Horatio was not a man who knew things.

"Yes, he was," I insisted, shooing a chicken away from my beer. "In our country the son is next to the father. The dead chief's younger brother had become the great chief. He had also married his elder brother's widow only about a month after the funeral."

"He did well," the old man beamed and announced to the others, "I told you that if we knew more about Europeans, we would find they really were very like us. In our country also," he added to me, "the younger brother marries the elder brother's widow and becomes the father of his children. Now, if your uncle, who married your widowed mother, is your father's full brother, then he will be a real father to you. Did Hamlet's father and uncle have one mother?"

His question barely penetrated my mind: I was too upset and thrown too far off balance by having one of the most important elements of *Hamlet* knocked straight out of the picture. Rather uncertainly I said that I thought they had the same mother, but I wasn't sure – the story didn't say. The old man told me severely that these genealogical details made all the difference and that when I got home I must ask the elders about it. He shouted out the door to one of his younger wives to bring his goatskin bag.

Determined to save what I could of the mother motif, I took a deep breath and began again. "The son Hamlet was very sad because his mother had married again so quickly. There was no need for her to do so, and it is our custom for a widow not to go to her next husband until she has mourned for two years."

"Two years is too long," objected the wife, who had appeared with the old man's battered goatskin bag. "Who will hoe your farms for you while you have no husband?"

"Hamlet," I retorted without thinking, "was old enough to hoe his mother's farms himself. There was no need for her to remarry." No one looked convinced. I gave up. "His mother and the great chief told Hamlet not to be sad, for the great chief himself would be a father to Hamlet. Furthermore, Hamlet would be the next chief: therefore he must stay to learn the things of a chief. Hamlet agreed to remain, and all the rest went off to drink beer."

While I paused, perplexed at how to render Hamlet's disgusted soliloquy to an audience convinced that Claudius and Gertrude had behaved in the best possible manner, one of the younger men asked me who had married the other wives of the dead chief.

"He had no other wives," I told him.

"But a chief must have many wives! How else can he brew beer and prepare food for all his guests?"

I said firmly that in our country even chiefs had only one wife, that they had servants to do their work, and that they paid them from tax money.

It was better, they returned, for a chief to have many wives and sons who would help him hoe his farms and feed his people: then everyone loved the chief who gave much and took nothing – taxes were a bad thing.

I agreed with the last comment, but for the rest fell back on their favorite way of fobbing off my questions: "That is the way it is done, so that is how we do it."

I decided to skip the soliloquy. Even if Claudius was here thought quite right to marry his brother's widow, there remained the poison motif, and I knew they would disapprove of fratricide. More hopefully I resumed. "That night Hamlet kept watch with the three who had seen his dead father. The dead chief again appeared, and although the others were afraid, Hamlet followed his dead father off to one side. When they were alone, Hamlet's dead father spoke."

"Omens can't talk!" The old man was emphatic.

"Hamlet's dead father wasn't an omen. Seeing him might have been an omen, but he was not." My audience looked as confused as I sounded. "It *was* Hamlet's dead father. It was a thing we call a 'ghost.'" I had to use the English word, for unlike many of the neighboring tribes, these people didn't believe in the survival after death of any individuating part of the personality.

"What is a 'ghost'? An omen?"

"No, a 'ghost' is someone who is dead but who walks around and can talk, and people can hear him and see him but not touch him."

They objected. "One can touch zombis."

"No, no! It was not a dead body the witches had animated to sacrifice and eat. No one else made Hamlet's dead father walk. He did it himself."

"Dead men can't walk," protested my audience as one man.

I was quite willing to compromise. "A 'ghost' is the dead man's shadow."

But again they objected. "Dead men cast no shadows."

"They do in my country," I snapped.

The old man quelled the babble of disbelief that arose immediately and told me with that insincere, but courteous, agreement one extends to the fancies of the young, ignorant, and superstitious. "No doubt in your country the dead can also walk without being zombis." From the depths of his bag he produced a withered fragment of kola nut, bit off one end to show it wasn't poisoned, and handed me the rest as a peace offering.

"Anyhow," I resumed, "Hamlet's dead father said that his own brother, the one who became chief, had poisoned him. He wanted Hamlet to avenge him. Hamlet believed this in his heart, for he did not like his father's brother." I took another swallow of beer. "In the country of the great chief, living in the same homestead, for it was a very large one, was an important elder who was often with the chief to advise and help him. His name was Polonius. Hamlet was courting his daughter, but her father and her brother…[I cast hastily about for some tribal analogy] warned her not to let Hamlet visit her when she was alone on her farm, for he would be a great chief and so could not marry her."

"Why not?" asked the wife, who had settled down on the edge of the old man's chair. He frowned at her for asking stupid questions and growled, "They lived in the same homestead."

"That was not the reason," I informed them. "Polonius was a stranger who lived in the homestead because he helped the chief, not because he was a relative."

"Then why couldn't Hamlet marry her?"

"He could have," I explained, "but Polonius didn't think he would. After all, Hamlet was a man of great importance who ought to marry a chief's daughter, for in his country a man could have only one wife. Polonius was afraid that if Hamlet made love to his daughter, then no one else would give a high price for her."

"That might be true," remarked one of the shrewder elders, "but a chief's son would give his mistress's father enough presents and patronage to more than make up the difference. Polonius sounds like a fool to me."

"Many people think he was," I agreed. "Meanwhile Polonius sent his son Laertes off to Paris to learn the things of that country, for it was the homestead of a very great chief indeed. Because he was afraid that Laertes might waste a lot of money on beer and women and gambling, or get into trouble by fighting, he sent one of his servants to Paris secretly, to spy out what Laertes was doing. One day Hamlet came upon Polonius's daughter Ophelia. He behaved so oddly he frightened her. Indeed" – I was fumbling for words to express the dubious quality of Hamlet's madness – "the chief and many others had also noticed that when Hamlet talked one could understand the words but not what they meant. Many people thought that he had become mad." My audience suddenly became much more attentive. "The great chief wanted to know what was wrong with Hamlet, so he sent for two of Hamlet's age mates [school friends would have taken long explanation] to talk to Hamlet and find out what troubled his heart. Hamlet, seeing that they had been bribed by the chief to betray him, told them nothing. Polonius, however, insisted that Hamlet was mad because he had been forbidden to see Ophelia, whom he loved."

"Why," inquired a bewildered voice, "should anyone bewitch Hamlet on that account?"

"Bewitch him?"

"Yes, only witchcraft can make anyone mad, unless, of course, one sees the beings that lurk in the forest."

I stopped being a storyteller, took out my notebook and demanded to be told more about these two causes of madness. Even while they spoke and I jotted notes, I tried to calculate the effect of this new factor on the plot. Hamlet had not been exposed to the beings that lurk in the forests. Only his relatives in the male line could bewitch him. Barring relatives not mentioned by Shakespeare, it had to be Claudius who was attempting to harm him. And, of course, it was.

For the moment I staved off questions by saying that the great chief also refused to believe that Hamlet was mad for the love of Ophelia and nothing else. "He was sure that something much more important was troubling Hamlet's heart."

"Now Hamlet's age mates," I continued, "had brought with them a famous storyteller. Hamlet decided to have this man tell the chief and all his homestead a story about a man who had poisoned his brother because he desired his brother's wife and wished to be chief himself. Hamlet was sure the great chief could not hear the story without making a sign if he was indeed guilty, and then he would discover whether his dead father had told him the truth."

The old man interrupted, with deep cunning, "Why should a father lie to his son?" he asked.

I hedged: "Hamlet wasn't sure that it really was his dead father." It was impossible to say anything, in that language, about devil-inspired visions.

"You mean," he said, "it actually was an omen, and he knew witches sometimes send false ones. Hamlet was a fool not to go to one skilled in reading omens and divining the truth in the first place. A man-who-sees-the-truth could have told him how his father died, if he really had been poisoned, and if there was witchcraft in it; then Hamlet could have called the elders to settle the matter."

The shrewd elder ventured to disagree. "Because his father's brother was a great chief, one-who-sees-the-truth might therefore have been afraid to tell it. I think it was for that reason that a friend of Hamlet's father – a witch and an elder – sent an omen so his friend's son would know. Was the omen true?"

"Yes," I said, abandoning ghosts and the devil; a witch-sent omen it would have to be. "It was true, for when the storyteller was telling his tale before all the homestead, the great chief rose in fear. Afraid that Hamlet knew his secret he planned to have him killed."

The stage set of the next bit presented some difficulties of translation. I began cautiously. "The great chief told Hamlet's mother to find out from her son what he knew. But because a woman's children are always first in her heart, he had the important elder Polonius hide behind a cloth that hung against the wall of Hamlet's mother's sleeping hut. Hamlet started to scold his mother for what she had done."

There was a shocked murmur from everyone. A man should never scold his mother.

"She called out in fear, and Polonius moved behind the cloth. Shouting, 'A rat!' Hamlet took his machete and slashed through the cloth." I paused for dramatic effect. "He had killed Polonius!"

The old men looked at each other in supreme disgust. "That Polonius truly was a fool and a man who knew nothing! What child would not know enough to shout, 'It's me!'" With a pang, I remembered that these people are ardent hunters, always armed with bow, arrow, and machete; at the first rustle in the grass an arrow is aimed and ready, and the hunter shouts "Game!" If no human voice answers immediately, the arrow speeds on its way. Like a good hunter Hamlet had shouted, "A rat!"

I rushed in to save Polonius's reputation. "Polonius did speak. Hamlet heard him. But he thought it was the chief and wished to kill him to avenge his father. He had meant to kill him earlier that evening...." I broke down, unable to describe to these pagans, who had no belief in individual afterlife, the difference between dying at one's prayers and dying "unhousell'd, disappointed, unaneled."

This time I had shocked my audience seriously. "For a man to raise his hand against his father's brother and the one who has become his father – that is a terrible thing. The elders ought to let such a man be bewitched."

I nibbled at my kola nut in some perplexity, then pointed out that after all the man had killed Hamlet's father.

"No," pronounced the old man, speaking less to me than to the young men sitting behind the elders. "If your father's brother has killed your father, you must appeal to your father's age mates; *they* may avenge him. No man may use violence against his senior relatives." Another thought struck him. "But if his father's brother had indeed been wicked enough to bewitch Hamlet and make him mad that would be a good story indeed, for it would be his fault that Hamlet, being mad, no longer

had any sense and thus was ready to kill his father's brother."

There was a murmur of applause. *Hamlet* was again a good story to them, but it no longer seemed quite the same story to me. As I thought over the coming complications of plot and motive, I lost courage and decided to skim over dangerous ground quickly.

"The great chief," I went on, "was not sorry that Hamlet had killed Polonius. It gave him a reason to send Hamlet away, with his two treacherous age mates, with letters to a chief of a far country, saying that Hamlet should be killed. But Hamlet changed the writing on their papers, so that the chief killed his age mates instead." I encountered a reproachful glare from one of the men whom I had told undetectable forgery was not merely immoral but beyond human skill. I looked the other way.

"Before Hamlet could return, Laertes came back for his father's funeral. The great chief told him Hamlet had killed Polonius. Laertes swore to kill Hamlet because of this, and because his sister Ophelia, hearing her father had been killed by the man she loved, went mad and drowned in the river."

"Have you already forgotten what we told you?" The old man was reproachful. "One cannot take vengeance on a madman; Hamlet killed Polonius in his madness. As for the girl, she not only went mad, she was drowned. Only witches can make people drown. Water itself can't hurt anything. It is merely something one drinks and bathes in."

I began to get cross. "If you don't like the story, I'll stop."

The old man made soothing noises and himself poured me some more beer. "You tell the story well, and we are listening. But it is clear that the elders of your country have never told you what the story really means. No, don't interrupt! We believe you when you say your marriage customs are different, or your clothes and weapons. But people are the same everywhere; therefore, there are always witches and it is we, the elders, who know how witches work. We told you it was the great chief who wished to kill Hamlet, and now your own words have proved us right. Who were Ophelia's male relatives?"

"There were only her father and her brother." Hamlet was clearly out of my hands.

"There must have been many more; this also you must ask of your elders when you get back to your country. From what you tell us, since Polonius was dead, it must have been Laertes who killed Ophelia, although I do not see the reason for it."

We had emptied one pot of beer, and the old men argued the point with slightly tipsy interest. Finally one of them demanded of me, "What did the servant of Polonius say on his return?"

With difficulty I recollected Reynaldo and his mission. "I don't think he did return before Polonius was killed."

"Listen," said the elder, "and I will tell you how it was and how your story will go, then you may tell me if I am right. Polonius knew his son would get into trouble, and so he did. He had many fines to pay for fighting, and debts from gambling. But he had only two ways of getting money quickly. One was to marry off his sister at once, but it is difficult to find a man who will marry a woman desired by the son of a chief. For if the chief's heir commits adultery with your wife, what can you do? Only a fool calls a case against a man who will someday be his judge. Therefore Laertes had to take the second way: he killed his sister by witchcraft, drowning her so he could secretly sell her body to the witches."

I raised an objection. "They found her body and buried it. Indeed Laertes jumped into the grave to see his sister once more – so, you see, the body was truly there. Hamlet, who had just come back, jumped in after him."

"What did I tell you?" The elder appealed to the others. "Laertes was up to no good with his sister's body. Hamlet prevented him, because the chief's heir, like a chief, does not wish any other man to grow rich and powerful. Laertes would be angry, because he would have killed his sister without benefit to himself. In our country he would try to kill Hamlet for that reason. Is this not what happened?"

"More or less," I admitted. "When the great chief found Hamlet was still alive, he encouraged Laertes to try to kill Hamlet and arranged a fight with machetes between them. In the fight both the young men were wounded to death. Hamlet's mother drank the poisoned beer that the chief meant for Hamlet in case he won the fight. When he saw his mother die of poison, Hamlet, dying, managed to kill his father's brother with his machete."

"You see, I was right!" exclaimed the elder.

"That was a very good story," added the old man, "and you told it with very few mistakes. There was just one more error, at the very end. The poison Hamlet's mother drank was obviously meant for the survivor of the fight, whichever it was. If Laertes had won, the great chief would have poisoned him, for no one would know that he arranged Hamlet's death. Then, too, he need not fear Laertes' witchcraft; it takes a strong heart to kill one's only sister by witchcraft."

"Sometime," concluded the old man, gathering his ragged toga about him, "you must tell us some more stories of your country. We, who are elders, will instruct you in their true meaning, so that when you return to your own land your elders will see that you have not been sitting in the bush, but among those who know things and who have taught you wisdom."

CHAPTER 2

Spatial Locations

How do we situate or locate ourselves in space? Are notions of space "universal" or are they shaped by culture? This chapter explores these questions from macro to micro contexts, including discussion of maps, nations, segregation, public spaces, invisible spaces, and that space that is no place: cyberspace.

Spatial Locations

Space is, perhaps, our primary means of orientation in the world – physically, socially, and cosmologically. The need for spatial orientation is universal among humans, but the meanings of space are not. Space is neither empty nor neutral; it is filled with things and with meanings. Why is it, for example, that even when the physical distance is the same, it seems shorter when you go to visit a friend than when you have to run an odious errand? Physical space is rarely only that; it also encodes social meanings and values. In *Return to Laughter* (noted in chapter 1), Elenore Smith Bowen describes this very well:

> Some walks overtaxed my own strength. … One "not far" excursion put me to bed for a couple of days after a twenty-five-mile round trip without food or water, whereafter I set out on a "far" journey equipped with lunch and water, only to find it less than four miles in all. At first I thought their use of these words was incontrovertible evidence that they had no idea of distance. Then I figured out that "far" referred not only to space, but to time and social distance as well. ([1954] 1964: 52)

What does it mean if someone says, "Give me space!" What would or should your reaction be? Or, in a relationship, how do you feel if you are on the receiving end of a comment such as "I need some space"? Does it mean that the person needs a bigger room or a few acres to plant vegetables? No! It usually implies that the other person is feeling emotionally caged in, trapped, perhaps a little claustrophobic. Does it mean you are being too possessive? Personal space is also very much a matter of culture.

Americans tend to stand quite far apart when talking. If someone gets too close to us, we tend to take a step backward. We feel they are invading our "bubble" of private space – that pocket of air surrounding our body. In some cultures, speakers get so close you can

Investigating Culture: An Experiential Introduction to Anthropology, Second Edition.
Carol Delaney with Deborah Kaspin.
© 2011 Carol Delaney. Published by Blackwell Publishing Ltd.

feel and smell their breath. To many Americans, this would be offensive except in intimate situations or with an infant.

In this chapter we will explore a number of different levels of spatial organization and their effects on everyday life. Providing some ground under our conceptual feet, we will first look at spatial coordinates on earth and then briefly move to their wider cosmological moorings before coming back to earth to discuss the spatial divisions of nations and regions, the public spaces of work and leisure, and the more personal spaces of home and the very rooms we occupy. Finally, we will take a look at the new space that is no place, cyberspace, and consider the implications for rearrangements of space in the future.

Maps

When we enter another culture, we enter another world – not totally, of course, but to a greater or lesser extent. This is true even if it is another regional culture or the culture of a different ethnic group in one's own country. We need to orient ourselves and get our bearings. We need maps and guidebooks to tell us *what* is there and the *significance* of what we are seeing. It is difficult to get your bearings in a new city or new country without a map, even more so if you do not know the language, and especially if you do not know the writing system and, therefore, cannot even read the signs. For example, as an English speaker you could recognize the letters in French or German and could ask someone for a particular street address; but what if the signs were in Arabic or Chinese and you did not know those scripts? You couldn't even read the signs to be able to ask someone. In many of the cultures that anthropologists have studied, maps and guidebooks are scanty or nonexistent, and no one hands anthropologists an orientation packet. Each of us has to make our own mental map.

Even with a map, it can be difficult if the orientation is different from what is familiar. Conventionally, north is at the top of contemporary maps, but on the map of the Stanford University campus, north is at the bottom. No wonder people get lost! But why is north conventionally at the top? Who decided that, and what are the consequences? From the standpoint of outer space, there is no north. It depends on perspective, but whose? Ali Mazrui, Kenyan-born professor at both the University of Michigan and the University of Jos in Nigeria, and host of a nine-part television series on Africa, asked, "Is Europe *north* of Africa? Is Europe *up* and Africa *down* in geographical location, as well as in income, power, and global status? Of course, the maps say Europe is north of Africa (and therefore *up*). But that decision was arbitrary and made primarily by European mapmakers" (quoted in *Dial*, September 1986: 21–22). European mapmakers also distorted the size of continents. The Mercator map, which in various versions has been in common use since the sixteenth century, has had insidious consequences. Mazrui comments, "The visual memories of millions of children across generations have carried distorted ideas about the comparative physical scale of northern continents in relation to southern ones" (p. 22). For on that map North America is shown to be one and a half times the size of Africa, whereas Africa is three and a half times the size of North America! He suggests that

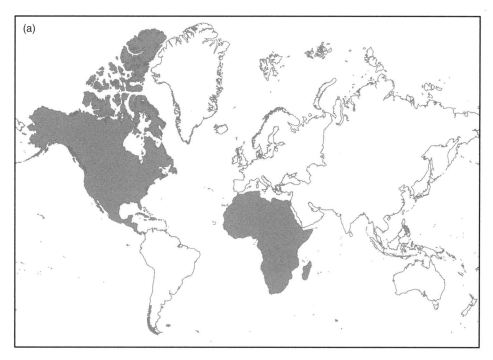

Figure 2.1a Mercator map. North America and Africa are shaded. Lynn Carlson, GISP, Brown University.

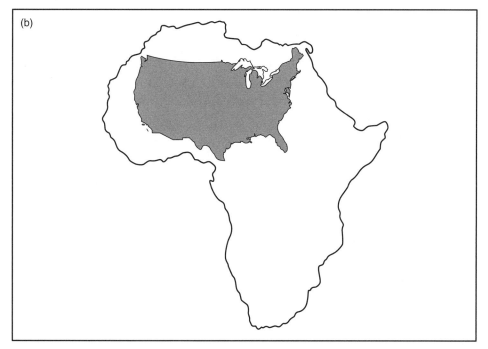

Figure 2.1b Africa, with the United States superimposed. Reprinted by permission of Waveland Press, Inc., from Bohannan, *Africa and Africans*, 4th ed. (Long Grove, IL: Waveland Press, Inc., 1995). All rights reserved.

every class ought to experiment with turning the world upside down. (See figures 2.1a and 2.1b.)

Similar things can be said about east and west, because what is east to one is west to another. I spent most of my life on the east coast of the United States; to me, "large body of water" (the Atlantic) was east and west always meant the Wild West – the high mountains of Colorado and Wyoming. When I moved to California, I got very disoriented. If someone gave me directions to go east, I naturally headed in the direction of "large body of water" (i.e., the Pacific), and when they told me to go west, I headed inland in the direction of Wyoming and Colorado. In my own mental map I had never really considered California part of the west – it was beyond the pale, another place altogether. Once our mental maps are ingrained, they are very difficult to dislodge. The artist Steinberg expressed this visually in his humorous map of the world from the perspective of a New Yorker, where known places beyond the Hudson River were few and their locale vague. Others, such as Mark Fiore, have made their own versions (see figure 2.2).

When l lived in California, I had to go west to get to the Far East. Somewhere over the Pacific a line was drawn determining our spatial and temporal coordinates, so that in crossing the Pacific, you enter not only the "East" but also a new day; it is also where we

Figure 2.2 Post-9/11 version of Saul Steinberg's *View of the World from 9th Avenue*, by Mark Fiore. Published in *San Francisco Chronicle* (September 30, 2001). © Mark Fiore.

entered the new millennium. The placing of that line was and is arbitrary; it was made not just by human decision but also by the decision of a few people. Maps, then, are not just physical guides but also ideological ones. Think of the meanings we have invested in "East" and "West," "Western culture," "the Orient," and the "Middle East." These meanings have become incorporated in our notions of the way the world *is*. Yet we need to ask why is the area that is now occupied by Israel and a number of Arab nations called the "Middle East," or the "Near East"? For whom is it "near" or "middle"? Whose view of the world is being imposed, and what are the implications? (Cf. Said 1979: 19 for a detailed discussion.)

Cosmology

Such meanings may be more obvious in medieval maps of the world, *mappae mundi* as they are called (see figure 2.3). On these maps, heavily influenced by a Christian worldview and often made by monks, east, not north, was generally at the top because that is where Paradise (the Garden of Eden) was presumed to be. In that worldview, there were only three continents, Asia, Africa, and Europe, and each was populated by the descendants of one of Noah's three sons, Shem, Ham, and Japheth (Genesis 9:18–19). Maps like these shaped the imaginations of medieval Europeans, including Christopher Columbus, who, when he landed in the new world, thought he had reached an island at the periphery of Asia.

Figure 2.3   T-O type, Mappae Mundi. Lynn Carlson, GISP, Brown University.

Humans everywhere have cosmic concepts. They are oriented not only on the earth but also in a universe or cosmos, although maybe even the notion of *uni*-verse is not universal since it implies one world organized by the same principles. We speak of four directions, four cardinal points, four *corners* of the globe. But there can be no corners on a round earth. Over the last half-century, we have seen what our planet looks like from outer space. In the photographs taken by astronauts, our planet looks blue and is swathed in clouds and floating in space. This space is imagined as relatively empty, not layered as in ancient and medieval worldviews. *Empty* also implies devoid of meaning. We think of the planet as physical material that can be explored scientifically, an idea we think came from the Greeks, yet it also derives from the biblical worldview. It was precisely the belief in the separation of the Creator from Creation, the simplification of power to one dynamic principle, and the lawful organization of matter that allowed early modern scientists to think they were investigating God's laws embedded in the material (nature) he supposedly created. The scientific notion of nature is, thus, intimately involved with a biblical worldview. In this worldview, there is a distinction between the divine and the material (supernatural vs. natural); not only do they stand in hierarchical relation, but also there is felt to be no divine *in* nature and vice versa. This is not the case in other cosmologies, other worldviews. While the cosmos can be explored scientifically, it depends upon a *prior* notion of cosmos that is, itself, derived from a religious worldview. The separation of divine from physical is peculiarly Western and has all kinds of implications for the way we imagine our lives and our place in the world. It has implications for our exploitation of resources and the disdain that we often exhibit toward people with very different cosmologies.

Cosmic concepts are not dependent on what is personally seen or experienced. Instead, by symbolic means, humans construct and live in spatially coordinated worlds that transcend personal or individual experience. Today people talk with ease about "outer space," even though only a few have ever been there and not very far. And there are competing theories about how it is shaped and how far it extends, and these theories are first and foremost based on mental images – images that by and large have been constructed in a particular cultural milieu. By planting the American flag on the moon, were the astronauts staking a claim to that territory? Some people think they can colonize "outer space," that they can create boundaries and shields that will keep certain things in and other things out. But by what right? Still others have begun to think about finding new planets to inhabit once we have destroyed this one, an idea that no doubt influenced and was popularized by *Star Trek*.

In the medieval Christian worldview, the Garden of Eden and Heaven and Hell were imagined as if they existed in physical space. Some people still hold this view. Regardless, no one except Adam and Eve (if you believe they existed) has ever seen or experienced the Garden of Eden, yet some people are looking for the archaeological remains of it, which they believe are in modern-day Bahrain. Hell, as a physical place, has surely fired the imaginations of millions of people and helped to keep them on the straight and narrow path – a moral concept that is, nevertheless, spatially expressed.

Cosmology, then, is not just the science of the stars but also, as I use it, a term for worldview in its widest cultural meaning. It gives us a sense of where we are and what kind of world we live in. Conversely, cultural notions of what kind of world it is also influence the mental images that scientific cosmologists turn into theories. It is a two-way exchange.

Nations and Regions

Between "outer space" and "inner space," there is a wide range of spatial concepts that order and organize our lives – from the nation and region, to public spaces, parks, buildings, houses, and rooms. First, let us think about the nation. We take it for granted that nations are the natural, obvious way to divide up the world – but only because we have been born into a world that is divided into nations. The notion of a nation as a *bounded territory* is a very Western and relatively modern idea; *nation* (from *natio* or birth) used to mean a people identified by language and religion rather than a specific piece of land.

Arabs, too, have had a very different notion of land. Borders were unimportant, maybe nonexistent. This made perfect sense in an area that was mostly desert and that had to be crossed in order to get someplace – to the oases, water, and people. So they did not have borders around their territories. The lines drawn in the sand, literally, by the British at the end of World War I created the nations of Iraq, Lebanon, Syria, and Palestine. These bounded territories had little to do with the inhabitants' notions of land. Not surprisingly, the lines have been contentious ever since. The one drawn between Iraq and Kuwait, for example, divided what had been one territory under the control of the Ottomans. Not only that, but also it created tensions over the land bordering the Arabian Gulf – especially when it transected the oil fields and left Iraq a tiny exit to the sea. The Gulf War of 1991 was fought to maintain the line. Another line, drawn after World War II, has been a continuous source of friction that portends to draw not just the Middle East but also the whole world into a conflagration – that is, the line that created the state of Israel from Palestinian land.

Other people, too, have very different notions of land and territory. Some think it a very strange idea that individuals can *own* a piece of the planet, enclose it for their own use, and even defend it at gunpoint. They think of land as a resource for all humans, or at least for those who have rights of usufruct. And where land ownership is recognized, it can vary widely in scope and meaning. When the United States was founded, land ownership entitled white men to vote, in a sense giving them – and only them – status as real people. In the United States today, land ownership is no longer a prerequisite for voting rights, but it does confer tax benefits that homeless people and renters (arguably those who need them most) cannot claim.

Nomadic peoples as a rule do not accept the notion of bounded territory. They are accustomed to traversing a wide area in search of pasture for their animals. While they often visit the same places in their yearlong cycle, they do not have a permanent residence. When the land they were accustomed to crossing was divided between different nations, the issue of borders became volatile, leading governments to take measures to force nomadic peoples to adopt sedentary lifestyles. Gypsies also roam far and wide, not so much to pasture animals as to trade and do odd jobs. They, too, make "nations" very nervous, since they cross borders and do not give allegiance to any nation in particular. Migrant workers also move across land in search of work. They, too, confound a system that assumes permanent residence and a permanent place of work, making it difficult for them to get health and social security benefits or to enroll their children in school. All of these groups are examples of what British anthropologist Mary Douglas calls "matter out of place." In her book *Purity and Danger* (1966), she argues that anything that confounds a particular system of order is "matter out of place." Because the boundaries or lines of the system have been sullied, the offending matter is culturally perceived as polluting, as dirt.

Even more than migrants, nomads, or gypsies, the homeless confound the social order. With no place to call their own, they are forced to live "on the street," spectacularly exemplifying Mary Douglas's notion of "matter out of place." No wonder they are so often considered polluting. City officials try to move them to get them out of sight, and people walking down the street often turn their heads away, pretending not to see them. Perhaps they fear contamination. Or perhaps they are too discomfited by such palpable evidence of social *dis*order to acknowledge that homeless people exist.[1] The social invisibility of these people-out-of-place is poignantly and powerfully illustrated by the fate of homeless children, who, when they die,

> are buried in an unmarked grave in a ditch at a place called Potter's Field. Potter's Field is New York City's public burial ground, it's on an island in Long Island Sound, it's part of a prison colony. The children are brought there from hospital morgues and buried by prison inmates. No ceremony memorializes their existence. Their mothers can't attend their burial, and that may be just as well. It wouldn't be consoling. Half the people buried in Potter's Field since 1981 are infants. A lot of them the children of the homeless. (Kozol 1989: 13)

Spatial Segregation

Australian aborigines, tenants on that continent for 40,000 years, had a very unusual notion of their land. Their land is fairly barren; to our eyes there are few distinguishing markers to orient and direct us. But for them it was filled with signs derived from their cosmology and from their stories about the Ancestors who had traveled across the vast territory *singing* about the sites and thus naming them. These "songlines … created ways of communication between the most far-flung groups. … A 'song' … was both map and direction-finder. Providing you knew the song, you could always find your way across the country … [for] the distance between two … sites can be measured as a stretch of song" (Chatwin 1987: 13). The late Bruce Chatwin was a travel writer, not an anthropologist, yet, after the time he spent with the aborigines, he was able to convey their notion of space and land better than many of the anthropologists. The aborigines, he said, "could not imagine territory as a block of land hemmed in by frontiers: but rather as an interlocking network of 'lines' or 'ways through'" (p. 56), that is, the songlines. This is not to say they were, therefore, landless or had no system of ownership. He explained that

> everyone inherited, as his or her private property, a stretch of the Ancestor's song and the stretch of country over which the song passed. A man's verses were his title deeds to territory. He could lend them to others. He could borrow other verses in return. The one thing he couldn't do was sell or get rid of them. (p. 57)

When the British arrived, they took over the aborigines' land, put them on reservations, or sent them to work on cattle ranches. The indigenous population was decimated by European diseases and by the despondency created as their way of life and their identity were destroyed. Recently, however, some groups are attempting to restore their culture and reclaim certain specific sites.

Similar things happened to the aboriginal population of the Americas. While there is much debate over the estimates of the indigenous Caribbean population before the arrival of Columbus and the Spaniards, it is believed there were somewhere between 1 and 8 million people living in the islands. Within thirty years of the Europeans' arrival, about 80 percent of them had died, mostly from diseases like smallpox to which they were not immune. Although he was not often there when atrocities occurred, Columbus has been blamed for what is, most definitely, an enormous tragedy.

In North America, things were not so different. The settlers (invaders) apparently assumed they had a divine right to the land as their "manifest destiny," since they were bringing true religion and civilization to the "naked" savages. They often justified their actions with biblical quotes, such as "Ask of me, and I shall give thee, the heathen for thine inheritance, and the uttermost parts of the earth for thy possession" (Psalm 2:8), and "Whosoever therefore resisteth the power, resisteth the ordinance of God: and they that resist shall receive to themselves damnation" (Romans 13:2). The number of Native Americans who perished during the conquest has been subject to considerable research, but current scholarship places the rate of extermination at 98% to 99%. This "vastly exceed[s] that experienced by the Jews of Europe under the Nazis ... [and] represents a scale and scope of genocide without parallel in recorded human history" (Jaime 1992: 7). Those who survived often had their land taken by broken treaties or by being "relocated" onto reservations that, not surprisingly, had the least arable land. The social problems that resulted from this devastation were subsequently blamed on the victims.

The pattern of disinheriting Native Americans continues to the present day. The most recent example concerns Yucca Mountain in Nevada. This mountain, which is sacred to both Western Shoshone and Paiute groups, is located on Western Shoshone land that is supposedly guaranteed by treaty. Yet in 2002, President George W. Bush pushed through legislation that designated it as the dump site for nuclear waste, thereby abrogating the treaty. In 2006, the newly Democratic Senate blocked construction of the project, and in 2009, the Obama administration proposed to eliminate all funding for it. But Congress has not enacted this proposal. For now, the Yucca Mountain project is delayed but not defunct, and Native Americans continue their fight to regain some of their lands or the benefits from it.

The removal of Native Americans to reservations was one form of racial-spatial segregation. So, too, was apartheid in South Africa. Although that system has been dismantled, lines are still drawn that keep blacks separate from whites. Inferior education, formidable housing costs, and job segregation contribute to the separation. The same institutionalized segregation was and is practiced in the United States. Until relatively recently, there were separate places for blacks and whites – bathrooms, lunch counters, neighborhoods, churches, and schools – the space of the South divided up between different groups of people. The inner-city ghettos in the North are another outcome of that legacy as blacks escaped from the confines of the South.

But spatial divisions do not always divide people who are racially or linguistically different. The "Berlin Wall," first erected during the night of August 12–13, 1961, eventually extended not only 28 miles through Berlin but also an additional 75 miles around West Berlin, effectively making it an island in the middle of East Germany. The Wall divided people who considered themselves a nation in the sense of a people of the same "stock" (another term that means something very similar to race), language, and religion. The Wall was a structure that not only separated East from West, but also became a major source of orientation both spatially and temporally for all Berliners, albeit from two different perspectives. It provided a physical frame for the construction of different narratives within which the individuals on both sides made sense of their lives. The physical division into two countries for almost 30 years created two different peoples with different histories; they lived with different ideologies that permeated their life experiences. The assumption that they were really the same people (race, ethnic group) created problems during the so-called unification after the Wall came down in the fall of 1989, and the problems of cultural division continue. And yet, despite the evidence that the Berlin Wall created more problems than it solved, governments continue to erect walls to secure territories and populations, and to solidify cultural cohesion on one side – their own side – of them. Witness Israel's "security fence" – or "apartheid wall" as Palestinians see it – dividing Israel from parts of the West Bank, and the United States' "security fence" dividing Texas from Mexico.

While states sometimes build barriers to wall off their territories from outsiders, they – or their citizens – also build barriers to separate social groups within their territories. Americans call these internal divisions *ghettos*, a term that originally referred to sections in European cities set aside for Jews, and today refers to areas of American cities where poor people or minorities live. The *barrios* in Brazil and the *gecekondu* in Turkey are similar phenomena. But there are also ghettos for the middle class and the affluent. I used to live in what was called "the faculty ghetto" at Stanford because it was a place on the campus where *only* faculty could live. At one time, this was a facetious and somewhat derogatory name because of all the beautiful homes there. But in the 1980s, because of the enormous increase in housing costs in the surrounding Silicon Valley, it became one of the few places where faculty could afford to live. The recent development of "gated communities" is, perhaps, a better example. These are "ghettos" of the rich; they keep out "unwanted elements" and keep in "desirable" people like themselves. Some of these communities make further distinctions when they are designed expressly for singles or for retired people.

We have seen how spaces are divided by race, ethnicity, and income, but they are also divided by gender, age, occupation, and habit. In a book called *Women and Space: Ground Rules and Social Maps*, the editor Shirley Ardener notes that

> any restricted area such as a club, theatre or nation-state has rules determining its boundary,
> how it shall be crossed, who can occupy that space. In order to do so one must meet certain
> kinds of criteria (become a member, buy a ticket, get a visa, pass a citizenship test) and each
> has a gate-keeper whether that is a porter, usher, or Immigration Officer. (Ardener 1981: 11)

It is important to recognize how space keeps certain people in and out. Prisons and mental hospitals are obvious examples, but courts, churches, offices, government buildings, and even public parks also regulate the people who enter and exit them. Who has freedom of movement? In a classroom, who can walk about? In an office, which people are "chained to their desks"? Who feels safe walking in a city at night or in a large park alone? A number of years ago when I was living in Cambridge, Massachusetts, the mayor put a curfew on women after dark because there had been an increase in the number of attacks and rapes. I called and asked why not put the curfew on men since they were the ones creating the problem. Why not let women, for once, have free use of the streets? (My request was not instituted.) The same idea seems to have inspired the "Take Back the Night" events that began in England in the late 1970s but quickly became international in scope, although organized by local communities. Women, men, and children march to protest violence against women and families and to make it safe to walk at night. Very few men, I think, understand the restricted spaces in which women can move easily and freely and the effects of this on their lives (cf. Massey 1994).

In many places in the world, there are spaces divided by gender – the "men's house," for example, in a number of cultures we label "primitive." But the same is true for certain places in the so-called civilized, industrial world; in Turkey, men can sip tea in the *çayhane* but women are excluded, and there have been (and still are) men's clubs in Britain and the United States. Silvia Rodgers (1981) compared the Iatmul men's house in New Guinea with the British House of Commons, with striking results. Throughout most of its history, the House of Commons *was* a men's house. "The classification of physical space," Rodgers claims, "derives from the cultural map of political power" (1981: 53). The speaker of the house sits at the front, and members of the party currently in power sit in front of him on his right, the opposition on the left. After his ceremonial entry, the speaker's prayers both open the session and make a direct link to the sacred power of the church. "A member's entry and exit into the chamber is marked by a bow towards the Chair" (1981: 53). Since all of these positions have traditionally been held by men, it is not too surprising that it was very difficult for them to accept women in their midst; they appear to be "matter out of place." Since 1919, women have been able to be elected to Parliament, yet there are still very few female members, in part because of the pervasive atmosphere and veiled hostility. One seemingly trivial way they were "told" they did not belong concerned the bathrooms. The women's bathroom was clearly marked "Private, Lady Members Only," while the men's room had emblazoned on the door, "Members Only." "Does this demonstrate the implicit assumption that in the symbolic ordering of the British political system the members of the House are men?" (p. 55). No doubt very similar things could be said about the US Congress, especially the Senate, where there are so few women.

Spaces in Cities

Cities developed in the ancient Near East around 4000 BC – Erech and Ur in Sumer, now Iraq, are thought to be the oldest cities. Although cities are a very efficient way to consolidate power, they are extremely dependent on those outside it, unlike peasant villages or nomadic encampments, which are much more self-sufficient. Think of what is necessary for a city to come into being and to maintain itself. Primary, of course, is a source and control of water and a system to provision inhabitants with food; both of these imply political organization, consolidation of power, and thus hierarchy. In addition, there must be certain kinds of building materials and styles of housing that can accommodate large numbers of people in a smaller space. And yet, despite the material needs of cities, those needs do not dictate their design. This is an artifact of culture.

Edward Hall has noted that in Europe, there are two major systems for patterning space. One of these, found primarily in France and Spain, is the "radiating star," while the other is the grid that traveled from Asia Minor (ancient Turkey) with Caesar to England (Hall 1966: 137). The contrast becomes obvious if you compare the Place de la Concorde in Paris with the numbered streets in New York, Chicago, or San Francisco. Hall claims that the "French-Spanish system connects all points and functions … [while] the grid system separates activities by stringing them out" (p. 137). It is something worth pondering, especially his further claim that the former is sociopetal while the other is sociofugal; in other words, one brings people together, while the other tends to disperse them.

Cities are also generally divided up into a variety of sections by activity, such as the business or financial section, the shopping section, and the theater district. They are also divided by ethnic group and by income category.[2] Look around your city or the one closest to you and try to figure out who lives where, and who does what where and when. In the not too distant past, cities were the major places to shop. Even if you lived outside the city, you had to go to the city, indeed "downtown," to shop for a new dress, a coat, or a pair of shoes. It was an outing, a special occasion. Downtown areas in cities, and Main Streets in towns, began to decline in the 1960s when a very different phenomenon began to appear – the shopping mall. A mall is set outside the city and even outside the town. At first, people wondered who would go there. There is nothing there! Today, it is probably where most people do their shopping. Shopping malls are thought to provide the variety of the city with the convenience of the country since it is much easier to park the car at a mall than "downtown." They are also self-contained worlds – there are not only department-type stores but also numerous specialty shops featuring items such as shoes, jewelry, toys, children's clothes, sporting goods, and evening wear. Many also have flower shops and grocery stores as well as coffee shops, restaurants, beauty parlors, spas, movie theaters, video game halls, and even places to leave the children for a couple of hours while adults shop. It is a totally artificial environment, not rooted to any place in particular, although there are variations and differences related to the wealth of the communities around them. But it is this environment that has become especially popular as a "meeting place" for young people among whom a whole "mall culture" has sprung up. Investigations of this phenomenon have begun to yield insights not just about adolescents but also about the effect of space on notions of self and consumer versus citizen.

It is also interesting to consider the difference between an American mall and the shopping areas in Middle Eastern cities. In the Middle East, each shopping area has numerous shops selling the same kind of things rather than a variety of things in one place. That means that in one area or street you will find only leather goods, in another kitchenware, or carpets, or wedding clothes, or goldsellers. Each shop has the very same kind of items, for example, gold bracelets, earrings, and necklaces; there may be a slight variation in styles but basically the same items are sold in each shop. This arrangement may have the unintended consequence of keeping the shopkeepers relatively honest, because if one of them began to charge exorbitant prices, he could lose customers to his neighbors who are not. The reasons you patronize one rather than another is not so much because of the difference in the items sold as because of social connections, because it is run by a relative or a friend, or it was recommended by one. Generally, each shopping excursion has a specific purpose in mind. There are exceptions, of course. For example, in some Middle Eastern cities there are "passages" – spaces between buildings or underground where a variety of small shops coexist. This is also true in the Grand Bazaar (*Kapılı Çarsı*, or Covered Bazaar) in Istanbul, perhaps the world's first shopping mall, established soon after the Muslim conquest of the city in 1453. Today, there are about 4,000 tiny shops selling a variety of goods under its roof. Nevertheless, they are still arranged in different "streets" according to the type of item sold, for example, "the goldsellers' street."

Public Places

All cities, towns, and even villages have public places where numbers of people can gather, not only for ceremonial displays or protests but also where more informal meetings can take place. There are public squares such as Red Square in Moscow, Trafalgar Square in London, or Times Square in New York, as well as parks and green spaces – the Mall in Washington, DC; Hyde Park in London; and Central Park in New York. While parks such as these also serve as major public gathering places, they are used more informally as well – for reading the newspaper, for picnics, for pushing the baby carriage, or for jogging. Not only do they break up the monotony and oppressiveness of buildings, but they also provide a breathing space for the city's inhabitants. Nevertheless, different cultures have very different ideas about what a park is and what it should look like. In Paris, for instance, the parks are very well manicured and are often filled with formal gardens, fountains, statuary, and artificial pools of water. People keep to the graveled paths and sit on park benches. The whole thing is extremely decorous. In contrast, in Berlin, there are many parks scattered all over the city and some of them are quite wild – lots of woods and bushes and natural ponds. People ride their bikes and even horses on the paths and sit or lie down on the grass or ground. It gives Berliners a feeling they have been able to get into the countryside even in the heart of the city. I taught in Berlin for a semester, and at first I was quite wary of going into these parks alone because of my enculturation in the United States, where entering such a place can be extremely risky for women. But this does not seem to be the case in Berlin; I never heard of any assaults against women in parks. This is not to say they did not or never happen, but it would be an unusual event, and I saw many women walking alone, sitting and reading alone, and even sunbathing topless alone. They seemed to have the feeling that they had as much right to the use of the parks as men – at any time. More importantly, the men did not seem to feel this as an infringement on *their* space. What do you think accounts for this difference? More importantly, what do you think is necessary to make it safe for women to walk in parks day or night? What other ways do you think the space of the city is felt and used differently according to gender?

In the United States, at the other end of the spectrum from city or town parks are state parks and national parks. These are away from cities and towns and demand a more extended excursion. They are not just a place to stroll at lunchtime or after the evening meal. Although they are public, they are usually not free but require an entrance or use fee. State parks are meant primarily as recreational spaces for their citizens; they are designed for family activities – swimming, boating, games, and some camping. State parks tend to be more domesticated, while national parks were designed to protect "wilderness" areas from human traffic. "In wildness is the preservation of the world," said Henry David Thoreau,[3] who not only gave expression to a vigorous but suppressed religious belief in the effects of nature (cf. Albanese 1990) but also, unknowingly, gave inspiration for a movement to preserve the United States' wilderness areas for posterity.

Yet, despite the image of wilderness, national parks are well controlled. There are designated places for tourists, normally on the periphery, so they might get some sense of the natural beauty; but except for these places there are few domestic amenities in national parks. Those who wish to enter the "wild" must usually get permission and enter at their own risk. These parks provide a space for wild animals and dwindling numbers of endangered species. While it is also a place for some people to escape, for a brief period of time, the intrusions, especially the noise, of modern life, the park often displaced the people who had been living there. National parks are also often the site where certain people play out the cultural myths of "returning to nature," often with dire consequences. An especially poignant story is told in *Into the Wild* by Jon Krakauer (1996), which was made into a hit movie in 2007.

Other Public Spaces

Sporting arenas and museums can also be considered public spaces since generally anyone who can afford a ticket can enter that space. And they are also considered public because they are often, but not always, supported by public taxes. Further along this continuum are such places as movie theaters, cafés, and pubs. These are privately owned, sometimes by corporations, but public insofar as anyone who can pay the price of admission or is of the appropriate age can enter.

Restaurants, too, are semipublic spaces. Some are extremely exclusive due to prohibitive cost, and others attract only a young boisterous crowd. Women often feel "out of place" if they go alone, and sometimes are made to feel that way, while the lone male diner rarely experiences the same stigma. Some American restaurants have "family sections" to separate adults with babies and children from adults who wish to dine by themselves. Consider by contrast the "family restaurants" in Turkey. There, at least in some towns, it is felt to be inappropriate for women unaccompanied by men to be seen in restaurants, so "family restaurant" means a place where women can eat with or without their children.

Almost every American restaurant now has a smoking section, segregating people by their habit, and recently, some restaurants have set aside separate sections for cell phone users. What other kinds of sections or divisions do you find? A restaurant is a good place to examine social divisions. Look closely at who is occupying which spaces. Who is working behind the scenes? Who is in the dining area? While it is true that these very same people might change places in another location, or at another restaurant, the social divisions still remain.

Let us return, briefly, to the subject of bathrooms. In the United States, bathrooms in public places are generally segregated by sex. If there is just one bathroom, each sex would use it separately. That is not what I found in what I considered staid Belgium. There the toilets are often unisex, which means that both men and women use the same bathroom at the same time. I found it a bit disconcerting. In American public bathrooms, there are now often tiny places for changing baby diapers – but they are generally only in the women's bathrooms, a subtle indication that American culture views diaper changing a woman's job. In Scandinavian countries, in contrast, there are such areas in both men's and women's bathrooms. What different notions of gender are being expressed?

Work Space

When you enter a large office, aren't you immediately aware of the status of the person sitting at the desk? Or at least you make assumptions about it. The status is communicated not just by the plush carpets, the view, and the furnishings, but also from the sheer size of the office. The size of an office, even if the difference is only a few square feet, can create all kinds of personnel issues and conflicts. In academia, which is the place I know best, there is a pecking order for who gets what office and it would be an insult if you were more senior but got a smaller office than a new assistant professor. In Turkey, professors generally have to share offices. Meanwhile, in France, professors generally do not have offices at all! They work at home and meet students in cafés. How do you think status would be communicated there? In American business, a president, vice president, or chief executive officer will normally have a large office with a view, often on a different, usually higher, floor. But even the head of a particular department will have a private office – often in a corner or place somewhat away from the other workers. By contrast, "the man in charge of a French office can often be found in the middle – with his minions placed like satellites on strings radiating outward from him" (Hall 1966: 138). In Britain, when Hall's book was written, the members of Parliament had no offices but apparently "conduct[ed] their business on the terrace overlooking the Thames" (p. 130). How do you think American congress members would have reacted to that?

We spend a great deal of our time working, so therefore work space is important for how we feel about ourselves. Different occupations demand different kinds of spaces: scientists need laboratories; architects need large tables, chefs need kitchens, and so on. But if the space is designed only for efficiency without taking into consideration workers' needs, they will probably not be very efficient. In factories, priority is given over to machines; how do you think that affects how workers view themselves and their work, especially when a foreman is watching from a platform above the workfloor? When you visit a business, observe how the space is arranged. Where do the clerical staff sit, and what kind of space are they allotted? Who has an office? Are there separate spaces for eating, for recreation, and for child care? What can you tell about the business just by the spatial arrangements?

Houses and Rooms

Forms of shelter, or what I shall call *houses* for purposes of simplification, are enormously varied – not just across the world, but also across time and region. This is a huge and interesting subject that we can only touch upon. Houses express who we are, both as individuals and as peoples. They vary not just in the materials used but also in square footage, layout, and design – in other words, their use of space. In an extraordinary book, *The Material World* (Menzel 1994), a photographer set about the task of making portraits of people and their possessions in different parts of the world. He was interested to get a "representative" family, that is, a family that represented the statistical average. In Mali, for instance, a family of seven live in an adobe (mudbrick) house that is 540 sq. ft.; in South Africa, the same number of people live in a cement block house of 400 sq. ft. In Mongolia, a family of six live in a *yurt* (a one-room round tent) that is only 200 sq. ft., while in Kuwait a family of the same size has 4,850 sq. ft. to move around in. The average in the United States was a family of four living in 1,600 sq. ft. In all of these countries, there is obviously a wide variation in wealth, family size, and house size, but the averages, nevertheless, tell a great deal about the "normal" lifestyle and spatial values in each cultures.

I thought a lot about this when I spent a year in the Groot Begijnhof in Leuven, Belgium. Established in AD 1230 for a group of *béguines* (pious laywomen) who devoted themselves to charitable work, it was taken over by the Katholieke Universiteit te Leuven in 1962 as a residence for faculty and visiting scholars. The Begijnhof was a beautiful, quiet place cut off from the traffic and noise of the city by a surrounding wall. There were streams and tiny footbridges connecting different parts of it; the houses were of brick and half-timber – the size and scale depending on each woman's circumstance – and each one had a tiny garden and a view. What really struck me, however, was the exquisite and careful design of the facility that could consolidate many residents without sacrificing their privacy. In that tiny enclosed space, even though houses were right next to or across from each other, you could not see into your neighbor's home.

Turkish example

Turkish living space varies considerably from city to village. In the cities, and even now in towns, very few people live in houses anymore. Most people live in apartment buildings of four to eight stories. While there are significant differences regarding luxury, especially size and materials, most are fairly similar in design: generally, each apartment has three to four bedrooms, and there are only four apartments on each floor, with each commanding a corner. It is assumed that people have children and even newly married people generally live with their parents until they can afford to buy their own flat. The few people who live in separate houses are either the very rich who, for example, live in villas along the Bosphorus in Istanbul, or the very poor who live in makeshift houses in the *gecekondu* (literally, built in a night) areas on the outskirts of the city, or in villages.

In the village where I conducted my fieldwork, most of the people lived with their extended family in traditional houses made of mudbrick. Today, many villagers are constructing houses of cement block, which are considered "modern." However, cement blocks do not provide as good insulation as mudbrick, which stays warm in the winter and cool in the summer. There was also a fairly standard design for the living space, called *karnıyarık*, which means "split womb." Such a house is meant to accommodate several families: ideally of brothers, but often including their parents. The house I lived in was only half a *karnıyarık*; but the example (seen in figures 2.4 and 2.5) shows two typical *karnıyarık* designs and also a half. In the middle house there is a central hallway, called *hayat*, which means life. Each room is, in theory, considered to be an entire house (perhaps evoking memories of the Turks' nomadic past, when they lived in tents), though today some rooms are distinguished by function (i.e., bedroom, kitchen, or sitting room). Often, however, the sitting room is multifunctional: people sleep there, cook there, eat there, bathe there, and sew and knit and card wool there. I once even saw the carcass of a whole cow being cut up for various forms of meat. Divans are placed against the walls all around the room, and possessions are stored underneath. Rarely is there a table or chairs. The major large piece of furniture is a cupboard in which the television is placed and other important mementos such as photographs or postcards. A relatively small room in a Turkish village house can easily accommodate 20–50 people for dancing during wedding activities, for example. In the same-sized room, most Americans would begin to feel uncomfortable if there were more than five people occupying that space – so filled are our rooms with large pieces of furniture. Today, however, when young Turkish villagers get married, they are requesting living room, dining room, and bedroom "sets" that represent to them a more "modern" lifestyle.

In the village, people generally live on the second story of their houses; the ground floor is for animals, machinery, and storage space for food, and is often the place where bread and cheese are made. Animals are typically sheltered beneath the living quarters so that their warmth also warms the house. The house complex is surrounded by a wall, part of which actually is a house wall. A gate, however flimsy, marks a very important boundary – it signifies that the house area is private. Anyone who enters must call out. Women are freer to enter houses because the house is the woman's place. An unrelated man must wait at the gate or just inside the entrance to the courtyard. Not surprisingly, *thresholds* carry symbolic importance – the entrance not only to the complex but also to the house proper. Before entering a house, people must remove their shoes.

Inside the house, the space is not neutral but is meaningfully (culturally) coded. Every child knows implicitly what the *seating arrangements* are. Old men sit on the divan near the window and farthest from the door. Other men sit next to them, while women sit on the floor or on other divans. A person's rank and relative value are expressed in these arrangements. When a group gathered, I formed a boundary between male and female. I was in a "liminal" space, "betwixt and between" the categories of honored guest and woman (an honorary man in some instances).

Once outside the house, the space is also coded. Because the lanes and paths between houses are considered public, and therefore dirty, people throw their garbage there. It is expected that the dogs, goats, and other animals that pass by will eat it. As the house is the primary preserve of women, the streets are men's space, and women are not as free to move around there. In the village a woman needed permission from her father or husband to visit another woman in the village, even if she lived just across the street, and normally she

Figure 2.4 Plan of "my" house – half a *karnıyarık*. Drawn by Oya Aksoy.

Figure 2.5   Typical *karnıyarık* layout. Drawn by Oya Aksoy.

had to be accompanied. Although it took less than 10 minutes to walk from one end of the village to the other, women did not walk around alone. To leave the village was impossible without permission, and, besides, everyone would see you. Moreover, there were miles of "wild" space between the village and the nearest town (40 kilometers away), and that space was for shepherds, their flocks, and the vicious dogs who are trained to attack intruders. Young men did not need permission to walk around the village – that was their domain – but they did need it to leave the village in order to go to town.

You can understand how my relatively free movements were unsettling for the villagers. They often asked me, "Who gave you permission to come to our village?" "Was it your father, your university, or your government?" It became an issue every time I left the village – to get supplies or to visit friends in the city and pick up my mail. Since the teachers and the midwife (who were outsiders) needed to have government permission to leave, didn't I? I solved this problem by informing the *muhtar* (headman) every time I was planning to leave and when I was planning to return so that he could answer their inquiries and not have his honor called into question.

The inside–outside dichotomy was replicated at other levels of structure. Inside and outside the village had many of the same meanings as the inside and outside of the house. Villagers thought of their village as *kapalı* (closed), which is the same word used to refer to women who cover their hair. The headscarf symbolizes that the women are *kapalı*, closed, off limits.[4] They are enclosed by the honor and protection of their menfolk. Although there was no wall around the village, there might just as well have been. Outsiders could be seen approaching the village and would be scrutinized. For insiders, entering the village felt similar to entering a home: you felt as if you were entering a place of refuge and protection.

Inside and outside the nation carries similar connotations. At the collapse of the Ottoman Empire, Atatürk was able to rally the people to the nation's honor that had been defiled by the capitulations the Ottomans made to outside powers. He felt called upon to establish the borders of the nation, to keep outsiders out and fellow citizens in. For Muslim Turks, the whole world should be under the protection of God; they think of non-Muslims as living in Dar el Harb (The Place/Space of War), while they themselves live in Dar es Islam (The Abode of the Muslims, i.e., those who *submit* to God).

What is not often noticed is that these physical places are symbolically coded as female, while their rulers and representatives are male. Thus men rule over and represent the household in public records and gatherings; the elected headman of the village rules the village and represents it to the government; and a man has always been president (although there has been one female prime minister, Tansu Çiller) who rules over and represents the nation to the rest of the world. And ultimately, God, also symbolically male, rules over all (see figure 2.6).

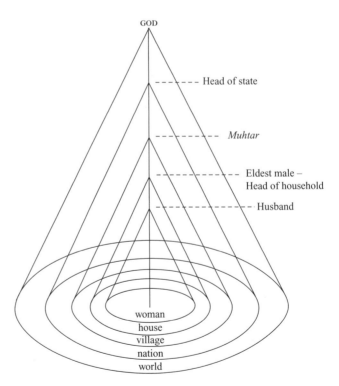

Figure 2.6   The structure of traditional Turkish authority relations as they are symbolically gendered (Delaney 1991). The female symbolizes the physical, unregenerate aspects of cultural entities – the house, the village, the nation, and the world. The male encloses, represents, and forms the generative relations between them. In this role, he stands in line with the divine.

"The American home"

Because the United States has always been multiethnic or multicultural, and because it is such a large country with a number of very different regions, there is no such thing as a typical American house (cf. Foley 1980). There are certain styles of house that one associates with New England, such as the "Saltbox colonial." When you see such a house in California, you would say, "There's a New England-style house." However, it is unlikely you would find an adobe-style New Mexico house in Vermont. The different styles may derive in part from the materials available and weather, but they also shed light on the concepts and values of the different regions and ethnic groups. At the same time, commonalities in house styles draw upon and express wider American values.

Unlike the Turkish village, where all the houses are together and the fields and land surround the village, the American dream has been for each family to have its own house set in the middle of its own land – at least since the days of the pioneers. This is as true in the farming country of the Midwest, where houses are few and far between, as it is in suburbia, where each house is set on a tiny plot of land. We are said to value our individualism and our privacy; we don't want neighbors peering in our windows or overhearing our arguments. In a Turkish village, however, that very proximity creates a brake on domestic violence. Back in the United States in the past, especially on the east coast, houses normally had several stories and there were separate rooms for separate functions, each with a door. And that was the case not just for the rich but also for the working class.

In the 1950s, a new trend toward more open space swept across the nation – rooms without boundaries, rooms that were multifunctional or at least blended one into another. Dining room and kitchen, or dining room and living room, or kitchen and living room; bathroom and bedroom or sleeping loft; study and guest room or television room or "family room"; and even hallways became more open as they often were combined with stairs on split levels. "Ranch houses" became popular. Not modeled on any real ranch house, the term referred to a house built all on one sprawling level.

In the past, a "house was thought of as the repository of a family's history," a place where family heirlooms and other memories were displayed (Carol Vogel, *New York Times Magazine*, June 28, 1987). Today, according to research conducted by the Joint Center for Housing Studies (at MIT and Harvard), houses are seen not as family museums, but as financial investments. And what people are "interested in purchasing [is] a life style, with all the modern conveniences of affluent urban life – such as security and maintenance services – minus the crime and dirt" (Vogel, *New York Times Magazine*, June 28, 1987).

Although house size has increased with middle-class affluence, the two-income couples who live there hardly have any time left to spend in them since they are generally working (more than) full-time. No wonder they desire "bringing some semblance of resort living into [their] everyday lives" (Vogel, *New York Times Magazine*, June 28, 1987), referring to the desire for swimming pools, hot tubs, tennis or squash courts, and even golf courses in their planned communities. The emphasis is no longer on unique individual houses but on luxury and comfort in the upscale housing developments that cater to this kind of lifestyle.

"Good fences make good neighbors"

So said Robert Frost in a poem about neighborliness (or lack thereof) in rural New Hampshire. A neighbor insisted on rebuilding a wall even though there was no ostensible need. Frost (1915) quips,

> Before I built a wall I'd ask to know
> What I was walling in or walling out,
> And to whom I was like to give offense.

Yet Americans seem to love fences – picket or ranch, chain link, tall filigreed iron, or stockade; fences are another expression of the desire for privacy and possession. They announce: this is my property, my castle, however humble; keep off until or unless invited in. Fences like these create a kind of buffer zone between the privacy of the house and the public area of the street or sidewalk. The distance seems similar to the distance we like to keep between ourselves and the person we are speaking to.

Porches used to perform the function of "buffer zone," according to Sue Beckham in "The American Front Porch: Women's Liminal Space" (1988; and see figure 2.7). The author associates the porch mania that flourished in the century between 1840 and 1940 with the rise of the industrial revolution and the era (at least among the middle classes) when men went off to work in a factory or business and women were increasingly confined to the home. During this time, the home came to be regarded as a sanctuary and identified as women's space. But the porch became a symbol of women's resourcefulness in overcoming the isolation they were experiencing (p. 88) – it was "betwixt and between" the private inside of the house and the public arena dominated by men.

> For women, kept at home by children in need of care and the labor necessary to keep a household going, the porch functioned as a social place – their own space – at home yet not inside – a space simultaneously work place and salon – where they could visit, keep track of neighborhood activities and exchange news flashes from passers by while they watched their children and performed the more portable and sedentary chores. (p. 74)

My mother, who as an adolescent lived in Brooklyn, New York, during the 1920s, described how she and her mother would "freshen up" to sit out on the porch after the evening meal and the dishes were done. It was a place not just to cool off but also to visit with the neighbors as they walked by or came up to sit with them for a while. This was a place young men could court the girls, for the rules were more relaxed on the porch than in the parlor. Porches were often equipped with swings and hammocks and rocking chairs – adding to the languid atmosphere of the place. The custom has not vanished completely. My daughter and her husband recently bought an old house in the Boston area with a small open front porch. When they and the children are out there, the neighbors do drop by to chat.

I also recall spending many happy hours on the wraparound porch of a farm in New York State where we spent several summers. Not only was it the place where the grownups sat and smoked or did their mending, but it was also the place where we children shelled peas, shucked corn, and snapped beans in preparation for canning. Today instead, people

Figure 2.7   An American porch, 1945. Photo Irene Jordan/Detroit News.

tend to prefer patios and decks, generally situated at the back, and more private, side of the house. But what is lost when we shift to the back or when we enclose porches with screens or glass or move inside where it is air-conditioned?

Perhaps dogs perform some of the same functions in neighborhoods today as porches did half a century and more ago. Walking your dog around your neighborhood allows you to talk to the neighbors and exchange news and gossip without having to invite them into your house. We think of dogs as members of the family, and, like children, they permit us to talk to people, even strangers, on the street. They, too, provide that "liminal" space "betwixt and between" the privacy of our homes and the public place of work. At the same time, according to Constance Perin in *Belonging in America: Reading between the Lines* (1988), dogs can also destroy the sense of community in a neighborhood by digging up gardens, despoiling sidewalks, continually barking, and occasionally biting. And they can also be used to create barriers – "Keep Out: Guard Dog."

Rooms and Spatial Arrangements

The size of rooms, like house size, varies tremendously. Arabs, apparently, like huge rooms with ceilings so high they do not "impinge on the visual field; and in addition there must be an unobstructed view" (Hall 1966: 162). In conversations with Arabs, Edward Hall said that the "term 'tomb' kept cropping up in conjunction with enclosed space. … [They] don't mind being crowded by people but hate to be hemmed in by walls" (p. 162). Furniture is generally placed on the periphery, leaving the center of the room empty. Americans, he noted, felt very uncomfortable in such rooms, accustomed as we are to filling them with furniture.

Victorian houses had parlors or sitting rooms where guests were received. Guests did not go wandering around the house and only on occasion were invited into the dining room. Wealthy people who had servants also had hidden corridors and stairways so that they would not be found in the same spaces with the family or the guests – two almost entirely separate groups of people occupied the same house.[5] Social differences once again are marked by spatial arrangements.

From the 1950s on, the "family room" took over the functions of the living room so much that many people hardly ever use their living rooms except on formal occasions. The family room was the place to watch television and to promote family "togetherness." In the new millennium, this may be a thing of the past, gone the way of the family meal, since it is far more likely that each family member watches his or her favorite programs on his or her own television. Kitchen counters with stools or "breakfast nooks" are, today, more likely to be the places where people eat rather than dining rooms. Even though fewer and fewer people are doing much cooking, kitchens among the affluent have, nevertheless, become large and equipped with all the latest appliances. They give a semblance of the ideal American family but are more symbolic than real. "Houses don't always reflect the way we really live, often they represent fantasies of the way we'd like to live" (Vogel, *New York Times Magazine*, June 28, 1987, quoting New York architect Robert Stern).

Spatial arrangement refers not only to the size and layout of stove, sink, refrigerator, and so on, but also to where each person decides to put things. Have you ever noticed, when you are trying to use another person's kitchen, how difficult it can be to find anything? Everything is in its place, but clearly that place is different from the one that you would assign. Each of us has our own sense of order. Nevertheless, this sense has been influenced by our culture and by the region where we grew up; by the ethnic, educational, and economic background of our parents; and by the times in which we live.

No doubt, every one of you has had some experience in moving furniture around. Many of you have moved from one house or apartment to another, some many times. No doubt you discovered that different spaces demand different arrangements, even different types of furniture. But even if you lived in the same place all your life, you probably changed your room as you moved out of childhood into adolescence. Not only did you want different furniture or colors, but also you probably wanted a different arrangement of your space. And even if your own room is a mess with piles of clothes and books scattered about, you can probably tell if someone has been in it. Something will be out of place; even the slightest movement of an object will signal trespass.

Americans typically think that every child should have a private bedroom right from birth. In many other cultures, people think it cruel to make an infant sleep alone in a room, rather than in the same room – indeed, in the same bed – with the mother. Of course, Americans do depart from the ideal of "a room of one's own": many children share rooms with siblings, and some families – adults and children – sleep together in the same room, following the cultural norms of their ethnic group. But these aberrations have created controversy among adoption agencies, child protective services, housing authorities, and rental agents (Pader 1994), revealing that the cultural ideal has social consequences.

If you are boarding at college, you were assigned a room and probably a roommate. Was one of your first conversations about the use of space? Who would have which bed, and on which side? Or did you think of making bunk beds to create extra space? A number of my students have confided to me that when they first arrive as freshmen, they wanted to duplicate as closely as possible their room at home. They filled it with the same things; but when they returned as sophomores, they wanted their rooms to be entirely different. Why do you think that is? I also heard of a very creative and unusual arrangement that would probably not be allowed in some places. A group of six students, male and female, who had a three-room suite decided to use one room for communal sleeping, another for study, and the third for a living room! In many colleges and universities today, dormitories are co-ed, something that was simply unimaginable when I went to college. Men could visit in the parlor only on certain days and times, and were never permitted on our floors, let alone in our rooms.

Feng Shui

Feng Shui is the Chinese art of "auspicious placement" of houses, rooms, furniture, and other objects in order to create a balance between the lived environment and the natural world. The goal is to let the *chi*, the life energy that animates all things, flow without obstruction. According to this art, the house is like a second body and so it is very important to get both in "sync." Feng Shui has become very popular in the United States in recent years, as witnessed by the numerous books available, consultants and workshops, but it is often detached from the wider philosophy/cosmology/worldview to which it is deeply connected. Nevertheless, it has created more awareness of the use and meaning of space.

Author unknown.

Each of us has an idea about our spatial arrangements, but rarely do we try to analyze our underlying assumptions. In some cultures, however, spatial arrangements are a matter of explicit and extended discourse. "In the West, we are taught to perceive and to react to the arrangements of objects and to think of space as 'empty' [whereas] … the Japanese are trained to perceive the shape and arrangements of spaces" (Hall 1966: 153). They even have a word for this, *ma*, which means interval. *Ma* "is a basic building block in all Japanese spatial experience. It is functional not only in flower arrangements but apparently is a hidden consideration in the layout of all other spaces" (p. 153). One need only think of Japanese rock gardens, which are merely the arrangement of a few rocks on sand or gravel and yet have a stunning effect. Space as a meaningful and integral part of the overall design is also reflected in their paintings by the term *yohaku*, which means "white space." The background space was as important a part of the overall effect as the brush strokes.

Chinese philosopher Lao Tzu, who lived in the sixth century BC, also captured this idea in chapter 11 in the *Tao Te Ching*:

> Thirty spokes converge on a single hub,
> but it is in the space where there is nothing
> that the usefulness of the cart lies.
> Clay is molded to make a pot,
> but it is in the space where there is nothing
> that the usefulness of the clay pot lies.
> Cut out doors and windows to make a room,
> but it is in the space where there is nothing
> that the usefulness of the room lies.

Therefore,

> Benefit may be derived from something,
> but it is in nothing that we find usefulness.
> (Lao Tzu 1990: 70)

Invisible Spaces

So far we have discussed spaces for living – macro and micro. Yet there are other spaces we often do not think about unless, or until, we have to go there. These are spaces that are somewhat hidden from our daily lives, such as hospitals, nursing homes, mental institutions, prisons, and cemeteries, in other words, places for the ill, the criminal, the dying, the dead, and anything else we do not like to contemplate. Hospitals are, perhaps, the least hidden of these, located not too far from living areas to be accessible, but not too close to be unavoidable. In other words, they are places we visit only when we must. Perhaps that is why "hospital space is at a premium," and there never seem to be enough "beds." But beds don't take up very much room, and in the grand scheme of things they are not expensive! It is a way of talking about other things, about social values and priorities – the facts that medical schools restrict the number of MDs they produce, and that the greed of managed care companies not only reduces the number of nurses and other support staff but also keeps their salaries low.

Most of us are generally not familiar with nursing homes, mental institutions, and prisons unless we work there or know someone who is in one. Not only are they often hidden from the spaces and places of routine daily life, but also the people in them become invisible, hidden from the view of the general public. What values about the old and the infirm are expressed by their spatial location? Why are they as invisible as criminals? What message is conveyed? Even here, because of the limitations on space (!), they will not get the attention they deserve, but it is important to include them so that they will not be left out of our account of space.

In stark contrast to the spaces for the living are the spaces for the dead. Cemeteries are places that house the dead. They can be vast and fairly impersonal, or small, intimate, and very local; they can be sites of national mourning and ritual, such as Arlington National Cemetery, or sites of pilgrimage for family members and devotees. For example, rock music lovers visit the Cimetière du Père Lachaise in Paris, where Jim Morrison, the lead singer of the Doors, is buried, and thousands have gone to view the burial place of Princess Diana. The differences in cemeteries and in memorial services at cemeteries often reflect the social statuses of the dead and the bereaved. But all cemeteries serve the same essential purpose: to separate the dead from the living, while preserving the connection of the dead to the living. The Turkish villagers I knew expressed this dual purpose through their own burial practices. They place their cemeteries on the periphery of their villages, outside but in view of their communities. All the dead are interred there, and all the living expect to join them on the occasion of their own deaths. This pathway is so important that even Turks who die abroad are returned to their natal town or village for burial. So, too, they refuse to fly in airplanes, lest the planes crash, which would incinerate their bodies and leave nothing of their physical selves to restore to their families.

Space That Is No Place: Cyberspace

We cannot leave this discussion of space without talking about *cyberspace*. According to science writer Margaret Wertheim, this term first appeared in 1984 in William Gibson's novel *Neuromancer*, although at the time "few people outside the military and the academic field of computer science … were even aware that 'cyberspace' existed" (Wertheim 1999: 225). By the end of the twentieth century, "the World Wide Web (the most public component of the Internet) … [had] over 300 million pages … [and was] growing by a million pages a day … [making it] the fastest-growing 'territory' in history" (1999: 226, 228). This amounts to a new creation that, like the "Big Bang" of scientific cosmology, is expanding exponentially. And yet unlike the physical universe that the Big Bang produced, cyberspace does not exist in a material sense. It came "out of the blue" and "out of left field," and lies "beyond the space that physics describes." As such, "[I]t is not subject to the laws of physics, and hence it is not bound by the limitations of those laws" (p. 228). If, then, cyber*space* is more metaphorical than material, does it make sense to include it in this chapter? The answer is yes, because, like physical space, it is the foundation of multiple social fields and processes, and because it profoundly transforms our experience of physical space and its limitations.

Since its inception in 1989, the Internet has become an essential medium for a wide range of communicative purposes: gathering and disseminating information, creating and maintaining social networks, seeking employment opportunities, creating new personas, and, on the shady side, finding targets to defame, defraud, and assault. As a consequence, growing numbers of people are spending increasing amounts of time in cyberspace and, consequently, less time engaged with the people immediately around them. This led recently to the identification of "Internet addiction" as a syndrome to which children and adolescents are especially susceptible. But the trend was already apparent in 1999, when William J. Mitchell, dean of the School of Architecture at MIT and author of *e-topia*, speculated on the impact of the Internet not on developing children but also, more pervasively, on the fabric of social life. His remarks begin innocuously with the problem of meeting places:

> Where will we get together? What sorts of meeting places, forums, and markets will emerge in the electronically mediated world? What will be the twenty-first-century equivalents of the gathering at the well, the water cooler, the Greek agora, the Roman forum, the village green, the town square, Main Street and the mall? (1999: 85)

Today the answer to this question is obvious: electronic meeting places have proliferated in reach and type from the formalized MySpace, Facebook, and YouTube, to the idiosyncratic sites of the blogosphere, to a variety of instant-messaging services that require only a handheld device – we can walk down the street and text people a world away, while ignoring the ones right in front of us. Even e-mail – probably the most common use of the Internet – disrupts our sense of location. This became obvious and distressing to me when I was in Europe, e-mailed my housesitter in Stanford, and had no idea that she was e-mailing me back from Brazil.

Mitchell's real concern was not, however, the meeting places per se, but the effect of inhabiting networks that are not rooted in a physical location. Specifically, the Web reinforces "sociocultural boundaries and categorical identities … [since it] typically provides efficient means for linking up like-minded people rather than for confronting differences." As such, it limits rather than expands our cultural horizons, by consolidating people of common outlook and effectively creating new versions of the gated community.

The importance of electronic communities is clear when they mobilize political movements that confront entrenched sites of power. On the positive side, this includes the Tiananmen Square struggle of 1989 and the Zapatista rebellion of 1994, both of which were witnessed and perhaps buoyed up by world audiences, thanks to local participants who could access global media. Similarly, the 2009 Iranian opposition to President Ahmadinejad relied on electronic communication both to orchestrate street protests and to broadcast the events to the world at large. On the negative side, the Internet has also broadened the reach and recruiting capacity of organizations whose motives are – at least from an American perspective – far more worrying. Al Qaeda relied on electronic communications and money transfers to plan and implement the 9/11 attacks in 2001. More recently Jihadists, like the Nigerian Abdulmutallab (the "underwear bomber"), have found their way to Islamist militants via Internet websites. It is little wonder that governments around the world – from the United States to Iran to the People's Republic of China – enlist hackers to investigate their electronic adversaries, and erect electronic barriers to keep other hackers at bay. Evidently "security fences" and "superspies" now exist in cyberspace as well as in the physical world.

Still, despite its spatial reach and its centrality in American life, we must not assume that the Internet is a pervasively public medium, overriding all distinctions of culture and location. In fact, access is still limited to specific sectors of the world's populations. For example, although Internet cafes can be found in dirt-road small towns in Turkey, the only people in them are adolescent boys, a reflection of the cultural mores concerning gender segregation and discrimination. Similarly, old people have mostly been left out of the "digital revolution," a function perhaps of their invisibility to Internet entrepreneurs who court a younger – sometimes much younger – clientele. This is unfortunate since the Web could ease the loneliness that often afflicts older people and provide an interesting use of their time.

On a brighter note, the Internet could have positive effects on some local communities. According to Mitchell, the digital revolution may put back together what the industrial revolution split apart, namely, work and home, and as a result make people more, not less, concerned about their local environment. Unlike the commuters who leave their bedroom communities behind when they go to work, the cybercommuters will presumably become more involved in the communities in which they live *and* work. Beautiful, historic cities that were economically sidelined, like Venice, Bath, and Savannah, can again become vital because work will no longer require one to live near the centers of industry and finance (Mitchell 1999: 77). As an architect, Mitchell is aware that this new kind of space that is no place will have an enormous impact on the design of living spaces, both domestic and public; however, at this point in time, it is too early to tell just how.

Returning to where we began this chapter, it is clear that cyberspace will also have an enormous impact on cosmology and perceptions of the world. Wertheim is perhaps an avatar, for she claims that "with each shift in our conception of space also comes a commensurate shift in our conception of our universe – and hence of our own place and role within that universe. ... In a very real sense, we are the products of our spatial schemes" (1999: 308). What will be the personal, social, and cosmological consequences of cyberspace? What notion of the self, of society, and of the universe will emerge? She thinks that we are

> in a similar position to Europeans of the sixteenth century who were just becoming aware of the physical space of the stars, a space quite outside their prior conception of reality. Like Copernicus, we are privileged to witness the dawning of a new kind of space. What history will make of this space, appropriately enough, only time will tell. (p. 308)

What better place to turn to an investigation of time and the way it informs and is informed by culture.

Notes

1. Penelope Leach, a British psychologist and pediatrician, has written eloquently about the breakdown of the social contract in her groundbreaking book, *Children First: What Our Society Must Do – and Is Not Doing – for Our Children Today* (1994). She points out that although the stereotypic image of the homeless is the drug-addicted man or woman, more than a quarter of a million (300,000) of the homeless are children

under the age of 10 (p. 173). She believes that the "principal problems of rich societies … are not a shortage of money but of political will" (p. 174).

2. See the work being done by Saskia Sassen (1995) and Manuel Castells (1989) about the way the global economy is affecting different groups living in the city.

3. It is also the title of a Sierra Club book with photographs by Eliot Porter (1962).
4. That is, spatial boundaries are projected onto bodies. See Douglas (1966) and Boddy (1982, 1989).
5. The British television series *Upstairs, Downstairs*, as well as the film *Gosford Park*, give good portrayals of this.

EXERCISES

2.1. A Map of Campus

A.   Draw a map of your college or university that reflects the places that are important to you. It may be sketched in broad strokes and need not be very detailed. Do not use a campus map as your guide.

B.   After completing your map, take a trip around campus – on foot or by bike, car, or bus (depending on which applies) – and pay attention to the way space is organized. Write about two pages, addressing the following three questions:
   •   What kinds of spatial divisions are noticeable? *Hint*: think about the differences between "town and gown," between study and leisure, and so on.
   •   How does the space relate to different categories of people, for example male and female, children and elderly, faculty and students, or clerical staff and other workers? Who has freedom of movement in these spaces, when, and where?
   •   In what ways are activities classified by space, for example, sleeping, eating, and so on? (They are also related to time, but that is another topic.)

2.2. A Room of Your Own

Think (but don't write) about the criteria by which you organized the space in your room. Did you discuss this with your roommate (if applicable)? Could you tell if someone had moved something of yours?

2.3. Space as Metaphor

In your notebook, begin to keep track of spatial metaphors in everyday speech. For example: warm *up*, cool *down*, *high* society, and *lower* class.

Bibliography

Albanese, Catherine (1990) *Nature Religion in America: From the Algonkian Indians to the New Age.* Chicago: University of Chicago Press.

Ardener, Shirley, ed. (1981) *Women and Space: Ground Rules and Social Maps.* New York: St. Martin's Press.

Beckham, Sue (1988) "The American Front Porch: Women's Liminal Space." In *Making the American Home: Middle-Class Women and Domestic Material Culture, 1840–1940*, ed. Marilyn F. Motz and Pat Browne. Bowling Green, OH: Popular Press.

Boddy, Janice (1982) "Womb as Oasis: The Symbolic Context of Pharaonic Circumcision in Rural Northern Sudan." *American Ethnologist* 15(1): 4–27.

Boddy, Janice (1989) *Wombs and Alien Spirits: Women, Men, and the Zar Cults in Northern Sudan*. Madison: University of Wisconsin Press.

Bohannan, Paul (1995) *Africa and Africans*, 4th ed. Long Grove, IL: Waveland Press.

Bowen, Elenore Smith ([1954] 1964) *Return to Laughter: An Anthropological Novel*. New York: Doubleday.

Carroll, Raymonde (1988) "Home." In *Cultural Misunderstandings: The French-American Experience*. Chicago: University of Chicago Press.

Carsten, Janet, and Hugh-Jones, Stephen (1995) *About the House: Lévi-Strauss and Beyond*. Cambridge: Cambridge University Press.

Castells, Manuel (1989) *The Informational City: Information, Technology, Economic Restructuring, and the Urban-Regional Process*. Oxford: Blackwell.

Chatwin, Bruce (1987) *The Songlines*. London: Jonathan Cape.

Delaney, Carol (1991) *The Seed and the Soil: Gender and Cosmology in Turkish Village Society*. Berkeley: University of California Press.

Douglas, Mary (1966) *Purity and Danger: An Analysis of the Concepts of Pollution and Taboo*. London: Routledge & Kegan Paul.

Foley, Mary Mix (1980) *The American House*. New York: Harper & Row.

Frost, Robert (1915) *North of Boston*. New York: Holt.

Hall, Edward (1966) *The Hidden Dimension*. Garden City, NY: Doubleday.

Hall, Edward (1983) *The Dance of Life*. Garden City, NY: Doubleday.

Hallowell, A. Irving (1977) "Cultural Factors in Spatial Orientations." In *Symbolic Anthropology: A Reader in the Study of Symbols and Meanings*, ed. Janet Dolgin, David S. Kemnitzer, and David Schneider. New York: Columbia University Press.

Jaime, M. Annette, ed. (1992) *The State of Native America: Genocide, Colonization, and Resistance*. Boston: South End Press.

Kozol, Jonathan (1989) "Adrift in America." *Texas Observer*, February 24, pp. 10–14.

Krakauer, Jon (1996) *Into the Wild*. New York: Villard.

Lao Tzu (1990) *Tao Te Ching*, trans. Victor H. Mair. New York: Bantam.

Leach, Penelope (1994) *Children First: What Our Society Must Do – and Is Not Doing – for Our Children Today*. New York: Alfred A. Knopf.

Massey, Doreen (1994) *Space, Place, and Gender*. Minneapolis: University of Minnesota Press.

Menzel, Peter (1994) *Material World: A Global Family Portrait*, text by Charles Mann, intro. Paul Kennedy. San Francisco: Sierra Club Books.

Mitchell, William J. (1999) *e-topia*. Cambridge, MA: MIT Press.

Motz, Marilyn F., and Browne, Pat, eds. (1988) *Making the American Home: Middle-Class Women and Domestic Material Culture, 1840–1940*. Bowling Green, OH: Popular Press.

Pader, Ellen-J. (1994) "Spatial Relations and Housing Policy: Regulations that Discriminate against Mexican-Origin Households." *Journal of Planning Education and Research* 13(2): 119–35.

Perin, Constance (1988) *Belonging in America: Reading between the Lines*. Madison: University of Wisconsin Press.

Porter, Eliot (1962) *In Wilderness Is the Preservation of the World*. San Francisco: Sierra Club Books.

Rodgers, Silvia (1981) "Women's Space in a Men's House: The British House of Commons." In *Women and Space: Ground Rules and Social Maps*, ed. Shirley Ardener. New York: St. Martin's Press.

Said, Edward (1979) *Orientalism*. New York: Vintage.

Sales, Kirkpatrick (1990) *The Conquest of Paradise*. New York: Alfred A. Knopf.

Sassen, Saskia (1995) "Analytic Borderlands: Race, Gender and Representation in the New City." In *Re-Presenting the City: Ethnicity, Capital and Culture in the Twenty-First Metropolis*, ed. Anthony D. King. London: Macmillan.

Sobel, Dava (1995) *Longitude*. New York: Penguin.

Wertheim, Margaret (1999) *The Pearly Gates of Cyberspace: A History of Space from Dante to the Internet*. New York: Norton.

Zinn, Howard ([1980] 1990) *A People's History of the United States: 1492–Present*. New York: HarperCollins.

READING

The American Front Porch: Women's Liminal Space
Sue Bridwell Beckham

Sitting on the Porch
An event, in those days
for which one freshened up.
The houses were close to the street
and to sit on the porch
meant to be accessible
to visit, to chat and receive,
to be public and on display.
My grandmother did not
sit on the porch
before four o'clock
but sometimes stayed there
through sweet summer evenings.
And when I was with her
I thought of it as
an occasion. (Easter 15)

Every evening of a summer, after supper dishes were done, my mother-in-law insisted that the whole household gather on the front porch to "cool off." The ritual made good sense before her husband persuaded her to let him install air conditioners in their Mississippi home, but long after the house was kept at a comfortable 70 degrees, Ms. Beckham continued to insist that we all troop out on the porch after supper to cool off. Whenever I tried to beg off because I wished to read a book or watch a television show, the lady was convinced that nothing less than a rift with some family member would keep anybody indoors. And she was equally certain that whatever pique there was would disappear once I occupied a rocker on the front porch and communed with the group. Clearly, her faith in the ministry of the porch went deeper than relief from the heat. The porch for my mother-in-law was, as it was for Mary Easter, author of the poem above, and her grandmother, a ritual space. For those women, it was a space which met certain largely female needs, a space which, like a church, required compliance with certain forms for maximum benefit – and also, like a church, permitted the casting off of other social forms in order to realize a largely hidden self.

While virtually all American porches owe their architectural being to forms developed in other cultures, the American front porch is a peculiarly American institution. The earliest porches in recorded history were ceremonial. Porticoes on Greek temples and on the ceremonial buildings of America's Mississippian Indians alike blurred boundaries between the populace outside and the high priests performing their rituals in the inner sanctum. They were bridges between the sacred and the profane from which the highly revered could speak with the lowly and on which they could perform public rites for untutored – or unsanctified – audiences on the outside. It is far in space and times from Greek temples and pre-Columbian Indians to the porches on American houses and yet, unless the function were somewhat similar, my mother-in-law would not have placed so much faith in her porch and its restorative power. Nor would Mary Easter have recalled the ritual of freshening up at the appropriate time of day for the "occasion" of sitting on the porch.

Those authors, particularly women, who write of the American experience have long been aware that a ritual significance attaches to the front porch; the absence of direct allusion to that significance, however, suggests the realization to have been subconscious. In *The Ballad of the Sad Cafe*, for example, Carson McCullers recounts the peculiar use her protagonist, Miss Amelia Evans, made of her porch. Having lost her mother in early childhood and her father at the vulnerable age of nineteen, Miss Amelia, six feet tall and utterly masculine in build, had not learned – or chose to acknowledge – the womanly virtues, but implicitly she understood the proprieties of a woman living alone. In the daytime, she admitted men to the store on the ground floor of her house where they bought necessities such as feed, fertilizer and snuff. In the evening, when male visitors inside would have been improper, she sold men her moonshine through the kitchen door – liquor she would never permit to be consumed in her house or her store.

Miss Amelia did, however, permit the men to drink her liquor on her front porch. The porch was Miss Amelia's property, readers are told, but this intensely possessive woman "did not regard [it] as her premises; the premises began at the front door and took in the entire inside of the building" (118). Clearly Miss Amelia understood the porch to be neither her home nor public property. She allowed the men to consume her liquor on the porch and to enjoy a certain amount of social interchange, but all the time she remained standing in the doorway guarding the inner sanctum and presiding over the proceedings. For this woman and for the town in which she lived, the porch was a space "betwixt and between" private and public, and once we consider the special properties attributed to the liquor consumed there, it becomes a place for ritual communion as well:

> For the liquor of Miss Amelia has a special quality of its own. It is clean and sharp on the tongue, but once it is down a man it glows inside him for a long time afterward. And that is not all. It is known that if a message is written with lemon juice on a clean sheet of paper there will be no sign of it. But if the paper is held for a moment to the fire then the letters turn brown and the meaning becomes clear. Imagine that the whisky is the fire and that the message is that which is known only in the soul of a man – then the worth of Miss Amelia's liquor can be understood. (107)

It was night on the front porch when, after consuming the liquor of self knowledge, Miss Amelia first encountered love and did the most ill advised and spiritually significant act of her life: She shared the liquor with a total stranger and *invited him into her house*. The fictional Miss Amelia and her creator Carson McCullers clearly sensed the front porch as a space of ritual significance. So did Russell Baker. In his autobiography, *Growing Up*, Baker's grandmother Ida Rebecca, had a very different ritual use for her porch.

In the 1920s, women of rural towns were generally proscribed from the exercise of public power. Despite feminist movements that thrived in the cities, the heady power of getting the vote waned, and the reprieve from domesticity provided by World War I was history. The majority of women were once again housebound, and their accepted authority was only over furniture and children. Women, however, found socially acceptable ways to circumvent their public limitations. Whatever the mores of her time, Ida Rebecca, mother of twelve strapping sons and one daughter, was the acknowledged head of "a sprawling empire" and the unacknowledged ruler of the small Virginia town of Morrisonville. Baker's earliest and most vivid memories of his grandmother reveal her "sitting in state in the front porch rocker that served as her throne." Whether she was waiting for a son to bring home a prospective bride, presiding over the mandatory Sunday family gatherings, or surveying her domain, Baker recalls her sitting in that rocker, on that porch situated on a rise that put her at one end of and a few feet above the rest of Morrisonville. And in Morrisonville, "everybody said, 'It's her way or *no* way'" (28–32).

Whether or not Ida Rebecca thought of her porch as a mystic space from which she as high priest would preside, that is certainly the way it impressed young Russell and the citizens of Morrisonville. And why not? Forbidden by her motherhood to run for public office or to engage in business enterprises as Miss Amelia did, forbidden by custom and, as we have recently learned, by fearful male clergy, to seek the ministry, forbidden then to have an official office or temple, Ida Rebecca devised her own space from which to rule, and if we are to believe her grandson, she did it with aplomb. For Ida Rebecca, then, the front porch must have been a space betwixt and between the dwelling to which she had been condemned and the public arena in which she was forbidden to function, between the sanctity of the home and the profanity of the marketplace.

The porch for Miss Amelia and Ida Rebecca – and for millions of women from the mid-nineteenth century to the mid-twentieth – was a sort of "liminal space." Anthropologist Victor Turner speaks of a "liminal state" which occurs in those more primitive cultures studied by anthropologists – a time when the participants in a ritual are "betwixt and between" two cultural states – neither completely inside the culture nor yet outside it since their position is a transitional one.[1] Among those Turner describes as liminal are stone age peoples undergoing puberty rituals and medieval squires practicing the rites preparatory to knighthood. Two comparatively modern female liminal states are experienced by women who have declared their availability for marriage but who have not yet been claimed (debutantes, for example) and engaged women – both betwixt and between the protection of their parents and that of their husbands.

During their liminal period, such people are neither children nor adults, neither aspiring nor fully achieving. Using Tuner's model, the front porch becomes a liminal space – neither sanctified as the hearth nor public as the road. One must be *invited* to sit on the porch, but, on the other hand, one has the right to *expect* that invitation because a person sitting on the porch has declared herself "to be accessible/to visit, to chat and receive/to be public and on display." Occupants of a porch are betwixt and between because they are neither fully sheltered from the elements nor fully exposed to them – neither fully a part of the workings of the public sphere nor fully excluded from them.

Although every structural feature of the porch is borrowed from another culture, the domestic front porch is an American institution – owing its origin to the Southeastern climate and gradually spreading into the fabric of American life in all geographic regions. While it was English settlers and African slaves who conceived of and built the first American front porches early in the seventeenth century, they borrowed concepts from the Indian bungalow, the Haitian "shotgun" house, and the French side and back "galleries."[2] Later, wealthier English stock tempered the practical porch with majestic columns and ornate porticoes borrowed from the ancient Greeks. While those formal porches testify to the architectural genius of such men as George Washington and Thomas Jefferson, and even the more humble porches of the common people were usually conceived and built by men, one suspects that women had something to do with their proliferation and their pervasiveness by the mid-nineteenth century.

The widespread use of the domestic front porch in the United States came at a time when the functions of male heads of households and of their female counterparts were being redefined. Late in the eighteenth century and early in the nineteenth, the industrial revolution for the first time made working away from home the order of the day for great numbers of people. Before that, soldiers and adventurers left home for months on end, hunters for shorter periods. Wealthy Europeans, perhaps, maintained multiple dwellings and moved freely among them as they do today. But the masses of the earth's people lived and worked together in exceed-

ingly small geographic areas. While their chores were often delineated by sex, both men and women were involved in work in or near the dwelling – even when, as with nomads, home itself moved seasonally. Families and groups of families could count on social intercourse and highly valued work. In the western world of the nineteenth century, however, all that would change. Particularly in the United States, the industrial revolution and unbridled capitalism brought about for all classes a departure from traditional ways of life. And it brought about corresponding changes in domestic architecture. One historian of American domestic architecture characterizes the new culture of the American mid-nineteenth century this way:

> The dynamics of this entire era was nothing less than the industrialization of America. … Life itself was harder and more cynical. The old Jeffersonian vision of an agrarian democracy, of independent men, rooted in the security of their own land or their own handicraft skills, had become more dream than actuality. The ruptures, dislocations, and insecurities of wage work and absentee ownership were increasingly the realities of American life.
>
> But with these miseries came also the optimism that was part of a period of phenomenal growth. It was the opening of an age of untrammeled *laissez-faire* capitalism, of rugged individualism, of unparalleled opportunity. … America felt herself to be the inheritor of all the riches of the historic past and scientific present, claiming furthermore an inalienable right to do with her inheritance exactly as she wished. This was true no less in architecture than in the mining, lumbering, and marketing conquest of a continent. (Foley 163)

American men may certainly have enjoyed that sense of unparalleled opportunity and the inalienable right to do with their political inheritance exactly as they wished. Women, however, are notably absent from that female writer's concept – and with good reason. With the industrial revolution and the rise of the middle class in European and American societies, it became possible for large numbers of families to "enjoy the luxury" of sending their men out to earn a living while the women stayed home and "enjoyed" the pleasures of domestic life. Wealthy women, of course, still could employ servants to handle domestic chores and carriages to move about in society. At the other end of the spectrum, every able bodied member of less fortunate families was required to work for wages just to keep food on the table.

But increasingly, the class which could neither afford servants nor needed the proceeds of every member's work to survive became the dominant class. What developed was a caste of women whose roles kept them largely indoors and solitary during the day. These women were to engineer domestic bliss, "influence" the children in Christian virtue, and act as moral guides to their men. Much has been written about the stress and frustration women suffered in this period because of their isolation and the gradual devaluation of their work. And much has already been written about ways they devised to deal with it. But one strategy women used to maintain contact with the community remains unconsidered.

The author of the quote above who celebrated the unparalleled opportunity for American men and the accompanying effervescence in domestic architecture of the period includes in her book dozens of drawings of representative American houses built between 1860 and 1941. And virtually every one of those examples has a front porch of some sort. And yet, like the women of the period she celebrates, the porches seem to be invisible. As in most other histories of American architecture, porches are virtually unmentioned in this book and, while architecture is seen as indicative of the consciousness which spawned it, no quarter is given to implications of ubiquitous porches.

It is probably impossible to prove that women had any direct influence on the porch mania that swept America from this period through the early 1940s. But it is a notable coincidence that, in the era in which the house became woman's domain and man exited to the market place, porches blossomed with an unprecedented abandon and pervasiveness. Before that time, American porches were confined to the Southeast where climate demanded the indoor–outdoor space. Beginning in the 1850s, however, virtually every domestic structure was built with a porch. And to those whose builders failed to catch on to the trend soon enough, porches were sure to be added. A careful look at older residential sections of almost any American community reveals a healthy sprinkling of appended porches among the more common houses on which the porches are integral.

Whether or not women were responsible for the explosion of porches spanning three generations, there can be no doubt that indoor/outdoor living space became for them a way of countering domestic isolation, at least during the warm months. For women, kept at home by children in need of care and the labor necessary to keep a household going, the porch functioned as a social place – their own space – at home yet not inside – a space simultaneously work place and salon – where they could visit, keep track of neighborhood activities and exchange news flashes with passers by while they watched their children and performed their more portable and sedentary chores. Middle-class women could – and did – sit on the porch swing to prepare vegetables and fruits for cooking, even for preservation. Shelling peas, peeling apples and peaches, snapping beans, shucking corn – all were acceptable porch activities. So were hand sewing, endless mending, knitting in preparation for the colder indoor months and the more leisurely "fancy work." And while women performed those chores, they could keep an eye on the children – those middle-aged people who today remember the porch as partially sheltered playground.

The more fortunate women who had a back porch as well could do their more strenuous and less presentable chores in the back. Their poorer sisters, however, often actually canned those peeled apples and shelled peas on the front porch. The cramped kitchen would have been just too hot. The porch also served as summer laundry room. Today, adults from the South especially recall playing the familiar automobile game of "counting washing machines on the front porch" in the late thirties, the forties and into the fifties. Those washing machines had replaced earlier boilers and washtubs.

Porches did make heavy chores more pleasant in hot weather, and they did offer the opportunity to take quieter tasks into the semi-public, but the most liberating use women found for the porch, one imagines, was social. On the porch, the casual visitor, the maid separated from the family by class and caste, the family itself experienced "communitas." One characteristic Turner ascribes to people in a liminal state is "communitas" – the temporary but vital attachment that only people caught between cultural states can establish. Communitas, according to Turner, is "undirected, equalitarian, direct, nonrational, existential." Thus behavior in the liminal space is "spontaneous, immediate, concrete." The rules that apply to relationships and behavior in the structured environment on either side of the liminal space do not apply within it. So it is with the porch. There, betwixt and between absolute private and absolute public, relationships that would be impossible elsewhere can flourish for however brief a time – and they can be spontaneous. Thus, bashful and protected youth in the first flush of intimacy are free to experiment with new relationships; thus, caste and class can be suspended and commonality explored; thus the boundary between friend and stranger breaks down; thus, the powerless are empowered; and thus, established relationships are freed from the constraints and tensions of business on the outside and busy-ness indoors to commune and, if my mother-in-law is to be taken seriously, to heal.

The communitas established on the porch has contributed to the transmission of culture from generation to generation. In the evening, when whole families gathered on porches, family lore was passed in the guise of stories of old times. On my grandfather's porch, in the long televisionless summer evenings, I learned family history – and family legend. But in the day, with my grandmother, I learned my proper place. The turn-of-the-century girl child in the illustration learns from a female family retainer how to sweep a porch – and the importance of keeping it swept. At the turn of the century, at the height of Jim Crow, she also learned that it was sometimes socially acceptable for blacks to sit with whites – at least with white children – on porches, but never in living rooms. On some porches white female employers could indulge the friendships they formed with black employees without public censorship. It was my mother-in-law's custom to invite her maid for a mid-morning Coke on the screened part of the front porch – and again in the mid-afternoon. Ida Rebecca Baker's realm was more strict. Her black maid and lifelong friend Annie was permitted the sanctity of a porch rocker only in times of sickness or death and then only, like the woman in the illustration, in the

company of children. (Baker 42) It was a reward for service rendered.

The porch also provided a setting within which blacks could maintain social relationships with whites. A white woman who would never have entered her black friend's living room unless it was to impart some matriarchal service could sit on the black woman's porch with impunity. When he filmed *The Color Purple*, Stephen Spielberg retained Alice Walker to advise him on cultural mores with which he was unfamiliar. In the film he illustrated proper decorum for whites visiting blacks. When Sophia's white employer brought Sophia to spend the day with her relatives, she could not start the car to return home. One of Sophia's sisters, eager not to have her celebratory dinner interrupted while her menfolks ministered to the white woman's car, offered to fix her a plate of food and serve it on the porch. While the white woman refused the proffered gift, it is clear that eating "colored" food on the porch was permissible. The liminal porch was clearly a place where the color barrier could be weakened if not destroyed.

The sex barrier was also weakened on the front porch. In literature and the popular arts, as in life, the porch was the place for innocent courting. Young men have always been more or less able to come and go as they please. Not so young women. Traditionally, they must wait for men to come along, men to make the first move toward courtship, men to suggest marriage.

Most of us know that while women did often initiate acceleration of a relationship, the myth of the male initiator was a charade that had to be maintained, and it was maintained with the help of the porch. Since it was inappropriate for women to go into the public arena in search of potential mates, they needed a way to shop and to sample before making a selection – while all the time seeming to acquiesce in a male decision. Thus the porch, betwixt indoors and out, between public and private, became a sexual market place where the woman seemed to be on display but where she actually sampled wares presented before her.

The nineteenth century was a time, it must be remembered, when peddlers sold house to house, when dressmakers brought their bolts and patterns to the consumer, when fruits and vegetables were delivered to the back door. So it was with men. While Amanda Wingfield in Tennessee Williams' semi-autobiographical *The Glass Menagerie* does not mention her front porch, we are rather certain her living room would not have contained the seventeen gentlemen callers who visited her one fateful Sunday afternoon. And both Margaret Mitchell and David O. Selznik opened *Gone With the Wind* with Scarlett surveying masculine wares on the front veranda. Incidentally, Selznik was at least subconsciously aware of the ritual significance of a porch. While Scarlett is at her feminine best, the veranda is intact. When she returns to Tara to take over the man's job of running the place and even working in the fields, the porch is gone. We are led to believe that Yankees destroyed it, but the subtext is that a gritty female farmer has no use for the accoutrements of a girl whose only responsibility was to snare a husband.

It was for good reason that the porch was the place to entertain gentlemen callers. Inside the rules of propriety and chaperonage were restrictive. On the porch, neither in the parents' parlor nor in the forbidden public arena, certain rules could be broken. A girl on her mother's porch was properly chaperoned, but so long as her mother was inside, she could steal a touch or even a kiss and, in the cover of night, she could talk of subjects inappropriate indoors.

Conversely, while the porch offered relative freedom for the protected young lady, for unchaperoned women it was itself protection from men who thought *they* were doing the shopping. In the movie *Judge Priest*, set sometime around 1910, the principal female character was an orphan condemned to live alone in her inherited house. While she could never invite gentlemen callers indoors, this young woman could entertain the occasional male guest on her porch secure in the knowledge that, were he to get out of line – and one did – she was in the hearing of Judge Priest next door. And she could hardly have become the subject of gossip when she entertained in full view of the street.

Not only had women the right to expect such protection from male neighbors – their virtue was the responsibility of such neighbors. An incident that Amory, Mississippi, residents would almost as soon forget illustrates the extremes to which that obligation extended. Early one sweltering summer eve in the 1920s, dentist and respected Amory citizen Dr. I. W. Beauchamp (pronounced Bee-chum) sat on the porch of his ornate Victorian house on Amory's Fifth Street with his wife

and his two visiting and virginal nieces. Dr. Beauchamp was secure in the knowledge that his young charges would witness nothing unseemly from the sanctity of his porch, but that particular steamy evening as the women and the man sat decorously fanning, chatting, and observing events on Fifth Street – usually few and commonplace – the unspeakable and the anti-social happened. Across the street in the less stately home at 105 S. Fifth Street lived the Frashes, a large family with several adult married sons. All of the Frash boys including one "Billy" known to be "not quite right" and his brother "Jim" worked for the Frisco Railroad maintaining engines.

Having guests the Beauchamps probably sat on the porch later than usual. On the other hand the working men across the street had to be up with the sun and opted for an early bedtime. Billy went to his room to prepare for bed as usual – except this time he veered from the norm. He forgot to lower the shade over the large front window to his bedroom! The japonica that now provides a degree of privacy even for forgetful people had not yet reached window level. The result was the virginal nieces learned more about male anatomy than was ever customary before marriage. The nieces may have secretly been delighted, but Dr. Beauchamp was enraged. He was entitled to entertain female guests in his outdoor sitting room confident that their innocence would not be violated. The willing compromise to privacy one accepts by sitting on the porch in full view of the street does not extend to being forced to witness indecent exposure.

In the humid dawn of the next day, after what was probably a night of trying in vain to sleep on sticky sheets in a ninety degree plus bedroom, Dr. Beauchamp made his angry way to the roundhouse in search of his neighbors. Unfortunately, the first Frash he came upon was Jim – entirely innocent of all wrong doing. Equally unfortunately, Jim bore a strong family resemblance to his forgetful brother. Thinking he had found his man, Dr. Beauchamp collared his prey, threw him against the wall and shot Jim – not Billy – dead. And he was never brought to trial![3]

The incident makes a good story – amusing, shocking and tragic, even gothic – but its real significance is what it reveals about the culture of porches. Nobody today remembers much about the legal proceedings following the shooting. What they know, however, is what Dr. Beauchamp and the Mississippi legal system knew then – that young women had the right to sit on porches and expect the community to protect their virtue. That right, in fact, was so sacred that men were justified in going to any extreme to assure that it was maintained – even to the point of shooting the wrong man.

While Dr. Beauchamp could avenge his nieces' loss of innocence if he could not protect them from it, the dead parents of the protagonist in Bobbie Ann Mason's short story "Residents and Transients" were entirely helpless to protect her from her own instincts. Mason creates an entirely 1980s version of the liminal nature of porch entertaining when Mary Sue, left at loose ends while her husband is away on extended business obligations, relies on her inherited porch, and perhaps the spirits of her parents, to protect her from her own darker desires. Bored and confused about her place in her culture and her marriage, Mary Ann is surprised one afternoon when her *dentist*, seeing her on her porch, stops for a friendly chat. Nothing unseemly in that – except that the porch is the back porch! Since hers is a farmhouse, the back porch faces the road and functions as front porches usually do, but for Mason the fact that it is a back porch offers the chance for ambiguous messages. While no taboos forbid men to visit women on front porches, back porches, with their suggestion of privacy and even secrecy, are something else again. Thus, the character herself is in the ambiguous position of not knowing whether she is being unfaithful or merely friendly.

The dentist's first visit grows into a custom with which Mary Sue can live – so long as they are visible from the road, the couple have not done anything technically anti-social. The crucial step in the relationship is not taken until the dentist crosses the threshold into the inner sanctum of the house. Then, just as when Miss Amelia took the stranger into her house after dark, an irreversible and fateful step has been taken. It is Mason's custom not to make reading her stories easy for the reader by resolving them, but the reader knows that once the visitor is inside, Mary Sue can no longer refrain from confronting her own ambiguities.

Mary Sue's dilemma is definitely a twentieth-century problem with well-articulated options once she inter-

prets her own feelings. In earlier decades women confused about their place in the world had no clearly delineated choices. But they did have porches, understood – subconsciously at least – as places where rules could be suspended. In *The Awakening*, when Kate Chopin's protagonist, Edna Pontellier, begins to awaken to the limiting nature of her role as a Creole wife, much of the action takes place on the porch of her summer cabin. Vacations are suggested by Turner to be liminal periods when the vacationers temporarily move outside the expectations of their culture. Resorts, then, must be themselves liminal spaces. Thus Edna, summering at a vacation spot where many of her daily routines are suspended, is outside her culture enough to examine her lifestyle. And she doesn't like what she sees.

Edna's culture, however, has not taught her fulfilling alternatives. Even so, timidly at first, she begins to experiment. One experiment she tries is flirtation. At the resort, that is entirely acceptable. When she entertains her chosen gentleman friend on her own porch, her husband remarks how pleased he is that she has the young man to keep her amused while he is away during the week attending to business. It is only when, back in the city in colder weather, Edna invites her guests *indoors* in her husband's absence that family and friends perceive something untoward in her search for self.

But receiving gentleman callers is not the most significant indication that Edna – and Chopin – perceive the front porch to be a liminal space. On the night that Edna first awakens to her intense dissatisfaction with her life, the night that she begins a long campaign to declare her independence, she does it on the porch. Edna is accustomed to honoring her husband's every nighttime whim whether it be for a sexual encounter or to leave her bed to check on children who are obviously sleeping peacefully. On this particular night, however, she refuses to come in from the porch when her spouse announces it is time for bed. Throughout the night, she continues to reject any ruses her husband devises to attract her indoors where his rule is supreme. Subconsciously, at least, she realizes that, on the porch, she is subject neither to the rules that govern her performance in her husband's house and nor to those of the public domain.

Edna, of course, becomes acutely aware that her life thus far has been a series of command performances. In

The Presentation of Self in Everyday Life, Erving Goffman outlined his now classic contention that in their everyday lives virtually all people present themselves to others in full-fledged performances that include costume, setting and, most of all, acting. Thus, the place where people act becomes a stage and the witnesses an audience. Preparation for such a performance, of course, demands a backstage. In his chapter on "Regions and Regional Behavior," Goffman discusses "front places" and "back places" (106–40). A front place is where performances are staged. A back place, on the other hand, is not only where the actor prepares for performance, but where she can be herself. For women and their porches, a strange reversal of back and front sometimes occurs. We have already seen that for Edna Pontellier, the front porch in full view of friends and neighbors – the audience – is where she feels most free to try being herself. Indoors, in the bedroom, one of the most back places for Goffman, with only her husband for audience, Edna must act the role of perfect wife and mother.

In *Their Eyes Were Watching God*, Zora Neale Hurston suggests a variation on the reversal theme when her protagonist Janie tries to free herself from the restrictions of her role as wife. In earlier times, before the advent of air conditioning, businesses were often equipped with porches, but these public porches were gathering places for men. Women were unwelcome. So it was with the store Janie ran with her husband. Janie was expected to mind the store for the occasional customer when groups of men – and sometimes unattached women – gathered on the store porch. To Janie, excluded in the dark store – merely a spectator to the camaraderie in front,

> When the people sat around on the porch and passed around the pictures of their thoughts for the others to look at and see, it was nice. The fact that the thought pictures were always crayon enlargements of life made it even nicer to listen to. (81)

When Janie moved to join the tempting revelry on the porch, her husband told her in no uncertain terms that her place was inside, and when finally, in defiance, she engaged her husband in a game of insults on the porch, it was an act of rebellion that was to destroy the marriage. A wife sharing his porch with him was not part

of the role Janie's husband wanted to play. That happened in the middle of Janie's story. After taking the reader with Janie on a strenuous journey into genuine love and self knowledge, Hurston involves her protagonist and the reader in another porch scene. Having learned that she need not conform to society's artificial rules for her, Janie exchanges pictures of her spiritual journey with her bosom friend on the porch of her own house. The porch for Janie was symbolic of both her limitations and her freedom. While the store porch was a front place for Janie's husband, for her it had been a back place from which she was excluded. In the store, she acted the role of dutiful wife; on the porch she broke the rules and learned something about herself. And on the house porch, another back place located on the front, Janie experienced communitas with her female friend.

Goffman, writing in the 1950s, had an interesting view of women – a view possible only in a patriarchy. While in his examples, drawn primarily from the workplace, women have roles every bit as important as men, he sees the places where women get together alone as "back places" – no concept that they might perform for each other since he seems to consider women alone as "back people." With some accuracy he cites Simone de Beauvoir to bolster his position. What both he and de Beauvoir miss is that in the same chapter from which he quotes, de Beauvoir mentions situations in which women present themselves for women.[4] Surely when women decorated their houses, collected china, glassware and other paraphernalia for entertaining, they did not do it to impress men. And surely, when they decorate their porches they do it neither purely for personal satisfaction nor to impress some all-male world.

Nineteenth- and early twentieth-century women seem to have been more free to be themselves on porches than any place else. They could enjoy the communion of passers by and chance visitors on the porch while they watched children and did some of their more portable chores. And they could keep up with community news via casual exchanges with people on the street. As a matter of fact those people on the street were very important in building a porch culture. The porch served a dual role as stage and orchestra for Goffmanesque performances. As Mary Easter indicates, sitting on the porch at certain times of day, was "an occasion." People planned it; people freshened up for it. Women retired to their porches after demands of the protestant work ethic had been met to see and be seen. From their perch above the street, they could look down on passers by, wave, greet, and, after the passer had gone, comment. Each new event on the street was occasion for new stories or for dragging out old ones. And at the same time, those who walked by were audience for the performance on the porch.

Except at resorts and vacation cottages, the stage function of the porch seems to have been the only part of women's porch culture to survive into the 1980s. True, people do still sit on porches – when they have them – in the spring and fall, but it seems usually to be a sentimental harkening to days gone by. When it gets really hot, they huddle indoors with their air conditioning. Women, equipped with cars and telephones, no longer need to sit outdoors to maintain social contact. Television supplies continuous undemanding entertainment for those who are bored. And most women of the eighties are too busy performing the superwoman roles today's society has assigned them to have time to sit outdoors to greet and be greeted. In our frenetic society, a new need for "privacy" demands that what serious outdoor activity remains be relegated to decks at the rear of newer homes. And houses are seldom built with porches any more.

At the end of *The Ballad of the Sad Cafe*, Miss Amelia, bereft of the love who appeared one night on her front porch, waits three years on the same porch for his return, but no longer is there any communion on that porch, and finally she shuts herself inside – away from all society. So it seems in the American summertime as row upon row of tightly shut-up air-conditioned houses suggest that communion is unwelcome, that the pedestrian is an intruder. Many of the porches that remain have been enclosed to provide indoor living space. Like Miss Amelia, female residents in these houses have shut themselves inside away from communion with their neighbors. And the porches that remain outdoors have often been partially enclosed with unsightly screens – allowing occupants to be indoors and outdoors at the same time but denying access to passers by. Traces of the porch as stage remain, however, to show that women reluctantly relinquish the liminality of the porch.

In the South, where porches provided indoor/outdoor living space for most of the year, new houses are built with rudimentary vestiges of the once grand veranda. With spindly columns and scarcely three feet of width, these so called porches are furnished as carefully as the living room within, but not as if to be used. Women spend hours scouting to find the correct antique mammy's bench, wickerwork cradle or hand caned rocker to suggest that any minute now a woman in hoop skirts, baby in hand, will come out to sip iced tea and wave at the neighbors. Untold thousands are spent on wrought iron furniture never intended for the derriere to suggest gracious living in a time just past. Blossoming plants tended as the babies once were extend the garden a little closer to the seldom used front door – people today enter through the attached garage, never seeing the outdoors as they emerge from their air-conditioned cars. Those fortunate enough to own older homes, north and south, furnish their porches with comfortable traditional swings and rocking chairs, but often they reveal the merely decorative nature of the furniture by placing them so close to the walls that rocking or swinging would be disastrous.

Those remembrances of community past are amusing and often even attractive. Other porches, however, seem almost tragic in the longing they reveal for a time of greater neighborliness. Women deprived of self actualization, not by today's mores but by their age and the era in which they grew, sometimes decorate their porches as if they were their last mute contact with other people. It is not unusual to find a single porch sporting wind chimes, all-season wreaths, plastic flora and fauna, concrete plant urns and […] even a wine bottle or two. Even more heart rending for me, however, are the houses with no porch at all.

Once air conditioning made porches expendable, people for whom home ownership itself must have been a dream come true put the money that might once have gone for a porch into window units. The result was what I call a "mean little house" – mean in the sense of stingy, giving only what must be given, begrudging even that. These unadorned dwellings seem often to occupy lots with few or no trees, and equally often they seem to house older people – people who were once part of porch culture. And in front of or beside these houses, older women can often be seen huddled under the eave on a kitchen chair, or in the car port, knowing, regardless of an air-cooled interior, the need to "cool off" on the porch just as my mother-in-law did.

Last summer I visited my home town in Kentucky to show my children where I grew up and, incidentally, to photograph porches. As we strolled by one of the grandest houses from my day – the house of the federal judge – I was telling my children how excited I had been when the judge's granddaughter invited me to play with paper dolls on that very porch when we noticed in the corner of that great front porch, a tiny, shriveled-up woman. Her live-in companion confirmed that the woman on the porch was the judge's wife and grandmother of my childhood friend and invited me to speak with her, warning me she wouldn't know me. True, she did not recognize me, but she would never forget the ritual of the porch. Strapped in her chair so that she wouldn't fall, bereft of most of the knowledge she had accumulated in ninety-odd years, she greeted me as she had hundreds of other visitors to her porch over all those years – as if it were once again 1951, and she had yet to have a car of her own, the only air conditioning was to be found in movie houses, televiewing was relegated to those who had a stomach for professional wrestling, and the ritual of the porch had never ended. She had freshened up to sit on the porch, she was "assessable, receiving," and I was a neighbor who passed on the street and stopped to chat.

Women of her era, often foggy about the present, have no difficulty recalling the porch's meaning for women for over a century of American history. For her, for me, and for countless other women the front porch will remain an artifactual testimony to the isolation women once experienced and the resourcefulness with which they overcame it.

Notes

1. All information on Turner's liminality and communitas is drawn from Victor Turner, *Dramas, Fields and Metaphors: Symbolic Action in Human Society*, Chapters 1 and 7, although he has written of the concepts in many of his writings.
2. Material on the actual history of porches is difficult to find, and most of what is available is impressionistic – as is this article. The most serious scholarship on the front porch as significant domestic architecture to date is a mere two pages by John Michael Vlach. In *The Afro-American Tradition in Decorative Arts*, Vlach has carefully documented the African and Caribbean origins of the traditional American front porch (136–8). In "The North Carolina Porch: A Climactic and Cultural Buffer," Ruth Little-Stokes reported the same origins but her essay is primarily interpretive. Davida Rochlin's essay, "The Front Porch," reports the social significance of American porches but eschews history. In his classic history of architecture, Sir Bannister Fletcher acknowledges the ancient European origins of the "grand porticoes" and galleries of the early American Southeast, but porches *per se* are beneath his concern. Other sources have undoubtedly mentioned perfunctorily the appendages on American houses, but the architectural history of porches is most significant for its invisibility.
3. This story, very difficult if not impossible to track down through newspapers of the day, was related by T. H. Beckham, 86-year-old lifetime resident of Amory and Beauchamp's neighbor after 1940 when he bought and moved into the house at 105 S. Fifth Street.
4. Goffman quotes de Beauvoir when he quite accurately demonstrates that women alone are often freed from the restraints of social performance (125). In *The Second Sex*, a startling new book when Goffman wrote *The Presentation of Self in Everyday Life*, Simone de Beauvoir also shows that women perform for other women as well as for men although she appears unaware that she is describing performers when she describes women's behavior among themselves (528–45).

Works Cited

Baker, Russell, *Growing Up*. New York: Congdon and Weed, 1982.

de Beauvoir, Simone, *The Second Sex*. New York: Alfred A. Knopf, 1953.

Easter, Mary, "Sitting on the Porch." *Absorb the Colors: Poems by Northfield Women Poets*. Ed. Beverly Voldseth and Karen Herseth Wee. Northfield, Minnesota: privately published, 1986.

Fletcher, Sir Bannister, *A History of Architecture*, 17th ed. New York: Charles Scribner's Sons, 1983.

Foley, Mary Mix, *The American House.* New York: Harper and Row, 1980.

Goffman, Erving, *The Presentation of Self in Everyday Life.* Garden City, NY: Doubleday, 1959.

Hurston, Zora Neale, *Their Eyes Were Watching God.* 1937. Urbana, Illinois: University of Illinois Press, 1980.

Little-Stokes, Ruth, "The North Carolina Porch: A Climactic and Cultural Buffer." *Carolina Dwelling.* Ed. Douglas Swaim.

Mason, Bobbie Ann. "Residents and Transients." *Shiloh and Other Stories.* New York: Harper, 1983, pp. 121–31.

McCullers, Carson. *The Ballad of the Sad Cafe. Seven Contemporary Short Novels.* 3rd ed. Ed. Charles Clerc and Louis Leiter. Glenview, Illinois: Scott, Foresman and Company, 1982.

Rochlin, Davida, "The Front Porch." *Home Sweet Home: American Domestic Vernacular Architecture.* New York: Rizzoli, 1983.

Turner, Victor, *Dramas, Fields and Metaphors: Symbolic Action in Human Society.* Ithaca: Cornell University Press, 1974.

Vlach, John Michael, *The Afro-American Tradition in Decorative Arts.* Cleveland, Ohio: The Cleveland Museum of Art, 1978.

CHAPTER 3

All We Have Is Time

Time is another major way we orient ourselves. What does it mean to be on time, out of time, or in time? This chapter discusses different cultural notions of time, the development of measuring time and clocks, the construction of the Western calendar and its rootedness in a sacred worldview, and birthdays and other markers of time.

All We Have Is Time

"Time is money."

With that simple statement, Benjamin Franklin captured the spirit that would transform America. The quotation is a very condensed summary of what has been called the *Protestant ethic*. This ethic, according to Max Weber, fueled the beginnings of capitalism in the sixteenth century. In *The Protestant Ethic and the Spirit of Capitalism*, Weber characterized the ethic as "this-worldly asceticism" in contrast to the more typical kind of asceticism that focuses on the next world. It was ascetic because it frowned upon luxury and consumption and encouraged thrift and saving in order to build up capital; the accumulation of wealth for its own sake should not be the motive, "but the attainment of it as a fruit of labour in a calling was a sign of God's blessing" (Weber [1904–5] 1958: 172). Today, this ethic, in an age of consumption and prodigal spending, seems very distant, especially its religious underpinnings, but it set the stage for the widespread transformation of the way our lives would be conducted and our time used.

The Protestant ethic became more entrenched with the industrial revolution in Europe and the United States in the nineteenth century. While seemingly unrelated to Protestantism or to ethics, time was, nevertheless, part of both. People had to change their perception and relation to time. Time became a commodity to be used (well) rather than the medium in which life is lived. It had to be used for work, not pleasure; and any time spent not working meant less money. Work began to be strictly plotted against the clock so that workers were paid by the hour; thenceforth, each hour became equivalent to a specific amount of money. So much is the equivalence taken for granted that the language we use for time is the same that we use for money: we save it, we spend it, we borrow it, we waste it, and we budget it. This notion of time now seems so natural that it is difficult

Investigating Culture: An Experiential Introduction to Anthropology, Second Edition.
Carol Delaney with Deborah Kaspin.
© 2011 Carol Delaney. Published by Blackwell Publishing Ltd.

for most of us to imagine other ways of thinking about it. The idea that time is money also implies that it comes in different quantities, not nickels, dimes, and quarters, but seconds, minutes, and hours. Time, thus imagined, is also like a ruler (in both senses of the term); not only does it reign over us, but also it is calibrated like inches, feet, and yards. Each of the time segments is equal to all others in the same category; that is, each second is equal to every other second. Time is imagined as something outside of ourselves against which we measure our work and days. But what if time was considered a gift? What different metaphors would describe it? How might such a different conception of time affect your daily life?

86,400 Seconds per Day

Imagine there is a bank that credits your account each morning with $86,400. It carries over no balance from day to day. Every evening it deletes whatever part of the balance you failed to use during the day. What would you do? Draw out every cent, of course! Each of us has such a bank. Its name is TIME. Every morning, it credits you with 86,400 seconds. Every night it writes off, as lost, whatever of this you have failed to invest to good purpose. It carries over no balance. It allows no overdraft. Each day it opens a new account for you. Each night it burns the remains of the day. If you fail to use the day's deposits, the loss is yours. There is no going back. There is no drawing against "tomorrow." You must live in the present on today's deposits. Invest it so as to get from it the utmost in health, happiness, and success! The clock is running. Make the most of today.

> To realize the value of ONE YEAR, ask a student who failed a grade.
> To realize the value of ONE MONTH, ask a mother who gave birth to a premature baby.
> To realize the value of ONE WEEK, ask the editor of a weekly newspaper.
> To realize the value of ONE HOUR, ask the lovers who are waiting to meet.
> To realize the value of ONE MINUTE, ask a person who missed the train.
> To realize the value of ONE SECOND, ask a person who just avoided an accident.
> To realize the value of ONE MILLISECOND, ask the person who won a silver medal in the Olympics.

Treasure every moment that you have. And treasure it more because you shared it with someone special, special enough to spend your time. And remember that time waits for no one. Yesterday is history. Tomorrow is mystery. Today is a gift. That's why it is called the present! (life-cycles-destiny.com n.d.)

Cosmological Time

Time, like space, is one of the major ways we orient ourselves in the world. Although we talk about it all the time, it is also something we take very much for granted. Time and space, we assume, are given in the human condition and, therefore, universal. While true, we must ask a further question. Paraphrasing linguist Benjamin Lee Whorf (1956: 138):

Are our concepts of time and space and matter given in substantially the same form by experience to all people? Or are they conditioned by the particularities of language and culture?

Is the *experience* the same worldwide and then conceptually warped or channeled differently due to local custom? Or, is the very experience itself shaped and molded by culture? This chapter is not intended to provide answers but rather to raise awareness of the issues involved. In this first part, we will consider the widest, cosmological aspects of time – clocks and calendars. In the second part, we focus on lived time, that is, the myriad ways that time forms the context and parameters of our lives.

Relativity of time

Ever since Einstein, we have been taught that time is relative even if we do not understand his theories. Time is relative to space, neither is absolute, they are mutually constitutive; nor is there any independent standpoint for measurement. While the theory of relativity involves sophisticated mathematical knowledge and calculations, even a child becomes aware that time is relative to space as soon as he or she tries to call a grandparent living in another time zone.

Still, this is a different sense of the relativity of time from what I am getting at, namely, that the concepts and experience of time are also relative. Surely even in your own lives you are aware of different experiences of time – sometimes it flies by, and at other times it drags and seems to stand still. We remember our childhoods as slow and seemingly endless; as we enter our forties and fifties, time seems to speed up, and the years begin to flip over very fast. Our clocks and calendars are unable to represent even this common experience.

What notions of time does Octavio Paz (1984), the Mexican poet, capture in this excerpt from his poem "Hymn among the Ruins"?

> Day, Round day
> luminous orange in 24 sections
> all filled with the same sunny sweetness …

Clearly, he had the roundness of the earth, the roundness of the sun, and the roundness of a clock dial in mind. Between them, he seems to say, a homology exists. The poem was obviously composed before the invention of "digital" clocks. Although the word *digital* refers to fingers, and thus evokes a "hand," making all clocks "digital," it has come to refer to a very specific kind of clock or watch invented in July 1970. Digital clocks and watches became affordable and widespread in the 1980s (see figure 3.1 for a humorous take on this). Until then, clocks and watches were most commonly in the form of a circle with hours 1–12 set around the dial. Two hands, one for the hour and one for the minutes (and occasionally a third one to mark the seconds), moved "clockwise" around the dial. On digital clocks and watches the exact time, for example 3:23, flashes in the window. The numbers are alone, not set in the context of the round of hours, as on a clock face.

Figure 3.1   Worldly Wit cartoon by Mike Scott © 1989 Cartoonists and Writers Syndicate.

Today when I ask someone what time it is, I usually get an answer more exact than I want so that I have to pause to figure it out according to my time frame. I have a mental model of the round clock face and am used to hearing someone say, "It's ten past four," not "4:11," or "Quarter to six," not "5:48." Time has become linear in the extreme and calibrated to the second. Children today are being brought up not only with a much more linear view of time but also one timed to the precise moment. They are also being made more aware of time at an earlier age because of television, for they quickly learn that they will miss their favorite programs if they don't know how to tell time. Not only are they learning how to tell time, they are also being trained early to think of it as something external – as something against which to coordinate their activities. We do not yet know the long-term effects of this on their lives.

Some people think of time as a *RIVER* – it flows on and on – and Heraclitus, an ancient Greek philosopher, made the comment that you can never step into the same river twice. Other people think of time as a *PENDULUM* – back and forth, tick-tock, representing the alternation of night and day. Still others think of time as *CYCLICAL*, that it goes round and round, with the continual return of the seasons.

Our view of time is that it marches on relentlessly and impersonally. We live with a mechanical sense of time because our culture is so dominated by machines – the "clock-work universe." Yet there are other models of time. One former student imagined the following possibilities: agriculturalists and peasants, he thought, must live with a seasonal view of time, and people in fishing societies live with a tidal view of time. No doubt, surfers do too!

But these are not the only alternatives; some groups live by flower time – the Australian aborigines, who traditionally were hunters and gatherers, kept time by the type of flower in bloom and, thus, when to expect honey and certain kinds of fruit. And in *Return to Laughter* (see chapter 1), Bowen says something similar: "there was the season of yams, of guinea corn, and of millet" ([1954] 1964: 69). Your grandparents surely had some sense of this because of the seasons when certain fruits and vegetables would be available, for example, spinach, Brussels sprouts, blueberries, tomatoes, grapefruit, and oranges. Do you know what seasons they traditionally appeared in? While it is wonderful to have all things available all the time (from someplace), do we lose that sense of anticipation? Is it possible our senses get blunted?

Time before clocks

> Time – the time that we know through clocks and calendars – was invented.
>
> *Encyclopedia Britannica* (n.d.)

Most of us think about time in terms of clocks; they are so pervasive in our lives it is difficult to think of life without them. But many people live and have lived their entire lives without clocks. They lived by the diurnal rhythms of the sun and the alternation of the seasons. Elenore Bowen (Laura Bohannan) well captured her own struggle with the time sense among the people she studied in Africa. After only 10 weeks "in the field," she said that

> already time had taken on a more individualistic and yet more seasonable aspect than I had been used to. Already the days of the week and the month were no more than a heading printed on my diary pages. I did try to keep count; old habit made me feel I ought to know the date. Yet, in July, when I went back to the station for supplies, I found I had lost three days. ([1954] 1964: 68)

She went on to say that it was easier to give up the idea of "right time of day" and instead went on her own time zone. In order to maintain some kind of schedule, she decided that "dark and seven by the clock were to coincide. Every few weeks for the rest of my stay in the bush, I readjusted the clock."

> I learned to forget months and to live by moons: to anticipate the full moon for its dances and storytelling; to fear the dark of the moon when witches were abroad.

Cutting through the moons was, for me, a complicated combination of weeks. First there was the cook's seven-day curry week, highlighting Saturdays. Then there was the five-day cycle of markets by which everyone made engagements. Finally there was the seven-day-beer-brewing week. … There was no year, merely a succession of seasons and agricultural activities uncorrelated with moons or markets. The rains began when it began to rain; when it began to rain people started to plant. One could say that a man had done his planting late, but not that the rains had come late. (p. 69)

Evans-Pritchard, a well-known British anthropologist, said something similar about the Nuer, a different African group he studied.

The Nuer have no expression equivalent to "time" in our language, and they cannot, therefore, as we can, speak of time as though it were something actual, which passes, can be wasted, can be saved, and so forth. I do not think that they ever experience the same feeling of fighting against time or of having to co-ordinate activities with an abstract passage of time because their points of reference are mainly the activities themselves, which are generally of a leisurely character. Events follow a logical order, but they are not controlled by an abstract system, there being no autonomous points of reference to which activities have to conform with precision. ([1940] 1976: 103)

The Nuer, he concludes, are fortunate. For us time is the enemy, we are always fighting against it. Ultimately, of course, it is a battle we will lose. Might our conception of time have anything to do with the frantic pace and anxiety that have come to characterize our lives? Perhaps this anxiety is related to the current interest in Eastern philosophies and techniques of relaxation and meditation. However, these practices, in the West, are taken out of context, unhinged from the worldview or cosmology that produced them.

Time's beginning and end

Where or when does time start and where or when will it end? Ali Mazrui, whom I discussed in chapter 2, also asked why it is that Greenwich in Britain is "the mean time for the alarm clocks of the human race. The clocks of the world have responded to that choice. Even when we say 'universal standard time' we are really predicating it on Greenwich mean time. A spot on the British Isles has changed the clocks and watches of the world" (quoted in *Dial*, September 1986: 21). He noted how that was a political act. It had to do with Britain's domination of the world, when it was an Empire over which the sun never set, that is, when it had a colony in every time zone.

The International Dateline

The idea for the international dateline came about when Greenwich mean time was accepted as the universal prime meridian, that is, the point from which longitude was calculated and world time was set. This was decided in 1884 at a conference in Washington, DC, attended by representatives of 25 nations but, at that time, was accepted by only 22. The international dateline, which set the time zones of the planet, was to be halfway round the world, at 180 degrees, in the mid-Pacific. Not all countries accepted this at first; the last two nations were Saudi Arabia, 1962, and Liberia, 1972.

Author unknown.

Clocks were introduced beginning in the fourteenth century; at that time they were primarily installed in church towers and were used to ring out the time of *matins* and *vespers* – morning and evening prayers. But clocks were not very accurate and people continued to use sundials, even to set the clocks, in the seventeenth, eighteenth, and nineteenth centuries. Most towns ran on their own time, setting the clocks at high noon. The impetus for a *standard* for time was the railroad, and it was a Canadian, Sanford Fleming, who came up with the idea.[1]

Actually, the clocks of the world are no longer set according to Greenwich mean time. Since 1972, we have gone onto UTC (Coordinated Universal Time) calculated by the atomic clock(s) at the US Naval Observatory. Time is no longer "measured by the motion of the earth in space but by the oscillations at the atomic level of a rare, soft, bluish-grey metal called *cesium*" (Duncan 1998: 290). And it is based on the measure of a *second* rather than minutes, hours, or days. "Our second is now determined by the difference in energy state of the cesium-133 atom when its nucleus and outer electron spin in the same or opposite direction" (Barnett 1998: 167). There are officially 86,400 seconds in each day (see the box at the beginning of this chapter); however, every now and again "leap seconds" have to be added because there is a gap between the atomic clock and the earth's rotation! The atomic clock is too perfect for this wobbly and flawed earth.

In accordance with the theory of relativity, atomic clocks do not keep uniform time, but depend on the gravitational field where they happen to be placed. Their running also varies with the latitude of the place, the height above sea level, the distance of the earth from the sun, the distance of the moon, etc. But all of these variations can be calculated and allowed for, thus arriving at a suitable scale of time. (Fraser 1966: 411)

Suitable for whom? Fortunately, most of us do not yet need to calculate our lives according to nanoseconds or picoseconds but can get by with conventional clocks and watches.

Calendars

Calendars, like clocks, help us keep track of time – they mark not the minutes and the hours but the days, weeks, months, and years. Most of us have calendars not only on our walls or on our desks and in our computers but also in our purses, bookbags, and briefcases – whether they are Filofaxes or PalmPilots. We carry them with us so we can schedule appointments and keep track of our activities. Calendars also situate us in the world and history, for we plot world events according to the calendar. We characterize history in terms of decades and centuries – the 1960s, for example, or the nineteenth century. We know we are living in the twenty-first century and are poised to compare it with centuries past.

Calendars construct time in the same way that maps construct space, embedding cultural schemas in the foundation of "reality" and vice versa.[2] Thus the Western calendar – which is now the dominant world calendar – reflects a specific cultural history by dating it from the year of Christ's birth. It is – insert current year – AD (*anno Domini* – in the year of Our Lord).[3] Some people have begun to use CE (common era) instead of AD as a more "politically correct" form. But just *whose* common era? Jews preceded Christians by at least a millennium, and the two religions have surely not merged despite the hyphen in Judeo-Christian. I find *common era* a euphemism because it still begins with Christ's birth and, thus, subordinates the Jewish calendrical system—and those of every other non-Christian people who rely on the Western calendar—to the Christian.

Jews do have their own calendar; at the Christian year 2000, the Jewish calendar recorded 5,760 years since the *world* began. The traditional Chinese calendar was lunar and the year 2000 was, for the Chinese, 4698. When Mao Zedong accepted the Gregorian calendar in 1949, the Chinese people lost 2,649 years! However, they continue with their 12-year cycles of animals (the year 2000 was the year of the Dragon). Muslims also have their own calendar; I will describe it in somewhat more detail because I know a little more about it and it is unfamiliar to non-Muslim Westerners.

The Muslim calendar

Although Islam is one of the Abrahamic religions – because it goes back to the founding story of Abraham – and shares much with both Judaism and Christianity, its calendar is different from both. It does not begin with Creation, as the Jewish calendar does, nor does it begin with the birth of Muhammad, as the Christian calendar begins with the birth of Jesus. Instead, it begins with a specific event that was critical for the establishment of the new Muslim community: Muhammad's migration (*Hijra*) from Mecca to Medina. According to Christians, this occurred in AD 622, but according to Moslems, this is year 1 AH (after the *Hijra*). This places in their temporal schema what prayer practices, pilgrimages, and, recently, their cars' Global Positioning Systems enact in their spatial schemas: the Muslim world begins in Mecca.

The Muslim calendar further differs from the Western calendar by marking lunar cycles instead of solar, creating a discrepancy of about 10 days between them which can be reconciled only through a complicated calculation. Thus the Muslim calendar consists of 354 or 355 days divided into 12 lunar months of, alternately, 29 and 30 days. Each month begins with the new moon, an important symbol of Islam, which is why it is found on the flags of Muslim nations. Furthermore, because lunar cycles do not coincide with seasons, Muslim holidays – unlike Christian and Jewish holidays – also do not coincide with seasons. Instead, every year they fall about 10 days earlier on the Western calendar than they did the previous year, and complete an entire circuit on the Western calendar every 33 years. For example, Ramazan or Ramadan, the month of fasting, will begin 10 days earlier this year than it did last year. One is supposed to fast from dawn (when you can distinguish a white thread from a black) to about an hour after sunset. During the time I was in Turkey, Ramazan fell at the worst possible times, August and July respectively, which meant that people fasted – ate nothing and drank nothing – for up to 18 hours every day.

This movement of the festivals through the year communicates a subtle message. Their lack of attachment to earthly seasons points *beyond them* to emphasize the distinction between the earthly and divine realms. It also helps to highlight the mutability and transitoriness of earthly life and the immutability and eternity of the divine realm. Thus the calendar, itself, incorporates meanings of cosmological and spiritual significance.

So, too, does the call to prayer (*ezan* in Turkish), which is intoned five times a day from a minaret, the slender tower adjacent to a mosque. Each *ezan* has a specific name, and the intervals between them are not equal. The longest intervals are the ones between the late-night *ezan* and the one when first light appears, and between that *ezan* and the one at midday. In addition, the daily schedule changes from summer to winter since the timing and therefore the intervals depend on the hours of daylight. The intervals are shorter in winter and longer in summer. Regardless, five times a day Muslims are oriented toward Mecca – an unseen point on the horizon – which is the earthly symbol of their original and final destination. The call to prayer orients Muslims temporally, spatially, and spiritually.

Calendar changes   We think of the calendar as a neutral kind of chronological record-keeping mechanism, but it is actually a highly political institution. For example, after the fall of the Ottoman Empire, Atatürk changed the country's calendar to coincide with that of the West. This was meant as a secularizing, modernizing, and Westernizing reform, but it is, of course, also the Christian calendar. Not surprisingly, a number of devout Turks resent this change for, to them, it means living by the time of the infidels. However, Atatürk was not the first to change his country's calendar.

French revolutionary calendar   After the French Revolution, a new calendar was instituted. "The count of the years would begin with 1792; and the New Year's Day would be 22 September – the equinox" (Aveni 1989: 144). Anthony Aveni, an astronomer who became fascinated with anthropology, wrote a splendid book, *Empires of Time: Calendars, Clocks, and Cultures*, which gives a brief account of the French revolutionary calendar. It was to be very "rational" and designed to counteract the "irrational" elements inherent in religion, specifically to break the hold of Christianity over the people. The new calendar consisted of a 10-day week with three weeks to a month. Each day had 10 hours of 100 minutes each and each minute had 100 seconds. Each day was named numerically rather than after celestial bodies and the Norse gods that represented them, as are the English days: Sun day is obvious; Moon day = Monday; Tiw's day = Tuesday; Woden's day = Wednesday; Thor's day = Thursday; Fria's day = Friday; and Saturn day = Saturday. In the French revolutionary calendar, months were named after the kinds of weather characteristic of the time, for example, mist, frost, and snow. The year had 360 days, and the five or six extra were given special names and became days of festivity. Most of the people hated the new calendar because, after a while, it became difficult to know what day was Sunday and, thus, what day to go to church, make confession, take the sacrament, and receive blessing. It lasted only 14 years; the old (Gregorian) calendar was reinstated after Napoleon took power.

Soviet Union revolutionary calendar

Another attempt to change the calendar was made by Russian revolutionaries. In 1929 the Soviet Union embarked on a five-day continuous production week – four days for work and the fifth was free. There were six weeks in a month and, although the Gregorian names of the months were retained, the days of the week were numbered. Each worker was assigned to a particular day and each day had a particular color. Some people would begin their workweek on day 1 and work for four days then have a day off, others would begin on day 2, work for four days and have a day off, still others would begin on day 3, and so forth. That is what made it a *continuous production* week, but the social consequences were significant. First, only one-fifth of the population was off on any given day. It became very difficult to remember when various friends and relatives had their day off. Would their day off coincide with yours? Would you ever be able to go on an outing together? Since no more than a fifth of the population would be free at the same time, it became difficult for people to mobilize for protests and demonstrations. The calendar was, clearly, a measure of social control, but it, too, was implemented expressly to destroy "the opiate of the people," that is, their addiction to religion. Like the French revolutionary calendar before it, the Soviet version also faced strong resistance from the people. A number of changes were made, but it was finally abandoned in 1940, when the Soviets, too, returned to the Gregorian calendar.

The Gregorian calendar

The Gregorian calendar itself marked a significant change from the Julian calendar that preceded it. The motive for change was that the Julian calendar was out of sync with the solar year, so that Easter and other religious holy days were falling at the wrong times. So, "in 1582, Pope Gregory XIII officially revised the accepted length of the year to 365.2422 days, adjusted the leap-year rule, and lopped off the 10 extra days" (*Encyclopedia Britannica*, n.d.)! This brought the calendar into harmony with the cosmology and strengthened the hold of Catholicism on the routines of social life. Of course, this also created discrepancies in the historical records that scholars must continually reconcile: dates recorded before 1582 are out of phase with those recorded after. But most of us are unaware of this "wrinkle in time" that lies within our own historical records, a reflection of how completely we have internalized the Gregorian calendar as simply the way time is.

The week

So many of us take the seven-day week for granted that we probably assume it is "natural." Yet the Romans had an eight-day week, and other peoples have had "weeks" consisting of 3 to 10 days. But why bother with weeks? Couldn't we get along just fine with days, months, and years? British anthropologist Edmund Leach claims that people need to punctuate the seamless flow of time, to give order and rhythm to their lives.

> We talk of measuring time, as if time were a concrete thing waiting to be measured; but in fact we *create time* by creating intervals in social life. Until we have done this there is no time to be measured. (Leach 1961: 135)

Knowing what day it is is often the first thing we think of when we get up, because we do different things on different days. So says Eviatar Zerubavel, a sociologist who has written a fascinating book on the history and meaning of the week, *The Seven Day Circle* (1985). Ordinarily, there is an alternation between "sacred" time and "profane" time, one day is a holy day (holiday) or festival day or, as in the Soviet calendar, a day of rest breaking up the week of labor. You have different classes on different days; you have sports practice on Mondays, say, or theater group on Thursday mornings. Knowing what day it is is "indispensable for transcending our subjectivity and participating – at least mentally – in a social, rather than a merely personal world" (Zerubavel 1985: 2). Each day of the week also has its own distinct "feel." Friday afternoons, for example, have a very different feel than do Monday mornings (except if you happen to be a museum employee, since museums are usually closed on Mondays). Weekends, for most of us, are completely different from the workweek – a time for relaxation, for shopping, for sports, for a movie, or for church. The differing meanings of the days become apparent to those who do not have a Saturday night date or, at least, some alternative plan.

Some of you may never have thought about where our week comes from; others are probably well aware that it is intimately related to religion. It is the legacy of Genesis, the first book of the Bible, common to both Jews and Christians. In Genesis it is stated that God created the world in six days and rested on the seventh day. Our workweek, then, is a dim reflection of the work of Creation. This rhythm of days has been going on since the times of the ancient Hebrews:

Six days shalt thou labor, and do all thy work but the seventh day is the sabbath of the Lord thy God; in it thou shalt not do any work – thou, nor thy son, nor thy daughter, thy manservant, nor thy maidservant, nor thy cattle, nor the stranger that is within thy gates. For in six days, the Lord made heaven and earth, the sea and all that is in them, and rested the seventh day: wherefore the Lord blessed the sabbath day and hallowed it. (Exodus 20: 8–11)

Even for nonbelievers, or for believers of other faiths, each week reenacts the biblical event. For those of you who think that religion is something private, a personal individual decision, it is important to realize how a religious tradition creates worldviews and influences attitudes, values, and even notions of time and space that affect everyone regardless of their private, personal beliefs. We don't use the calendar we do because it is better. The use of a specific calendar is deeply political – the result of battles, of power and politics, and of the domination by one particular segment of the world's population.

Clearly, calendars can be changed – after all, they are arbitrary – but it is very difficult because they have important meanings to the people whose lives are conditioned by them. The secular calendars have been resisted for a number of reasons, but the primary one was because they were seen as sacrilegious, they transgressed the sacred rhythm of days ordained by God and laid down in Genesis, at the beginning.

The year, as well as the week, also has a religious foundation – not from Genesis but from Christianity. What of the recent millennium? Whose millennium is it? It signifies 2,000 years of Christianity. What about people who do not or did not have a seven-day week or the same calendar? Do you think they should adopt it because the Christian calendar is better? More accurate? Or, do you think they have been forced to adopt it because of political domination? In my opinion, the millennium offered an opportunity to begin again. For, despite its Christian roots, the entire world did acknowledge and celebrate it. We could have started with year 0 to avoid the problems the Christian calendar created because it began with year 1. We could have called it Global Calendar or GC for short. Even though it would be built on the Christian calendar, it would quickly become separate from it since Christians could continue with their own calendar just as Jews, Muslims, Hindus, Chinese, and others already do, but a Global Calendar might gain worldwide consent as long as it was separate and distinct and used for secular, communicative, and business purposes.

Our notions of time, not just calendars, also have religious roots that are entangled with the concept of Creation. While this discussion may challenge or even offend those who believe strongly in the monotheistic God of Judaism, Christianity, or Islam, it is important to think about. Stephen Hawking, perhaps the most famous contemporary physicist-cosmologist, is well aware of the relation between religious concepts and time. In his book *A Brief History of Time*, he said,

> So long as the universe had a beginning, we could suppose it had a Creator. But if the universe is really completely self-contained, having no boundary or edge, it would have neither beginning nor end; it would simply be. What place, then, for a Creator? (1988: 140–1)

While all peoples have myths of origin, not all stories of origin are stories of creation and, thus, not all have a notion of a creator. Some origin myths recount transformations of one thing into another, or describe emergences from underground, or even portray the world as dream or illusion. Some peoples may have a variety of origin myths to explain and account for the variety of phenomena. A culture influenced by monotheism has a tendency to search for monocausal explanations – for example, the current search by physicists for a "grand unified theory" – one theory to explain how the universe (and everything in it) came into being.

We tend to think of time as linear, universal, and quantifiable, yet we know this view is not universal. Our notion of time incorporates a specific teleology – the idea that there is a purpose, goal, or reason inherent in it; but that idea, itself, derives from a particular *mythos*, a legacy from the Judeo-Christian worldview. I quote Johannes Fabian, a Dutch anthropologist, from his book *Time and the Other*:

> In the Judeo-Christian tradition [and I would add Islamic tradition], Time has been conceived as the medium of a sacred history. Time was thought, but more often celebrated, as a sequence of specific events that befell a chosen people. Much has been said about the linear character of that conception as opposed to pagan, cyclical views of Time as an *eternal retour*. Yet such spatial metaphors of temporal thought tend to obscure something of more immediate

significance. … Faith in a covenant between a Divinity and one people, trust in divine providence as it unfolds in a history of salvation centered on one Savior, make for sacred conceptions of Time. They stress the specificity of Time, its realization in a given cultural ecology – the Eastern Mediterranean, first, and the circum-Mediterranean with Rome at its hub, later. [For Muslims it is Mecca, and for all three religions, Jerusalem is a sacred city they fight over.] (Fabian 1983: 2; my remarks in square brackets)

Fabian continues,

Decisive steps toward modernity, those that permitted the emergence of anthropological discourse, must be sought not in the invention of a linear conception, but in a succession of attempts to *secularize* Judeo-Christian Time by generalizing and universalizing it. (p. 2; my italics)

What he is saying is that *our* (Western) time became the time of all others. On the surface that sounds inclusive, but, in fact, it denies or effaces other people's senses of time. Because of political power, our sense of time has become the truth and the way for understanding others. (See figure 3.2.)

The notion of Creation implies a beginning – not just of the universe but also of time – symbolized in the Bible by the "Fall" when Adam and Eve left the Garden of Eden. We might easily imagine that the scientific theory of the "big bang" origin of the universe is a *secularization* of the notion of Creation at a specific moment, though cosmologists might take exception. The notion of a *beginning* to time also affects ideas about history, which recounts events that unfold in time, and are not repeatable. This, too, is a legacy from a specific religious tradition.

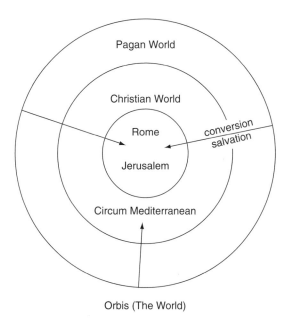

Figure 3.2 Premodern time–space: incorporation (Fabian 1983).

> The early Christian writers stressed the importance of individual historical events that would not be repeated. History, they said, did not move in cycles. On the contrary, there had been a Creation at a particular point in time. Christ had died on the Cross but once, and had been resurrected from the dead on but one occasion. Finally, at some point in the future, God's plan would be completed, and He would – once and for all – bring the world to an end. (Morris 1984: 11)

From this perspective, one could not imagine, as some cultures do, time as a deep-layered phenomenon in which the present moment was not just the end result of all that preceded it but also contained all of what went before. "Past," in that view, is "co-present"; whereas for us past is past, over and done with. We are oriented toward the future, so much so that we send "time capsules" into the future so that those who come after us might get some sense of what we were like. For example, each year at graduation, Stanford students place a time capsule under a pavement stone in the main quad that has the year's date engraved on it; it will be opened 100 years hence. At the same time, they dig one up from 100 years ago. Time capsules have been made elsewhere in the country, some intended to come due in 1,000, or even 5,000, years.

The linear view of time permitted the rise of notions of advancement and progress, and also of evolution. But it can also imply degeneration and collapse (entropy), and these ideas have figured prominently in theories and interpretations of human culture. In the nineteenth century when the issue of human evolution was first raised, theorists divided into two camps. *Monogenists* believed that modern humans all have the same origin. This basically recapitulates the Adam and Eve story in scientific dress. *Polygenists,* on the other hand, believed that there were different origins for the different races. According to this view, some of the peoples encountered might not be quite human. But monogenists could also espouse racist theories, for when they encountered "primitives," they often assumed they had degenerated from an earlier, more advanced, state and thus had to be recivilized.[4] Variants of these positions are still circulating.

Cultures inspired by religious traditions that are not monotheistic or even theistic do not, then, have a Creator god or gods who create the variety of things. They would have very different notions of time, of history, and the course and meaning of life.[5]

The assumption of a general, universal, and secular time underpinned, and continues to underpin, the project to create a universal history which is, at the same time, imagined as a *natural history* rather than the particular Christian history of salvation. This was, in

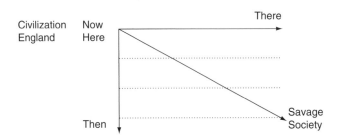

Figure 3.3 Modern time–space: distancing (Fabian 1983).

part, accomplished in the nineteenth century by the demise of Bishop Ussher's calculation, based on the genealogies in Genesis, that the world began in 4004 BC, and its replacement by theories of geological time. In the middle of the nineteenth century, according to anthropologist Thomas Trautman, the bottom "door" of time dropped out, that is, it extended backward not just by thousands but by millions of years. This radical transformation of Western notions of time and the rupture in the context of people's lives has hardly been appreciated. No longer was history divided into just ancient, medieval, and modern but a new category, "prehistory," was invented.

Prehistory came *before* ancient history; prehistory also implies nonliterate. When Europeans encountered peoples without written texts, they dubbed them "preliterate" and, therefore, "primitive," and placed them at the bottom of the evolutionary scale – implying that there is a teleology to literacy. These peoples were relegated to the rim of civilized space and the dawn of history. We refer to some of them as *stone-**age** peoples*, and imply by such a term that they are like people who existed long *before* us in the very distant past. *Stone-**tool** peoples*, focusing on their technology and way of life, is a better way of describing such people who are our contemporaries. We have imagined ourselves at the (advanced) center, they are at the edge, that is, earlier in time and peripheral in space. Time was not only naturalized, generalized, and secularized, but also spatialized. People living *far* from the center of "civilization" were *lower* on the evolutionary ladder. The closer to the beginning, the *lower* on the evolutionary scale. No wonder we call them aborigines, from *ab origine* meaning at the origin. We have thought that these ways of looking at others are scientific, but perhaps we have not really understood the mythical foundation of some of our basic scientific concepts. (See figure 3.3.)

The notion of progress (perhaps the secular version of salvation) and the naturalization and secularization of time were essential for the emergence of theories of evolution. Theories of *social* evolution (that some people are more advanced than others) were around long before Darwin developed his theory of *biological* evolution (that species change, through random mutation and natural selection, over time). As Darwin's theory became increasingly persuasive, proponents of social evolution appropriated his language, arguing that "progress" is propelled or obstructed by the biological capacity of different peoples. The result was some very dangerous beliefs and projects, such as the eugenics movement in the early twentieth century and, more recently, sociobiology. Both of these theories stress innate endowment over culture and environment as the source of human variation and achievement, and give natural selection an intention and purpose that Darwin never claimed. As such, they have converted the Calvinist notion of "divine election" – the belief that God has preordained who is saved and who is not (Yanagisako and Delaney 1995: 5) – into its secular equivalent, by seeing evolution as progress, and progress as the inevitable (or at least probable) trajectory of some people.

The transformation in time sense is also intimately related to the emergence of the academic disciplines of geology, archaeology, history, anthropology, economics, comparative religion, and probably others. They would not have arisen without these linear notions of time, and most are unable (or unwilling) to break free of them. This is not to disparage these intellectual accomplishments but to make you more aware that they have been achieved *within* the frame of a specific temporal-cosmological view. As such, they have come with certain costs, most notably an inability to imagine otherwise, and to assume our way is the only way and is both right and true. By the same token, intellectual break-throughs – or paradigm shifts – in academic disciplines do, at times, occur. This was certainly the case with American anthropologist Franz Boas and his students, who would make the first effort to study human and cultural variation in a way that did not reduce difference to developmental points on a linear timeline.

Lived Time

Thus far we have discussed the cosmological concepts of time – notions of beginnings and endings, calendars and clocks, and their religious underpinnings. These notions form the widest context in which we live our lives. We will now narrow our focus to the specific ways that concepts of time shape our daily lives and vice versa. Our concern here is summed up by the American author Sinclair Lewis, who wrote in his novel *Main Street* (1920):

> The greatest mystery about a human being is not his reaction to sex or praise, but the manner in which he contrives to put in twenty-four hours a day. It is this which puzzles the longshore-man about the banker, and the Londoner about the bushman [and no doubt your professor about you, and vice versa].

In other words, the experience of time is related to a particular form of life – to one's occupation, gender, age, class, and race – all of which are felt personally and are embedded in a larger culture and its history.

Consider, for example, your own past and future. The fact that you are in college or university means that in the past you spent time studying, so that you would get the grades necessary for admission. Decisions about how you spent your time were made long ago. You gave up some of your free time because you thought, or were told, that your future depended on it, that you could not get the job you want without a college education. Some of you may also have worked at odd jobs to earn spending money or to help support your family. That cut down on your study time and put you at a disadvantage to someone who did not have to work. Of course, a lot of young people from affluent families don't spend their time studying either, but they might be able to get a private tutor when it is necessary.

By contrast, inner-city youth, according to some sociologists, get into so much trouble not just because of poverty but also because they do not have (an idea of) a *future* that would be significantly different from their present. Similar statements have been made about young people who join terrorist groups. Without a sense of, and hope for, the future, people tend to see and use each day as if it might be their last, and for too many it is. This expectation is supported by the following statistics published in "Moments in America" by the Children's Defense Fund in 1991, also stated within the idiom of time. In the United States, every 5 hours a 15- to 19-year-old is murdered; every 35 seconds an infant is born into poverty; every 64 seconds an infant is born to a teenage mother; every 2 minutes an infant is born to a mother who received late or no prenatal care; every 14 minutes an infant dies in the first year of life; and every 14 hours a child younger than 5 is murdered (Sidel

1992: ix). Still others – more often than not, inner-city boys and men – *do time* in jail. What exactly does that mean? Why do you think the overwhelming majority of them are minorities? Do you think there is something inherent *in* them that predisposes them to criminal activity? Or, do you think their rate of incarceration has to do with cultural assumptions about race, and the political and economic arrangements that reinforce them? What are some of the ways that class and race affect how you spend your time?

Class and race are two of the variables that affect how we spend and think about time. In the rest of this chapter, we will focus on two arenas of lived time – lifetimes and work times – and consider how our experience of them is inflected by our statuses as men and women, as young and old, as affluent and indigent, as office worker and peasant, and so on.

Lifetimes

We begin with the lifetime, because it is a recurring framework in which all of us contend with the impact of time on our circumstances and possibilities. We believe we "have one life to live," as the soap opera says, and thus we want to make the most of it. But how much time do we have and how shall it be filled? In the United States, and most industrialized countries, life expectancy has increased dramatically over the past century, even in the last 50 years. For example, in 1950 the average life span, regardless of race or gender, was 68.2 years, whereas in 2001 it was 77.3 years (from US Department of Health and Human Services, in *Almanac and Book of Fact*, 2002). Of course, that doesn't mean all of us will reach those ages, but in general, people are living a longer time than in the past. In Third World countries there is more variation: in Kenya, for example, in 1950, life expectancy for both genders was 41 years, then it reached a high of around 60 in 1990, but has been declining ever since, so that in 2000 it was only 49 years (United Nations n.d.). Meanwhile, in Turkey, which has been considered a Third World country, the increase has been from 43.6 in 1950 to more than 70 in 2000! The gender disparity is in favor of women in industrialized nations, but shifts in favor of men in the Third World. What, do you think, might be responsible for this difference?

While we can all imagine a life span, we tend to think of it not as a straight path from birth to death, but as a curve ascending until maybe 40 or so and then it's "downhill all the way." We also break it up into phases – infancy, childhood, adolescence, young adulthood, adulthood, middle age, and elderly or just plain old – and punctuate it further with life cycle rituals or *rites de passage* that mark transitional events such as birth, marriage, and death. Some life events tend to coincide with calendrical cycles. June, for instance, is the favored month for weddings; births peak in late summer; and deaths in northern countries tend to occur in the winter. Even divorce rates betray a temporal logic, as most occur within four years of marriage. And we are profoundly disturbed when life events take place out of sequence – when, for example, a child dies, or when someone has a child long before or long after the "appropriate" age of parenthood.

In addition, people everywhere attach significance to particular dates (*times*). In the United States, for example, one such date is "sweet sixteen"; in many states, it is also the age at which you can legally drive. Other important ages are 18, when you can vote, buy lottery tickets or a gun, join the army, and get legally married; and 21, when you can drink legally. What other ages do you consider milestones? What significance, if any, do you give to turning 30, 40, 50, and 60? In the United States, 65 used to hold meaning when it was the mandatory age of retirement; but, citing ageism, the law was repealed and now people can work for as long as they want. Yet, under the aegis of ageism, there are many people who will feel guilty if they don't keep working. Perhaps it was better when the decision was out of individuals' hands and was the same for all.

Birthdays   Americans typically mark their journeys (to use a spatial metaphor) through their lives by celebrating birthdays. Yearly birthday celebrations are especially important to children – it is their special day – and many would feel bereft if they did not have a party. Parties are normally made for children, though adults celebrate certain of them, 60 and 65 being fairly popular. But as we age, our ambivalence about our advancing years is reflected in our reticence to publicize our birthdays with parties. For women especially, each year passed can be cause for depression, not celebration. This reflects the fact that age is differently gendered: in American culture, as in many others, older men are still imagined as attractive and vital, while older women are imagined as "old crones," are the butt of jokes, or are ignored. Still, 75 and 100 seem to be birthdays worth celebrating for both men and women: perhaps this is to salute their victory over the many hazards encountered along the path of a long life.

While we tend to mark and celebrate birthdays, people in many other cultures value them differently or not at all. In South Korea, the first birthday is the most important and is lavishly celebrated with special food and clothes, while the rest are downplayed or ignored. And in Turkey, as noted in chapter 1, people celebrate death days, perhaps because that is the day a person is born into the next, and better, world. Thus the celebration includes the recitation of the *Mevlud*, a poem that commemorates the birth of Mohammed, and by association links the death of the person to the birth of the prophet. Those who have become westernized have picked up the custom of celebrating birthdays, but many villagers did not know their birthday, only the year in which they were born.

Death, of course, is the end of a lifetime, and is socially marked everywhere, although more elaborately by some peoples than by others. In fact, death rituals are often seen as an indicator of culture, one that is found not only in all human societies, but also in the fossil remains of Neanderthals and even in some nonprimate mammals, such as elephants. For human societies, the way death is conceptualized and dealt with, especially the way the body is disposed of, reflects cultural beliefs concerning the constitution of the person. Does anything of the person persist after death? Is there a soul? If so, what happens to it? Americans tend to be in a state of "denial" about death;[6] as a culture we fear it, do not mention it, and do not set aside a time for mourning as is so common elsewhere. Maybe that is why we have so enthusiastically embraced birthdays.

School time   Our lifetimes are structured in a profound way by our educational system that commits us to years of schooling in preparation for adulthood. In most industrialized countries, people must go to school until they are 16, but since World War II the length of time Americans spend in school has grown dramatically. We finish high school (usually by 18), and then go on to other kinds of schools – trade schools; art, music, and dance schools; technical schools; colleges and universities; and then beyond to law school, business school, graduate school, or medical school. Some of you began school before you were 6 – perhaps as young as 2 or 3 – having attended infant day care or nursery school. And some of you will continue in school until you are over 30. That is a long time waiting for and preparing for the future. The long apprenticeship is premised on a belief in a long life, as well as on the assumption that complex skills and credentials are necessary to lead a successful life. Of course, we are living while we are preparing, but we often do not think of it that way; we say, "When I begin real life" or "When I enter the real world."

One of the "life skills" we learn in college is time management itself. Many freshmen have told me that learning to manage their own time was one of the most difficult things they encountered as college students. As a high school student, you went to school in the morning, at 8 A.M. or so, and finished in the afternoon sometime around 3 P.M. Then you either went to a part-time job, an after-school activity, or home. Time was managed for you. Even time for homework was often decreed by parents. Suddenly, at college, no one is monitoring your time; no one is checking to see if you go to class, do your homework, eat your meals, get enough sleep, or get your papers in on time. (You are probably not aware that the term *deadline* originally meant "a boundary line in prison that prisoners can cross only at the risk of being shot" [*American Heritage Dictionary*, 2007].) You are the one who has to decide *how to spend your time*. What are your priorities? Why? Where did they come from? What other activities besides schoolwork eat into your time? How do you spend your free time? And how do you decide when "task time" is finished and "free time" has begun – and vice versa?

The lengthening of school time has also changed American marriage practices. Before World War II and for a time after, it was normal for young people to marry soon after they graduated high school. In fact, in most states girls could legally marry without parental permission as young as 16 and in some states as young as 13. Furthermore, if a woman wasn't married by 21, she was "an old maid," and if a man wasn't married by 30, he was a "bachelor." Today, most adults think teenagers are too young for marriage, a shift in values that coincides with the additional years they are expected to spend in school.

As such, college has become a time to experiment with one's sexual possibilities and identity – concepts that did not even exist when I was in college in the 1960s. Many of you will meet the person with whom you intend to spend the rest of your life, while many others will decide to postpone that search until later. Many of you will argue at length with your friends about the relative value of marrying at all, remaining single, or living with a partner without marriage. Still others will decide that they want to marry someone of the same gender – an option that was, for all intents and purposes, impossible a generation or two ago. And college is also a time of romantic disappointments. According to research conducted by Zick Rubin, Charles T. Hill, and Letitia Peplau, romantic relationships between college students tend to break up during May/June, September, or December/January, that is, during times before or after holidays when they might have been separated ("Natural Rhythms," n.d.).

Holidays   Because we are in school so long, school time lays down a kind of rhythm to our days that in later life is difficult to erase. In fact, school shapes our sense of annual cycles more profoundly than the calendar, because it dictates our activities for two decades – the first two – or more of our lives. The school year was originally molded by the farm cycle, which demanded the most labor during the summer months. Although few Americans today are farmers, we are acclimated—even wedded to—the coordination of the school year with the seasons: it begins in the fall, runs through winter and spring, and closes for the long summer vacation.

The school year is also the backdrop for our core experience of the holidays, because they break up the long school term with days and weeks off, with special themed activities, and—what teachers and school administrators know too well—with educational thresholds and deadlines. Thus the school year begins, in most places in the United States, with Labor Day—an ironic name for the end of summer vacation—and then is interrupted by Columbus Day, Halloween, Veterans Day, Thanksgiving, and Christmas. Christmas and New Year together mark the long break between semesters, and then school resumes, interrupted by Martin Luther King Day, Valentine's Day, Presidents' Day, spring break (once called Easter vacation), and Memorial Day. Summer vacation itself is bookended by Memorial Day and Labor Day, with the Fourth of July marking its midpoint. Although we also learn that each holiday has a particular meaning, we sense their importance through their disruptions of our routine with special activities, foods, gifts, or simply the opportunity to relax.

Of course, the holiday cycle is not about the school cycle—although it is interesting to see how often working adults must make their own work and holiday schedule conform to those of their school-aged children. But the cultural meanings of holidays are to be found elsewhere, in the separation of "sacred" time and "profane" time (see Leach 1961) and in the collective identities the holidays assemble and celebrate. Labor Day, for example, commemorates working people – the "backbone" of the United States – while Memorial Day commemorates our fallen soldiers. According to Caplow and Williamson, the different holidays draw together different arenas of social solidarity: "National solidarity is celebrated on Independence Day, Memorial Day, and Washington's birthday; family solidarity on Thanksgiving, Mother's Day, and Father's Day, and (with a special nuance) Valentine's Day; neighborhood solidarity on Halloween and New Year's; and civic solidarity on Memorial Day" (1980: 222–3). Religious solidarity is implied by Christmas and Easter, though they argued that both holidays have considerable secular aspects. And religious and ethnic minorities celebrate their own solidarities through holidays—like Passover, Kwanzaa, and Ramadan—that are not part of the American, presumptively Christian mainstream and, therefore, not official holidays established by government. Similarly, in England some schools celebrate Hindu and Muslim holidays, but the government does not recognize them as national holidays or grant children days off from school.

What is behind the more recent trend to name days, weeks, and months for certain causes such as World Peace Day, National Cheese Day, Women's History Month, AIDS Awareness Day, and so on? What social forces must be mobilized to steer these through legislation?[7]

Work versus leisure

As important as school systems are in shaping our experience of time, work systems are more important, since they define, and often disrupt, the rhythms of our adult lives and of our society as a whole. In fact, school time is dictated to a great extent by the needs of working parents who must free themselves of child care in order to go to work. The evidence lies in the exceptions, such as cancellation of school for snow days, which forces parents to either forfeit a workday or pay another adult to take care of their children.

As a cultural system, work time encompasses both labor and leisure, that is, the alternation of toil and relaxation daily, weekly, yearly, and over the course of our lives. Thus for many of us, daily life is ordered by work hours versus off-work hours, and by workdays versus weekends, while our yearly schedule is ordered by work weeks versus holidays and vacations. In addition, we expect to spend a certain amount of our life*time* working, and hope to, at some point, retire and enjoy a life of prolonged leisure. The distinction between work and leisure is also spatialized; normally we work in one place and take our leisure in another place.

But were these distinctions always like this? If not, how did they come about? Anthropologists have long been puzzled over why hunters and gatherers would ever switch to agriculture since the former work, at most, about 20 hours a week to supply all their needs. In his article "The Original Affluent Society" (1972), Marshall Sahlins, a well-known anthropologist at the University of Chicago, turns upside down the conventional view that also drives Western economic theory. That view assumes that in "primitive" society, there are scarce resources so the people must be working all the time just in order to survive. That was never the case; instead, Sahlins shows that they worked fewer than 2–3 hours a day and that most of their time was spent in leisure, social activity, and ceremonies. He explains that affluence is a relation between wants and the means to satisfy them; hunter–gatherer wants were in *proportion* to their ability to satisfy them, thus they could feel affluent and express this sentiment in their behavior. Rather than hoarding goods because of scarcity, people were generous, even profligate. This behavior continually mystified the explorers and missionaries who came in contact with them. In contrast, our wants are out of proportion to our ability to satisfy them; they are unlimited, and new ones are created every day. This imbalance intensifies the feeling of scarcity.

Agricultural labor is arduous, time-consuming, and risky, yet people still retain control over their time and the products of their labor. Agricultural work is also episodic, that is, there are times of intense labor (normally in the summer) and times of great leisure (generally in the winter). British social theorist E. P. Thompson noted that "the work pattern was one of alternate bouts of intense labour and of idleness, wherever men were in control of their own working lives" (1967: 73). He goes on to say that this "pattern persists among some self-employed – artists, writers, small farmers, and perhaps also with students" and wonders if this is not a more "natural human work-rhythm." This was certainly my experience living in the Turkish village for two years (see "Village Time," this chapter). And even as a student and professor, I alternated between periods of intense academic work and periods of, if not of idleness, certainly nonacademic activity.

In addition, "for an academic or artist, money is time," claimed anthropologist Lawrence Rosen, overturning the epithet that opened this chapter. In order to devote oneself to painting or writing, one needs time – lots of it. The trick is to find a way to get the money to provide that time. Although artists and writers and some others devote many, many hours to their work and struggle over it, the time is often not *felt* as work. Not only that, work and leisure alternate more organically and many do not *go out* to work. This is definitely not the work rhythm most of us experience. Some people, of course, may prefer working outside the home from 9 A.M. to 5 P.M. and then have the rest of the time for themselves, for leisure. But we need to ask if this kind of work schedule is really necessary – why should anyone have to work like that? Why should life be so sliced up? Germans, for example, get many more vacation days, at least a month, than Americans. In addition, most stores close at noon on Saturday and remain closed all day Sunday. The idea is to encourage more family time. However, it also assumes a stay-at-home housewife or, if she works, it puts an added burden on her since she would have to do the shopping during lunch hours or after work. The French, too, as of January 2000, have a 35-hour workweek and more than a month of holiday time.

Industrial time …   People in our modern industrialized and postindustrial capitalist societies are working longer hours than ever before in human history. According to a report released by the International Labor Organization at the United Nations on Labor Day, 2001, Americans were working more in 2000 than they were just 10 years earlier; indeed, they are working more than people in other industrialized nations and have fewer vacation days than anywhere else. Just in the decade of the 1990s, they added an extra week of work. And that seems to have escalated: "According to the International Labor Organization, Americans now work 1,978 hours annually, a full 350 hours – nine weeks – more than Western Europeans" (de Graaf, *New York Times*, April 12, 2003). To point this out dramatically, John de Graaf coordinated the national "Take Back Your Time Day" scheduled for October 24, 2003, exactly nine weeks before the end of the year!

Although the official hours of work each day and week have decreased over the past century, many people today are working more than the standard 8 hours per day. This is as true of professionals as it is of lower-income people working *overtime* or working two jobs (*New York Times*, September 3, 2001). With so-called progress, shouldn't we be working less? What happened? How did we come to have the kind of work time we do?

E. P. Thompson claims that "the transition to mature industrial society entailed a severe restructuring of working habits" (1967: 57), which in turn involved a change in notions of time. Once clocks became available to individuals, not just churches and government offices, employers were able to use them to *discipline* workers, not in the sense of punishment but in the sense of regimentation. In order to get paid, workers had to check in *on time*; their work was *timed* according to the clock, and they were released at a specific *time*. Their time was no longer their own, it belonged to the employer. If they wanted to keep their jobs, they had to conform to employers' schedules, and they had to perform in relation to the external measure – the clock. It did not take much intelligence to realize that "time is money."

... And domesticity   The industrial revolution in the nineteenth century changed the way we work. One of the biggest social consequences was the separation of work from home. No longer was work just part of sustaining the family as in farming communities, or piece-work taken into the home and paid for by the piece, or a family business attached to the home. Instead, one went out to work for a certain period of time and then returned home for "leisure" time. Work and home became antinomies, opposites. And they were gendered. "Work" became identified with men, and the "home" with women. Men were paid a "family wage" in order to be able to keep their wives at home to attend to children and housework. Not only did this rhetoric disguise the fact that many women did go out to work, thus ignoring the issues of race and class, but it also made women's work in the home invisible.

In middle-class families especially, women were increasingly confined to the home, where they were expected to provide the rest and respite from the working world their men went out to battle each day. Despite all the work women were actually doing, it was no longer seen as work that contributed to the gross national product (see Folbre 1991 for fuller discussion), even though the industrial economy would collapse without it. So too, women were regarded less as "helpmates" who kept the household going, and more as "dependents" who, like children, were supported by men rather than giving support to men.

Not surprisingly, women rebelled. Organized resistance began at the Seneca Falls Convention in 1848, when women gathered to protest slavery and marriage, the latter which, given the laws at the time, they described as a form of slavery. The political move-ment they initiated gathered momentum and eventually bore fruit, the most important being the ratification of the 19th Amendment in 1920, which gave women the right to vote. But women were still regarded as the house-bound dependents of men. These restrictions were loosened briefly during World War II, when the recruitment of men into the military coupled with the expansion of the armaments industry drew women out of the home and into the labor force.[8] But when the war ended and GIs reentered the workforce, women were once again pushed out of their jobs and into their homes, or rather, out of paid labor and into unpaid.

This set the stage for the second wave of the women's movement. The 1950s saw the resurgence of the "cult of domesticity" or the "cult of true womanhood," now coupled with an array of new "time-saving" devices – washing machines, vacuum cleaners, mix masters, and so on. These devices lulled women into their new roles for a time, or at least the advertisements made it seem so. But isolated in their new suburban homes for most of the day, women grew bored and fell ill with "the problem that has no name," as Betty Friedan called it in *The Feminine Mystique*. In the 1960s, they began to push once again for eco-nomic parity with men, focusing increasingly on career opportunities, financial independ-ence, and reproductive rights.

... And career women   Today more women are working outside the home than ever before, but the underlying conflict that industrialization created – the separation of work and home – persists, as does the problem of caring for children, the sick, and the aged. The solution, it seems to me, is not to send women back home, or to create even more

institutionalized care such as day care centers, hospitals, and nursing homes, but to begin to change our notions of time, work, and life goals. One place to begin involves the very notion of a "career."

A career is a profession or occupation that has a trajectory that is measured against time. It is believed that intellectual achievements, like athletic ones, come relatively early in life. But they do not just happen; in order to achieve, you have to put in a lot of time. When people comment how few women "geniuses" there are, or composers, or artists, or whatever, they ignore the way in which time has been, and continues to be, gendered. In her article "Inside the Clock-Work of Male Careers" (1975), Arlie Hochschild examines the gendered timetable. Although her example is an academic career, the same holds true for most others. "The classic profile of the academic career is cut to the image of the traditional man with his traditional wife" (1975: 49). What she means is that if you want to become a full professor one day, you must begin by getting into the best graduate school possible, you must choose a topic early so that you do not *waste time*, and make your work your top priority so that you do not take too much *time* to finish. You must take the best job you can get, then spend what remains of your twenties and definitely your thirties writing articles and books, giving papers at conferences, getting your name known, and getting tenure. Then you must write more articles and books so you can be advanced to full professor. Although Hochschild's article was written a quarter of a century ago, it rings (almost) as true today as then. What are some of the problems with this scenario?

To concentrate on your work with the zeal required, it surely helps if you have someone taking care of the housework, the cooking, the shopping, the laundry, and the cleaning, not to mention the children. Already you can see why this typical pattern, designed with men's lifetimes in mind, disadvantages women before they even start. In the past, women were told that if they wanted a career they better not marry. Today, instead, we hear women say, "I need a wife."

To be fair, I must admit that my own case is an anomaly. I was 36 when I went to graduate school in 1976, the oldest person the department had ever admitted. Not only that, I had a child and was on welfare. I was told (by the chair*man* of the department) that the program was very rigorous, and was asked what I intended to do with my child while I was studying. I was also told that by the time I finished I would be ready to retire! Clearly, older students, especially women, were not taken very seriously. The burden to prove them wrong was heavy, and so it was with great glee I informed them about my job at Stanford.

Still, the fact that I succeeded despite, and not because of, the expectations of my department confirms Hochschild's conclusion, "the very clockwork of a career system … seems to eliminate women not so much through malevolent disobedience to good rules, but through the making up rules to suit half the population in the first place" (p. 59). But why shouldn't we all have the opportunity to pursue a career and also enjoy the benefits of love, marriage, and children if we want? Why shouldn't everyone be required to spend part of their time caring for others – whether children, the sick, or the elderly, and regardless of whether they are one's own relatives or not? After all, we have all been cared for by others.

Some people see salvation in the computer for it enables more and more people to work at home and thus offers the possibility of, once again, combining work and leisure into a more organic life rhythm. Personally, I am doubtful. For 150 years now, industrialism – also known as the "machine age" – has placed everyone in the thrall of breakthrough technologies, expecting that new devices – from combines to cars to computers – will reduce our work load and increase our leisure. But new technologies never actually save us time. As syndicated columnist Ellen Goodman writes in "Time Is for Savoring," they "merely allow us to do more in the same number of minutes, leaving us with full schedules and the need to find more ways to save time" (1977).[1] Here Goodman echoes the prescient words of John Stuart Mill made over a century and a half ago: "It is questionable," he said, "if all the mechanical inventions yet made have lightened the day's toil of any human being" ([1848] 1985: 90). Marx added that they may have lightened the toil of the rich.

… And family time This is a good point to consider the impact of industrial work-time on family time. Most, if not all, children in the United States – whether rich or poor – have less time with their parents than did children in the past. Of course, wealthy parents can provide substitutes in the form of nannies and private tutors and time-filling activities such as piano (and other) lessons, while children of poor parents are often left alone, or with inadequate supervision, or on the streets. British pediatrician Penelope Leach (1994) says that parent–child time has decreased by 40 percent since 1975. Part of this can be attributed to the fact that in many families today, both parents are working – some because they cannot support a family on just one income, and others because both parents also want to engage in a fulfilling career. At the same time, the number of one-parent families is growing. In that case the parent, normally the mother, is doing the job of two, and too often she is working long hours at low wages with few, if any, benefits. With so many parents working, a likely time to spend with family would be dinner times. But that is not the case: in the United States, families eat together "one-third less often than in the mid-1970s" (*San Francisco Chronicle*, September 24, 2000). Many families never have the evening meal together; instead, each family member is off doing his or her "own thing." How often did you (or do you) eat dinner with your family?

One of the students who helped me with some of the research for this book spent the year between high school and college in France. Living with a French family, she became very aware of different cultural patterns and values. One of the things she cherished about that experience was that the whole family (which at that time included her) ate dinner together every night. When she came back home, she tried to institute it with her own family, but it was not possible. Everyone had his or her own schedule.

The decrease in the amount of time parents spend with their children is a social change that signifies a major change in values. In *Children First* (1994), Penelope Leach has written eloquently on the need for changing our priorities so that we might begin to change the way we work *and* care for children. Children are suffering from this lack of *time* with their parents. To make up for this deficit, psychologists introduced the concept of "quality time." The amount of time a parent spends with his or her child is held to be not as important as the "quality" or meaningfulness of the interaction. The concept sounds good, but there is a major flaw: the time a parent has available may not coincide with the times the child really needs parental attention. Not only that, but also parents miss the chance to shape the child's values and leave that job to whoever is with the child most of the day. For values are instilled not just verbally, not just during the moments of "quality time," but also subtly by actions and by modeling of behavior. No doubt the concept of "quality time" has helped to assuage the guilt of many working mothers. But why not of working fathers? Why is it *women's time* that is at issue? Here we encounter an example of the way that time is gendered. The old adage that "a woman's work is never done" is just as true now as ever, maybe more so as so many women are working what Arlie Hochschild calls "the second shift" of housework and child care work after a full day at the office (Hochschild 1975).

Village time   The Turkish villagers' sense of time was the most difficult thing for me to get accustomed to. I am not sure I ever got the hang of it. I could not incorporate (literally, to bring into my body, corpus) their tempo and daily rhythms, and that affected my speech, my behavior, and my style of movement. My *sense of timing* was off, I could feel my rough edges, and my gait was all wrong. One does not rush in the village; it is undignified.

Sometimes I would ask when we were going to do something and the answer would be: *şimdi* – which means now. But *now* could mean anywhere from immediately to a few minutes to a few hours, and sometimes was simply a way of letting the matter drop eventually. I could never really tell when something was going to start – a wedding, for example. For us, such a major event is announced well in advance and the date and time are specified on the invitation. If you are late, you will miss it completely. In the village, even when a wedding was announced formally (invitations were newly being introduced and had become a kind of status symbol) and the day and time specified, that information did not have much meaning. The wedding would begin when enough people had gathered. How many is enough? I don't know, and the number varied for each occasion. But on each occasion, at a certain magical moment, everything would begin.

Visiting forms one of the major components of village life, and hospitality is a primary virtue. Unlike Americans, who often say "Drop in anytime" but really don't mean it (cf. Varenne 1986), Turks would say its equivalent and *mean it*. People can and did drop in anytime. You are *honored* by a visit – at any time – and you are expected to drop whatever you are doing and welcome your guests. You cannot say, "I am really busy now; could you come back later?" Social life in the village presumes that someone (a woman) will be at home to receive visitors and to prepare the tea to refresh them.

In the village, work was integrated into social life and daily activities. First, no one worked alone, for there were always household members, friends, or relatives to help with any task. Second, work took place at a *leisurely* pace; there was no hurry and no time clock. Thus even agricultural tasks – what villagers and outsiders alike see as the backbreaking work of peasant life – were interspersed with frequent respites for tea and relaxation (all the tea implements were carried to the fields, including a portable gas burner, glasses, and sugar). As a result, the work days cycled comfortably between periods of exertion and rest.

Predictably I had a difficult time convincing the villagers that work for urban Americans could also be hard: after all, the physical demands of my work pale by comparison with the physical demands of theirs. Instead, our work is hard because of the need to rush in the face of constant pressure and to adopt a pace determined by external demands and external clocks that conflict with our own rhythms and even the tasks at hand. Still, what my words could not convey, my work habits did, as villagers kept chiding me, "Çok har-cayorsun" – you're exerting yourself too much. You're spending yourself; you're wasting energy.

This perhaps is the crux of the difference between the Turkish villagers' mind-set and my own about time and work. For me one wastes *time*, but for them, one wastes *oneself*. For me, time can be used wisely or well, but for them, time was not an object, much less a commodity that can be wisely invested or foolishly thrown away. Instead, their experience of time was much more like what French anthropologist Pierre Bourdieu described in his article "The Attitude of the Algerian Peasant toward Time":

> Inwardly felt, as the very movement of life rather than as a constraining limit, time cannot be dissociated from the experience of activity and of the space in which that activity takes place. Duration and space are described by reference to the performance of a concrete task; e.g. the unit of duration is the time one needs to do a job, to work a piece of land. (1963: 60)

In Turkey, the term that describes a parcel of land is a *dönem*. Today it is a specific meas-urement, but it derives from the amount of land a man was thought to be able to work in a day, that is, before tractors and mechanical plows were introduced. Space and time were not only related but also equivalent, and both were dimensions of a specific activity. This is called *task orientation*, which, according to E. P. Thompson, has three major qualities: (1) "it is more humanly comprehensible than timed labour"; (2) there is "the least demar-cation between 'work' and 'life'"; and (3) to outsiders who work under the clock, it "appears to be wasteful and lacking in urgency" (1967: 60), all of which fit my experience in the village.

While villagers complained about the heavy work, some who had tried working in town talked of how monotonous and boring most of it was. All day long one had to do the same kind of thing, whereas in the village they do many different kinds of tasks and see them through the whole process – such as building a house, which begins with gathering stones for the foundation and making mud bricks; caring for the fields and fruit trees, which involves planting, harvesting, and preserving their own food; and caring for animals and processing their meat, their milk, and their wool or (goat) hair.

Work in the village was an occasion for social activity and people were not alienated from their labor, that is, they saw the process from beginning to end and benefited from the end products. Many of you might not find this kind of life appealing because you want to develop and use other talents and capacities. But you should also keep in mind that in our industrial and postindustrial world, it is the fortunate few who are really able to work in a nonalienated way. You may not end up working in a factory (though millions do), but you may end up spending all day at an office at a desk in front of a computer.

Peasant labor is changed irrevocably when work is no longer primarily for subsistence but is geared toward production for the market. Given villagers' attitude to life and to work, it is not difficult to imagine the *ambivalence* generated by the shift from subsistence to production for the market. Machines have reduced the arduousness of some of the work and greatly increased the amount of land under cultivation. The extra cultivated land is not necessary for their own needs but is intended to produce the food to feed the urban population. The cash income generated from the surplus food nevertheless makes them indebted, especially for the machines and also for the additional seeds and fertilizer. They end up working more, and their sociability is being destroyed. How do you think villagers were convinced to produce for the market? What forces might have been exerted? In what ways do you think their sense of time changed?

In Islam there is a belief that your lifetime is already determined at your birth but only God knows its length. While there were some fairly old people in the village, the average life expectancy was much lower than in the United States. They remarked on my age and the fact that although I had a child, I was still in school; "here we just keep having children, and then we die." It is very important to have children; that is what establishes you as an adult. Sons are especially important because it is through them that the family line will continue. But it is also important to have children because they are expected to take care of you in your old age in return for the care you gave them when they were young. As a person grows from child to adult there is a kind of backward look, toward the parents, whereas in the United States children are pointed always toward the future. Most Turks, rural or urban, frowned on the American habit of putting their parents in retirement homes or nursing homes.

Although there is a backward look to a life span, the goal is toward the "other world," which is your original, true, and final home. Mecca, believed to be the place where the first land appeared upon the waters, is felt to be the closest to the "other world" one can get in this life; it is the *axis mundi* (the navel of the world). Making the *hajj* (pilgrimage) to Mecca at least once in a lifetime, if at all possible, is incumbent upon Muslims. But rather than a going forth as exemplified in John Bunyan's *Pilgrim's Progress* (1678), this pilgrimage is a return, back to the source. This, too, I believe, gives a very different feeling to time (and space) and a lifetime from that of people raised in a country dominated by Christianity.

A common wall hanging in villagers' homes included a saying attributed to the medieval Muslim scholar al-Ghazali. It went like this:

> What are you? Where do you come from? Where are you going? Whether your life span be short or long, the world is but a brief lodging (a guesthouse), so take care to make provisions for the eternal home.

Unlike the Protestant ethic with its focus on "this-worldly" asceticism, the Muslim ethic, at least in this saying, encourages an asceticism that focuses on the "other world." For while the reward in both cases is Heaven, Protestants were also encouraged to save in this world so that they could launch a thousand ships, gain capital for business, and bequeath the riches to their children. This does not mean that villagers went around in a pious state all the time, but they made a big distinction between "this world" and the "other world," and the "other world" was very real. For example, they would say, "I have three children in this world, and two in the other world," meaning two children had died. Villagers were very much involved with life in this world and curious about material things. But there was also a sense in which they were not so identified with their things; they did not seem to depend on them as much as we do. With so few material possessions, you would think they would be more, not less, concerned about them, but that was not the case at all. They were very generous in sharing whatever they had, and giving away a treasured possession was not uncommon. They also seemed to possess a sense of humor about the vicissitudes of life that I found unusual and refreshing (cf. Sahlins 1972) – perhaps because they were confident about the rewards awaiting them. For the villagers, death—and not baptism, as in Christianity—was the means to the second birth. And the next life, especially for men, who will have anywhere from 7 to 70 *houris* (virginal maidens) waiting on them, is expected to be a life of ease and comfort.

Notes

1. For those interested in the story, I recommend Clark Blaise's *Time Lord: Sir Sanford Fleming and the Creation of Standard Time* (2001).
2. The word *calendar* comes from *calends*, the beginning of the month when religious leaders would announce that month's festal days.
3. For an accessible investigation of the calendar, see David Ewing Duncan's book, *Calendar: Humanity's Epic Struggle to Determine a True and Accurate Year* (1988). He claims that the AD dating system was devised by Dionysius Exiguus ("Little Dennis") in the year AD 531, although how Dionysius decided that he was living 531 years after the birth of Christ is a mystery, especially since the date of "Christ's birth is unknown and a matter of immense controversy even today" (Duncan 1998: 91–2).
4. See Stocking (1968) and Gould (1981).
5. A scathing account was published by Jessica Mitford, *The American Way of Death* (1963).
6. For example, see Caplow and Williamson (1980).
7. For a classic analysis of Memorial Day, see Warner (1953).
8. See, for example, the film *Rosie the Riveter* (1980).

3.1. Signs of the Time

Make a list of all the ways we are reminded of time in our daily lives. Try to have at least 15 different ways.

3.2. Time as a Thing

What would it mean to say, "Time is a gift"? How different is "time as a gift" from "time as money"? How might such a view change our lives? Can you think of any negative aspects to this view of time?

3.3. Time Schedules

Make a detailed account of your own use of time through a 24-hour time period. Specify both how you intend to divide up the day and how you actually do. Then compare your schedule with that of someone you know who is not a student.

Bibliography

The American Heritage Dictionary of the English Language, 4th ed. (2007) Boston: Houghton Mifflin.

Aveni, Anthony F. (1989) *Empires of Time: Calendars, Clocks, and Cultures*. New York: Basic.

Barnett, Jo Ann (1998) *Time's Pendulum: The Quest to Capture Time – from Sundials to Atomic Clocks*. New York: Plenum.

Berger, John (1979) *Pig Earth*. New York: Pantheon.

Blaise, Clark (2001) *Time Lord: Sir Sanford Fleming and the Creation of Standard Time*. New York: Pantheon.

Bourdieu, Pierre (1963) "The Attitude of the Algerian Peasant toward Time." In *Mediterranean Countrymen*, ed. J. Pitt-Rivers. Paris: Mouton, pp. 55–72.

Bowen, Elenore Smith ([1954] 1964) *Return to Laughter: An Anthropological Novel*. New York: Doubleday.

Bunyan, John (1678) *Pilgrim's Progress*. London: Ponder.

Campbell, Jeremy (1986) *Winston Churchill's Afternoon Nap: A Wide-Awake Inquiry into the Human Nature of Time*. New York: Simon & Schuster.

Caplow, Theodore, and Williamson, Margaret Holmes (1980) "Decoding Middletown's Easter Bunny: A Study in American Iconography." *Semiotica* 32(3/4): 221–32.

Children's Defense Fund (1991) "Moments in America." www.childrensdefense.org/child-research-data-publications/moments-in-america-for-children.html.

Duncan, David Ewing (1998) *Calendar: Humanity's Epic Struggle to Determine a True and Accurate Year*. New York: Avon.

Encyclopedia Britannica (n.d.) "Clockworks." www.britannica.com/clockworks/article.html.

Evans-Pritchard, E. E. ([1940] 1976) *The Nuer: A Description of the Modes of Livelihood and Political Institutions of a Nilotic People*. Oxford: Clarendon.

Fabian, Johannes (1983) *Time and the Other: How Anthropology Makes Its Object*. New York: Columbia University Press.

Folbre, Nancy (1991) "The Unproductive Housewife: Her Evolution in Nineteenth-Century Economic Thought." *Signs* 16(31): 463–84.

Fraser, J. T. (1966) *The Voices of Time: A Cooperative Survey of Man's Views of Time as Expressed by the Sciences and by the Humanities*. New York: George Braziller.

Goodman, Ellen (1977) "Time Is for Savoring." Boston Globe, October.

Gould, Stephen Jay (1981) *The Mismeasure of Man*. New York: Norton.

Hawking, Stephen (1988) *A Brief History of Time*. New York: Bantam.

Hochschild, Arlie (1975) "Inside the Clock-Work of Male Careers." In *Women and the Power to Change*, ed. Florence Howe. New York: McGraw-Hill, sponsored by the Carnegie Commission on Higher Education.

Holy Bible, New International Version (1973) Colorado Springs, CO: Biblica.

Leach, Edmund (1961) "Two Essays Concerning the Symbolic Representation of Time." In *Rethinking Anthropology*. London: University of London, Athlone Press.

Leach, Penelope (1994) *Children First: What Our Society Must Do – and Is Not Doing – for Our Children Today*. New York: Alfred A. Knopf.

Lewis, Sinclair (1920) *Main Street*. New York: Harcourt Brace.

life-cycles-destiny.com (n.d.) "86,400 Seconds per Day." www.life-cycles-destiny.com/for/time-living-present-integration.htm.

Mill, John Stuart ([1848] 1985) *Principles of Political Economy: With Some of Their Applications to Social Philosophy*, books IV and V, ed. and intro. Donald Winch. Harmondsworth: Penguin.

Mitford, Jessica (1963) *The American Way of Death*. New York: Buccaneer.

Morris, Richard (1984) *Time's Arrows: Scientific Attitudes toward Time*. New York: Simon & Schuster.

"Natural Rhythms" (n.d.) www.trinity.edu/~mkearl/time-1.html.

Paz, Octavio (1984) *Selected Poems*. New York: New Directions.

Sahlins, Marshall (1972) "The Original Affluent Society." In *Stone Age Economics*. Chicago: Aldine-Atherton.

Sidel, Ruth (1992) *Women and Children Last: The Plight of Poor Women in Affluent America*. New York: Penguin.

Steel, Duncan (2000) *Marking Time: The Epic Quest to Invent the Perfect Calendar*. New York: John Wiley.

Stocking, George W., Jr. (1968) *Race, Culture, and Evolution: Essays in the History of Anthropology*. New York: Free Press.

Thompson, E. P. (1967) "Time, Work-Discipline and Industrial Capitalism." *Past and Present* 38: 56–97.

United Nations (n.d.) "United Nations Statistics Division." http://unstats.un.org.

US Department of Health and Human Services (2002) *Almanac and Book of Fact*. Washington, DC: Author.

Varenne, Hervé (1986) "'Drop in Anytime': Community and Authenticity in American Everyday Life." In *Symbolizing America*, ed. Hervé Varenne. Lincoln: University of Nebraska Press, pp. 209–28.

Warner, William L. (1953) "An American Sacred Ceremony." In *American Life*. Chicago: University of Chicago Press, pp. 1–26.

Weber, Max ([1904–5] 1958) *The Protestant Ethic and the Spirit of Capitalism*, trans. Talcott Parsons. New York: Scribner.

Whorf, Benjamin (1956) "The Relation of Habitual Thought and Behavior to Language." In *Language, Thought and Reality*. Cambridge, MA: MIT Press.

Yanagisako, Sylvia, and Delaney, Carol (1995) *Naturalizing Power: Essays in Feminist Cultural Analysis*. New York: Routledge.

Zerubavel, Eviatar (1985) *The Seven Day Circle: The History and Meaning of the Week*. New York: Free Press.

R E A D I N G

Time Is for Savoring

Ellen Goodman

A few months ago, when a preening French official descended from his Concorde into Washington, he bragged to Tip O'Neill that he saved four, count 'em, four hours traveling supersonically.

At that point the Speaker turned and asked him, benignly, what he had done with the four hours he'd saved. The official, as the story goes, was taken aback, right aback into silence. This exchange stuck in my mind, and not because I'm snooping into the Frenchman's activities. I'm not that sort of reporter.

But it occurred to me that O'Neill's response was a nice healthy challenge to the time-saving obsession of our lives. I guess the Concorde is as good a place to begin as any.

It has taken the accumulated wisdom of centuries to build this plane, and what have we got? For one thing, a noisier airplane which uses more fuel to carry fewer people in less comfort from one continent to the other at greater expense. We call this peculiar achievement "progress" for only one reason: It does all this absurd stuff in a shorter amount of time than a conventional plane.

Saving time, it seems, has a primacy that's too rarely examined. From the Concorde to the microwave oven to the Speed Reading class, we value saving time more than the way we spend it and more than the values we may sacrifice to it. At times we behave like the efficiency

expert in *Pajama Game* whose rationalization for his life was simple: "For a time-study man to waste time / is a crime."

We tell ourselves that we are all busy people. Our lives are geared to the school bells and alarm clocks and factory whistles outside of our control. But on the whole, the time-saving devices – both mechanical and personal – that are supposed to help us save time, don't. They merely allow us to do more in the same number of minutes, leaving us with full schedules and the need to find more ways to save time.

With the aid of the plane, the official and the businessman can turn a two-day trip into a one-day trip. But they are usually faced with two one-day trips. The people who learn to Speed Read don't spend less time reading; they just read more in the same time.

The machines that make it possible for us to do things that we could never do before – like cook a roast in a half hour – also make it more likely that we will do things we never would have done before. Like cook that roast.

These things don't save time, any more than the assembly line saves the worker time.

There is actually no way to bank our minutes away. The best we can do, with the most sophisticated machinery products, is to redistribute those minutes. And, like the French official, we don't always do a good job of that. We have even become so addicted to saving time that we forget to differentiate between the things we like to do (dining with our families, for example) and the things we hate to do (cleaning the oven). We efficiently shorten them all.

At the end of a busy day, families often get dinner "down to a science": the science of convenience foods, mixes, and fifteen-minute "gourmet" recipes. In some houses, dinner goes from the refrigerator to the dishwasher in less than an hour. Then, having saved all these minutes, rather than spending them with each other, we drop them like quarters in a television slot machine.

Either we spend more and more energy processing ourselves through our days, doing more and more in the same amount of time, or we throw away our "free time" like Daddy Warbucks.

It's not that I want to go back to ox carts, let alone wooden washtubs, but it seems to me that we ought to make some personal judgments about the machines that are pushed on us in the name of the clock. We have to ask: Is it really going to save time? *My* time? Is it going to cut down unpleasant time, or pleasant time? And, as the Speaker would say, what am I going to do with the time I save?

Ultimately, time is all you have and the idea isn't to save it but to savor it. Like the man on the record, James Taylor, says, "The secret o' life is enjoying the passage of time."

CHAPTER 4

Language: We Are What We Speak

Is language quintessentially human or do some other animals possess it? Communication versus language. Writing. The symbolic function and metaphor: different languages, different worlds? The social function: what information do you obtain from a person's speech? How are race, class, and gender inflected in language?

Language: We Are What We Speak

We are what we speak in more ways than one. Speech is what makes us human; no other species speaks. When you hear someone speak and have no visual clues, such as on the telephone, think of all the things you can immediately grasp, or at least infer, about that person: gender, nationality or ethnicity, region of origin, age, emotional attitude (anger, fear, sadness, or elation), mental state (confident, anxious, or confused), physical state (just waking up, cold, or drunk), class, education, and often relationship to the hearer. All of this information is perceived almost without thinking, but it predisposes you to respond in a certain way. The way this information is evaluated – the meaning given to it – is, of course, heavily influenced by your culture.

There is yet another way we are what we speak. Edward Sapir, a famous American linguist, captured it well:

> Human beings do not live in the objective world alone, nor alone in the world of social activity as ordinarily understood, but are very much at the mercy of the particular language which has become the medium of expression for their society. It is quite an illusion to imagine that one adjusts to reality essentially without the use of language and that language is merely an incidental means of solving specific problems of communication or reflection. The fact of the matter is that the "real world" is to a large extent unconsciously built up on the language habits of the group. No two languages are ever sufficiently similar to be considered as representing the same social reality. *The worlds in which different societies live are distinct worlds, not merely the same world with different labels attached.* (Sapir 1949: 69; emphasis mine)

This idea may be startling to you, for most of us are brought up believing that the "real world" is quite separate and distinct from language; we simply assume that language merely

Investigating Culture: An Experiential Introduction to Anthropology, Second Edition.
Carol Delaney with Deborah Kaspin.
© 2011 Carol Delaney. Published by Blackwell Publishing Ltd.

reflects that world. Language, in that view, presumes a kind of transparency or direct connection between words and things. This commonsense assumption has been called the *Adamic view of language* because that is how the biblical Adam in Genesis went around giving names to things.

> And out of the ground the Lord God formed every beast of the field, and every fowl of the air; and brought *them* unto Adam to see what he would call them: and whatsoever Adam called every living creature, that *was* the name thereof. And Adam gave names to all cattle, and to the fowl of the air, and to every beast of the field. (Genesis 2:19–20; emphasis in original)

In this "Adamic" view of language, names or words are like labels hung onto things (whether those "things" are concrete objects or "feelings"). For a pointed but amusing attack on this view, see the short story by Ursula LeGuin (daughter of American anthropologist Albert Kroeber) included with this chapter (LeGuin 1987). In addition, words are assumed to refer to things; thus, all we need to do is to point to something and we will get the name for it. This view is reinforced because it appears to us that that is the way babies learn language. René Magritte, the surrealist painter, poked fun at this simplistic notion of language in his paintings where he tried to disrupt the association of word and thing, noting that "an object is never so closely attached to its name that another cannot be found that suits it better."[1] (See figure 4.1.) Michel Foucault picked up this theme in his book *This Is Not a Pipe* (1982), titled after one of Magritte's paintings, which depicted a pipe. Learning a language is far more complicated than learning the names for things, as those of you who have tried to learn another language are keenly aware. Knowing the words for things does not allow you to speak properly or to get the sense of what someone is saying.

The commonsense view of language is both that it is a reflection *of* reality and that it *refers* primarily *to* reality. Since most of us assume that language is a transparent medium primarily for the purpose of communication, it is difficult to accept the idea that our thoughts, feelings, and descriptions are conditioned, even shaped, by the possibilities of our language. Yet the bilingual (or trilingual or more) among you know that no two languages are really equivalent; not only does each have a different feeling and tone, but also the structures are different (some have no verb tenses, and others put the subject at the end of the sentence), the vocabulary is different, and there are some things you simply cannot say in some languages. Translation, therefore, is a matter of not just finding the corresponding words in the other language, since sometimes there are no equivalents, but also trying to convey the sense and meaning. This can be exceedingly difficult. For example, you cannot say, "I had a lot of fun," in Russian, because there is no word that translates as *fun*. In addition, "Russian has a single word for 'happiness' and 'luck,' suggesting that happiness is more a matter of good fortune than an inalienable right" (Lourie and Mikhalev 1989). Nor is it possible to say something like "Starting one's own business can be quite a challenge," since there is no word that translates "challenge" in that sense. On the other hand, Lourie and Mikhalev predict that the transformation of the Russian economy will provide ample opportunity to invent such a word.

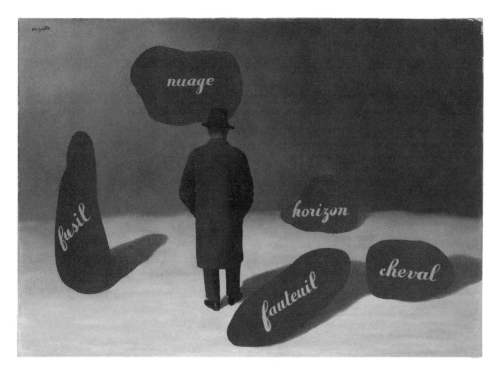

Figure 4.1   René Magritte, *Personnage marchant vers l'horizon* (1928–9). Collection of Staatsgalerie Stuttgart, Stuttgart. © ADAGP, Paris and DACS, London 2010.

Translation has often been a metaphor for what anthropologists do – they are thought to translate one culture into the terms of another (i.e., the anthropologist's own). While accurate in a very broad sense, it also assumes that culture is like a text, "out there," and readily available for translation.[2] Yet, it is important to realize that the construction of a cultural text derives from the anthropologist's own experience of interaction and collaboration with the people among whom he or she is living.

This chapter, like the preceding ones, is divided roughly into two parts. In the first part we will examine theories of language and, although I will indicate some of the ways they have been used by anthropologists to develop models for thinking about culture, you should be able to make some analogies on your own. In the second part, we will move into the area of *sociolinguistics* – basically, how people use language. This division coincides to some degree with the distinction made by Ferdinand de Saussure, an enormously influential French linguist who had a significant impact on anthropology, particularly through the *structuralism* as developed by Claude Lévi-Strauss. Language, according to Saussure, is divided into *langue* and *parole*; *langue* is the systematic aspect of language, but it exists only in individual speaking acts, *parole*. Unlike other linguists of his era and before, he was not concerned with origins, grammar, or etymology; instead, he was fascinated by the systematic aspects of language.

Theories of Language

Saussure was the first to realize that "language is a system of interdependent terms in which the value of each term results solely from the simultaneous presence of the others" (1959: 114). It must be a system, otherwise our speaking would make no sense. However, the system as a whole is not accessible; it does not exist some*place*, but instead we must infer it from individual acts of speaking. It is the job of the linguist or analyst to make the system more explicit. By analogy, this is how some people have come to think about culture. Culture, like language, does not exist some*place*, but must be inferred from nonverbal behavior as well as speech, otherwise social life would be incomprehensible.

Language is a symbolic system

Each of us inherits a language; we learn it as babies, which is why our native language is often called our *mother tongue*. "No society, in fact, knows or has ever known language other than as a product inherited from preceding generations" (Saussure 1959: 71). It is through and through a *social* invention and a social institution – no one person invented it. An artificial language such as Esperanto[3] has not been fully adopted by any society, and if it were put into circulation it would be "transmitted according to laws which have nothing in common with those of its logical creation. … [It] would be borne along, willy-nilly, by the current that engulfs all languages" (p. 76). Computer "languages" are also artificial languages; they are not at all like natural languages because their significations are fixed.

Language is not just a system; it is a completely *symbolic* system. There is no necessary connection between a sound (word) and the concept signified; different languages have different words for the same concepts. This means that the relation is arbitrary and symbolic; each word *represents* a concept. Rather than representing or reflecting the world, each language represents a conceptual scheme. The origins of language lie in the misty past and may never be known; but what has become clear is that the capacity for symbolic thought was a major ingredient in the transformation of *Homo sapiens* from its hominid ancestors. According to philosopher Suzanne Langer, "[I]t is not the essential act of thought that is symbolization, but an act *essential to thought*, and prior to it" ([1942] 1979: 41). Humans are symbol-making creatures. We did not first arrive at a fully complete, large-brained, and erect human body, and then create language and culture; they were essential parts of our *physical* evolution (see Geertz 1973).

Furthermore, contrary to popular belief, language appears to have developed not for practical reasons – not so humans could bring things to their hand or mouth – but "to bring things *into their minds*" (Langer [1942] 1979: 121) and be able to ruminate about them *in absentia*. Langer gave the example of Helen Keller, a deaf and blind young woman who finally learned language not when she *needed* something, like water, but when she realized that "water" symbolized or stood for the cool liquid flowing over her hands. Language is what allows us to think. "Real thinking is possible only in the light of genuine language" (p. 63).

Thinking is done with concepts or ideas. But ideas do not exist readymade before words – the words and the concepts coincide. Words unite "not a *thing* and a name, but a concept and a sound-image" (Saussure 1959: 66). Not only does this challenge our commonsense belief that words *mean* things, but also it should remind us that words are composed not of letters but of sounds. Writing comes much later and will be discussed shortly. A word, or *sign* in Saussure's usage, is like a sheet of paper. One side is the sound and the other the concept. Clearly, this relationship is arbitrary – there is no intrinsic reason to relate a specific slice of sound with a specific concept.

However, and maybe even more important, the meaning of that particular sign does not exist by itself but emerges *only* in relation to all the other signs, not the external world. Words are defined by other words; that is what a dictionary does. *Meaning*, therefore, is a function of an environment of signs, according to Saussure. Meaning, as we shall see later, is also a function of *context*. To get an idea of what Saussure meant, think about the nuances and differences between the words *afraid*, *fear*, *terrified*, and *dread*. We can distinguish between a present fear, in different degrees (*afraid*, *terrified*), and an anticipated fear (*dread*). The relation between *afraid* and the other two is one of intensity, and that would be removed if there was no word *afraid*; the meaning would have to be divided between the other two. Think also of words for edibility – *appetizing*, *tasty*, *delicious*, *juicy*, *luscious*, and *succulent*. They mutually condition each other and have slight variations in meaning that would be absent if we had only one word. (Why is it that all of these words can also be used to describe women? Does it mean that women are edible? We shall get to this kind of metaphoric transfer in a moment.) The issue here is that each word evokes and is conditioned by the range of synonyms and antonyms. Theories of language are a complicated subject, but, for our purposes, the main points are as follows:

1. Language is a symbolic system.
2. There is no transparent relationship between words and things.
3. Meaning is not the same as reference.
4. The system is relatively arbitrary.

How does this change your thinking about language? Can you see the implications for theories of culture?

If there are no preexisting concepts but these are constructed simultaneously with language, then it is somewhat easier to understand why no two languages are exact equivalents. For example, the Japanese concept *ma*, discussed in chapter 2 (in the section entitled "Feng Shui"), has no meaningful equivalent in English: it can be translated as "interval," but this does not convey its significance as an element of spatial arrangements. Similarly, some languages do not have abstract nouns for things like "time," but have a number of different words that characterize different qualities of what we call *time*. Our language allows us to talk about time as if it is a concrete thing, as we discussed in the previous chapter. How could one philosophize about "the good, the true, and the beautiful" if there were no abstract nouns to symbolize these concepts? This, clearly, has major implications for philosophy, the practice of which is conducted, to a very large extent, in abstract terms and assumes a kind of universality to its thought. Yet different social groups have conceptualized things differently even though there might be considerable overlap between some of them. As a child, you learn the conceptual structure of the language you are taught. This doesn't mean that you can't learn other languages, but your native language will always remain your ground.

Communication versus language

There are no simple or incomplete languages. Languages that do not have abstract nouns (see "Language is a symbolic system," above) are not more rudimentary; they are just different. Hunters and gatherers have as grammatical and complete languages as do people living in contemporary New York. But "[b]etween the clearest animal call of love or warning or anger, and a man's least, trivial *word*, there lies a whole day of Creation – or in modern phrase, a whole chapter of evolution" (Langer [1942] 1979: 103). This is not to say that animals don't communicate, for they do. Some of them can understand some language; for example, my cat seems to know her name and comes when I call her, and she responds to a number of other questions, commands, and terms of endearment.

There is a great deal of communication that goes on between humans and other animals. But communication is not the same thing as possessing language. The major questions about whether some animals have language concern the differences between (1) comprehension and performance, (2) sign using and symbol using, and (3) being able to communicate and being able to express a worldview. *Sign* in this instance does not have the same meaning that Saussure gave it; here it means something more like signal. (The confusion has to do with the difference between French and English.)

Linguist Emile Benveniste takes up the issue of "Animal Communication and Human Language" (1971) in his article of that title. His example is bees rather than hominids, whom we will discuss momentarily, for it has long been noticed that bees have some form of communication between each other. If one bee finds honey, it can go back to the hive and apparently "tell" the others where it is. That bee does not have to lead them to the honey; the directions, communicated by means of some kind of dance, are sufficient. "The message passed on contains three items of information … the existence of a source of food, its distance, and its direction" (1971: 52). This is clearly a significant form of communication. But what it lacks, according to Benveniste, are the following: the message is relayed without voice, there is no dialogue or reply, and the message cannot be reproduced by another bee that has not seen whatever the first one saw. It is a "signal code," highly sophisticated, but not a language.

Perhaps the most striking thing that differentiates bee communication from human language is that bees cannot sit around discoursing about honey as "nectar of the gods," or use it as a term of endearment. Bee communication lacks the metaphorical possibilities of language. The difference, in Suzanne Langer's terms, is the mind. The mind is not just a transmitter – not just a switchboard to relay messages – but also a transformer. The process of symbolization enables us to express a conception of life and of the world. Some symbolic ability seems also to be true of some of our nearest hominid neighbors.

Apes and language   Experiments teaching language to different kinds of hominids have included Koko, a gorilla; Washoe and Lana, chimpanzees; and Kanzi, a bonobo chimpanzee, to name only a few of the most famous. Not only do they understand some language but also they can communicate with some level of symbolic performance. They have been taught Ameslan (American Sign Language), a sign language for the deaf, and appear to be using it "in many of the ways that humans use it – to construct a world, to obtain desirables, and to regulate the behavior of others" (Hill 1980: 337). Hill, who summarized the findings of a number of experiments, said that some of these hominids have also creatively elaborated the signs that they know. For example, "Washoe produced 'water-bird' on first seeing ducks; … Lana used 'coke which is orange' for Fanta orange drink … and Koko signed 'finger bracelet' for ring, 'white tiger' for zebra" (p. 140). Koko has also been able to report on "her inner states of happiness, sadness, fear, and shame" (p. 341, citing Koko's trainer).

As of the year 2010, Koko is about 40 years old and appears to have an understanding of, and ability to use, about 1,000 words according to the people who work with her, but the process has been extremely time-consuming and demanded incredible patience. A baby understands quite a lot of words before he or she is a year old and often talks in sentences by the age of two. Due to the lack of vocal equipment that enables humans to speak, Koko, for all her remarkable achievements, cannot talk, and she does not appear to be able to transmit her facility with language to her offspring.

Since Hill's report, more recent work has been conducted with bonobo chimpanzees, and the results are even more haunting. Sue Savage-Rumbaugh, who has been working with some of these animals since 1980, developed a keyboard with a variety of signs for words. The chimps learned the meanings and could press the keys to "talk" to her and her assistants. Her primary subject was Matata, an adult female. Even after Matata gave birth to Kanzi, Savage-Rumbaugh continued to focus her teaching on Matata with the idea that she would start with Kanzi when he was about two. However, it turned out that Kanzi was learning all along simply by listening and watching, just as human children do. One day, his mother was taken away for mating purposes; Savage-Rumbaugh expected to use that time to "begin more systematic instruction with Kanzi, making certain that he could both use and understand symbols" (Savage-Rumbaugh, Shanker, and Taylor 1998: 23). But to their astonishment, his secret skill erupted. On the first day after his mother left, Kanzi "produced 120 separate utterances" (p. 22) and used them correctly. Nor was it simply an accident, for he continued to "talk" and expand his knowledge and ability. As Savage-Rumbaugh et al. noted,

I was in a state of disbelief. It was several weeks before I and others working with Kanzi began to accept the fact that he had really learned to talk even though we had not been attempting to teach him. … It was not just that I had successfully taught him how to use symbols to stand for things. … I had not intentionally taught Kanzi anything, nor had I been able to teach his mother what he had somehow learned, even though I had been trying to do so for two years. (p. 25)

This remarkable achievement threw a wrench into her theories about teaching chimps to "talk" and forced her to develop new ones. From that time on, she "decided to abandon all instruction and focus attention instead on what was *said to Kanzi* rather than on what we could teach him to say" (p. 27).

These examples are truly poignant signs of simian intelligence which should give pause to those who so easily kill these animals or put them in cages to be gawked at. Or, in Hill's words, "[I]t seems clear that the experiments, while holding out the possibility of apes as particularly refined human surrogates, at the same time cast serious doubts on the ethics of using them in that role" (1980: 351).

In spite of the strides in these experiments with hominid language, many linguists still have doubts, believing that these animals are merely imitating their human trainers, or that the trainers are imagining hand signs when they do not exist. The recent studies using computers and/or keyboards with symbols and icons representing things and concepts raise questions about whether the animals have simply been taught to respond to certain cues without really using language. Savage-Rumbaugh et al. (1998) think part of the reluctance of linguists to accept animal language is because they have reified language and taken it out of the social contexts in which it is embedded. This is possible in literate societies, where written language is separable from such contexts (1998: 195). Clearly, the argument about whether some animals possess, or can be taught, language will continue, and the verdict is still open.

The one thing that nonhuman primates are *not* doing is speaking, and that is surely one of the first definitions of language – that it is primarily sound. An exception to this definition is, obviously, sign language, which is a fully human language even though it is neither spoken nor heard. A second, and perhaps more perplexing, exception is the vocal ability of parrots and other talking birds, whose speech, though perfectly intelligible to human ears, has long been dismissed by animal behaviorists and linguists as meaningless imitation. The recent work of animal psychologist Irene Pepperberg has cast doubt on this assumption. She worked for 30 years with an African grey parrot called Alex, who not only spoke many English words but also could use them appropriately to answer questions, make demands, invent new words and phrases, and express his feelings – whether anger, fear, or anxiety. He also told Pepperberg, "I love you," on numerous occasions, although according to her this was less a declaration of sentiment than an effort to coax her into doing something for Alex that she did not want to do. As such, it is a very inventive and calculating use of speech. (See "Alex & Me" 2009; Carey 2007; Pepperberg 2009.)

Orality versus literacy

When we think of language, we generally think of the written word. When we learn a new language, we generally start with a textbook. Yet, as noted above, language is primarily an oral and aural phenomenon, that is, it is composed of intelligible *sounds*. Living, as we do, in a primarily print culture, we too easily forget this essential fact. Through the work of Walter J. Ong, specifically his book *Orality and Literacy: The Technologizing of the Word* ([1982] 1999), we will look briefly at some of the features of oral cultures and the social implications of literacy.

It is extremely difficult, says Ong, for us to put ourselves in the place of someone in a primary oral culture – "a culture where no one has ever 'looked up' anything" (Ong [1982] 1999: 31). If you were brought up in an oral culture, you could not look up a word, nor could you *see* it in the mind's eye; a word would not be a visual thing. Speaking is an *event*, and one that is evanescent. "Sound exists only when it is going out of existence. … [T]here is no way to stop sound and have sound. … [I]f I stop the movement of sound, I have nothing – only silence" (p. 32). There are no texts, so there can be no document to contradict a spoken statement or claim. At the same time, there are ways to aid memory in oral cultures:

> In primary oral culture, to solve effectively the problem of retaining and retrieving carefully articulated thought, you have to do your thinking in mnemonic patterns, shaped for ready oral recurrence. Your thought must come into being in heavily rhythmic, balanced patterns, in repetitions or antitheses, in alliterations and assonances. (p. 34)

Knowledge of the world and the history of the group are communicated in poetic, narrative, and aphoristic form but are very much contextualized and communal. Generally, you speak *to* someone or a group of people. Speaking, therefore, assumes a response, what Ong calls an *agonistic* quality; there is an interaction between speaker and hearer. "Oral communication unites people in groups. Writing and reading are solitary activities" (p. 69). Writing distances and objectifies. It is writing that fosters the notion that words are merely labels hung onto things.

Writing

People were speaking for thousands of years before the invention of writing. And it is an invention; it is completely artificial, and it is neither necessary nor inevitable. Therefore, Ong suggests we ought not to call oral cultures *illiterate*, because of the pejorative sense of the term, or *preliterate*, which suggests an evolutionary trajectory, but simply "oral cultures." Writing was first invented sometime around 3500 BC by the Sumerians in ancient Mesopotamia. The impetuses seem to have been urbanization and the need to control people, collect taxes, and plan projects, that is, for some kind of record keeping (see Schmandt-Besserat 1986).

The first writing, called *cuneiform*, was iconic, that is, it employed pictographs that had some resemblance to what was represented. Gradually these signs became more symbolic and abstract (see figure 4.2). But a "script in the sense of true writing … does not consist of mere pictures, of representations of things, but is a representation of an *utterance*, of words that someone says or is imagined to say" (Ong [1982] 1999: 84). Ong goes on to say that writing "was and is the most momentous of all human technological inventions. It is not a mere appendage to speech. Because it moves speech from the oral-aural to a new sensory world, that of vision, it transforms speech and *thought* as well" (p. 85; emphasis mine). In other words, it has transformed human consciousness. He claims we could not think as we do, particularly long, involved analytic formulations, without writing. Our thought patterns and our speech patterns have now been conditioned by the technique of

Figure 4.2   A clay tablet impressed with cuneiform script, from the Baghdad Museum, Iraq. © David Lees/CORBIS.

writing. Writing is, to a certain extent, context free; it need not have a present interlocutor or audience even though one must be imagined. But it is surely context dependent in terms of culture and era, and the age, ethnicity, gender, education, and religious background of the writer.

Writing was further enhanced by the invention of the alphabet and then by print.

> The most remarkable fact about the alphabet no doubt is that it was invented only once. It was worked up by a Semitic people or Semitic peoples around the year 1500 BC, in the same general geographic area where the first of all scripts appeared, the cuneiform, but two millennia later than the cuneiform. (Ong [1982] 1999: 89)

The Egyptians had used symbols for sounds but mixed them up with pictographs; it was the people living in the Levant who are believed to have invented the alphabet. Then the Phoenicians carried it to the Greeks, who added vowels, and from them all modern alphabets derive. The phonetic alphabet makes writing much easier to learn and thus more democratic than it had been. Some writing systems such as Chinese are not alphabetic but have elaborate characters representing words, concepts, and even whole phrases, and take many years to master.

The invention of moveable print type by Johannes Gutenberg in the fifteenth century further enhanced the possibilities of the written word. No longer were manuscripts copied by hand by elite scribes, but they could be mass produced for a mass reading public. The Bible not only was the first book to appear in print, but also was printed in vernacular languages and no longer in the Learned Latin that had been the possession of the elite. People could finally read and interpret the Bible for themselves rather than having it mediated by priests, and this was a major factor contributing to the Protestant Revolution now known as the Reformation.

In Europe, Learned Latin had been the language not just of the church but also of school and of international exchange. It was also a language of men. Although it had once been a mother tongue,

> for well over a thousand years, it was sex-linked, a language written and spoken only by males, learned outside the home in a tribal setting which was in effect a male puberty rite setting … it had no direct connection with anyone's unconscious of the sort that mother tongues, learned in infancy, always have. (Ong [1982] 1999: 113)

Latin was isolating and exclusive and, thus, extremely powerful. Only certain privileged males were initiated; most of the great scientists and philosophers did their thinking and writing in Latin. Although some women learned to read and write, they were excluded from this kind of education; when some of them began to put their thoughts on paper, they wrote in the vernacular and tended to focus on events and relationships in the domestic sphere to which they were generally confined. Ong believes that women's very different life experience led to the invention of the novel.

Writing was suspect when first invented, especially since it was the preserve of the elite. But there were other reasons. In *Phaedrus*, Plato has Thamus, the king of Egypt, say the following to Theuth (the Greek spelling of the Egyptian *Thoth*), the god who invented letters:

> [T]his invention will produce forgetfulness in the minds of those who learn to use it, because they will not practice their memory. Their trust in writing, produced by external characters which are no part of themselves, will discourage the use of their own memory within them. You have invented an elixir not of memory, but of reminding; and you offer your pupils the appearance of wisdom, not true wisdom, for they will read many things without instruction and will therefore seem to know many things, when they are for the most part ignorant and hard to get along with, since they are not wise, but only appear wise.[4]

Similar criticism has been leveled at the use of computers. People already complain that with the avalanche of email and other electronic information, they cannot remember things. In addition to handheld devices like PalmPilots and smartphones, many people now depend on the computer *memory* to store what they need to know, assuming they can retrieve it at will. Like writing, computers have also transformed the way we think. I know very well that I write quite differently if I sit down with a pad of paper and a pencil than if I sit in front of the computer screen. It is also far different from a typewriter, even an electric one, because I can revise, erase, and move sentences around at will: sometimes, when I do that, I notice that I lose track of the meaning.

Children are now often learning to type on the computer keyboard before they can write; indeed, one wonders whether the art (or technique) of writing will soon disappear. Perhaps, in the near future, we may revert to oral composition. Computers and telephones, for example, have "voice recognition," and computer technology is becoming increasingly adept with voice simulation. Very soon, I believe, someone will speak into the computer, and it will either transfer the message into print or forward it by voice. Clearly this will be a boon to millions of nonliterate people around the world, but what will be the effect on literate cultures? Will writing and print become a quaint artifact of the past?

Language, culture, and reality

We assume everyone sees the same things, and that perception is, itself, the apparatus that permits us to see. Yet, we see what we are trained to see, what we are socialized to see. Each of us is born into a particular culture and language, as well as into a particular family, birth order, sex, class, ethnic group, and religion. Our parents or parental surrogates who guide our interactions and interpretations, and hence our experience, socialize us. They tell us what is there, what to look for, how to look for it, how to feel about it, and what to think about it – in short, what it means. Language (and culture) is what mediates between us and the world or "reality"; in other words, perception is not direct but always mediated. This is as true of what are called the *empirical sciences* as it is for ordinary everyday perception.

> Observation has become almost entirely indirect; and *readings* take the place of genuine witness. The sense-data on which the propositions of modern science rest are, for the most part, little photographic spots and blurs, or inky curved lines on paper. These data are empirical enough, but of course they are not themselves the phenomenon in question; the actual phenomena stand behind them as their supposed causes. Instead of watching the process that interests us, that is to be verified – say, a course of celestial events … – we really see only the fluctuations of a tiny arrow … and *calculate to the "facts" of our science*. What is directly observable is only a sign of the "physical fact"; it requires interpretation to yield scientific propositions. Not simply seeing is believing, but *seeing and calculating, seeing and translating*. (Langer [1942] 1979: 20)

These "facts" are through and through symbolic, for "facts" exist only in relation to a (conceptual, and therefore language-based) theory. Langer goes on to say that "the triumph of empiricism in science is jeopardized by the surprising truth that *our sense-data are primarily symbols*," and, indeed, "the edifice of human knowledge stands before us, not as a vast collection of sense reports, but as a structure of *facts that are symbols* and *laws that are their meanings*" (p. 21). If sense perception is guided by language, then it should be becoming clearer that we live in symbolically constructed worlds – a situation I have heard described as "an inverted pyramid in which only one block rests on the ground"!⁵

If this is somewhat difficult to accept, let's try another tack. Benjamin Whorf, who, along with Sapir, became one of the most famous linguists of the twentieth century, began his career as an investigator for a fire insurance company. What ignited his interest in linguistics was his observation that people acted on the basis of linguistic cues. One of his most memorable examples involved the storage of gasoline drums. When workers were told that the drums contained fuel, they exercised great caution around them; but when they were told that the drums were empty, they smoked and threw their cigarette butts around, and were surprised when there was an explosion. Most of us today now realize that vapor from "empty" gasoline drums is just as dangerous, perhaps more so, than containers full of gasoline.

Such examples in which just one word seemed to trigger behavior led Whorf to wonder about the full extent of a given language to model behavior. Like anthropologists who usually study other cultures before turning to their own, Whorf felt that the "best approach [to the study of language] is through an exotic language, for in its study we are at long last pushed willy-nilly out of our ruts. Then we find that the exotic language is a mirror held up to our own" (1956: 138). Consequently, he went on to study Native American languages, particularly Hopi. Almost at once he noticed important differences between Hopi and what he called Standard Average European (SAE).

One of the first things that struck him was the different representations of time in the Hopi language. In English, we can say "10 men" and "10 days" as if they are somehow similar, standing in a row. Our language objectifies or quantifies time. In Hopi one cannot say "10 days" but only something like "He left on the eleventh day." We make nouns out of temporal phenomena and then assume that these are somehow objective units that we can stand in a row. In Hopi, summer or morning are not nouns but something like adverbs: "when it is the morning phase" or "when conditions are hot." But nothing influences our thought about time more than the "three-tense system of SAE verbs" (1956: 143). Whorf says that if "we inspect consciousness we find no past, present, future … [instead] everything is in consciousness": what we call the "present" is really the sensuous aspect – seeing, hearing, touching; what we call the "past" is the nonsensuous aspect of memory; and the future is the non-sensuous aspect of belief, intuition, and uncertainty (pp. 143–4). What we do experience is that everything gets later and later, but we lose this sense because of the way our language predisposes us to think about time. Quite a few languages have only two verb tenses – *earlier* and *later* – and some have no verb tenses at all but express these aspects of time with other linguistic modifiers.

We objectify time and assume it is a kind of "thing" divisible into measurable units – it is another example of the way our language persuades us to think in terms of formless matter and form: a *glass* of water, a *cup* of coffee, a *moment* or *hour* of time. At the same time (!), Whorf notes that our "objectified view of time is, however, favorable to historicity and to everything connected with the keeping of records," whether these are diaries, histories, calendars, or projections. Whereas, for the Hopi, for whom "everything that ever happened still is [presumably in consciousness] … there is less incentive to study the 'past'" (p. 153).

In effect, we *spatialize* time or duration as well as other modalities. "All languages," says Whorf, "need to express durations, intensities, and tendencies" but "it is characteristic of SAE … to express them metaphorically. The metaphors are those of spatial extension, i.e., of size, number (plurality), position, shape, and motion" (p. 145). For example, Whorf says that we

> express duration by long, short, great, much, quick, slow, etc.; intensity by large, great, much, heavy, light, high, low, sharp, faint, etc.; tendency by more, increase, grow, turn, get, approach, go, come, rise, fall, stop, smooth, even, rapid, slow; and so on through an almost inexhaustible list of metaphors that we hardly recognize as such, since they are virtually the only linguistic media available. (p. 145)

In other words, peoples with SAE languages tend to spatialize even the most nonspatial situations, and we do not recognize this tendency as metaphoric and imaginary. Think, for example, of such common phrases as *high* society, *lower* class, that's *deep*, getting *high*, warm *up*, cool *down*, *far out*, *shallow*, *uppity*, *down*town, *up*town, fooling *around*, hang *out*, the *in* crowd, and so on. To most of us, these seem to characterize the situation as it *is*; we think these are normal, hardly metaphoric, statements.

The idea, proposed by both Sapir and Whorf, that language massively influences culture became known as the *Sapir–Whorf hypothesis*. While there have been a number of critiques and most linguists and anthropologists no longer accept it *in toto*, it has, nevertheless, been extremely productive. Their primary focus was the *structure* of languages rather than the characteristic *ways* of saying things in each particular language. It is quite difficult to prove that there is a correlation between language structure and culture. But the idea that each language is a different conceptual system, and that there are characteristic ways of interpreting and expressing things ("fashions of speaking" in Whorf's terminology) that have an impact on culture, is a correlation that holds up very well. Perhaps it is not in the structure of language but in the metaphors utilized in each culture that habitual ways of thought, behavior, and worldview are best glimpsed.

Metaphor

George Lakoff and Mark Johnson imply the importance of metaphor in our lives by the title of their book, *Metaphors We Live By*. "If our conceptual system is largely metaphorical, then the way we think, what we experience, and what we do every day is very much a matter of metaphor" (1980: 3). This was recognized long ago by Aristotle, who claimed, "The greatest thing by far is to be master of metaphor" (Aristotle, *Poetics*, 1459a). So too did Rousseau: "As man's first motives for speaking were of the passions, his first expressions were tropes. Figurative language was the first to be born" (1781, in Moran and Gode 1967: 12). Suzanne Langer, whose influential theories about language and symbolization affected symbolic anthropology, felt keenly the constructive power of metaphor:

The use of metaphor can hardly be called a conscious device. It is the power whereby language, even with a small vocabulary, manages to embrace a multimillion things; whereby new words are born and merely analogical meanings become stereotyped into literal definitions. … [S]peech becomes increasingly discursive, practical, prosaic, until human beings can actually believe that it was invented as a utility, and was later embellished with metaphors for the sake of a cultural product called poetry. ([1942] 1979: 141–2)

She calls attention to the popular view that language is primarily for utilitarian communication rather than for expression (of a worldview). However, her discussion of Helen Keller and of dreams, ritual, and artistic creation challenges that view, and suggests that language enables the creation of a world to live in, that is, a culture.

Nevertheless, despite these advocates of the power and importance of metaphor, it has not fared very well in modern times. Instead, it is more commonly regarded as the "fancy dress of language" that covers up the "real, true, bones" of whatever is at issue. As Lakoff and Johnson state in the first paragraph of their book,

Metaphor is for most people a device of the poetic imagination and the rhetorical flourish – a matter of extraordinary rather than ordinary language. Moreover, metaphor is typically viewed as a characteristic of language alone, a matter of words rather than thought or action. For this reason, most people think they can get along perfectly well without metaphor. We have found, on the contrary, that metaphor is pervasive in everyday life. (1980: 3)

The first example they use to illustrate their point is that we tend to think about argument as war. They say that

we don't just *talk* about arguments in terms of war. We can actually win or lose arguments. We see the person we are arguing with as an opponent. We attack his positions and we defend our own. We gain and lose ground. We plan and use strategies. If we find a position indefensible, we can abandon it and take a new line of attack. Many of the things we *do* in arguing are partially structured by the concept of war. Though there is no physical battle, there is a verbal battle, and the structure of an argument – attack, defense, counterattack, etc. – reflects this. It is in this sense that the ARGUMENT IS WAR metaphor is one that we live by in this culture; it structures the actions we perform in arguing. (p. 4)[6]

The authors ask the reader to imagine a culture in which "arguing" took the form of a dance. The structure would be different and so would the outcome, so much so that we would not see what they were doing as "argument." Lakoff and Johnson go on to stress that it is not just the words that are metaphoric, but also the concept of what an argument, in essence, *is*. In this case, as in many others, the metaphors are not some cover-up or "fancy dress" but constitute reality for us.

In "Anthropological Aspects of Language: Animal Categories and Verbal Abuse," British anthropologist Edmund Leach analyzes the metaphoric construction of terms of abuse. "Why," he asks, "should expressions like 'you son of a bitch' or 'you swine' carry the connotations that they do, when 'you son of a kangaroo' or 'you polar bear' have no meaning whatsoever?" (1964: 29). What is the relationship between animal categories and terms of abuse? His answer, quite ingenious and somewhat complicated, depends on the widespread association between eating and sexual intercourse, even though what is eaten and who is an appropriate sexual partner can vary cross-culturally. Leach shows how the British classification of animals, in terms of distance from oneself, is homologous with a classification of both living environments and kinship relationships. Starting with the self and proceeding outward, Europeans and Americans classify kin in the following manner: (1) the closest are the nuclear family – the people with whom sexual relations, except those between the married couple, are taboo; (2) next are kin but not as close – the category of first cousins – with whom marriage is forbidden or strongly disapproved of, yet it is still permitted in 26 of the United States (*New York Times*, April 4, 2002; cf. Ottenheimer 1996) and is also practiced in parts of the Middle East, including Turkey; (3) neighbors (friends) who are not kin but potential affines (e.g., in-laws), the category from which one might expect to obtain a husband or wife; and, finally, (4) distant strangers – people known to exist but with whom no social relations exist.

Analogously, the English, Leach claimed, "put most of their animals into four very comparable categories: (1) those who are very close, i.e., pets; you do not eat your pet dog; he is almost one of the family, and "man's best friend"; (2) those who are tame but not very close, i.e., farm animals who are edible if immature or castrated; (3) field animals, i.e., "game" – animals who live under human protection but are not tame – and who are edible only at certain set times of the year; and, finally, (4) remote wild animals deemed inedible. Terms of abuse derive from animals that are closest to us, and so too do terms of endearment, for example we can say "you bitch" or "lamb"; furthermore, some of them "serve as near obscene euphemisms for unmentionable parts of the human anatomy" (e.g., cock, ass, and pussy) (1964: 49–50). While the homology is not exact, and Leach did not answer the question of why the terms for female animals are the ones most commonly used as terms of abuse, the exercise revealed a number of important cultural beliefs.

Sexual metaphors   In my own work I have discovered that sexuality, particularly related to procreation, forms a massive metaphorical area that influences the way we think not only of men and women, but also of such seemingly unrelated areas as education and cosmology, whether scientific or religious. For thousands of years, the dominant *folk* theory of procreation in the West is what I have called the "seed-soil" theory (Delaney 1986, 1991). This theory is inscribed in some of our most influential texts: the Bible, the work of Plato and Aristotle, the writings of early and medieval Christian theologians, and Freud's work, for example, and it persists even today on television, in popular songs and poems, and in turns of phrase. In this theory, the male is imagined as the one to plant the seed (*inseminate* literally means to put the seed in), which renders the woman analogous to the nurturant, or possibly barren, *soil*. This seemingly simple and innocuous agricultural metaphor is a very important example of what Sylvia Yanagisako and I mean by "naturalizing power" (Yanagisako and Delaney 1995), because it attributes the creative, engendering, identity-giving role to the male; he *begets*. The child, in essence, is in the seed. The female is not imagined as co-creator; she *bears*. Her role is secondary and supportive; she merely nurtures the seed-child and brings it forth. The folk theory of procreation symbolically allies men with the creative, life-giving ability of God, and women with what was created *by* God

(Nature). This analogy constitutes a metaphoric (and hierarchical) relationship between cosmology and humans.

As cosmological metaphor, these meanings amplify the Catholic Church's position on birth control, abortion, and homosexuality. In a major document about human sexuality, *Humanae Vitae*, promulgated in 1968, the church stated that each marriage act (read heterosexual intercourse) must be open to the *transmission* of life. This clearly recapitulates the ancient idea that that life (or soul) is transmitted via semen. Biochemically, life is not transmitted at all; it is a process that begins when ovum and sperm merge and mitosis begins – a process that normally takes place *inside* the woman's body (or today, occasionally, on a petri dish). But for the church, seed and life are transmitted through heterosexual congress, hence too homosexual acts and masturbation "spill the seed," waste life, and therefore are sinful.

Although the Catholic Church does not have the ideological reach it once had, similar meanings persist in our common ideas about procreation. Think of the different images and meanings evoked by the phrases *to father* and *to mother*, *paternity* and *maternity*, and *patrimony* and *matrimony*. These images and meanings were established long ago, long before the science of genetics emerged whereby we now believe that both male and female, through sperm (from *sperma*, meaning seed) and ova, provide half the genetic endowment, half the *seed*, so to speak, to each child. In addition, of course, the woman also continues the nurturing role while the child is in the womb and after it is born. Until very recently that is the role that defined *mother*, yet a mother's role has now been fragmented into birth mother, surrogate mother, and genetic mother.

We think of the process of procreation as *reproduction*, a word that was not introduced to refer to the process until the mid-nineteenth century and, at the time, was considered a quaint metaphor. Until then the biblical *begetting* and *bearing, generation*, or *procreation* were used. To my mind, *reproduction* is not an improvement for it conjures images of churning out copies, like a Xerox machine. Because our gender definitions are so deep and independent from scientific theory, it is very difficult to change them unless conscious effort is expended to do so, and that will involve developing different metaphors and images.

The relation between the theory of procreation and the monotheistic view of Creation seems quite clear. But that is religion, what does it have to do with science? Yet scientific cosmologists have been searching for the grand unified theory (i.e., *one* "mono-theory" to explain the coming into being of the universe) and also to conceptualize the origin of the universe as a "single seed smaller than an atom" yet "so potent it blossomed into everything there is" – the single seed that exploded in the Big Bang.[7] Do you think people with different cosmologies and different theories of procreation would come to the same conclusions?

The same theory of procreation is carried into the area of education. Why do we have *fields* of study, *bodies* of knowledge? I believe that the *body* of knowledge is symbolically female because women have been associated with nature, that which is to be explored, subdued, penetrated, and exploited.[8] The explorer, scientist, "knower" is symbolically male, while that which is explored and known is symbolically female; this may derive from the biblical notion that to have sex was "to know." Similarly, the word *conceive* can refer to both intellectual and physical conceptions. *Seminal* ideas are defined as original and creative; women can have them, but the language suggests that creative thought is masculine in character. We do not hear of *ovulul* ideas, and *pregnant* ones, while auspicious, are merely potential. Because high-quality thinking is characterized as seminal and penetrating, do you think there might be some correlation to why women thinkers and scholars have not been taken as seriously as their male counterparts? What about the gendering of the "hard" versus "soft" sciences, or, more basic – the sciences versus the humanities? Can you think of other gendered metaphors pertaining to the acquisition of knowledge?

The sexual metaphors have also shaped the image of the anthropologist in doing *field-work*. Clifford Geertz characterized anthropological work as follows: "In the study of culture, analysis penetrates into the very body of the object" (1973: 15). Why must analysis "penetrate"? Why is culture imagined as a body? What kind of body? Why is the body passive and inert, an object (to be penetrated) rather than an active, living participant-subject? Regardless of the *sex*, the analyst's *gender* is inherently masculine. The question is as follows: are these merely words, or do they shape the way we think and go about our studies? Philosopher Paul Ricoeur, who has written extensively on metaphor, considers it to be the supreme creative act, which carries cognitive import and expands knowledge, like Aristotle before him and anthropologist Marilyn Strathern[9] after him. Yet Ricoeur also perpetuates the sexual connotations, for, to him, "metaphor is an idyll with a new partner who resists while giving in" (1976: 56).

Language in Use

The previous section has briefly introduced you to theory about language and its consequences; in this section, I would like to shift to the more "sociolinguistic" aspects of language. Sociolinguistics is the study of the social uses of language – or language in use. Scholars interested in this side of language tend to study not just slang and regional variations of speaking but also the way gender, race, and class are indexed, which is closely related to the ways power and dominance are enacted linguistically. Since my own work has focused more on gender, that will get somewhat more attention here.

Language and gender

The word *gender* was first and foremost a linguistic term, referring to the way some languages classify words according to sex. For example, the articles *le* and *la* in French both mean *the*, but *le* modifies masculine nouns, as in *le soleil* (the sun), while *la* modifies feminine nouns, as in *la lune* (the moon). The gender of the noun also determines the indefinite article ("a"), as in *un* and *une*.

The use of the word *gender* to refer to the social and cultural meanings of male and female developed in the 1970s. Until then, most people simply assumed, and were socially encouraged to think, following Freud, that "biology is destiny." This meant that your biological sex, defined in relation to your role in reproduction, determined your social role.[10]

However, if that is true, then you would expect that sex roles and definitions would be the same worldwide. But anthropologists had long known that the definitions of male and female, and the social roles they were expected to perform, varied considerably cross-culturally (e.g., Mead 1928, 1935, 1949). By the early 1970s, feminist anthropologists adopted the word *gender* to highlight that awareness and to utilize ethnographic knowledge to challenge mainstream Euro-American definitions of masculinity and femininity.[11] While sex and gender are surely related in some way, exactly how has not yet been conclusively determined. Instead, it has become clearer that gender is inextricably entwined with cosmology, religion, language, culture, economics, and kinship, as well as with sex and biology.

Once the anthropological concept of gender was invented, it was adopted and elaborated by scholars in a number of different fields, and it should be obvious that it does not apply just to women. The concept of gender has also helped men to question stereotypical definitions and roles of masculinity, and opened up a wider discussion that includes issues of homosexuality and transgender (see chapters 5 and 8). However, the word (and the concept) *gender* does not exist in many languages. It does not exist in French, for example, and French feminists have not tried to adopt it; instead, their strategy is to use only *sex* but try to show that it is not just about biology. For all their sophistication on the topic, particularly the relation between sex and language, the use of *sex* continues to plague their analyses.[12] *Gender* does not exist in Turkish either, and I was forced to use the word for *sex* (*cinsiyet*) in the Turkish translation of my book, *The Seed and the Soil: Gender and Cosmology in Turkish Village Society* (Delaney 1991), thus undermining my intention.

Pronouns   One of the first linguistic issues concerning gender had to do with pronouns, namely the use of *he* to stand for both *she* and *he* similar to the way that the generic *man* is intended to stand for both men and women, or what Wendy Martyna, among others, calls "He/Man" language (1980). Although we assume that men and women are covered by the general pronoun, it is not immediately obvious. Sometimes it does include both, but just as often it is intended to refer only to *males*. The US Constitution says, "All men are created equal," but women were not necessarily, or always, included; otherwise, there would be no need for the Equal Rights Amendment, which, to this day, has still not passed. Once you are sensitized to the question of inclusiveness of pronouns, reading can become difficult as you try to ascertain in each instance whether or not you are included. Through the consciousness-raising movements of the late 1960s and early 1970s, women began to hear themselves excluded in the very language around them, for example when a teacher said to a mother of a daughter, "every student must do *his* own homework," or when a politician said that "every voter must follow *his* own conscience in the stance *he* takes on the transportation bond issue" (Morton 1972: 181–2; emphasis mine). Nelle Morton, one of the first to write about this phenomenon, commented, "The prevalence of male terminology in the common speech appeared insignificant and even funny at first. Everybody knew that everybody did not mean literally male and that was that: *Then there came a time when it ceased to be funny*. Women began hearing themselves shut out of their own traditions" (p. 182). At first, many people thought the issue of pronouns was silly; indeed, in 1971, the linguistics faculty of Harvard criticized an attempt by a theology class to eliminate sexist language from its discussions: The fact that the masculine gender is the unmarked gender in English … is simply a feature of grammar … there is really no cause for anxiety or pronoun-envy on the part of those seeking such changes. (Martyna 1980: 483)

They would soon have to eat those words, for it became more and more obvious that the language was pervasively sexist. It is worth noting that the language issue became politicized first in religion and theology classes, in this case at Harvard Divinity School, which during the 1970s exploded with feminist critiques of theological language. (I know because I was there.) The critiques began with language but did not stop there; they went on to criticize the institutional structure and personnel of the organized religions, and then launched a wider critique of the society influenced by the monotheistic religions. In this, they echoed the first "wave" of the women's movement in the mid-nineteenth century, the spokeswomen of which critiqued the gendered language in the Bible, rewrote some biblical stories, and published them as *The Woman's Bible* (Stanton et al. [1898] 1974). It was quickly banned and not republished until 1974.

The problems hit close when we turn to the law:

Where a statute imposed duties or penalties on persons, where the masculine form was used it was asserted that women were included. … Yet where a statute imposed privileges or benefits upon persons, the opposite was the case: courts held that women were not intended to be included. (Hamilton, Hunter, and Stuart-Smith 1992: 341)

It is quite disturbing to think that the law, which is assumed to be impartial, can be so selectively used.

The "pseudogeneric" *he*, as Debora Schweikart calls it, has not always been prescriptively used in the law, but only became so in the past 150 years. In Britain it was mandated in an Act of Parliament in 1850. The idea was first proposed by J. Kirkby in 1746, but perhaps reached its most explicit form in the following statement of grammarian Goold Brown:

The gender of words, in many instances, is to be determined by the following principle of universal grammar. Those terms which are equally applicable to both sexes (if they are not expressly applied to females), and those plurals which are known to include both sexes, should be called masculine in parsing; for, *in all languages, the masculine gender is considered the most worthy,*† and is generally employed when both sexes are included under one common term. Thus *parents* is always masculine.

† The Supreme Being (*God*, …) is, in all languages, masculine; in as much as the masculine sex is the superior and more excellent; and as He is the Creator of all, the Father of gods and men. (Schweikart 1998: 2, citing Brown, 1851; first emphasis mine)

It is clear that Brown did not know many languages or cultures for not all languages have gender, and surely not all religions have a masculine god, or even a god at all, as in the case of Buddhism and numerous others. But the statement is very telling about the relationship between gender, religion, and societies influenced by the Abrahamic religions (Judaism, Christianity, and Islam).

The issue of the pronoun can have serious consequences, as a number of legal scholars have begun to point out. For example, Hamilton et al., in an article about jury instructions, ask, "Can a woman claim self-defense when 'he' is threatened?" (1992: 340). In the language of the court, it actually becomes difficult to determine just who is the assailant and who the victim. In a case where a woman killed someone, allegedly in self-defense, these were part of the verbatim instructions to the jury:

> when there is no reasonable ground for the person attacked to believe that *his* person is in imminent danger of death or great bodily harm, and it appears to *him* that only an ordinary battery is intended and is all that *he* has reasonable grounds to fear from *his* assailant, *he* has a right to stand *his* ground and repel such an assault. But *he* has *no right* to repel a threatened assault by the use of bare hands or a deadly weapon, unless *he* believes, and has reasonable grounds to believe, that *he* is in imminent danger of death or great bodily harm. (p. 342; gendered pronouns italicized and other emphasis in original)

One begins to think that the assailant was the victim of the attack. This case was used in a study to determine the effect of the masculine generic *he* in comparison with *he and she*, or just *she*, as would have been appropriate in this case, and concluded that the results of the study "indicate that the most important decisions before the jury in many murder trials, the decision concerning self-defense, might potentially be affected by the pronoun used in jury instructions" (p. 346). That is serious business. Part of the problem has to do with the idea and ideal of the "reasonable man," that is, what would a reasonable man do in similar circumstances? But in situations of physical threat, it is not reasonable to compare women's behavior with men's.

The linguistic changes wrought by the twentieth-century women's movement have been far reaching and have become embedded in "normal" language, so much so that those of you reading this in the twenty-first century must think it all very odd and antiquated. For my part, it is difficult to communicate the intensity of discussions about pronouns that took place in the media, academia, and across the kitchen table, let alone in the bedroom, during that not-so-long-ago time.

Along with the discussion of pronouns came the awareness that a woman's marital status, but not a man's, was linguistically indicated. Two forms of address, *Miss* and *Mrs.*, contrast with just one, *Mr.*, for men. In order to change this unequal treatment, women campaigned for *Ms.* to apply to all women, but it has met with only limited success. In addition, married women's identity is further erased when they are addressed as Mrs. John Smith. Other words distinguish gender in English, for example, *actor* and *actress*, *waiter* and *waitress*, and *poet* and *poetess*.

Gendered language, even something as seemingly neutral as a pronoun, creates images in the mind that are difficult to supplant. They affect the way we imagine things to be, and that affects the way we respond. What happens to girls when the books they read use only the male pronoun to refer to doctors, lawyers, archaeologists, or professors, and the female pronoun only in reference to nurses, teachers, or librarians? In addition, gendered language affects the way we imagine, reconstruct, and display the past, for example in theories of "Man the Hunter," or exhibits in museums of natural history, where men are portrayed as the actors (see, for example, Hager 1997; Haraway 1989; Landau 1991; Zihlman 1991). The gender critique of language did not stop with pronouns and forms of address.

Gendered talk   Other scholars were interested in the way that language is used by each gender, noticing that "gender hierarchies display themselves in all domains of social behavior, not the least of which is talk" (Ochs 1992: 336). Girls are socialized to talk differently than boys. As a result, women's talk is more tentative and does not command the same attention as men's speech, in part because of rising intonation (at the end of sentences that are not questions), "hedges" (as in "I kind of wanted to go"), qualifiers ("That was so very, very nice of you"), distinction phrases ("Oh dear, I dropped the house keys"), and tag questions ("That looks okay, doesn't it?") versus direct commands (see Robin Lakoff's *Language and Woman's Place*, 1975). Others such as Deborah Tannen (1990) suggest that women speak to maintain connections, give support, preserve intimacy, and avoid isolation, whereas men speak to preserve independence, negotiate hierarchy, give information, and avoid failure. It has been claimed that children recognize gendered language by the time they reach first grade (Edelsky 1976).

In a study that contrasted the white middle-class American style of mothering with that of Samoan women, Elinor Ochs concluded that the verbal strategies used by American mothers helped to "construct a low image of themselves" (1992: 347). They did this by prioritizing the child's point of view and excluding their own participation in helping a child accomplish certain tasks. "Mother," Ochs says, "is underrated because she does not socialize children to acknowledge her participation in accomplishments. 'Mother' is ignored because through her own language behavior, 'mother' has become invisible" (p. 355). The devaluation of motherhood in American society is not solely dependent on mothers' *language*, but Ochs's study does indicate that American mothers are complicit in devaluing their status by their linguistic style. At the same time, we should not forget that mothers, too, have been socialized by their culture and child care experts in communicating with babies and young children.

At college, it has been noticed that men tend to dominate classroom discussions, or perhaps professors tend to pay more attention to them. No doubt this relates to the discussion above that women's mode of talking does not command the same kind of attention as men's, but it might also have something to do with the way "the knower," knowledge, and the pursuit of knowledge are characterized. Do these dynamics hold in your classes? What about outside of class?

Language and race

It is not necessary to repeat all the horrible epithets that have been used to put down people on the basis of race – whether the people in question are black, Jewish, Asian, Irish, Hispanic, Italian, or some other. You might have noticed that not all of the categories mentioned are what are normally counted as "racial"; instead, some refer to "ethnic" groups. Nevertheless, members of these groups have all been the butt of the same kind of linguistic behavior. As children, we are taught that "sticks and stones will break my bones, but words will never hurt me." But they do.

Anthropologists have long argued that there is no such thing as race, that the overlap between people whose surface physiognomy appears different is so great as to make the category of "race" meaningless. Recent breakthroughs in genetics, DNA, and the human genome only confirm this. We are all one human race; in fact, we are 98 percent chimpanzee – we share 98 percent of our DNA with chimps.[13]

Although there is overwhelming biological and anthropological evidence that race as a *natural* category does not exist, it nevertheless exists as a *social* category – one that wields enormous power and causes enormous strife and suffering. The concept of race is created by people as a way to draw boundaries between a "we" and a "they." Rather than dismiss the notion of race, as the biological and genetic data would dictate, it is important to investigate its construction. As a social category, race "denotes a particular way in which communal differences come to be constructed and therefore it cannot be erased from the analytical map" (Anthias and Yuval-Davis 1992: 2). In their book *Racialized Boundaries*, Anthias and Yuval-Davis suggest that we understand "racisms as modes of exclusion, inferiorization, subordination and exploitation that present specific and different characters in different social and historical contexts" (p. 2). That is, racism is not just one thing; it takes different forms in different times and places. Their analytical framework includes the overlapping but somewhat different category of ethnicity and its corollaries, nation and nationalism; in addition they suggest that the way in which racism operates on both gender and class also needs to be investigated. In *Orientalism* (1979), Edward Said examined the racist attitudes of Europeans toward Orientals (who, in that context, were Middle Eastern Arabs). What he did not show was the sexist metaphors in which this construction was made, that is, the Orient was imagined as veiled, seductive, and sexual, and in need of "mastery" by the white Europeans who were symbolically, and often literally, male. How did these images prefigure encounters with Arabs, and how did they affect Arab women and men?

It is not the purpose of this chapter or this book to attempt an account of the construction of race or of racism; however, we will briefly look at a couple of ways race and racism are expressed and enacted linguistically. One simple, or seemingly simple, way involves the label that gets attached to a particular group, for example in the linguistic nomenclature that extends from *Negro* to *black* to *African American*. *Negro* now appears to belong to discredited racial theories; *black*, in contrast, became a label of self-definition during the 1960s with the Black Power movement, while *African American* is seen as an ethnic designation similar to Italian American or Irish American that focuses on one's cultural heritage. One can say black British, but it is far more difficult to say African British or African German. Linguistically, *American* does not carry the same racial-ethnic load that either *British* or *German* does, though in practice it does. In Britain, some South Asians (from India) have identified themselves with the category *black* as a political statement (cf. Baumann 1996).

As another example, ethnicity is also indexed by the labels attached to Spanish-speaking people in the United States, especially in the Southwest. "Speakers of Spanish, regardless of geographical origin or citizenship, were traditionally called 'Mexicans' by Anglos. In the 1960s many Americans of Mexican heritage adopted 'Chicano', but the term remains controversial among Spanish speakers in the region" (Hill 1993: 169n1). Hill goes on to say that some prefer *Latino*, while others feel that term "applies only to Spanish speakers from the Caribbean. 'Hispanic' is ... essentially a 'race' term introduced by the US Justice Department to include Puerto Ricans, Cubans, Spaniards, Mexicans, Salvadorenos, Colombians, etc." (p. 169 n. 1).

In her article "Hasta La Vista, Baby," Hill (1993) discusses the way that the misuse of Spanish words and phrases by Anglos is one method that racism is enacted linguistically. The title is a good example of what she is getting at; the phrase "Hasta la vista" means "Until we meet again" and is a "rather formal farewell, uttered sincerely to express hope for the pleasure of a future meeting" (p. 145). When Arnold Schwarzenegger used the phrase, adding "baby," in *Terminator 2*, it was a parody and became an expression of contempt as "he blows the bad terminator away forever (he thinks)" (p. 145).

Another example of a possible linguistic "put-down" presented itself as Hill had breakfast in a hotel restaurant. All of the employees were Hispanic, but the placemat that greeted her said *Buenas Dias* rather than *Buenos Dias*. A simple mistake, but it could so easily have been avoided. Did the owner of the restaurant check the spelling? Did the workers notice the misspelling? If so, how did they feel about it? By itself, this may seem an insignificant example, but added up, they can create a hostile work environment. Hill argues that in the Southwest, Anglo uses of Spanish are strategic: they are part of the construction of a "regional political economy based on racial hierarchy, that requires Anglos to produce and reproduce the subordination of Spanish-speaking and Native American populations who have a prior claim to the resources of the region," reducing them to "a profound marginality from which recovery is only just beginning" (p. 147). A good bilingual education for both Spanish speakers and English speakers might help in this recovery.

Bilingual education   Bilingual education, however, is a hotly debated issue in the United States, where, next to English, Spanish is the most widely spoken language. Nevertheless, the bilingual education issue is not just about Spanish, nor did it begin with it. In 1974, the US Supreme Court decided that the San Francisco School Department had violated the civil rights of a Chinese American student to obtain a public education. The court determined that this child, and other students like him with limited proficiency in English, were denied access to equal public education because they could not understand the language of instruction. This case, *Lau v. Nichols*, would turn out to be the landmark case in bilingual education. After the decision in support of Lau, Congress passed the Equal Education Opportunity Act, and school districts across the country scrambled to come up with programs for children who did not speak English. In San Francisco, this could mean accommodating over 90 different languages spoken by primary-grade schoolchildren.

Bilingual education is not a uniform system by any stretch of the imagination. Inextricably linked to race and class, it has come to mean different things in different states, school districts, and parts of the country. In some school districts, students with limited English proficiency (LEP in educational parlance) must take English as a Second Language before being "mainstreamed" with native speakers at their grade level. In others, students participate in "double immersion" or "two-way" programs that provide English speakers with an opportunity to learn a second language while ensuring that speakers of the other language (such as Spanish or Cantonese) learn English. In others, it means students receive most of their instruction in their native language (perhaps French or Korean) while learning English at a slower pace; this is the method most people associate with "bilingual education."

Advocates of bilingual education argue that children should have at least some of their classes in their primary language because they will more quickly gain knowledge and literacy in that language. Once you learn to read – in any language – it is apparently easier to learn to read in another language, thus the transition to English may be smoother. In addition, becoming literate in one's native language and gaining knowledge through that language would also give these children the confidence to succeed in school.

Opponents of bilingual education, including some native Spanish speakers (e.g., Richard Rodriguez), say that such a policy holds back children and prevents them from achieving success in the English-speaking world. They argue that the best, if not the only, way to teach a language is total immersion, and that the only language that really matters in the United States is English. They argue that many LEP students end up languishing in bilingual classrooms for years without ever learning enough English to be "mainstreamed."

Today, bilingual education is a hot button topic. Ballot initiatives funded by California millionaire Ron Unz asked voters in California, Arizona, Massachusetts, and Colorado to overturn decades of bilingual education policy and submit all children to the "sink-or-swim" approach. The initiatives passed in all states but Colorado. Massachusetts voters approved the most draconian initiative of all, which included a provision stating that teachers could be sued for using a child's native language. This hit close to home since my oldest grandson began his education in a bilingual public school that opened for the first time in fall of 1999. Half of his class were native Spanish speakers, the other half were native English speakers, and classroom time was spent equally in Spanish and English.

From my own observations and from anecdotal evidence, it seems to be working very well for the Spanish-speaking kids but not as well for the English-speaking kids. After all, English is the ambient language; the native Spanish speakers hear it in the stores, on television, and in the gym and lunchroom. English speakers may, nevertheless, gain status among their peers and teachers by mastering a second language like Spanish or Chinese. But to succeed in school and the workplace in the United States, Spanish speakers, like speakers of Chinese or Vietnamese, *need* English. Beyond this, however, is a much bigger philosophical issue to consider: the way in which language is tied up with the nation-state and nationalism. Why should there be only one national language? Wouldn't it be better if all of us could speak at least two if not more languages as many people in Europe already do? And aren't bilingual employees more sought after than those who speak only one language?

Ebonics   Ebonics, or African American Vernacular English, is spoken by vast numbers of African American youngsters. There are many people who think it is merely slang, a lazy or defective language, and this affects how they think about those who speak it. Linguist John Rickford, and others, argue that it is a structured, systematic, grammatical, and rule-governed language like any other, and for many African American children it is their primary language. Rickford and other like-minded linguists were able to persuade the Linguistics Society of America to recognize it as such. In January 1997, the society passed a resolution to that effect and also pronounced the decision of the Oakland school board – where the debate over Ebonics first erupted – to take it into account when teaching Standard English "linguistically and pedagogically sound" (Rickford 1998). While it could be considered a dialect of English, it is important to realize that the distinction between a dialect and a language is made on social and political grounds, not linguistic ones. Rickford gives the example of Norwegian and Swedish, which are considered two separate languages although speakers can understand each other, whereas speakers of a variety of Chinese dialects cannot. While there is not a move to *teach* Ebonics, the recognition of it as a legitimate language helps make the teaching of Standard English easier. On this issue, the controversy over Ebonics is clearly intertwined with that about bilingualism.

Language and class

Class has to do with differences in status, power, and birth, not just wealth. Members of traditional upper classes can tell immediately who is *nouveau riche* by his or her pronunciation, grammar, and vocabulary.

> Bankers clearly do not talk the same as busboys, and professors don't sound like plumbers. They signal the social differences between them by features of the phonology, grammar, and lexical choice, just as they do extralinguistically by their choices in clothing, cars, and so on. (Guy 1988: 37)

People are judged by the way they speak, and the judgments determine how others will respond, if at all.

American Tongues is an excellent film that demonstrates the range of regional differences in American English and raises the question of why certain ways of speaking – a Brooklyn or South Boston accent – are disparaged. Speaking voice and perfect grammar are expected of mainstream, prime-time newscasters – maybe it is part of the job description. Why do you think there is no one with a deep Southern drawl as host of a major network news program? In what other ways do you think your manner of speaking might affect your social life and job possibilities?[14]

While the speaking voice is a marker of class, so too is grammar. In recent years I have noticed an increase in grammatical mistakes even among educated people. One of the most glaring mistakes is the confusion over when to use *I* and when to use *me*. I frequently hear statements like the following: "She brought the video to Tim and I" rather than "She brought the video to Tim and me," or "Do you want to go to the movies with Jane and I?" rather than "Do you want to go to the movies with Jane and me?" Are children no longer being taught the different parts of speech in grammar school? Do they not know the difference between the subjective and objective cases, or that prepositions such as *at, in, to, from*, and *with* always take the objective case? Do they even know what a preposition is? Another mistake is using *good* when it should be *well*, as in "I am good, thanks," rather than "I am well, thank you," or *real* when it should be *really*, as in "That was a real good dinner" instead of "That was a really good dinner." A third type of mistake is the mispronunciation of words – saying *nukular* instead of *nuclear* (this apparently began with President Jimmy Carter, but George W. Bush also mispronounced it regularly), or *breakfrist* for *breakfast*. The use of *like* not as a comparative but in constructions such as "like, you know?" or "He was, like, cool," or "She, like, completely ignored me" is becoming widespread. This "filler" word seems to indicate an inability on the part of speakers to express what they mean.[15] Additionally, many people are using *whatever* as a way of being noncommittal or deferring a decision, such as when someone asks whether you want to go to the movies or rollerblading and you answer, "Whatever." It is also used when one's facts or logic are challenged; using "whatever," said Theodore Roszak, "means not even arguing the point because truth is beside the point" (*San Francisco Chronicle*, July 16, 2000); it is a weary response that seems to say, "Who cares?" It is also another instance of the dumbing down of the United States to the lowest common denominator rather than encouraging all to speak well.

What does it mean when the American editors of the Harry Potter books changed not only the spelling of many words but also the words themselves? For example, they substituted *gray* for *grey*, *color* for *colour*, and *flavor* for *flavour*, and they changed *lorry* to *truck*, *post* to *mail*, *Hoover* to *vacuum*, *fortnight* to *two weeks*, and *crumpets* to *English muffins*. "Are we afraid that when presented with new vocabulary, children will shrink away?" asks Peter Gleick in a *New York Times* op-ed piece (July 10, 2000). Isn't it more interesting for children to read about English children having tea and crumpets instead of English muffins? Wouldn't that stir their curiosity and spur them to ask, "What are crumpets?" or, heaven forbid, to consult a dictionary and thus expand their cultural horizons? "By insisting that everything be Americanized," Gleick argues, "we dumb down our own society rather than enrich it." "Dumbing down" also involves the issue of class. Did the editors think that no one would understand the English words, or did they think that the words sounded too pretentious and uppity?

Language is, clearly, about much more than communication. Recall the passage from Sapir:

> No two languages are ever sufficiently similar to be considered representing the same social reality. The worlds in which different societies live are distinct worlds, not merely the same world with different labels attached. (1949: 69)

Thus, we live in different worlds, and it behooves all of us to get some sense of them. Language is an extremely important means for investigating culture; you cannot possibly understand a culture without knowing the language. At the same time, it is very important to realize that language and culture are not necessarily isomorphic, that is, "language, culture, and race do not form a single package but, rather, each element pursues a different historical trajectory" (Briggs 2002: 483). After all, people of different ethnicities can learn the same language, and people of the same ethnicity can learn different languages, just as they can learn other cultures, and learn to function in them.

Nevertheless, it is important to become more aware of the way the language you use conditions what you think and what you perceive. That is the anthropological legacy from Sapir. Another aspect of language, however, concerns how people use language to influence others and achieve power. That is the anthropological legacy from sociolinguistics.

Turkish

Turkish is a very unusual language. It is not related to any of the major language groups such as Indo-European or Semitic. Consequently, you will probably not find any cognates unless they have been directly borrowed. Some scholars think Turkish is related to Uralic-Altaic languages or to Finnish, others say that the structure, although not the words, is similar to Japanese. In part it is an agglutinative language, which means that significant aspects (tense, negation, and interrogative) of a word occur within or are attached to the word rather than, as in English, simply multiplying the number of words. For example, "I am going" = *gidiyorum*; and "I am not going" = *gitmiyorum*. The *I* is not a separate word but is the *-um* ending, and the negative *not* is the tiny part in the middle, *-mi-*. Direct and indirect objects are indicated by the endings that are attached to the nouns or pronoun. *Prepositions in English, that is, words like *with*, *to*, *from*, *at*, and *in*, are *postpositions in Turkish, and are attached at the end of the noun, for example *Ankara'ya* = to Ankara; and *Ankara'da* = in or at Ankara.

The verb and subject come at the end of the sentence preceded by all kinds of phrases and modifiers. Consequently, you learn about the context and conditions before you know *who* is involved or affected. Similarly, you cannot say in Turkish "I am hungry" but rather *karnım aç* – my stomach is open; not "I have a headache" but *kafam ağrıyor* – my head aches. It is not *I* who desires food or complains of pain, but the particular body part involved. I am not clear to what extent this may help relieve one of responsibility for one's desires or dissociate oneself from pain. In the village, pregnant women who craved certain sweets were generally indulged because it was thought to be the baby who required and desired them, and no one would deny a baby.

Turkish is also a vowel-harmonic language, which means that all the vowels in a word have to agree, that is, if one is a front vowel, the other vowels must also be front vowels, and if one is a back vowel, then all must be. During the Ottoman period, Turkish was written in Arabic script even though Turkish is not at all related to Arabic. In addition, Arabic script was totally unsuited to Turkish since Arabic, like Hebrew, does not indicate vowels in its script! Because of this, Turkish, or *Osmanlıcı* (Ottoman) as it was called, was extremely difficult to read or write, and most of the people were illiterate.

When World War I ended and the Ottoman Empire collapsed, Mustafa Kemal Atatürk established the Republic of Turkey in its wake and introduced a new language policy as one of his first major reforms. He decreed that Turkish would no longer be written in Arabic script but would switch to Latin letters. Newspapers were given only a few weeks to make the switch, one that many thought would or should take years. Atatürk himself went around the country with a blackboard instructing the people in the new script. With this sweeping reform, millions of people learned to read and to write their own language. Nevertheless, this change angered devout Muslims who believed that Arabic (and Arabic script) was sacred since the Qur'an was delivered from God to Muhammad in Arabic. They believed that Atatürk had switched to the language of the infidels.

Although the people were able to read and write more easily, the change also cut them off from their history. Today if a Turk wishes to read Ottoman documents, he or she must take courses in Ottoman in order to do so; it is, apparently, like learning a foreign language. But even Turkish written in Latin letters has changed since the 1920s, as substantially as the difference between Chaucerian English and modern English (Henze 1982).

Another part of Atatürk's language reform was to establish the Turkish Language Association. This association was mandated to study the history of the Turkish language, which Atatürk believed was the Ur language. He also wanted to purge Turkish of foreign loan words, especially Persian, Arabic, and French ones, and requested the association to seek Turkish replacements. Every few years the association has published numerous lexicons of the new words. Although they are referred to as *Öz Türkçe* (or real, true Turkish), they are actually new compositions created from Turkish roots.

Turkish, as it is spoken in Turkey today, is one form of a number of Turkic languages that are spoken in Mongolia and some of the former provinces of the Soviet Union. Within Turkey itself, there are regional variations in pronunciation and some differences in form, for example villagers use slightly different forms from those used by the urban educated elite. But they have no trouble understanding each other. Turkish spoken in Istanbul is held to be the standard, as a generalized midwestern accent is the standard in the United States, especially for radio and television news reporters. But there is a difference by gender; elite Istanbul women speak in a distinct style that includes a particularly high pitch of the voice and the use of exceptionally polite forms much like Japanese women do (cf. Inoue 2002).

Because Turkish is not widely studied outside of Turkey, many Turks also learn English, French, or German throughout school so they can converse with their European neighbors and American visitors. Some use these linguistic skills when they continue their education abroad, but even at a number of (the most prestigious) universities in Turkey, English is the language of instruction. And most professors write in English, as well as in Turkish, so that their work will reach an international audience. But it is hardly only the well educated who are bi- or trilingual; many taxi drivers, restaurant owners, rug merchants, and ship captains speak very passable English and/or German.

The dominance of English around the world surely makes it easier for Americans abroad, but it is not because it is an easy language. Think about how and why English has come to dominate the linguistic world. Do you think English *should* become the world language? Why? Why is it that Americans are so bad at learning languages, and why does the study of foreign languages have such a low priority in schools? Do you think endangered languages should be preserved? Is the loss of them equivalent to the loss of endangered species? What might it mean for life on the planet?

Notes

1. Attributed to Magritte, *La Révolution Surréaliste* (1929), but cited at an exhibition of his work at the San Francisco Museum of Modern Art in 2000.
2. E.g., Bruner (1984), Clifford and Marcus (1986), and Rabinow and Sullivan (1979).
3. Esperanto, meaning *hopeful*, was invented in 1887 by Ludwik L. Zamenhof, a Polish physician and oculist. Although there are alleged to be about 100,000 speakers in 83 countries, it has not really taken off as a worldwide language (*Encyclopedia Britannica* n.d.).
4. Plato (1960: 563).
5. It seems likely that this image was provided by Langer, Sapir, or Whorf, but it could have been said by my teachers Sahlins or Schneider. I have scoured their works and cannot find it. I don't think I invented it, but if so, it captures the import of what they are saying.
6. George Lakoff wrote and circulated a paper on the Internet during the Gulf War entitled "Metaphor and War: The Metaphor System Used to Justify War in the Gulf" (1991a, 1991b).
7. These quotes are taken from a film, *Creation of the Universe*, in which scientific cosmologists, including several Nobel Prize winners, are discussing the origin of the universe. It was shown for the first time on PBS on November 20, 1985. The narrator is Timothy Ferris, a science writer and professor at the University of Southern California.
8. Brian Easlea examines some of the precursors of this idea, especially Francis Bacon's "The Masculine Birth of Time," and the fearful implications in the manufacture of nuclear weapons in his *Fathering the Unthinkable: Masculinity, Scientists, and the Nuclear Arms Race* (1983). See also Carol Cohn's "Sex and Death in the Rational World of Defense Intellectuals" (1987).
9. In an article on the use of certain metaphors to discuss new reproductive technologies (NPRs), Marilyn Strathern claims, "Culture consists in the way analogies are drawn between things, in the way certain thoughts are used to think others" (1992: 33).
10. In the 1950s–1970s, women who rejected or rebelled against their sex role were made to feel that there was something wrong with them. They were sent to psychiatrists and psychologists for therapy, and were also prescribed tranquilizers to help them accept and adjust to their role. See Betty Friedan's *The Feminine Mystique* (1963) for a description of those times.
11. See, for example, the trailblazing volumes *Women, Culture, and Society*, ed. Michelle Rosaldo and Louise Lamphere (1974); *The Anthropology of Women*, ed. Rayna Reiter (1975), and *Nature, Culture, and Gender*, ed. Carol MacCormack and Marilyn Strathern (1980).
12. Most French feminist discussions of language and sex draw upon the work of Jacques Lacan, a Freudian psychoanalyst, and focus on the *phallus* as a key signifier but reject the idea that it has anything to do with the penis. Instead, I would argue that it has everything to do with what the penis has meant, namely, that it was imagined as the organ through which *life* was transmitted, via seed. See the work of Julia Kristeva, Luce Irigaray, Hélène Cixous, and Monique Wittig.
13. See *What It Means to Be 98% Chimpanzee: Apes, People, and Their Genes* (Berkeley: University of California Press, 2002) by biologist Jonathan Marks.
14. Penny Eckert's book *Jocks and Burnouts: Social Categories and Identity in the High School* (1989) is a lively ethnography of the ways in which class among high school students is expressed and reinforced not just by clothing, drug use, and activities, but also by the difference in linguistic use.
15. Linguists make a distinction between "prescriptive" and "descriptive" grammar, the first having to do with the prestige variety of a language while the second is the study and analysis of language in use. Don Brenneis, a linguistic anthropologist, also explained to me that some of what I call *mispronunciations* may reflect regional dialect differences (see also Macaulay 1994, 1997).

EXERCISES

4.1. Spatial Metaphors

A. You were asked to keep track of spatial metaphors (e.g. "warm up") that occur in everyday speech. List at least 20 of such phrases and give a short definition.

B. Select three or four of the above. Following the point made by Sapir (see the first page of this chapter), what do these metaphors say about our culture? What values are encoded? How do they structure and influence the way we perceive reality?

4.2. Conversational Style

How does your conversational style change depending on whether you are talking to another student or with a professor? Think of as many aspects of communication as possible – not only verbal ones – that differentiate your conversations with fellow students from those with professors.

Bibliography

"'Alex & Me': The Parrot Who Said 'I Love You'" (2009) *NPR*, August 31.

Anthias, Floya, and Yuval-Davis, Nira, in association with Harried Cain (1992) *Racialized Boundaries: Race, Nation, Gender, Colour and Class and the Anti-Racist Struggle*. London: Routledge.

Aristotle (n.d.) *Poetics*. www.perseus.tufts.edu/hopper/text?doc=Perseus%3Atext%3A1999.01.0056%3Asection%3D1459a.

Baumann, Gerd (1996) *Contesting Culture: Discourses of Identity in Multicultural London*. Cambridge: Cambridge University Press.

Benedict, Ruth ([1946] 1976) *Chrysanthemum and the Sword: Patterns of Japanese Culture*. New York: Meridian, New American Library.

Benveniste, Emile (1971) "Animal Communication and Human Language." In *Problems in General Linguistics*. Coral Gables, FL: University of Miami Press.

Briggs, Charles L. (2002) "Linguistic Magic Bullets in the Making of a Modernist Anthropology." *American Anthropologist* 104(2): 481–98.

Bruner, Edward M., ed. (1984) *Text, Play, and Story: The Construction and Reconstruction of Self and Society*. Prospect Heights, IL: Waveland Press.

Carey, Benedict (2007) "Brainy Parrot Dies, Emotive to the End." *New York Times*, Sept 11.

Clifford, James, and Marcus, George, eds. (1986) *Writing Culture: The Poetics and Politics of Ethnography*. Berkeley: University of California Press.

Cohn, Carol (1987) "Sex and Death in the Rational World of Defense Intellectuals." *Signs* 12(4): 687–719.

Delaney, Carol (1986) "The Meaning of Paternity and the Virgin Birth Debate." *Man* 21(3): 494–513.

Delaney, Carol (1991) *The Seed and the Soil: Gender and Cosmology in Turkish Village Society*. Berkeley: University of California Press.

Dolgin, Janet, Kemnitzer, David S., and Schneider, David, eds. (1977) *Symbolic Anthropology: A Reader in the Study of Symbols and Meanings*. New York: Columbia University Press.

Douglas, Mary (1966) "The Abominations of Leviticus." In *Purity and Danger: An Analysis of the Concepts of Pollution and Taboo*. London: Routledge & Kegan Paul.

Easlea, Brian (1983) *Fathering the Unthinkable: Masculinity, Scientists, and the Nuclear Arms Race*. London: Pluto Press.

Eckert, Penny (1989) *Jocks and Burnouts: Social Categories and Identity in the High School*. New York: Teachers College Press.

Edelsky, Carole (1976) "The Acquisition of Communicative Competence: A Recognition of Linguistic Correlates of Sex Roles." *Merrill-Palmer Quarterly* 22(1): 47–59.

Encyclopedia Britannica (n.d.) "Esperanto." www.britannica.com/EBchecked/topic/192713/Esperanto.

Foucault, Michel (1982) *This Is Not a Pipe*. Berkeley: University of California Press.

Friedan, Betty (1963) *The Feminine Mystique*. New York: Norton.

Geertz, Clifford (1973) *Interpretation of Cultures*. New York: Basic.

Guy, Gregory (1988) "Language and Social Class." In *Linguistics: The Cambridge Survey*, vol. 6, ed. Fredrick J. Newmeyer. Cambridge: Cambridge University Press, pp. 37–63.

Hager, Lori (1997) *Women in Human Evolution*. New York: Routledge.

Hamilton, Mykol C., Hunter, Barbara, and Stuart-Smith, Shannon (1992) "Jury Instructions Worded in the Masculine Generic: Can a Woman Claim Self-Defense When 'He' Is Threatened?" In *New Directions in Feminist Psychology*, ed. Joan C. Chrisler and Doris Howard. New York: Springer, pp. 340–7.

Haraway, Donna (1989) *Primate Visions: Gender, Race, and Nation in the World of Modern Science*. New York: Routledge.

Henze, Paul (1982) "Turkey: On the Rebound." *Wilson Quarterly* 6(5): 108–25.

Hill, Jane (1980) "Apes and Language." In *Speaking of Apes: A Critical Anthology of Two-Way Communication with Man*, ed. Thomas A. Sebeok and Jean Umiker-Sebeok. New York: Plenum, pp. 331–51.

Hill, Jane (1993) "Hasta La Vista, Baby." *Critique of Anthropology* 13(2): 145–76.

Inoue, Miyako (2002) "Gender, Language, and Modernity: Toward an Effective History of Japanese Women's Language." *American Ethnologist* 29(2): 392–422.

Lakoff, George (1991a) Part I: Metaphor and War: The Metaphor System Used to Justify War in the Gulf (Part 1 of 2). *Viet Nam Generation Journal & Newsletter* 3(3): http://www2.iath.virginia.edu/sixties/HTML_docs/Texts/Scholarly/Lakoff_Gulf_Metaphor_1.html.

Lakoff, George (1991b) Part II: Metaphor and War: The Metaphor System Used to Justify War in the Gulf (Part 2 of 2). *Viet Nam Generation Journal & Newsletter* 3(3): http://www2.iath.virginia.edu/sixties/HTML_docs/Texts/Scholarly/Lakoff_Gulf_Metaphor_2.html.

Lakoff, George, and Johnson, Mark (1980) *Metaphors We Live By*. Chicago: University of Chicago Press.

Lakoff, Robin (1975) *Language and Woman's Place*. New York: Harper & Row.

Landau, Misia (1991) *Narratives of Human Evolution*. New Haven, CT: Yale University Press.

Langer, Suzanne ([1942] 1979) *Philosophy in a New Key: A Study in the Symbolism of Reason, Rite, and Art*. Cambridge, MA: Harvard University Press.

Leach, Edmund (1964) "Anthropological Aspects of Language: Animal Categories and Verbal Abuse." In *New Directions in the Study of Language*, ed. Eric Lenneberg. Cambridge, MA: MIT Press, pp. 23–63.

LeGuin, Ursula (1987) "She Unnames Them." In *Buffalo Gals and Other Animal Presences*. New York: Plume.

Lourie, Richard, and Mikhalev, Aleksei (1989) "Why You'll Never Have Fun in Russia." *New York Times*, June 18.

Macaulay, Ronald K. S. (1994) *The Social Art: Language and Its Uses*. New York: Oxford University Press.

Macaulay, Ronald K. S. (1997) *Standards and Variations in Urban Speech: Examples from Lowland Scots*. Philadelphia: John Benjamins.

MacCormack, Carol, and Strathern, Marilyn, eds. (1980) *Nature, Culture, and Gender*. Cambridge: Cambridge University Press.

Magritte, René (1929) *Enquête sur l'amour'* [Inquiry on Love]. *La Révolution Surréaliste* (12).

Marks, Jonathan (2002) *What It Means to Be 98% Chimpanzee: Apes, People, and Their Genes*. Berkeley: University of California Press.

Martyna, Wendy (1980) "Beyond the 'He/Man' Approach: The Case for Nonsexist Language." *Signs: Journal of Women in Culture and Society* 5(3): 482–93.

Mead, Margaret (1928) *Coming of Age in Samoa: A Psychological Study of Primitive Youth for Western Civilization*. New York: William Morrow.

Mead, Margaret (1935) *Sex and Temperament in Three Primitive Societies*. New York: William Morrow.

Mead, Margaret (1949) *Male and Female: A Study of the Sexes in a Changing World*. New York: William Morrow.

Moran, John H., and Gode, Alexander, trans. (1967) *On the Origin of Language: Jean-Jacques Rousseau, Essay on the Origin of Language; Johan Gottfried Herder, Essay on the Origin of Language*. New York: Ungar.

Morton, Nelle (1972) "The Rising Women's Consciousness in a Male Language Structure." *Andover-Newton Quarterly* 12: 177–90.

Ochs, Elinor (1992) "Indexing Gender." In *Rethinking Context*, ed. A. Duranti and C. Goodwin. New York: Cambridge University Press, pp. 335–58.

Ong, Walter J., S.J. ([1982] 1999) *Orality and Literacy: The Technologizing of the Word*. New York: Routledge.

Ottenheimer, Martin (1996) *Forbidden Relatives: The American Myth of Cousin Marriage*. Urbana: University of Illinois Press.

Pepperberg, Irene (2009) *Alex & Me: How a Scientist and a Parrot Discovered a Hidden World of Animal Intelligence – and Formed a Deep Bond in the Process*. New York: Harper.

Plato (1960) *Phaedrus*, trans. Harold North Fowler, Loeb Classical Library. Cambridge, MA: Harvard University Press.

Rabinow, Paul, and Sullivan, William M., eds. (1979) *Interpretative Social Science*. Berkeley: University of California Press.

Reiter, Rayna, ed. (1975) *The Anthropology of Women*. New York: Monthly Review Press.

Rickford, John (1998) "Using the Vernacular to Teach the Standard." From California State University, Long Beach, Conference on Ebonics, March 25. www.stanford.edu/~rickford/papers/VernacularToTeachStandard.html.

Ricoeur, Paul (1976) *Interpretation Theory: Discourse and the Surplus of Meaning*. Fort Worth: Texas Christian University Press.

Ricoeur, Paul (1977) *The Rule of Metaphor: Multidisciplinary Studies of the Creation of Meaning in Language*. Toronto: University of Toronto Press.

Rosaldo, Michelle, and Lamphere, Louise, eds. (1974) *Women, Culture, and Society*. Stanford, CA: Stanford University Press.

Rousseau, Jean-Jacques (1781) *Essay on the Origin of Language*. Paris.

Said, Edward (1979) *Orientalism*. New York: Vintage.

Sapir, Edward (1949) *Culture, Language, and Personality*. Berkeley: University of California Press.

Saussure, Ferdinand de (1959) *Course in General Linguistics*. New York: McGraw-Hill.

Savage-Rumbaugh, Sue, Shanker, Stuart G., and Taylor, Talbot J. (1998) *Apes, Language, and the Human Mind*. Oxford: Oxford University Press.

Schmandt-Besserat, Denise (1986) "An Ancient Token System: The Precursor to Numerals and Writing." *Archaeology* 39(6): 32–9.

Schweikart, Debora (1998) "The Gender Neutral Pronoun Redefined." *Women's Rights Law Reporter* 20 (Fall–Winter): 1–9.

Singer, Milton (1984) *Man's Glassy Essence: Explorations in Semiotic Anthropology*. Bloomington: Indiana University Press.

Stanton, Elizabeth Cady, et al. (1898) *The Woman's Bible*. New York: European Publishing. (Republished by Seattle Coalition on Women and Religion, 1974).

Strathern, Marilyn (1992) *Reproducing the Future: Essays on Anthropology, Kinship, and the New Reproductive Technologies*. Manchester: Manchester University Press.

Tannen, Deborah (1990) *You Just Don't Understand: Women and Men in Conversation*. New York: Morrow.

Whorf, Benjamin (1956) *Language, Thought and Reality*. Cambridge, MA: MIT Press.

Yanagisako, Sylvia, and Delaney, Carol (1995) *Naturalizing Power: Essays in Feminist Cultural Analysis*. New York: Routledge.

Zihlman, Adrienne (1991) "Mechanism and Meaning of Reproduction: Myths of Paternity, Realities of Maternity." Paper prepared for Wenner-Gren Symposium.

R E A D I N G

She Unnames Them
Ursula LeGuin

Most of them accepted namelessness with the perfect indifference with which they had so long accepted and ignored their names. Whales and dolphins, seals and sea otters consented with particular grace and alacrity, sliding into anonymity as into their element. A faction of yaks, however, protested. They said that "yak" sounded right, and that almost everyone who knew they existed called them that. Unlike the ubiquitous creatures such as rats or fleas who had been called by hundreds or thousands of different names since Babel, the yaks could truly say, they said, that they had *a name*. They discussed the matter all summer. The councils of the elderly females finally agreed that though the name might be useful to others, it was so redundant from the yak point of view that they never spoke it themselves, and hence might as well dispense with it. After they presented the argument in this light to their bulls, a full consensus was delayed only by the onset of severe early blizzards. Soon after the beginning of the thaw their agreement was reached and the designation "yak" was returned to the donor.

Among the domestic animals, few horses had cared what anybody called them since the failure of Dean Swift's attempt to name them from their own vocabulary. Cattle, sheep, swine, asses, mules, and goats, along with chickens, geese, and turkeys, all agreed enthusiastically to give their names back to the people to whom – as they put it – they belonged.

A couple of problems did come up with pets. The cats of course steadfastly denied ever having had any name other than those self-given, unspoken, effaninef-fably personal names which, as the poet named Eliot said, they spend long hours daily contemplating – though none of the contemplators has ever admitted that what they contemplate is in fact their name, and some onlookers have wondered if the object of that meditative gaze might not in fact be the Perfect, or Platonic, Mouse. In any case it is a moot point now. It was with the dogs, and with some parrots, lovebirds, ravens, and mynahs that the trouble arose. These ver-bally talented individuals insisted that their names were important to them, and flatly refused to part with them. But as soon as they understood that the issue was pre-cisely one of individual choice, and that anybody who wanted to be called Rover, or Froufrou, or Polly, or even Birdie in the personal sense, was perfectly free to do so, not one of them had the least objection to parting with the lower case (or, as regards German creatures, upper-case) generic appellations poodle, parrot, dog, or bird, and all the Linnaean qualifiers that had trailed along behind them for two hundred years like tin cans tied to a tail.

The insects parted with their names in vast clouds and swarms of ephemeral syllables buzzing and stinging and humming and flitting and crawling and tunneling away.

As for the fish of the sea, their names dispersed from them in silence throughout the oceans like faint, dark blurs of cuttlefish ink, and drifted off on the currents without a trace.

None were left now to unname, and yet how close I felt to them when I saw one of them swim or fly or trot or crawl across my way or over my skin, or stalk me in the night, or go along beside me for a while in the day. They seemed far closer than when their names had stood between myself and them like a clear barrier: so close that my fear of them and their fear of me became one same fear. And the attraction that many of us felt, the desire to smell one another's smells, feel or rub or caress one another's scales or skin or feathers or fur, taste one another's blood or flesh, keep one another warm, – that attraction was now all one with the fear, and the hunter could not be told from the hunted, nor the eater from the food.

This was more or less the effect I had been after. It was somewhat more powerful than I had anticipated, but I could not now, in all conscience, make an excep-tion for myself. I resolutely put anxiety away, went to Adam, and said, "You and your father lent me this – gave it to me, actually. It's been really useful, but it doesn't exactly seem to fit very well lately. But thanks very much! It's really been very useful."

It is hard to give back a gift without sounding peevish or ungrateful, and I did not want to leave him with that impression of me. He was not paying much attention, as it happened, and said only, "Put it down over there, OK?" and went on with what he was doing.

One of my reasons for doing what I did was that talk was getting us nowhere; but all the same I felt a little let down. I had been prepared to defend my decision. And I thought that perhaps when he did notice he might be upset and want to talk. I put some things away and fiddled around a little, but he continued to do what he was doing and to take no notice of anything else. At last I said, "Well, goodbye, dear. I hope the garden key turns up."

He was fitting parts together, and said without looking around, "OK, fine, dear. When's dinner?"

"I'm not sure," I said. "I'm going now. With the –" I hesitated, and finally said, "With them, you know," and went on. In fact I had only just then realized how hard it would have been to explain myself. I could not chatter away as I used to do, taking it all for granted. My words now must be as slow, as new, as single, as tentative as the steps I took going down the path away from the house, between the dark-branched, tall dancers motion-less against the winter shining.

READING

Seeing Is Believing

Alan Dundes

Whether from early memories of playing "peek-a-boo," "showing and telling" in school, or learning the opening phrase of the national anthem – "Oh, say can you see" – the primacy of vision in American culture is affirmed again and again as infants grow to adulthood. Americans are conditioned from childhood to believe that "what you see is what you get."

There is more to such a phenomenon than immediately meets the eye. That Americans rely more on vision than on other senses doesn't mean that they are aware of it. Nor does it mean that it is a peculiarly American trait. People everywhere rely on their senses to perceive their world and order their experiences, but since my data are derived from American folk speech, I cannot speak about others. In any case, because I have been taught to mistrust hearsay, I have decided to take a look at the evidence for a visual bias and to see for myself.

In Western thought, a distinction has commonly been made between sensory perception and reasoning. The power of reason is presumably the superior of the two. According to Aristotle, there are five senses – sight, hearing, smell, taste, and touch – which provide data generally deemed less trustworthy or, at least, frequently illusory, compared to the information that is provided by the faculties of rational thought. Subjective versus objective and body versus mind are other expressions of this distinction between the sensory and the rational. If we assume, however, that reasoning cannot take place without some reference to metaphor, then it is certainly possible that much American logic and reasoning is closely tied to metaphor in general and to visual metaphor in particular.

The allegedly inferior sensory experiences seem to be ranked according to how effective or reliable a given sense is assumed to be. In American culture, the sense of sight is normally the first of the five senses to be listed. However, whether sight is actually more useful or crucial for perception than the other senses is a moot question and, in fact, does not require an answer to show that a cultural bias for the sense of sight really

exists. In the present context, it is not the literal meaning of sight that is important, but the metaphorical. I believe that, metaphorically speaking, Americans tend to *see* the world around them, rather than hear, feel, smell, or taste it. It may be no accident that Americans *observe* laws and holidays.

American speech provides persuasive evidence to support the notion that "vision" is used as a metaphor for "understanding." Consider, for example, the classic punning proverb, "'I see,' said the blind man, as he picked up his hammer and saw." The oppositional structure in this text is produced by the juxtaposition of sight and blindness. Here is a clear distinction between literal and metaphorical seeing. Literally a blind man cannot see, but figuratively he certainly can.

Americans consistently speak of "seeing" the point of an argument when, in fact, an argument is not really seen but comprehended. Intellectual positions, or "perspectives," are frequently referred to as points of *view*. When articulated, they may be introduced by such formulas as, "As I see it" or "It all depends on how you look at it."

American culture is pronouncedly concerned with empiricism, and this empiricism is explicitly visual. "Seeing is believing" and "I'm from Missouri" (which means "you've got to show me") are indications of the emphasis on seeing something for oneself and the tendency to distrust anyone else's report of a given event. "I saw it with my own (two) eyes" is a common authenticating formula, as is the invitation to "see for yourself."

Without sight, there may be disbelief or lack of faith: "I'll believe it when I see it," "That I've got to see," or "I can't picture that." Even though the reliability of vision may be questioned – "There's more to this than meets the eye" – in general, people tend to believe what they see. Thus, when something is really out of the ordinary, we say, "I couldn't believe my eyes." Something that is incredible or unbelievable is termed "out of sight," a phrase dating from before the end of the nineteenth century.

Imagination is sometimes called "the mind's eye," but why should the mind have an eye? Probably for the same reason that patients want doctors "to see them." Telephone conversations or other purely oral–aural channels are not considered entirely satisfactory. Actually, the patient is probably relieved by *his* seeing the doctor. Seeing the doctor, in turn, is part of the widespread cultural insistence upon interviews. Literally, the word *interview* refers to A seeing B and B seeing A.

Consider the nature of American tourist philosophy – sightseeing. To "see the sights" is a common goal of tourists, a goal also reflected in the mania for snapping pictures as permanent records of what was seen. Typical travel boasting consists of inflicting an evening of slide viewing on unwary friends so that they may see what their hosts saw.

This is surely a strange way of defining tourism. Visiting a foreign locale certainly involves all of the sensory apparatus. There are exotic smells and tastes, and the opportunity to savor new foods and experience the "feel" of a foreign setting is as important in understanding a country and its people as seeing them. One reason Americans frequently fail to enjoy touring as much as they might may be their almost compulsive tendency to see as many sights as possible. The seeing of many sights is, of course, consistent with a tendency to quantify living, and, specifically, with the desire to get one's money's worth.

When shopping, whether in foreign countries or at home, Americans are reluctant to buy anything "sight unseen." They prefer "to look something over," "to walk into something with their eyes open." A thorough inspection theoretically allows one to "see through" a pretense or fake. And obviously, a product can only "catch a person's eye" if he sees it.

Public "images," too, are part of the visual pattern. But why, after all, should a person have to be depicted in a term such as image? Even though looks may be deceiving ("Never judge a book by its cover"), it seems clear that packaging that appeals to visual esthetics is equally effective whether one is hawking cigarettes or automobiles or selling political candidates.

The reduction of persons or events to purely visual terms is also evident in the use of the popular slang phrase for a detective: "private eye." By the same token,

sleep is commonly referred to as "shut-eye," which obviously singles out only one aspect of the dormant state. Furthermore, this suggestion that sleep is shut-eye also implies that the waking state is marked chiefly by having one's eyes open.

As I collected examples of folk speech, I soon found that comparison of vision with the other senses reaffirmed the superiority of sight. That a "seer" can make predictions by gazing into a crystal ball, for example, suggests that vision is more effective than the other senses in fore*seeing* future events.

The same bias in favor of the visual is found in American greeting and leave-taking formulas. Examples include: "See you around," "I'll be seeing you," or "I haven't seen so-and-so in ages." Greetings may also be couched in visual terms. "It's good to see you," Americans say, rather than, "It's good to hear, smell, or feel you."

There seem to be relatively few complimentary references to hearers, smellers, talkers, and touchers. "Look, but don't touch" hints at a delight in gawking (girl-watching), and possibly at a cultural distaste for body contact. Someone who is "touchy" is not pleasant to have around. A "soft touch," which sounds as if it should have a positive connotation, is a slang term for a dupe or easy mark.

One of the most interesting pieces of evidence supporting the notion of visual superiority over the other senses is that the original version of "Seeing's believing" was presumably "Seeing's believing, but feeling's the truth." That most Americans have dropped the second portion of the proverb does not seem to be an accident. Rather, it reflects a definite penchant for the visual in contrast to the tactual. Originally, the proverb denigrated "seeing" in favor of "feeling."

Comparisons between the visual and the aural are the most common, however, with hearing considered second best. Consider "Believe nothing of what you hear and only half of what you see." Although caution is urged against believing everything one sees, seeing is surely depicted as being more reliable and trustworthy than hearing. Compare the following two statements: "I hear that X has just moved to Miami," and "I see that X has just moved to Miami." The first statement is possibly true, possibly not true: there is an element of doubt. The second, in contrast, seems to be a statement of fact.

Other instances are found in legal parlance. Although judges hear cases, there is no doubt that *hearsay*, that is, aural–oral, evidence is not in the same league as that offered by an eyewitness. Actually, the word *witness* indicates that the person was physically present during an event and saw with his own eyes the activities in question. If so, then the term *eyewitness* is redundant. Strangely enough, at *hearings* there is an insistence that *hearsay* evidence be rejected and that only *eyewitness* testimony be accepted. On the other hand, it is interesting to recall that Justice is depicted as being blind. Justice cannot see and presumably blindness guarantees fairness. But of course, sometimes even an innocent man may be guilty "in the eyes of the law."

The eye is also more powerful than the ear insofar as it is regarded as an active rather than a passive agent. The eye looks, peers, or gazes. There is seductive power in the eye, as in "giving a girl the eye," and the malevolent power of the eye is manifested in "the evil eye." The ear, by contrast, is a passive receptacle. There is little evidence of evil ears. Remember also that "big brother is watching you," not listening to you, although bugging rooms with microphones makes listening more likely than watching. Note also that voyeurs, such as Peeping Toms, are considered to be worse than eavesdroppers. The active versus passive with respect to seeing and hearing may also be implied by the connotative differences between "spectators" and "audience."

Marshall McLuhan and his followers have suggested that the oral–aural channels of preliterate, or rather, nonliterate man may be enjoying a renaissance. According to this view, as man becomes literate, written language – which must be seen to be read – takes priority over the oral. Recently, however, radio and television have created postliterate man, whose world is once more primarily oral–aural. Many Americans learn the news of the day by hearing it on the radio rather than by reading it in newspapers. Even on television, the argument says, the news is mainly told, not shown. Then, too, telephone conversations are replacing letter writing more and more.

One can contend, however, that television has replaced radio, and thus the visual still supersedes the purely aural. Americans still prefer to get agreements in writing rather than to trust a gentleman's handshake (a tactile sign) or take someone's word or say-so (oral sign)

for a contract. Once an agreement is down in black and white, Americans watch out for, and read, the small print, with an "eye" toward avoiding an unfavorable set of conditions.

If Americans do have a deep-seated penchant for the visual sense, as I have tried to suggest by examining American folk speech, the question of what it means remains to be answered. It is not just a matter of being able to see more clearly why Americans tend to look for men of vision to lead them. Much more important is the influence of folk metaphors on scientific thought. American science is not culture-free, no matter how devoutly American scientists wish that it were or think that it is.

As an anthropologist, I am struck by the fact that American anthropologists insist upon being participant observers (no voyeurs!) when they go into the field so as to gain insight into the world-views of other cultures. Why "insight"? Do all examples of problem solving by insight actually involve visual perception? And why world-view?

Anthropologists do not always agree whether man is active or passive with regard to world-view. Bronislaw Malinowski, for example, tended to consider man passive: he depicted man as being molded by the impress of a culturally patterned, cookie cutter kind of world-view, which imposed its structure upon human minds. "What interests me really in the study of the native," Malinowski said, "is his outlook on things, his *Weltanschauung*. Every human culture gives its members a definite vision of the world." In contrast, Robert Redfield, by defining world-view as "the way a people characteristically look outward upon the universe," suggested that man was a more active participant. In any case, whether man passively accepts a culturally determined world-view or actively creates a world-view system, the visual bias in the very search by anthropologists for world-view is evident.

It has been observed that for Americans the universe is essentially something they can draw a picture or diagram of. But surely a person's world is felt, smelled, tasted, and heard as well. This propensity for visual metaphorical categories may produce distortion in attempts to describe facets of American culture. It is unlikely that such distortion would even be noticed, since the distortion, like beauty, is strictly in the subjective eye of the beholder. But what happens when Americans or American scientists seek to describe features of other cultures or the features of the natural world?

It is at least possible that by looking for the worldview of other peoples, we run the risk of imposing our own rank-ordering of the senses upon data that may not be perceived in the same way by the people whose cultures are being described. If we are truly interested in understanding how other peoples perceive reality, we must recognize their cognitive categories and try to escape the confines of our own.

The history of man is full of instances of one group's conscious or unconscious attempts to impose its particular set of cognitive categories upon another group. The imposing group typically claims that its categories represent the true nature of reality (as opposed to the categories of the victimized group, which are deemed odd at best and false at worst). Whether it is nineteenth-century American linguists searching in vain for Latin cases (for example, the dative or accusative) in American Indian languages, or a modern Western physician, imbued with the number three, trying to persuade an American Indian, who believes in the sacredness of the number four, that only three doses or inoculations are sufficient (as in a series of three polio shots), the issue is the same.

This is why it is essential for Americans (and for other peoples as well) to become aware of their dependence upon cognitive categories such as the visual metaphorical mode I have been talking about. Armed with this awareness, it is possible to appreciate more fully the aptness of the visual metaphor Ruth Benedict used to explain why so many social theorists failed to notice custom or culture: "We do not see the lens through which we look." A conscious recognition of our visual bias may help make the lens visible. We must never forget the possible relativity of our own sensory perception categories.

Inventories of the same or similar sense categories found in other cultures may help. Clifford Geertz reports, for example, that the Javanese have five senses (seeing, hearing, *talking*, smelling, and feeling), which do not coincide exactly with our five. The delineation of such differences may teach us just how culture-bound or culture-specific our own observations of nature may be. We tend to delude ourselves into thinking we are studying the nature of nature, foolishly forgetting that we cannot observe raw or pure nature. We can perceive nature only through the mediation of culture, with its panoply of culturally relative cognitive categories.

Much of the study of "natural history" often turns out to be "cultural history" in disguise. Theories and ideas about the natural world are invariably couched in terms of a specific human language and are based upon data obtained from human observation. With human observation expressed in human language, one simply cannot avoid cultural bias. Searching for culture-free descriptions of nature may be a worthwhile goal, and perhaps man will one day succeed in achieving it. In the meantime, we must be wary of mistaking relatives for absolutes, of mistaking culture for nature. Cross-cultural comparisons of sense categories may not only reveal critical differences in the specific senses, but also whether or not the apparent priority of vision over the other senses is a human universal. For the moment, we can do little more than wait and *see*.

CHAPTER 5

Relatives and Relations

Notions of kinship and kinship theory: to whom are we related and how? Is there any truth to the idea that "blood is thicker than water"? What constitutes a family? This chapter also discusses different meanings of friendship, romantic relationships, and parent–child relationships.

Relatives and Relations

Social relationships are at the heart of anthropology, just as they are at the heart of life. We are social beings; we exist in a web of social relationships that shape who we are. In this chapter we will look at a variety of relationships we experience and how we define them. We will also explore how cultural meanings are expressed in and through our relations with others. When you hear the word *relationship*, you probably first think about romance, as in "They're in (or having) a relationship." Romantic relationships are a very important kind of relationship, especially among people of college age, for that is the socially sanctioned time for young people to explore their identity, sexual and otherwise. College is also the place where many young people hope to find a mate. We will, therefore, start with courtship and romantic relationships before moving to a discussion of *kinship*, which was for a long time a major focus of anthropology.

Courtship

Ideas and practices of courtship vary considerably around the world. In the West, there is a long romantic tradition that there exists only one person ideally suited to you – a "soul mate." This concept emerged primarily in the medieval period, although it also resonates with Plato's idea that each person seeks his or her other half. In this cultural scenario, you may meet this "other half" by chance, or you may have to overcome obstacles for true love to flower. Romantic novels, poems, songs, and movies express these formulaic themes. These ideas about romance color our expectations of a romantic relationship, even among those who believe the expectations are unrealistic.

Investigating Culture: An Experiential Introduction to Anthropology, Second Edition.
Carol Delaney with Deborah Kaspin.
© 2011 Carol Delaney. Published by Blackwell Publishing Ltd.

Although the background assumptions about romantic relationships in the United States have remained relatively unchanged, courtship rituals have changed a great deal since the middle of the last century. Then, as now, young people met each other primarily at school and work, but parents and friends took a much larger role in introducing them. Social elites devised what were called "coming-out parties" intended to introduce young women to "society," that is, to eligible young men. In many places, this traditional "rite of passage" is fast disappearing, although in others, like the Filipino community in San Francisco, it is being revived. In an analogous ritual, the *quinceañera*, 15-year-old girls in some Latin American societies are presented to their community. The ritual is a way to announce that a girl has reached sexual maturity and is, theoretically, eligible for marriage. Apparently, getting tattooed used to perform a similar function for girls and boys from Samoa, Hawaii, and Tahiti (*San Francisco Chronicle*, December 30, 2001).

College, for those who can attend, has long been considered the primary place for finding a mate, but the means have changed since the early 1960s, when I was in college. Then, women's dormitories had what were called *parietals*, which meant that women had to be in the dorm by a certain hour at night, usually around 10 P.M. on weekdays and midnight on Saturday. You had to sign out, give the name of your date, and specify where you were going. And when you returned, you had to sign in, or an administrative official would go in search of you. As far as I know, men did not have parietals and had more freedom than women, but their dating behavior was also restricted. Men were expected to call women for dates at least a week in advance. They could not just drop by, but were permitted to visit the women's dorm only on certain days and only in the sitting room. Women could not go away for the weekend without parental permission. The school, in other words, was acting *in loco parentis* (in place of parents) by taking on the responsibility for their daughters. If this sounds like the dark ages, it was in the 1960s, just before everything changed. I know because I was expelled from Simmons College in 1961 for staying out beyond the curfew. In the mid-1960s, many colleges abandoned parietals and began to allow men to visit in the dorms and even in the bedrooms.

We never dreamed that a few decades later, there would be co-ed dorms and even co-ed floors and bathrooms. But this is probably the context in which many of you are living. Clearly, there are ample opportunities for men and women to meet each other. Ironically, co-ed dorm living has had the effect of diminishing romance rather than fostering it. You get to see each other's habits – messy rooms, wet towels on the floor, hair in rollers, and so on – rather than the public *persona*. Dorm mates apparently become more like siblings than possible partners; indeed, I have heard the term *dormcest* to refer to a romantic relationship that springs up between dorm mates. While dorm mates often go out together as friends or in groups, they usually look elsewhere for someone to date.

What is a date?

A *date* is a focal point for romantic relationships. The concept of a date is so commonplace that probably few of you have thought about defining it. Everyone simply knows what it is. As budding anthropologists, however, you need to step back and ask about these commonplace items of your culture, for that is how you will discover the cultural values embedded in them. Here are a few questions you should ask to find out what a date is: does the word *date* refer to the person, to the event, or to both? How many people are involved in a date? Is it assumed they are heterosexual, or can they be homosexual? How is going out on a date different from going out with a friend or friends? How is it different from other kinds of appointments? Answers to these questions shed light on the concept *date* as well as on the differences between categories of people. The concept of a date also relates to different categories of time, since dates normally occur in the evenings, with Saturday night being a preferred date time.

The concept and experience of dating are unknown to a large portion of the world's youth. So what makes dating possible? At minimum, it requires the means to contact the person you wish to ask out, usually a telephone or access to email. Second, it requires a degree of independence of the two parties, who do not need parental permission either to ask someone out or to accept an invitation. This, in turn, involves a specific notion of individual autonomy and responsibility. Third, it requires that the individuals have their own money, so they can go to the movies, take the subway, or go out for coffee or dinner. Fourth, and perhaps most important, it requires a culture which encourages romantic relationships between young people, permits young people of opposite sexes to be in public together, and offers places where they can go. Most cultures expect young people of the same sex to pal around together, so even if they are romantically involved, being seen together does not raise the same kinds of concerns. But opposite-sex dating requires numerous social underpinnings, without which such pairings are not possible.

Besides the framework of a date, what are the expectations? What is a date supposed to accomplish? You might say that a date is just a date, something to do for fun. But it is also the means by which young people discover themselves and what they seek in a relationship. Physical attraction plays a large part, at least initially, in coupling. But people also stress feeling comfortable and being able to talk to the other person. One student told me that finding someone you can talk to is the most important thing in a relationship: "What often begins a relationship is that the two of you discover you can talk to each other, that you have some interests or ideas in common, and you end up staying up late, sometimes all night, just talking." Talking together is the primary way we grow comfortable with another person. We learn what they believe in, what they value, and what their personal and political goals are.

The Saturday Night Date by Margaret Atwood

Ten years ago, I had a girl of 15 ask me: *what was your social life like when you were my age?*

I counted back: that would have been the 50's. "Well," I said, "first the boy would call you up ahead of time and ask you for a date."

Really? she said. (Young people her age did not go on dates by that time. They traveled in schools, like fish, on the spur of the moment.)

"Then he would ring the doorbell, wearing a shirt and tie – *Really?* – and you would ask him in and introduce him to your parents, who were usually your actual biological mother and father – *No kidding!* – and they would all make nervous conversation while you put the finishing touches on your hair." (The hair part was understood.)

What did you wear?

"If you were going to a formal dance, you might have a strapless gown – two melons made of wire, and a skirt that looked like a varnished lettuce. If it was to the drive-in – *The what?* – you'd wear a circle skirt with a crinoline, a cinch belt and white buck shoes with triple-rolled white cotton socks (these all needed explanations), but if it was a more formal occasion, then high-heeled shoes, nylons with seams and a panty girdle. *A what?*

("I remember those," said a male friend of my vintage. "The rubber ones. It was steamy in there, like a Turkish bath – and once you got your hand in, you couldn't get it out.")

"Then," I continued, "the boy would escort you to the car, open the door and assist you into it – *ohmigawd!* – and he would park, and extract you from the car, and you would go to the movie, and he would pay." *Really?*

There were many never-stated but well-understood rules for what went on after the movie – a set of complex handholds and bodily movements as stylized as judo, incarnating at least 4,000 years of assumptions about men and women and how they should behave when so entangled – but I didn't go into those, teenagers being notoriously prudish.

We're all flies in amber. Up to the minute, out of date, flavor of the month – these are the pins that fix us into place, and also into time. What a difference a day makes, not to mention a thousand years! Will you – dear readers, inheritors of the future – be able to understand a single word of this? Not if you are giant cockroaches, as some predict. But even if you're still human, you'll have trouble. There's one page of the Talmud that is entirely commentary on a single word of text. And so it is with the Saturday Night Date. A small thing in itself, but what a once-living, now-drowned universe it bodies forth. (Margaret Atwood, "An Encyclopedia of Lost Practices: The Saturday Night Date," *New York Times*, December 6, 1999, sec. 6, p. 148)

If you were Apache, however, you would not speak to your girlfriend or boyfriend for weeks or months, even though you are already holding hands and going places together. According to anthropologist Keith Basso (1970), Apache are sparing of words and feel that "there are types of situations" in which, as one of his consultants commented, "it is right to give up on words" (p. 217). A typical situation is when you encounter a stranger for the first time, while another is courtship. Basso described a work group in which one of the members was an outsider. No one spoke to him until they had ample time to observe what kind of man he was. He notes that their "verbal reticence with strangers is directly related to the conviction that the establishment of social relationships is a serious matter that calls for caution, careful judgment, and plenty of time" (p. 217). This is quite different from the American practice of chatting with strangers in, for example, the check-out line at the supermarket. But given the Apache attitude toward social relations, it is not surprising that words are not risked in courtship in the initial stages. Said one boy of 17,

> It's hard to talk with your sweetheart at first. She doesn't know you and won't know what to say … you get very bashful … so you just go around together and don't talk. At first, it's better that way. Then after a while, when you know each other, you aren't shy anymore and can talk. (p. 219)

Some of you might wonder, how *do* they get to know each other? And what do they learn about each other while keeping silent? You might want to give it a try. Although it is quite likely that Apache courtship practices have changed since the 1960s, when Basso did his research, his findings still provide an interesting contrast to standards of courtship behavior in your own community.

In the United States, people expect compatibility – sexually, intellectually, and emotionally – with another person *before* they would even consider a committed relationship. How different from Turkish youth in the village where I worked. There it was assumed that compatibility and love would develop *after* marriage. Women wanted a husband who did not swear or drink and who would be a good provider; men wanted a wife who was a virgin, a good worker, and agreeable to his mother. Physical attraction was rarely mentioned as a prerequisite for a marriage relationship, although a pleasant personality was. Most of the marriages were "arranged," that is, they were initiated by the parents of the boy, who discussed it with the parents of the girl. When presented with the offer, the young woman usually, but not always, had veto power. In many ways, this manner of contracting a marriage makes sense in a society where the woman usually moves into the home of her husband's family and must get along with his mother, with whom she would be sharing the work of the household.

Urban, elite Turkish youth tend to follow American and European modes of relationship and dating. They go out together – in couples and in groups – to clubs and movies, to malls and snack shops, and to sports events and concerts. Their style is quite sophisticated, especially in Istanbul. Yet there are millions of urban Turks who follow village custom. These Turks are poor and often recent migrants from rural parts of Turkey; some are nominally Muslim, and others are quite fundamentalist and do not allow young men and women to mix socially.

In the United States we expect young people to find their own mates. While Americans extol the notion of *free choice*, our practice also has its costs. Many young people do not find a partner before they enter intense careers which leave them little time for social activities. There was more leeway in the 1960s, when college graduates did not have to rush into a career path, but could work part-time, still pay rent and live decently, and have time to explore. Today everything is much more expensive, and essentials, like rent, are unaffordable without a full-time salary. With so little time to find and explore relationships, people now turn to the many dating services and "personals" that have sprung up in newspapers and on the Internet. Such services were uncommon, even laughable, 20 or 30 years ago, but, like all formalized courtship rituals, offer clear benefits: not only do they introduce people who would not otherwise meet, but also they govern these introductions with clear rules and procedures. This prevents (or reduces) misunderstandings that can lead to disappointment, conflict, and even violence.

Couples

Dating sometimes leads to the formation of a "couple," when two people decide to be together in some form of a committed or exclusive relationship. While most of you are probably aware that dating and mating rituals vary cross-culturally, you probably also assume that there are some qualities that are universally expected in a couple relationship, or at least among our European contemporaries. Yet, Raymonde Carroll, a French woman married to an American man, both of whom are anthropologists, feels quite differently. In her book *Cultural Misunderstandings: The French-American Experience* (1988), she discusses a number of important differences expected in the behavior of couples.

In France, if a couple joins a group of friends, it is expected that "the group has priority over the couple and does not admit an exclusive relationship … the group must make sure (often by playing little games or tricks on the lesser known partner) that my couple relationship does not affect or threaten my other relationships" (1988: 63). In addition, she claims, French couples show with words rather than with their bodies and gestures that they are a couple. Often this includes banter that would make many Americans uncomfortable. Carroll reported a typical response:

> [W]hen we are with others, in the presence of friends, my partner and I can gently poke fun at each other. … [W]e can contradict each other, have "violent" discussions, or take opposing sides on an issue. We can "intervene" (Wouldn't you be better off not having another drink?) … ; we can become exasperated with each other … and even get angry without worrying our friends in the least. … In fact, I would go so far as to say that one would probably be wary of a couple who always seemed to be in perfect agreement. (pp. 63–4)

She believes this type of behavior would be unacceptable among most American couples.

American couples, she claims, show that they are a couple visibly – by standing close to each other, holding hands, and other physical contact. Furthermore,

> the ideal American couple always agrees. No contradictions, and especially no "corrections" … no admonition, no intervention, no advice, no disagreement, no radically different opinions, no fighting, no frowns, no disapproving silences, no reproaches, no anger, and especially, no yelling. All conflict, all threat of conflict or suggestion of conflict, is a bad sign: the couple has problems and probably will not last. (p. 65)

This is somewhat of an exaggeration, but it does, I believe, capture some major differences in what people expect in a couple relationship. But why do these differences exist? Carroll outlines what she believes are the *cultural* premises that underpin the differences.

1. *French*: "The stability of the couple is created by the possibility (the freedom) to be myself, to be accepted as I am with my faults as well as my strong points" (p. 68).
    American: "The stability of the couple is created by the fact that my partner encourages me to be as I would like to be. … [C]riticism, reproach, disagreement, and contradiction are therefore, by definition, destructive" (p. 69).
2. *French*: "Our affective ties and our conduct are separate; one is not necessarily the reflection of the other. Thus, we can easily accept that a couple may spend their time fighting but that this doesn't prevent them from loving each other. … Affective ties are not necessarily synonymous with harmony" (p. 68).
    American: "Affective bonds and behavior reflect each other. … Affective bonds are the equivalent of harmony" (p. 69).
3. *French*: A "couple's relationship is considered to be a relationship of equality or, rather, of equilibrium in its complementarity" (p. 69). Except for the sexual aspect, she feels it resembles more the relationship between siblings.

American: Because "each person needs the other to satisfy his or her desires (encouragement, sympathy, support), the couple's relationship can only be a relationship of interdependency, or of alternating dependency" (pp. 69–70). Again, except for the sexual aspect, Carroll feels that American couple relationships are modeled more on parent–child relationships, especially because we do not expect the ideal parent to criticize, correct, or humiliate us in public but to encourage and support (p. 70).

Whether or not you agree completely with these characterizations, Carroll does point to some major areas of difference in couples' expectations of each individual in a committed relationship. Any of you who have been involved in a heterocultural relationship no doubt have your own examples of how these implicit, unvocalized assumptions can cause puzzlement, anger, resentment, and hurt. Unless they are confronted and analyzed, the relationship will probably not last.

Greeting and leave taking

Couple behavior is often quite distinct from that between friends or family. How can you tell who is greeting whom? Try to imagine the kinds of behaviors that are expressed when a lover is greeting or leaving a lover, a parent is greeting or leaving a child, a male friend is greeting or leaving a male or female friend, a host is greeting a guest or a guest is leaving the host, and so on. Then, as an exercise in observation, you might go out to some busy meeting place and observe greeting and leave-taking behaviors.

This is just what a group of social psychologists at the University of California, Davis, did when they conducted a study of couple behavior at airports (Aproberts, *San Francisco Chronicle*, December 12, 1999, p. C-6). Some of the couples were asked to answer a questionnaire about their relationship; others were simply observed. Airports are ideal places to observe all kinds of emotional dramas, for they highlight in a very concrete way the more mundane activities of meetings, reunions, and leave taking. The researchers observed numerous reunions and partings and began to categorize behaviors, such as "the goodbye hug," "contact seeking" (various forms of stroking, hand holding, and leaning heads on shoulders), and "grooming behavior" where a man might smooth a woman's hair or a woman might pick lint off a man's jacket, that the couples engaged in. Soon they were able to surmise something about the type and quality of the relationship by the kinds of behaviors exhibited.

But such a study does not stop with mere description. Analysis begins when you start to ask *why* certain kinds of behaviors occur with different kinds of persons. In answering that question, you would also need to consider notions of personhood, gender, relationship, age-related behavior, power and authority, and respect and deference. How are these notions given visible form? Are there definite cultural and ethnic differences in expression? In France, friends generally kiss each other on both cheeks when they meet and when they part; in Belgium, this is extended to three kisses – left, right, and left again! In Turkey women embrace and kiss women, and men embrace and kiss men when they meet, but, except among the urban elite, such behavior is not acceptable *between* the sexes. In the United States friends merely wave, give a "high-five," or possibly shake hands. A student from Iowa – a place that seemed as exotic to many of my students as New Guinea – said that a typical wave in greeting is two fingers off the steering wheel as you pass each other on the road. Some women in the United States, but rarely men, embrace when greeting or leaving each other. Greeting and leave taking are emotionally charged events (after all, we do not know if or when we will see that person again); we recognize this by the various rituals that, ironically, because they are ritualized, seem to minimize their importance.

Marriage

Until fairly recently, the expected outcome of a couple relationship was marriage, so before we move on to other options, let us think for a moment about a conventional marriage in the United States and other Western nations. It closely follows Van Gennep's three-part schema for rites of passage discussed in chapter 1. When you marry you *separate* yourself from your friends, at least to some extent. You are meant to "cleave only unto" your spouse. The formation of a new social unit is what, in part, the wedding ceremony accomplishes. The *liminal* period, for those who can afford it, is the "honeymoon" – a trip away from family and friends that allows you to adjust to each other and the new state of being married. Upon return you take up residence together, often in a new home, and are *reintegrated* back into society as a new entity – a married couple. These public rituals formalize and give legitimacy to the new social state, which is one reason why gays and lesbians want to be able to legally marry. It is also why many people spend so much money and even go into debt for the clothes, food, décor, and gifts for their wedding day.

Most societies recognize a period of time – sometimes only a night, but more often several days or weeks – when a new couple is becoming a social entity. In the Turkish village on the morning of the wedding, the bride is surrounded by her family and girlfriends as she gets prepared (elaborate bath, hair braiding, and getting dressed). Once she is ready, she is taken from her home, heavily veiled, to the home of her husband and his parents. There she sits "in state" all day, not speaking to the friends and relatives of her husband's family who come to view her. After the marriage is formalized by the *imam*, the couple can retreat to their own room. Although they wake up in the husband's household, their new marital status is not fully recognized for 40 days, at the end of which they finally take up their roles and chores as a couple in the village.[1]

Today in Europe and in the United States, there are a number of other options for couple behavior. Children in middle and high school "go steady" and begin to engage in sexual relationships much earlier than my peers did in the 1950s. Couple relations such as these are not expected to end in marriage, but are experiments or trials, although they are often emotionally costly. In some regions of the United States, notably large cities in the Northeast and the west coast, young couples can live together as unmarried partners more freely than in the past. These relationships, however, are expected to lead ultimately to marriage, as evident in the many social benefits – health care, social security, inheritance, and so on – that they can claim only as married partners. This is another reason why gays and lesbians seek the right to marry.

Among all groups and nations, there are restrictions on whom one can marry, yet the rules vary considerably. Almost everywhere marriage is forbidden with the closest relatives, although sexual relations with them, such as father–daughter incest, are not that unusual (Herman 1981; McKinnon 1995). In some places, notably parts of the Middle East, marriage with a first cousin is the preferred type of marriage, especially between the children of two brothers. In the village in Turkey where I did my fieldwork, half of the marriages contracted while I was there were between relatives, and one quarter of those were between first cousins on either the mother's or father's side (Delaney 1991: 108).

In the United States, cousin marriages were fairly common in the eighteenth and nineteenth centuries, especially in Boston and New York. Lewis Henry Morgan, who was a lawyer in upstate New York in the nineteenth century and is considered the founder of kinship studies, married his first cousin. Even today, marriage with a first cousin is permitted, with certain restrictions, in 26 states including New York, California, and Massachusetts, according to a report in the *New York Times* (April 4, 2002). Martin Ottenheimer's *Forbidden Relatives* (1996) discusses the issue at length.

Among Australian aborigines, people are assigned to "marriage groups" at birth. There are several types, but for purposes of exposition let us look at an eight-class system shown in table 5.1. This is the way it works: If you are a male *Panunga*, you must marry a female in the *Purula* group, and your children (male or female) will be *Appungerta*. But if you are a male *Purula*, you must marry a female in the *Panunga* group, and then your children (male or female) will be *Kumara*. An *Appungerta* must marry an *Umbitchana*: if male, the children will be in the *Panunga* group; and if female, they will be assigned to the *Panunga* group.[2] All that you need to know is which group you belong to and which group you must take a partner from.

Both the Australian and American examples assume heterosexual couples, as does the French example that Carroll describes. This raises the following questions: do homosexual couples follow the same patterns as heterosexual couples in each culture, or do they develop their own patterns? Why, for example, do homosexual couples in the United States seek marriage? Is it primarily for the benefits just mentioned, or is it for the cultural legitimacy that marriage confers to a committed relationship? Why have so few states allowed it? Do homosexual couples in other cultures seek to marry?

One issue here is the *meaning* of sexual orientation. In the United States and many other Western societies today, heterosexuality and homosexuality are seen primarily as identities, that is, internalized senses of self from which patterns of attraction and emotional attachment emerge. In other societies – and in United States in the past – sexual acts in all possible

Table 5.1 Australian aboriginal marriage groups

I	II	III	IV
Panunga	Purula	Appungerta	Kumara
Uknaria	Ungalla	Bulthara	Umbitchana
Bulthara	Kumara	Uknaria	Purula
Appungerta	Umbitchana	Panunga	Ungalla

forms (heterosexual, homosexual, masturbatory, voyeuristic, and so on) are only acts and, as such, have no bearing on one's suitability or need for marriage, the purpose of which is the establishment of a household and not sexual or emotional gratification.[3]

Another issue here is the *meaning* of marriage, a culturally specific term. Although we find conjugal relationships between men and women and family-type relationships all around the world, *marriage*, as most Americans understand it, is not universal, and *family* does not mean the same thing everywhere. First, the Western notion of marriage derives primarily from a Christian heritage that prescribes heterosexuality: according to the Bible, male and female were created for each other and for the purpose of procreation. For this reason, the Catholic church and many Protestant churches are loath to condone homosexuality, which they consider a sin. Second, Christianity understands the conjugal relation as a *union* of a man and a woman – "and the two shall become one" – with the couple forming a single entity under the authority of the man. This is not the case with many other peoples. Turkish villagers, for example, insist that marriage is not a union, but a contractual relationship for economic and sexual benefits. This means that the spouses are distinct individuals who assume and value their separateness.

I discovered that one of the unexpected benefits of an arranged marriage, at least for the woman, is that she is not identified with her husband. This leaves her psychologically and emotionally much freer than her American contemporaries who, from my observation, often merge into the identity of their husbands. This makes sense, since American women choose their husbands and therefore are implicated in their behavior. But in the Turkish village, if a husband does something stupid, it does not reflect on the woman, because his behavior has nothing to do with her. On the other hand, her behavior does seriously reflect on him: she can tarnish his honor if she raises suspicions that she has looked at or talked with another man. As a result, her freedom to move about is quite circumscribed. In American culture, where individual freedom and choice are highly valued, the institution of arranged marriages would not have a chance. Yet I cannot say that Turkish village marriages are any less happy than American marriages.

Divorce

About half of American marriages end in divorce. Perhaps it is because Americans expect too much from marriage and are disappointed by reality. Or perhaps it is because Americans receive little instruction about marriage and therefore have very little idea of what it is. The conventional romantic notion is that marriage should last "until death us do part." This is a Christian idea – part of the marriage vows – and is not a universal belief or expectation; indeed, many Americans no longer anticipate this kind of commitment. Still, no one enters marriage with the expectation of divorce, so we must ask why divorce is so common. Why, for instance, do most divorces occur after the birth of a first child? Many couples do not know how drastically child raising will change their lives. As one person told my daughter and her husband when they were expecting their first child, "It is as if a bomb fell on your marriage." That turned out to be good advice for it warned them that dramatic changes were about to occur.

For couples who do not weather the storm and split up, the usual result is that a man's standard of living rises while the woman's falls. This is a function of income and custody. Thus "when a couple with children breaks up, frequently the man becomes single, while the woman becomes a single parent" (Pearce 1990: 267). Furthermore, "[F]or most women and children divorce means precipitous downward mobility – both economically and socially" (Okin 1989: 161). Single fathers do not suffer the same falling fortunes for the following reasons. First, they typically earn more money than their ex-wives. Second, they are more apt to find sympathetic women to help with child care. And, third, they tend to remarry far sooner than single mothers.

Divorce exposes the reality that marriage is not, and cannot be, an equal partnership. While many young couples today say they want to share child-rearing and domestic tasks, this is rarely possible, because their choices are already socially constrained. If marriage is to become an equal partnership, then wider societal changes are necessary, including variable work times, job sharing, flexible career arcs (see chapter 3), and more widespread and accessible child care and health care.[4] Instead, women usually end up working the "second shift" (Hochschild 1989) of housework and child care in addition to their wage-earning jobs. Political scientist Susan Okin, among others, has addressed this issue in a chapter titled "Vulnerability in Marriage" in her book *Justice, Gender, and the Family* (1989):

> The division of labor within marriage (except in rare cases) makes wives far more likely than husbands to be exploited both within the marriage relationship and in the world of work outside the home. To a great extent and in numerous ways, contemporary women in our society are *made* vulnerable by marriage itself. They are first set up for vulnerability during their developing years by their personal (and socially reinforced) expectations that they will be the primary caretakers of children, and that in fulfilling this role they will need to try to attract and to keep the economic support of a man, to whose work life they will be expected to give priority. They are rendered vulnerable by the actual division of labor within almost all current marriages. They are disadvantaged at work by the fact that the world of wage work, including the professions, is still largely structured around the assumption that "workers" have wives at home. They are rendered far more vulnerable if they become the primary caretakers of children, and their vulnerability peaks if their marriages dissolve and they become single parents. (1989: 138–9)

I had firsthand experience of this. When I got divorced and became a single parent, my daughter was only a year old. I received minimal child support payments for about a year, and then they stopped. It was difficult to collect the payments as the courts were, and still are, ill equipped to deal with the demand. I was able to earn only slightly more than I had to pay a babysitter. There was no day care then, but it wouldn't have helped, since day care is extremely expensive, often taking half of a woman's take-home pay.

The realization of my vulnerability radicalized me. I realized that no matter how much I worked, I would be unable to pay the babysitter and also pay for rent, food, medical bills, and clothes, let alone some toys and entertainment. This inspired me to investigate our cultural assumptions about gender and family. Even though I was divorced, I was still a mother and wanted very much to be involved with my daughter's care and upbringing. Is it more socially valuable to have all single mothers of young children working full-time, or would it be better for the children and for society if they spent at least part of their time with their children?

At that time, the only option for me was to go on welfare, for which I was very thankful: it allowed me to give up the futile attempts to collect child support, to spend more time with my daughter, and to move on with my life. However, welfare in the United States was then and remains today highly stigmatized and punitive. Out of 17 industrialized nations, the United States ranks as one of the lowest in its "family support" program, with only Israel and Ireland ranked lower. According to several studies, more than half the women on welfare were once married, and most had worked or were working, but they could not earn enough money to support their families. There were more white women than black on welfare, and most had only one or two children. Nevertheless, President Reagan's caricature of the "welfare queen" – a lazy black woman driving around in a Cadillac with her many illegitimate babies – persisted through the welfare debate during the Clinton administration. We never heard about the welfare mothers who went on to become senators, congresswomen, reporters, lawyers, doctors, entrepreneurs, and professors like myself. While the U.S. government was willing to spend $40,000 to $60,000 per year to keep a child in foster care, and $73,000 per year to keep a young man in prison, it balked at giving a mother $10,000 per year[5] to allow her to care for her own children and keep them out of trouble. Many scholars agree that providing adequate support for all children in the United States is economically possible. What is lacking is the public recognition that single mothers are systematically disadvantaged, and that collective remedies are necessary and feasible.[6]

Beyond that, girls need to be raised to think they will have to support themselves and possibly a family; instead, however, the old romance tales continue to fire girls' imaginations and condition their prospects. In the United States, romance novels such as the Harlequin books are read by more than 20 million people, mostly girls and women. In 1981 Harlequins accounted for about 12 percent of the paperback market in the United States, and 28 percent in Canada, apparently because they met a need for both excitement and security (Jensen 1984: 15). "The basic plot is that the hero and heroine meet and fall in love but there is an obstacle to their love," thus providing the excitement. "The barriers are removed in the last chapter and the hero and heroine are allowed to unite" and live happily ever after. "Any variation unfolds itself within this structure" (p. 76), thus making readers secure in the knowledge that love conquers all. Through novels like these and other social influences, girls are conditioned to become sexually attractive to some male who will fall in love with them and support them. While the realities do not support this script, parents, guidance counselors, and other authority figures perpetuate this scenario.

And these are the realities. Today, almost a century after women were granted the right to vote, women's salaries are still significantly lower than men's, with women earning 77 cents for every dollar a man earns. Certainly this is an improvement from a generation ago, when women earned only 59 cents on the dollar, but today's wage disparities reveal that inequities in the work economy persist. Identifying their source is not, however, easy. Certainly gender bias in hiring and promotion persists in many professional arenas, especially in the corporate world. But in many instances, women disable themselves. For example, women typically seek indoor jobs as receptionists, office staff, and so on, which lie at the lower end of the income ladder, and ignore outdoor jobs as drivers, groundskeepers, and the like which lie at the higher end. So, too, women rarely negotiate for high starting salaries, pay raises, and promotions from their employers, while men in the same jobs do. Finally, many women enter the workforce only to exit it or scale back to raise children, and in so doing forfeit not only their salaries in the short term, but also the pay raises they would have otherwise received over the long term. As a consequence, when they rejoin the work force, they do so at a lower pay level than their counterparts who never left it. All of these forces together depress the average earnings of women relative to men.

The solutions, then, are not simple. Some lie in legislation to prohibit gender discrimination in the job market, such as the Lilly Ledbetter Fair Pay Act which President Obama signed into law in 2010. Some lie in training girls to be more effective self-promoters, so that they seek jobs with higher starting salaries, whether or not they see other women in them, and negotiate for more pay and benefits from their employers. However, the most difficult problems concern the persistent and inevitable conflicts between work life and home life: someone has to care for the children, the sick, and the elderly, and as long as women's incomes are, on average, lower than men's incomes, women will most often assume this responsibility, depressing their incomes even further. The choice facing the United States (and other highly industrialized nations) is to create new and better bridges between workplaces and home places that allow women and men to pursue meaningful careers and to provide nurturance for children, the ill, the elderly, and each other.

Family

Family, like marriage, is another term we use freely, assuming it to be a natural entity necessary to the survival of the human race. As a natural entity, we further assume it is universal. However, it is precisely these self-evidently natural concepts and social forms that should be scrutinized. Although humans generally live in domestic groups, this doesn't mean that the *family* is universal. Rather, it has a particular meaning and history in Western culture. Etymologically, the word *family* comes from the Latin *familia* and *famulus*, which meant all those dependent on a male head, including a wife, children, slaves, and servants. The concept of the male-headed family also has biblical roots, as in Genesis when God tells Eve that Adam shall rule over her. Throughout Western cultural history, the male is the established head of the family and the one who *has* a family. The persistence of this notion today is revealed in the reluctance of government officials, among others, to refer to single women with children as families instead of *female-headed households* or possibly *broken families*. If they were considered whole or complete families, perhaps there would be less stigma and more social support and concern for them.

In United States, the notion of family is usually assumed to mean a heterosexual couple, their biological children, and sometimes the grandparents, especially if they are living under the same roof. There are, however, many other family types. There are cohabiting adults without children, single adults with children, and couples and single adults with adopted children. In the case of adoption, there is no "blood" connection between the parents and the child, although the ideal family form is affirmed (or its breach is concealed) if the adopted child is of the same race or ethnic group. Interracial and transnational adoptions present a greater challenge to the biological notions of family and can provoke hostility from the surrounding community. My second grandson was adopted from Korea and does not look like his parents or his brothers. My daughter reported one nasty encounter at the supermarket when a woman walked up to her and in front of her son asked, "He is not your *real* son, is he?" Then, "He's Chinese, isn't he?" When she said, "No, he is from Korea," the woman replied, "Oh, it's all the same thing anyway!" Some Native American groups do not want *their* children to be adopted outside of the community, and some countries will not permit transnational adoptions for fear the children will be used for their organs.[7]

Same sex couples also confound the normative family. In some cases, they are raising the biological children of one of the two partners, and in some states they are able to adopt children. Some lesbian couples opt to have children through sperm donation, although often the partner who is not the biological mother finds she cannot adopt these children to become their legal parent.[8]

Should all of these different groupings be considered *family*, or should the term be restricted to its conventional sense of a heterosexual married couple and their biological children? This question is provocatively addressed in an article titled "Is There a Family?" by anthropologists Collier, Rosaldo, and Yanagisako, who ask if the family is, indeed, universal. Reviewing the anthropological literature on the family, they pointed out how its universality was simply assumed, and how the logic for that assumption was circular: "because people need nurturance, and people get nurtured in The Family, then people need The Family" (1992: 41). But nurturance can be provided in a number of ways and by people other than family. They show that when the idea of "nurturance" is scrutinized, it becomes clear that it means more than

> the provision of food, clothing, and shelter required for biological survival. What is evoked by the word *nurturance* is a certain kind of relationship: a relationship that entails affection and love, that is based on cooperation as opposed to competition, that is enduring rather than temporary, that is noncontingent rather than contingent upon performance, and that is governed by feeling and morality instead of law and contract. (p. 42)

As the site of nurturance, the family represents to many of us a place of refuge, where people love and care for you no matter what. This idealized conception of the family creates expectations and longings that persist throughout our lives.

The reality, for many people, however, is just the reverse: the family may not be a place that provides support and nurturance, and may, in fact, be a place of terrible emotional and physical violence. But because the family is sacrosanct and the ultimate *private* sphere, it has been off limits for the law. So too, police and child welfare workers are hesitant to interfere, and often allow serious problems to go undetected for a long time. Such was the case with Phillip Garrido, who kidnapped an 11-year-old girl in 1991, held her captive in a backyard compound in California for 18 years, and bore two children with her. Although Garrido already had a criminal record for rape and kidnapping, and his neighbors reported suspicious activities at his home to the police, no police action was taken until 2009, when Garrido himself approached the FBI and the campus police of University of California, Berkeley, about his own history of sex crimes.[9]

Collier, Rosaldo, and Yanagisako argue that the idealized view of the family emerged historically as industry was separating from the home; thus, "what gives shape to much of our conception of The Family is its symbolic opposition to work and business, in other words, to the market relations of capitalism" (1992: 42). Although many assume that the family is a distinct and separate unity, particularly when facing the world, inside it there are often conflicting goals and desires. For example, there may be conflicts over the way the household money is spent, the way chores are allocated, or who has the burden of income earning, housework, and child care.

This brief discussion has, I hope, convinced you to seek the definitions and meanings of various social groups and relationships from, as anthropologists often say, "the native's point of view." We will explore the importance of viewpoint in the next section on kinship, which has long been a major focus of anthropology.

Kinship: Relatives and Relations

Kinship is an area of social relations that has preoccupied anthropologists since the discipline emerged in the nineteenth century. Kinship concerns *kin* or people we call *relatives* – those people to whom we are related biologically or by marriage, or, in anthropological jargon, by *consanguinity* (common blood) and *affinity* (marriage). Early anthropologists were confounded by the significant differences in the *kinship systems* of different societies, and set out to investigate and explain them.

Lewis Henry Morgan

Lewis Henry Morgan, considered the "founding father" of kinship studies, noticed that the Iroquois who lived near him in upper New York State had a very different kinship system from that of Anglo-Americans. While we have two different words for father and father's brother (that is, *father* and *uncle*), the Iroquois have one word. And while we have two different words for mother and mother's sister (that is, *mother* and *aunt*), the Iroquois have one word. Furthermore, while we have different words for our siblings and our cousins, the Iroquois use the same words for their siblings, their mother's sister's children, and their father's brother's children, and another set of words for their mother's brother's children and their father's sister's children.

The more Morgan learned about the Iroquois, the more perplexed he became. If the biological facts of reproduction are the same everywhere, aren't family relations also the same? He began to wonder if all Native American peoples had the same kinship system as the Iroquois. To find out, he designed a questionnaire asking for the native words that corresponded to our words for mother, father, sister, brother, aunt, uncle, cousin, grandmother, and so on, and filled out this questionnaire every time he visited a Native American group. Then he wondered about the variety of kinship systems in different parts of the world. So he gave the same questionnaire to missionaries, explorers, and government officials who were posted around the world and asked them to collect the same data from the native peoples there. All of this material, along with his discussion and theorizing of it, was

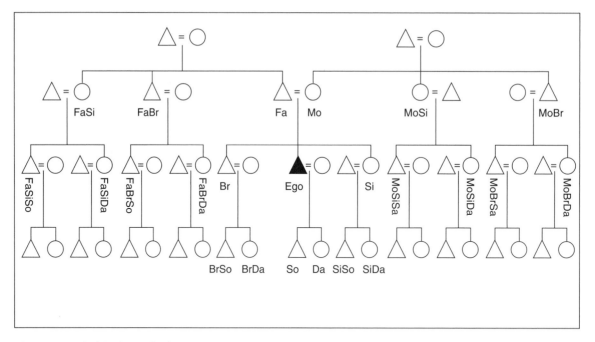

Figure 5.1   Kinship chart: The descriptive system.

compiled and included in the largest and most expensive book the Smithsonian had ever published, *Systems of Consanguinity and Affinity in the Human Family* (1871).

Morgan discerned two primary types of kinship systems, each with numerous variations. The two major types he called *classificatory* and *descriptive*, examples of which are shown in figures 5.1, 5.2, 5.3, and 5.4. For those of you who have not seen a kinship chart, *Ego* is you, and the relations and terms are from your perspective. Triangles are the symbols for men, and circles for women; the equal sign means marriage, horizontal lines link sibling groups, and vertical lines show the children from each parental couple.

1.   The *classificatory* type of system *classifies* a whole group of relatives under a single term. For example, all the men one generation above you (your "father's" generation) on your "father's" side are called by the same term (let's say *tama*), and all the men of that generation on your "mother's" side are called by another term (let's say *vungo*). The same principles are used to classify all the women one generation above you. In some systems, such as the "Hawaiian," all of the men in each generation (one above yours, your own, and one below yours) are called by the same terms and are not divided into the father's side and the mother's side.

2.   A *descriptive* system uses separate words to *describe* (or recognize) each distinct relationship. The Euro-American system is primarily a descriptive system, although it occasionally conflates several relationships into one kinship category; for example, we refer to both our mother's sister and our brother's sister as *aunt*. The Turkish system, in contrast, is more descriptive because it has different words for each of those

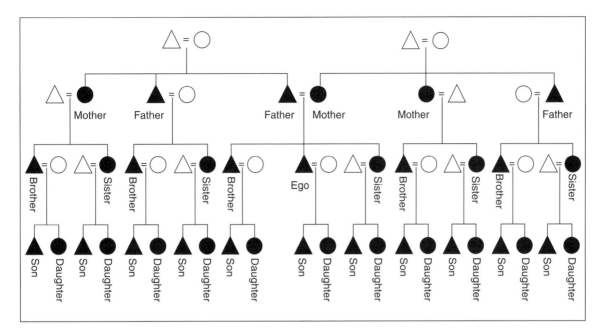

Figure 5.2 Kinship chart: Classificatory system.

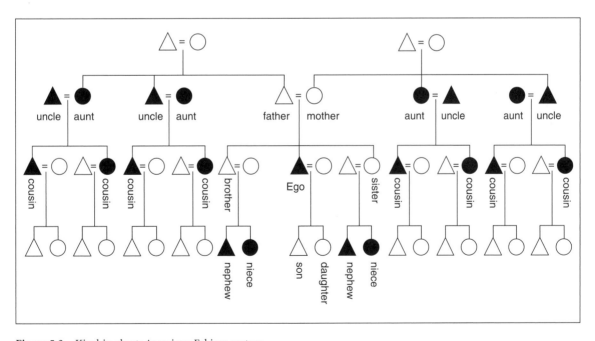

Figure 5.3 Kinship chart: American Eskimo system.

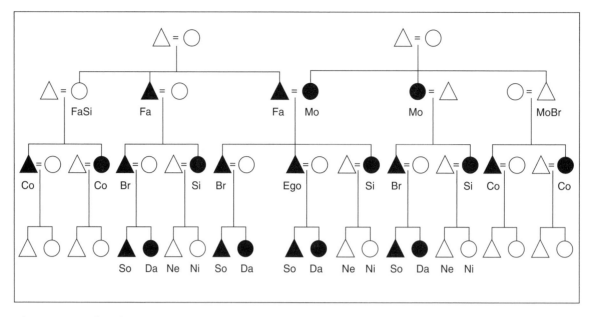

Figure 5.4 Kinship chart: Iroquois system.

relations: *teyze* (mother's sister) and *hala* (father's sister). For Morgan, the descriptive system was the true and correct system. Here is his famous definition:

> As a system it is based upon a true and logical appreciation of the natural outflow of the streams of blood, of the distinctiveness and perpetual divergence of these several streams, and of the difference in degree, numerically, and by lines of descent, of the relationship of each and every person to the central *Ego*. It is, therefore, a natural system, founded upon the nature of descents, and it may be supposed to have been of spontaneous growth. But it manifestly proceeds upon the assumption of the existence of marriage between single pairs, and of the certainty of parentage through this marriage relation. Hence it must have come into existence after the establishment of marriage between single pairs. (1871: 468–9)

Morgan decided further that the different kinship systems corresponded to different stages in the development of society. He arranged each society in evolutionary sequence from the most primitive to the most advanced, with those using classificatory kinship systems on the primitive side, and those with descriptive systems on the advanced. Not surprisingly, he placed European and American societies at the most advanced end, even though their kinship systems were not the most descriptive systems in his sample.

Morgan's evolutionary model of kinship and cultures was worked out primarily in *Ancient Society*, published in 1877. His theories were adopted by Marx and Engels in *The Origin of the Family, Private Property and the State* ([1884] 1972), since he claimed that the change from classificatory to descriptive kinship systems was driven by the rise of private property. This he believed would *naturally* be in the hands of men, who, just as naturally, would want to pass it down to their "legitimate" heirs. Morgan's theories remained the basis of Soviet social science until the collapse of the Soviet Union in 1991.

Morgan's entire corpus of work was masterful for its grasp of a very large body of data and for the concise schemes he derived from it. But it was based on an underlying and unproven assumption: that kinship terms reflect the biological facts of reproduction. Thus, when he first encountered classificatory systems, he assumed that the societies in question did not practice pair bonding and allowed promiscuous intercourse and group marriage instead; as a consequence, no one knew who among one's kinsmen was one's biological father. So, too, descriptive kinship systems arose when societies demanded sexual exclusivity (at least from women) making it possible to trace paternity. In both types, kinship terms reflected the "streams of blood" that flow from one generation to the next and the ability of each society to recognize them. People with classificatory kinship terms are simply ignorant of the facts of sex and generation and, therefore, are primitive.

Many scholars did, in fact, challenge some of Morgan's facts and inferences. John McLennan, for example, said that kinship terms did not refer to specific relationships, but were merely forms of address used to differentiate group members from outsiders.[10] Later generations disputed Morgan's evolutionary model, arguing that kinship terminologies reflected not stages of development, but the fundamental social structures of each society. Some anthropologists concentrated on issues of *descent*, focusing primarily on *lineages* as the foundation of social organization, while others concentrated on *alliance*, that is, the bonds created between kin groups (like lineages) through intermarriage. Much of this work was based on research in Africa and formed the core of British social anthropology from the 1940s through the 1960s.[11] Still, for all of their critical advances beyond Morgan, no one disputed Morgan's core belief that kinship meant sex, blood and pedigree.

Finally, in the 1970s, the biological basis of kinship was called into question. In a short but influential article titled "Kinship Systems" (1973), A. M. Hocart confronted the problem of translation that lay at the heart of kinship studies, beginning with Morgan's questionnaire. As Hocart observed, if an anthropologist asked a Melanesian man, "Who is your *tama*?" he often pointed to his father, leading the anthropologist to record *father* as the meaning of *tama*. Soon, however, the anthropologist realized that many other men were also called *tama*. According to Hocart, he should have dropped the first translation and found a new one to cover its range of usage, but instead he retained "father" as the primary meaning and assumed it was extended as a metaphor to encompass a widening pool of people. As a consequence, the anthropologist failed to recognize that *tama* and similar terms "do not express consanguinity, as we have unfortunately been accustomed by Morgan to believe, but … fix the place of any relative according to generation and side" (1973: 175). Hocart extrapolated further, "All our difficulties spring from a preconceived idea that kinship terms everywhere try to express the same thing as they do in Aryan and Semitic languages, and that in those languages they show the place on the family tree" (1973: 176).

David Schneider, an anthropologist at the University of Chicago, worked in parallel with Hocart to dislodge the Western cultural models that were entrenched in the anthropology of kinship. He first sensed the inadequacy of kinship theory in the 1940s, when he did fieldwork on the Pacific island of Yap, but he later realized that a "Morganian" approach could not explain American kinship either. Americans, after all, often count their pets or roommates as family members, and exclude some people who are clearly genealogical kin: consider the phrases "He is no brother of mine!" and "You are no longer my son!" Rather than compiling questionnaires, genealogies, and family profiles, Schneider conducted open-ended interviews to access the natives' understandings of their own kin universe. In this case, the natives were Americans.[12]

Schneider discovered that for Americans, "blood" is a recurring and dominant symbol of profound social connection, as in the phrase "Blood is thicker than water." In fact, he said, it is difficult "to convince an American that blood as a fluid has nothing in it which *causes* ties to be deep and strong" (Schneider 1972: 48; emphasis mine), in other words, that blood *symbolizes* kinship relations, but does not create them. With this point of entry, Schneider found his way into a wider cultural universe – a system of symbols and meanings – that shape how Americans understand their social world and their position within it. A recurring theme throughout this system is the centrality of biology – an essential nature – that is the core of our individual and collective being.

Nature, Culture, and Folk Biology

Schneider's work on kinship opened the door to new work on biology as a Western cultural system and its manifestations in gender ideology. This included research on gender roles and identity, health and immigration policy, and even obstetrics and gynecology. But before these specialized concentrations took shape, several anthropologists confronted a core belief linking biology and gender in the Western imagination: that women are, by virtue of their sexual biology, allied with animals and with nature. These ideas crystallized in Simone de Beauvoir's book *The Second Sex*, which argued that women are devalued because they merely reproduce the species, while men produce monuments of culture. In effect, she equated women with *nature* and men with *culture*.

Anthropologist Sherry Ortner took exception to this in a (now) famous article, "Is Female to Male as Nature Is to Culture?" (1974). She argued that women's secondary status is rooted not *in* nature, but in cultures that seek to dominate nature and that associate women with nature. Reproduction, we have assumed, is a matter of nature and is therefore universal; it is devalued both because it is associated with nature, not culture, and with women rather than men. Marilyn Strathern, a British anthropologist, then sought a contrary example in the non-Western world. In "No Nature, No Culture: The Hagen Case" (1980), she demonstrated that the nature–culture dichotomy, long held to be universal, was not how the Hagen of New Guinea conceptualized their world. They see a major division between the "wild" and "domesticated," and while this dichotomy is related to their ideas about gender, it does not easily map onto a Western worldview.

How, then, are we to understand Western notions of nature, culture, and gender? Our current views of nature are interlaced with our understanding of biology, but while biological science is a modern discipline, our commonplace notions about biology – our "folk biology" – are embedded in a much older mythological and cosmological tradition. This cultural tradition confounds and confuses much of what biological science actually tells us.

This is illustrated by what I have called the "seed-soil" theory of procreation, a theory rooted in the Bible, the Qur'an, and influential Greek texts that still, despite modern science, dominates our common understanding of gender and parenthood (Delaney 1986, 1991, 1998). In this theory, the man creates (or begets) the child with his *seed*, while the woman nurtures that *seed*-child in her womb and after she gives birth to it. Thus, in the Qur'an, men are told, "Women are given to you as fields; go therein and sow your seed" (Sura 2: 223), while women are either fertile or barren, like the fields the farmers plow. As the sole procreator, the man is symbolically allied with the Creator, the male-imaged God who created the world without a partner. The woman, in turn, is identified with the earth and is subordinate to the man, just as the earth is subordinate to God. This seed-soil theory pervades Genesis, even though the New Revised Version of the Bible has replaced the word *seed* with the word *progeny*. But this effort to use gender-neutral language cannot erase the import of the mythology: men beget children, and women bear them.

The biblical account of procreation has been thoroughly disproven in the biological sciences. Today we know that the man and woman contribute equal kinds and quantities of material – 23 genes each – to the embryo through the combination of ovum and sperm, and that the developing fetus obtains additional gestational material from the mother's body through the placenta and the uterine environment. But our words, images, metaphors, laws, and social arrangements have not caught up with the science of procreation. We still say that a man impregnates a woman, and that a woman gets pregnant or is impregnated. Consider also the meanings associated with *father* and *mother*. *Fathers* create, invent, and found, as Bill Gates is the father of Microsoft, and our fore*fathers* founded a great nation. *Mothers*, in contrast, nurture, support, and sustain, as Mother Theresa nurtured the orphans of Calcutta and the motherland sustains the nation. There is nothing in our biological nature that prevents men from nurturing and women from creating, but our cultural models say otherwise.

To use words like *father* and *mother* as translations for kinship terms in other cultures surely distorts other people's notions of relatedness as it continues to obscure our own notions from ourselves.

New forms of kinship and kinship studies

The study of kinship continues to be an important part of the anthropological enterprise, but in recent years the focus has shifted dramatically. Feminist anthropologists have pointed out that conventional kinship studies were based on assumptions about gender. While anthropologists had long known that *male* and *female* are defined differently in different societies and also that their roles differ, they did not follow through with this realization. It took feminist anthropologists like Jane Collier and Sylvia Yanagisako to

argue that gender and kinship have been defined as fields of study by our folk conception of the same thing, namely, the biological facts of sexual reproduction. Consequently, what have been conceptualized as two discrete fields of study constitute a single field that has not succeeded in freeing itself from notions about natural differences between people. (1989: 15)

They do not deny

> that men and women are different, just as individuals differ, generations differ, races differ, and so forth. Rather, we question whether the particular biological difference in reproductive function that our culture defines as the basis of difference between males and females, and so treats as the basis of their relationship, is used by other societies to constitute the cultural categories of male and female. (p. 48)

Perhaps somewhere gender differences are defined by the differential distribution of hair on the body or by breasts or the lack of them. But even if procreation is a salient aspect of the definitions, different cultures understand this process very differently. It matters whether the man or the woman is the sole creator, whether both are creators, or whether the entire process is in the work of ancestral spirits and not the two persons intimately involved.

The work of Collier and Yanagisako is primarily a critique of past and prevailing theories of kinship with suggestions for unifying future studies of gender and kinship. Other voices working on that edge have begun to be heard: (1) gays and lesbians who question the heterosexual bias of kinship and gender studies; (2) people who feel a kinship bond because they have the same genetic disease – a biological relationship, to be sure, but not one based on consanguinity; (3) groups of adoptive parents, who argue that kinship is about care and nurturance, not sex and blood; and (4) those who have used the new reproductive technologies (NRTs) which fragment the roles (e.g., sperm donor, egg donor, biological mother, surrogate mother, birth mother, and so on).[13] All of these people have been challenging the taken-for-granted notions of kinship and forging new definitions that we are only beginning to understand and accommodate socially and culturally. One thing is clear: kinship is not and never has been stable; it is not something given "in the nature of things" but is constructed in particular cultures in particular ways around particular notions of person and cosmos.

Friends

How do we define a friend? Often people become friends because they live in the same neighborhood or go to the same school.[14] They discover they share similar interests or responses to things. Among girls and young women, telling secrets to each other is the seal of a friendship, and betraying those secrets usually signals the end of the friendship. What is friendship, and how is it similar to or different from love?

Raymonde Carroll was forced to rethink her beliefs about friendship after an experience that occurred when she was doing her initial fieldwork on the Pacific atoll of Nukuoro. She elected to stay "at home" while the villagers had gone out sailing. She looked forward to a period of quiet, of not having to concentrate on the language, and just being alone. That was not to be the case. Very soon she was visited by a village woman who, once she noticed that Raymonde was staying behind, decided to come keep her company so she wouldn't be alone! The woman refused to abandon Raymonde despite her subtle hints that she actually wanted to be alone. In addition, the local woman declared herself a *friend*, and said that friends brought each other gifts (she had brought a coconut) and that, as a friend, she would teach and correct Raymonde's use of the language. Raymonde wrote,

> What seems particularly important to me is the shock that this incident brought to my concept of friendship. This woman declared herself my friend point blank, without even asking me, in a way that I guessed would be irrevocable. What is more, she seemed to be according me an extraordinary favor. Where I come from, dear lady, I thought to myself, one does not unilaterally declare oneself someone's friend. One "becomes" a friend, and this is based on mutual (though tacit) agreement. (Carroll 1988: 72)

Something very similar happened to me early during my fieldwork in the Turkish village. The midwife with whom I stayed the first week or so asked, "Do you love me?" I was shocked and wondered, at first, if this was some kind of lesbian overture. Then she asked if I would be her friend. I was just as surprised as Raymonde Carroll and thought to myself, "I don't even know you! She doesn't understand what it means to be a friend, and moreover, I don't want to be her friend, I don't particularly like her." But when I asked a sophisticated, well-educated, urban Turk, he explained the assumption behind her query: "Once the declaration has been made, you will *become* friends. It is a relationship that is taken seriously and often lasts throughout one's life, and it doesn't matter if you are very different." Most Americans, I think, want their friends to be like them, to confirm their feelings and agree with their views.

The issue becomes, perhaps, even more difficult when friendship occurs between people who come from what we so easily assume are similar cultures, such as France and the United States. Raymonde Carroll notes, in fact, that at the descriptive level, the conception of friendship in the two countries is almost identical. But, she says, "it is not the category that proves to be the source of cultural misunderstanding but rather the presuppositions that enter into this category, which can be very different" (p. 78). Friends, she says, are the people who understand us; but what they *do* to show how much they understand us will be very different. Not unlike her characterization of couples, Americans tend to seek friends who are supportive, who, when you do something stupid, will try to make you "feel better by finding extenuating circumstances, by reminding" you of your good qualities. A French friend, in contrast, will help you see more clearly the stupid thing you did and help you "find a means to patch things up. ... This means that my friend understands me because he or she is another me ... in the sense that he or she is the half of me that remains reasonable" (p. 79). She claims that such friends can show you what you did wrong without judging you and still remain your friend.

In Turkey, France, and many other places, it is normal for women friends or men friends to walk arm in arm. This behavior does not signal a homosexual relationship but merely friendship. But in the United States it is rarely done. Why do Americans have such a phobia about touching, particularly between people of the same sex? A personal experience may be illustrative. When my daughter was in eighth grade (and about 13), she was about as tall as I am. We got along very well, and sometimes when we were walking around Cambridge, Massachusetts, where we lived at the time, I used to take her arm. She didn't like it; it simply wasn't done. Not only did it suggest that we were not mother and daughter – a distinction she wanted to be obvious since many people took us for sisters – but it also implied that we were lesbian lovers, an impression she also disliked. When she was 16 she visited me in Turkey, and then we fell quite easily into this habit. It seemed natural there since everyone else was doing it and it was a pleasant way to walk and talk. Later, when I returned to Cambridge and she was in college, we again took up the practice – just strolling around, walking and talking. People made rude remarks that surprised us both. But by that time, she let them pass over her; the experience in another culture made her aware that there was nothing intrinsic about the behavior that gave it meaning but rather the way it signified specific things in a specific culture. And by this time, she didn't care what such people thought.

In Praise of Manners

Social relations are made smooth because of conventional, ritualized practices of interaction and behavior. These practices are sometimes referred to as *manners* or *etiquette*. From an early age, children are inducted into the society's rules of etiquette. In the United States, this training was once supplemented by books on the topic. I remember a truly horrid children's etiquette book called *Slovenly Peter* (Hoffman, 1848) that told of terrible things that would befall you if you neglected your manners. In addition, such books answered questions about situations that were outside of everyday experience, or that occurred rarely in one's own life such as weddings and funerals.

Today, books of etiquette and manners seem to be going the way of white gloves and crinolines, symptomatic, perhaps, of a widespread rejection of social formalities as unnecessary pretensions. Thus on April 4, 2002, the *New York Times* and Peter Jennings's ABC news program reported that, according to a sociological study, Americans' manners had deteriorated considerably since the 1950s. This erosion of etiquette suggests a society where individualism has gone awry, where people feel no need to conform to social norms or to smooth social relations. It is a society that is unaware of itself as a society, as something that conditions and shapes the lives of its members. But while Americans today are testing the limits of social *mis*behavior, they are doing so within the parameters of social norms, norms that value "doing one's own thing" but do not want such freedoms taken too far. "Flipping off" close friends and distant strangers may be tolerable gestures of rudeness, but flipping off your employer or your teacher is simply not done.

Manners remain important. Having socially accepted and widely known forms of etiquette actually makes social life easier, because everyone knows what is expected in particular circumstances. Manners are primarily the responsibility of parents who teach and train their children. Other adults such as grandparents and other relatives, teachers, counselors, and coaches can also help, especially as a child grows, but the major responsibility belongs to parents.

Parents' responsibilities

Please and thank you   In past generations, according to my mother-in-law, children were taught to say *please* and *thank you* at very young ages; sometimes they were the first words a child was taught. This conveyed, very early on, a sense that there were others out there to consider and to respect. From my observations of parents and children in the United States today, it appears that children are no longer being taught these simple but important phrases. Children do seem ruder and more selfish. They are not being taught to consider others, let alone have any respect for authority, including their parents. Instead, from this observer's point of view, it seems they are being taught to fight for themselves, individually. Has our world really become so Hobbesian? Has our world become so individualistic? Perhaps it ought not to be so surprising that theories of utilitarianism, social Darwinism, and its latest form – sociobiology – have all emerged in English-American societies. This is not the way it is in France, according to Raymonde Carroll.

> As soon as I become a parent in France, I must answer to society for my behavior toward the child. As a parent, my role is to transform this "malleable, innocent, impressionable, and irresponsible" creature into a social being, a responsible member of the society. ... [T]his means that on becoming a parent, it is first and foremost to the society that I incur an obligation, a debt, rather than to my child, who comes second. If I give priority to my child, I isolate myself from this society. (1988: 47)

She goes on to say that to

> understand the American situation, one need only in a sense reverse all the signs. When I (an American) become a parent, I incur an obligation to my children rather than to society, which comes second. My obligation is not to teach my children the rules and practices of society, but above all to give them every possible chance to discover and develop their "natural qualities," to exploit their gifts, and to blossom. (p. 49)

No doubt, these are somewhat exaggerated stereotypes, but nevertheless they do indicate very different ideas about society and its value.

Not surprisingly, France was the home of the great social thinker Emile Durkheim, who was the first really to think of society as something *sui generis*, that is, not just the sum of all the individuals in it but also something with its own characteristics and requirements. His insights provided the basis for the field of sociology. In the United States, in contrast, our behavior expresses a deep belief and adherence to notions of individualism and individual freedom to pursue our own desires and goals. Our social policy, too, tends to perpetuate this; we have much less of a safety net for people than does France or any other European nation. In the United States, you sink or swim on your own.

Table manners   It is obvious that table manners vary from time to time and place to place. Europeans tend to use their knives and forks differently from Americans. They cut their meat the same way Americans do, but they raise it to their mouths on an overturned fork held in the left hand; Americans generally put the knife down, switch the fork back into the right hand, and use it right side up.

In the United States and Europe, dinner conversation is expected, but in the Turkish village people were not expected to carry on conversation when eating; that was reserved for after dinner, when people sat upon the divans and drank tea. While different cultures have different norms for table manners, in each particular culture there are still norms or rules of behavior, and, with training, these become habitual. These habits allow the dinner to proceed without incident. But what happens if someone goes against the norms? All attention is turned to that person; his or her behavior disrupts the dinner and makes people uncomfortable. Although I have heard young people in the United States say they should be able to eat as they wish because "it's a free country," they do not realize that their behavior is really an attention-grabbing maneuver. It also communicates the message that they do not care what other people think. In turn, the other people might then decide that person is not worth caring about. All of this goes on without one word being spoken, but such behavior can have serious consequences in terms of both romance and careers. When everyone is taught how to eat, how to cut their meat, and which fork or knife to use for which items, then social life proceeds smoothly, and one can concentrate on the food, on one's dinner partners, and on the conversation rather than on someone's execrable manners.

Ms. Manners, Ann Landers, and so on

In a country where there is so little consensus about manners and etiquette, it is understandable why advice columns such as Ann Landers and Ms. Manners and advice talk shows on radio and television are so popular. People, quite often, simply do not know how to act in certain situations and do not know what to expect from others; they can, therefore, offend the people they are trying to please and get offended and hurt by actions they do not understand. They need advice from experts. But experts in what? Etiquette and manners, of course! They are performing the function that the etiquette books used to perform: they let brides know they have to send thank-you letters for gifts received or whether they can exchange wedding gifts; they tell parents when it is appropriate to intrude and interfere with their children's choice of friends or their marriages, and when it is not; they tell some people what forks or soup bowls to use and when you can dispense with them; they tell what kinds of sexual actions are inappropriate for what ages, and whether you have the right to say no; they tell people how to respond to their mothers- or fathers-in-law, what to wear to a funeral, and so on.

Americans are often proud that we have so few social rules and think that "anything goes" here, but it doesn't, as too many learn the hard way. Despite the help Ann Landers and Ms. Manners can offer, the need for such advice experts reveals a widespread confusion about social mores, or, perhaps a breakdown in their transmission from one generation to the next. This creates holes in the American social fabric, which are themselves important sites for cultural investigation.

Turkish social relations

From more than 30 years of acquaintance with Turks and Turkish society, I feel I can say that Turks, in general, are extremely gracious and hospitable people; indeed, hospitality is a national value and a primary virtue. This is as true, if not more true, among peasant villagers as among the urban elite. They possess a kind of civility and grace that contradict the image of the fierce and warlike Turk, for so long promulgated in European literature and imagination. They are not as suspicious of strangers as are most Americans, and often invite total strangers into their homes and give them tea and some food.

The majority of parents in the United States are child directed, that is, their focus is the child and his or her future. They try to push and promote the child forward, and provide whatever support they can to launch him or her into the world. In Turkey, parents surely care deeply for their children, but children are brought up to consider and respect their parents in a way that American children are not. Turkish youth assume they will have to take care of their parents in their old age. In the village, women's nursing of their infants establishes "milk rights" that require their children to nurture them in their old age as they nurtured their children in infancy.

Young men did not smoke in front of their parents, especially their father; it was considered an affront to his dignity and authority. In the village, they needed their father's permission to leave and go to town; young women needed it simply to visit a friend at the other side of the village. Both needed parental permission to continue school beyond the then mandatory requirement of fifth grade. (Currently, children are required to complete junior high school or the eighth grade.)

Not only did children do what they were told, but also they did it without the complaining that is so common among American children, especially teenagers. I remember very vividly one occasion when many villagers were going to a wedding in the next village. This was greeted as a special outing, a time to meet new people and just get out of the village. My next-door neighbors were planning to go, but at the last minute the husband-father decided to stay home. But he could not stay home alone (who would fix his meals?), so his teenage daughter was told to stay home with him. She did so without a murmur. When I asked her if she was disappointed, she smiled and said she had to care for her father. He was hardly a typical patriarch, but her acquiescence clearly demonstrated submission to patriarchal ideology. Still, she also knew she had much to thank him for, since he allowed her to attend the middle school in the village (and was one of only three girls to do so). Later, when she finished at the top of her class, he allowed her to attend high school, even though this meant she had to leave home and live with relatives in town.

Notes

1. For a full description of Turkish marriage and wedding practices, see Delaney (1991).
2. This information is taken from Spencer and Gillen (1899: 72).
3. For the historical emergence of homosexuality as an identity, see Bayer (1987), Foucault (1990), and Weeks (1989).
4. See Hochschild (1975). Despite the date, the material in the article is just as relevant today.
5. The figure $10,000 per year is an extrapolation from the $200 per week that women received in welfare payments and is included here to demonstrate the cost differences for foster care, imprisonment, and welfare subsidies. In reality, few women received welfare for a full year.
6. See Delaney (1998: 241–7); the *New York Times*, August 14, 1995, citing the Luxembourg Income Study; Carnegie Foundation (1994); Handler (1995);

Kamerman (1984); Kamerman and Kahn (1984, 1989); Katz (1986); Leach (1994); and Sidel ([1986] 1992, 1996).

7. For excellent work on these topics, see Gailey (2000), Howell (2001), Modell (1994), and Strong (2001).

8. In her book *Families We Choose: Lesbians, Gays, Kinship* (1990), anthropologist Kath Weston writes about the way gays and lesbians go about constructing families, especially when their own families of origin shun them.

9. A summary of this case can be found at en.wikipedia.org/wiki/Kidnapping_of_Jaycee_Lee_Dugard (Wikipedia, 2010).

10. For "McLennan as well as for Morgan, 'kinship' was about marriage, about the facts of procreation and conception, about blood-ties and genetic relationships as they could be known or were knowable, about the ties that arise out of the biological facts of human reproduction; for McLennan, rights and duties, succession and estates followed blood-ties, not kinship terms" (Schneider 1972: 35).

11. The classics of African kinship studies in British social anthropology include Radcliffe-Brown and Forde (1951); Evans-Pritchard (1951), and Fortes (1945, 1959).

12. See Schneider (1968).

13. All of these issues are taken up in Franklin and McKinnon (2001). For further references, see their bibliography.

14. Penny Eckert, a linguistic anthropologist, studied the way young people begin to classify each other – a process that began in junior high school but continued into high school – and how these identifications affect the rest of the students' lives. I have included a chapter from her book *Jocks and Burnouts: Social Categories and Identity in the High School* (1989) in this chapter. While *jock* or *burnout* might not be the lingo you used during that time of your life, you will be able to make analogies.

EXERCISES

5.1. Family Ethnography

A. Describe the composition of your family, that is, its members and their relationships to each other.

B. Arrange these people in a diagram that shows their relative closeness to you. *Note*: you can devise any kind of chart you like, as long as it reflects what to you determines closeness and distance.

C. Describe the allocation of tasks and duties within your family. In other words, who does what for the family as a whole, and who does what for their own satisfaction or maintenance?

5.2. Reproduction

Devise a way to explain to a child the basic facts of reproduction – that is, where babies come from – that is not inappropriately graphic but does not use misleading metaphors like *seed* and *soil*. Feel free to try other metaphors.

5.3. Work and Home

Propose some strategies whereby American society can better integrate home life and work life, so that the distribution of domestic work and income earning between men and women is more equitable.

Bibliography

Basso, Keith (1970) "To Give Up on Words: Silence in Western Apache Culture." *Southwest Journal of Anthropology* 26(3): 213–30.

Bayer, Ronald (1987). *Homosexuality and American Psychiatry*. Princeton, NJ: Princeton University Press.

Boellstorf, Tom (2005). *The Gay Archipelago: Sexuality and Nation in Indonesia*. Princeton, NJ: Princeton University Press.

Carnegie Foundation (1994). "Starting Points: Meeting the Needs of Our Youngest Children." Princeton, NJ: Author.

Carroll, Raymonde (1988) *Cultural Misunderstandings: The French-American Experience*. Chicago: University of Chicago Press.

Collier, Jane, and Yanagisako, Sylvia (1989) *Gender and Kinship: Toward a Unified Analysis*. Stanford, CA: Stanford University Press.

Collier, Jane, Rosaldo, Michelle, and Yanagisako, Sylvia (1992) "Is There a Family?" In *Rethinking the Family: Some Feminist Questions*, ed. Barrie Thorne and Marilyn Yalom. Boston: Northeastern University Press.

Degler, Carl (1980) *At Odds: Women and the Family in America from the Revolution to the Present*. New York: Oxford University Press.

Delaney, Carol (1986) "The Meaning of Paternity and the Virgin Birth Debate." *Man* 21(3): 494–513.

Delaney, Carol (1991) *The Seed and the Soil: Gender and Cosmology in Turkish Village Society*. Berkeley: University of California Press.

Delaney, Carol (1998) *Abraham on Trial: The Social Legacy of Biblical Myth*. Princeton, NJ: Princeton University Press.

Eckert, Penelope (1989) *Jocks and Burnouts: Social Categories and Identity in the High School*. New York: Teachers College Press.

Evans-Pritchard, E. E. (1951) *Kinship and Marriage among the Nuer*. Oxford: Clarendon.

Fortes, Meyer (1945) *The Dynamics of Clanship among the Tallensi*. London: Oxford University Press.

Fortes, Meyer (1959) *The Web of Kinship among the Tallensi*. London: Oxford University Press.

Foucault, Michel (1990) *The History of Sexuality*, vol. 1. New York: Random House.

Franklin, Sarah, and McKinnon, Susan, eds. (2001) *Relative Values: Reconfiguring Kinship Studies*. Raleigh, NC: Duke University Press.

Gailey, Christine Ward (2000) "Race, Class and Gender in Intercountry Adoption in the U.S." In *Intercountry Adoption: Developments, Trends, and Perspectives*, ed. Peter Selman. London: Skyline House/British Agencies for Adoption and Fostering.

Handler, Joel (1995) *The Poverty of Welfare Reform*. New Haven, CT: Yale University Press.

Hebdige, Dick (1981) *Subculture: The Meaning of Style*. New York: Routledge.

Herman, Judith Lewis (1981) *Father–Daughter Incest*. Cambridge, MA: Harvard University Press.

Hocart, A. M. (1973) "Kinship Systems." In *The Life-Giving Myth*. London: Tavistock.

Hochschild, Arlie (1975) "Inside the Clock-Work of Male Careers." In *Women and the Power to Change*, ed. Florence Howe, sponsored by the Carnegie Commission on Higher Education. New York: McGraw-Hill.

Hochschild, Arlie, with Machtung, Anne (1989) *The Second Shift*. New York: Avon.

Hoffman, Heinrich (1848) *Slovenly Peter*, trans. Mark Twain. New York: Warne.

Howell, Signe (2001) "Self-Conscious Kinship: Some Contested Values in Norwegian Transnational Adoption." In *Relative Values: Reconfiguring Kinship Studies*, ed. Sarah Franklin and Susan McKinnon. Raleigh, NC: Duke University Press.

Jensen, Margaret Ann (1984) *Love's Sweet Return: The Harlequin Story*. Toronto: Women's Press.

Kamerman, Sheila (1984) "Women, Children, and Poverty: Public Policies and Female-Headed Families in Industrialized Countries." *Journal of Women in Culture and Society* 10(21).

Kamerman, Sheila, and Kahn, Alfred (1984) "Social Policy and Forms of Family in Europe." *International Social Security Review* 47(3–4).

Kamerman, Sheila, and Kahn, Alfred (1989) "Single-Parent, Female-Headed Families in Western Europe: Social Change and Response." *International Social Security Review* (January).

Katz, Michael (1986) *In the Shadow of the Poorhouse*. New York: Basic.

Leach, Penelope (1994) *Children First: What Our Society Must Do – and Is Not Doing – for Our Children Today*. New York: Knopf.

Lévi-Strauss, Claude ([1949] 1969) *The Elementary Structures of Kinship*. Boston: Beacon Press.

Marx, Karl, and Engels, Frederick ([1884] 1972) *Origin of the Family, Private Property and the State*, ed. and intro. Eleanor Burke Leacock. New York: International.

McKinnon, Susan (1995) "American Kinship/American Incest: Asymmetries in a Scientific Discourse." In *Naturalizing Power: Essays in Feminist Cultural Analysis*, ed. Sylvia Yanagisako and Carol Delaney. New York: Routledge, pp. 25–46.

Modell, Judith (1994) *Kinship with Strangers: Adoption and Interpretations of Kinship in American Culture*. Berkeley: University of California Press.

Morgan, Lewis Henry (1871) *Systems of Consanguinity and Affinity in the Human Family*, Smithsonian Contributions to Knowledge No. 17. Washington, DC: Smithsonian.

Morgan, Lewis Henry (1877) *Ancient Society*. New York: Holt.

Okin, Susan Moller (1989) *Justice, Gender, and the Family*. New York: Basic.

Ortner, Sherry (1974) "Is Female to Male as Nature Is to Culture?" In *Women, Culture, and Society*, ed. Michelle Rosaldo and Louise Lamphere. Stanford, CA: Stanford University Press.

Ottenheimer, Martin (1996) *Forbidden Relatives: The American Myth of Cousin Marriage*. Urbana: University of Illinois Press.

Payne, Kay E. (2001) *Different but Equal: Communication between the Sexes*. Westport, CT: Praeger.

Pearce, Diana (1990) "Welfare Is Not *for* Women: Why the War on Poverty Cannot Conquer the Feminization of Poverty." In *Women, the State, and Welfare*, ed. Linda Gordon. Madison: University of Wisconsin Press.

Radcliffe-Brown, A. R., and Daryll Forde, eds. (1951) *African Systems of Kinship and Marriage*. London: Oxford University Press.

Schneider, David (1968) *American Kinship: A Cultural Account*. Englewood Cliffs, NJ: Prentice Hall.

Schneider, David (1972) "What Is Kinship All About?" In *Kinship Studies in the Morgan Centennial Year*, ed. P. Reining. Washington, DC: Anthropological Society, pp. 32–63.

Sidel, Ruth ([1986] 1992) *Women and Children Last: The Plight of Poor Women in Affluent America*. New York: Penguin.

Sidel, Ruth (1996) *Keeping Women and Children Last: America's War on the Poor*. New York: Penguin.

Spencer, W. B., and Gillen, F. J. (1899) *The Native Tribes of Central Australia*. London: Macmillan.

Stacey, Judith (1996) *In the Name of the Family: Rethinking Family Values in the Postmodern Age*. Boston: Beacon Press.

Strathern, Marilyn (1980) "No Nature, No Culture: The Hagen Case." In *Nature, Culture and Gender*, ed. Carol MacCormack and Marilyn Strathern. Cambridge: Cambridge University Press.

Strong, Pauline Turner (2001) "To Forget Their Tongue, Their Name, and Their Whole Relation: Captivity, Extra-Tribal Adoption, and the Indian Child Welfare Act." In *Relative Values: Reconfiguring Kinship Studies*, ed. Sarah Franklin and Susan McKinnon. Raleigh, NC: Duke University Press.

Tylor, E. B. (1889) "On a Method of Investigating the Development of Institutions: Applied to Laws of Marriage and Descent." *Journal of the Anthropological Institute* 18: 245–72.

Waring, Marilyn (1990) *If Women Counted*. San Francisco: Harper.

Weeks, Jeffrey (1989) *Sex, Politics, and Society: The Regulation of Sexuality since 1800*. London: Longman.

Weston, Kath (1990) *Families We Choose: Lesbians, Gays, Kinship*. New York: Columbia University Press.

Wikipedia (2010). "Kidnapping of Jaycee Lee Dugard." en.wikipedia.org/wiki/Kidnapping_of_Jaycee_Lee_Dugard.

Young, Iris (1995) "Mothers, Citizenship, and Independence: A Critique of Pure Family Values." *Ethics* 105: 535–56.

R E A D I N G

Symbols of Category Membership
Penelope Eckert

WHAT MAKES SOMEBODY A BURNOUT?

You know, maybe somebody who smokes all the time, you know, smokes marijuana and stuff, but you know, everybody does that. You could call me a Burnout. You know, I've did that … maybe, maybe it's the way they dress. It's a lot of things, I think. Your look, you can wear these leather – and these wallets with chains and look really bad, you know – lot of people say, "Oh, that guy's got to be a Burnout."

The Jock and Burnout categories emerge upon entrance to junior high school, where they develop in mutual opposition through a rapid foregrounding and differentiation of selected values, behavior, and symbols. Unstructured differences that have developed through elementary school are imbued with significance as they are thrown into opposition, and the opposition itself gains hegemony as it absorbs more and more aspects of everyday life. In an effort to differentiate themselves, the two categories progressively separate their worlds, developing opposing territories, appearances, demeanors, and activities. The underlying ideologies that separate Jocks and Burnouts are in turn strengthened by the increasing range of external manifestations associated with them.

The differences between Jock and Burnout social structure and norms are not very apparent in the daily business of life. In fact, by the time the cohort reaches graduation, Jocks and Burnouts know precious little about each other. What everyone knows of their differences is what shows – the symbolic manifestations of category affiliation. Ask high school students or recent graduates about the social categories in their school, and they will begin with how they dress, where they hang out, or what substances they use. Clothing and other forms of adornment, ways of speaking, territory, and even substance use and school performance all have symbolic value in the adolescent context. However

subconsciously, they all stand for deeper cultural differences that may themselves not be accessible to all who participate in the symbolic system. Differences in symbolic behavior are commonly taken as the only differences between the categories – and such things as clothing differences are regarded as if they had social value in themselves rather than simply in association with an evaluation of the people who wear them. Category symbols attain their value from association with clear differences in both form and content, developing around salient social differences between the categories and maximizing distinctness in visible form.

Clothing and adornment is perhaps the most powerful symbolic subsystem in the Jock–Burnout opposition. An individual's bodily adornment is seen simultaneously with the individual and thus provides the guarantee that the individual will not be separated from his or her social identity. To the extent that they are inseparable from the person, other portable symbols, such as books, radios, cigarettes, and sports paraphernalia, are also effective indicators of social identity, as are cars. Musical taste can be unambiguously displayed through the use of radios. Styles of demeanor and movement rely to a great extent on action and interaction, as does language. Finally, territorial and activity displays are limited to specific settings. All of these areas of behavior are fully exploited to express social category affiliation, and because adornment is the only ever-present symbolic subsystem, it is manipulated to incorporate as many of the elements of other subsystems as possible. Musical tastes can be displayed on T-shirts; activities, on activity-specific clothing (such as motorcycle boots or football jerseys); language style and demeanor, in action and in messages on buttons and T-shirts; territory, on jackets (such as the DETROIT jackets worn by some Burnouts).

Just as the Jock and Burnout categories develop in mutual opposition, so do their symbols. Elements of behavior that come to represent one category will be rejected by the other, and they may be exploited by the other category through the development of a clearly opposed element. Thus the Burnouts not only avoid the pastel colors that characterize Jock clothing, but they consistently wear dark colors. (This opposition could, of course, be expressed in reverse – the Jocks avoid dark colors and consistently wear pastels.) At the same time, these colors have positive significance: Pastel colors are associated in our society with youth, innocence, and gaiety, while dark colors are associated with sombreness, age, and sophistication – all qualities that are associated with the categories that wear them.

Many Jock and Burnout symbols stand above all for differences in economic means, perception of life stage and adult domination, and school and local orientation. Jocks are locally oriented both to the school and to the local community, while Burnouts are oriented away from the school, toward the neighborhood, and toward Detroit. Jocks embrace adult norms for the adolescent life stage, while Burnouts constantly lay claim to adult status. Finally, Jocks associate themselves with the middle class and its relative affluence, while Burnouts associate themselves with the working class and its relatively limited material means.

School Territories

Jock and Burnout use of school facilities is symbolic of differences in attitudes toward the school and in orientation to the adolescent life stage. The Jocks accept the facilities provided by the school and use them in rough conformity to school expectations – they store their coats and books in lockers, use the bathrooms for their intended purpose, and eat in the cafeteria. Burnouts, on the other hand, express their counter-cultural position in the school by transforming the school facilities to suit their needs and identities (see Willis, 1977, for a discussion of such transformation). To a certain extent, their use of the school is built around cigarette smoking, which, as will be discussed later, is a key symbol in the Jock–Burnout split. In schools across the country, Burnouts' smoking leads them to hang out in doorways and stairwells, parking lots, bathrooms, breezeways, and loading docks. This use of marginal areas has added

significance in its representation of Burnouts' more generally marginal place in the school. This marginalization not only is imposed through the school's rejection of Burnout values, but is embraced by Burnouts in their rejection of the school as a comprehensive social institution. While the Jocks center their social lives in the school and accept the school as a "home away from home," the Burnouts energetically deny any such function of the school. The Jocks embrace whatever facilities the school offers them. In contrast, the Burnouts pick and choose. They use facilities that reflect recognition of their adult status and needs – the courtyard, vocational classrooms, parking lot. They shun those that reflect the school's parental role of providing food and living space, namely, lockers and the cafeteria. Those they cannot shun – the bathrooms – they transform into alternative smoking areas.

Lunchtime Territories

In addition to seeking marginal spaces, Burnouts reject school facilities that represent the school's in loco parentis role. One such facility is the cafeteria. Although the food in the Belten cafeteria is quite good, the Burnouts are overwhelmingly critical of it. The common Burnout claim that cafeteria food has made people sick implies a rejection of not only the school's right but its ability to assume a parental role. The few Burnouts who do eat in the cafeteria occupy the most marginal table in the room – a table off to the side and next to the rear exit, where they can be "half in and half out" of the cafeteria and separate from the main cafeteria activity.

DO YOU EAT IN THE CAFETERIA?

Sometimes. … When it looks edible. When it doesn't look like it's moving around at you.

OH GOD. WHO DO YOU EAT WITH USUALLY?

All the Burnouts, you know, just anybody who comes along and sits at the table … right next to the first line. We just sit there and chow down, and talk.

Many Burnouts do not eat lunch at all, and of those who do the overwhelming majority limit themselves to packaged food, which they can carry out to the courtyard. The Belten cafeteria provides two hot food lines leading from the main entrance and a fast-food line leading from a side hall (and emptying near the Burnout table referred to above), where Burnouts buy their cookies or potato chips. One Burnout demonstrated the norm against eating in the cafeteria, in her reaction to a friend's insistence that she did eat there, and her proud denial of engaging in legitimate transactions with the school.

DO YOU EVER EAT IN THE CAFETERIA?

In there? Huh-uh.
[friend speaking] Yeah, you do.
Bullshit. I never eat in there.
[friend] Come on.

NOT EVEN WHEN THE WEATHER IS REAL BAD?

No, I used to chow in the hall. Or I don't eat at all.

BUT DO YOU EVER, LIKE, BUY FOOD THERE AND THEN GO OUT INTO THE COURTYARD?

Yeah. Well, I don't buy food. … Everybody rips off from them. I remember one time I went up to the chip rack, you know. I had Linda and them stand behind me, and when they weren't looking I'd whip chip bags back there. And they're cramming them in their purse. We'd walk out, we were munching down.

High school cafeterias everywhere show strict territorial specialization. A high school in a neighboring town shows a stratified use of the cafeteria, with the Burnouts (called "Freaks" in this school) eating near the outside doors at the bottom of the cafeteria so they can slip out for a smoke, and the Jocks at the top of the cafeteria – an area actually elevated above the rest. The "In-betweens" occupy the middle area. The Belten cafeteria is set up with long tables along three walls and round tables in the middle. The human geography of the cafeteria varies between lunch periods and semesters, but by and large the Jocks occupy the tables on the west wall and an occasional round table, while the fast-food line and the Burnout table are on the east wall. Some people refer to the tables along the west wall as the "Jock tables."

Burnouts are not the only ones who eat elsewhere than in the cafeteria. Members of the choir, which rehearses before and after lunch, frequently eat in the choir room; those who work in the student store sometimes eat in the room behind the store; many on the yearbook staff eat in the yearbook room; ROTC members sometimes eat in the ROTC room; and a few people eat in various classrooms and faculty spaces. Lunch periods are so routinized that I knew exactly where to find most people during that time. People always eat in the same place with the same people, and if they don't stay there for the whole period, they retire to a specific place to wait for the bell to ring. In-between people who smoke may go to the courtyard, a few go to the library or to the room where their next class meets (if they can get past the hall monitors), and many stand, always in the same place, in the cafeteria lobby and the gym hall. The Jocks who are not in any of the specialized areas stand directly in front of the main entrance to the cafeteria and in front of the student store opposite, the Burnouts who are not in the courtyard stand in the hall by the radiator at the courtyard's main entrance, and the In-betweens congregate between the two areas. Students clearly see this after-lunch standing around as a significant activity, and some remain in the cafeteria expressly to avoid it.

AFTER LUNCH, DO YOU STAY IN THE LUNCHROOM?

Mm hmm. I hate standing out in the hall. I feel like I'm on exhibit. Bothers me. You just stand there, and everybody else looks around, it's all crowded. Don't like it. I'd rather just sit.

The Courtyard

The locus of Jock–Burnout territorial separation is the courtyard. Whereas the cafeteria is in the public domain, the courtyard is Burnout territory by virtue of its designation as the authorized smoking area. The close association between Burnouts and the courtyard comes out repeatedly in conversation, as Burnouts are commonly described as "the people who smoke" and "the people in the courtyard." One Jock accounted for his split-up with several junior high friends in the following way:

Like there's a few others … who also go here who I don't hang around with at all any more, I mean, not that I, you know, wouldn't want to, it's just, we just went different ways in tenth grade and ever since.

HOW DID YOU GO DIFFERENT WAYS?

They went into the courtyard and I went into the student government.

Burnouts who do not smoke go regularly to the courtyard, but few other nonsmokers do, since smoking is the only legitimate excuse for a non-Burnout to be in Burnout territory. Those non-Burnouts who do go into the courtyard are apt to be labelled as Burnouts by many of the people in the school, both because of their use of the courtyard and because they smoke. These people stick to the southwest corner of the courtyard, which is recognized among those in the courtyard as neutral – a distinction not recognized by those who do not frequent the courtyard. The courtyard is the one place in the school that the Burnouts consider their own, and their care for the courtyard contrasts with the graffiti found on the walls that lead to it. This care was described by one In-between smoker who frequents the southwest corner of the courtyard.

I've always, I've always liked it out here. It's just, just, besides the litter. But there's not really that much, because, um, like people, you know, a lot of, most of the Burns come out here, you know, the Burnouts that think they're real cool and stuff. They come out here, and, um, and, you know, if they see litter, believe it or not, they'll pick it up. Because, you know, like they, they, this is the one part they can say is theirs, you know, because all the really popular people really don't come out here. … It, it really is nice, you know, it's big, and, I don't know, it's nice. They have, they have flowers, and people really don't pick the flowers and stuff, you know, like, and they don't step on the little, like we plant trees in here sometimes, and they don't pick them and everything, you know, and throw them away, and just. … I think a lot of people take care of it because they look, they look at other high schools, and, you know, like they have nothing at all.

Smoking and the courtyard (probably because of its association with smoking) are the most widely recognized Burnout symbols and are therefore the most carefully maintained areas of differentiation. Presence in the courtyard is recognized as an unambiguous social statement. One In-between gave the following explanation for why she and her best friend do not go into the courtyard:

DO YOU EVER GO IN THE COURTYARD?

No.

ANY PARTICULAR REASON?

I've well, let's see. Julie and I are, you might say we party. I mean, there's Jocks and Jells like that. But we don't smoke cigarettes. And I think – I don't know – I get the impression that if people who don't smoke cigarettes go out there, everybody automatically thinks, "Oh, they want to be a Jell." So I wouldn't want every body saying, "Oh, what are you, um, trying to be a Jell now?" or something.

Avoidance of the courtyard incurs considerable inconvenience, because the courtyard provides a shortcut between classes and from classes to the cafeteria. Some In-betweens will use this shortcut between classes but will not go there during lunch:

I don't go out in the courtyard because [of] all the smokers and stuff. … I'll go outside and walk through it, probably, but I won't stay out there.

Most Jocks go through their high school years without ever setting foot in the courtyard. Some say this is because of the smoke, although in a large outdoor area like the courtyard, it is easy to avoid other people's smoke.

AND WHEN YOU'RE CHANGING CLASSES, DO YOU EVER WALK THROUGH THE COURTYARD TO TAKE A SHORTCUT?

No. No, I don't … even if it were longer inside, I'd stay inside. Because there's a lot of that smoke, you know, and stuff, especially near the areas where people are allowed to smoke. And it gets in my hair and I have to wash it. That's the only reason. It smells bad, it really reeks.

Others cite the Burnouts themselves as a reason not to go into the courtyard.

DO YOU EVER GO INTO THE COURTYARD?

Hm mm. Something might bite us. ... They're dangerous animals. They're so funny. It's like watching prehistoric man out there. It's so funny, because one time we saw, these two guys were acting like "Kung Foo Joe" you know, and me and Sally were, "I don't believe it."

Many cite fear of ridicule as the main reason for avoiding the courtyard. A few say that because presence in the courtyard implies smoking, they would run the risk of expulsion from a team if they were seen there. The following Jock, who prides himself on his ability to get along with Burnouts, evoked the more general significance of territory in his account of why he never goes into the courtyard. The confusion of his account reflects the fact that his behavior toward the courtyard has been so strongly dictated by social norms that he has not incorporated it into his personal ideology.

I think I've walked through the courtyard twice, and both the times, it was like after school and nobody was around. I never walk through the courtyard.

EVEN TO CHANGE CLASSES AND STUFF, YOU DON'T DO THAT?

Nope.

HOW COME?

Well, for one thing, there's other ways to get around, you know, if you want to walk through. And when it's cold, I can't see people standing out in the courtyard, that doesn't make sense. But just being out in the courtyard has a lot of significance. When people see you out there, even if you're out there just to walk by and everything, if somebody walks by, you catch their attention, if you've never been out there

before, and, you know, somebody sees you, they might think something. I think, you know. But it – that's not why. Because I really, I really don't care what people think about me, as long as, you know, I do what I think is right. But it's just the idea of having – having to walk through there. It doesn't, you know, it doesn't make sense. If you want to get somewhere, you don't have to walk through the courtyard. It's – I don't know, I don't know how to explain it. It's like, it's territory which you don't have to go through. If it's going to cause problems, why – you know, avoid it. ... I think it – I think when you walk through the courtyard, you're easily – it's easy to get a label ... and if you talk to the people out there that have the reputation of, you know, always around drugs, or, you know, having any kind of influence with drugs, then you're going to get labelled that way. I mean, if you're inside the building, that's a different story, you know, if somebody walks by and sees you talking to somebody that, you know, is around drugs, they're not going to think too much about it because they'll say, "Well, maybe they're just talking about a class or something." They don't know what you're talking about. But once you're outside, it's like, you're in his shop. He can tell – you know, it's like you're working with him on his type of you know, his thing, so, I don't know.

Because cigarette smoking is a universal Burnout symbol, Burnouts across the country occupy high school smoking areas: In one California high school, the Burnouts are called "Sectioners" by virtue of the fact that they hang out in the smoking "section." Most schools that permit smoking designate unattractive outdoor areas in the back for this purpose, and one school in the Detroit area co-opted the Burnouts' choice of territory by tearing out the fixtures and stalls from one boys' and one girls' bathroom and designating them as sex-segregated smoking areas. The central location and attractiveness of the courtyard in Belten provides an unusually habitable and nonmarginal Burnout territory. I have been told by students from the wealthier Neartown high school that the proof that Belten has a "Burnout problem" is that it allows this category its own territory. However, while the courtyard is Burnout territory, almost the entire rest of the school is Jock territory. As a number of Burnouts have pointed out, "the Jocks own the school." The Jocks can afford to have their territory defined residually in relation to the Burnouts', because they dominate so much of the functional area of the school. They can regularly be found during their free time in the student activities office, in the various areas of the athletic department (gym, multi-purpose room, faculty offices), in the music rooms, and in classrooms and teachers' offices. Territorial disputes do not arise in Belten, probably because there is adequate territory for both categories. In a nearby town, where Burnouts hang out in stairwells and vestibules, the "Freaks" occasionally invade the opulent central lounge that is known as Jock territory. The invasions have taken place on boys' varsity game days, when symbolism is at its height and Jocks are wearing their game day "uniforms": uniforms for cheerleaders and pompom girls, jackets and ties for players.

Lockers

Just as the courtyard is home base for the Burnouts, the Jocks' home base is their lockers. Each class is assigned lockers in a specific area of the school, and with seniority each class graduates from the least to the most prominent location in the school – freshman and sophomore lockers in the back halls, junior lockers in the upstairs front hall, and senior lockers in the front hall on the main floor. Lockers serve as age-segregated gathering places, each area named for the class it houses: "Senior Hall," "Junior Hall," "Sophomore Hall." It is significant that Burnouts do not acknowledge these names. Two people are assigned to a locker at the beginning of the school year. Jocks generally visit their lockers between classes and spend a lot of time "fooling around" at their lockers before and after school. One peripheral junior Jock described her feelings about Junior Hall in much the same way that Burnouts describe the courtyard:

> I like that hall too, because I know everybody. Junior Hall. I can say "Hi" to everybody. I don't feel left out.

In one school in the Detroit area, the senior Jocks are particularly territorial about Senior Hall, and most underclasspeople take detours rather than risk harass-

ment by walking down it. The lockers in this hall are elaborately decorated – some Jock boys have carpeted the insides of their lockers, and joke about installing stereos. They spend long periods of time sitting against the wall opposite their opened and impressively adorned lockers. At Belten, Jocks decorate the outsides of locker doors for important events: birthdays, performances, and games. For Valentine's day, girls anonymously decorate the lockers of the boys' starting varsity basketball team. The location of prominent people's lockers is important information and is frequently essential to the interpretation of the signs that appear on them, such as "Nice going, Joe!"

Locker sharing, virtually always among members of the same sex, is as close as Jocks can come to living together and as such is an important sign of friendship. People frequently affirm the importance of a friendship by pointing out that the friend is their "locker partner." In keeping with the Jock norm against limiting themselves to a "best friend," … many share a locker with as many as five people.

> And now it's like all three of us, and Laurie Smith is good friends with us too. We all share a locker. All four of us. It doesn't have a lock on it either.
>
> DO THEY USUALLY ASSIGN LOCKERS TO FOUR PEOPLE OR DO YOU JUST – THEY ASSIGN IT TO A COUPLE OF PEOPLE AND EVERYBODY ELSE MOVES IN?
>
> Two. Two people for each locker, and like we, "this isn't even anybody's locker, I don't think." We just kind of, "Oop, no one's in this locker."
>
> IS THAT REALLY IMPORTANT, WHO YOUR LOCKER PARTNER IS?
>
> It is, because I wouldn't see Alice during the day if we weren't locker partners. I wouldn't – I'd see Laurie a couple of times, but not, you know, I wouldn't see Alice at all. Because we don't have any classes or even lunch or anything.

This girl's pride at not having a lock on the locker is reminiscent of pride at living in a "good neighborhood," and contrasts with the Burnouts' claim that stuff gets stolen from lockers.

The first week of school brings almost a total reshuffling of lockers, as people move into lockers with their friends and as rows of lockers are taken over by networks. By virtue of this reshuffling, the Jocks in each grade occupy a specific area of lockers in their hall. The locker houses not only school paraphernalia, but personal effects. The insides of lockers are frequently decorated with signs and pictures.

Burnouts do not keep much in their lockers, rarely visit them, and never "fool around" at them. Because they go into the courtyard between classes, Burnouts do not have time to go to their lockers, and scorn those who do. But they also claim that lockers are unsafe, that the locks never work, and that things get stolen from them. This claim, along with their claim that cafeteria food is bad for you, amounts to a denial of the adequacy of the school's parental ability, further justifying their rejection of the school's claim to a parental role. Adding to the Burnouts' hostility toward lockers is the school's reservation of the right to examine lockers for drugs – a right that Burnouts argue against strongly, claiming that lockers should be private space and inviolable. Since the lockers are not to be treated as adult living space but as the living space of a child subject to parental supervision, the Burnouts will not use them.

Looking and Acting Different

Smoking

Drugs and alcohol have come and gone as symbols of rebellion for adolescents, but the one classic and enduring magical substance is tobacco. While the Burnouts may be named for drug use, their key symbol is – as it was for the hoods of the 1950s and the greasers of the 1960s – the cigarette. Cigarette smoking is the pivotal issue in the beginning of seventh grade and remains the key symbol (Ortner, 1973) of the Burnout category throughout high school, even after more potent symbols of rebellion, such as drugs, became part of the opposition. The Burnouts are most frequently described as "the people who smoke," and Jocks continue to shun cigarettes, even after a number of them begin to smoke pot covertly. The cigarette's symbolic value within the ado-

lescent culture undoubtedly arises from its condensation of referents and its portable, displayable, consumable, and quasi-illicit properties. The cigarette is most commonly interpreted as a symbol of adulthood, but is also associated with rebellion, machismo, sophistication or "coolness," independence, and vice. Burnouts display cigarette packages rolled in T-shirt sleeves or protruding from shirt pockets or purses, and requests for cigarettes or elaborate craving gestures are common forms of greeting. In keeping with the Burnouts' norms of sharing, … cigarette sharing with an extended network serves to solidify social relations. Cigarettes are the ideal commodity for such a system of exchange, since they are relatively inexpensive and carry additional value in themselves as a symbol of Burnout identity. Several Burnouts report having used cigarette exchange as a way of making friends when they first arrived at Belten.

HOW DID YOU MEET?

She comes up to me, "Got a smoke?" I go, "Yeah." And then, then the other day, "You got a smoke?" And then, and one day, a couple days later, I go, "Hey, you," because I didn't have no smokes, I go, "You, you owe me a couple smokes." She goes, she goes, "Oh, really?" Then I don't know, I don't know how I got to know her.

I usually, when I come into a new school, I've learned to make friends real quick because I've moved so many times, so I just walk up to someone, you know, "You want a cigarette?" "Yeah," and start talking, and "yeah, check out that girl over there," or something, you know, just get something going.

The symbolic status of smoking for the Burnouts is reflected in and matched by the Jocks' vocal and passionate opposition to smoking. Jocks overwhelmingly do not smoke: Of 49 Jocks asked, only 2 reported being smokers, and neither smokes at or near the school or at school functions; of 38 Burnouts, 35 reported being smokers. Of 20 In-betweens, 9 reported being smokers. Opposition to smoking is an important Jock norm, and Jocks join the school in its campaign against smoking. One of the prestigious extracurricular activities at Belten is the "Smoking Committee," a group that gives anti-smoking presentations in elementary schools around the area. The status of this committee and other anti-smoking activities as part of the institutional structure of the school brings the Jock alliance with the school squarely into the Jock–Burnout opposition (Eckert, 1983). The Jocks and the school, together, condemn and oppose the Burnouts in this "unhealthy," "smelly," and "self-destructive" behavior. One girl's account of how one of her teachers helped shepherd her back into the fold illustrates the symbolic value of smoking.

In junior high I was really bored with like, you probably experienced this too, it just, you just get really bored with the whole situation … and, um, and like the Burnouts always seemed like they were, they had so much fun, you know, they were always the neat people to be with, so I started getting mixed up with them a little bit. And so, um, I got my first D that I ever got in math. And my math teacher always like teased me in front of the class, you know. And like we'd draw like, um, geometric figures, and one time there was one like this, I'll never forget, like a, a cigarette box with a, a cigarette sticking out, and he said, "Denise, what does that look like to you?", you know. And then this one guy said, "A pack of cigarettes," and like they'd always, like, because they were all like really straight kids in AP math. And so I think that helped me a lot, though, to have all of that, because it, it made me, I don't know, it just kind of made me realize what was going on.

Clothing

The stranger to the high school notices a variety of clothing, but just as the geography of the school becomes meaningful only when one begins to see how various people use the building, the clothing styles take on meaning as one begins to notice that certain patterns of clothing appear in certain parts of the school, and eventually as one comes to know the social significance of these patterns. Clothing is a particularly powerful social maker because it is regularly renewed and never separated from the individual in public situations. Just about every component of external clothing has indexical or symbolic value in the category system.

Throughout society, clothing style signals economic means, access to information, and specific group identity. Economic means are reflected both in a rapid turnover of clothing – exhibited through wardrobe size and swift style changes – and in the quality and expense of individual items. Within any social group, the specific items and combinations of items one chooses reflect group consensus. These subtler differences, which can be achieved only through private information, are the ultimate indication of group membership. The relative paucity of an outsider's or a marginal individual's information may prevent that individual from even knowing that he or she is not completely "in style" with the target group. Each group's style is thus a function of specific identity, information (including both verbal information and exposure), economic means, practical needs, and an ideology based on all of these. As a social marker of group membership, clothing style is closely associated with the social and cultural characteristics of groups and can elicit powerful emotional reactions. Style is not interpreted simply as an indication of social affiliation but as a direct and intentional expression of group values, a marker of group boundaries, and thus a rejection of alternative values. Failure to conform to group style, therefore, is taken to signal lack of solidarity.

The significance of clothing is not equal for men and women. In American society, women are expected to pay more attention than men to clothing style. Women's style encompasses a wider range than men's, and even includes much of men's style. In general, women wear more accessories than men, and their clothes include a wider range of colors and of cuts. The difference between women's informal and formal wear is greater, and women's adornment extends beyond clothing and accessories to cosmetics and labor-intensive hair styles. Differences in adornment serve as simple gender markers, but women's greater stylistic elaboration is also an indication of their greater reliance on symbolic means of signalling social status in a society that denies them equal access to social mobility through action. Adolescent girls have to work harder to achieve social status and are far more constrained by physical attractiveness than boys. In addition, girls are more constrained by social distinctions than are boys and must take greater care to signal the appropriate identity through the full range of symbolic means. Just as boys are freer than girls to cross category boundaries, they are less bound by category-specific clothing styles.

Jock and Burnout clothing is clearly differentiated on the basis of cost. Jocks, particularly girls, strive for a good number of outfits and consciously avoid wearing the same thing too closely in succession. Expense of clothing is apparent in the quality of cut, fit, and fabric, and in the more obvious designer labels. Most Belten Jock girls shop, frequently in pairs or groups, in the mid- to somewhat higher-priced stores in major shopping malls in the Detroit suburban area. Burnouts, much of whose solidarity is based on relative lack of economic means, pride themselves on not being concerned with clothing as a status symbol and maintain somewhat more limited and inexpensive wardrobes. Even those Burnouts who can afford to dress on a Jock scale tend not to, as an expression of solidarity with those who cannot. Lack of means is in itself a positive value, and Burnouts criticize Jocks for what they see as unnecessarily expensive and competitive dressing. The Burnout taboo on competitive dressing reflects not only solidarity in lack of means, but the more general disapproval of social competition. ...

Many Jocks' enhanced economic status is indeed reflected in their ability to follow the fashions and in their emphasis on "designer" clothing, particularly Calvin Klein jeans and Izod shirts. The economic aspects of Jock clothing, like the social value of economics in general, are not absolute but geared to the dominant means of the main Jock group. While in some wealthier schools around the Detroit area, Jocks wear entire Izod outfits, it is frowned upon in Belten to wear more than one Izod item at a time or even to own more than one or two. The preppy look, therefore, is not adopted with abandon at Belten. The stigmatization of "preppy Jocks" as conspicuously wealthy extends to the entire preppy look, as reflected in one Jock boy's strong reaction to one group of girls' habit of wearing their collars up.

> Like some of the people are wealthy, you know, and I hate Preppies, I mean, I hate people who wear their collar up and stuff, like, you know, that's totally stupid, I mean, if so many people do it, I guess it's

not stupid, but it looks dumb, I don't know why they do it. And there's one girl ... she'll ah, wear her collar up, and whenever you say anything, or happen to mention "Preppy," she'll make sure it's up – you know, make sure it's really good and up there.

Burnout fashion includes some elements that spread from working class urban areas and some outmoded elements of Jock style. In the early 1980s, Burnouts were wearing the bell-bottomed jeans popular among Jocks five years before, and Burnouts boys' long hair styles are another throwback to that era. In 1986, Burnout girls were wearing the straight-legged jeans and feathered hair style fashionable among Jocks in the early 1980s, while Jocks had moved on to short, pegged jeans and permed hair styles. The chronological relation between certain Jock and Burnout styles is not an indication that fashions simply pass from Jocks to Burnouts, for Burnouts' current jeans and hair styles correspond also to current young adult working class fashion and to the fashions currently worn by certain hard rock and country music stars. Just as Jocks follow mainstream adult influence in clothing, Burnouts follow the fashions of working class adults and the entertainers that appeal to them. Certain elements of style never adopted by Jocks reflect "country" influence, such as the buckskin "squaw boots" popular among Burnouts in the early 1980s and still popular today.

Bell-bottoms were a particularly strong Burnout index in the early 1980s and, of all the Burnout indices, the greatest object of disparagement among Jocks. Bell-bottoms are the most salient, and the first mentioned, item of Burnout fashion at Belten. This is reflected in one In-between's characterization of the lower socioeconomic school in Neartown as a place where "they wear bell-bottoms 10 feet wide." This reference to the specific width of the bell-bottoms reflects the significance of the width continuum. Jeans in the early 1980s ranged all the way from the wide bells of the early 1970s through the slightly more conservative flares, to the mainstream straight legs, and finally to the new and very fashionable pegged baggies. Among the latter two cuts, the prestige hierarchy of designer names had become an additional element of style. Even ignoring brand name, the casual observer could notice before long that jean leg width and school territory were closely related, particularly in the distribution of jeans in after-lunch territories in Belten (see Eckert, 1982). The geographic continuum from the lobby directly in front of the cafeteria (Jock territory), down the gym hall, and into the courtyard (Burnout territory) corresponds to a striking continuum in jean leg width. As one moved from the Jock to the Burnout territory, the average jean width gradually increased.

This distribution reflects not simply an opposition between bells and straight legs, but a width continuum corresponding to the social continuum. Just as the school population boasts a mass of In-betweens in addition to Jocks and Burnouts, the cut of jeans presents in-between alternatives. Not only are there more bells in the courtyard and more straight legs in the cafeteria lobby, but there are more flares in the transitional area. This continuum is repeated in the styles worn by students who spend time together. Quantitative observations of casual groups of students showed that people walking together commonly wear the same cut of jeans. However, pairs and groups also show combinations within a limited range of the jeans continuum: bells with flares, flares with straight legs, straight legs with baggies. Virtually no groups or pairs reflect jumps in the continuum.

While Jocks wear polo shirts, button-down shirts, and crew-neck sweaters, Burnouts overwhelmingly wear rock concert T-shirts. These T-shirts have the double symbolic value of displaying lack of means and of advertising the Burnout taste for hard rock. Burnouts girls wearing sweaters do not sport the "preppy" look of woolen crew necks, but opt for patterned sweaters frequently made of synthetic materials.

The most richly symbolic element of Burnout upper body wear is the jacket. The Burnouts signal their peripheral relation to the school – the fact that they are "just passing through" – by wearing their jackets all day in school. They say that they wear their jackets because they go into the courtyard between classes, because their lockers are not safe to keep anything in, and because it facilitates skipping out on the spur of the moment. The jacket worn in school very closely signals all of these elements of Burnout culture.

Certain elements of Burnout clothing also symbolize urban identification. Some Burnout boys signal their affiliation with Detroit by wearing black jackets with DETROIT written in white on the back. This urban style stands in clear opposition to the frequent Jock letter jacket, which indicates local and school orientation and participation in sports. In the early 1980s, most Burnout boys wore lined jeans jackets, which gradually gave way to the current urban fashion of hooded sweatshirts under unlined jeans jackets. Familiarity with and competence in the tougher and more crime-ridden urban environment is also symbolized by two elements of male style – metal studs, particularly on leather jackets and wrist bands, and chains attaching the wearer's wallet to his belt loop.

Sports

Sports present a complex picture in the Jock–Burnout opposition. Many Burnouts are good athletes and pride themselves on their physical abilities. Their resentment that the Jocks' involvement in school sports implies athletic superiority, and the fact that some good Burnout players defected from school teams, gives rise to considerable competition wherever Jocks and Burnouts come into contact in an athletic context. As one Burnout said:

God, in gym, man, it's Jocks against the Burnouts whatever you're doing, man. That's where, you know, it gets let out a little bit.

During junior high, there was at least one Jock–Burnout game, but, as one Jock describes below, the school tried to discourage such competition:

Like when we were in Rover we used to have a Jock–Burn football game, Jock–Burn baseball game and stuff, you know. … Like they'd come up and ask one of our – you know, one of the guys from the football team, "Hey, you want to have a game?" You know, "You guys think you're so great." They're just, not really mean, they're just, you know, goofing around. Just, you know, for something to do. So, I don't know, it's just anybody, just some – they get an idea or we get an idea and we. … Except our coach found out and he goes, "Yeah, I'm gonna be driving down, driving by [the park] today, and if I see any of you guys out there, uh, don't be – don't be coming back to practice" or something.

WHY?

I don't know, it's just, he didn't want no one getting hurt and stuff, you know how that goes, and he just thought it was a dumb thing to do to have a – he just thought it was dumb having a distinction too, you know. But if some of the Burnouts, or whatever, would have just played football, we could have been a lot better, so he was kind of mad because they'd – they'd stay away just because, you know, kind of peer pressure.

While Burnouts were on school teams, particularly football, in junior high, their numbers fell off as they reached high school. Several factors contributed to this disaffection. Since the Jocks' corporate mentality leads them to form social networks around school activities, school sports enhance their social lives. The Burnouts, on the other hand, for whom social networks are primary, found that the time taken up by afternoon practices threatened the solidarity of their peer groups and excluded them from group activities. Coaches' disciplinary actions were another factor: Burnouts who missed practices or were caught using forbidden substances were suspended and dropped from teams. In keeping with their hostility toward the school's parental presumptions, Burnouts came to consider school athletics as a threat to their personal autonomy. One Burnout explained that the coaches' attention to substance use contradicted meritocratic selection – that a coach should be concerned simply with the individual's athletic performance regardless of his or her life-style. Eventually, Burnouts began to feel that they were being discriminated against, in team selections and in interactions with their teammates, on the basis of their category affiliation. As a result of all these factors, most Burnouts confine their athletic activities to city and commercial teams and to informal games.

Co-ed pickup games in neighborhood parks are a common Burnout activity in good weather. These games are as much social activities as athletic events, and all levels of skill are accepted. Particularly significant in these games are the cigarette breaks. On several occasions in games in which I participated, play was interrupted while a "runner" ran onto the field to pass a cigarette around to players stranded on base – a clear affirmation of Burnout solidarity in an activity that might otherwise be identified as "Jock."

Language

Perhaps the strongest evidence of the depth of the difference between Jocks and Burnouts lies in their use of language. There are the obvious, conscious differences – the Burnouts' more frequent and public use of obscenities and of specialized vocabulary such as drug-related slang. On a somewhat less conscious level, there are differences in routine expressions such as greetings. While Jocks tend to use the common short greeting "hi" when they come across a casual acquaintance, Burnouts overwhelmingly use the longer "how 'ya doin'." These particular greeting differences are repeated in the larger society between middle class and working class speakers. While such differences are not consciously maintained, they are recognized when pointed out to speakers.

Grammar is a conscious marker of Jock and Burnout affiliation – both in recognition and in use. The Burnouts are overwhelmingly seen as speaking "ungrammatically," that is, as using nonstandard grammar. Standard grammar is the grammar used by the powerful society's mainstream and embraced by its institutions, including the school. Its forms are not necessarily more conservative historically, nor is it any more systematic, logical, or beautiful. The use of standard grammar simply signals one's membership in and identification with the national mainstream. At times the use of nonstandard grammar may reflect sufficient isolation from the mainstream to prevent significant exposure to standard language, but its more important mechanism is its social symbolic value in the local non-mainstream community. And as with any symbolic material, the use of nonstandard grammar can reflect rejection of mainstream society and identification with the local non-mainstream community.

The multiple negative (such as *I don't know nothing*) is among the most commonly cited features of nonstandard grammar. (Multiple negation has been absurdly associated with a variety of cognitive shortcomings, with which it was never connected in the sixteenth century, when it was standard in English.) All the students in Belten High have access to standard negation; all of them use it at least some of the time, but many of them also use multiple negation. The Burnouts use far more multiple negatives than Jocks. The Burnouts used multiple negation in their tape-recorded speech with a probability of .720, while the Jocks used it with a probability of .280 (sig. = .006). None of the speakers in either category used multiple negatives all the time. The variable use of multiple negation may mean that the speaker uses standard negatives when he or she is speaking carefully but multiple negation is more natural. It may also mean the opposite: that standard negation is more natural but the speaker intentionally uses multiple negation on occasion. Finally, it may mean that the speaker's usage depends on the situation and the kind of impression he or she is trying to make or the connotations he or she wants to give to the utterance. No doubt all of these apply within the community of speakers at Belten. There is certainly no question that much of the Burnouts' use of multiple negation, and the Jocks' use of standard negation, is symbolic of category affiliation and of the relation to schooling associated with that affiliation.

While vocabulary, greetings, and grammatical patterns function on a relatively conscious level, there are also patterns of pronunciation that differ between Jocks and Burnouts. Some of these are used almost entirely unconsciously. One such pattern is in the pronunciation of several vowels that are in the progress of undergoing historical change in the Detroit area, almost entirely without the awareness of the speakers who are actually implementing the change. For example, there is a tendency in the Detroit area for speakers to back the vowel that occurs in *lunch* so that is sounds more like the vowel in *launch* (there are many such pairs – punch/paunch, but/bought, cut/caught). This change is spreading outward from the urban area, and in Neartown as in other suburbs around the Detroit area the Burnouts lead significantly in this change. In a sample that includes only people who grew up in Neartown, not recent arrivals from Detroit, the Burnouts back this vowel with significantly greater frequency than the Jocks. (This change is discussed in detail in Eckert, 1988.)

Together, these kinds of linguistic features differentiate the Jocks and the Burnouts and serve as powerful symbols of category membership. They are not simply class markers picked up in the neighborhood or the home. It is well known that children acquire their dialects from their peers rather than their parents, and that dialects tend to settle in the preadolescent years – in fact, at the very time that the Jock and Burnout categories are forming. The clearest indication that these linguistic features are acquired as a function of category affiliation, though, is the fact that while they correlate statistically with category affiliation, they do not correlate with parents' socioeconomic class. That is, there is sufficient class crossover in the categories … so that the effects of home can be separated from the effects of peer affiliation.

The Growth of Symbolic Oppositions

In seventh grade, the Burnouts aggressively display their counter-school values through the adoption of distinct public behavior with clear symbolic value related to claims on adult status and to orientation to the school. Smoking, drinking, occupation of the illicit smoking area adjacent to the school, and gathering outside of dances and roller skating rinks to smoke and drink are unambiguous in their meaning. The Jocks' development of strong and vocal norms against all of these activities, and their central participation in school social activities (as opposed to hanging out at the periphery), comes to signal opposition to the Burnouts' behavior. This symbolic behavior is supplemented as increasing domains of everyday life are incorporated into the set of oppositions. The clear association of any piece of behavior with one category will lead to the adoption of opposing behavior by the other. As more domains and details of behavior are incorporated as category symbols, the oppositions become mutually reinforcing, developing a structured symbolic system with its own impetus. Clothing, territory, substance use, language, demeanor, academic behavior, and activities all ultimately serve as conscious markers of category affiliation. In each of these areas, the behavior of one category is carefully opposed to that of the other, and one can see clearly that the two sets of behavior have grown in relation to each other. This ever-enlarging set of oppositions strengthens the hegemony of the category system in adolescent life and increasingly restricts individual perceptions and choice.

The elaboration of the system of oppositions exerts increasing constraints on individual behavior, narrowing individuals' personal options and view of the world. Since the two categories develop in mutual opposition, behavioral choices are typically binary, offering alternatives that are seen as opposites and excluding other choices altogether from the range of accepted behavior. As rock concert T-shirts and polo shirts become associated with Burnouts and Jocks, respectively, the choice of a third alternative, such as a frilly blouse, becomes anomalous and is taken to indicate that the individual wearing it does not know the adolescent clothing system. The limitation to the binary choices associated with the category system is reinforced by the adolescent need to deny parental domination of personal behavior, particularly behavior, such as clothing choice, that does not have a clear "good" or "bad" association in the real world. This denial must take the form of participation in the system of socially meaningful choices offered within the adolescent community.

The oppositional system also focuses attention on those areas of behavior that it has made salient, making attention to other areas anomalous. Lunch, for instance, is either bought in the cafeteria or brought in an inconspicuous paper bag. An individual who chose to bring lunch to school in a conspicuous and carefully chosen container would be viewed as paying attention to the wrong things and thus as not knowing what is important in adolescent society. It would also suggest that the individual is participating in some system outside the local adolescent community. In the case of the lunch container there might also be a childish connotation carried over from elementary school lunch boxes, while an individual who carried a newspaper in school would be viewed as trying to look excessively adult. The system of oppositions is further strengthened by the links established among the binary choices, encouraging an association among otherwise independent areas of behavior. The value of smoking and rock concert T-shirts as Burnout symbols links them in an implicational relationship, so that the individual who wears rock concert T-shirts will be assumed also to smoke. This is also apt to be true, because those in need of a clear social identity are likely to make the entire range of choices consonant with one or the other category.

Thus, in the development of the system of oppositions, individual traits lose their independence and form a network of associations, resulting in an increasingly powerful system. As the system of oppositions develops, each pole becomes increasingly specified and constrained. The consequences can be far-reaching, because the oppositions dominate not only temporary behavior, such as clothing, but choices with lasting implications, such as curriculum choice, academic effort, and substance use.

The Jock and Burnout categories represent the two extremes in relation to adults, and the oppositions associated with each term of the Jock–Burnout split represent choices that adolescents and preadolescents see themselves confronted with in the process of disengagement from the family. Ambivalence over disengagement leads to confusion over a variety of decisions, particularly those that involve the assumption of adult roles and rebellion against parents. These decisions are played out in the continual exercising of oppositions, which set up the social world in terms of binary choices and simplify the appearance of the choices to be made. At the same time, the category system provides group support for these choices: The decision to smoke is no longer an individual transgression, but is condoned and supported not only by individuals in one's group but by the existence of a social category characterized by these choices. The institutionalization of the opposition provides social sanction for either choice. Thus the decision not to smoke, if it appears to be simply obedience to one's parents, is at least as threatening to one's image as the decision to smoke. Status within a category characterized by non-smoking allows the individual to feel independent from the family while choosing parentally approved behavior.

The simplification of choice within the category system leads to oversimplification of values, and the overwhelming judgments of "good" and "bad" associated with the categories prevent individuals from recognizing the independence of many of the decisions they are faced with. The close association of traits within either category is powerful enough to force individual decisions, not on the merits of the issues at hand, but as a simple requirement and expression of category affiliation and participation in adolescent society. Thus a Burnout will find it difficult to avoid smoking or to participate in a school activity, while a Jock will feel pressured to invest in a wardrobe and to participate in activities that he or she may find uninteresting.

Obviously not everyone in Belten High School describes himself or herself as a Jock or a Burnout. In fact, only about 30 percent or 40 percent of them do. But this does not make these categories any less powerful in the social structure of the school. The fundamental status of these categories is underscored by the fact that almost all those who are not professed Jocks or Burnouts describe themselves and are described as "In-betweens."

> When people go into classifying, you know, you got the Jocks and the Jells, and then there's the In-betweeners, or whoever you want to say, you know.

The status of In-between is a by-product of the oppositional system, dominated by the same binary choices that constitute the opposition between Jocks and Burnouts. Most of the In-betweens do not choose alternative behavior, but simply mix Jock and Burnout choices. People who choose alternatives are generally referred to as "weirdos" or "nerds." The In-betweens describe themselves in terms of which choices they share with either category, and sometimes as occupying a place in a continuum between the poles, defined by the number of traits chosen from either pole. As the cohort matures, the population of the school increasingly constitutes such a continuum, but retains a significant cluster of people near each pole. There is continuous feedback of the separation and hostility between the categories and the symbolic oppositions that develop in association with them. This feedback increasingly isolates the members of each category, so that by the time the cohort reaches eleventh grade, they know relatively little about each other. As one Burnout said in his junior year:

> I don't know the Jocks any more. I don't have anything to do with them. It's hard to remember their names.

References

Eckert, P. (1982). "Clothing and Geography in a Suburban High School." In C. P. Kottak (ed.), *Researching American Culture* (pp. 139–44). Ann Arbor: University of Michigan Press.

Eckert, P. (1983). "Beyond the Statistics of Adolescent Smoking." *American Journal of Public Health*, 73, 439–41.

Eckert, P. (1988). "Sound Change and Adolescent Social Structure." *Language in Society*, 17, 183–207.

Ortner, S. B. (1973). "On Key Symbols." *American Anthropologist*, 75, 1338–46.

Willis, P. (1977). *Learning to Labour*. Westmead, Farnborough, Hants, England: Saxon House.

R E A D I N G

Kinship Systems
A. M. Hocart

When we explore a new language, we infer the meaning of words from the objects to which they are applied. The first object gives us a preliminary definition. That may chance to be right, but further experience may compel us to revise it. Thus I may first hear the word "table" used of a list of facts in a book, and so translate it "page." By degrees I shall learn better.

This caution is generally borne in mind by students of literary languages, but it is too often lost sight of in the study of non-literary languages. A great many investigators never get beyond the first use of the word that happens to come their way. Miss Lucy Mair has produced a striking example in the *Bulletin of the School of Oriental Studies*, vii, 918. An investigator heard the Uganda word *obuko* applied to palsy. He entered it in his dictionary as "palsy." It really refers to marriage rules, to a breach of which palsy is the consequence.

One of the most flagrant cases is the translation of the so-called classificatory kinship terms. The person most commonly called *tama* in Melanesia, the one most in evidence, is a man's father. He is the man who will be named if you asked, "Who is your *tama*?" So *tama* has been duly set down as "father." The same has been done with other kinship terms in Melanesia and elsewhere. It was soon noticed, however, that other men besides the father are called *tama*. By all rules the first translation should have been dropped, and a new one found to cover all the different *tamas*, and thus express the essence of *tama*-ship. Unfortunately, no single word can do so, and it has remained in the literature of the South Seas as "father," with the proviso that it is "extended" to cover father's brother, father's father's brothers' sons, and so on. Ever since we have been racking our brains to explain how Melanesians can call their uncles, and even remote cousins, "fathers."

The effect on theory has been disastrous. The order in which we have learned the uses of *tama* and similar words has been confused with the order of development in actual history. Because we first took it to mean father we slip unwittingly into the assumption that it meant father originally.

This fallacy has now received official expression in the term "kinship extensions." That expression implies that the meaning father is primary and that all other uses result from extending the term to an ever-widening circle of kinsmen.

It is curious that this doctrine, which is historical since it describes a process of development in the past, is championed most stoutly by those who are forever gibing at origins, evolution, historical reconstruction. This is a historical reconstruction, or what is?

The only way of proving that a process has taken place in the past is by recognized historical methods: either produce documents or resort to the comparative method. It is perhaps fortunate in this case that we have little documentary evidence and so must rely on the much more reliable comparative method.

Before we can apply it we must get our facts right. To that end let us forget all we have ever been told about the meaning of classificatory terms and rediscover the language, taking Fijian as an example. Evidently *tama* cannot mean father since it includes cousins to the *nth* degree, even cousins too young to have children; in fact,

a man is born a *tama*. We notice, however, that all those cousins have one thing in common: they are once removed; in other words, they are of the generation next to Ego, and, to be more precise, to the one immediately before. Not all the members of this generation, however, are *tama*. There are two sides to that generation, the father's and the mother's; only those on the father's side are *tama*. That is evidently the meaning of *tama*, so our final definition will run:

> *tama* = all males of the previous generation on the father's side.

Repeating the process we go on.

> *vungo* = all males of the generation immediately above and below Ego on the mother's side;
>
> *tavale* = all males of the same generation on the mother's side.

And so on. When our list is complete we find that all the terms fall into two sets, one set belonging to the father's side, the other to the mother's. Each term refers to a particular generation within one side. In short, these terms do not express consanguinity, as we have unfortunately been accustomed by Morgan to believe, but they fix the place of any relative according to generation and side. If I call a man *tuaka* it is clear that he is of my generation on my father's side, and senior to me; a *wati* is a woman of my generation on the side from which my mother comes.

This last term affords an excellent illustration how a particular use is mistaken for the true one, and the true one comes to be looked upon as an improper one. A Fijian introduces his wife as *wati*, so the word is noted as "wife." When it is found there are hundreds of *watis* who are not his wives, the first translation is not abandoned, but all other uses are explained as extensions: these women, it is explained, are called wives because he might marry any of them if the family so decided; they are wives by anticipation, "potential wives." Upon this muddled lexicography has been built up a whole edifice of primitive promiscuity.

Exactly the same usage exists in Arabic. Arabic-speaking husbands can often be heard addressing their wives as *bint 'amm*; but they also call their paternal uncles' daughters *bint 'amm*. We do not translate "wife," "potential wife," because we know that *bint* is daughter, and *'amm* is paternal uncle; therefore *bint 'amm* means "cousin on the father's side." When a man marries his cousin, as it is best to do, he goes on calling her "cousin" as he has been accustomed to since childhood. The Fijian and the Ashanti do exactly the same.

We can remember the time when an English youth would refer jocosely to his father as "The Governor." No one has ever suggested that this was primary and that the word has been extended to colonial administrators.

All our difficulties spring from a preconceived idea that kinship terms everywhere try to express the same thing as they do in Aryan and Semitic languages, and that in those languages they show the place on the family tree. The result is that in a certain African language the term *nana* is rendered father's father, father's father's brother, and so on through thirty-four European relationships, and then it does not exhaust all the possibilities. And what is the outcome of all this painstaking? We have a list of cases, but we have not got the meaning. It is as if a dictionary under "hot" told us "the sun is hot, pepper is hot, *A*'s temper is hot, the discussion is hot," and left it at that. If we go to the trouble of extracting the meaning of *nana* from the cases we find it simply means "any relative two generations above or below."

At this point we may be asked what evidence have we that the people themselves understand kinship terms in this sense. The same evidence as we have for the meaning of any word, what is common to the cases in which it is used.

As regards the Chinese system we have more, we have the definite statement of a Chinaman. Mr H. Y. Feng produces documentary evidence that the Chinese system was once a cross-cousin system, and so it is akin to the Fijian. As in cross-cousin systems the kinsfolk are still divided into two: those of the same patronymic, and those of another. These sides he chooses to call "sibs." Besides this vertical division, there is a horizontal one into generations. "These two factors, sib and generation," he sums up, "not only pervade the whole system but regulate marriage." A man marries a woman of another patronym of the first generation.[1]

The hill tribes of Viti Levu, Fiji, indicate very clearly what their kinship terms mean to them. Every hillsman assumes all other hillsmen to be his kinsmen. He is not concerned how near or how far related a stranger may be; he does not search the pedigrees to find out how they are related. All he wants to know is their respective generations. That is easy, because the whole population is divided into two alternate generations called *tako* and *lavo*. If both are *tako* or both *lavo* they are of the same generation, and then the senior is *tuka*, the junior *tadhi*, terms which have unfortunately been translated (by myself among others), as elder and younger brother. Evidently they mean nothing of the kind, since a man's grandfather is his *tuka* as well as his elder brother. The words simply mean "of the same one of the two generations, on the same side, senior," or "junior," as the case may be. If one man is *tako*, the other *lavo*, then they are related as *tama* and *luve* – that is as one generation to the other. In the case of relatives who are known, and whose side is therefore known, two sets of terms exist, just as in all cross-cousin systems. The line and the generation is what the Fijian looks for in his kinship system, not propinquity.

Why should he be so interested in the generation and so little in the nearness of kin? Because nearness is of little importance in public affairs; generation and line are all important. If a chief, chieftain, or priest dies it is not the next of kin that succeeds, as with us, but the next senior of his generation, no matter how distant; if the deceased was the last of his generation, then it goes to the most senior of the next. A Lauan expresses the rule thus: "X was not made chief, because his *tama* was living." We are not rendering the meaning at all by translating *tama* "father," because X's father was dead. What is meant is that X could not succeed because there was still a member of the previous generation on his father's side to come before him.[2]

We now understand why members of the same generation and side are so carefully distinguished as senior and junior (commonly rendered "elder brother and younger brother, classificatory"). The order of seniority is all important. With us only one of a group of brothers has to have his status made clear in royal and titled families; so among such families he bears a special title "heir" which singles him out; the rest are lumped together as brothers, for their seniority is normally of little importance, since they drop out of the succession. It is only when the holder has no issue that the seniority of his younger brothers need be remembered.

It is not the whole of a generation that succeeds, but only those in the male line. Therefore the female line has to be distinguished from the male by special terms. Since the female line is completely excluded, seniority does not come into consideration at all in their case, so no distinction is made between senior and junior.

Generation, line, and seniority decide not only succession, but everyday behavior. The duties in the ritual are fixed in the same way.[3]

In short, what we seek most is the next of kin, and so we run up and down the family tree. The Fijians (and the Australian aborigines, and the rest) do not, because there is no point in doing so. All they want is such information as will enable them to place each man on the correct side in the right generation. An inquiry proceeds thus: "How are you related?" "Of the same side and generation." "Why?" "Because our fathers were of the same side and generation." Or else: "We belong to successive generations on opposite sides, because he is of my mother's side and generation."

If the users of classificatory systems can get on without pedigrees, surely the field-worker can. He would be all the better for it in working out the system. He would cease to see the system thus:

Tama = tina		*Vungo*
Tuaka	*Ego = wati*	*Tavale*
Luve		*Vungo*

and learn to see them thus:

	Tama	*tina*	*Vungo*
Tuaka	*Ego*	*wati*	*Tavale*
	Luve	*Vungo*	

I do not mean that pedigrees are useless. There are many investigations that are impossible without them, but they have exercised a pernicious influence on the theory of classificatory systems.

Some systems are more complicated, some less, than the typical cross-cousin system from which our illustrations have been drawn, but the principle remains the same. It is all a matter of how many lines and how many generations are distinguished.

Since classificatory terms have no real equivalents in our language we must either use cumbrous circumlocutions or condensed symbols. We must choose between saying: "A boy is circumcised by a man one

generation up on the opposite side"; or else represent that man by something like this: I leave it to others to work out something on these other lines. It would be easy enough but for the Australian systems. Anyhow we cannot go on identifying these classificatory terms with our kinship terms which mean something quite different.

We are now in a position to examine more fruitfully the theory of kinship extension. In a paper of this dimension it is only possible to outline the evidence, and the more so as nothing has been done to deal systematically and comparatively with the problem, except in the case of Aryan languages. I can only sum up here the results of bringing up to date Delbruck's survey of Aryan kinship terms. The reader will find a detailed discussion in the *Ceylon Journal of Science*, sec. G, i, 179; ii, 33.[4]

The conclusion is that our own kinship terms appear to have once been used in a classificatory sense. The word father, for instance, meant originally not the procreator, but any man who conferred life on another, whether by sacramental intercourse with the mother or by some other ritual act, but not by the mere unconsecrated infusion of semen. It also applied to all the kinsmen of the father's side and generation, because they are ritually interchangeable with the father. At a very early date, before the splitting up of the parent Aryan tongue, this and other terms were narrowed down to their present use; but the original use still persists in connection with ritual, e.g. godfather, lay brother, etc. The present usage is thus a result of contraction, not of extension, and is based on modern physiology, not on a theory of sacraments.[5]

The Semitic evidence wants working out in detail, but a superficial examination provisionally points the same way.

Are we to believe that speakers of Aryan and Semitic started with a classificatory system and ended with a genealogical one, while the rest of the world reversed the process, extended terms which meant properly begetter, bearer, begetter's begetter, and so on, to cousins so distant that kinship is only presumed? It is hardly probable, but if anyone believes it happened so, let him produce some evidence.

He might point out that classificatory terms are constantly used like ours, that in Melanesia *tama* is often understood to mean the father and no one else. Is this the original use, as is constantly assumed by the "exten-sionists," or is it the beginning of contraction? Only definite cases can decide this question.

If a Fijian asks, "Have you a *wati*?" it is obvious he cannot mean, "Have you kinswomen of your generation on your mother's side?" because, where kinship is unbounded, no man is without such kinswomen. What is meant is "Do you own such woman?" – in short, "Are you married?" There is not a boy who has not got kins-women two generations before him, so the statement "he has a kinswoman two generations up" can only refer to one of them, the nearest. The meaning is: "He is a boy who has been much under the care of his grand-mother, and so known a good deal of old women's lore." This is an excellent example how the meaning of words is filled in by the rest of the sentence and by custom. Here custom narrows down the dictionary meaning not only to one person, but to one characteristic of that person. If a Frenchman talks of "ma femme" he refers to one woman only, not any woman connected with him, not his servant, or even his mistress, but the one with whom he has contracted a permanent alliance rec-ognized by the state, and possibly by the Church. No one has ever suggested this is the original meaning of the word, and that it has been extended to all women. It is not always necessary to have a possessive. If an Englishman says "The King," everyone understands he means the King of England. It does not follow that originally the title meant that king only, and has been extended to other kings.

In all these cases words designating whole classes of men are restricted by the singular, the definite article, or some other sign of definiteness to one person, the context and custom further define who that one person is. "My *tama*" is the *tama* of the family circle; "the Captain" is the commander of the speaker's company; "herself" is the speaker's wife. It is easy to see how, as the household emancipates itself from the clan or kindred, kinsmen outside the household drop more and more into the background, the direct line father-grand-father monopolizes the attention, and so the kinship terms. The father always stands out among the men of his generation; but he stands out more than ever when the household forms a closed body with its own house-hold cult. That cult now no longer descends from brother to brother, but from father to son, so that the

other members of the father's generation can no longer be regarded as being on the same footing as the father.

In the use of *tama* to mean "father," *wati* to mean "wife," we have the germ, not the survival of a genealogi-cal system.

A short review of the facts thus raises a presumption that the classificatory terms are not due to extension, but that our habit of denoting nearness of kin is the result of contraction.[6] Finally, to establish this presump-tion it would be necessary to show that it fits all the facts, not only of kinship, but of social organization generally. Among the most important facts are the ritual functions of kinsmen. The first task is to collect them all and to try and find the underlying principle why it is, for instance, that the men of the father's side and generation provide the regalia for initiation, while the men of the mother's generation and side carry out the operation. Until that has been done all discussions as to the ultimate meaning of classificatory systems, or indeed of kinship systems in general, must remain idle guesswork.

Note. – Miss Margaret Mead has made a very inten-sive study of these functions in the Admiralty Islands.[7] Only a comparative study, however, can explain.

I only know of one serious attempt to prove the extension theory, that is, if I have understood Prof. E. E. Evans-Pritchard aright. In his paper on "The Nature of Kinship Extensions"[8] he shows with admirable objectivity how the Azande child learns to extend the terms and the behavior from the immediate family circle to wider circles. Presumably these children are repeating the phylogenetic evolution. But our children begin by calling all adult men *dada*, and are taught to limit it to one man. There is obviously a flaw in an argument that leads to contradictory results. The flaw is that the conditions under which a child learns a lan-guage, or behavior, generally do not reproduce those under which evolution has taken place. As Vendryes says: "Children only teach us how an organized lan-guage is acquired; they do not give us an idea what language can have been at the beginning of its evolu-tion." Substitute "behavior" for "language," and the statement remains equally true. Biologists have for some time recognized the fact that the growth of the human body does not exactly reproduce the evolution of the race. The chief merit of Prof. Evans-Pritchard's paper is that it gives us the Azande point of view in their own words and actions, and does not romance about what is going on inside their minds.

Notes

1. "Teknonymy and the Chinese Kinship System," *Amer. Anthr.*, 1936, p. 60.
2. These remarks apply equally to the Aranda who have the same system of succession, according to Strehlow. It is also found in Ceylon where the classificatory system prevails (*Ceylon Journal of Science*, sec. G, i, 75; Geigler, *Culavansa*, i, 20ff.).
3. See my *Lau Islands*, pp. 35ff., and *The Progress of Man*, pp. 259ff.
4. R. S. Rattray made a move in the right direction by dividing up his kinship terms into generations; but he stopped half-way. *Ashanti*, pp. 24ff.
5. Supplemented by my *Progress of Man*, pp. 261ff.
6. From a manifesto by Infante Don Alfonso Carlos and King Alfonso's reply it appears that the Royal House of Spain can use "Uncle" and "Nephew" of second cousins once removed, as in classificatory systems.
7. "Kinship in the Admiralty Islands," *Anthr. Papers of the American Museum of Natural History*, vol. xxxiv, Pt. ii, 20ff.
8. *Man*, 1932, p. 7.

CHAPTER 6

Our Bodies, Our Selves

Are we our bodies or do we *have* bodies? Different concepts of the body, the gendered body, the physical body, the social body. Techniques and modifications of the body. Tattoos. Body parts and organ transplants. Traffic in body parts. Body image, advertisements, and eating disorders. Bodies before and after death.

Our Bodies, Our Selves

The title of this chapter is also the title of a book by the Boston Women's Health Collective. Appalled by the lack of information about their bodies available to women in the 1960s, this "consciousness-raising" group gathered the information, pooled their knowledge, and published it in 1973. That first edition was a thin booklet on newsprint; the 1992 edition had a commercial publisher and is heavy with 752 pages. It remains a highly acclaimed resource. Our bodies *are* ourselves.

Our bodies allow us to occupy space, experience the sensual world, and interact with others. We take them for granted as coextensive, coexistent with ourselves; indeed, they are so much a part of us that our bodies and selves seem inseparable. Yet the way we often think and speak of them implies something different. Each of us *has* or *is* a body – but there is a world of difference between the choice of verb. Do I *possess* my body? Or *am* I my body? Who is the *I* who *has* a body? How am *I* distinguished from *my* body? If I *have* a body, does that imply *I* am somehow separate from it? Alternatively, if I *am* my body, what does that imply about my mind, about my soul? Is my mind subsumed by my brain? Is the *mind–body problem*, as it is known, a problem confronted by people everywhere, or is it the result of a particular philosophical tradition? Is it the secularized form of Christian *body–soul* dualism? These are important issues dealt with primarily by philosophers and theologians. I forefront them here to alert you to the way notions of the body, and treatments of it, are embedded in wider cultural frames of meaning.

Anthropologists have always been interested in the ways that peoples around the world think about and treat their bodies – about the different features acknowledged, emphasized, or muted; about techniques and rituals of the body; about bodily adornment (see chapter 8); about sex and gendered bodies; about diseased and dead bodies; about the ways societies discipline and subject bodies; and about the symbolic uses of the word *body* in terms such

Investigating Culture: An Experiential Introduction to Anthropology, Second Edition.
Carol Delaney with Deborah Kaspin.
© 2011 Carol Delaney. Published by Blackwell Publishing Ltd.

as the *social body* or the *body politic*. Books have been written about each of these aspects of the body; in this chapter, I wish only to point out some of the terrain for your exploration. But before we begin, there is a major point, rarely made, that appears to undermine the entire enterprise – *there is no such thing as "the body."*

It is undeniable that each of us has or is a body, and share certain aspects of bodiliness such as flesh, blood, and bones as well as a susceptibility to illness, aging, and death. Although bodiliness is part of what it means to be human, to speak of it in general terms, even within a specific culture, is to miss a crucial point – that there is no such thing as "the body," because all societies make a distinction between bodies that are female and those that are male. "The body" is an abstraction – one made possible by a particular kind of language (see Whorf 1956; and, chapter 4, this volume). This kind of abstraction and nominalization is something that is not possible in all languages. This shorthand allows those of us who speak Indo-European languages to construct whole theories about abstractions like *the body*, *truth*, and *beauty*.

Because there is no such thing as "the body," male and female bodies have different meanings. One or the other may be more associated with the very notion of bodiliness. For example, in Western cultures the female body is more closely associated with bodiliness, as in the phrases *mother earth* and *earth mother*, despite the fact that all of us, male and female, are equally "embodied" and therefore equally susceptible to the ravages of corporal existence. Why that association? In the West we tend to think of bodies as natural entities, as part of animal nature, but it is women's bodies, in particular, that become associated with nature. This is so because reproduction is considered a natural phenomenon, and women are the ones primarily associated with reproduction (see Ortner 1974). But, as we saw in chapter 5, this was not always the case. Clearly, these associations are cultural, not natural.

Bodies surely have physical limits as well as potentialities that cannot be ignored, but they exist in complex matrices of meaning, desire, and power. Bodies are not, and cannot be, solely natural, self-evident entities, for there is no such thing as a "natural" body outside the grip of culture. Rather, as Susan Bordo reminds us, "We are creatures swaddled in culture from the moment we are designated one sex or the other, one race or another" (Bordo 1993: 36). Bodies are molded and shaped by culture – not only by what we eat, or how we sleep or walk, but also how we experience our bodies (with pride, disgust, confidence, or pain, and by images and cultural icons) – which includes the social control and discipline exerted on them.

Body Experience

Our sense of our body begins so early that we have no conscious memory of it; but whether we were welcomed into the world or unwanted and emotionally rejected, whether we were held often with love or left alone for long periods, and whether we were fed when we cried or cried because we were starving – these are the bedrock upon which both our bodies and our self-images are built. Then we are taught how to walk, how to eat, and how to comport ourselves – instructions infused with cultural images of appropriate behavior. We are praised, criticized, shamed, or blamed for our ability or inability to live up to the cultural prescriptions. So much of our early training has to do with control of our bodies and their functions. Why do people in some cultures insist on early toilet training, while others assume it will happen when the child is ready? Why do people in some cultures swaddle their babies, while others barely cover them? Why is it acceptable in one culture that the whole family sleep together and experience bodily warmth and skin contact, whereas in another culture, among the dominant group in the United States for example, such practice is thought to impede the development of independence and have deleterious effects on psychological and sexual health? Almost any bodily practice you can think of will have contrasting evidence from another culture – a clear indication that different societies have very different notions about bodies and bodiliness.

A child care guide, like the popular manual of Dr. Spock, is an excellent guide to beliefs about appropriate bodily practice and discipline held by a majority of people in the United States, even though it is couched in universalistic language. But what if Dr. Spock had been born in Bali? What advice would he have given then? These questions inspired Judy DeLoache and Alma Gottlieb to develop a book that would make alternative forms and norms of child rearing explicit and thus show there is no *natural* way to accomplish this task. By providing other examples of successful child rearing, they also highlighted the ways in which our own practices are deeply embedded in a particular cultural milieu. Since many cultures do not have a tradition of child care manuals written by experts, they asked anthropologists, historians, and psychologists to write guides from the point of view of the cultures they had studied – *as if* they were the local expert(s). The resulting book, *A World of Babies* (DeLoache and Gottlieb 2000), is a collection of such imagined but culturally accurate child care guides. In my own contribution, I took on the persona of the grand-daughter of the village midwife recording her views about child care for posterity – a role not so different from my anthropological one. Here are a couple of examples from my fieldwork. In the Turkish village where I worked (and in many others I visited), babies were tightly swaddled, even in summer. People told me they do this to make a baby feel more secure and to protect him or her from drafts, which are thought to bring illness. They were aghast when I told them that in hot weather, Americans often dress their babies only in a shirt and diaper and that their little legs and arms are left free. Americans (and their doctors) believe that babies must crawl in order to lay down pathways in the brain that affect eye–hand coordination. I never saw a baby crawl in the Turkish village, but they seemed to have no difficulty with such coordination.

In Europe and the United States, child care guidebooks are common, yet many cultural values of bodies and norms of bodily behavior are conveyed implicitly by nonverbal means. We are instructed by words as well as actions how to experience our bodies; our bodily experience is also conditioned by images of bodies that are held up as ideal in a society.

Body Image

Images of bodies come from many sources – parents and other caretakers, siblings, relatives, and friends, and later from peer groups, the media, cultural icons, and heroes. In the past, images of culturally valued bodies might simply have been pointed out among the group of people, or in sculptures or paintings, but the invention of photography and other visual media has released a flood of images. Today, in modern industrialized nations, it is primarily from these media that people derive their images of ideal bodies and attempt to conform to them. While these images affect both men and women, they affect them differentially. I will discuss women first because women, much more than men, have been valued *for* their bodies – for how they look more than for what they do. Female attractiveness, we are told, is what will "get the man." We live in a culture where "a woman with an IQ of 180 who is not lovely is likely to marry ugly, be paid modestly well and secretly despise herself until the day she dies. A woman with an IQ of 100 and beauty in the 99th percentile is likely to marry a physician or an investment banker, have a maid and be admired by all her neighbors" (psychologist Rex Beaber, quoted in *People*, October 30, 2000, p. 108). No doubt this comment is an exaggeration, but stereotypes do encode important cultural notions. Even if partially true, it is a sad commentary on our culture, which does not know how to value women's intelligence, and on those men who are conditioned to prefer beauty to brains and to choose women who are their intellectual inferiors.

Women display male wealth and prestige on and by their bodies. In the West it is the thin, elegant woman who displays the wealth and prestige of her husband. The same is true among the urban educated elite in Turkey. But in the rural areas, it is the round, plump woman who demonstrates for all to see that she is provided for and has enough to eat. This confers honor and prestige to her husband. Fat is also beautiful among numerous groups in Africa. At a festival in Niger, women "compete to become the heaviest. They train for the beauty contest by gorging on food, especially millet, and drinking lots of water on the morning before the contest" (Onishi, *New York Times*, February 12, 2001). Some of them have even resorted to using steroids to build bulk. "The world is a funny place," commented a doctor in Niger. "In America, you are rich, you have everything, and the women there want to become so thin as if they had nothing. Here in Africa, we have nothing, the women who buy these products [steroids and other weight-inducing drugs] have nothing, but they want to become fat as if they had everything." Despite the differences in the ideal of beauty, the "motivations appear the same: seeking men's approval."

Women will struggle with body image until the hold of that motivation is broken, and men as well as women must help in this endeavor. "Fathers can help daughters in the body-image battle," proclaimed another article in the *New York Times* (September 18, 2000), perhaps more than mothers who are struggling with the same issues as their daughters. One father, concerned about what his teenage daughters confronted every day in the media, in movies, and from peers, started an organization "dedicated to enhancing fathers' relationships with their daughters, but also, more specifically, to girls' relationships with their bodies." Girls need to be educated and supported in this area; boys need to learn how to appreciate girls and women for all of their attributes, not just those that conform to an ideal body type.

Images of female attractiveness vary over time, even in the same culture. To understand that, we do not need to go back to the rounded, fleshy bodies painted by Rubens or even Renoir; all we need to do is to take a look at movies from the 1950s. At that time in the United States, the idols of feminine beauty were Marilyn Monroe, Ava Gardner, and

Elizabeth Taylor; these women were buxom and curvaceous. Since then, the ideal has changed dramatically – from US size 10 or 12 (UK size 12 or 14) to US size 2 or 4 (UK size 6 or 8). What has happened in just 40 years? More importantly, *why* has this change occurred?

Growing up in the 1950s, my friends and I were certainly concerned about our looks, and it was clear we would never measure up to the film idols mentioned above. However, we focused more on skin and hair, and how to develop larger breasts. No one I knew ever went on a diet or purposefully "worked out." We had gym class, of course, and played field hockey, basketball, volleyball, or softball because we had to. Some played on the high school teams, and others simply swam, hiked, or skied because we enjoyed it. Even in college, I knew only one or two women who dieted, and they were thought by the rest of us to be a little strange. We never heard of anorexia or bulimia; if they existed then, they must have been extremely rare.

Today, at the beginning of the twenty-first century, they appear to be epidemic.

According to the National Association of Anorexia Nervosa and Associated Disorders, roughly 7 million American girls and 1 million boys struggle with eating disorders. The mortality rate from anorexia – estimated between 10 and 20 percent – is the highest of any mental disorder. (*People*, October 30, 2000, p. 109)

A poll conducted in 1996 showed that "young girls are more afraid of becoming fat than they are of nuclear war, cancer, or losing their parents" (Council on Size and Weight Discrimination n.d.). Such a perspective on life bodes ill for the future of our society, at least among middle- and upper-middle class white girls and women – those who "have everything" – where the myopic fixation on the body is particularly strong. No wonder it seems like self-indulgence to those who do not enjoy such luxury.

This focus on the body prevents these girls from becoming involved in larger social and political issues, and sometimes also detracts from their studies. Their energy is channeled into their bodies rather than into projects to protect the environment or to eliminate nuclear weapons; that is, they "make the body into an all-consuming project in ways young women of the past did not" (Brumberg 1997). According to Brumberg, no one

could foresee that as American women shed their corsets, they would adjust their waistlines to a different set of expectations and constraints that would be even harder and tougher than cotton laces and whalebone stays. Over the course of the twentieth century, girls' bodies have been a critical index of our social and economic life, in ways that we are just beginning to understand. (p. 213)

For many young women, the "body project" continues in college. College is seen by many women as the means to get a man, rather than a career, and the way to get a man is through the body. In my "Investigating Culture" classes I ask students, anonymously, to write a page describing how they feel about their bodies, whether they ever dieted, whether they ever tried to make their body conform to some ideal. In general, the men say they are satisfied, although a few admit they work out to "tone up." But the papers of the women make me want to cry. "I am very dissatisfied with my body and have been ever since I was a little girl." "I hate myself, I hate my stomach and my arms. … I wish I was shorter. I wish my tummy was firmer and I wish my hips were smaller." A more serious case: "I used to play five to ten hours of tennis a day and not eat … well I'd eat once or twice a week (an apple and some carrot sticks, maybe some pretzels). … I'd play all summer and I'd pass out on the courts and my friends would have to carry me home." A few confessed that they were becoming somewhat more accepting of their bodies. The black women, generally, seemed to have fewer problems with eating and were much more accepting of their bodies. While I know many female students who are not so preoccupied with body image, even the brightest and most ambitious tell me that practically everyone they know is on a diet, and that some of them have been dieting since grammar school. When they go through the cafeteria line in the dorm, they feel everyone else is watching the kind and quantity of food they are putting on their plates. In this era of unprecedented freedom for women, they are being policed by themselves and their peers.

The origin of the ideal of the very thin body is often attributed to the British model Twiggy (*née* Leslie Hornby) who, in 1966, became an overnight sensation and changed the image of female attractiveness. At 16, Twiggy was 5 ft 7 in, rail thin, and flat-chested, and weighed only 87 lbs – an impossible weight for most women, since the average American woman at the time was 5 ft 3 in, weighed 140 lbs, and wore a size 14 dress (Council on Size and Weight Discrimination, n.d.).[1] However, over the past few decades, the ultrathin body has become the ideal, and in order to reach it, young women have been starving themselves, literally. Many of the diets they follow have fewer calories than were allotted to women in concentration camps (see Wolf 1991: 195); indeed, the women with the most severe cases of anorexia look as if they *were* in a concentration camp. Naomi Wolf also notes that in India, "the very poorest women eat 1,400 calories a day, or 600 more than a Western woman on the Hilton Head Diet" (p. 193).

Anorexia nervosa, the medical term for this disease of self-starvation, is often not recognized as a disease, and that, as well as uncertainty over its causes, make it difficult to treat. No doubt many of you are aware of this health concern and may know someone who is anorexic. A number of theories have developed to account for this illness. Early theorists assumed that the young women were retreating from womanhood – that they resented the changes in their bodies and wanted to remain prepubescent. They accomplished this by starving themselves to the point that they ceased to menstruate. They also thought that the young women feared sex and became emaciated to prevent unwanted sexual advances. In other words, the illness was a sign that women were being forced to be sexual too early.

This perspective invites comparison with Darwin, who believed that female beauty and sex appeal were evolutionary strategies for procuring male partners for reproduction. If true – and there is considerable debate about it – what does the current ideal of the ultrathin, almost boyish, and often infertile female body convey about femininity, masculinity, and reproduction?

Other theories trace anorexia to the mother–daughter relationship or to a "dysfunctional family," while more socially oriented theories argue that it must be analyzed in a fuller cultural and social context. The disease has to be a combination of individual and social factors, if for no other reason than that the individual must carry out the regime prescribed by the culture. That involves her volition and will.

Dieting and becoming extremely thin obviously take an enormous amount of willpower. This can bring a great deal of satisfaction to the person who can do it. It shows that you have discipline and control, that you can overcome the temptations of ice cream, chocolate, and other delicious foods depicted in the advertisements and displayed in the stores. I have actually witnessed anorexic women I know in upscale gourmet markets feasting their eyes on the food displays, and then walking away without buying anything. However, this *experience* of power and control needs to be placed in a wider framework of the cultural demands put on women to be thin; while *felt* as powerful, the practices are really training them in docility to cultural ideals (see Bordo 1993: 27). Instead, we need to ask what is this denial all about? Why is there such a vilification of plumpness, flab, or fat? Where does it come from? Who is creating these images, and for what purposes? Who is hurt by them, and who profits?

The hatred of the flesh has, admittedly, a long history in Christianity, where flesh is imagined as a snare that imprisons the soul. Those who aspired to be saintly often mortified the flesh, but the ways were different for men and women. In the fifth to seventh centuries some of these men, known as *stylites* (see chapter 1), went into the desert and sat atop pillars; others made pilgrimages on their knees while flagellating themselves. Women, in contrast, tended to deny themselves food, as a way to deny the appetites of the body and achieve spiritual illumination.[2] "Fasting, aimed at spiritual purification and domination of the flesh, was an important part of the repertoire of Christian practice in the Middle Ages" (Bordo 1993: 185). The aim was the development of the soul, not the elimination of fat. Indeed, it is interesting that so many spiritual exercises actually focused on the body. While some encourage acts of excess and license, most focus on quelling the body's movements, appetites, and/or desires, and this is true whether the religious practice is Christian, Buddhist, or Hindu. The body, however, is not the object. Instead, the goal is to forget or ignore the body.

Anorexia has occasionally been compared to these medieval practices, but there is an important difference. The modern practices of denial have been detached from formal religious institutions and rituals and inserted into the routines of secular life. As such, we

> have elevated the pursuit of the fat-free, lean body into a new religion. It has a creed: 'I eat right, watch my weight and exercise' … [and] in following the creed, one is guaranteed beauty, energy, health, and a long successful life. (Seid 1994: 4)

Perhaps it *is* the religion of late capitalism.

> On the one hand, as producers of goods and services we must sublimate, delay, repress desires for immediate gratification; we must cultivate the work ethic. On the other hand, as consumers we must display a boundless capacity to capitulate to desire and indulge in impulse; we must hunger for constant and immediate satisfaction. The regulation of desire thus becomes an ongoing problem, as we find ourselves continually besieged by temptation, while socially condemned for overindulgence. (Bordo 1993: 199)

As women have been turned more into consumers than producers, they are being asked to consume more and more of all the products, including a rich variety of foods not available in the 1950s. At the same time, they are being given a contradictory message that to be beautiful and attractive they must be thin, and this demands denial. One way of promoting these contradictory claims is very seductive: you can have both at once – *fat-free* chocolate decadence! Of course, fat-free does not necessarily mean low-calorie; however, you can always burn off the calories by using a new exercise machine.

No one will deny that health and fitness are important goals. The concern has to do with the *obsession* to be thin and the narrowing of *focus* on the self, the body, and food. The authors who write most eloquently about the contemporary obsession with food and with slenderness have often had personal experience of it (see especially Kim Chernin 1981; Naomi Wolf 1991; Susan Bordo 1993).

But none of us is immune from the dictates of culture. Not all of us will become anorexic, but many, maybe most, women struggle with their body image. Even the staunchest feminist knows that a slim, toned body has more respect, will be listened to, and gets more attention than a fat, soft, flabby body. During the summer of 2000, when I began to write this book, I decided that I did not want to be a plump old lady. If I didn't lose the weight then, I might not be able to do so later. I had six months before I would turn 60. I wanted to give a big dance party and had always wanted to wear a black sequin dress. I joined Weight Watchers, lost 25 lbs., gave the party, and wore the dress. I can't deny that I felt and looked much better and that this *does* affect one's attitude, which carries into all areas of one's life. Because of my success, I was asked to work for Weight Watchers! I imagined myself the next duchess of York featured in Weight Watchers television ads. So, ironically and quite coincidentally (or is it?), I wrote this chapter on the body while I was also working part-time for the local branch of Weight Watchers. (Of course, I can legitimate it as part of my research.) Surely, it has given me more insight into the terrible anxieties that women of all ages and sizes have about their weight. People are impatient and want change fast; rather than changing their relation to food and watching what and how much they eat, many try fad diets, drugs, or surgery in an attempt to shed the pounds quickly. The evidence of numerous studies shows that people who do that tend to gain back all they lost and more. Nevertheless, all weight reduction programs – with their meetings, dues, books, and foods – make billions off of women's dissatisfaction (over $40 billion a year, according to the Council on Size and Weight Discrimination [n.d.]). The diet industry feeds women's dissatisfaction in order to continue to reap the profits. They are collusive, and this should give women pause.

"A Body to Die For" was the title of a special report in the October 30, 2000, issue of *People* magazine. The cover screamed, in large letters, "DYING TO BE THIN." The report told the poignant "stories of six people who, like so many, were consumed by the battle to lose weight. Three sought help from liposuction, two took pills, one starved herself – and all paid with their lives" (p. 109). The one who starved herself was a bright and very attractive college student who had everything to live for, but became anorexic; her 5 ft. 7 in. frame wasted to 88 lbs. As she was slipping in and out of consciousness, she told her heart-sick parents, "I don't want to be fat. I want to die" (p. 111). Fatness was a sin worse than death.

Male Bodies

When we think about bodies and struggles over body image, we generally think of women. But increasingly in contemporary American society, and perhaps somewhat less so in Europe, men are becoming concerned not just with weight but also with their bodies. "Why are men so much more concerned about their bodies today than they were 50 years ago?" This question was the first line in a *New York Times* article, October 7, 2000. It was also the question that provoked a research project at Harvard Medical School, whose findings are discussed in *The Adonis Complex: The Secret Crisis of Male Body Obsession* (Pope, Phillips, and Olivardia 2000). The authors noted that

> men of the 1950s or 1960s didn't worry about their muscularity; they didn't pour money into gym dues or protein supplements or weight machines for the basement. Similarly, male eating disorders, such as binge eating and vomiting, were almost unknown. Most men hadn't even heard of a body fat measurement, nor did they worry greatly about how much body fat they had. And for all practical purposes, there was no such thing as a "personal trainer." (p. 27)

Since the 1960s, men's dissatisfaction with their body image has grown dramatically. According to a 1997 study, "*43 percent – nearly half* – of the men in this survey reported that they were dissatisfied with their overall appearance" (Pope et al. 2000: 27; emphasis in the original). These researchers attribute this growing concern to a number of factors, notably to the use and display of male bodies in advertisements, the use of steroids, and boys' action toys.

The changes in G.I. Joe since his first appearance in 1964 are illustrative (see figure 6.1). The original doll, if he were a man, would be "5 feet 10 inches tall, he would have a 32-inch

Figure 6.1   The evolution of G.I. Joe, from *The Adonis Complex* by Harrison G. Pope, Katharine Phillips, and R. Olivardia (New York: Free Press, 2000), p. 41. Courtesy Simon & Schuster/Zachary Shuster Harmsworth.

waist, a 44-inch chest, and a 12-inch bicep – a perfectly respectable physique" (p. 41). Since then, he has gone through a number of transformations, each one becoming more and more muscular until the arrival of G.I. Joe Extreme in the mid-1990s. If he "were full-sized, he would have a 55-inch chest and a 27-inch bicep … bigger than that of most competition bodybuilders" (p. 42). The same kinds of changes have occurred in other action toys for boys – characters from *Star Wars* and those with names like Gold Ranger, Iron Man, Batman, and Wolverine. "All have physiques suggestive of steroid-using bodybuilders" (p. 43). If these are the models that toy makers present to our young boys, we should not be surprised that so many of them feel physically inadequate. More and more men are afraid to go to the beach or appear in public without a shirt because they do not measure up (see Steven Hall, "The Troubled Life of Boys: The Bully in the Mirror," *New York Times*, August 22, 1999). They fear being judged on the basis of their bodies.

There are societies that stress male beauty and attractiveness, a situation that Darwin's theory of sexual dimorphism and evolution, mentioned above, does not explain. David Gilmore, in "The Beauty of the Beast: Male Body Imagery in Anthropological Perspective," discusses societies in which men are the objects of desire and display their bodies for public viewing. The Fulani of Africa, for example, "stage male beauty contests with women judges" (Gilmore 1994: 197), with the men adorning their bodies, applying makeup, preening, strutting, and displaying themselves before the women who rate them.

In the West, too, there have been times when males exhibited the cultural ideals of beauty and attractiveness. Ancient Greece is a notable example, as the numerous sculptures of nude males amply display. The male form epitomized the ideal. "The Platonic association of the 'beautiful' with the 'good,' the belief that physical beauty is a sign of interior or spiritual beauty, originates with the Greeks and runs as a thread throughout Western Christian civilization" (Gilmore 1994: 212). In eighteenth-century Europe, men of the elite classes adorned themselves with velvet coats, wigs, makeup, perfume, gold jewelry, and elegant shoes, hose, boots, and hats. This is not to imply that women during that time were drab creatures. They, too, wore elaborate costumes and powdered wigs, but what is unusual is that men were similarly objects of beauty. Male bodies were also idealized in Nazi Germany, as we shall see below.

However, today's increasing focus on male bodies represents not a shift of the cultural ideal of beauty from women *to* men, but rather the objectification of both women and men as desirable things. At one time, it was primarily women's bodies that were used in advertisements to sell anything from cars to vodka (see figure 6.2). When men appeared in ads as, for example, the Marlboro man, their sexiness was due not to their nakedness, but to their activities and personae. Since the 1950s "the percentage of ads depicting women in some state of undress remained relatively stable. … By contrast, the percentage of ads depicting undressed men rose sharply, from less than 5% in 1950 to as much as 35% in the 90s" (Pope, quoted in Emily, Eakin, "In This Woman's World, What's a Guy to Do? Sweat," *New York Times*, October 7, 2000, p. 19). The ads for the perfume Obsession are emblematic: not only does the female model resemble an emaciated waif, but also the naked male torso is on display.

From one perspective, men are finally getting to feel what women have endured for a very long time. However, it doesn't seem to make them more sympathetic, nor have they

Figure 6.2 An advertisement for vodka that uses a woman's body to sell the product. Reproduced by permission of Swardlick Marketing Group.

launched a crusade comparable to the women's movement to oppose the cultural models and the exploitation. Instead, more of them desire to reach the ideal. To add bulk and develop muscles, and especially to gain the "six-pack" abs depicted on so many of the ads, they must work out. And they seek these attributes, whether or not women actually find them attractive.

Like women, men have also become too focused on their bodies, dieting, and working out to pursue other projects and goals. Referring to one of the men they interviewed, Pope said, "He puts all his hopes and dreams into his workouts and not into his daily life" (Pope et al. 2000: 7). Pope and his associates discuss the very poignant case of a young man who gave up a promising career because he needed more time to work out. Instead, he became a personal trainer in a gym because "it was the only job I could think of that gave me enough time to do my own training" (p. 8). He admitted to the researchers that during the day, 90 percent of the time his thinking

> would have something to do with either my weightlifting, my diet, or the way I look. I can't go past a mirror without posing just for a minute to check out my body – as long as I'm sure nobody's watching. I even check myself out when I see my reflection in a store window or car

window. … Sometimes when I'm in a restaurant, I even study my reflection in the back of a spoon. (p. 9)

It is often said that men spend 99 percent of their time thinking about sex; now, instead, many are thinking about their bodies. What has happened? This man's obsession with his body wrecked a very satisfactory relationship with a woman because he had no time left to spend with her after his hours at work and workouts.

The researchers conclude that the "Adonis complex" has arisen primarily because of "two sociocultural factors that distinguish the present generation from every generation before it: the availability of anabolic steroids and the increasing parity of women" (p. 60). "As women have entered the work force and become heads of families, men have had to relinquish their traditional roles as fathers, soldiers and breadwinners … which leaves their bodies as the only way to demonstrate their masculinity" (*New York Times*, October 7, 2000). Surely there are other ways to conceive of masculinity. Conclusions that blame the women's movement and women's entrance into traditional male occupations could be used to push women back into the home and sabotage the gains women have earned in the past 30 years. These researchers fail to consider how "feminist thought and conversation has created room for alternatives to traditional masculinity" (Hall 1999), nor even listened to those conversations.

Although they decry the ads and the toys, Pope et al. do not consider the role of capitalism in the deformation of roles as well as bodies. Their research lacks a critique of an economy that has made it imperative that both men and women work in order to consume the products (and the lifestyle) that fuel the economy. Nor do they imagine a more egalitarian model in which women and men can be sexy and be parents; can work outside the home and do the "dependency work" (Kittay 1996: 219) of caring for children, the sick, the disabled, and the elderly; and can be breadmakers as well as breadwinners. This is obviously much more difficult; not only would it demand a change in the definition of male roles, but also it would require a total restructuring of the economy and of the ways in which we live and work; it would demand a change in institutions and in values.

Body Modifications

Dieting and "working out" are two common ways in which men and women attempt to modify and transform their bodies. They are not the only ways: corsets or girdles are another, as are breast implants, liposuction, Botox injections, and straightening teeth. Because some of these practices are (or have been) widespread, they seem almost "normal," while those of others are exoticized and deplored, such as the use of neck rings to elongate the necks of Padung women of Burma (Myanmar) or the Chinese practice of binding women's feet (to be discussed in chapter 8). These are only a few examples by which women's bodies are molded to cultural norms of feminine beauty. These forms are externally accomplished, but there are other ways in which the bodies of women and men are transformed – ways that involve the skin (like scarification, piercing, and tattooing), and still others that change or remove parts of the body to accomplish the cultural ideal (such as the filing or removal of teeth, the removal of a finger joint, subincision, circumcision, infibulation, and castration). I cannot discuss all of the forms here but mention a few that you or your friends may practice and some that have received international attention.

Tattooing and scarification

These might more logically be considered under the category of bodily adornment dealt with in chapter 8, but will be briefly noted here since they do involve penetration of the skin. Scarification is practiced among a number of peoples, such as the Nuer and Dinka in Africa, whereby designs are created on the body by scars that are ritually applied at specific times like puberty initiation. Tattooing is an ancient practice among a number of peoples: the faces and hands of Muslim women in the southeastern part of Turkey and among some Bedouin groups are tattooed. These designs are generally geometric and abstract and in deep blue and red. A very different kind of tattooing occurs among a dwindling number of Japanese men: a full body tattoo. Called *horimono* from the word *hori* meaning "to carve," this practice is quite ancient but today is frowned upon. This art that seems to cry out for display is, ironically, concealed. The men who get such tattoos cover them up, do not venture to beaches or steam baths, and a few have even been able to keep the knowledge from their colleagues, their wives (by changing and bathing in the dark), and their children (*San Francisco Chronicle*, September 1, 2002). Nevertheless, it forms a bond between these men who expose them to each other on their annual pilgrimage to a shrine outside of Tokyo. (See figure 6.3.)

These forms of tattoo are not at all like the hearts and flowers, ships, pinups, crosses, or "Mother" that are common among some Americans; they are an ancient cultural form traditionally prescribed by the culture, even though today the Japanese men are choosing to continue it. In the United States, tattoos are no longer associated with sailors or motorcyclists, but have, since the 1990s, become popular with many high school and college-age men and women. Tattoos are no doubt desired for purposes of identity and possibly for sexual titillation; they may also, like piercing, be interpreted as symbols of rebellion against parents or what they stand for, namely, bourgeois society. More recently, a number of people, including firefighters, have gotten tattoos to remember someone they lost during the attack on the World Trade Towers on September 11, 2001 (see, e.g., figure 6.4). A photograph exhibit, "Indelible Memories: Sept. 11 Memorial Tattoos Photographed by Vinnie Amessé," was held at the Staten Island Historical Society during the spring of 2003.

While many people have small tattoos – a flower on the breast or a snake at the base of the spine or a "bracelet" around the ankle – others are going in for much more ostentatious and provocative forms of tattooing, scarification, and piercing. For example, law enforcement officials in Utah and California noticed a marked increase in tattoos among prisoners who join white supremacist groups while they are in prison. Such tattoos either proclaim "white power" or depict hate slogans against targeted groups (Madigan, *New York Times*, April 5, 2003).

Some extreme practices of marking the body can be interpreted as a means of rebellion; however, according to one advocate, "the most important thing you learn is that you are not your body, you just live in it" (Vale and Juno 1989: 29).[3] These *modern primitives*,

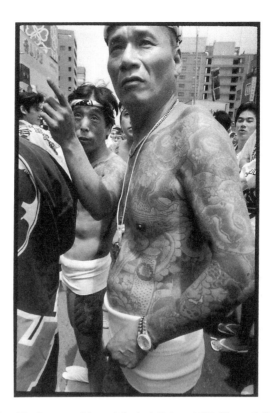

Figure 6.3 Example of *horimono* at Matsuri festival, Tokyo, 1998. Photo © Bruce Gilden/Magnum Photos.

as they are called, are of the opinion that you *have* rather than *are* your body. Overcoming pain and daring to step outside of conventional society are expressed in terms of *control* in the only place where they feel they can exercise it – the body (not unlike explanations given by anorexics). Some of them also feel that their practices are part of a spiritual process that puts them in touch with authentic primitives and the types of rituals they have had to endure. However, as British cultural analyst Christian Klesse (2000) notes, the modern primitives have idealized and romanticized "primitive society," which is decontextualized, dehistoricized, universalized, and essentialized. They take only one aspect of it (bodily modification) to represent that society. Furthermore, they perpetuate the dichotomies not only of primitive and modern but also of nature (in this case, the body) and culture.[4]

Body piercing

Body piercing has also been widely practiced cross-culturally but, again, the meaning must be explored in each culture. In her book *The Body Project*, Brumberg notes that "unlike aboriginal societies, where the part to be pierced is determined by long-standing ritual and

Figure 6.4   George Henrique showing the tattoo of his daughter Michelle, who died in the 9/11 disaster. Photo by Vinnie Amessé.

tradition, contemporary teens face an array of piercing options" (1997: 131). Yet we should not forget that the notion of *choice* is a very longstanding and important tradition in the United States, even as our choices are quite narrowly confined; for example, we can choose between Lancôme, Estée Lauder, or Max Factor, but they are all cosmetics, are made of the same ingredients, and do a very similar job. Marketed as choices, they really reflect status, identity, and lifestyle.

In the United States, piercing used to be limited to ear piercing and was desired so women could wear earrings without the fear of losing them as was so common with screw-ons or clip-ons. In the mid-1960s I wanted to have pierced ears but was afraid both of the pain and the mess I would make of it. People I knew were piercing their ears themselves – with an ice cube and a needle. I tried one, but it got infected and so I dropped the whole idea. Years later when my daughter was in eighth grade and all her friends were getting their ears pierced, I reconsidered. By then, professionals performed the brief operation with a stapler-like machine that inserted a gold stud as the hole was being pierced. I went with my daughter, who was braver and went first. Then I grit my teeth, held her hand, and had mine pierced too.

In contrast, today many young women (and a few men) have their ears pierced, some have multiple ear piercings; in addition men as well as women have nose, eyebrow, lip, tongue, and navel piercings. Some indicate sexual orientation, others are said to increase sexual pleasure, and some border on S/M practices. Those referred to as *modern primitives* engage in even more intimate body piercings – of the nipples, penis, labia, and clitoris – that seem to play along the boundaries of more institutionalized torture and mutilation,[5] and thus could be seen as trivializing those practices.

Circumcision

Another widespread, and seemingly quite normal, form of body modification is circumcision. Although it is practiced among a number of peoples, I will discuss, briefly, only that prescribed for Jews and Muslims. Both attribute the practice to Abraham, who instituted it after his sojourn in Egypt (see Genesis 17:10–14). Jews circumcise boys when they are babies (traditionally, on the eighth day), because Isaac was a baby when he was circumcised. Muslims, who trace their descent from Abraham's son Ishmael, prefer to perform it between the ages of 7 and 13, because Ishmael was already a grown boy when he was circumcised. This means that Muslims often see circumcision as a test of manhood.

Some biblical scholars claim that the circumcision of Jewish boys is related to sacrifice, especially the sacrifice of the firstborn: "Sanctify unto me all the first-born, whatsoever openeth the womb among the children of Israel, both of man and of beast. It is mine" (Exodus 13:2; see also Exodus 22:29). Jewish scholar Jon Levenson goes further when he sees circumcision "as a sublimation for child sacrifice in ancient Israelite religious practice" (1993: 51), that is, as a *pars pro toto* (a part for the whole – the foreskin for the child). I disagree with this interpretation, first because there is no evidence that child sacrifice was practiced by either the ancient Israelites or their neighbors (see Delaney 1998). More importantly, circumcision was a sign of the covenant that God made with Abraham, the context of which is fruitfulness and procreation, not sacrifice:

> And I will make thee exceedingly fruitful, and I will make nations of thee, and kings shall come out of thee. And I will establish my covenant between me and thee and thy seed after thee in their generations for an everlasting covenant. (Genesis 17: 5–8)

Howard Eilberg-Schwartz, a scholar of ancient Judaism, agrees, and thinks that language such as "uncircumcised trees" offers a clue – that "cutting away the foreskin is like pruning a fruit tree ... both increase the desired yield. One might say that when Israelites circumcise their male children, they are pruning the fruit trees of God" (1990: 152). What neither he nor most other scholars have asked, however, is why the covenant between God and humans is signed on *male* flesh. Why is the male sexual organ seen as *the* organ for the transmission of life? For me, the answer is in the word *seed* – the ancient, though still prevalent, notion that the male "seed" contains the child and that the female is merely the nurturing medium (soil) in which it is planted (see Delaney 1991, 1998). In any case, circumcision was clearly a distinguishing mark that separated one people – the people of Abraham – from all others.

The medical, as opposed to ritual, circumcision of male babies has been routinely practiced in the United States for decades for supposed hygienic reasons. Today, however, many people oppose the practice, since there is no convincing evidence that it reduces infections or cancer more effectively than proper habits of cleanliness. In addition, many people, doctors included, feel that it *is* painful and that serious accidents do happen through mistakes in cutting and cauterization and through infection.[6]

Female genital cutting

Female genital cutting (FGC), also referred to as *female genital mutilation* (FGM),[7] is sometimes called *female circumcision*, although it differs significantly from male circumcision. Male circumcision does not impede sexual pleasure, while FGC – primarily, the excision of the clitoris – is designed to eliminate it completely. The most severe form of FGC is called *infibulation* or *pharaonic circumcision* and involves cutting off the clitoris and the labia minora, sewing shut the labia majora, and leaving only a small opening for urine and menses.[8] Sex initiated at marriage is usually extremely painful and often leads to infections and other serious health problems that can make birth very difficult. Estimates suggest that 100 million women are now living with FGC and another 2 million girls (between the ages of 5 and 6) every year are at risk. Although the majority of FGCs are done in 28 countries across the mid-belt of Africa, it also occurs among immigrants from those countries in Europe and North America. And although it is primarily associated with African Muslims, the practice itself is pre-Islamic and has been practiced by African Jews and Christians as well as those who follow other religious traditions. Westerners have been appalled by the practice and have lobbied to get it included, under the concept of the right to bodily integrity, in the International Bill of Human Rights. Only recently in the United States has asylum been granted to women who want to avoid FGC.

In many cultures, including our own (at certain times), female sexuality is culturally construed as rampant, uncontrollable, and in need of constraint. While not explicitly focused on the sexual organs, some practices such as "covering" (i.e., veiling), home confinement, foot binding, and so forth seek to contain female sexuality and ensure paternity of the children. Female circumcision is only the most extreme.

Yet it would be wrong to assume that such operations have been practiced only in other, particularly African, cultures. While many Western women protest these "surgical" procedures, they are often unaware of the history of this practice in Europe and the United States. During the nineteenth and well into the twentieth centuries, clitoridectomy was performed on thousands of women, because of masturbation, mental imbalance, or retardation. Again, these surgical procedures were performed because of beliefs about female sexuality and the idea of hysteria (literally, "wandering womb") (see Ehrenreich and English 1973, 1979).

While Western feminists have been appalled by female genital cutting, they often act like cultural imperialists without any sensitivity to the local meanings and understanding. Insisting that cultural practices are wrong only creates defensiveness and resistance; hence, to change practices, one must work from the meanings and values that the practitioners find in them.[9] Anthropologists often go to the other extreme: while they generally support the "rights of people to pursue their traditional practices and values" (Gruenbaum 2001: 29), they sometimes fail to ask whose interests these practices serve. It is easy to blame men for FGCs, but the practices are more often enforced by older women who insist that uncircumcised girls are not desirable as marriage partners. Ultimately this means that the practice aims to make women valuable to men, but ending it requires dislodging the consensus view of feminine desirability. Perhaps there is a lesson to be learned from the way the Chinese ended foot binding. They formed "pledge societies" whereby the parents of girls pledged they would not bind the feet of their daughters while parents of boys pledged they would not let their sons marry girls with bound feet. First, of course, they had to be convinced that the practice was harmful.

Another way is through the medium of humor. Sia Amma, a Liberian native, staged a humorous performance inaugurating the First Annual International Clitoris Celebration in Oakland, California, in March 2003 as part of her effort to end the practice of female genital cutting. She also founded "Global Women Intact," a nonprofit organization devoted to educating African people about the practice, and every year she returns to Liberia and Senegal to give a class, "Clitoris 101," to girls and women there.

Castration

One of the most extreme measures ever taken to control sexuality concerns men. This is castration, the surgical removal of the testicles. Like women who have undergone FGC, castrated men are more docile and are thus useful as guards of female quarters such as the *harem* (which refers not to the women themselves but to their living quarters). The institution of *eunuch* (from the Greek "keeper of the couch") guards reached its epitome in the Byzantine court in Constantinople, from which it was adopted by the Ottomans with whom it is usually associated, and it was an element in the slave trade (Ringrose, 1994). During the sixteenth century the practice entered Europe in the form of *castrati* – men who underwent the operation before puberty – whose voices remained soprano or rich contralto needed for choirs and operas, since women were banned from performing on stage. This practice should be distinguished from what some called *chemical castration*, which was proposed in the mid-1990s for sex offenders in the United States. In no way does it resemble physical castration, since the process can easily be reversed by withdrawing the medication.

Sex change

Sex change surgery is probably the most dramatic form of body modification to emerge over the last half-century. For this reason it must be acknowledged here, even though it is far beyond the scope of this book to give more than a passing nod to the topic and to some of the questions it raises for cultural anthropologists. Sex change means the transformation of male bodies into female, and females into male, through plastic surgery, hormone treatment, voice modification, and considerable effort to learn new body techniques – that is, styles of walking, sitting, gesturing, and so on. (Body techniques are the topic of the next section.) Some of the earliest efforts at surgical sex reassignment were performed on infants with ambiguous genitalia, and as these techniques improved, so too did the possibility of offering them to adults with gender identity disorder. But as sex researchers and their clients soon discovered, gender identity disorder is not only, or even primarily, about genital anatomy. Rather it concerns a constellation of issues such as an internalized sense of self; patterns of sexual arousal and attraction; and gender role conformity and nonconformity. So too, solutions to gender atypicality do not always – or even usually – involve sex reassignment surgery, since it is costly, time consuming, risky (as is all surgery), and irreversible. Instead, treatment options unfold on a cline, with episodic transvestitism at one end, total surgical and hormonal reassignment at the other, and a variety of intermediate accommodations in between. The Turkish singer Bulent Ersoy pursued several options as a transgendered man before finally choosing surgery. His case is discussed in greater detail in chapter 8.

For anthropologists, sex change surgery raises several questions, which may ultimately prove to be unanswerable, but are nevertheless worth pondering. First, what is the source of gender identity and gender identity disorder? Are they inborn, are they learned, or are they a combination of the two? Most sex and gender researchers claim that they are both, but proceed to offer explanations that focus entirely on one side of the equation at the expense of the other. Very few have made any effort to integrate the innate with the acquired, leaving the interplay of nature and nurture unexplained.

Second, is gender identity *disorder* a condition that emerges from the person, or is it a dilemma that emerges in a society that cannot tolerate certain types of nonconformity? In American society today, only two sexes – male and female – are legally recognized, while the population at large insists that gender behavior conform to masculine and feminine types. This leaves few options for gender nonconformists except to force themselves into male or female typicality. In other societies, such as the Zuni of the American Southwest, institutionalized forms of cross-genders are permitted and even celebrated, giving greater flexibility for at least some forms of gender bending. Would sex reassignment surgery even be an issue in societies that don't require its members to be either masculine men or feminine women?

Third, does a sex change procedure fundamentally turn someone into the opposite sex, or is this simply an exercise in deception? In other words, is gender identity immutable, notwithstanding the transformations of the body? Underlying this question is the same issue that informs much of this chapter: am I my body, or do I have a body?[10]

Techniques of the Body

I first began to think about techniques of the body when I found I could not squat with my feet *flat* on the floor or the ground as could the Turkish villagers among whom I lived. Even the elderly could squat comfortably for long periods of time. They squatted while they prepared food for cooking, did the dishes, or waited for someone, or simply while watching the world go by. I practiced and eventually was able to do it, but it was not comfortable and quickly became painful. It occurred to me that one had to develop this technique from childhood, training the tendons and muscles to keep them from tightening.

I do not know why this practice developed among Turks – perhaps it relates to their nomadic past, when chairs were not used. Even today, village Turks do not often use chairs, although they are becoming *de rigueur* as part of the trousseaux of the young. Instead, they sit on cushions on the floor or on a *divan* (a kind of day bed set against the walls with firm cushions lined along the back edge) where they can draw their legs up and under them.

Marcel Mauss, French anthropologist and nephew of Emile Durkheim, published a groundbreaking article in 1934 titled "Techniques of the Body." In it, he commented that one "can distinguish squatting mankind and sitting mankind … people with chairs and people without chairs" ([1934] 1973: 81). He was the first anthropologist to draw attention to the variety of bodily techniques and propose they be studied systematically. He noticed how swimming techniques had changed even in his lifetime and were quite different elsewhere. Although he recognized the biophysical limits and individual idiosyncrasies of body movement and posture, he claimed that there were significant cultural patterns that were transmitted by example and explanation. Bodily techniques "are assembled by and for social authority" and become habitual. Mauss used the word *habitus* – a kind of acquired ability but more than habits. Later Pierre Bourdieu turned the word into a key concept as a system of "durable dispositions" that are taught by word, example, and imitation. He states this quite eloquently when he says, "The book from which children learn their vision of the world is read with the body" (Bourdieu [1972] 1977: 90). This concept was quite useful to me in the village as I watched how Turkish children moved or were allowed to move, how they learned to become not just Turkish but also a Turkish girl or boy. As young children, both girls and boys could roam around their neighborhoods quite freely; however, since boys were more socially valued, they were supposed to conduct themselves with decorum, while girls could run about, shriek, and act silly. This behavior changed drastically as they approached adolescence. Then boys were expected to be *delikanlı* (crazy-bloods), while girls had to become *kapalı* (covered), which meant covering their hair with headscarves, covering their bodies with voluminous clothing that also restricted their movements, and enclosing themselves in the house.

There is usually no question that *training* in bodily techniques is involved when the issue is yoga, tai chi, or sports, but people are generally more skeptical when the focus is an ordinary activity like walking. Yet there are very different ways of walking, not only among the Maori, where mothers supposedly train their daughters to walk with a "loose-jointed swinging of the hips" – a walk that has a special name – but also between the French and the British (Mauss [1934] 1973: 72). Europeans claim they can spot Americans by the way they walk, and Deborah Kaspin noted that, as a graduate student, she could easily distinguish black men from white men on the streets of Chicago by their outlines and movement when they walked.

Mauss's classification of bodily techniques included

1. those of birth and obstetrics: why, for example, is it considered normal in the United States to give birth lying down where in many other societies it is done squatting or even standing?
2. those of infancy: here he discussed methods of carrying babies, and also distinguished societies with and without cradles. What, I wonder, are the implications of a crib?

3. those of adolescence: issues relating to puberty such as techniques for removing facial and body hair, of ejaculation, and of menstruation. This is also a time when youths in some societies are initiated into techniques of sexual behavior including kissing, intercourse, and so on. Although "[n]othing is more technical than sexual positions, very few writers have had the courage to discuss" them, yet because they vary considerably cross-culturally, they might provide interesting insight into the culture.

Under techniques of "adult life," Mauss included bodily techniques such as sleeping that actually span age groups. He distinguishes "between societies that have nothing to sleep on except the 'floor,' and those that have instrumental assistance … people with mats and people without … people with pillows and those without" (p. 80), and those, like Japanese and some African groups, that make a kind of "bench" to support the neck. "The Masai can sleep on their feet," others can sleep on horseback, and Mauss acknowledges that he learned to sleep standing up, or on rocks, during World War I. There are techniques of dancing, jumping, climbing, pulling, lifting, throwing, coughing, spitting (a great example was in the film *Titanic*), and bodily hygiene, such as bathing, teeth cleaning, hair washing, and so on (see Miner 1956). All of these techniques are inflected by gender, age, and efficiency.

Body Orientation

The cultural values and beliefs illuminated by techniques of the body are still largely unstudied. But the meanings of body orientation, especially right–left polarization, have been extensively analyzed. Here, Robert Hertz was prescient. His groundbreaking article "The Pre-Eminence of the Right Hand: A Study in Religious Polarity," originally published in 1909, was included in Needham's 1973 volume *Right and Left: Essays on Dual Symbolic Classification* and is now an anthropological classic. It begins,

> What resemblance more perfect than that between our two hands! And yet what a striking inequality there is! … Every social hierarchy claims to be founded on the nature of things. … Aristotle justified slavery by the ethnic superiority of the Greeks over barbarians; and today [keep in mind this was 1909] the man who is annoyed by feminist claims alleges that woman is *naturally* inferior. Similarly, according to common opinion, the pre-eminence of the right hand results directly from the organism and owes nothing to convention or to men's changing beliefs. But in spite of appearances the testimony of nature is no more clear or decisive, when it is a question of ascribing attributes to the two hands, than in the conflict of the races or the sexes. ([1909] 1973: 3)

The idea that inequality is bound up with systems of classification which are, at root, symbolic, cultural, conventional, and thus humanly constructed is an idea of utmost importance, yet it is one that few people seem to have learned since Hertz first articulated it over a century ago. His response to studies that claimed we are right-handed *because* we are left-brained could still be used today. Even if there is a strong correlation between right-handedness and left-hemisphere brain development, we can easily turn the claim around and argue that "we are left-brained because we are right-handed" ([1909] 1973: 4). It is a good example of a chicken-and-egg problem.

Even if there is a slight inborn preference for the right hand, this is "not enough to bring about the absolute preponderance of the right hand if this were not reinforced and fixed by influences extraneous to the organism" (p. 5). If the left were, indeed, naturally weaker, that should be reason to develop and strengthen it. But this does not happen. Historically American children were trained to use the right hand by punishing them for using the left hand and sometimes attaching restraining devices so they could not. My sister, who is left-handed, recalls that during the year we spent in Catholic school – when she was just a first grader – the nuns repeatedly hit her left hand. Rather than letting children develop either or both hands, many, if not most, cultures prescribe that the right be developed, and the left thwarted, repressed, or given only the most odious tasks. In Turkey and India, for example, the left hand is used to wash the genital area after defecation and cannot be used to handle food.

In the United States, there has been a gradual loosening of prescriptions to use the right hand at school, but it has not disappeared. My daughter was fully ambidextrous as a child, but this so disconcerted her teachers and doctor, all of whom believed that ambidexterity would confuse or scramble brain development, that they insisted she choose one hand as her preferred hand. Although she learned to use the right hand for writing and some other tasks, she "freaks people out" when she plays tennis or ping pong because she can switch hands with ease. I do not know if this would be allowed in professional sport matches.

Some research suggests that left-handed people die younger than right-handed people, primarily because of accidents in a world built to accommodate right-handed people: "Everyday implements, such as scissors, gearshifts and can openers, even the direction in which the threading of screws is angled, [are] biased toward right-handed use" (*New York Times*, August 29, 1989). I recall the difficulties in trying to teach my left-handed sister to knit. The researchers also claimed less obvious examples such as the following: "traffic patterns are designed to utilize the clockwise turning bias of the right hander." Whether the same is true for the British, who drive on the left with the gearbox on their left, is something they will have to answer.

The very words for *left* and *right* carry loaded meanings: *dexterity* comes from the Latin *dextra* for right hand, while *sinister* comes from *sinistra* for left hand. French for left, *gauche*, has become *gawky* in English, while right, *droit*, means the law. In Turkish right is *sağ* and left is *sol*; *sağ* is used in all kinds of expressions such as *sağ olsun* – may you be well. In Chichewa and other Bantu languages, the right hand is called the male hand, and the left hand the female. One need hardly mention how right and left are used for political leanings and parties or that Jesus sat on the *right* hand of God. Although today, *left* and *right* signify secular values and political orientations, Hertz argues that the polarity itself, like so many other things we have discussed, has theological underpinnings; that is, the meaning of polarity – the opposition of right and left – derives from and is justified by recourse to something beyond the *nature* of the two hands.

The Social Body

Anthropologists, among others, are quite familiar with the notion of society as a "body." Herbert Spencer, an influential nineteenth-century social thinker, noted, "A dim perception that there exists some analogy between the body politic and a living individual body, was early reached, and from time to time re-appeared in literature" (cited in McGee and Warms 2000: 13 [1860]), but it had not been scientifically explored. He argued that the social organism was like individual organisms in at least three ways: (1) they augment in mass (grow bigger), (2) there is increasing complexity of structure, and (3) the various parts gradually acquire mutual dependence. This idea was adopted by Emile Durkheim, who wanted to know what held modern society together. Durkheim theorized that there are two basic types of social solidarity that relate to the division of labor: "organic" and "mechanical." Modern, industrialized societies, he believed, functioned "organically"; each sector was devoted to only one kind of labor, only a part of the functioning whole. In primitive societies, he believed that the division of labor was far less differentiated, with everyone performing the same essential tasks. I think the nomenclature is deceptive since modern societies are dominated by machines, primitive societies are closer to the organic world, and the latter typically divide labor by gender, age, and other criteria. Still, the underlying point is valid: in order to be a *society*, the population itself has to be regulated and the tasks have to be both distributed and integrated for the society to function. Bodies are shaped not only by cultural values and ideals, and by families and peers, but also in a more forceful way by governments – whether chiefs, tribal councils, kings, or the modern state – all of which attempt to regulate and subject individual bodies to the social order.

Mary Douglas, a famous British anthropologist working in the Durkheimian tradition, suggests that the "body is a model which can stand for any bounded system. Its boundaries can represent any boundaries which are threatened or precarious" ([1966] 1999: 116). She goes on to say that we

> cannot possibly interpret rituals concerning excreta, breast milk, saliva, and the rest unless we are prepared to see in the body a symbol of society, and to see the powers and dangers credited to social structure reproduced in small on the human body" (p. 116)

This was and continues to be a highly creative and useful suggestion. However, it also reveals basic differences between British social anthropology and American cultural anthropology. While I agree with Douglas that the body is a rich source of symbols, we cannot assume that their meaning is naturally determined or universal. That is, I do not assume that the human body and its various parts are perceived the same way in all societies, or even that there is consensus about what is "natural." Thus, the body's use as a model for society cannot be assumed *a priori* but must be investigated in each case.

Furthermore, Douglas does not specify which kind of body – male or female – shall stand as the model for the society. In Turkey, only the male body is thought to be "bounded" and self-contained, while the female body is relatively unbounded: it sprouts breasts, its belly distends in pregnancy, and it leaks in menstruation and lactation. It is imagined as naturally "open," especially to sexual advances from men, and, thus, must be bound and contained by social practices. As noted above, this is symbolized by various forms of "covering."

But while the male body is the symbolically bounded body, the female body provides the model for the society, perhaps because of the symbolism linking women and land: thus the word *Anavatan* means Motherland. Because of the cultural understandings of the openness and vulnerability of the female body, "[b]oundaries thus become a focus of anxiety, and exits and entrances are controlled and under surveillance" (Delaney 1991: 278). This is true whether the boundary is the female body, the house, the village, or the nation. Outside influences, whether the presence of foreigners at the center of Ottoman economy, or the seductive attractions of the West, have been imagined as corrupting the country in the same way an illicit relationship pollutes and corrupts a woman. The economic "capitulations" demanded by the foreign powers prior to World War I were felt by Turks as forced prostitution. When the country was going to be dismembered and the parts given to the Allies, Mustafa Kemal rallied the people to fight to save the "Motherland." In the nation he created, he was given the name Atatürk, which means Father Turk or Father of the Turks. The gendered symbolism intensifies the meaning of the patrol and control of Turkey's borders and points of entry, especially over the Dardanelles and the Bosphorus – the narrow waterways leading straight to the heart of the country, Istanbul. They patrol the "Motherland" as they patrol and surveil (protect) *their* women – mothers, sisters, and daughters.

Body and Nation

The Turkish example shows how easily the "social" body can blend with the "national" body.[11] But again, we must ask, "Which bodies?" Women often *symbolize* the nation – its physical land mass and boundaries – but men (or symbolic men, as in the case of the "Iron Maiden" Margaret Thatcher) usually *represent* it both as heads of state and as its defenders. When nations were formed in Europe, female bodies symbolized them as Britannia, Germania, and Marianne (for the French Republic). In the United States, although Columbia was proposed at the Columbian Exposition in Chicago in 1893, it is really "Lady Liberty" (the Statue of Liberty) that has assumed this place. (We will return to this in chapter 9.) But beyond these representations, bodies and nations are intertwined in other ways.

In Nazi Germany, the state developed a cult of the body, especially the nude male body, which was imagined as "the temple of manliness" (Mosse 1985: 46). Germany was to become a *manly* nation, an ideal achieved through fresh air, exercise, and a natural diet.

> The stereotyped embodiment of manliness was modeled on an ideal of male beauty born in the eighteenth-century Greek revival, while the image of the woman in German or English national iconography was frequently fashioned after traditional portrayals of the Virgin Mary. (Mosse 1985: 23).

The ideal woman was wholesome and chaste until marriage, and only those deemed suitably Aryan were encouraged to reproduce the nation. At the heart of Nazi ideology, though relatively unknown, was the Lebensborn movement. *Lebensborn* means "source," and it was to be the fountain that would supply the revitalized nation with its vital new citizens. Young women with the proper Aryan background and features were encouraged to mate with similarly approved SS officers. They did not need to get married, because the Führer was the putative father and the children would be raised in state-run homes. The film *Of Pure Blood* discusses some of the features of the movement and tells the stories of some of the children raised there. They are heartrending – many died, deprived of the close nurturing care more typical of families, while others became listless and retarded. At the end of the war, those still alive suffered from not knowing who their parents were. The idea of a "pure" blood that constitutes the nation clearly has racist implications. "Aryan" Germans were encouraged to marry only other "Aryans," for otherwise they would be polluting the pure blood of the nation (see Linke 1999: 198ff.).

Reproduction, while seemingly a private issue, is intimately tied to building the nation and to nationalism. Women are recruited to reproduce the nation, that is, to produce its citizens. However, only certain kinds of women are sought for this project. France, for example, encourages "French" women to get pregnant and give birth to children, and pays them stipends if they do; it is not happy when North Africans proliferate because most of them are not citizens. In 1983, Israel, fearful that its Jewish population was declining, passed "the Law on Families Blessed with Children … giving a whole range of subsidies to families with more than 3 children" (Yuval-Davis 1987: 83). Of course, only Jewish women married to Jewish men were eligible. In addition, in many countries, only male citizens are able to pass on citizenship to their children. For example, if a Turkish woman living in Turkey is married to a French man, their children are not automatically Turkish. Children born *in* the United States are citizens, but children born abroad are subjected to different rules, depending on the gender of the citizen-parent. A child born abroad before 1934 to an American mother and a foreign father is not a citizen, but one born abroad to an American father and foreign mother is, and has been since 1855. As stated in *Montana v. Kennedy* (366 US [1961]),

> The court ruled that a child born abroad prior to May 24, 1934, to an American citizen mother did not acquire American citizenship at birth, since at that time citizenship at birth was transmitted only by a citizen father. Although subsequent legislation conferred upon American women the power to transmit citizenship to their children born abroad, such legislation was not retroactive and did not bestow citizenship on persons born before the enactment of such legislation.

And even then, citizenship would not descend until the child returned and resided in the United States for a five-year continuous period prior to his or her eighteenth birthday.

There are other ways in which bodies are deeply entwined with the nation. In times of war, for example, governments have been able to commandeer (male) bodies to fight and be killed. The modern nation-state has literally been built on the bodies of men. In his influential book *Imagined Communities* (1983), Benedict Anderson described the nation as an "idea" for which countless people have willingly sacrificed their lives. Although many civilians lost their lives in the creation of nation-states, it is usually male bodies that are conscripted to fight and die for them. The use of their bodies has been legitimated through rhetorics of honor and glory so they will not seem to have died in vain. Today, with the threat of nuclear weapons and other varieties of modern warfare, the collateral damage to human bodies is enormous. It is clear that the nation controls our bodies in many ways, some of which we are not aware of or only become aware of when that control impinges on us personally.

Rights in our bodies and rights to our bodies

Citizens of the United States assume that we possess our bodies, but this is true only to a limited extent. The state, by deciding who shall receive health care and who shall have access to good food and housing, literally shapes the bodies of its inhabitants. It can decide who can do what kinds of work and how many people are allowed to occupy an apartment, house, or bedroom, disciplining the spaces bodies can occupy. It can scrutinize and even block certain kinds of bodies from entering the country, such as bodies with disabilities, AIDS, mental deficiencies, and particular kinds of sexual orientation. Finally, it has the power to discipline the bodies of those who transgress its rules and regulations.

Although the United States is said to be a multicultural society, it nevertheless discourages some groups from reproducing and has in the past sterilized members of stigmatized racial groups and the genetically impaired. Today, poor women are the target for state population control policies. Believing that poor women reproduce only to gain added, but extremely minimal, welfare benefits, the United States is one of the most punitive of all industrialized nations with regard to "welfare" for single or poor mothers.

> Poor children in the United States are poorer than the children in most other Western industrialized nations … only in Israel and Ireland are poor children worse off than poor American youths. (Keith Bradsher, reporting on the Luxembourg Income Study, *New York Times*, August 14, 1995; see also an op-ed piece by Richard Russo, same day)

This was confirmed independently by a three-year study financed by the Carnegie Foundation entitled "Starting Points: Meeting the Needs of Our Youngest Children" (1994).

Although it takes two to make a child (with conventional methods), only women are the targets of birth control devices and programs, despite the fact that the majority of out-of-wedlock teenage pregnancies are the result of intercourse with men who are over the age of 21 and therefore have much easier access to such devices. In addition, "virtually all sterilization abuse (as well as proposals for less drastic bodily invasions, such as the use of Norplant) is directed against women on welfare" (Bordo 1993: 76). There was a vociferous public outcry when chemical sterilization (erroneously called *chemical castration*) of convicted male sex offenders was proposed; it was held that their reproductive rights could not or should not be infringed. But there was little objection to the forced sterilization of welfare mothers through Norplant and methods.

In the United States, where individual freedom is assumed and where state intervention into personal lives is generally abhorred, women's control over their bodies is quite limited. Philosopher Susan Bordo argues that two different traditions have influenced both law and medicine concerning individual rights: "one for embodied subjects, and the other for those who come to be treated as mere bodies despite official rhetoric that vehemently forswears such treatment of human beings" (1993: 72). Bodily integrity is held in such high regard that "judges have consistently refused to force individuals to submit without consent to medical treatment even though the life of another hangs in the balance" (p. 73). In other words, you cannot be forced to donate bone marrow to save the life of your already born and living child. But many of these same judges are eager to see the repeal of *Roe v. Wade*, which would force women to carry pregnancies to term and give birth against their wishes. Bordo decries the way women's bodies are imagined as "fetal incubators"; in some of the rhetoric, the fetus's *personhood* takes precedence over that of the woman involved. We must ask, as the title of Bordo's article does, "Are Women Persons?"

Traffic in Body Parts

When we think about "the body" we generally think of the whole body. Although our language distinguishes different body parts – arms, toes, heart, liver, and so on – they are integral parts *of* the body; they are continuous with and connected to it. We do not normally think of them as separate and partible. Yet, due to recent technical advances in medical practice, we also know that some of these body parts are partible. For example, a living person is able to give half a lung or a kidney to another person without dying in the process. But science has also developed techniques for "harvesting" organs such as hearts, livers, and eyes from cadavers, and preserving them until they can be transplanted into living people who need them. People are encouraged to donate their organs when they die. In the United States, people are given forms to sign when they get or renew their driver's licenses, so that if they are involved in a fatal accident, their organs can be taken.

This technology is, obviously, lifesaving for many people, but there is a dark specter looming behind it – the traffic in body parts. There is a long tradition in the West of separating the body from market transactions; hence, selling the body – whether into slavery or prostitution – is against the law. Selling *parts* of the body is also against the law

in virtually every country (Iran is perhaps the only exception) and has been condemned by all of the worlds' medical associations. In the United States, the National Organ Transplant Act, passed in 1984, calls for as much as a $50,000 fine and five years in prison if a person is convicted of buying or selling human organs. … Yet in Israel and a handful of other nations, including India, Turkey, China, Russia, and Iraq, organ sales are conducted with only a scant nod toward secrecy. (Michael Finkel, "This Little Kidney Went to Market: Complications," *New York Times Magazine*, May 27, 2001, pp. 26–59, p. 28)

However, since it is normally poor people who sell their organs, some people think they should be paid. This includes doctors like Michael Friedlaender, who performs transplant operations at Hadassah University and argues that "everyone else in the transaction profits – the doctors, the hospital, the nurses and of course the recipient. 'Why,' he wonders, 'does the person losing the most have to do it for free?'" (Finkel 2001: 32). There is a certain logic to his point.

However, others, such as Lawrence Cohen and Nancy Scheper-Hughes, medical anthropologists at the University of California, Berkeley, and cofounders of Organ Watch, strongly disagree precisely because the donors tend to be the poorest and most vulnerable people (Cohen 1999; Scheper-Hughes 2000). According to Scheper-Hughes, "[T]he flow of organs follows the modern routes of capital: from the South to the North, from Third to First World, from poor to rich, from black and brown to white, and from female to male" (2000: 193). The traffic in organs replicates global inequalities and works to further enforce them. It is very difficult to maintain the line (or fiction) between voluntary donation and coercion in such cases since poor people are vulnerable to coercive tactics and rhetoric, whether within the family or from outside. For example, in India, where Cohen has conducted extensive fieldwork, it is mostly women who "donate" a kidney. Husbands "made it clear that if the men had to do heavy labor, it was only fair that the women contribute to the family income by selling a kidney." But, he went on, "in none of the cases did selling an organ significantly improve the family's fortune in the long run" (Cohen, cited in Finkel 2001: 33). There is even a slum outside the city of Chennai that is "nicknamed 'Kidneyvakkam' because so many of the residents had undergone the operation" (Cohen 1999: 137).

Are the bodies of poor people going to be viewed as commodities, as resources for spare parts? It seems they already are, according to Japanese social theorist Tsuyoshi Awaya, who has coined the term "neo-cannibalism" to describe the phenomenon. "We are now eyeing each other's bodies greedily as a source of detachable spare parts with which to extend our lives" (Awaya, cited in Scheper-Hughes 2000: 198). Condemned and executed prisoners in China have already been used in this way; and there are fears that certain groups such as street children are also being used for this purpose (e.g. the film *Central Station*). Whether these fears are grounded in fact I do not know. But even as rumors, as "weapons of the weak" – that is, as a form of protest by those most vulnerable – they have had a powerful effect. A friend who was adopting a baby from a third-world country heard that people were reluctant to allow international adoption, lest the children be harvested for their organs. Clearly, international guidelines for obtaining and transplanting organs need to be developed and enforced to stop the trafficking in body parts. More importantly, there has to be a better way to solve the problem of poverty than by dismembering the poor.

If you believe that you *are* your body, who are you if you have parts from someone else? If you believe the body should be buried (or burned) intact, what is the status of a body from which an organ (or organs) has been removed? What are the implications for death (Lock 2002)? Different religions and religious people have different feelings about this. Judaism and Islam, for example, believe the body should be buried intact, and religious officials seem more ambivalent about donating organs than they are about receiving them. Surprisingly, Christianity does not seem to have such qualms (Finkel 2001: 28).

Or maybe it is not so surprising, since there was a "trafficking in holy body parts" (Bynum 1995: 327) among Christians during the Middle Ages. "By the twelfth century," according to medievalist Caroline Walker Bynum, "the faithful were enthusiastically fragmenting bodies … so that parts could be given to religious communities that wished to share in the saint's power and presence" (p. 201). In addition, there seemed to be a hierarchy of parts – hearts went to abbeys, and entrails to lesser churches. Sometimes the parts were buried, and thus the same saint could be buried in two (or more) places. But more often they were "divided up to provide relics" (p. 201). At first reliquaries were elaborate constructions in the shape of churches and made of gold encrusted with gems; later they came to resemble the part that they housed, like the hand of John the Baptist that I have seen in the collection at Topkapı Palace, Istanbul. Because of the enthusiasm for fragments of saints' bodies, it sometimes happened that a particular saint ended up with more parts than he or she had in life. In a sense, the "enthusiasm for bodily partition was made possible by the confidence in ultimate victory over it" (p. 213), for God would reunite all the parts at resurrection. Despite the view that the earthly body was a house of rot and corruption, it would be wrong to conclude that the practices of fragmentation and partition suggest "either dualistic rejection of the body or the equation of self with soul" (p. 328). Instead, the whole person, the true person, is the resurrected body.

Dead (and Dying) Bodies

The way we think about and treat dead bodies very much depends on what we think about bodies more generally. At issue is whether we believe, as poet Erica Jong poignantly put it, "Flesh is merely a lesson. We learn it and pass on" (1979: 24). The way we treat dead bodies depends on whether we believe that we are merely our bodies, that our bodies are the casing for the soul or spirit, or that these aspects of the person are inseparable. Americans are particularly squeamish about death. For a society so focused on youth and fitness, the deterioration of the body is a terror to be avoided at all costs, and the idea of death is anathema. As noted in chapter 2, elderly dying people are often shunted away out of sight – to nursing homes or hospitals. Except for those who routinely tend to the dead and dying, most people rarely see a dead body. In the United States, the body is treated as so much dead matter, whisked away as quickly as possible and delivered to a funeral home to be prepared for burial or cremation. Personally, I find something quite barbaric in this treatment, and at the death of one of my parents I postponed informing the attending staff so that I could sit with the body for a time.

Is Life the Incurable Disease?

> Is life the incurable disease:
> The infant is born howling
> & we laugh,
> the dead man smiles

& we cry,
resisting the passage,
always resisting the passage,
that turns life
into eternity.

Blake sang alleluias
on his deathbed.
My own grandmother,
hardly a poet at all,
smiled
as we'd never seen her smile
before.
Perhaps the dress of flesh
is no more than a familiar garment
that grows looser as one diets
on death, & perhaps discards it
or gives it to the poor in spirit
who have not learned yet
what blessing it is
to go naked?

Erica Jong, in *At the Edge
of the Body* (1979)

There are some societies where the family and close friends sit with the body for quite a while after death to let the spirit adjust to its new condition, fearing that haste will bring misfortune on the living. The *Tibetan Book of the Dead*, for example, suggests a period of 33 days to allow the spirit to negotiate the different levels of *bardo* existence. Then the body is exposed to let birds of prey pick the flesh clean, leaving the bones to be collected, cleaned, and placed in jars.

During my fieldwork I became quite preoccupied with death because the villagers were gravely concerned about their responsibilities if I died there. I had never really given it much thought, but confronted with it daily I was forced to try to clarify my beliefs. In the end, I dealt with it by giving the headman the telephone number of the American Embassy. People have different views in different contexts, and I was no exception. Still, this preoccupation helped me to learn about their views.

When a person dies in that Muslim village, everyone is immediately aware of it, because the *ezan* (call to prayer) is broadcast from the minaret outside of its regular schedule and floats over the village. Everything happens very quickly because the dead must be buried within 24 hours. The corpse is washed, usually by the oldest female relative, and its orifices are plugged with cotton wool. Then it is immediately wrapped in a length of white cloth called a *kefen*. The body of a man is first taken to the mosque, where all the men of the village have gathered to pray for him, while the body of a woman is taken directly to the cemetery. Women do not go to the mosque but gather, instead, at the home of the deceased's family, where they mourn by singing tales about the dead person, cry and wail, and comfort the survivors.

Bodies must be buried intact because villagers believe the dead will be interrogated by an angel before they may enter Paradise. The questions are simple, and all villagers have memorized the answers in Arabic, the language of the Prophet and the Qur'an. What is your religion? Who is your prophet? Did you keep *oruç* (the fast of Ramazan)? Did you perform *namaz* (daily prayers)? And, for women, did you keep your hair covered? It is said that for every strand of hair exposed, a woman will burn 90 days in hell. Not surprisingly, hell is thought to be occupied primarily by women.

Turks will not countenance cremation, and many of the village Turks would not fly in an airplane because it could crash and incinerate the passengers in the ensuing fire. Instead they traveled in buses, even when they went on the *hajj* to Mecca. Of course, many urban and even some village Turks have flown, and Turkey, like all Muslim countries, has a national airline, several private ones, and a number of modern airports. When a Turk who has been working in Europe dies, quite often the body is flown home to be buried in the soil of that person's natal village.

In the contemporary United States, there are a number of options for dead bodies, and the choice is often related to the person's religious beliefs. Jews and Christians, generally, believe the body should be buried intact. Although the phrase "ashes to ashes, dust to dust" could easily include cremation, it is not a common practice in the United States. When it is chosen, the bereaved must decide how to treat the ashes. Some choose to bury them, others house them in urns, and still others scatter them in places that held special meaning for the deceased. Some people, like my mother, donate their dead bodies to hospitals so that students may learn from them; others donate parts so that others might live.

Immortality and Cryonics

For the devout believer, Christianity takes away the sting of death (1 Corinthians 15:55) by promising a continued existence in Heaven. But in a secular society influenced by Christianity, there are some who seek an earthly immortality to be achieved by cloning or by cryonics.[12] The word *cryonics* was coined in 1965 and refers to "the freezing of people for future revival" (Alcor Life Extension Foundation [1989] 1993: 6). Although the idea is not particularly new, the ability to put it into practice is. Today there are several facilities where this technology is available, with about 100 people frozen and stored at one of these facilities. This practice received considerable attention in July 2002, when the body of baseball hero Ted Williams was delivered to Alcor. Some clients have elected to have only their head and brain frozen, believing that their unique personality is stored in the brain rather like information in a computer.

In part, the beliefs and practices of the cryonicists came about with the realization that there are several clinical definitions of death – when the heart stops beating, when a person stops breathing, or when brain activity stops – all of which can sometimes be reversed with modern technology. According to Robert Ettinger, a founder of the movement, a person "dies little by little usually, in imperceptible gradations, and the question of reversibility at any stage depends on the state of medical art" (1964: 3). In other words, death is like gestation – a process, rather than an event – and has numerous possible outcomes. He proposed that if the (allegedly) dead body could be frozen quickly enough, it could remain in a state of "suspended death" until the technology is developed to reanimate it and the treatments – medicines, cloning, and cell revitalization – are available to cure the disease that killed it in the first place. Death, in their new jargon, is merely "deanimation" awaiting "reanimation." Cryonicists also discuss the possibility of "suspended animation" or "suspended life" for people who are old or feeble and want to be frozen before they die. But is this euthanasia and therefore illegal? Perhaps a more interesting issue is why most of the participants involved in the cryonics enterprise are white, middle class, and male. Is it simply because they have the resources to do so, or are they more dissatisfied than the rest of us with a life of mortal limits? How would notions of time change if the possibility for immortality existed? Why is life not enough?

Notes

1. "Barbie," a doll invented by Ruth Handler and introduced in 1959, is bustier than Twiggy and closer to the ideal body type of the 1950s. But she is still an impossible model for a woman to emulate. Her shape if transferred to a human female would be 39–21–33, and her legs are out of proportion with the rest of her body.

2. See especially Bynum (1987) and Bell (1985).

3. Vale and Juno's book *Modern Primitives* (1989) is a documentary of a variety of these contemporary practices.

4. See Kuper's *The Invention of Primitive Society* (1988) for a discussion of the way the notion of "primitive society" was invented in the mid-nineteenth century in an evolutionary framework as a mirror to Western society. We have already talked of the way the body (nature) is constructed within culture and does not exist outside it.

5. See, for example, Elaine Scarry's book *The Body in Pain* (1987).

6. Probably the most notorious case in recent history was that suffered by David Reimer in 1966, when, as an infant, his penis was obliterated beyond surgical repair during a circumcision procedure. The account of the accident and the subsequent attempt to raise him as a girl are told in John Colapinto's book, *As Nature Made Him: The Boy Who Was Raised as a Girl* (2006). Numerous other circumcision accidents, from mutilation to death from infection, have been reported in the press.

7. The term *female genital mutilation* is offensive to Sudanese women (and others) because it is not seen as mutilation. The English speakers among them use *circumcision*, while others prefer the term *female genital cutting* (e.g., Gruenbaum 2001).

8. Infibulation is practiced primarily in the Sudan, Somalia, Eritrea, and Djibouti. The procedure and its cultural meanings are described extensively by Janice Boddy (1989).

9. For culturally sensitive accounts that at the same time do not condone the practice, see especially the work of anthropologists Janice Boddy (1982, 1989) and Ellen Gruenbaum (2001). For an Egyptian doctor's perspective, see Nawal El Sadaawi's *The Hidden Face of Eve* (1980).

10. For a readable, if controversial, account of transsexualism, see Michael Bailey (2003)

11. Recently, an enormous literature has developed on this topic. See, for example, Anthias and Yuval-Davis (1992); Linke (1999); Mosse (1985); and Parker, Russo, Sommer, and Yeager (1992).

12. My information about cryonics was supplied by Tiffany Romain, a graduate student in my department, who is making this study the basis of her doctoral dissertation.

Exercises for Chapter 6   239

E X E R C I S E S

6.1. Advertising Images

Cut out two advertisements from any popular magazine, one that features a man and one that features a woman. For each ad, do three things:

A. Describe the person in the ad: body image, stance, expression, and so on.
B. Discuss why you think this particular image helps to sell whatever product is being advertised.
C. Discuss how this particular image communicates something about the culture's notions of males and females. You might ask a couple of friends to comment on the photos as well and include their comments in your analysis.

6.2. Self-Image

Can you think of an example in your own life when you were aware of trying to make your body, or part of it, conform to the cultural norm or standard? How did you do it? If you cannot readily think of such an example – or would prefer not to share it – ask someone else if they'd be willing to tell you about such an experience in their life.

Bibliography

Alcor Life Extension Foundation ([1989] 1993) *Cryonics: Reaching for Tomorrow*. Scottsdale, AZ: Author.

Anderson, Benedict (1983) *Imagined Communities*. London: Verso.

Anthias, Floya, and Yuval-Davis, Nira, in association with Harried Cain (1992) *Racialized Boundaries: Race, Nation, Gender, Colour and Class and the Anti-Racist Struggle*. London: Routledge.

Bailey, Michael (2003) *The Man Who Would Be Queen: The Science of Gender-Bending and Transsexualism*. Washington, DC: Joseph Henry Press.

Bell, Rudolph (1985) *Holy Anorexia*. Chicago: University of Chicago Press.

Bettelheim, Bruno (1954) *Symbolic Wounds: Puberty Rites and the Envious Male*. New York: Free Press.

Blacking, John, ed. (1977) *The Anthropology of the Body*. London: Academic Press.

Boddy, Janice (1982) "Womb as Oasis: The Symbolic Context of Pharaonic Circumcision in Rural Northern Sudan." *American Ethnologist* 15(1): 4–27.

Boddy, Janice (1989) *Wombs and Alien Spirits: Women, Men, and the Zar Cults in Northern Sudan*. Madison: University of Wisconsin Press.

Bordo, Susan (1993) *Unbearable Weight: Feminism, Western Culture, and the Body*. Berkeley: University of California Press.

Boston Women's Health Book Collective ([1973] 1992) *The New Our Bodies, Ourselves*. New York: Simon & Schuster.

Bourdieu, Pierre ([1972] 1977) *Outline of a Theory of Practice*, trans. Richard Nice. Cambridge: Cambridge University Press.

Brownmiller, Susan (1984) *Femininity*. New York: Fawcett Columbine.

Brumberg, Joan Jacobs (1997) *The Body Project: An Intimate History of American Girls*. New York: Random House.

Bynum, Caroline Walker (1987) *Holy Feast and Holy Fast: The Religious Significance of Food to Medieval Women*. Berkeley: University of California Press.

Bynum, Caroline Walker (1995) *The Resurrection of the Body in Western Christianity, 200–1336*. New York: Columbia University Press.

Carnegie Foundation (1994) *Starting Points: Meeting the Needs of Our Youngest Children*. New York: Author.

Chernin, Kim (1981) *The Obsession: Reflections on the Tyranny of Slenderness*. New York: Harper & Row.

Cohen, Lawrence (1999) "Where It Hurts: Indian Material for an Ethics of Organ Transplantation." *Daedalus* 128(4): 135–65.

Colapinto, John (2006) *As Nature Made Him: The Boy Who Was Raised as a Girl*, rev. ed. New York: Harper.

Council on Size and Weight Discrimination (n.d.) "Facts and Figures." www.cswd.org/docs/facts.html.

Delaney, Carol (1991) *The Seed and the Soil: Gender and Cosmology in Turkish Village Society*. Berkeley: University of California Press.

Delaney, Carol (1998) *Abraham on Trial: The Social Legacy of Biblical Myth*. Princeton, NJ: Princeton University Press.

DeLoache, Judy, and Gottlieb, Alma, eds. (2000) *A World of Babies: Imagined Childcare Guides for Seven Societies*. New York: Cambridge University Press.

Disch, Estelle (1997) *Reconstructing Gender: A Multicultural Anthology*. Mountain View, CA: Mayfield.

Douglas, Mary ([1966] 1999) *Purity and Danger: An Analysis of the Concepts of Pollution and Taboo*. London: Routledge & Kegan Paul.

Ehrenreich, Barbara, and English, Deidre (1973) *Complaints and Disorders: The Sexual Politics of Sickness*. Old Westbury, NY: Feminist Press.

Ehrenreich, Barbara, and English, Deidre (1979) *For Her Own Good: 150 Years of the Experts' Advice to Women*. New York: Anchor.

Eilberg-Schwartz, Howard (1990) *The Savage in Judaism: An Anthropology of Israelite Religion and Ancient Judaism*. Bloomington: Indiana University Press.

El Sadaawi, Nawal (1980) *The Hidden Face of Eve: Women in the Arab World*, trans. and ed. Sherif Hetata. London: Zed Press.

Ettinger, Robert C. W. (1964) *The Prospect of Immortality*. New York: Doubleday.

Featherstone, Mike, ed. (2000) *Body Modification*. London: Sage.

Gilmore, David (1994) "The Beauty of the Beast: Male Body Imagery in Anthropological Perspective." In *The Good Body: Asceticism in Contemporary Culture*, ed. Mary G. Winkler and Letha B. Cole. New Haven, CT: Yale University Press, pp. 191–214.

Gruenbaum, Ellen (2001) *The Female Circumcision Controversy*. Philadelphia: University of Pennsylvania Press.

Hertz, Robert ([1909] 1973) "Pre-Eminence of the Right Hand: A Study in Religious Polarity." In *Right and Left:*

Essays on Dual Symbolic Classification, ed. Rodney Needham. Chicago: University of Chicago Press.

Jong, Erica (1979) *At the Edge of the Body*. New York: Holt, Rinehart & Winston.

Kittay, Eva (1996) "Human Dependency and Rawlsian Equality." In *Feminists Rethink the Self*, ed. Diana Tiejtens Meyers. Boulder, CO: Westview Press.

Klesse, Christian (2000) "'Modern Primitivism': Non-Mainstream Body Modification and Racialized Representations." In *Body Modification*, ed. Mike Featherstone. Thousand Oaks, CA: Sage.

Kuper, Adam (1988) *The Invention of Primitive Society: Transformations of an Illusion*. New York: Routledge.

Levenson, Jon (1993) *The Death and Resurrection of the Beloved Son: The Transformation of Child Sacrifice in Judaism and Christianity*. New Haven, CT: Yale University Press.

Linke, Uli (1999) *Blood and Nation*. Philadelphia: University of Pennsylvania Press.

Lock, Margaret (2002) *Twice Dead: Organ Transplants and the Reinvention of Death*. Berkeley: University of California Press.

Mascia-Lees, Frances E., and Sharpe, Patricia (1992) *Tattoo, Torture, Mutilation, and Adornment: The Denaturalization of the Body in Culture and Text*. Albany: State University of New York Press.

Mauss, Marcel ([1934] 1973) "Techniques of the Body." *Economy and Society* 2(1): 70–88.

McGee, Jon, and Warms, Richard (2000) *Anthropological Theory: An Introductory History*. Mountain View, CA: Mayfield.

Miner, Horace (1956) "Body Ritual among the Nacirema." *American Anthropologist* 58: 503–7.

Mosse, George L. (1985) *Nationalism and Sexuality: Middle-Class Morality and Sexual Norms in Modern Europe*. Madison: University of Wisconsin Press.

Ortner, Sherry (1974) "Is Female to Male as Nature Is to Culture?" In *Women, Culture, and Society*, ed. Michelle Rosaldo and Louise Lamphere. Stanford, CA: Stanford University Press.

Ottenheimer, Martin (1996) *Forbidden Relatives: The American Myth of Cousin Marriage*. Urbana: University of Illinois Press.

Parker, Andrew, Russo, Mary, Sommer, Doris, and Yeager, Patricia, eds. (1992) *Nationalisms and Sexualities*. New York: Routledge.

Pope, Harrison G., Jr., Phillips, Katharine A., and Olivardia, Roberto (2000) *The Adonis Complex: The Secret Crisis of Male Body Obsession*. New York: Free Press.

Ringrose, M. (1994) "Living in the Shadows: Eunuchs and Gender in Byzantium." In *Third Sex, Third Gender: Beyond Sexual Dimorphism in Culture and History*, ed. Gilbert Herdt. New York: Zone.

Scarry, Elaine (1987) *The Body in Pain: The Making and Unmaking of the World*. New York: Oxford University Press.

Scheper-Hughes, Nancy (2000) "The Global Traffic in Human Organs." *Current Anthropology* 41(2): 191–224.

Seid, Roberta P. (1994) "Too Close to the Bone: The Historical Context for Women's Obsession with Slenderness." In *Feminist Perspectives on Eating Disorders*, ed. Patricia Fallon, Melanie A. Katzman, and Susan C. Wooley. New York: Guilford.

Suleiman, Susan Rubin, ed. (1986) *The Female Body in Western Culture: Contemporary Perspectives*. Cambridge, MA: Harvard University Press.

Turner, Bryan (1984) *Body and Society: Explorations in Social Theory*. Oxford: Blackwell.

Vale, V., and Juno, Andrea (1989) *Modern Primitives: Tattoo, Piercing, Scarification: An Investigation of Contemporary Adornment and Ritual*. London: Re/Search.

Whorf, Benjamin (1956) *Language, Thought and Reality*. Cambridge, MA: MIT Press.

Wolf, Naomi (1991) "Hunger." In *The Beauty Myth: How Images of Beauty Are Used against Women*. New York: Anchor Doubleday.

Yuval-Davis, Nira (1987) "The Jewish Collectivity and National Reproduction in Israel." In *Women in the Middle East*. London: Khamsin.

READING

Body Ritual among the Nacirema
Horace Miner

The anthropologist has become so familiar with the diversity of ways in which different peoples behave in similar situations that he is not apt to be surprised by even the most exotic customs. In fact, if all of the logically possible combinations of behavior have not been found somewhere in the world, he is apt to suspect that they must be present in some yet undescribed tribe. This point has, in fact, been expressed with respect to clan organization by Murdock (1949: 71). In this light, the magical beliefs and practices of the Nacirema present such unusual aspects that it seems desirable to describe them as an example of the extremes to which human behavior can go.

Professor Linton first brought the ritual of the Nacirema to the attention of anthropologists twenty years ago (1936: 326), but the culture of this people is still very poorly understood. They are a North American group living in the territory between the Canadian Cree, the Yaqui and Tarahumare of Mexico, and the Carib and Arawak of the Antilles. Little is known of their origin, although tradition states that they came from the east.

According to Nacirema mythology, their nation was originated by a culture hero, Notgnihsaw, who is otherwise known for two great feats of strength – the throwing of a piece of wampum across the river Pa-To-Mac and the chopping down of a cherry tree in which the Spirit of Truth resided.

Nacirema culture is characterized by a highly developed market economy which has evolved in a rich natural habitat. While much of the people's time is devoted to economic pursuits, a large part of the fruits of these labors and a considerable portion of the day are spent in ritual activity. The focus of this activity is the human body, the appearance and health of which loom as a dominant concern in the ethos of the people. While such a concern is certainly not unusual, its ceremonial aspects and associated philosophy are unique.

The fundamental belief underlying the whole system appears to be that the human body is ugly and that its natural tendency is to debility and disease. Incarcerated in such a body, man's only hope is to avert these characteristics through the use of the powerful influences of ritual and ceremony. Every household has one or more shrines devoted to this purpose. The more powerful individuals in the society have several shrines in their houses and, in fact, the opulence of a house is often referred to in terms of the number of such ritual centers it possesses. Most houses are of wattle and daub construction, but the shrine rooms of the more wealthy are walled with stone. Poorer families imitate the rich by applying pottery plaques to their shrine walls.

While each family has at least one such shrine, the rituals associated with it are not family ceremonies but are private and secret. The rites are normally only discussed with children, and then only during the period when they are being initiated into these mysteries. I was able, however, to establish sufficient rapport with the natives to examine these shrines and to have the rituals described to me.

The focal point of the shrine is a box or chest which is built into the wall. In this chest are kept the many charms and magical potions without which no native believes he could live. These preparations are secured from a variety of specialized practitioners. The most powerful of these are the medicine men, whose assistance must be rewarded with substantial gifts. However, the medicine men do not provide the curative potions for their clients, but decide what the ingredients should be and then write them down in an ancient and secret language. This writing is understood only by the medicine men and by the herbalists who, for another gift, provide the required charm.

The charm is not disposed of after it has served its purpose, but is placed in the charm-box of the household shrine. As these magical materials are specific for certain ills, and the real or imagined maladies of the people are many, the charm-box is usually full to overflowing. The magical packets are so numerous that people forget what their purposes were and fear to use them again. While the natives are very vague on this point, we can only assume that the idea in retaining all the old magical materials is that their presence in the charm-box, before which the body rituals are conducted, will in some way protect the worshipper.

Beneath the charm-box is a small font. Each day every member of the family, in succession, enters the shrine room, bows his head before the charm-box, mingles different sorts of holy water in the font, and proceeds with a brief rite of ablution. The holy waters are secured from the Water Temple of the community, where the priests conduct elaborate ceremonies to make the liquid ritually pure.

In the hierarchy of magical practitioners, and below the medicine men in prestige, are specialists whose designation is best translated "holy-mouth-men." The Nacirema have an almost pathological horror of and fascination with the mouth, the condition of which is believed to have a supernatural influence on all social relationships. Were it not for the rituals of the mouth, they believe that their teeth would fall out, their gums bleed, their jaws shrink, their friends desert them, and their lovers reject them. They also believe that a strong relationship exists between oral and moral characteristics. For example, there is a ritual ablution of the mouth for children which is supposed to improve their moral fiber.

The daily body ritual performed by everyone includes a mouth-rite. Despite the fact that these people are so punctilious about care of the mouth, this rite involves a practice which strikes the uninitiated stranger as revolting. It was reported to me that the ritual consists of inserting a small bundle of hog hairs into the mouth, along with certain magical powders, and then moving the bundle in a highly formalized series of gestures.

In addition to the private mouth-rite, the people seek out a holy-mouth-man once or twice a year. These practitioners have an impressive set of paraphernalia, consisting of a variety of augers, awls, probes, and prods. The use of these objects in the exorcism of the evils of the mouth involves almost unbelievable ritual torture of the client. The holy-mouth-man opens the client's mouth and, using the above mentioned tools, enlarges any holes which decay may have created in the teeth. Magical materials are put into these holes. If there are no naturally occurring holes in the teeth, large sections of one or more teeth are gouged out so that the supernatural substance can be applied. In the client's view, the purpose of these ministrations is to arrest decay and to draw friends. The extremely sacred and traditional character of the rite is evident in the fact that the natives return to the holy-mouth-men year after year, despite the fact that their teeth continue to decay.

It is to be hoped that, when a thorough study of the Nacirema is made, there will be careful inquiry into the personality structure of these people. One has but to watch the gleam in the eye of a holy-mouth-man, as he jabs an awl into an exposed nerve, to suspect that a certain amount of sadism is involved. If this can be established, a very interesting pattern emerges, for most of the population shows definite masochistic tendencies. It was to these that Professor Linton referred in discussing a distinctive part of the daily body ritual which is performed only by men. This part of the rite involves scraping and lacerating the surface of the face with a sharp instrument. Special women's rites are performed only four times during each lunar month, but what they lack in frequency is made up in barbarity. As part of this ceremony, women bake their heads in small ovens for about an hour. The theoretically interesting point is that what seems to be a preponderantly masochistic people have developed sadistic specialists.

The medicine men have an imposing temple, or *latipso*, in every community of any size. The more elaborate ceremonies required to treat very sick patients can only be performed at this temple. These ceremonies involve not only the thaumaturge but a permanent group of vestal maidens who move sedately about the temple chambers in distinctive costume and headdress.

The *latipso* ceremonies are so harsh that it is phenomenal that a fair proportion of the really sick natives who enter the temple ever recover. Small children whose indoctrination is still incomplete have been known to resist attempts to take them to the temple because "that is where you go to die." Despite this fact, sick adults are not only willing but eager to undergo the protracted ritual purification, if they can afford to do so. No matter how ill the supplicant or how grave the emergency, the guardians of many temples will not admit a client if he cannot give a rich gift to the custodian. Even after one has gained admission and survived the ceremonies, the guardians will not permit the neophyte to leave until he makes still another gift.

The supplicant entering the temple is first stripped of all his or her clothes. In everyday life the Nacirema avoids exposure of his body and its natural functions. Bathing and excretory acts are performed only in the secrecy of the household shrine, where they are ritualized as part of the body-rites. Psychological shock results from the fact that body secrecy is suddenly lost upon entry into the *latipso*. A man, whose own wife has never seen him in an excretory act, suddenly finds himself naked and assisted by a vestal maiden while he performs his natural functions into a sacred vessel. This sort of ceremonial treatment is necessitated by the fact that the excreta are used by a diviner to ascertain the course and nature of the client's sickness. Female clients, on the other hand, find their naked bodies are subjected to the scrutiny, manipulation and prodding of the medicine men.

Few supplicants in the temple are well enough to do anything but lie on their hard beds. The daily ceremonies, like the rites of the holy-mouth-men, involve discomfort and torture. With ritual precision, the vestals awaken their miserable charges each dawn and roll them about on their beds of pain while performing ablutions, in the formal movements of which the maidens are highly trained. At other times they insert magic wands in the supplicant's mouth or force him to eat substances which are supposed to be healing. From time to time the medicine men come to their clients and jab magically treated needles into their flesh. The fact that these temple ceremonies may not cure, and may even kill the neophyte, in no way decreases the people's faith in the medicine men.

There remains one other kind of practitioner, known as a "listener." This witch-doctor has the power to exorcise the devils that lodge in the heads of people who have been bewitched. The Nacirema believe that parents bewitch their own children. Mothers are particularly suspected of putting a curse on children while teaching them the secret body rituals. The counter-magic of the witch-doctor is unusual in its lack of ritual. The patient simply tells the "listener" all his troubles and fears, beginning with the earliest difficulties he can remember. The memory displayed by the Nacirema in these exorcism sessions is truly remarkable. It is not uncommon for the patient to bemoan the rejection he felt upon being weaned as a babe, and a few individuals even see their troubles going back to the traumatic effects of their own birth.

In conclusion, mention must be made of certain practices which have their base in native esthetics but which depend upon the pervasive aversion to the natural body and its functions. There are ritual fasts to make fat people thin and ceremonial feasts to make thin people fat. Still other rites are used to make women's breasts larger if they are small, and smaller if they are large. General dissatisfaction with breast shape is symbolized in the fact that the ideal form is virtually outside the range of human variation. A few women afflicted with almost inhuman hypermammary development are so idolized that they make a handsome living by simply going from village to village and permitting the natives to stare at them for a fee.

Reference has already been made to the fact that excretory functions are ritualized, routinized, and relegated to secrecy. Natural reproductive functions are similarly distorted. Intercourse is taboo as a topic and scheduled as an act. Efforts are made to avoid pregnancy by the use of magical materials or by limiting intercourse to certain phases of the moon. Conception is actually very infrequent. When pregnant, women dress so as to hide their condition. Parturition takes place in secret, without friends or relatives to assist, and the majority of women do not nurse their infants.

Our review of the ritual life of the Nacirema has certainly shown them to be a magic-ridden people. It is hard to understand how they have managed to exist so long under the burdens which they have imposed upon themselves. But even such exotic customs as these take on real meaning when they are viewed with the insight provided by Malinowski when he wrote (1948: 70):

> Looking from far and above, from our high places of safety in the developed civilization, it is easy to see all the crudity and irrelevance of magic. But without its power and guidance early man could not have mastered his practical difficulties as he has done, nor could man have advanced to the higher stages of civilization.

References Cited

Linton, Ralph (1936) *The Study of Man*. New York: D. Appleton-Century.

Malinowski, Bronislaw (1948) *Magic, Science, and Religion*. Glencoe: Free Press.

Murdock, George P. (1949) *Social Structure*. New York: Macmillan.

CHAPTER 7

Food for Thought

What constitutes food? What makes a meal? What does it mean to say that "food is love"? Relation of food to the environment. Fast food, slow food, genetically modified food ("Frankenfood"). Food and sex. Food and civility. Food and religion. Cooking.

Food for Thought

> *A hundred years from now anthropologists and other descendants, upon looking back on our best-selling reading lists, will be curious to know just when it was that food and chefs and things culinary, and books about them, replaced sex as our main sensuous nourishment.*
>
> Martin Arnold ("Food Beats Sex in Best Sellers," *New York Times*,
> May 24, 2001, p. B3)

Introduction

You may not agree that food has usurped the place of sex in American culture, but the ascendance of interest in food, cooking, chefs, and restaurants cannot be denied. The journalist quoted above was struck by the number of books about food on the best-seller list – three as he wrote, one just off the list after 15 weeks, and others soon to appear on it. Tastes in reading, like tastes in food, change with the times and provide an interesting avenue for investigating a culture. In addition to books about food, more than 2,000 cookbooks were published in the year 2000 alone. Surely, this is food for thought. Ruth Reichel, one of the best-selling authors and the last editor of *Gourmet* magazine,[1] suggested that the explosion of interest in food is a sign that we are finally "getting away from our Puritan roots and no longer are embarrassed about thinking about food" (cited in Arnold 2001), that is, we are able to view food sensually and aesthetically rather than merely as a source of energy and survival.

In this chapter I lay out a smorgasbord of ideas about the ways food shapes culture and culture shapes food. It is not a chapter about the nutritional value of food – about vitamins,

Investigating Culture: An Experiential Introduction to Anthropology, Second Edition.
Carol Delaney with Deborah Kaspin.
© 2011 Carol Delaney. Published by Blackwell Publishing Ltd.

minerals, and food as an energy source – but about the culturally constituted nature of food and meals. These are interlarded with issues of classification, religion, identity, civility, pleasure, economics, and the environment. Throughout, be attentive also to the way this topic draws on the topics from the previous chapters – space, time, language, social relations, and body.

1. Regarding space, for example, think of all the places where you can obtain food and the spaces needed to grow food, which includes the pasturing of animals. *Consuming Geographies: We Are Where We Eat* (Bell and Valentine 1997) is organized around social spaces of food consumption – body, home, community, city, region, nation, and, finally, the globe.

2. The temporal dimension not only is indicated by the specific seasons when certain food becomes available, but also is present in the times of our daily meals. Each meal has a different meaning, as do the meals of different days of the week, let alone holiday meals associated with the ritual calendar.

3. Linguistically, there is an enormous lexicon of terms for food, beginning, one might say, with the raw and cooked – also the title of a book by French anthropologist Claude Lévi-Strauss[2] – and roasted, boiled, broiled, baked, grilled, sautéed, and steamed, to mention only a few.

   Roland Barthes, a French structuralist, sees all foods as "signs in a system of communication" ([1957] 1972: 63). The messages expressed by means of food can involve love or disdain, profligacy or stinginess, tradition or *avant garde*, ideas about gender, and the condition of, or concern for, health. As with language, there are rules of combination and substitution – that is, what goes with what, the order of the components, and what are suitable substitutes. Moreover, food terms are used metaphorically to speak of other things; for example, a person who asks, "Have you got any bread on you?" is not asking for food but to find out how much money you have in your pocket. "What's your beef?" does not mean what cut of meat you want but what is your gripe.

4. "Eating together lies at the heart of social relations" (Counihan 1999: 6); it is a kind of training ground in civility (Flammang 2009). The etymology of the word *companion* has to do with breaking bread with someone.

5. Finally, and obviously, food is essential for our bodies and, as we have just seen, it is also intimately related to our body image. Food is a consuming passion.[3]

We Are What We Eat

Food is a very strong cultural marker and thus an integral part of a person's identity. In 1825, Jean Anthelme Brillat-Savarin, a French politician-gourmet, said, "Tell me what you eat, and I will tell you who you are."[4] The statement referred less to ethnic identity than to the stage a nation had reached on the scale of civilization, a scale which, at that time, was assumed to be unilinear and progressive. Naturally, France, with its subtle, refined, and sophisticated cuisine, was thought to epitomize high civilization. Today, anthropologists are far more likely to approach food as an index to culture, not in the sense of "high" versus "low" culture, but as particular cultures and ethnicities. Nevertheless, elements of cultural ascendancy, even snobbishness, persist in statements like the following: "French subtlety of thought and manners is said to be related to the subtlety of their cuisine, the reserve of the British to their unimaginative diet, German stolidness to the quantities of heavy food they consume, and the unreliability of the Italians to the large amounts of wine they drink" (Farb and Armelagos 1980: 40). Despite these stereotypes, food is a quintessential symbol of *identity* – we are what we eat – both individually and culturally. "A people's cuisine, or a particular food, often marks the boundary between the collective self and the other, for example, as a basis of discrimination against other peoples" (Ohnuki-Tierney 1993: 3), or merely just a distinguishing trait, as in the case of Marmite.

> Marmite is a brownish vegetable extract with a toxic odor, saline taste and an axle grease consistency that has somehow captivated the British. ... They buy it at a 24 million-jar-per-year clip that has enshrined it as a national symbol right up there with the royal family and the Sunday roast. (Hoge, *New York Times*, January 24, 2002)

Indeed, so much is it a symbol of being British that several "members of Parliament asked the Commons to affirm the Britishness of Marmite," especially because of "its lack of appeal for the majority of the world's population" (*New York Times*, February 27, 2002). When I was working on an archaeology project sponsored by the British Institute of Archaeology in Turkey, Marmite was the spread of choice among all the British members. Americans, on the other hand, brought peanut butter.

Clearly, one of the most important ways that people reproduce themselves as British, or Turkish, or Chinese, or American is by the food they eat. This is something often ignored by biologists, developers, and aid planners, and the absence of such awareness has had a number of embarrassing, and in some cases tragic, consequences. During a particularly bad famine in part of Africa some years ago, the United States sent an enormous supply of wheat to ease the hunger. However, it turned out that the people did not eat wheat and didn't know what to do with it, so the starving continued. Americans, I think, would balk if they were suddenly told they had to eat grubs – unless they were a contestant on the television show *Survivor*. There are many species of plants and animals that are edible, but only some of them become food. Those that become food vary cross-culturally. Why is it that Germans eat pork, while for Jews and Muslims it is forbidden? Why is beef the heart of a meal for many British and Americans, but sacred and not eaten in India? Why is the dog elevated to sacred status in Britain and the United States, but eaten in Vietnam and elsewhere? All of these meats are edible; it is culture that deems them edible or inedible. Eating is not just about surviving, about getting a certain amount and kind of nutriments; what we eat is who we are as a people. People "survive in a definite way. They reproduce themselves as certain kinds of men and women, social classes, and groups, not as biological organisms or aggregates of organisms ('populations')" (Sahlins 1976: 168).

Because of the strong association between food and identity, some people find it difficult, for instance, to sample food from a culture very different from their own, because the food will be unfamiliar, and they do not like to try new things. That was certainly true among many Turks I met. Turkish cuisine is considered to be one of the great cuisines in the world, and Turks have strong feelings about it. They do not, or did not, see the point of trying foods of different cultures or ethnicities, perhaps because they thought it would dilute their Turkishness. Until very recently, there were few restaurants featuring foods of other nations; indeed, Turkey was not really a restaurant culture. Today, this is changing rapidly, partly in response to tourism, so now, at least in the major cities, one can find all kinds of ethnic restaurants as well as French cafés, pizza parlors, Chinese takeout, sushi bars, as well as the ubiquitous McDonald's. Food may be globalized and creolized, but people's attachments to their own local, regional, and national dishes remain remarkably strong.

The French notion of *terroir* is related to these sentiments. Although there is no exact English equivalent, it means that an agricultural product carries with it something of the "flavor" of the place where it was grown. "For terroir's most ardent promoters, it is axiomatic that the finest fruits and vegetables are those truest to their roots; those whose taste reflects the interplay of soil, climate, topography, and ritual" (Steinberger, *New York Times*, April 14, 2001). Although normally the term is applied to wine making, where the specific region, light, soil, and type of vine are all thought to contribute to the distinctive style of the wine produced in that place, it can, nevertheless, be applied to any agricultural product. Not surprisingly, the French have a very ambivalent attitude to the commercialization and globalization of foodstuffs.

Because food is an important symbol of identity, "a nation's diet can be more revealing than its art or literature" (Schlosser 2001: 3). Italians, according to Alessandra Farkas, a correspondent for Italy's leading newspaper, are identified not just with pasta but also especially with the meat and tomato sauce called *ragù*. "The sauce is the center of everything, it's like a cultural force. … [I]t's like chicken soup for American Jews – it holds generations together" (Asimov, *New York Times*, November 3, 1999). Meanwhile, people in Argentina eat steak "as if it were a national obligation" (Christian, *New York Times*, May 28, 1988) and eat more of it than any other people in the world. For the Japanese, it is rice.

This is the thesis of Ohnuki-Tierney's well-researched discussion of *Rice as Self: Japanese Identities Through Time* (1993). "The symbolic importance of rice has been deeply embedded in the Japanese cosmology both of the elite and the common folk: rice as soul, rice as deity, and ultimately rice as self" (p. 8). Rice is the symbol of commensality – of eating together – whether in a feast for the gods or in daily meals among humans. It is also a kind of sacred medium of exchange. It is relatively easy for Japanese to distinguish themselves from Westerners (meat eaters and bread eaters), but they also distinguish themselves from other rice-eating peoples. At issue is not the *type* of rice, since the Japanese are vehemently opposed to the importation of rice from California even though its short-grain variety is very similar to their own and is much cheaper than the home-grown variety. In fact, Japanese will pay the additional cost to have *Japanese* rice grown in Japanese rice paddies. The issue is that rice is both a symbol of the self and a symbol of the land – its spatial and temporal dimensions – with territorial and historical meanings. "As a metaphor of self, rice paddies are *our* ancestral land, *our* village, *our* region, and ultimately, *our* land, Japan" (p. 10). By ingesting Japanese rice, one incorporates the spirit of Japan, creating an identity between self and nation.

Similar studies can be done for other cultures. A public furor erupted in India when the United States tried to patent a type of basmati rice. Protesters accused the US firm of "bio-piracy and theft of indigenous plant wealth" (*New York Times*, May 25, 2001) and felt that the term should only be applied to rice grown on "Indian soil [and] irrigated by waters from the Himalayan rivers," much as "champagne" can only be applied to sparkling wines from grapes grown in the Champagne district of France.

While rice may be a "key symbol" (Ortner 1973) of Japanese identity, anthropologist Anne Allison argues that such identity reveals an "ideological state apparatus," that is, institutions that "exert power not primarily through repression but through ideology" (1991: 196). While the primary purpose of schools is assumed to be education, educational practices are also ways "of indoctrinating people into seeing the world a certain way and of accepting certain identities as their own within that world" (Allison 1991, quoting Althusser). It is similar to what Sylvia Yanagisako and I have called "naturalizing power," "the ways in which differentials of power come already embedded in culture … for power appears natural, inevitable, even god-given" (Yanagisako and Delaney 1995: 1): it is simply the way the world is.

> [O]ne look at a typical child's *obento* – a small box packaged with a five- or six-course mini-aturized meal whose pieces and parts are artistically arranged – would immediately reveal [that] no food is "just" food in Japan. What is not so immediately apparent, however, is why a small child with limited appetite and perhaps scant interest in food is the recipient of a meal as elaborate and as elaborately prepared as any made for an entire family or invited guests. (Allison 1991: 196)

The state apparatus has made it seem normal for Japanese mothers to devote their time, skill, and money on tiny, beautiful morsels for the lunch boxes of their nursery school children, while the children, even if they do not appreciate the artistry, learn that they deserve such attention. In this way, the state forms particular kinds of people by means of the food they eat.

Some people revel in trying different kinds of food; they consume the culture, literally. And some take this to extremes. "The idea that you are what you eat has been enthusiastically promoted for years by Den Fujita, the eccentric billionaire who brought McDonald's to Japan three decades ago. 'If we eat McDonald's hamburgers and potatoes for a thousand years,' Fujita once promised his countrymen, 'we will become taller, our skin will become white, and our hair will be blonde'" (Schlosser 2001: 231). Americans, apparently, take a different approach. Playing with Brillat-Savarin's dictum, Donna Gabaccia, in her book *We Are What We Eat: Ethnic Food and the Making of Americans* (1998), thinks that

> our food reveals that we are cosmopolitan and iconoclasts; we are tolerant adventurers who do not feel constrained by tradition. … What unites American eaters culturally is how we eat, not what we eat. As eaters, all Americans mingle the culinary traditions of many regions and cultures within ourselves. We are multi-ethnic eaters. (pp. 225–6)

My Turkish friends did not put such a positive spin on this mingling. They said that by eating anything and everything, we reveal we have no culture. The multiethnic mixtures in our stomachs turn us into mongrels.

What Is Food?

While seemingly obvious, what counts as food is far more problematic than one might think. According to best-selling writer Michael Pollan most of the items in contemporary American supermarkets don't deserve to be called food. Instead he refers to our overprocessed concoctions designed by food scientists as "edible foodlike substances" filled with excess salt, high fructose corn syrup, and numerous chemicals to enhance flavor and prevent decay (Pollan 2009, p 5). He suggests that we eat nothing that our great-grandmothers would not recognize as food.

But even that is not so simple. Take, for example, the artichoke. Who, coming upon this thorny thing for the first time, could ever have imagined eating it? Indeed. I was 20 when I first saw and ate an artichoke; my first meeting with an artichoke coincided with the first meeting of my Bostonian (soon-to-be) in-laws. I do not know which was more intimidating.

We need food to survive, that is a given, but what counts as food? Food, in the United States, has until recently been classified into four food groups: (1) meat, fish, and poultry; (2) grains; (3) dairy products; and (4) fruits and vegetables. In 1991 a physicians' group recommended that this be completely changed and that four new groups be substituted: (1) fruits, (2) legumes (including beans, peanut butter, and soybeans), (3) grains, and (4) vegetables, with meat and dairy products being options. This is also known as a *vegan* diet. While this was not officially adopted, the United States Department of Agriculture (USDA) was in the process of changing its recommendations for a healthy diet, including reducing significantly the role of meat and dairy products in it. On April 24, 1991, the USDA sent its proposal, the Eating Right Pyramid, to the printer to replace the food wheel used since the 1950s; the next day, the Agriculture Secretary, Edward R. Madigan, cancelled it. Although he denied it, it is widely suspected that the reason was "because meat and dairy producers objected to what they felt was the pyramid's negative depiction of their products" (Burros, *New York Times*, May 8, 1991). The Department of Agriculture is clearly in a double-bind, since it must promote both the health of the nation and the wealth of the meat and dairy industries. Meat and dairy products are now included in the revised Food Pyramid just below fats, oils, and sugars, implying they should be eaten sparingly (see figure 7.1).

Regardless, the old "meat and potatoes" definition of a main meal is surely changing. After the debacle over the Food Pyramid, nutritionists began to refer to the healthy diet as the "Mediterranean diet," which is essentially the same one originally proposed by the USDA. "The characteristics of the Mediterranean diet [are] simple 'peasant' food, with emphasis on pastas and breads, grilled fish, fresh fruit and vegetables, red wine, and especially olive oil" (Bell and Valentine 1997: 156). This diet, celebrated in Britain as well as in the United States in restaurants, in advertisements, and on supermarket shelves, is thought

THE FOOD GUIDE PYRAMID
Number of servings per day

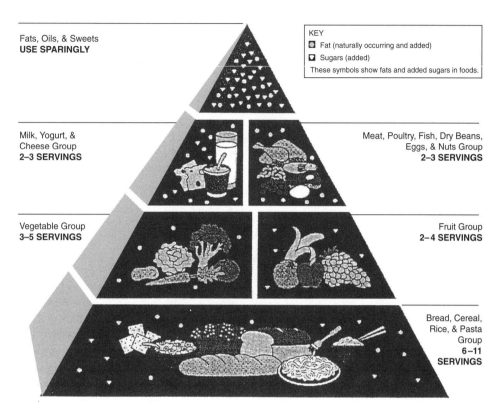

Fats, Oils, & Sweets
USE SPARINGLY

KEY
▣ Fat (naturally occurring and added)
❏ Sugars (added)
These symbols show fats and added sugars in foods.

Milk, Yogurt, &
Cheese Group
2–3 SERVINGS

Meat, Poultry, Fish, Dry Beans,
Eggs, & Nuts Group
2–3 SERVINGS

Vegetable Group
3–5 SERVINGS

Fruit Group
2–4 SERVINGS

Bread, Cereal,
Rice, & Pasta
Group
**6–11
SERVINGS**

Figure 7.1 The USDA Food Pyramid. The newest version of the Food Pyramid is multicolored and visually arresting, but does not reproduce well in black and white. It contains the same essential information as the version presented here.

to be far healthier than what the British and Americans have been eating, and it is also thought to be responsible for the longevity of the Mediterranean peasantry. The popularity of this diet began as more and more British and Americans toured the Mediterranean area, but it is also credited to the well-known British food and cookbook writer Elizabeth David, who was the first to bring a bit of culinary sunshine to the colder northern climes. Nevertheless, it is worth pointing out, as did Bell and Valentine, that the notion of a "Mediterranean" diet is a *construction*, because it ignores significant variation in national, ethnic, and local cuisines. The only things that North African, Syrian, and Greek cuisines have in common are the ingredients, not the culturally distinctive ways they are used to make particular dishes and meals.

Clearly, food is more than a matter of calories, vitamins, and minerals. It is a matter of culture and, within that, of individual preference. What is considered food by one person or culture is considered inedible to another. "One man's meat is another man's poison," as the old adage succinctly states.

Classification systems

What counts as food in any particular culture, and what foods are preferred or forbidden, is intimately related to a system of classification that, in many cases, has roots in religious prescriptions. According to Genesis, for example, humans as well as animals were originally vegetarian.

> Behold, I have given you every herb bearing seed, which is upon the face of all the earth, and every tree, in which is the fruit of a tree yielding seed; to you shall it be for meat.
>
> And to every beast of the earth, and to every fowl of the air, and to every thing that creepeth upon the earth, wherein there is life, I have given every green herb for meat: and it was so. (Genesis 1: 29–30)

Not every fruit was given as food, for eating the apple changed the human condition forever (Genesis 3). But only after the Flood, when Noah saved the animals, did God offer them as food.

> Every moving thing that liveth shall be meat for you; even as the green herb have I given you all things. But flesh with the life thereof, which is the blood thereof, shall ye not eat. (Genesis 9: 3–4)

The last sentence could still be seen as an injunction against eating warm-blooded animals, but is, instead, interpreted as an injunction against eating blood. Thus kosher and halal meat has had the blood drained from it. So too, some contemporary vegetarians believe that we might return to Eden if we would only return to the original vegetarian dispensation.

Leviticus 11: 1–32, 39–47 – Clean and Unclean Animals

And the LORD said to Moses and Aaron,[2] "Say to the people of Israel, These are the living things which you may eat among all the beasts that are on the earth.[3] Whatever parts the hoof and is cloven-footed and chews the cud, among the animals, you may eat.[4] Nevertheless among those that chew the cud or part the hoof, you shall not eat these: The camel, because it chews the cud but does not part the hoof, is unclean to you.[5] And the rock badger, because it chews the cud but does not part the hoof, is unclean to you.[6] And the hare, because it chews the cud but does not part the hoof, is unclean to you.[7] And the swine, because it parts the hoof and is cloven-footed but does not chew the cud, is unclean to you.[8] Of their flesh you shall not eat, and their carcasses you shall not touch; they are unclean to you.

9 "These you may eat, of all that are in the waters. Everything in the waters that has fins and scales, whether in the seas or in the rivers, you may eat.[10]But anything in the seas or the rivers that has not fins and scales, of the swarming creatures in the waters and of the living creatures that are in the waters, is an abomination to you.[11] They shall remain an abomination to you; of their flesh you shall not eat, and their carcasses you shall have in abomination.[12] Everything in the waters that has not fins and scales is an abomination to you.

13 "And these you shall have in abomination among the birds, they shall not be eaten, they are an abomination: the eagle, the vulture, the osprey,[14] the kite, the falcon according to its kind,[15] every raven according to its kind,[16] the ostrich, the nighthawk, the sea gull, the hawk according to its kind,[17] the owl, the cormorant, the ibis,[18] the water hen, the pelican, the carrion vulture,[19] the stork, the heron according to its kind, the hoopoe, and the bat.

20 "All winged insects that go upon all fours are an abomination to you.[21]Yet among the winged insects that go on all fours you may eat those which have legs above their feet, with which to leap on the earth.[22] Of them you may eat: the locust according to its kind, the bald locust according to its kind, the cricket according to its kind, and the grasshopper according to its kind.[23] But all other winged insects which have four feet are an abomination to you.

24 "And by these you shall become unclean; whoever touches their carcass shall be unclean until the evening,[25] and whoever carries any part of their carcass shall wash his clothes and be unclean until the evening.[26] Every animal which parts the hoof but is not cloven-footed or does not chew the cud is unclean to you; every one who touches them shall be unclean.[27] And all that go on their paws, among the animals that go on all fours, are unclean to you; whoever touches their carcass shall be unclean until the evening,[28] and he who carries their carcass shall wash his clothes and be unclean until the evening; they are unclean to you.

29 "And these are unclean to you among the swarming things that swarm upon the earth: the weasel, the mouse, the great lizard according to its kind,[30]the gecko, the land crocodile, the lizard, the sand lizard, and the chameleon.[31]These are unclean to you among all that swarm; whoever touches them when they are dead shall be unclean until the evening.[32] And anything upon which any of them falls when they are dead shall be unclean, whether it is an article of wood or a garment or a skin or a sack, any vessel that is used for any purpose; it must be put into water, and it shall be unclean until the evening; then it shall be clean. ...

39 "And if any animal of which you may eat dies, he who touches its carcass shall be unclean until the evening,[40] and he who eats of its carcass shall wash his clothes and be unclean until the evening; he also who carries the carcass shall wash his clothes and be unclean until the evening.

41 "Every swarming thing that swarms upon the earth is an abomination; it shall not be eaten.[42] Whatever goes on its belly, and whatever goes on all fours, or whatever has many feet, all the swarming things that swarm upon the earth, you shall not eat; for they are an abomination.[43] You shall not make yourselves abominable with any swarming thing that swarms; and you shall not defile yourselves with them, lest you become unclean.[44] For I am the LORD your God; consecrate yourselves therefore, and be holy, for I am holy. You shall not defile yourselves with any swarming thing that crawls upon the earth.[45] For I am the LORD who brought you up out of the land of Egypt, to be your God; you shall therefore be holy, for I am holy."

46 This is the law pertaining to beast and bird and every living creature that moves through the waters and every creature that swarms upon the earth,[47] to make a distinction between the unclean and the clean and between the living creature that may be eaten and the living creature that may not be eaten.

I will return to the issue of vegetarianism below, but for now direct you to the biblical classification of permitted and tabooed foods first outlined in Leviticus 11 and Deuteronomy 14. The meaning of the lists has perplexed numerous commentators for centuries. A major question is why were Jews forbidden from eating pork? Was it a matter of hygiene, a recognition that occasionally people became ill from eating the meat, or because of the scavenging habits of pigs? Anthropologist Mary Douglas, in her famous 1966 essay "The Abominations of Leviticus," took issue with people who explained the prohibitions in terms of hygiene – that is, that there is an underlying medical reason for the prohibition. Douglas calls such people "medical materialists" (1966: 33).

> For Maimonides himself, the great twelfth-century prototype of medical materialism, although he could find hygienic reasons for all the other dietary restrictions of Mosaic law, confessed himself baffled by the prohibition on pork, and was driven back to aesthetic explanations, based on the revolting diet of the domestic pig. (p. 32)

But that is *not* the reason given in the Bible. Indeed, "nothing whatever is said about its dirty scavenging habits" (p. 56). Pig is forbidden because it does not fit into the categories of the classification system – namely, those of cloven-hoofed, cud-chewing animals. Douglas's argument places the food prohibitions in a context of a system of classifications: certain animals are ambiguous or anomalous – they do not fit the system of classifications – and thus are tabooed. While "cloven-hoofed, cud-chewing ungulates are the model of the proper kind of food for a pastoralist," a pig is cloven-hoofed but not ruminant. That "is the only reason given in the Old Testament for avoiding the pig" (Douglas 1966: 56). Since it does not fit the classification, it is outlawed. The primary issue about kosher rules is holiness and how to maintain a state of purity. "Holiness requires that individuals shall conform to the class to which they belong. … Holiness means keeping distinct the categories of Creation" (p. 54). Clearly, the pig transgressed those lines.

Hers is a very compelling and important argument and points out why people become morally exercised when others purposefully transgress cultural boundaries: it amounts to sacrilege. However, Douglas does not explain the system of classification itself, which, after all, is a human construct with no self-evident logic.[5]

In a very different vein, novelist Jorge Luis Borges poked fun at the seeming naturalness of Western classifications when he suggested that any "creature, instead of belonging to groups like 'insects' or 'amphibians,' could be classified in one of these categories: 1) belonging to the Emperor, 2) embalmed, 3) tame," and so on (Rothstein, *New York Times*, May 12, 2001, p. A19). While fantastic to our modern scientific sensibilities, this classification does force us to think about how Europeans and Americans categorize the natural world. "Do we create a narrative account, giving each animal a proper place, as in the biblical story of creation? Is there a hierarchy in our orderings, in which we judge animals by their usefulness to us or by their place in an evolutionary ladder?" (p. A19). Why should humans be at the top of the ladder? Do other people organize the world this way? If not, why not, and what are the implications?

British animals

Edmund Leach, another British anthropologist, made an attempt to decipher the classification of animals, not of Genesis, but of the British. Although the focus of his article "Anthropological Aspects of Language: Animal Categories and Verbal Abuse" (1964), discussed in chapter 4, is on the issue of taboo, his analysis depended on the classification of food. He noted that while there is "a vast range of materials which are both edible and nourishing, … only a small part of this edible environment will actually be classified as potential food. Such classification is a matter of language and culture, not of nature" (1964: 30–1). He went on to distinguish three major categories:

1   Edible substances that are recognized as food and consumed as part of the normal diet.
2   Edible substances that are recognized as possible food, but that are prohibited or else allowed to be eaten only under special (ritual) conditions. These substances are *consciously tabooed*.
3   Edible substances that by culture and language are not recognized as food at all. These substances are *unconsciously tabooed* (Leach 1964: 31).

The difference between 2 and 3 is illustrated by the Jewish prohibition against eating pork and the English objection to eating dog. In the first case, it is admitted that pork is food but Jews will not eat it, while the second case depends on a categorical assumption that dogs are *not* food (p. 32), even though they are perfectly edible and, in some places, are bred for food. Marshall Sahlins, an American anthropologist, does a *cultural* analysis of animals and food.

American logic

Animals who share our beds and table are "one of the family," hence to eat them is unthinkable. According to Sahlins,

> America is the land of the sacred dog. … They roam the streets of major American cities at will, taking their masters about on leashes and depositing their excrements at pleasure on curbs and sidewalks. A whole system of sanitation procedures had to be employed to get rid of the mess. … Within houses and apartments, dogs climb upon chairs designed for humans, sleep in people's beds, and sit at table after their own fashion awaiting their share of the family meal. All this in the calm assurance that they themselves will never be sacrificed to necessity or deity, nor eaten even in the case of accidental death. (1976: 171–2)

His analysis of the American food system goes beyond the classificatory systems constructed by Douglas and Leach by considering the *meanings* of the categories and associations. His book *Culture and Practical Reason* (1976) is a major critique of economic explanations for cultural phenomena. One of the most telling examples he presents concerns food, specifically beef.

Why is beef, especially steak, the most prized and expensive cut of meat, even though "its absolute supply is much greater than that of tongue" (p. 176)? Doesn't this contradict one of the fundamental premises of economic rationality based on notions of supply and demand whereby scarcity is related to price? Steak is not the scarce item. Nor is there a natural desire for steak since many people(s) do not eat it and find it repulsive. "Taste," says Nick Fiddes in his book *Meat: A Natural Symbol*, "reflects rather than explains preferences" (1991: 6), and is related to an entire cosmology – distinctive views of how and what the world is.

According to Sahlins, "symbolic logic … organizes demand" (1976: 175), or to put it differently, economic rationality follows symbolic logic. For example, "innards" – liver, kidney, heart, and intestine – like tongue, are scarce in relation to steak, but they are cheap. Furthermore, we disguise the provenance of muscle meat with terms like steak, chuck, roast, and chops but refer to internal organs by the same terms we use for human organs. "Edibility is inversely related to humanity" (p. 175), Sahlins claims, thus people who eat innards – and are most often poor and most often black – are less human, while the entire meat system is a sustained metaphor on race, class, and cannibalism. "Black is in American society as the savage among us" (p. 176), with "us" referring to white middle-class Americans. Blacks, however, subvert and recoup this ascription when they rename innards *soul food*.

While there is always some play in the system, we must not be lulled into thinking that such classification systems are merely play, for "the symbolic scheme of edibility joins with that organizing the relations of production to precipitate, through income distribution and demand, an entire totemic order, uniting in a parallel series of differences the status of persons and what they eat" (Sahlins 1976: 176). That is, the scheme of edibility is a way of naturalizing and reinforcing class and ethnic differences.

The artichoke with which I began this section is a useful example of the way food can index status or class. In the 1960s when I first encountered one, artichokes were exotic and relatively rare on the east coast; I do not recall seeing them on the shelves of standard supermarkets. Being able to appreciate them, knowing where to find them, and how to cook and eat them were signs of elite status – of having what Pierre Bourdieu called "cultural capital." At that memorable luncheon, I was made aware, without any word being spoken, that I was clearly and obviously outclassed.[6]

What Makes a Meal?

Just as what counts as food is related to a classification system, so too are meals and menus. Is a hotdog a meal if it is bought from a street vendor and eaten on the street? What if you add french fries and a coke? What about pizza ordered in? In order to understand what a meal is, we must first consider all the other ways food can be obtained and eaten. Then we must consider the kinds of food that make a meal, the places where a meal can be eaten, and the people with whom a meal is shared. In "Deciphering a Meal" (1975), Mary Douglas began at home with her own family in Britain.

> Between breakfast and the last nightcap, the food of the day comes in an ordered pattern. Between Monday and Sunday, the food of the week is patterned again. Then there is the

sequence of holidays and fast days through the year, to say nothing of life cycle feasts, birthdays, and weddings. (Douglas 1975: 251)

The classification of meals consists not just in their order – in the day, the week, and the year – but also in the kinds of foods appropriate for each meal and the kinds of people with whom one "breaks bread."

In Britain there are, according to Douglas, "two major contrasted food categories … meals versus drinks. … Meals are a mixture of solid foods accompanied by liquids. With drinks the reverse holds" (pp. 254–5). Both the meal category and "drinks" category have names: breakfast, lunch, supper, cocktails, or tea. The drinks category is, appropriately, more fluid and is not nearly as structured as a meal. It also often involves standing rather than sitting at a table.

The food categories also correlate with social categories. "Drinks are for strangers, acquaintances, workmen, and family. Meals are for family, close friends, honored guests. The grand operator of the system is the line between intimacy and distance" (p. 256). As we noted in chapter 5, French people find the American custom of inviting new acquaintances home to dinner very odd, while Americans think the French are very cold and unfriendly because they rarely invite their new (American) friends to dinner in their homes. Being invited to a French home for dinner marks a significant shift in the quality of the relationship that might not be appreciated by an American guest for whom such behavior seems normal.

In India, caste membership will determine those with whom one may eat. Among the upper classes in England and France (and no doubt elsewhere), children do not regularly eat with their parents, and in quite a number of societies men and women do not eat together. In addition,

Meals properly require the use of at least one mouth-entering *utensil* per head, whereas drinks are limited to mouth-touching ones. … Meals require a *table*, a *seating* order, *restriction* on movement and on alternative occupations. There is no question of knitting during a meal. … (Furthermore), a meal is not a meal if it is all in the bland-sweet-sour dimensions. A meal incorporates a number of contrasts, hot and cold, bland and spiced, liquid and semi-liquid, and various textures. It also incorporates cereals, vegetables, and animal proteins. (Douglas 1975: 255–6; emphasis mine)

Before turning to the food and menus, let us briefly explore some of the conditions that make a meal a meal.

Setting the table

Douglas began with "mouth-entering utensil," of which chopsticks would qualify, but there are some peoples who use their fingers or bread to scoop food. The manner of eating will also indicate quite a lot about the cultural notions of proper food. However, for the purposes of this discussion, the example of a meal in my mind will be one familiar to Europeans and Americans and includes forks, knives, and spoons. That leads one to think

Figure 7.2   Formal place setting. © Image Source/SuperStock.

of the industries behind every meal. *First* are the manufacturers who produce the utensils, whether of stainless steel or sterling silver. Among the elite sterling silver is essential, a place setting includes far more than the three items above, and there is an intricate etiquette involved in the appropriate placing of each item. Among each type of flatware there are hundreds, if not thousands, of patterns, and a great deal of money is spent on advertising them. Women, in particular, are advised to choose a pattern, so that when they get married they can register it at various gift stores. (See figure 7.2.)

Second are the manufacturers of dinnerware, for in addition to utensils, you need dishes on which to put the food. Again, the distinctions and patterns are numerous and communicate a great deal about class, income, taste, and lifestyle. For example, many middle- and upper-class families have several sets of china – fine china for fancy dinner parties and pottery dishes for everyday fare. Some people are fortunate to be given or to inherit a set of china or silverware as a family heirloom, passed down from one generation to the next.

The *third* industry that provisions a dinner table is the makers of glassware – lead crystal versus ordinary glass, and stemware versus tumblers. *Fourth* are the makers of table linens, only some of which are actually made of linen, while most are made of cotton, synthetic fabrics, and, today, even plastic. In this category, there are tablecloths as well as placemats, and each denotes the level of formality.

The *fifth* industry involved in making a meal is furniture. Picnics notwithstanding, a proper meal generally demands a table: indeed, the phrase *picnic table* is an oxymoron. Some people eat at a table in the kitchen, while others eat on a different type of table in a dining room. In the 1950s, for instance, the big new thing was a Formica-topped kitchen table. Its selling point was that, unlike a wooden table, it wouldn't stain, didn't need polishing, and was easy to clean. At my house and among those of my acquaintances, dining rooms and dining tables were reserved for special holiday dinners or when other people were invited. Dining tables more typically are made of wood or sometimes glass.

Turkish villagers, at least where I worked, did not eat at tables. Instead, they sat on the floor around a large copper tray raised off the floor by a small round wooden support. A cloth was placed beneath the tray and each person picked up an edge to cover his or her legs and clothes; that is, it functioned as a napkin. Often we did not use plates, but each person had his or her own spoon or fork and simply took food from the communal dish. All family members sat around the tray, although in some villages men ate first, followed by the women and children.

Seating arrangements in American families (when they eat together) generally include every family member unless small children eat first and are put to bed before the grown-ups eat. A traditional seating plan has the head of the household, usually the father, sitting at the head of the table; most other family members have their regular seats. At a dinner party, the host or hostess often pays considerable attention to the seating plan and tries to put people with similar interests together, while also alternating by gender.

All this before we even get to the food. Nor have I mentioned the work in the background preparing and cooking the meal. There is a vast industry that supplies cooking utensils – the pots and pans and mixers and processors and stoves and microwaves. Not surprisingly these items, too, have many producers, prices, and designs, differences that often relate to class, income, lifestyle, and taste. There is no room to go into detail in this fascinating area; I state this merely to draw attention to the vast areas for research in relation to food besides the food itself. It is clear that what makes a meal a meal involves much more than merely food.

In addition to a table, the setting, and the seating, Douglas claimed there is a "restriction on movement and on alternative occupations." People are supposed to remain seated while at table, although children often get restive and are sometimes "excused" early. Douglas's definition seems to exclude those who listen to music or the radio or who watch television, as Turks (rural and urban) do while they eat. Would she consider it a meal if you eat alone? Would you?

The inclusion of a seating order in Mary Douglas's definition of a meal seems to imply that a real meal involves more than one person. Sociologist Janet Flammang is more explicit: "Table conversation is an art of give and take, where we think before we speak so we do not disrupt the pleasures and sharing of the group" (2009: 93). She believes that the "table is where we learn the art of conversation, especially across generations, learn to feel connected, and learn to trust ourselves and others." For her,

> [C]ivility at the table is a cornerstone of civil society and democratic process. … A democratic process is deliberative: people think and give reasons for what they think in trying to persuade others to agree with them. People will be more persuasive to the degree that they understand both what they think and what others think. This mutual self- and other-understanding comes primarily from conversations, (p. 93)

and people begin to learn this as children sitting with the family at mealtimes. This is clearly an idealistic view of the family dinner table, for there are numerous families where dinner times are tense and conversation is minimal. And there are numerous other families, where the family meal has disappeared completely, a function of conflicting work schedules and countless children's activities such as sports, scouting, music lessons, and so on. Still, Flammang's model conveys an important message at a time when American families spend little time together and rarely eat together. She believes there is a relationship between the breakdown in family dining and the breakdown in civility. Her book *The Taste for Civilization* explores the social costs and the possible alternatives that do not depend on putting women back in the kitchen or assume that women's lives have been improved by staying out of it. Instead, she advocates that we all need to become more involved with food and its preparation. Now that the table is set and the people are gathered around it, let us move on to the food, the actual components of a meal.

Menu

Any discussion of meals entails a discussion of the menu. Not only do menus vary considerably cross-culturally, but also "there is an implicit order governing the idea of what constitutes a meal both in terms of appropriate foodstuffs and the order of eating them" (James 1990: 676).

Breakfast around the World

What follows are traditional, or culturally dominant, breakfast menus in each culture. It by no means assumes that all people in each culture eat these meals, nor does it deny that many people go hungry and have no breakfast, let alone other meals.

United States

A common breakfast is orange juice, cold cereal with milk and sometimes fruit, and coffee. Alternatives: (a) toast or English muffin with butter and jam; (b) bacon and eggs and toast. (Some people get all of these combined in an Egg McMuffin.) On weekends Americans sometimes merge breakfast and lunch and call it *brunch*. This meal includes more elaborately prepared and presented foods: an omelet instead of just eggs, various cold meats or smoked salmon, and bagels and cream cheese. Some people serve champagne at this meal, sometimes mixed with orange juice and called a *mimosa*. Restaurants have capitalized on the craze for brunch and offer a veritable cornucopia of foods, lavishly presented.

Turkey

A *sine qua non* of a proper Turkish breakfast is bread, as it is of every meal. Indeed, food is equated with bread. Turks do not say, "Have you eaten (food)?" They say, "*ekmek edin mi?*" – have you eaten bread? In the city the *kapacı* (resident doorman) goes out for bread (crusty sourdough-type bread) every morning and delivers to each apartment in the building; in the village, round flat breads (like a large English muffin) are warmed up and eaten with white feta-like cheese, olives, tomatoes, and cucumbers in season. Sometimes in the village we would also have peppers, potatoes, and onions fried in olive oil—one of my favorites.

Japan

I was surprised to see a Japanese breakfast available at a hotel in Istanbul, Turkey. It consisted of miso soup, steamed spinach leaves, rice, grilled fillet of salmon, and green tea. I asked a Japanese anthropologist if this is a traditional Japanese breakfast. She said she would add eggs and pickles.

The Netherlands

Dark (wheat) bread, cold ham and a variety of cheeses, and butter and jam. One of my favorites is a honey-spice loaf cake, but now I hear it is intended primarily for children. Today my informants tell me that many people have shifted to cornflakes and other cereals.

Bhutan

A Bhutanese friend informs me that traditional breakfast among more well-to-do Bhutanese who live in the western part of the country is rice, dried yak meat, and butter tea (a mixture of tea, salt, butter, and baking soda). Farmers in the eastern part tend to be poorer and eat rice with pepper curry mixed with cheese. They only drink butter tea on special occasions because it is expensive and instead drink sugared tea without milk.

Ivory Coast

Among the Beng, breakfast could consist of leftover *foufou* (cooked yams pounded into a ball) with sauce or corn porridge sweetened with ripe bananas. If people have money, they might buy a loaf of French bread from a local trader and serve it with freshly made peanut butter.

We do not begin with dessert, as every child who wants ice cream first quickly learns. The order depends on the type of meal it is: a quick breakfast on a weekday or the "soup-to-nuts" menu (soup, fish course, meat course, salad, cheese, dessert, coffee, nuts, and cordials) appropriate for elite dinner parties. As a Fulbright fellow in Belgium, I was treated to several very elegant meals where the courses were separated by sorbets to cleanse the palate.

For each item in the order there are acceptable substitutions: for the soup course one might substitute a cream soup for consommé, and for the fish course one could have halibut, tuna, or salmon. All are equally fish, and each can be prepared in any number of ways. The same rule applies to all courses. Among some people color is important – one would not want every food in the meal to be the same color. I recall one home meal in Belgium where everything was kind of whitish – the soup, endive, rice, and white fish. Although it did not taste bland, it looked that way; I felt it was unappealing.

There are some meals where substitutions can only be made in a very narrow compass. Holidays have special foods though these may vary by region, ethnicity, and family. For example, my family always had roast beef and Yorkshire pudding for Christmas, but many others had duck or turkey. Some people have spring lamb at Easter, perhaps symbolic of the "paschal lamb," but others have ham, something that seems to me a direct affront to Jews, especially when Passover occurs near the same time. Gillian Feeley-Harnik, an anthropologist at the University of Michigan, explores the way food became an expression of the emerging theological differences between Jews and early Christians in her 1981 book *The Lord's Table: Eucharist and Passover in Early Christianity*.

Thanksgiving is a major holiday in the United States. The story we are told is that the Pilgrims instituted this to thank the Native Americans for helping them through a terrible winter. While they did have a harvest celebration in October 1621, there were hardly any Native Americans left around Plymouth because the Pawtuxet who lived there had been wiped out by an epidemic. Although the Pilgrims continued to hold harvest feasts, they did not become a national holiday until it was proclaimed by Abraham Lincoln in 1863. "It can be read as a first salvo in his re-election campaign … and of our bloody crucible as a people, [during] the Civil War" (Quinn, *New York Times*, November 24, 1994).[7]

The Thanksgiving meal has been represented by whole roasted and stuffed turkey along with gravy, cranberry sauce, pearl onions, yellow squash, a green vegetable, salad, and pumpkin pie. An article in the *New York Times* just before Thanksgiving in the year 2000 featured innovations made by different people around the country. A family in Georgia served *fried* turkey and turnip greens, while a Vietnamese family in California stuffed their *brined* turkey with shiitake mushrooms and lotus seeds, and a hip family in Massachusetts *replaced* turkey with a crown roast of pork stuffed with brandied dried fruit and sausage. The article concluded, "That's what makes the holiday so great. After all, this is America. You're free to create your own traditions" (Hesser, *New York Times*, November 15, p. B1). I am not so sure. Is it still Thanksgiving without a turkey?[8] Meanwhile, Chinese immigrants from Fujian Province now living in New York City use the day "for the new tradition of a Thanksgiving Day matrimonial marathon" (Sachs, *New York Times*, November 29, 2002) accompanied by traditional Chinese wedding banquets.

Main meal

Douglas's family rejected soup and pudding as a meal, because it has "a beginning and an end and no middle" (1975: 250); evidently, the main meal must consist of, at least, three courses. Meat is at the center of the main meal in both Britain and the United States. In Britain, according to Douglas (1975) and James (1990), meat could be fish, and both should be accompanied by two vegetables. In the United States, until recently, the main meal had to have "meat and potatoes" with vegetables or salad on the side. For many people in both Britain and the United States, a meal of only vegetables is not a meal at all. But why? The answer appears obvious, because meat is "high in strength-giving protein, and simply because when cooked it tastes good and is satisfying" (Fiddes, 1991: 1). And yet plenty of people flourish with little or no meat, and taste is surely a matter of culture and upbringing. Growing up in the 1940s and 1950s, I simply assumed that a proper evening meal consisted of meat (including occasionally fish or poultry), potatoes or other starch, and a vegetable. Once learned as a "proper meal," the habit is difficult to break, and to this day, I tend to follow that pattern except for occasional pasta dishes or a stew that would combine all in one dish. Dessert, in those days, at least at my house, was relatively simple – fruit, (often canned) or jello, and, when we got a freezer, ice cream.[9]

But why meat?

Many of us, and our society in general, consider meat eating normal; it is part of our *habitus*, what we take for granted. Yet recall the biblical injunction against meat eating (see p. 279). We tend to think that only vegetarianism is ideological, but in fact, meat eating is as well, since it embodies ideas, categories, and values that *go without saying*. Fiddes shows that vegetarianism is not substantively defined, but is defined only in relation to meat eating: it is the avoidance of meat eating.

Building on the work of Douglas, Leach, Sahlins, and others, Nick Fiddes argues that "our use of meat as food reflects our categorization of, and our relations towards, animal competitors, companions, and resources … that it tangibly represents human control of the natural world" (1991: 2). This idea has been with cultures influenced by the Bible for a very long time. Recall the biblical license: "Let them have dominion over the fish of the sea, and over the birds of the air, and over the cattle, and over all the earth, and over every creeping thing that creeps upon the earth" (Genesis 1:24). Fiddes continues, "Consuming the muscle flesh of other highly evolved animals is a potent statement of our supreme power" (1991: 2). Incorporating their flesh, we consume their power.

Of Meat and Men

"People with power have always eaten meat" (Adams 1991: 26), and that implies not just class distinctions but also gender. While Sahlins barely mentions the association of men and meat in his discussion, this is the main theme in the work of both Nick Fiddes and Carol Adams. I will focus here on two aspects of the relationship between gender and meat: first, the identification of women with meat, and second, the attribution to men of rights to meat. Although we cannot claim that either association is universal, they are both very common in many cultures.

Some of the gender symbolism of meat eating may have begun with "Man the Hunter," or at least the cultural myth and ideology of man the hunter. We do not eat lion meat, according to Fiddes, because it would blur the categories of Man the Hunter and Lion the Hunter. This seems a better reason than the one given by Leach, who said we don't eat lions because they are wild, beyond our pale. In any case, Man the Hunter is portrayed dragging home the meat. When this is combined with the idea that women are meat, we get the numerous cartoons of primitive man dragging home a woman by the hair. "Man is the hunter; woman is his game" (Tennyson, cited in Fiddes 1991: 144), a statement that casts all men as sexual predators or what we sometimes call *wolves*.

There are numerous words that can be applied indiscriminately to either food or women, such as appetizing, delicious, and succulent. Fiddes notes how Alex Comfort named his *Joy of Sex* after the classic American cookbook bible *The Joy of Cooking* (Rombauer and Rombauer Becker [1931] 1975), including chapter titles that continue the culinary metaphor: Starters, Main Courses, Sauces and Pickles (Fiddes 1991: 144). The symbolic equation of women with food, and specifically meat, can have violent implications. Adams tells how she came across what seemed at first glance to be a typical meat diagram in a Boston meat market – the kind that outlines where the rib, chuck, loin, and rump part of meat come from – but on closer inspection it proved to be a diagram of a woman's body. Might there be a connection, she asks, between the butchering and dismembering of animals and the killing and dismemberment of women's bodies by men? I recall that a cover of *Hustler* magazine depicted a woman's body going head first through a meat grinder.

Meat is associated with strength and virility, but if women *are* meat, then just whose strength are men incorporating when they eat it? Oddly, this contradiction was not noticed or commented on by the authors cited. But the associations between meat and masculinity may also be why some people think that vegetarian men are effeminate; after all, *Real Men Don't Eat Quiche* (Feirstein 1982). The association between men and meat is no doubt behind the prominence of meat on the training tables of athletes and soldiers. During World War II, for example, the consumption of meat by what Russell Baker called the "American warrior" was "about two-and-a-half times that of the average citizen" (Adams 1991: 32).

In patriarchal societies, men often eat their meals first and, thus, get "the lion's share" and the choicest cuts of meat, while women get the leftovers. Turkey is a patriarchal society, and in the village where I worked people ate little meat at regular daily meals – sometimes a bit of minced meat in a stew. Although it was a fairly prosperous village, most people could not afford to eat much meat. Since meat was intended for the market, whatever they ate meant that much less to sell and thus less income. But at special feasts such as weddings or before a *hajj* (pilgrimage) to Mecca, a number of sheep were slaughtered and roasted, and the whole village gathered for the meal. However, on these occasions, men ate together before the women who served them. The delicious smell wafted over the village, making everyone hungry for their share. Often, there was little left by the time the women and children were ready to eat. Having not had much meat for several months, I can still recall my lust as well as my guilt as I fell upon my portion of the roasted lamb that I, as an "honored guest," was served in their midst.[10]

When meat is scarce, it is usually women who go without, even when they are pregnant or nursing – a time when they need it more than men. Most of the women in "my" village were anemic. "Meat is a constant for men, intermittent for women, a pattern painfully observed in famine situations today. Women are starving at a rate disproportionate to men" (Adams 1991: 26; see also Fiddes 1991: 158ff.). In many countries, women do without meat, and in Britain and the United States, one occasionally hears news reports of "domestic abuse," that is, wife-beating, if the man of the house did not get meat for his dinner.

In addition to the supposed need of meat for strength, men are also thought to need it as "brain food." This idea and the statement below depend on the association of men with *head* work and women with *hand* work. George Beard, a nineteenth-century medical doctor influenced by Darwin, advocated,

> In proportion as man grows sensitive through civilization or through disease, he should diminish the quantity of cereals and fruits, which are far below him on the scale of evolution, and increase the quantity of animal food, which is nearly related to him in the scale of evolution, and therefore more easily assimilated. (Cited in Adams 1991: 30)

This ideological statement has little to do with nutrition, since humans assimilate plants more easily than flesh. Instead, his evolutionary schema seems to follow biblical valuations: recall that when Cain "brought of the fruit of the ground an offering unto the Lord" (Genesis 4:3), God rejected it, preferring Abel's offering of a "firstling of the flock." Cain became angry and, as the story goes, rose up and killed his brother. No reason is ever given for God's preference. Personally, I think that the story symbolizes the tension between the practices and beliefs of the agriculturalists of Mesopotamia and the nomadic pastoralists who were, through Abraham, to become the "chosen people" of God. The chosen food symbolized the people chosen.

Food and Worldview

Food is intimately related to religion and worldview whether it is biblical, Hindu, Buddhist, Hopi, or even that promoted by the "health food" movement. Anthropologist Jill Dubisch investigated the health food movement in the United States and claimed that the analysis of its "underlying world view reveals that, as a system of beliefs and practices, the health food movement has some of the characteristics of a religion" ([1981] 1997: 62). Its roots go back to mid-nineteenth-century "hygienists" such as Sylvester Graham, of graham cracker fame, who "preached that good health was to be found in temperate living. This included abstinence from alcohol, a vegetarian diet, consumption of whole wheat products, and regular exercise" (p. 63) – quite a contrast to Beard, who wrote somewhat later, after Darwin's work was published.

The health food movement resurfaced in the countercultural 1960s. According to Dubisch ([1981] 1997), becoming part of the movement often involves a kind of "conversion experience," perhaps one that includes healing from an ailment. Such an experience demands a reorganization of one's kitchen and also one's life; it demands a psychological reorientation – a different way of perceiving the world and one's own place in it. It

> means learning and accepting the general features of the health food world view. To begin with, there is great concern, as there is in many religions, with purity, in this case, the purity of food, of water, of air. In fact, there are some striking similarities between keeping a "health food kitchen" and the Jewish practice of keeping kosher. Both make distinctions between proper and improper foods, and both involve excluding certain impure foods (whether

unhealthful or non-kosher) from the kitchen and table. In addition, a person concerned with maintaining a high degree of purity in food may engage in similar behavior in either case – reading labels carefully to check for impermissible ingredients and even purchasing food from special establishments to guarantee ritual purity. (p. 64)

Devotees of health food categorize food either as *health food* or *junk food*. The former promotes well-being and bestows *mana* (a kind of beneficial power), while the latter is *taboo* and, if eaten, conveys malignant power. Foods that promote health are dark bread instead of white, honey instead of sugar, yogurt instead of ice cream, and tofu or soybeans in place of beef. Especially singled out for opprobrium are McDonald's hamburgers, french fries, and coke – the "all-American" favorites.

Health food is not just about achieving a healthy body: it is also a way to establish a healthy relationship with society and the universe. Growing your own food, baking your own bread, and perhaps raising a cow and making cheese are thought to foster independence and self-reliance – a pioneer ethos. Nutrition is thus linked to emotional, spiritual, and social problems, for cosmologically health food is allied with life-affirming nature, while junk food is associated with death-dealing culture (p. 67). In many ways the movement is nostalgic, for it harks "back to a 'golden age' which it seeks to recreate, assuming that many of the ills of the contemporary world are caused by society's departure from this ideal state" (p. 69) – Eden, once again. (See figure 7.3.)

Fast food

At the opposite end of the food spectrum from "health food" is "fast food." Fast food, itself, is not new, if one considers street kebabs in Turkey, fish and chips in Britain, noodles in China, and station box lunches in Japan (and see also figure 7.4). What is new is

Figure 7.3 Apples were once the quintessential health food, as in the phrase "An apple a day keeps the doctor away." Today food safety experts warn that the coating on apples is hazardous. Christian Darkin/Science Photo Library.

Figure 7.4   Food automat, 977 Eighth Avenue, Manhattan, 1936. Photo by Berenice Abbott/Museum of the City of New York. Horn and Hardart's "automat," which opened in 1902, might be considered fast food. The restaurant had tables and chairs, but its walls were lined with vending machines containing prepared food in little window boxes. There was a lot more choice in a typical automat than at a fast-food restaurant today. Automats were popular during the Great Depression and were still in operation when I was a child (in the 1940s) and visited them in New York with my grandmother.

standardization and automation. "During a relatively brief period of time, the fast food industry has helped to transform not only the American diet, but also our landscape, economy, workforce, and popular culture" (Schlosser 2001: 3). In his extraordinary book, *Fast Food Nation: The Dark Side of the All-American Meal* (2001), Eric Schlosser has meticulously documented the ways that the quintessential American meal, namely a hamburger and fries, has changed our relation to food, the environment, and each other. While most of us take "fast food" for granted and find it convenient, few of us know anything about the history and the darker side of the industry, and the consequences for our society as a whole.

The fast food industry began in late 1940s and early 1950s in California and was bound up with the increasing use of automobiles and, thus, the need for restaurants on the road and outside the city centers. Carl Karcher, the founder of Carl's Jr., began with a hot dog stand and later opened a drive-in restaurant, as did the McDonald brothers. But in 1948 the McDonald brothers transformed their operation. Not only did they reduce the number of items on their menu to, primarily, hamburgers, french fries, and milkshakes, but they also replaced dishes and glassware with paper cups and plates. In addition, they

> divided the food preparation into separate tasks performed by different workers. To fill a typical order, one person grilled the hamburger; another "dressed" and wrapped it; another prepared the milk shake; made the fries; and another worked the counter. For the first time, the guiding principles of a factory assembly line were applied to a commercial kitchen. The new division of labor meant that a worker only had to be taught how to perform one task. (Schlosser 2001: 20)

The de-skilling of workers spurred the expansion of the industry, since skilled cooks were more difficult to find and more expensive to hire. This and the Speedee Service system it facilitated caught the attention of Ray Kroc, who convinced the McDonald's brothers to sell him the franchise rights that would eventually spread McDonald's across the nation and the world. As McDonald's grew, Carl's Jr., Burger King, and Kentucky Fried Chicken followed suit, adopting the same methods of standardization and assembly-line labor to do so. But McDonald's came to symbolize the fast food phenomenon, as indicated by its use in new words such as McDonaldization, McWorld, McThink, McDollars, or, more caustically, McGarbage, McGreedy, and McProfits.

A new McDonald's opens every 3 hours, and there are now more than 30,000 in 119 countries.[11] "The company annually hires about a million people, more than any other American organization, public or private" (Schlosser 2001: 4). This is a depressing statistic that does not bode well for the future workforce. While some people deplore McDonald's food and work tactics, the behavior of numerous others, according to Conrad Kottak (1982), reveals that it functions not only as a place to get a fast meal, but also as almost a sacred site (with golden arches and, in some places, stained-glass windows), a pilgrimage destination, and a refuge, especially when one is in unfamiliar territory. I confess that once in Paris, the mecca of wonderful food, I slipped into a McDonald's just to feel "at home" – to hear English and to have a familiar "quarter-pounder with special sauce," a coke, and french fries. I also discovered that it had become, at least among young people, a trendy place to gather.

Despite McDonald's enormous success and increasing popularity, some people fear the "Americanization" of the world and worry that it "threatens a fundamental aspect of national identity: how, where, and what people choose to eat" (Schlosser 2001: 44). It counters this by being very pliable in the face of local tastes and producing new menu items, such as McDöner (Turkish döner kebab in Germany), McChao (fried rice in China), McLaks (grilled salmon in Norway), and Kosher Big Macs – that is, burgers with no dairy products – in Israel (Watson 1997).

Margaret Visser, a Canadian classicist who turned her attention to food in *Much Depends on Dinner* (1986), thinks the popularity of these "standardized mass-produced processed dishes" is an expression of democracy: "nothing more directly expresses our loathing for hierarchy than the pre-cut, pre-coated, ground and reconstituted portions – often compu-ter calculated to be *equal* – which we get as fast-food" (Visser, quoted in interview with

Trish Hall, *New York Times*, June 15, 1988). She may have a point, although this is a cookie-cutter image of democracy that confuses "equal" with "identical." Perhaps equal *access* to good food is a better expression of democracy.

In the year 2000, Americans spent more than $110 billion on fast food, more than they spend "on higher education, personal computers, computer software, or new cars. They spend more on fast food than on movies, books, magazines, newspapers, videos, and recorded music – combined" (Schlosser 2001: 3). Americans are hungry. Schlosser continues, "On any given day in the United States about one-quarter of the adult population visits a fast food restaurant," and so do millions of children who are, increasingly, the targets of advertising. Virtually all children in the United States know about McDonald's, and most have probably visited one many times, some several times a week. However, children who early on become accustomed to, if not addicted to, fast food do not easily abandon it. Obesity in children and in the general population has paralleled the growth of the fast food industry, and the same is true in other nations after they have introduced fast food. Schlosser does not claim fast food is the only cause, but it is certainly a contributing one; nevertheless, obesity contributes to and exacerbates numerous health problems which, in turn, contribute to rising health care costs. (See figure 7.5.)

The enormous demand for meat and potatoes, even in these new forms, has a concomitantly enormous impact on our environment. According to Sahlins, "The exploitation of the American environment, the mode of relation to the landscape, *depends on the model of a meal* that includes a central meat element" (1976: 171). Thus an enormous amount of land (80 percent of the arable land in comparison with a mere 3 percent taken up by cities) is devoted to feed grains for cattle and their pasturage, "[a]ll of which would change overnight if we ate dogs" (p. 171), became vegetarian, or adopted the diet recently proposed by the USDA.[12] In other words, there is nothing economically rational in the American use of land. Rather, the use is determined by the cultural logic of foods and meals and the meaningful distinctions and identities we create.

Another issue related to the land concerns how the fast food industry has changed the way the food is grown. In a very short period of time, a few companies have managed to

Figure 7.5 Cartoon by Pete Mueller: "I'm optional, you're optional, fries are not." © Pete Mueller.

buy out, take over, and dominate the production of both beef and potatoes, a process that has forced thousands of small farmers out of business or into virtual serfdom for the large agribusinesses. This in turn has driven many to suicide. In 1976 Sahlins reported that "the suicide rate among ranchers and farmers in the United States is now about three times higher than the national average" (p. 146). Decades later the problem continues, as Eric Ramirez found in his dissertation research on the Oklahoma farming crisis of the 1990s (Ramirez 2001).

Another human tragedy unfolds with the workers in "modern" slaughterhouses. No longer butchers, a highly skilled occupation, these workers have been demoted to manning one station in a long assembly line. It is now one of the most dangerous jobs in the United States, performed primarily by immigrants, who receive no benefits and risk life and limb every day. The speed of meat processing also increases the risk of contamination, primarily from spillage from intestines that can spread fecal bacteria to an entire line of meat. Such meat is not always disposed of, but can end up in restaurants and even schools, as we learn only after the fact, when incidents of food poisoning are reported in the news.

The human tragedy is paralleled by what happens to the cattle. Traditionally, cattle were raised in pastures that allocated 30 acres of grassland per head. Today, due in part to the rising cost of land and in part to the value of efficiency, most cattle are housed in pens where they can barely move. They are dosed repeatedly with antibiotics and hormones and fed a corn-based diet laced with chemical supplements and waste products. This can include the waste parts of animals, even the nerves and brains, which introduced bovine spongiform encephalopathy (BSE), otherwise known as *mad cow disease*, into the beef. When the cattle are fattened up, they are put on conveyor belts into the slaughterhouse, where one is killed and processed every minute. No wonder there are accidents and fecal contamination.

Where does all this automation and speed-up lead? Because of the way cattle are raised and processed, the food has little taste. Whatever taste it does have is derived from chemical additives, often made at perfume factories. The same is true for the fries. McDonald's used to fry their potatoes in 93 percent beef tallow, which gave them their distinctive taste. However, they did not disclose this fact, and after being sued by a group of vegetarians, they switched to vegetable oil, but continue to use chemical additives to simulate the smell of the former fries.

This overview is far too brief, but should be enough to whet your appetite for more information. Fast food has changed our lives. Not only has it changed *what* we eat, *how* we eat, and *where* we eat, but it has also damaged the farm economy, polluted land and waterways, eroded compassion for workers and animals, and erased the patterns of civility that accompany dining. In the long run the loss of civility may be its most deleterious effect, for this exacerbates the other concerns. Although it is true that families eat at McDonald's and other fast food chains, the experience is very different from that of families eating a home-cooked meal around the table and talking about the day's activities, or eating in a restaurant where thought is put into the selection and presentation of food, and where preparation is both a skill and an art. People who eat at fast food restaurants are generally people "on the run," people too busy to have a "normal" meal. Perhaps fast food is quintessentially American because it both symbolizes and embodies the value we place on speed and efficiency.

Anomalous Foods: Betwixt and Between

There are some edible things that are classified as non-food. In a health-conscious world, British anthropologist Allison James wonders why the consumption of confectionery, or candy as Americans refer to it, is actually increasing in Britain, despite the warnings about diets high in sugar and fat. In a report in 1988, Britons spent £3,285 million on confectionery but only £2,375 million on staples like bread, and only £650 million on cereals. It is not enough simply to say that Britons have a sweet tooth, for one still must ask why. James's explanation rests on a classification system which places confectionery in between "real" food and "junk" food. It is, therefore, "a 'liminal' foodstuff … [that] has the symbolic power both to mediate social relationships and to confer particular sets of social meanings" (James 1990: 666). Never part of a meal, yet still something to be eaten, it stands outside the major classifications and thus can act as go-between, sweetening the path of social relations. It makes an appropriate gift in place of flowers or wine when one is invited to dinner. Confectionery has become a symbol of love, not only between parents and children, but between men and women. Thus confectionery, especially chocolate, is an appropriate gift from men to women on Valentine's Day. The ability of candy to sweeten social relations depends first of all on the classification of sweet as good and pleasurable.[13]

Frankenfood

Just as we begin to understand what food is and is not, and what its meanings are, a new category emerges that confounds all the traditional classifications. These are the newly engineered, genetically modified foods, GMFs, or in a more ghoulish mode, *frankenfood*,[14] as the British refer to them (and see figure 7.6). These *transgenic* foods – the new chimera – fuse genetic material not only from two different kinds of plants (as occurs in hybrids) but also from two different species altogether. Thus we have tomatoes with fish genes, potatoes with chicken genes, tobacco with hamster genes, and corn plants with firefly genes (Rifkin 1998: 81). No wonder people are wary. Are these things safe to eat? Are they really foods? Will they have long-term effects on the environment? At a deeper level, the anxiety may be related to the belief that we are what we eat; if we eat transgenic food, the question looms: what will we become?

   The scientists who are developing these foods (or, more accurately, the seeds), emphasize their uses: they make plants resistant to bugs, they lace rice with vitamin-enriched bacteria, and they insert genes that prevent frost damage and thus, in principle, financial loss for farmers. All of these alterations will, they claim, help the starving peoples of the Third World. However, a *Nova Frontline* special (April 24, 2001) said that genetically modified food will not relieve world hunger but will, instead, make the third world more dependent on the companies that hold the patents on the seeds.[15] The developers seem not to have learned the lesson from the aid workers who, as we noted, discovered that even hungry

GENETICALLY MODIFIED SPECIALS

ODORLESS FISH

5⁹⁹ lb.

CAFFEINATED ORANGES
A perfect one-stop breakfast

78¢ each

HAMCHEESE
The multipurpose cold cut

2⁹⁹ lb.

NEW
Complete vitamin package bred right into meat!
MULTI VITAMIN LAMB SHANK

4⁷⁹ lb.

LASTING LETTUCE
Won't wilt for six months in or out of fridge
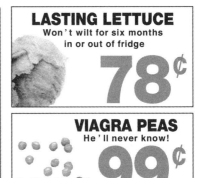
78¢

VIAGRA PEAS
He'll never know!
99¢

IBUPROFEN TOMATOES

89¢

PERSONAL-SIZED TURKEYS
Eat like quail!

3⁹⁹

BONELESS RABBIT
5⁹⁹

PINK BANANAS
Kids'll love 'em!

89¢ lb. NEW

PROTEIN POTATOES
Serve like meat!
1⁹⁹ lb.

SUPER JUMBO EGGS
6" (serves 4)
12" (serves 6)

5⁹⁹

RECTANGULAR ZUCCHINI Easy to grill!

1⁹⁹ lb.

GENOME SPECIFIC SALAD DRESSING
Pick the dressing that matches your DNA!

89¢

Figure 7.6 "Frankenfoods." Genetically Modified Specials, by Jesse Gordon and Knickerbocker Design. From *New York Times* (July 15, 2000). © Nicholas Blechman and Jesse Gordon.

people will reject edible food if it does not fit their classification system. Turkish villagers also told me that they rejected a new, "improved" strain of wheat because the flour made from it produced inferior bread.

If the main problem is not food scarcity but food distribution, as many economists believe, then there is no guarantee that genetically modified food can solve the problem of hunger. Most of the world's food is consumed by people living in the rich nations of the First World. We sample the world's smorgasbord while the rest of the world gets the crumbs. It is unlikely that a technological fix will solve what is essentially a social problem.

Consumers worry about what we are doing to our bodies and to the world's eco-system. Monarch butterflies apparently died eating genetically modified corn pollen (*Nova Frontline* special, April 24, 2001). Europeans demanded the labeling of all transgenic foods, but the United States, which is at the forefront of the development of these foods, decided it was unnecessary. In 2000–1 the fear that the genetically modified corn in Taco Bell tortilla shells could induce new allergies heightened public interest in GMFs. Still, the percentage of consumers involved in these issues is small, and many of them are not fully aware of the potential consequences of GMFs, especially that, once planted, the process is irreversible. These species cannot be contained within the boundaries of a field, for they can cross-fertilize and take over existing species, putting indigenous plants at risk of extinction. Some people are concerned about the consequent narrowing of the gene pool and feel it is presumptuous of scientists to "play God" by deciding which species will be preserved and which will perish. Are GMFs Lucifer in disguise?[16]

Farmers' markets

In response to the manufacturing of our food, whether as fast food or GMFs, some people clamor for farmers' markets in the hopes of finding a hint of the "authentic" tastes of their childhoods, when "a tomato tasted like a tomato." For some, this means "organic," foods grown without chemical additives and pesticides; for others, it means produce grown locally by small, traditional farmers. While farmers' markets and food stands with fresh local produce have been around for a long time, there has been increasing interest in them.

Alice Waters has been an important force in this development. She is the founder and owner of Chez Panisse, an upscale restaurant in Berkeley, California, and can rightly be called the new Julia Child because of the transformation she has brought about in notions about food and dining. But hers is a different kind of transformation from Child's. While Child was trained in the classic French tradition and emphasized recipes and method, Waters is more concerned with where and how our food is grown. Her "delicious revolution" has five component parts – land, food, meals, conversation, and community (Flammang 2009: 184). Rather than sampling the global smorgasbord, she emphasizes seasonal organic produce from *local* growers. At the celebration party for the 30th anniversary of Chez Panisse (in August 2001), there "was no caviar, no *foie gras*, no truffles, no shellfish, none of the luxury ingredients other lovers of fine food might have chosen" (Apple, Jr., *San Francisco Chronicle*, August 29, 2001). Good food need not be exotic.

An International School Lunch Tour 2003

Congress has vowed to take up the highly polarized issue of school lunches [in the spring of 2003] this spring with the reauthorization of the law that helps states pay for school lunches. The attention comes not a moment too soon. While school lunches have never approached haute cuisine, some of us can recall a time when trays of mystery meat and creamed corn offered a sort of bonding experience, something we suffered through together, like showers after phys. ed.

Today few children work up enough sweat in school to require a shower, and many are swapping the government-sanctioned "meat and two veggies" lunch for candy bars, ice cream and soda from the cafeteria vending machines. And who can blame them? Choosing soggy broccoli, gray pot roast and an apple over pizza, chips and chocolate cupcakes seems, well, almost un-American.

The problem, of course, is that American children are among the fattest in the world, and the readily available junk food has plenty to do with setting up unhealthy eating habits. Meanwhile, other nations focus on the basics: appetizing yet healthful, these lunches offer children all the choice they need.

Ellen Ruppel Shell, codirector of the Knight Center for Science and Medical Journalism at Boston University and author of "The Hungry Gene: The Science of Fat and the Future of Thin."

Russia

SCHOOL 1529, MOSCOW

On the Menu:

Beef
Potato and wheat soup
Boiled rice
Mandarin orange compote
Wheat bread
Rye bread
Fresh tomato
Whole grains and fresh fruit enliven this hearty selection.

France

ÉCOLE ÉLÉMENTAIRE, RUE ST. BERNARD, PARIS

On the Menu:

Ham with lentils
Salad with tomatoes, corn, soy and Gruyère
Yogurt with sugar
Baguette slices
Banana
Water
Four fresh vegetables and banana: French children get their "five a day" on a single tray.

Mexico

LÁZARO CÁRDENAS GRAMMAR SCHOOL, MEXICO CITY

On the Menu:

Meat
Rice, corn and squash
Horchata (water mixed with
oatmeal and sugar)
Apple
A big dose of starch, but very little sugar or fat.

South Korea

ELEMENTARY SCHOOL, TAEGU

On the Menu:

Rice
Chicken soup
Squid with hot sauce
Fried sweet potatoes
Radish kimchi
High in flavor, low in fat, and varied enough to keep even finicky eaters interested.

USA

SOUTH AVENUE SCHOOL, BEACON, NY

On the Menu:

Pot roast
Mashed potatoes
Broccoli
Apple
Milk
The gravy and chocolate milk may go down easy, but they don't do much to enhance the nutritional value of this fat-heavy meal. (Shell 2002)

In her search for fresh, local ingredients, Waters found and came to depend on a number of small-scale farmers and foragers with whom she established intimate relations unmediated by the middlemen of commercial food provisioning. She realized how much she and her restaurant were part of a wider interconnected community. As "a restaurant," she said, "we are utterly dependent on the health of the land, the sea, and the planet as a whole, and that this search for good ingredients is pointless without a healthy agriculture and a healthy environment" (Waters, in Clark 1990: 113). She has tried to show that "sustainable agriculture – a careful way of farming that maintains the quality of the soil for future generations – was possible and profitable" (Severson, *San Francisco Chronicle*, August 19, 2001).

As her philosophy developed, so did her political action. She worked with Catherine Sneed on the Garden Project whereby inmates from the San Francisco County Jail learned to work as organic farmers, a process that had a profound effect on their lives. It gave them "the kind of skills to nourish themselves physically and spiritually. And it shows that even the most difficult segments of society can find hope and self-worth if they're given just a small opportunity" (Waters, quoted by Ken Garcia, "Jail Sentences Reduced to Thyme Served: Unique Garden Program for Inmates," *San Francisco Chronicle*, April 17, 1999). At first they donated their produce to homeless shelters, but have since been allowed to sell directly to customers, which include many upscale Bay area restaurants.

This project gave Waters the idea for the Edible Schoolyard. After driving by a school with a large but unkempt yard and learning that it also had an abandoned kitchen and cafeteria (replaced by fast food concession stands on the playground), she decided to start a program similar to the Garden Project for the prisoners. Not only did the children learn how to grow vegetables and make them flourish, but also they became much more interested in the food they were eating. As Waters commented, "in about six weeks these kids go from saying 'I don't like salad' to saying 'You've gotta try the arugula!'" (see Flammang 2009: 201). The excitement they have in eating what they have grown is contagious and is passed along to family and friends; this may truly be the beginning of training in the civility that is, perhaps, the goal of the "delicious revolution."

The Edible School and other projects like it are now funded in part by the Chez Panisse Foundation set up in 1996, whose statement of purpose is "to support educational and cultural projects that promote sustainable agriculture, strengthen community, and reinforce self-esteem by creating opportunities for people to grow, prepare, and share their food" (quoted in Flammang 2009: 202).

In addition to the health food movement, organically grown food, and farmers' markets, there is an international movement called (appropriately) Slow Food that began in Italy in 1986. It now boasts more than 65,000 members in 45 countries, an indication that a reaction is setting in against fast food and the "fast life, which manifests itself through the industrialization and standardization of our food supply and the degradation of our farmland" (SlowFoodUSA.com, 2001). Not unlike Alice Waters (who is a member of a California branch), this movement "believes that pleasure and quality in everyday life can be achieved by slowing down, respecting the convivial traditions of the table and celebrating the diversity of the earth's bounty." Instead of creating fast, convenient foods for our fast-paced lives, they draw attention to the relation between food, social relations, the environment, and time. As we saw in chapter 3, time is the one thing Americans seem to have less and less of because we are working more than ever before. Are we really "getting away from our Puritan roots," as Ruth Reichel believes? Or are those roots becoming more exposed? What is the relation between them and the increasing interest in food, cooking, and cookbooks?

Cookbooks and cooking

In many parts of the world, traditional recipes are handed down from generation to generation. Where one learns by example, by helping to prepare meals, there is no need for a cookbook. In the Turkish village, for example, I was told there were only three ways to prepare green beans. In modern urban society where people do not live close to their parents or other relatives, and have often reached the age of maturity without learning to cook, cookbooks are a necessity. Obviously, they require a literate readership, for in order to use a cookbook, you have to know how to read. Beyond teaching the basics – how to boil, broil, bake, roast, or fry – cookbooks serve many purposes. For the neophyte cook, they help create menus that serve both to dissipate boredom and to ease the anxiety of entertaining. For immigrants displaced from the homeland, they can help keep alive the flavors and aromas of home while simultaneously helping them adapt to their new home. According to anthropology student Malindo Lo, Chinese cookbooks written by Chinese Americans are often quite nostalgic and attempt to evoke an authentic past which the immigrants may have never experienced (Lo 2001). For the more advanced cook, preparing meals from certain cookbooks is a means to impress friends. In the 1960s and 1970s, when I lived in Cambridge, Massachusetts, I remember the subtle competition among friends to reproduce the recipes from Julia Child's cookbooks.[17] Not only was Cambridge her home at the time, but also she had just launched the extremely popular television series *The French Chef*. (I used to walk by her house and liberate food magazines from her trash can!) She is certainly responsible for raising the level of appreciation of food and its preparation in the United States. Today, a number of other chefs have followed her lead: witness the proliferation of cooking programs on television. However, we do not know if viewers actually cook the recipes demonstrated on the programs, or if they watch them purely for entertainment. Nor do we understand exactly why it is entertaining. For that matter, we also don't know if people cook the recipes in their cookbooks, or if they just admire the beautiful illustrations in them.

Reading cookbooks can whet appetites and spur people to cook, but they can also provide vicarious pleasure – a culinary voyeurism or "food porn"[18] – for those who know full well they will never have the time or confidence to do so (see figure 7.7). This leads us back to the beginning of this chapter. Does the increased interest in cooking, food, and cookbooks indicate a revolution in our approach to food, or a nostalgia for the delicious, nutritious sensuousness of food that we have lost? Working so hard and so long has made people too tired for sex, so perhaps they have turned to food as the last resort, the last pleasurable refuge. Even though they do not have time to prepare the luscious meals they see in cookbooks or on television, they can still savor the simulacra of them.

Cooking, for Lévi-Strauss, represented the transition from nature to culture. It represented for him a major event in human evolution, distinguishing us from the animals. But it also symbolizes the transformation *of* nature, a magic trick we perform everyday. Even more important, cooking helps us to realize that there are other ways of transforming nature into culture besides domination and exploitation. Perhaps, as the only animal species that cooks its food, the lessons learned from cooking and the civility of the table are what make us fully human.

Bon appétit!

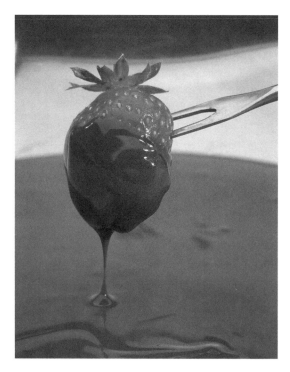

Figure 7.7   "Food porn." Photo © Food Features.

Notes

1. After 68 years in production, *Gourmet* magazine finally folded in 2009.

2. In it, he "argues that a universal feature of human thought involves linking the distinction between raw ingredients and cooked food with the fundamental distinction between nature and culture" (Beardsworth and Keil 1997: 61). Central to this distinction is his "culinary triangle," whereby raw food "becomes cooked food through a *cultural* transformation … [and] cooked food may be reclaimed by nature through the *natural* transformation of rotting" (p. 61; emphasis mine).

3. See the book of the same title by Peter Farb and George Armelagos (1980).

4. There are similar sayings among Hindus (see Parry 1985: 613), Germans, and others from the ancient past to the present (Ohnuki-Tierney 1993: 3).

5. In response to criticism from Bulmer (1967) and Tambiah (1969), Douglas revised her opinion (1975) and began an investigation of the relationship between metaphysical systems (or religions) and the classifications of everyday life.

6. Artichokes were a west coast vegetable introduced by Italians who immigrated to the area around Half Moon Bay, California, now known as the artichoke capital of the world.

7. See also Siskind (1992).

8. Turkey, the bird, also known as *Meleagris gullopavo* or *Americana sybestris auis*, is native to North America. Apparently the 1494 Tordesillas Treaty forged by the pope in Rome granted commercial enterprises to the Portuguese, who then brought the fowl to their colony in Goa, India, from whence it was taken to Egypt, then part of the Ottoman Empire. In Turkish, the bird is known as *hindi* (from India). When

Ottoman traders took some of these birds to the British Isles, it was designated *turkey*. Thus, according to H. B. Paksoy, a Turkish historian who wrote about this, the Pilgrims were already familiar with *turkey*. Benjamin Franklin suggested that it be designated as the symbol of the new republic, but instead the bald eagle was given the honor (Paksoy 1992, translated and sent to me by Levent Soysal).

9. In the 1950s home freezers changed the foodways of American households. I recall my mother ordering a "side of beef" to be cut into chops, steaks, and roasts in suitable portions for our family of six and put in the freezer until needed. Vegetables were no longer canned but frozen and soon could be bought in packages already frozen.

10. Not all patriarchal societies are meat eating, however. India is a patriarchal society, but, among Hindus, cows are sacred and are not eaten. A Hindu student made the interesting suggestion that the "mad cow disease" scare in Britain is a kind of revenge for the way they colonized and incorporated India in their commonwealth.

11. In 2003 there were reports that the number of franchises of McDonald's was decreasing and that some had also closed.

12. Frances Moore Lappé, author of *Diet for a Small Planet*, notes, "We feed almost half of the world's grain to livestock, returning only a fraction in meat – while millions starve. It confounds all logic" ([1971]

1991: xvii). Indeed, "*it takes 16 pounds of grain and soybeans to produce just 1 pound of beef in the United States today*" (p. 9).

13. See Mintz (1985), who discusses the dark side of the sugar industry. We will address this in chapter 9.

14. An excellent *Nova Frontline* special with this title was aired April 24, 2001, and can be ordered from PBS.

15. The Bush administration was attempting to force Europe to accept GMFs, claiming the European position is immoral because it leads to starvation in the developing world (Becker, *New York Times*, January 10, 2003). I think it is more a matter of having another market for US food products.

16. See also Kimbrell (2002).

17. During that time I, and many of my friends, saw no contradiction between cooking good food and preparing elegant dinners for our friends and marching for civil rights or against the war in Vietnam. Merry White, a close friend, and for a time my next-door neighbor, who was and is an excellent cook, has written several very good cookbooks, and is now a sociologist-anthropologist at Boston University, where she teaches courses about food and about Japan. I credit her with developing my interest in food.

18. I came across this term in an article by Anthony Bourdain in the *San Francisco Chronicle*, September 4, 2001; I do not know whether he is the originator of it.

EXERCISES

7.1. Supermarket

A. Go to a supermarket near you and describe the organization of the food and other goods inside it. What are the categories – represented in part by aisles – for classifying food? Does the store layout invite more costumer traffic in some areas than in others?

B. Go through the fresh produce aisle and figure out how many different places the fruits and vegetables come from. Indicate these locations on a map of the world. Are there any correlations between price and point of origin?

C. Choose a highly processed food item, such as a breakfast cereal or packaged snack item, and find out how many different ingredients are in it. Do you know what these ingredients are? See if you can figure out where they come from – that is, the actual farms, factories, and businesses – and where they were assembled into their final form before the finished food item is delivered to your supermarket. Indicate these locations on a map of the world.

7.2. Dinner

A. What, to you, makes dinner different from other meals and snacks? Define it in terms of food, preparation, location, time, and anything else that is important to you.

B. Describe some dinners that you have prepared for yourself and for different groups of guests. How does dinner change – that is, menu, presentation, time, and so on – depending on who is coming to it?

Bibliography

Adams, Carol J. (1991) *The Sexual Politics of Meat: A Feminist-Vegetarian Critical Theory.* New York: Continuum.

Allison, Anne (1991) "Japanese Mothers and *Obentos*: The Lunch-Box as Ideological State." *Anthropological Quarterly* 64(4): 195–208.

Barthes, Roland ([1957] 1972) *Mythologies.* New York: Hill and Wang.

Beardsworth, Alan, and Keil, Teresa (1997) *Sociology on the Menu: An Invitation to the Study of Food and Society.* London: Routledge.

Bell, David, and Valentine, Gill (1997) *Consuming Geographies: We Are Where We Eat.* London: Routledge.

Bulmer, R. (1967) "Why Is the Cassowary Not a Bird? A Problem of Zoological Taxonomy among the Karam of the New Guinea Highlands." *Man* 2: 5–20.

Clark, Robert, ed. (1990) *Our Sustainable Table.* San Francisco: North Point Press.

Counihan, Carole M. (1999) *The Anthropology of Food and the Body: Gender, Meaning and Power.* New York: Routledge.

Counihan, Carole M., and Kaplan, Steven L. (1998) *Food and Gender: Identity and Power.* Amsterdam: Harwood.

Douglas, Mary (1966) "The Abominations of Leviticus." In *Purity and Danger: An Analysis of the Concepts of Pollution and Taboo.* London: Routledge & Kegan Paul, pp. 42–58.

Douglas, Mary (1975) "Deciphering a Meal." In *Implicit Meanings: Essays in Anthropology.* London: Routledge & Kegan Paul, pp. 249–75.

Douglas, Mary (1984) *Food in the Social Order: Studies of Food and Festivities in Three American Communities.* New York: Russell Sage.

Dubisch, Jill ([1981] 1997) "You Are What You Eat: Religious Aspects of the Health Food Movement." In *Magic, Witchcraft, and Religion: An Anthropological Study of the Supernatural*, 4th ed., ed. Arthur C. Lehmann and James E. Myers. Mountain View, CA: Mayfield, pp. 62–70.

Farb, Peter, and Armelagos, George (1980) *Consuming Passions: The Anthropology of Eating.* Boston: Houghton Mifflin.

Feeley-Harnik, Gillian (1981) *The Lord's Table: Eucharist and Passover in Early Christianity.* Philadelphia: University of Pennsylvania Press.

Feirstein, B. (1982) *Real Men Don't Eat Quiche.* London: New English Library.

Fiddes, Nick (1991) *Meat: A Natural Symbol.* London: Routledge.

Flammang, Janet (2009) *The Taste for Civilization: Food, Politics, and Civil Society.* Chicago: University of Illinois Press.

Gabaccia, Donna R. (1998) *We Are What We Eat: Ethnic Food and the Making of Americans.* Cambridge, MA: Harvard University Press.

Goody, Jack (1982) *Cooking, Cuisine and Class: A Study in Comparative Sociology.* Cambridge: Cambridge University Press.

James, Allison (1990) "The Good, the Bad and the Delicious: The Role of Confectionery in British Society." *Sociological Review* 38(4): 666–88.

Kass, Leon R. (1994) *The Hungry Soul: Eating and the Perfecting of Our Nature*. Chicago: University of Chicago Press.

Kimbrell, Andrew, ed. (2002) *Fatal Harvest: The Tragedy of Industrial Agriculture*. Washington, DC: Island.

Kottak, Conrad, ed. (1982) *Researching American Culture*. Ann Arbor: University of Michigan Press.

Lappé, Frances Moore ([1971] 1991) *Diet for a Small Planet*. New York: Ballantine.

Leach, Edmund (1964) "Anthropological Aspects of Language: Animal Categories and Verbal Abuse." In *New Directions in the Study of Language*, ed. Eric Lenneberg. Cambridge, MA: MIT Press, pp. 23–63.

Lévi-Strauss, Claude (1966) "The Culinary Triangle." *Partisan Review* 33: 586–95.

Lévi-Strauss, Claude ([1968] 1978) *Mythologiques*, vol. 3: *The Origin of Table Manners*, trans. J. and D. Weightman. New York: Harper & Row.

Lo, Malinda (2001) "'Authentic' Chinese Food: Chinese American Cookbooks and the Regulation of Ethnic Identity." Unpublished paper, Department of Cultural and Social Anthropology, Stanford University.

Macbeth, Helen (1997) *Food Preferences and Taste: Continuity and Change*. Providence, RI: Berghahn.

Mintz, Sidney (1985) *Sweetness and Power: The Place of Sugar in Modern History*. New York: Viking.

Ohnuki-Tierney, Emiko (1993) *Rice As Self: Japanese Identities Through Time*. Princeton, NJ: Princeton University Press.

Ortner, Sherry (1973) "On Key Symbols." *American Anthropologist* 75: 1338–46.

Paksoy, H. B. (1992) "Türk Tarihi, Toplumların Mayası, Uygarlık." *Annals of Japan Association for Middle East Studies* 7: 173–220.

Parry, Jonathan (1985) "Death and Digestion: The Symbolism of Food and Eating in North Indian Mortuary Rites." *Man* 20: 612–30.

Pollan, Michael (2009) *Food Rules*. New York: Penguin.

Ramirez, Eric (2001) "Troubled Fields: Men, Emotions and the Oklahoma Farm Crisis, 1992–94." Ph.D. dissertation, Stanford University, Department of Cultural and Social Anthropology.

Rifkin, Jeremy (1998) *The Biotech Century: Harnessing the Gene and Remaking the World*. New York: Tarcher/Putnam.

Rombauer, Irma S., and Rombauer Becker, M. (1975) *The Joy of Cooking*. New York: Simon & Schuster. (Original work published in 1931)

Sahlins, Marshall (1976) *Culture and Practical Reason*. Chicago: University of Chicago Press.

Schlosser, Eric (2001) *Fast Food Nation: The Dark Side of the All-American Meal*. Boston: Houghton Mifflin.

Shell, Ellen Ruppel (2002) *The Hungry Gene: The Science of Fat and the Future of Thin*. New York: Atlantic Monthly Press.

Siskind, Janet (1992) "The Invention of Thanksgiving." *Critique of Anthropology* 12(2): 167–91.

SlowFoodUSA.com (2001). [Home page], September 4. www.SlowFoodUSA.com.

Tambiah, S. J. (1969) "Animals are Good to Think and Good to Prohibit." *Ethnology* 8(4): 423–59.

Visser, Margaret (1986) *Much Depends on Dinner*. Toronto: McClelland & Stewart.

Visser, Margaret (1991) *The Rituals of Dinner: The Origins, Evolution, Eccentricities, and Meaning of Table Manners*. New York: Grove Weidenfeld.

Waters, Alice (1990) "The Farm–Restaurant Connection." In *Our Sustainable Table*, ed. Robert Clark. San Francisco: North Point Press, pp. 113–22.

Watson, James L., ed. (1997) *Golden Arches East*. Stanford, CA: Stanford University Press.

Westwood, Sallie, and Bhachu, Parminder, eds. (1988) *Enterprising Women*. London: Routledge.

Yanagisako, Sylvia, and Delaney, Carol (1995) *Naturalizing Power: Essays in Feminist Cultural Analysis*. New York and London: Routledge.

Videos

American Eats: History on a Bun. A & E Home Video, August 21, 2001.

Babette's Feast, dir. Gabriel Axel, 1987.

Dim Sum, dir. Wayne Wang, 1985.

Eating: A Very Serious Comedy About Women and Food, dir. Nelly Alard, 1990.

Fast Food Nation, dir. Richard Linklater, 2006.

Food, Inc., dir. Robert Kenner, 2008.

Frankenfood, PBS *Frontline* special. April 24, 2001.

Julie and Julia, dir. Nora Ephron, 2009.

Our Daily Bread, dir. Nikolaus Geyrhalter, 2006.

Supersize Me, dir. Morgan Spurlock, 2004.

The Wedding Banquet, dir. Ang Lee, 1993.

You Are What You Eat: Religious Aspects of the Health Food Movement

Jill Dubisch

Dr. Robbins was thinking how it might be interesting to make a film from Adelle Davis' perennial best seller, *Let's Eat Right to Keep Fit.*

Representing a classic confrontation between good and evil – in this case nutrition versus unhealthy diet – the story had definite box office appeal. The role of the hero, Protein, probably should be filled by Jim Brown, although Burt Reynolds undoubtedly would pull strings to get the part. Sunny Doris Day would be a clear choice to play the heroine, Vitamin C, and Orson Welles, oozing saturated fatty acids from the pits of his flesh, could win an Oscar for his interpretation of the villainous Cholesterol. The film might begin on a stormy night in the central nervous system. …

Tom Robbins, *Even Cowgirls Get the Blues*

I intend to examine a certain way of eating, that which is characteristic of the health food movement, and try to determine what people are communicating when they choose to eat in ways which run counter to the dominant patterns of food consumption in our society. This requires looking at health foods as a system of symbols and the adherence to a health food way of life as being, in part, the expression of belief in a particular world view. Analysis of these symbols and the underlying world view reveals that, as a system of beliefs and practices, the health food movement has some of the characteristics of a religion.

Such an interpretation might at first seem strange since we usually think of religion in terms of a belief in a deity or other supernatural beings. These notions, for the most part, are lacking in the health food movement. However, anthropologists do not always consider such beliefs to be a necessary part of a religion. Clifford Geertz, for example, suggests the following broad definition:

a *religion* is: 1) a system of symbols which acts to 2) establish powerful, pervasive, and long-lasting moods and motivations in men by 3) formulating conceptions of a general order of existence and 4) clothing these conceptions with such an aura of factuality that 5) the moods and motivations seem uniquely realistic. (Geertz, 1965: 4)

Let us examine the health food movement in the light of Geertz's definition.

History of the Health Food Movement

The concept of "health foods" can be traced back to the 1830s and the Popular Health movement, which combined a reaction against professional medicine and an emphasis on lay knowledge and health care with broader social concerns such as feminism and the class struggle (see Ehrenreich and English, 1979). The Popular Health movement emphasized self-healing and the dissemination of knowledge about the body and health to laymen. One of the early founders of the movement, Sylvester Graham (who gave us the graham cracker), preached that good health was to be found in temperate living. This included abstinence from alcohol, a vegetarian diet, consumption of whole wheat products, and regular exercise. The writings and preachings of these early "hygienists" (as they called themselves) often had moral overtones, depicting physiological and spiritual reform as going hand in hand (Shryock, 1966).

The idea that proper diet can contribute to good health has continued into the twentieth century. The discovery of vitamins provided for many health food people a further "natural" means of healing which could be utilized instead of drugs. Vitamins were promoted as health-giving substances by various writers, including nutritionist Adelle Davis who has been perhaps the most important "guru" of health foods in this century. Davis preached good diet as well as the use of vitamins to restore and maintain health, and her books have become the best sellers of the movement. (The titles of her books, *Let's Cook It Right*, *Let's Get Well*, *Let's Have Healthy Children*, give some sense of her approach.) The health food movement took on its present form, however, during the late 1960s when it became part of the "counterculture."

Health foods were "in," and their consumption became part of the general protest against the "establishment" and the "straight" lifestyle. They were associated with other movements centering around social concerns, such as ecology and consumerism (Kandel and Pelto, 1980: 328). In contrast to the Popular Health movement, health food advocates of the sixties saw the establishment as not only the medical profession but also the food industry and the society it represented. Food had become highly processed and laden with colorings, preservatives, and other additives so that purity of food became a new issue. Chemicals had also become part of the food growing process, and in reaction terms such as "organic" and "natural" became watchwords of the movement. Health food consumption received a further impetus from revelations about the high sugar content of many popular breakfast cereals which Americans had been taught since childhood to think of as a nutritious way to start the day. (Kellogg, an early advocate of the Popular Health movement, would have been mortified, since his cereals were originally designed to be part of a hygienic regimen.)

Although some health food users are member of formal groups (such as the Natural Hygiene Society, which claims direct descent from Sylvester Graham), the movement exists primarily as a set of principles and practices rather than as an organization. For those not part of organized groups, these principles and practices are disseminated, and contact is made with other members of the movement, through several means. The most important of these are health food stores, restaurants, and publications. The two most prominent journals in the movement are *Prevention* and *Let's Live*, begun in 1920 and 1932 respectively (Hongladarom, 1976).

These journals tell people what foods to eat and how to prepare them. They offer advice about the use of vitamins, the importance of exercise, and the danger of pollutants. They also present testimonials from faithful practitioners. Such testimonials take the form of articles that recount how the author overcame a physical problem through a health food approach, or letters from readers who tell how they have cured their ailments by following methods advocated by the journal or suggested by friends in the movement. In this manner, such magazines not only educate, they also articulate a world view and provide evidence and support for it. They have become the "sacred writings" of the movement. They are a way of "reciting the code" – the cosmology and moral injunctions – which anthropologist Anthony F. C. Wallace describes as one of the important categories of religious behavior (1966: 57).

Ideological Content of the Health Food Movement

What exactly is the health food system? First, and most obviously, it centers around certain beliefs regarding the relationship of diet to health. Health foods are seen as an "alternative" healing system, one which people turn to out of their dissatisfaction with conventional medicine (see, for example, Hongladarom, 1976). The emphasis is on "wellness" and prevention rather than on illness and curing. Judging from letters and articles found in health food publications, many individuals' initial adherence to the movement is a type of conversion. A specific medical problem, or a general dissatisfaction with the state of their health, leads these converts to an eventual realization of the "truth" as represented by the health food approach, and to a subsequent change in lifestyle to reflect the principles of that approach. "Why This Psychiatrist 'Switched'," published in *Prevention* (September, 1976), carries the following heading: "Dr. H. L. Newbold is a great advocate of better nutrition and a livelier life style. But it took a personal illness to make him see the light." For those who have experienced such conversion, and for others who become convinced by reading about such experiences, health food publications serve an important function by reinforcing the conversion and encouraging a change of lifestyle. For example, an article entitled "How to Convert Your Kitchen for the New Age of Nutrition" (*Prevention*, February, 1975) tells the housewife how to make her kitchen a source of health for her family. The article suggests ways of reorganizing kitchen supplies and reforming cooking by substituting health foods for substances detrimental to health, and also offers ideas on the preparation of nutritious and delicious meals which will convert the family to this new way of eating without "alienating" them. The pamphlet, *The Junk Food Withdrawal Manual* (Kline, 1978), details how an individual can, step by step, quit eating junk foods and adopt more healthful eating habits. Publications also urge the readers to convert others by letting them know how much better health foods are than junk foods. Proselytizing may take the form of giving a "natural" birthday party for one's children and their friends, encouraging schools to substitute fruit and nuts for junk food snacks, and even selling one's own baking.

Undergoing the conversion process means learning and accepting the general features of the health food world view. To begin with, there is great concern, as there is in many religions, with purity, in this case, the purity of food, of water, of air. In fact, there are some striking similarities between keeping a "health food kitchen" and the Jewish practice of keeping kosher. Both make distinctions between proper and improper foods, and both involve excluding certain impure foods (whether unhealthful or non-kosher) from the kitchen and table. In addition, a person concerned with maintaining a high degree of purity in food may engage in similar behavior in either case – reading labels carefully to check for impermissible ingredients and even purchasing food from special establishments to guarantee ritual purity.

In the health food movement, the basis of purity is healthfulness and "naturalness." Some foods are considered to be natural and therefore healthier; this concept applies not only to foods but to other aspects of life as well. It is part of the large idea that people should work in harmony with nature and not against it. In this respect, the health food cosmology sets up an opposition of nature (beneficial) versus culture (destructive), or, in particular, the health food movement against our highly technological society. As products of our industrialized way of life, certain foods are unnatural; they produce illness by working against the body. Consistent with this view is the idea that healing, like eating, should proceed in harmony with nature. The assumption is that the body, if allowed to function naturally, will tend

to heal itself. Orthodox medicine, on the other hand, with its drugs and surgery and its nonholistic approach to health, works against the body. Physicians are frequently criticized in the literature of the movement for their narrow approach to medical problems, reliance on drugs and surgery, lack of knowledge of nutrition, and unwillingness to accept the validity of the patient's own experience in healing himself. It is believed that doctors may actually cause further health problems rather than effecting a cure. A short item in *Prevention*, "The Delivery is Normal – But the Baby Isn't," recounts an incident in which drug-induced labor in childbirth resulted in a mentally retarded baby. The conclusion is "nature does a good job – and we should not, without compelling reasons, try to take over" (*Prevention*, May, 1979: 38).

The healing process is hastened by natural substances, such as healthful food, and by other "natural" therapeutic measures such as exercise. Vitamins are also very important to many health food people, both for maintaining health and for healing. They are seen as components of food which work with the body and are believed to offer a more natural mode of healing than drugs. Vitamins, often one of the most prominent products offered in many health food stores, provide the greatest source of profit (Hongladarom, 1976).

A basic assumption of the movement is that certain foods are good for you while others are not. The practitioner of a health food way of life must learn to distinguish between two kinds of food: those which promote well-being ("health foods") and those which are believed to be detrimental to health ("junk foods"). The former are the only kind of food a person should consume, while the latter are the antithesis of all that food should be and must be avoided. The qualities of these foods may be described by two anthropological concepts, *mana* and *taboo*. *Mana* is a type of beneficial or valuable power which can pass to individuals from sacred objects through touch (or, in the case of health foods, by ingestion). *Taboo*, on the other hand, refers to power that is dangerous; objects which are taboo can injure those who touch them (Wallace, 1966: 60–1). Not all foods fall clearly into one category or the other. However, those foods which are seen as having health-giving qualities, which contain *mana*, symbolize life, while *taboo* foods symbolize death. ("Junk food is …

dead. … Dead food produces death," proclaims one health food manual [Kline, 1978: 2–4].) Much of the space in health food publications is devoted to telling the reader why to consume certain foods and avoid others. ("Frozen, Creamed Spinach: Nutritional Disaster," *Prevention*, May, 1979. "Let's Sprout Some Seeds," *Better Nutrition*, September, 1979.)

Those foods in the health food category which are deemed to possess an especially high level of *mana* have come to symbolize the movement as a whole. Foods such as honey, wheat germ, yogurt, and sprouts are seen as representative of the general way of life which health food adherents advocate, and Kandel and Pelto found that certain health food followers attribute mystical powers to the foods they consume. Raw food eaters speak of the "life energy" in uncooked foods. Sprout eaters speak of their food's "growth force" (1980: 336).

Qualities such as color and texture are also important in determining health foods and may acquire symbolic value. "Wholeness" and "whole grain" have come to stand for healthfulness and have entered the jargon of the advertising industry. Raw, coarse, dark, crunchy, and cloudy foods are preferred over those which are cooked, refined, white, soft, and clear (see table 7.1).

Thus dark bread is preferred over white, raw milk over pasteurized, brown rice over white. The convert must learn to eat foods which at first seem strange and even exotic and to reject many foods which are components of the Standard American diet. A McDonald's hamburger, for example, which is an important symbol of America itself (Kottak, 1978), falls into the category of "junk food" and must be rejected.

Just as the magazines and books which articulate the principles of the health food movement and serve as a guide to the convert can be said to comprise the sacred writings of the movement, so the health food store or health food restaurant is the temple where the purity of the movement is guarded and maintained. There individuals find for sale the types of food and other substances advocated by the movement. One does not expect to find items of questionable purity, that is, substances which are not natural or which may be detrimental to health. Within the precincts of the temple adherents can feel safe from the contaminating forces of the larger society, can meet fellow devotees, and can be instructed by the guardians of the sacred area (see,

for example, Hongladarom, 1976). Health food stores may vary in their degree of purity. Some sell items such as coffee, raw sugar, or "natural" ice cream which are considered questionable by others of the faith. (One health food store I visited had a sign explaining that it did not sell vitamin supplements, which it considered to be "unnatural," i.e. impure.)

People in other places are often viewed as living more "naturally" and healthfully than contemporary Americans. Observation of such peoples may be used to confirm practices of the movement and to acquire ideas about food. Healthy and long-lived people like the Hunza of the Himalayas are studied to determine the secrets of their strength and longevity. Cultures as yet untainted by the food systems of industrialized nations are seen as examples of what better diet can do. In addition, certain foods from other cultures—foods such as humus, falafel, and tofu—have been adopted into the health food repertoire because of their presumed healthful qualities.

Peoples of other times can also serve as models for a more healthful way of life. There is in the health food movement a concept of a "golden age," a past which provides an authority for a better way of living. This past may be scrutinized for clues about how to improve contemporary American society. An archaeologist, writing for *Prevention* magazine, recounts how "I Put Myself on a Caveman Diet – Permanently" (*Prevention*, September 1979). His article explains how he improved his health by utilizing the regular exercise and simpler foods which he had concluded from his research were probably characteristic of our prehistoric ancestors. A general nostalgia about the past seems to exist in the health food movement, along with the feeling that we have departed from a more natural pattern of eating practiced by earlier generations of Americans (see, for example, Hongladarom, 1976). (Sylvester Graham, however, presumably did not find the eating habits of his contemporaries to be very admirable.)

The health food movement is concerned with more than the achievement of bodily health. Nutritional problems are often seen as being at the root of emotional, spiritual, and even social problems. An article entitled "Sugar Neurosis" states "Hypoglycemia (low blood sugar) is a medical reality that can trigger wife-beating, divorce, even suicide" (*Prevention*, April 1979:

Table 7.1   Health food worldview

	Health Foods	*Junk Foods*	
cosmic	LIFE	DEATH	
oppositions	NATURE	CULTURE	
	holistic, organic	fragmented, mechanistic	
basic	harmony with body and	working against body and	*undesirable*
values	nature	nature	*attributes*
and	natural and real	manufactured and artificial	
desirable	harmony, self-sufficiency,	disharmony, dependence	
attributes	independence		
	homemade, small scale	mass-produced	
	layman competence and	professional esoteric	
	understanding	knowledge and jargon	
	whole	processed	
beneficial	coarse	refined	*harmful*
qualities	dark	white	*qualities*
of food	crunchy	soft	
	raw	cooked	
	cloudy	clear	
	yogurt*	ice cream, candy	
specific	honey*	sugar*	*specific*
foods with	carob	chocolate	*taboo*
mana	soybeans*	beef	*foods*
	sprouts*	overcooked vegetables	
	fruit juices	soft drinks*	
	herb teas	coffee,* tea	
	foods from other cultures:	"all-American" foods: hot	
	humus, falafel, kefir, tofu,	dogs, McDonald's hamburgers,*	
	stir-fried vegetables, pita	potato chips, Coke	
	bread		
	return to early American	corruption of this original	
	value, "real" American	and better way of life and	
	way of life	values	

* denotes foods with especially potent *mana* or *taboo*.

110). Articles and books claim to show the reader how to overcome depression through vitamins and nutrition and the movement promises happiness and psychological well-being as well as physical health. Social problems, too, may respond to the health food approach. For example, a probation officer recounts how she tried changing offenders' diets in order to change their behavior. Testimonials from two of the individuals helped tell "what it was like to find that good nutrition was their bridge from the wrong side of the law and a frustrated, unhappy life to a vibrant and useful one" (*Prevention*, May 1978: 56). Thus, through more healthful eating and a more natural lifestyle, the health food movement offers its followers what many religions offer: salvation—in this case salvation for the body, for the psyche, and for society.

Individual effort is the keystone of the health food movement. An individual can take responsibility for his or her own health and does not need to rely on professional medical practitioners. The corollary of this is that it is a person's own behavior which may be the cause of ill health. By sinning, by not listening to our bodies, and by not following a natural way of life, we bring our ailments upon ourselves.

The health food movement also affirms the validity of each individual's experience. No two individuals are alike: needs for different vitamins vary widely; some people are more sensitive to food additives than others; each person has his or her best method of achieving happiness. Therefore, the generalized expertise of professionals and the scientifically verifiable findings of the experts may not be adequate guides for you, the individual, in the search of health. Each person's experience has meaning; if something works for you, then it works. If it works for others also, so much the better, but if it does not, that does not invalidate your own experience. While the movement does not by any means disdain all scientific findings (and indeed they are used extensively when they bolster health food positions), such findings are not seen as the only source of confirmation for the way of life which the health food movement advocates, and the scientific establishment itself tends to be suspect.

In line with its emphasis on individual responsibility for health, the movement seeks to deprofessionalize knowledge and place in every individual's hands the information and means to heal. Drugs used by doctors are usually available only through prescription, but foods and vitamins can be obtained by anyone. Books, magazines, and health food store personnel seek to educate their clientele in ways of healing themselves and maintaining their own health. Articles explain bodily processes, the effects of various substances on health, and the properties of foods and vitamins.

The focus on individual responsibility is frequently tied to a wider concern for self-sufficiency and self-reliance. Growing your own organic garden, grinding your own flour, or even, as one pamphlet suggests, raising your own cow are not simply ways that one can be assured of obtaining healthful food; they are also expressions of independence and self-reliance. Furthermore, such practices are seen as characteristic of an earlier "golden age" when people lived natural lives. For example, an advertisement for vitamins appearing in a digest distributed in health food stores shows a mother and daughter kneading bread together. The heading reads "America's discovering basics." The copy

goes on, "Baking bread at home has been a basic family practice throughout history. The past several decades, however, have seen a shift in the American diet to factory-produced breads ... Fortunately, today there are signs that more and more Americans are discovering the advantage of baking bread themselves." Homemade bread, home-canned produce, sprouts growing on the window sill symbolize what are felt to be basic American values, values supposedly predominant in earlier times when people not only lived on self-sufficient farms and produced their own fresh and more natural food, but also stood firmly on their own two feet and took charge of their own lives. A reader writing to *Prevention* praises an article about a man who found "new life at ninety without lawyers or doctors," saying "If that isn't the optimum in the American way of living, I can't imagine what is!" (*Prevention*, May 1978: 16). Thus although it criticizes the contemporary American way of life (and although some vegetarians turn to Eastern religions for guidance—see Kandel and Pelto, 1980), the health food movement in general claims to be the true faith, the proponent of basic American-ness, a faith from which the society as a whole has strayed.

Social Significance of the Health Food Movement for American Actors

Being a "health food person" involves more than simply changing one's diet or utilizing an alternative medical system. Kandel and Pelto suggest that the health food movement derives much of its popularity from the fact that "Food may be used simultaneously to cure or prevent illness, as a religious symbol and to forge social bonds. Frequently health food users are trying to improve their health, their lives, and, sometimes the world as well" (1980: 332). Use of health foods becomes an affirmation of certain values and a commitment to a certain world view. A person who becomes involved in the health food movement might be said to experience what anthropologist Anthony F. C. Wallace has called "mazeway resynthesis." The "mazeway" is the mental "map" or image of the world which each individual holds. It includes values, the environment and the objects in it, the image of the self and of others, and the techniques one uses to manipulate the environment to achieve desired end states (Wallace, 1970: 237). Resynthesis of this mazeway—that is, the creation of new "maps," values and techniques—commonly occurs in times of religious revitalization, when new religious movements are begun and converts to them are made. As individuals, these converts learn to view the world in a new manner and to act accordingly. In the case of the health food movement, those involved learn to see their health problems and other dissatisfactions with their lives as stemming from improper diet and living in disharmony with nature. They are provided with new values, new ways of viewing their environment, and new techniques for achieving their goals. For such individuals, health food use can come to imply "a major redefinition of self-image, role, and one's relationship to others" (Kandel and Pelto, 1980: 359). The world comes to "make sense" in the light of this new world view. Achievement of the desired end states of better health and an improved outlook on life through following the precepts of the movement gives further validation.

It is this process which gives the health food movement some of the overtones of a religion. As does any new faith, the movement criticizes the prevailing social values and institutions, in this case the health-threatening features of modern industrial society. While an individual's initial dissatisfaction with prevailing beliefs and practices may stem from experiences with the conventional medical system (for example, failure to find a solution to a health problem through visits to a physician), this dissatisfaction often comes to encompass other facets of the American way of life. This further differentiates the "health food person" from mainstream American society (even when the difference is justified as a return to "real" American values).

In everyday life the consumption of such substances as honey, yogurt, and wheat germ, which have come to symbolize the health food movement, does more than contribute to health. It also serves to represent commitment to the health food world view. Likewise, avoiding those substances, such as sugar and white bread, which are considered "evil" is also a mark of a health food person. Ridding the kitchen of such items—a move often advocated by articles advising readers on how to "convert" successfully to health foods—is an act of ritual as well as practical significance. The symbolic nature of such foods is confirmed by the reactions of

outsiders to those who are perceived as being inside the movement. An individual who is perceived as being a health food person is often automatically assumed to use honey instead of sugar, for example. Conversely, if one is noticed using or not using certain foods (e.g., adding wheat germ to food, not eating white sugar), this can lead to questions from the observer as to whether or not that individual is a health food person (or a health food "nut," depending upon the questioner's own orientation).

The symbolic nature of such foods is especially important for the health food neophyte. The adoption of a certain way of eating and the renunciation of mainstream cultural food habits can constitute "bridge-burning acts of commitment" (Kandel and Pelto, 1980: 395), which function to cut the individual off from previous patterns of behavior. However, the symbolic activity which indicates this cutting off need not be as radical as a total change of eating habits. In an interview in *Prevention*, a man who runs a health oriented television program recounted an incident in which a viewer called up after a show and announced excitedly that he had changed his whole lifestyle—he had started using honey in his coffee! (*Prevention*, February 1979: 89). While recognizing the absurdity of the action on a practical level, the program's host acknowledged the symbolic importance of this action to the person involved. He also saw it as a step in the right direction since one change can lead to another. Those who sprinkle wheat germ on cereal, toss alfalfa sprouts with a salad, or pass up an ice cream cone for yogurt are not only demonstrating a concern for health but also affirming their commitment to a particular lifestyle and symbolizing adherence to a set of values and a world view.

Conclusion

As this analysis has shown, health foods are more than simply a way of eating and more than an alternative healing system. If we return to Clifford Geertz's definition of religion as a "system of symbols" which produces "powerful, pervasive, and long-lasting moods and motivations" by "formulating conceptions of a general order of existence" and making them appear "uniquely realistic," we see that the health food movement definitely has a religious dimension. There is, first, a system of symbols, in this case based on certain kinds and qualities of food. While the foods are believed to have health-giving properties in themselves, they also symbolize a world view which is concerned with the right way to live one's life and the right way to construct a society. This "right way" is based on an approach to life which stresses harmony with nature and the holistic nature of the body. Consumption of those substances designated as "health foods," as well as participation in other activities associated with the movement which also symbolize its world view (such as exercising or growing an organic garden) can serve to establish the "moods and motivations" of which Geertz speaks. The committed health food follower may come to experience a sense of spiritual as well as physical well-being when he or she adheres to the health food way of life. Followers are thus motivated to persist in this way of life, and they come to see the world view of this movement as correct and "realistic."

In addition to its possession of sacred symbols and its "convincing" world view, the health food movement also has other elements which we usually associate with a religion. Concepts of *mana* and *taboo* guide the choice of foods. There is a distinction between the pure and impure and a concern for the maintenance of purity. There are "temples" (health food stores and other such establishments) which are expected to maintain purity within their confines. There are "rabbis," or experts in the "theology" of the movement and its application to everyday life. There are sacred and instructional writings which set out the principles of the movement and teach followers how to utilize them. In addition, like many religious movements, the health food movement harkens back to a "golden age" which it seeks to recreate and assumes that many of the ills of the contemporary world are caused by society's departure from this ideal state.

Individuals entering the movement, like individuals entering any religious movement, may undergo a process of conversion. This can be dramatic, resulting from the cure of an illness or the reversal of a previous state of poor health, or it can be gradual, a step by step changing of eating and other habits through exposure to health food doctrine. Individuals who have undergone conversion and mazeway resynthesis, as well as

those who have tested and confirmed various aspects of the movement's prescriptions for better health and a better life, may give testimonials to the faith. For those who have adopted, in full or in part, the health food world view, it provides, as do all religions, explanations for existing conditions, answers to specific problems, and a means of gaining control over one's existence. Followers of the movement are also promised "salvation," not in the form of after-life, but in terms of enhanced physical well-being, greater energy, longer life-span, freedom from illness, and increased peace of mind. However, although the focus is this-worldly, there is a spiritual dimension to the health food movement. And although it does not center its world view around belief in supernatural beings, it does posit a higher authority—the wisdom of nature—as the source of ultimate legitimacy for its views.

Health food people are often dismissed as "nuts" or "food faddists" by those outside the movement. Such a designation fails to recognize the systematic nature of the health food world view, the symbolic significance of health foods, and the important functions which the movement performs for its followers. Health foods offer an alternative or supplement to conventional medical treatment, and a meaningful and effective way for individuals to bring about changes in lives which are perceived as unsatisfactory because of poor physical and emotional health. It can also provide for its followers a framework of meaning which transcends individual problems. In opposing itself to the predominant American lifestyle, the health food movement sets up a symbolic system which opposes harmony to disharmony, purity to pollution, nature to culture, and ultimately, as in many religions, life to death. Thus while foods are the beginning point and the most important symbols of the health food movement, food is not the ultimate focus but rather a means to an end: the organization of a meaningful world view and the construction of a satisfying life.

References

Ehrenreich, Barbara and English, Deidre (1979) *For Her Own Good: 150 Years of the Experts' Advice to Women*. Garden City, NY: Anchor Press/Doubleday.

Geertz, Clifford (1965) "Religion as a Cultural System." *In Michael Banton*, ed., *Anthropological Approaches to the Study of Religion*. ASA Monograph 3. New York: Frederick A. Praeger.

Hongladarom, Gail Chapman (1976) *Health Seeking Within the Health Food Movement*. PhD dissertation, University of Washington. (Xerox University Microfilms, Ann Arbor.)

Kandel, Randy F. and Pelto, Gretel H. (1980) "The Health Food Movement: Social Revitalization or Alternative Health Maintenance System." In Norge W. Jerome, Randy F. Kandel, and Gretel H. Pelto, eds., *Nutritional Anthropology*. Pleasantville, NY: Redgrave Publishing Company.

Kline, Monte (1978) *The Junk Food Withdrawal Manual*. Total Life, Inc.

Kottak, Conrad (1978) "McDonald's as Myth, Symbol and Ritual." In *Anthropology: The Study of Human Diversity*. New York: Random House.

Shryock, Richard Harrison (1966) *Medicine in America: Historical Essays*. Baltimore: Johns Hopkins.

Wallace, Anthony F. C. (1966) *Religion: An Anthropological View*. New York: Random House.

CHAPTER 8

Clothing Matters

Clothing does more than cover the body; it is also a cultural index of age, gender, occupation, and class. Is it then true that "clothes make the man"? Haute couture, sweat shops, clothing, and the economy.

Clothing Matters

"Man is born naked, but is everywhere in clothes."

This play on Rousseau's "Man is born free but is everywhere in chains" implies that we are imprisoned by clothes or "slaves to fashion."[1] It was also anthropologist Terence Turner's way of beginning an article describing the body adornments of the relatively naked Kayapo of South America (1980). The body, he argued, even among peoples regarded as "primitive," is never completely naked; everywhere humans have done something to modify the naked state, whether through the body paint of the Kayapo; the tattoos and body piercing of the new, urban tribalists; the boots and hats of American cowboys; or the full black veils worn by many Muslim women. Nudity is, therefore, no more natural than wearing clothes. Still, the fact that everyone everywhere (most of the time) wears clothes or their equivalent does not explain the variety and its meanings.

Clothes do not merely protect us from the elements, for they also express cultural meanings and identities and serve as markers of status, age, and gender as well as occupation, activity, degree of formality, and a host of other things. Like other nonverbal signs, these markers not only distinguish individuals and groups from each other, but also are a means for "placing" people in their social context. Walk down a busy street, and observe the clothes people are wearing. Based only on their clothes, what can you surmise about them?

Not only do clothes encode cultural values and social distinctions, but also they form a system – there is sense and reason behind the composition of an "outfit." Like sentences and meals (see chapter 7), clothing has a certain syntax, a lexicon of items and rules of combination for creating appropriate ensembles for different occasions. This was the conclusion reached by French semiotician Roland Barthes. Drawing on the work of linguist Ferdinand de Saussure, Barthes examines *The Fashion System* ([1967] 1983). Rather than

Investigating Culture: An Experiential Introduction to Anthropology, Second Edition.
Carol Delaney with Deborah Kaspin.
© 2011 Carol Delaney. Published by Blackwell Publishing Ltd.

conducting an ethnographic study, however, he investigated only the *discourse* about clothing, that is, the way clothing is discussed and written about in fashion magazines. This is surely an important aspect of the clothing system, but it leaves out the very aspects that most interest anthropologists, namely, the nonverbal way that clothes encode and reflect the wider cultural system.

Anthropologist Marshall Sahlins picks up where Barthes leaves off. Beyond the features emphasized in discourse, Sahlins observes that a host of perceptual differences – distinctions of style, texture, fabric, color, and line – encode cultural meanings that are drawn on to create a total ensemble. For example, certain fabrics can index class and gender: cashmere is a luxury wool associated with the upper class, while, more generally, wool is usually associated with men and silk with women. Women wear wool, of course, but its masculine connotations make it more business-like. Similarly, most of us have wondered why "[t]he overlap of a blouse, a jacket or a coat determines the sex of the article. By buttoning a garment on the right side, it becomes suitable for men only and definitely unsuitable for women. Whatever the quaint explanations of folklore are, the right side of the body has always been male, the left side female; this orientation survived despite its irrationality" (Sahlins 1976: 190, quoting Rudolfsky 1947; see also "Body Orientation" in chapter 6 on right and left as masculinity and femininity). The meanings of these orientations are common in Western societies, but whether they extend beyond them is open to investigation.

Turning to color, Sahlins observes that red is the most saturated and most advancing color: it catches the eye and commands attention. This in turn confers a variety of meanings on the people and things festooned in red. As a teenager in the 1950s, I was not allowed to wear red because the color was associated with prostitutes – presumably the only women who wanted to call attention to themselves. In other contexts and countries, red means danger, as indicated by its use in traffic signals. In still other contexts, red symbolizes blood, although the meanings of blood can vary. Thus in some instances, it refers to blood loss, killing, and death, and is therefore synonymous with danger. In other instances, it refers to the life blood of kinship relations. Hence in Turkey, red is the traditional color of the wedding dress, although a bride today might simply wear a red sash or red veil. In this context, red symbolizes the blood relation through males – the patriline – which, when she gives birth to a son, will continue.

Because clothes can represent so many things – about people, culture, and the economy – they are spectacular clues we can use for our sociocultural investigation.[2] In this chapter, we will briefly discuss why notions of modesty or protection are inadequate to explain the phenomenon of clothing, and then move on to what clothes accomplish besides a modest protection from the elements.

Modesty

Perhaps the earliest theory, at least in the West, to explain the adoption of clothes was rooted in the Bible. In Genesis, Adam and Eve "were both naked, the man and his wife, and were not ashamed" (Genesis 2:25). After eating the fruit from the "Tree of Knowledge of Good and Evil," which God had forbidden them, their eyes "were opened, and they knew that they were naked; and they sewed fig leaves together, and made themselves aprons" (Genesis 3:7). This theory attributes the origin and necessity of clothes to modesty. And just as some believe we can recreate Eden by adopting a vegetarian diet, others believe we can do so by abandoning clothing.

People in different societies feel quite differently about their bodies and its exposure, for, as cultural anthropology reveals, modesty is a learned behavior, not instinctual. "Australian aborigines, for example, are indifferent to their nakedness but are deeply embarrassed if seen eating" (Laver 1969, cited in Rubenstein 1995: 17). In addition, modesty is inflected very differently according to gender. Women in a number of societies are required to dress modestly, but what that means in practice varies considerably: in some places it means a long black veil that covers the entire body, while elsewhere it means dresses with sleeves, skirts to the knee, and shirts that cover the midriffs in school. Modesty has particular salience in cultures influenced by the monotheistic, Abrahamic religions – Judaism, Christianity, and Islam – and the definitions and meanings of gender embedded in them, but it is not a feature of a universal theory of clothing.

Another commonsense view is that clothing originated to protect us from the elements – from the extremes of temperature and from moisture. Without fur to keep us warm, we "borrow" it from those animals who do. This, then, would be the underlying rationale for the vogue of fur coats. While most of us want some protection from the elements and have devised all kinds of clothing to keep us dry in the rain, warm in the snow, and cool at the beach, it has long been noted that some peoples can withstand extreme changes in temperature even while relatively naked. Darwin reported that he and his crew huddled next to the fire and wrapped themselves in blankets, yet remained cold, while the people in Tierra del Fuego, "all naked, were some distance from the fire and yet perspiration streamed down their bodies" (Wulsin 1968, cited in Rubenstein 1995: 19). B. Spencer and F. J. Gillen, one a missionary and the other a government employee, spent many months among the Australian aborigines in the late nineteenth century and wrote that the aborigines, too, were able to withstand inclement weather and tolerate significant changes in the temperature without being greatly discomfited. Some practitioners of meditation and yoga claim that they, too, are able to ignore changes in temperature. Whether they actually ignore these changes or are able to make their bodies feel warm when they are cold and cool when they are hot, I am not sure, but in either case, it is an issue of mind over matter.

Even if modesty and protection are part of the rationale for clothing, they do not explain the variety of clothing around the world. Adaptationists would probably argue that people dress in accord with their environment, wearing few clothes where it is hot and more clothes where it is cold. However, I was disabused of this theory when I was travelling in a desert area near Haran, Turkey (allegedly Abraham's home) and the temperature was 120 degrees Fahrenheit. The people here were dressed in heavy woolen and thick velvet clothing in dark colors. Clearly, cultural factors – ideals of beauty, beliefs about gender, and, to be sure, local notions of modesty – determined what people wore.

Still another explanation is that people want to adorn themselves, whether for self-expression, to ward off the evil spirits, to create group identity, or, as some feminists claim, for the pure pleasure we derive from doing so. Adornment is an aspect – even a major aspect – of clothing. However, as a theory, it reduces the extraordinary variety of clothing and cannot account for what is culturally significant and meaningful. Rather than insisting on a universal theory to account for all clothing – something I am not sure is even possible – let's explore several issues that clothing and adornment raise.

Distinctions

One of the first things we can deduce about clothing is that it creates distinctions of status, age, gender, and activity. Some distinctions are, or seem, more obvious than others. Some are life-cycle statuses. For example, there is a difference between the clothing worn by children and that worn by adults. Yet this is a fairly recent phenomenon in the West, for if paintings from medieval times to mid-twentieth century can be taken as evidence, children once wore diminutive versions of adult clothing. In many cultures one can tell by her clothing if a woman is marriageable, married, or widowed. The only signifier in the West is the wedding ring, and not all married people wear one. In some societies people who have children or grandchildren have a special status that is indicated by their clothing or article of clothing. (When I became a grandparent, I longed for some sign that would display my new status – and my delight – to the world.) Mourning, too, is very often exhibited by special clothing. In the West, people in mourning often wear black at least to a funeral, while the Japanese traditionally wore white. In the past in Greece, widows wore black for the rest of their lives to indicate they were no longer marriageable.

Clothing matters especially at the highest social level. In Britain, at certain ceremonial occasions there is no mistaking who is queen: she is the one wearing a crown, a blue ribbon across her chest, and an ermine trimmed cape. The specially designed clothes and the elaborate hats that British royalty wear are also distinguishing marks. People want royalty to *look* like royalty and are willing to provide a great deal of money from the public purse so they can keep up their appearance. The president of the United States is not royalty but *primus inter pares* (first among equals), hence there are no sartorial signs to represent his status. Still he must look worthy of the job – in other words, he must look *presidential*. During the United States presidential election of 2000, the candidates' clothes were commented on in the newspapers and television almost every day. In an article titled "Read My Clothes,"[3] Bellafante and Trebay discussed the various "statements" that were made by the clothing choices of Mr. Bush and Mr. Gore. "With no conclusive vote count, the candidates have been forced to perform their roles symbolically … both have made numerous costume changes appropriate to their roles" (Bellafante and Trebay, *New York Times*, September 21, 2000); the authors note, however, that Mr. Gore's attempts at casual attire tended to backfire because they seemed forced, whereas George W. appeared comfortable in his ranch wear and cowboy hat. Perhaps it was Gore's clothes, and not the chads, that cost him the election.

In 2008, the unprecedented emergence of female candidates in both parties introduced a new wrinkle in presidential dress codes. When Hillary Clinton campaigned as the presumptive frontrunner for the Democratic nomination, media coverage focused repeatedly on her attire – the "ubiquitous" pantsuit – as an unconvincing attempt to appear both feminine and masculine. When Sarah Palin joined the Republican ticket as John McCain's running mate, media attention turned to her wardrobe and to the reported $150,000 lavished on clothes and cosmetics for her and her family. And when the Obama–Biden ticket campaigned for and won the presidency, media attention turned to Michele Obama, whose sense of decorum as First Lady was called into question by her preference for sleeveless dresses. In all three instances, media critics discredited politically powerful women by maligning their attire and, by implication, their suitability for high office and influence.

Certain professional statuses are denoted by clothing, especially those in religious orders, the judiciary, and the military. Among Catholics, there are distinct differences in the attire worn by those in monastic orders and those in priestly groups. Traditionally monks are clothed in simple homespun shifts tied with a piece of rope, minimizing differences in rank. But in priestly groups, the hierarchical differences are pronounced: the miter and white clothing of the pope, the red robes of the cardinals, the purple of bishops, green of abbots, and plain black of parish priests are visual signs of rank. (See figure 8.1.) Judges also don distinctive robes when they are in court, and in Britain they still wear white wigs. Academic robes, seen today only at graduation exercises, are emblazoned with school colors, emblems of highest degree, and branch of study.

Not surprisingly, the military distinguishes its different ranks by means of clothing, badges, and stripes, because it is an extremely hierarchical institution whose members must

Figure 8.1   Bizarro cartoon by Piraro, 1999, courtesy of Allsorts Media/King Features Syndicate.

know who, in any situation, is in command. Clothing also distinguishes the different branches, with the army, navy, air force, and marines each having distinctive uniforms. Military clothing can become a focus of intense controversy. For instance, in March 2001, when the US Army issued a new type of hat (a black beret) to every officer and soldier, the special branch called the Rangers, who, until then, were the only soldiers permitted to wear the beret, organized a march from Georgia to Washington, DC, in protest. If every soldier could wear the beret, the Rangers would have no badge of distinction (*New York Times*, March 12, 2001).

Although differentiations of rank are important elements of military dress codes, these distinctions cannot supplant the larger policy of uniformity and masculinity. And while the dress code is sometimes altered to accommodate the wider culture whence military recruits come, these changes are not allowed to jeopardize uniformity over all. Thus in 2002 the army updated its rules about appropriate attire. They determined that braids and cornrows were now permitted, but dreadlocks were not; that dyed hair must look "natural," and "baldness, natural or otherwise, is authorized"; that pale nail polish is permitted for women, but "fire-engine red, purple, blue, black" and camouflage are not; and that "men are not allowed to show body piercing on military installations." (It is unclear from the report if they can exhibit their body piercings while off base.) They further stipulated that women stationed in Saudi Arabia were no longer required to wear the chador when they go out. (These changes were reported in *New York Times*, January 9, 2002.)

Perhaps the most interesting disputes concern the effort to cultivate collective masculinity. For two decades, the US Navy debated whether "its men may carry umbrellas while in uniform" and finally decided they may. However for many of the top brass "a military man protecting himself from the rain with an umbrella looks too effete" (*New York Times*, November 11, 1987) and undermines the masculine image they wish to project. In an attempt to salvage some of the image, they issued strict rules about how and when an umbrella may be carried: "the Navy is requiring that umbrellas be plain black, that they cannot be carried in formations, that they must not be used as walking sticks and that they must be carried in the left hand to leave the right hand free for saluting" (*New York Times*, November 11, 1987).

The business suit, often called the uniform of the corporate world, creates a distinction between "white-collar" and "blue-collar" workers even though not all workers in either category wear only white or blue shirts. While the rules may be unstated, anyone applying for a "white-collar" job at a big company, whether in business or a law firm, better know them. You might think the only things that matter are brains, ability, training, and the résumé, but clothing matters too. Do you think a person who shows up for an interview in a sports coat, open shirt, and khaki pants will be hired? What would such behavior indicate to those hiring? College students, accustomed to casual attire, often need special classes to help them choose appropriate clothing for job interviews, because if they ignore their appearance, they project a lack of seriousness about the job. One guide (on the web) specifies what young men should wear: a single-breasted gray or navy suit with the jacket buttoned (except for the bottom button) when they enter the interview office, and unbuttoned when they sit down. Another website had several pages on pants – the proper length, pleats and creases, where the waistband should fall, and whether or not to have cuffs. A white, long-sleeved shirt with a straight point collar is advised, and on the matter of ties, stripes or small patterns are recommended; "small patterns in a tie are associated with the upper middle class and that is usually the group to which your interviewer belongs" (MansLife.com, 2001). Burgundy is a good color for a tie, and in any case it should have no more than three colors. "The tie should be long enough to reach your belt buckle, and don't forget the all important dimple – the indentation under the knot." The guide goes on to discuss shoes, socks, and belts as well as grooming tips. These rules should dispel women's beliefs that men's clothing seems simple compared with their own. Although the range is quite narrow, putting together a "dress for success" look takes time, attention to detail, and money. Furthermore, long after the interview, you must keep up the image if you wish to climb the corporate ladder. "If you want a promotion you must look like you deserve it and can fit into the post."[4]

In the 1950s, the corporate ideal was epitomized by *The Man in the Gray Flannel Suit*, a book about the compromises made by men in corporate America and played with style by Gregory Peck in the film of the same title. The suit and what it implied may have comprised one reason why so many of us in the 1960s rebelled against that image and the lifestyle that went with it. After that brief respite (the 1960s and early 1970s), the rules and corporate lifestyle returned with a vengeance.

All of the distinctions made by clothes discussed so far reflect authority: they don't just symbolize authority but also embody it. This is true even when the clothes are very casual, as in the case of the physicists that anthropologist Sharon Traweek studied at the Stanford Linear Accelerator (SLAC). She noted how easy it was "to distinguish between groups at the cafeteria. The physicists are dressed most casually, in shirts with rolled sleeves and jeans or nondescript slacks" (1988: 25), followed with increasing formality by engineers, technicians, administrators (in business suits), and secretaries. The people with the most authority and high status were able to wear the most casual clothing. Deborah Kaspin found a similar dress code in professional circles in Malawi: British and American expatriates routinely wear khaki shorts and opened collared shirts to work as management and professional personnel in government offices, NGOs, parastatals,[5] and universities, while Malawians in positions of similar and lesser status were obliged to wear suits and ties. Whether the business suit of the corporate world or the casual dress of physicists and postcolonial expats, the specific garments permit the wearer to display his authority. I use the word *his* purposely because authority has traditionally been (and remains symbolically) male.

When women began to enter professions that were predominantly male, they adopted a form of business suit to minimize their femininity and project an aura of authority. Today there are many guides to help women "dress for success" with tips on what to wear and not to wear to the office. In the film *Erin Brockovich*, based on the true story of a woman by that name, the lead character was criticized, especially by her female coworkers, for her sexy clothes, because the low-cut blouses exposing her cleavage, high heels, and miniskirts were deemed unacceptable attire in the law firm where she was hired and then fired. Only after her boss realized that she was investigating an important case did he rehire her. While Brockovich was able to get away with sexy clothes at her law firm, other women should not assume that they can follow her example.

Gender and Clothes

A major distinction created through clothing is gender. Everywhere men and women wear different kinds of clothes. In the contemporary United States, this begins at birth, when baby girls are dressed in pink, and baby boys in blue – a custom many will be surprised to learn developed after World War II (Garber 1992: 1). The color coding is not always strictly followed, for one can find gender-neutral colors for babies, such as white, yellow, and pale green. Still in general girls are associated with pink and boys with blue, and people respond differently to baby girls and boys when the only clues they have are the color and style of their clothing. Gregory P. Stone

> observed that dressing a newborn in blue begins a sequence of interaction that is different from the one experienced by a baby dressed in pink. … The color acts as a cue or stimulus that influences how people behave toward the child and how that child is expected to conduct himself or herself. It is the response of others to gender-specific attire that encourages gender-appropriate behavior. (Quoted in Rubenstein 1995: 83–4)

People use a different tone of voice, different words, and different ways of holding and handling a baby, depending on whether they think it is a boy or a girl, and generally use a softer, gentler tone and touch with girls than with boys. From these responses, repeated thousands of times over several years, a child develops a sense of the meaning of his or her gender which has very little to do with his or her genitalia.

Visit any department store and notice the differences in clothes for little girls and boys. Outfits for little girls often have frills or lace, and there are flowered dresses in baby and toddler sizes. Boys' clothes use more somber or saturated colors, are decorated with plaids and stripes instead of flowers, and are often small versions of adult clothes. In the United States, working-class families and those from certain ethnic groups will often dress their children in fancy and quite pronouncedly gender-specific clothes, while many middle-class parents have begun to dress their small children in gender-neutral clothing – pants and tops – made of material that is machine washable and does not need ironing. At adolescence, clothing is a marker that dramatically differentiates the genders.

The gender-specificity apparent in children's clothing is also elaborated in their games and toys. When my first grandson was around a year and a half old, he was very interested in babies (as many children are). I decided to get him a baby doll, so he could learn how to hold and play with one. I looked everywhere, hoping to find one that my grandson would assume was male. But all the dolls were dressed in pink, implying that the dolls were girls and, moreover, that only girls should play with them. I gave him a doll anyway, but when parents in his neighborhood saw him with it, they were aghast and would not let their sons play with him. They were already dressing their little boys in army camouflage and handing them copies of automatic weapons as toys.

Americans often believe that such gender typing in children's clothes and toys is natural, not cultural, but there is ample anthropological evidence to the contrary. In Turkish villages, for example, little girls and boys were dressed quite similarly in simple pants and tops. Ironically, in the United States, where we assume there is more gender equality than in Turkey, we mark the gender of children more strongly. For Turks, gender typing becomes increasingly marked when children advance to adult clothing. Thus, when a little boy started to play with a woman's headscarf, his mother shouted, "No, take that off. You are male, you are male."

A more basic question is why clothes are gendered in the first place. The differences cannot really be seen as functional, because the differences are neither constant nor universal. For example, in different times and places men have worn skirts (Scottish kilts, priestly vestments, Arab *jellaba*, and Greek/Albanian *fustanellas*) and women have worn pants (Turkish *şalvar*, and bloomers). But in any particular culture, there are clothes meant for women, and clothes meant for men, and if one does not conform, one is seen as unusual or deviant. Today, it is easier and more acceptable for western women to wear men's clothes than vice versa, but this was not always the case.

In Shakespeare's England, only men could be actors and perform on stage, thus men played women's parts and dressed accordingly. (The film *Shakespeare in Love* plays upon this convention cleverly.) Although not exactly cross-dressing, eighteenth-century noblemen wore clothing made in colors and of luxurious fabrics such as velvet and silk, adorned with lace, that today are symbolically feminine. In the mid-nineteenth century, two years after the first Women's Rights Convention in Seneca Falls (1848), Amelia Bloomer introduced a kind of trousers to be worn beneath dresses. The leaders of that first feminist movement – Elizabeth Cady Stanton, Susan B. Anthony, Lucy Stone, and Sarah and Angelina Grimké – wore them on their speaking circuits and advocated them as an alternative to conventional dress. Others felt "that trousers represented a usurpation of men's rights and prerogatives" and were vehemently opposed to them. Bloomer was not the first to suggest pants for women, since women in utopian, often socialist, communities like New Harmony or the Oneida had preceded her. However, in those communities, trousers were associated with free love and sexual license. Those meanings were projected onto the feminists' use of pants, and since that was not the image they wanted to convey, they soon abandoned them.

In contemporary Western society, many women wear pants much of the time and not just for leisure wear. As noted earlier in this chapter, Hillary Clinton has long been seen in pants while performing her duties as senator, presidential candidate, and secretary of state. Women's business suits now come with a skirt, pants, or both, and there are even tuxedos designed for women.

Cross-dressing

For women, there is clearly a continuum rather than a strict dichotomy between feminine and masculine dress styles: many women wear clothes that are fashioned to resemble men's clothes, others wear clothes that have actually been made for men, and still others are much more self-consciously dressing to pass as men. But women who wear men's clothes are unlikely to be seen as psychologically deviant, and may even seem sexy. One need think only of Katharine Hepburn, Marlene Dietrich, and Greta Garbo to realize the erotic undercurrent of women in men's wear. For men, the line is more strictly drawn. Men who wear

"At first it was just a disguise, but then I started to like it."

Figure 8.2 Wolf cartoon by Casey Shaw and Jason Whiton for *USA Weekend San Francisco Chronicle*, July 14, 2002. Why is this funny?

feminine clothes are assumed to have deep-seated problems and/or be gay. From observations in my grandsons' nursery schools, it was clear that little boys, like little girls, love to dress up in all kinds of clothes. When, how, and why is this beaten out of them? When men "cross-dress" and wear women's clothes, they, like the clothes, become a marked category with quite specific meanings and consequences.[6] Not only are they stigmatized and ridiculed, but also they are punished. Writing in the *San Francisco Chronicle* (July 22, 2001), Bruce Mirken said, "To hear people tell it, the greatest threat we face – working to undermine the very fabric of our civilization even as I write this – is men wearing dresses" – not terrorism, not nuclear war, not global warming.[7] Clearly, we have *Vested Interests* in our clothing categories, as Marjorie Garber eloquently discusses in her book of that title. (And see figure 8.2.)

Cross-dressing is, according to Garber (1992), a worldwide phenomenon with a long history. Sometimes one can cross-dress on specific occasions, such as on Halloween or at a masked ball, and it does not necessarily have any deep or long-term bearing on one's gender role; in other places, cross-dressing is a lifelong habit and coincides with a cross-gender role, whether or not a sexual role is also adopted. Then there are some people in some societies who dress in the clothing of neither one nor the other, but adopt elements of both male and female clothing. I will briefly mention a few of these. Because it is less well known, I give somewhat more space to the Albanian case.

"Sworn virgins of Albania"

According to a fascinating study by anthropologist Antonia Young, in Albania there are women who dress like men and take on all the rights, duties, and role of men except for sex. Once they take a vow to remain celibate and abstain from marriage, they are called "sworn virgins" and thenceforth live like men.[8] Those who take this vow and adopt this role sometimes do it to avoid an unwanted marriage, but more often it is done to retain the patrimony in the family, when there is no son to inherit it. Once they take these vows, they wear traditional men's trousers, shirts, and hats, although some of the younger, more urban ones have leather jackets and sunglasses. They become the heads of extended households over whom they have authority to make all major decisions concerning education, marriage, employment, and even clothing and the purchase of a rifle for any young man who comes of age. They also represent the family at village meetings. The division of labor is strict, and they, like all the other men, do all "heavy manual work: ploughing, hoeing, harrowing, manure spreading, chopping wood, scything, mowing, harvesting, watering and maintaining irrigation systems, protecting animals and property; it also includes being a host: talking to visitors, drinking and smoking with them, and avenging family honour" (Young 2000: 32). According to Young, this task takes precedence above all the others. Finally, they are buried as men.

Young makes clear that theirs is a social and not a sexual role. As far as Young and others have been able to ascertain, the "sworn virgins" are not lesbians; indeed, she believes the concept is alien to them. Nor do the concepts of "third gender," transsexual, transgender, or even cross-dresser help to illuminate what is going on here (p. 124). They differ in a number of ways from other "cross-dressers" not only because they take on the male role for life, but also because

> this change is in no way seen as deviant within their society; it is not the result of some psychological or physiological difference, but as a status within an orderly pattern of statuses. ... The accepted status is marked in a logical and regular fashion by the *adoption of appropriate dress.* (p. 113; emphasis mine)

Nor is there any question of a hidden sexual proclivity seeking expression. Young goes on to note that the role of the sworn virgin "is a dramatic illustration of the sociological concept of 'putting on a role,' rather than an occasion on which some inner self is permitted to 'come out'" (p. 113; thus, siding with the first opinion and challenging the second stated by Woolf, below).

Billy Tipton   Another case of one who cross-dressed for life is Billy Tipton, a jazz musician who was found at his death in 1989 to be a woman. He was married and had two (adopted) sons, and both his wife and sons never knew that he was a she underneath, so well did s/he accomplish the role. His adoption of men's clothing is often interpreted, as is the Albanian case, in terms of socioeconomic necessity. Garber challenges this and wonders why we must normalize transvestitism by "interpreting it in the register of socio-economic necessity. A patriarchal culture had ordained that jazz musicians were, or ought to be male; therefore, it is claimed, Billy Tipton cross-dressed" (Garber 1992: 69). Instead, she suggests that it is the transvestite who has the possibility of disrupting the rigid patriarchal binary (p. 70), the potential to loosen its hold and the damage it creates. Why, asks Garber, couldn't Billy Tipton's transvestitism be merely professional and public, one that could be left at the door of his house? What made him think it necessary to continue the charade at home?[9] At the same time, Garber gives short shrift to the different reasons women and men have for cross-dressing. It is quite reasonable that women might choose to wear men's clothing to obtain privileges only men have, such as travelling unmolested, as did Isabelle Eberhardt and many other women in the eighteenth and nineteenth centuries (see Blanch 1954); inheriting property, as in the Albanian case; or entering a profession closed to women, as did Billy Tipton. The reasons men choose to wear women's clothes are less obvious and thus in greater need of explanation.

Bülent Ersoy   Bülent Ersoy, one of the most popular singers in Turkey during the 1970s and early 1980s, is the reverse of Billy Tipton. An attractive man with somewhat feminine features, he decided not just to wear women's clothes and adopt a female persona, but also to undergo a sex change operation and become the woman he felt he was "underneath." However, once she did so, Parliament ruled that Ersoy could no longer work as an entertainer, because she was in their eyes a homosexual and as such was not allowed to perform in public. But was *he* really a homosexual man? Almost daily, there were articles in the newspapers describing how she was learning how to become a stereotypic woman by applying nail polish, doing her hair, and wearing heels, dresses, and women's underwear. Transvestitism was not well tolerated in Turkey; thus, whether Ersoy felt compelled to undergo the more drastic procedure to become a woman, or whether that was his or her own desire, is difficult to know.

"Third gender"   Some societies seem to tolerate a kind of intermediate status – neither male nor female. Rather than adopting the clothes and gender identity of one or the other, the person is able to don the clothes and personas of both and, in the process, create a kind of "third gender," at least for a period of time. This is what Norwegian anthropologist, Unni Wikan, claimed regarding the *xanith* in Oman, who are both male servants and homosexual prostitutes performing the passive role (1977: 305). In this extremely sex-segregated society, the *xanith* were able to move freely in the women's quarters and participate in their activities, although they do not wear the face mask (*burqa*) or other women's clothing:

> His clothes are intermediate between male and female: he wears the ankle-length tunic of the male, but with the tight waist of the female dress. Male clothing is white, females wear patterned cloth in bright colours, and transsexuals wear unpatterned coloured clothes. Men cut their hair short, women wear theirs long, the transsexuals medium long. (1977: 307)

Wikan goes on to describe how the *xanith*'s hairstyle, use of perfume and cosmetics, and gait follow neither the patterns used by men nor by women. While Wikan calls these men *transsexuals*, today we would reserve that term for those, like Bülent Ersoy, who actually change their anatomical sex. *Xanith*s are perhaps more appropriately called transgendered individuals or simply *xanith*. Unlike women, the *xanith* can move "about freely; but like women, he stays at home in the evenings, whereas men may spend their time in clubs and cafes" (p. 307). Despite being more like women and immersed in the women's area and activities, they retain their legal status as men and can revert to male status if they marry and perform the male role in intercourse. According to Wikan, "[i]t is the sexual *act*, not the sexual organs, which is fundamentally constitutive of gender" (p. 309).

The berdache of certain Native American groups is another, apparently intermediate gender. These are men and, more rarely, women who adopt many of the social roles and clothing of the opposite sex and are seen within their societies as neither male nor female, but a blend of both. Will Roscoe believes that "characterizations of berdaches … as men or women who 'assume the role of the "opposite" sex,' are reductionist and inaccurate" (1994) and argues for their place as third (for the male berdache) and fourth (for the female berdache) genders, who consolidate distinct identities by combining elements of maleness and femaleness. He also claims them as important resources for gay identity. In contrast, Ramón Gutierrez believes that the role of berdache arose in the context of conquest as a form of humiliation.[10] I would be curious to learn whether there are significant differences – in both the role and numbers of persons who take on that role – depending on whether they occur in matrilineal or patrilineal societies.

From these examples, can we decide whether clothes merely recognize and express an innate gender difference or do they create that image of difference? Virginia Woolf described these two perspectives in her novel *Orlando*, in which the title character goes through a series of changes from man to woman and back again. When Orlando puts on women's clothes, people respond to her in a certain way, treating her more delicately and paying her compliments, and s/he, in turn, begins to act like a woman. Woolf constructs a debate between two camps of philosophers. One side concludes that clothes "change our view of the world and the world's view of us … that it is clothes that wear us and not we them" ([1928] 1960: 122–3). The other side believes that "clothes are but a symbol of something hid deep beneath. It was a change in Orlando herself that dictated her choice of a woman's dress and of a woman's sex" (p. 123).

Contemporary versions of these positions are heard in the debates about sexual orientation and gender identity. I am not sure the issue can ever be resolved in favor of one position or another, perhaps, because the issue is too narrowly posed. In the West and in many Muslim societies, it is generally assumed that there are only two genders, and each corresponds with anatomical sex. Thus people should wear clothes appropriate to their *sex* and suffer punishment for deviating from the social norm. In recent years, these views have changed at least in some places, although the idea that there are more than two genders has been difficult to accept. Perhaps it is we in the West who have such limited imaginations that we continually force both people and clothing into only two categories.

> [A] major flaw in Western discourse on transgenderism is that we find it very difficult to break away from the basic dichotomy of male–female in our analysis of gender. Even within the

homosexual community we tend to see a breakdown according to traditional gender stereotypes, with one member of a partnership taking the 'active,' the other the 'passive' role. (Wood
1998, cited in Young 2000: 117)

Similarly, lesbian clothing aesthetics often divide into "butch" styles and "femme" styles. If
this is the case, then Sahlins is right to say that we have (at least) six sartorial genders.[11] In
another vein, geneticist Anne Fausto-Sterling claims that there are five naturally occurring
(that is, anatomical) sexes (1993) – male, female, and three intersexes. While some are more
rare than others, she asks why babies born intersexed are surgically "fixed" as male or female
before they are old enough to make a decision on their own behalf. In any case, if her claim
is true, then *cross*-dressing is a misnomer.

Clearly there are wide variations in definitions of gender and its expression in clothing.
If gender is culturally constructed and not just an either/or category immutably rooted in
nature, aren't we all "in drag"? We feel this more, perhaps, on formal occasions when it is
obvious we are "dressing up." But I also recall a similar feeling when I had to dress in a
certain way to go to work in an office. I felt like I was wearing a costume. Even now, I
continually try to figure out what is proper "professor" clothing. At the very least, we are
"dressing up" to our culture's definition of what is appropriate attire for men and women.

Women's clothing is the *marked* category in the sense that it stands out. This concept
comes from linguistics, which distinguishes words whose meanings are fixed from those
whose meanings are flexible. Thus the pronoun *she* is marked for gender, because it always
means *female*, while the pronoun *he* is unmarked for gender, because it sometimes means
male and sometimes is gender neutral. In the same way, female clothing is always female,
while male clothing can be male or neutral: hence women can wear men's clothes, but men
cannot wear women's. So, too, women's clothes absorb the meanings of the marked category as the second and inferior sex.

For some theorists, the implications are dire. Simone de Beauvoir saw fashion as enslavement, while the poet Adrienne Rich placed "dress codes" in the same category as purdah, foot
binding, and the veil (Gaines and Herzog 1990: 3). Other feminist theorists dispute this puri-
tanical view, observing that they, like many women, get a great deal of pleasure – both aesthetic
and erotic – from their clothes. Similarly, performance theorists like Judith Butler argue that
one can *try on* a variety of identities: thus clothes can be used to *épater la bourgeoisie* ("shock
the middle classes"), to project an image of power, to disrupt gender categorization, and to
impress and express many moods, identities, and whims. There is a lot of appeal in such a
theoretical stance, but it seems, also, to minimize the way identities and identifications are
ascribed and not just performed. That is, they have a history, are interwoven with other
domains and categories in a culture, and are not entirely under the control of the person
donning them. Does playing with the clothing of the other gender(s) really blur the boundaries of gender, or does it establish the genderedness of clothing even more forcefully?

Fashion

As the marked and supposedly inferior category, it is all the more surprising that women's
clothes today are the focus of extraordinary elaboration. As noted above, this was not

always the case in the West. From the sixteenth through early nineteenth centuries, men's clothes, at least those of the elite, were elaborate, made of luxurious materials, and the focus of attention. Although some of this attention to male clothing has returned, in general *haute couture* (high fashion) and the fashion industry are primarily concerned with female clothing. The fashion industry makes a fortune from the designing and selling of women's clothes, in short, from making *fashion*.

Haute couture, almost synonymous with Paris, was actually invented by a Londoner, Charles Frederic Worth, who moved to Paris in 1846 and set up his own dress-making business. He was also couturier to the court of Emperor Louis Napoleon, who believed "that the production of fashion was essential to the well-being of the nation" (Rubenstein 1995: 146). Napoleon "wanted to encourage the well-to-do members of the aristocracy to support the economy by spending money on clothes" (p. 146). In order to show off his designs to potential clients, Worth hit on the idea of what is known in the trade as the *fashion parade*, when supermodels strut down the "catwalk" showing off a designer's "models" – a term that applies to the dress, and not to the woman wearing it.

Worth also established the Syndical Chamber for Haute Couture, a group that decides which "houses" qualify for the label *haute couture*. Not every designer can qualify. In order to achieve this designation, a designer must meet the following criteria: "to employ a minimum of fifteen people at the workshops, to present to the press in Paris each season (spring/summer and autumn/winter) a collection of at least thirty-five runs consisting of models for daytime wear and evening wear" (Benaim, 2001). As of this writing, there are 18 houses that warrant the accolade of *haute couture*, including Dior, Balmain, Cardin, Chanel, and Givenchy.

Internally, an *haute couture* establishment is extremely hierarchical. At

> the bottom of the ladder are the *arpettes* or apprentices, who pin the fabrics and run from floor to floor. Next in line are qualified chief assistants, second assistants, fitters, chief and assistant sales staff. At the top of the pyramid is the designer. He is the great couturier and, in French, is always referred to by a masculine gender, regardless of whether the position is held by a man or a woman. (Jean-Louis Arnaud, www.france.diplomatie.fr, July 9, 2001)

And there were a number of well-known female designers, including Coco Chanel, who designed the "Chanel suit" and the famous perfume, Chanel No. 5; and Elsa Schiaparelli, known for her black and hot pink signature.

High fashion took off in the late 1940s and 1950s, following Christian Dior's "new look" of 1947 that emphasized fine shoulders and narrow waists and became the image of the ideal woman of all nationalities, not just the French (see figure 8.3). The high-fashion houses, providing extremely expensive, unique, luxurious clothes for a very few women, flourished until the 1970s. Although they still put out designs today, many have turned to *prêt-à-porter* (ready-to-wear) lines due, in part, to the social revolution of the 1960s with its ethic of equality and its disdain for extravagant displays by the ultrarich.

What is curious and calls out for research is why high fashion arose and flourished in the very places that sparked the great social movements for liberty, equality, and fraternity. In 1904 social theorist G. Simmel wrote that "fashion can only exist where social boundaries

Figure 8.3   A Dior evening dress, modeled by Barbara Goalen, 1947. © Hulton/Getty Images.

are permeable," for if boundaries are rigid, the clothing of each class becomes more like a uniform. This may be a partial answer, since there was more social mobility immediately after World War II, the same time period when haute couture was growing in popularity. Yet one could also argue that fashion emerged at this time, because the aristocracy did not want to let go of their class privilege so easily. A more aesthetic reason might be that high fashion, like art, is something that inspires, gives dreams, and adds glamour and sparkle to the more drab, domestic, complacent workaday world in which most people are enmeshed. And fashion often seems to "trickle down," as Emperor Napoleon recognized in the nineteenth century. Apparently he had Worth produce a new fashion "each season because everything the Empress wore created a demand first among upper-class women and then among the lower classes" (Saunders 1955, cited in Rubenstein 1995).

While high fashion continues to intrigue people, it is also increasingly difficult to justify the extraordinary cost of such clothes – from $20,000 for a women's suit to $60,000 and more for an evening gown – devoted to so few. At the 2001 Academy Awards, several movie stars admitted to borrowing dresses or buying high-fashion second-hands. Prior to World War II, 35,000 people were employed in the *haute couture* industry, while today there are only about 4,500 people, including seamstresses. There are fewer than 1,500 clients, down from more than 15,000, a change that is attributed by Benaim (2001) to a real change in lifestyles. The decline has also made it difficult for these houses to stay afloat, hence a number of them have folded, while others have been bought by conglomerates. Dior, for example, now belongs to the Louis Vuitton Moët Hennessy group (LVHM), thus placing haute couture under a single corporate umbrella with luggage, champagne, and brandy.

Subcultural Style

If the decline of high fashion is attributed to the social upheavals of the 1960s, so too is its reinvention, as it incorporated some of the styles bubbling up from the counterculture. Style was no longer dictated from the top, from *haute couture*, but arose from the psychedelic visions of the grassroots. In response to seeing themselves marginalized, designers of *haute couture* appropriated some of the style of the counterculture, such as Yves St. Laurent's *Rive Gauche* ready-to-wear line.

Hippies, as some of the people of this era were known, reacted against the button-down, buttoned-up shirts of the business world, adopted gauzy or tie-dyed shirts they made themselves, drawstring pants, and long flowing dresses. To the consternation of the "straight" world (at the time "straight" meant the conventional business world of the 1950s and was the opposite of "hippie"), men let their hair grow long, women went without bras, and both abandoned shoes or wore only sandals. At times everyone wore beads, feathers, and face paint, especially at the large "be-ins"[12] where people gathered to celebrate life and love.

Subcultural style did not actually begin with the hippie movement, for its immediate antecedent was the beats of the 1950s. Whether or not one went "on the road" like beat poet Jack Kerouac many of us longed to, for the idea underlay our outlook on life. At least we could express our affiliation with the beats by adopting its costume and signature color, black. Thus a black sweater was *de rigueur*, as was a black skirt or pants. We had to smoke, drink black coffee, and frequent dark smoky cafés, where we might discuss existentialism or the latest *avant-garde* poet.

There were other precursors to the hippie movement, such as the rock and roll styles of the late 1950s and early 1960s as well as the *zoot suiters* of the 1940s, and other theorists would, no doubt, project the history of subcultural style farther back. However, the 1960s seems to be a kind of watershed, perhaps because of the convergence of a number of social movements (civil rights, antiwar, communal, feminist, welfare rights, and drug-using and

-advocating groups) or, if not convergence, the fact that individuals participated in several of them at the same time. In addition, the movements were widespread, carried primarily by youth who seemed to be much more mobile and interconnected than in earlier periods of history.

One of the first and perhaps the finest attempts to confront and analyze subcultural style was made by Dick Hebdige, a British social theorist. In his book *Subculture: The Meaning of Style* (1979), he tracks the changes and the meanings of the clothing style of British youth from the 1950s to the late 1970s. But perhaps as a backdrop, he begins with the American beats and hipsters and shows that while both groups were "organized around a shared identity with blacks (symbolized by jazz), the nature of this identity, exposed in the styles adopted by the two groups, was qualitatively different" (1979: 48). Those stylistic differences spoke to social differences. Thus the hipster was typically

> a lower-class dandy, dressed up like a pimp, affecting a very cool, cerebral tone – to distinguish him from the gross, impulsive types that surrounded him in the ghetto – and aspiring to the finer things in life, like very good "tea," the finest sounds – jazz or Afro-Cuban … [whereas] … the Beat was originally some earnest middle-class college boy like Kerouac, who was stifled by the cities and the culture he had inherited and who wanted to cut out for distant and exotic places, where he could live like the "people," write, smoke and meditate. (Hebdige 1979: 48, citing Goldman 1974)

Hebdige continued this analysis in Britain where, again, blacks were the catalyst for the emergence of several white groups. During the 1960s, an immigrant black (mainly West Indian) population became "established in Britain's working-class areas, and some kind of rapport between blacks and neighboring white groups [became] possible" (p. 52). The various white youth cultures that emerged were influenced by their relation and reaction both to black subculture and to dominant working-class and bourgeous culture, represented by parents, teachers, police, and the workaday world.

Hebdige goes on to contrast the differences in style, in social position and class, and in music and philosophy between the Mods and Teddy Boys, between the skinheads and aficionados of Glam and Glitter rock, and finally punks, who combined "distorted reflections of all the major post-war subcultures" (p. 26), and whose primary target seemed to be bourgeois society. It is not possible here to examine the minute details of their styles and the way they play off each other and the "parent" or mainstream culture, nor to trace their interconnections. For those interested, such a diagram or flowchart can be found in the back of Ted Polhemus's wonderful book, *Streetstyle: From Sidewalk to Catwalk* (1994), which, along with spectacular photographs, also has brief descriptions of each group.

What was new in Hebdige's work was his attention not just to the myriad details of clothing and musical tastes that each group exhibited, but also to their class position and occupational possibilities. Building on the work of British social theorist Stuart Hall and others, he "interpreted the succession of youth cultural styles as symbolic forms of resistance; as spectacular symptoms of a wider and more generally submerged dissent which characterized the whole post-war period" (p. 80). At the same time, it was not just some kind of *general* dissent, but one "produced in response to different conjunctures which positioned them differently in relation to existing cultural formations (immigrant cultures, the parent culture, other subcultures, the dominant culture)" (p. 81).

Still, these subcultures, he argues, were not merely *responding*: they were embodying or *dramatizing* their dissent. With punks, their tattered clothes held together with safety pins, the black leather, and the sartorial elements of bondage worked to exhibit, as a kind of living gallery, the decay and tatteredness of British society and their own bondage to it in a life held precariously together. They *represented* the decline of British society and *presented* a challenge to it. Borrowing from a published interview with Sartre, Hebdige says he sought

> to acknowledge the right of the subordinate class (the young, the black, the working-class) to "make something of what is made of (them)" – to embellish, decorate, parody and wherever possible to recognize and rise above a subordinate position which was never of their choosing. (p. 139)

With their lack of options and narrow range of life choices in which many saw no future, it is hardly surprising their resistance and dissent were expressed so dramatically. What is surprising is that the violence of the clothes was not very often actualized. The Brixton race riots of 1980 in a section of London populated mainly by blacks were, according to social theorist Paul Gilroy, instigated in part because the police did not know how to interpret reggae sartorial and music styles and did not take seriously the deaths by fire of 13 young blacks who had attended a party (Gilroy 1987: 102–3). When blacks protested their handling of the case, the police instituted a "stop and search" operation, which apparently triggered the riots. The mostly white punks seemed to feel some sympathy and expressed "their hostility to both racist nationalism and nationalist racism in several records which recast reggae music in their own idiom" (p. 125), while their clothing symbolized their assault on the icons of Britishness – the Union Jack and the queen.

In today's period of late capitalism, even punk clothes have been co-opted and turned out as fashion. One can buy brand-name jeans, ripped and torn for inflated prices, as well as safety pin earrings, and a range of bondage gear that formerly could only be found in kinky sex shops or catalogs. In the meantime, several theorists complain that Hebdige gives too little attention to gender, aside from acknowledging that these spectacular subcultural styles were primarily male displays.

Nothing ever stays the same, especially in fashion. Some observers of the street scene in New York in the late 1990s noticed a strange shift in youth fashion. Kids were hanging out not in

> tattered jeans, worn leather coats, [or] combat boots [but in] puffy ski jackets, lots of polo shirts, lots of Gore-Tex and polar fleece. Designer logos (DKNY, Nautica, Ralph Lauren, North Face, Tommy Hilfiger) are de rigueur, as are bright Crayola colors. Industrial-strength sneakers and high-tech hiking boots are big; so are baseball caps and ski hats. The whole scene looks suspiciously like a tailgate party at an Ivy League football game. (Kakutani [1997], in Damhorst, Miller, and Michelman 1999: 398)

This was the *in* style worn, apparently, not just by affluent or "preppy" white kids "speaking fluent ebonics and doing their best to be black teenagers," but also by black ghetto kids "as a talisman of the better life they wish they had" (p. 399). Not addressed in the article, however, was the way one's class position and income affect the ease or difficulty in obtaining the latest fashion. Some teenagers have been known to kill in order to get a particular gold chain or pair of Adidas shoes, or have been killed while trying to climb the social ladder by means of clothes.

One poignant story that captures both the longing and the tragedy of wanting to mold one's own identity into the fashionable image of the moment is "Alienation" by Julio Ramón Ribeyro (1986). It is included as the reading for this chapter. Of course, not all stories of longing end as tragically as his; nevertheless, the path of alienation – from one's body, friends, and culture – is rarely a happy one.

Politics of Clothes

While the vagaries of fashion, especially *haute couture*, give the impression that clothing is frivolous, this would be a misinterpretation. Clothing, or particular articles of clothing, has enormous political implications. In this section I discuss two examples – first, how Gandhi's clothing symbolized and incited a revolution in India, and, second, the politics of headgear in Turkey.

Gandhi

Throughout his life Gandhi was very sensitive to the politics and implications of clothing. "No Indian leader took the problem of what to wear more seriously than Mohandas Karamchand Gandhi and probably no other leader changed his clothes so dramatically" (Tarlo 1996: 62). When he first went to England to study law, he tried to make sure he had obtained the appropriate clothes so as to blend more easily into his new surroundings. However, he had a number of embarrassing moments in this regard, beginning with his departure from the ship when he discovered that he was the only man in white flannels. Tarlo believes that the "psychological impact of these incidents may be measured by the fact that he bothered to record them nearly forty years later" (p. 65).

After numerous sartorial changes both in England and in South Africa that coincided with changes in his career, he returned to India determined to throw off the yoke of British colonialism. At the same time he began to throw off all items of European clothing and experimented with a variety of native clothes until finally, on September 22, 1921, he published his intention to wear only a simple loincloth made of cloth spun and woven by hand. He "proposed to wear a loincloth for a period of just over five weeks, until the allotted deadline for *swaraj*," home rule (Tarlo 1996: p. 72). It was not his intention to wear it for the rest of his life, since it was a protest against the British, a symbol of his desire for home rule, and a sign, also, of sympathy with the poor.

> I wish to be in tune with the poorest of the poor among Indians. … How can these poor people afford a long shirt with a collar? Who will give them a cap? If we wear so many garments, we cannot clothe the poor, but it is our duty to dress them first and then ourselves, to feed them first and then ourselves. (Gandhi, *Complete Works*, 24:456, quoted in Tarlo 1996: 75)

Once people took up spinning and weaving their own cloth and refused to import foreign cloth or wear clothes made from such cloth, Gandhi said he would revert back to his more "normal" clothes. When they did not do so, he continued to wear the loincloth as a sign of mourning "that the people had rejected his version of progress and national development" (Tarlo 1996: 77). Nevertheless, it was an extraordinarily potent symbol of the power of one small man to change the world, for it was never the same after Gandhi.

Turkish headgear

In his delightful book *A Fez of the Heart* (1995), Jeremy Seal recounts how headgear has paralleled political changes in the Ottoman Empire and the Turkish Republic. This was possible because Turkish "headgear has since time immemorial had a symbolic significance inconceivable in the West" (Seal 1995: 22). During the Ottoman period, the kind of clothes one could wear, the cloth and color of the clothes, and especially headgear were stipulated by law. Indeed, unlike other world powers, the Ottoman Empire made sure that persons of different gender, class, and professions had distinctive headgear, and some, like military and religious personnel, also displayed rank in the hierarchy. One could tell at a glance the group and rank to which a person belonged – an easy way to keep people under surveillance and, thus, under control.

In the early part of the nineteenth century, modernizing reforms were attempted, including reform of headgear. In 1826 turbans were banned and the fez, adopted from North Africa, was instituted by state decree. The changes in headgear and regimes were also immortalized on tombstones: before 1826 tombstones were decorated with a variety of turbans carved on top of the thin stone slabs, but after 1826, the fez became routine. Thus headgear differentiated the dead and their era. Up until the revolution that created the Republic of Turkey, the fez was the prescribed headgear for men. However,

> In 1925, the fez was outlawed and replaced by homburgs, panamas, bowlers, and flatcaps. And so a series of hats have provided the stepping-stones, the caravanserais, on the central theme of Turkish history, her great march westward toward the promised land represented by that ultimate measure of Westernization – the bare head. (Seal 1995: 21–2)

Approaching that ideal, the most common headgear among men today is the flatcap with a small brim in front. It is also highly functional. Because the cap can be turned around with the brim in back, its wearer can touch his head to the ground in prayer. Some devout Muslim men also wear embroidered skullcaps, similar to Jewish *yarmulkes*.

Women's headgear, not men's, is today the focus of heated controversy. The headscarf is an explosive issue not just in Turkey and other Muslim countries, but also in several

European nations with large numbers of Muslim immigrants. Some women have been killed for not wearing the veil. It is scarcely a frivolous issue. When Atatürk banned the fez, he also encouraged women to go bareheaded, but he banned the wearing of the headscarf only for government employees such as teachers, nurses, lawyers, and members of Parliament. Women in the villages continued to wear their headscarves, but many urban women abandoned them and adopted Western-style clothing.

Village women's headgear was never the long black covering mandated for women in Iran and Saudi Arabia. Instead, it consisted of different kinds of cloth depending on the circumstance. The most common was a small thin gauze scarf in a variety of colors, often printed with flowers or other designs and edged with lace, beads, or tatting which displayed the woman's handwork. The scarf was wound around the head so that some of it covered the shoulders, and was not tied under the chin like a kerchief. When visiting each other, some women would add a larger, longer white gauze scarf, and when going to town some of them, usually the older women, put on a large printed scarf that identified them as belonging to a specific area (see figure 8.4a and 8.4b). In winter this was replaced by a large woolen scarf. For a visit to the city, younger women have adopted the kerchief and long loose coat of religious Muslims. The long black veils which totally cover the body are a very recent urban phenomenon. Indeed, when I first saw them in Istanbul, I assumed the women were visitors from Iran or Saudi Arabia and was shocked to learn that some Turkish women had begun to wear them.

The polarization of Turkish society has intensified since the 1980s, and that polarization is mirrored in women's clothing, with each side provoking the other to greater extremes. Representing one extreme are young Western-oriented women who wear miniskirts, tight tops with spaghetti straps, and high-heeled sandals. Representing the other extreme are devout Islamist women who have adopted long coats and kerchiefs or the head-to-toe black veils. Although these women generally associate with others of like mind, occasionally one can see these two drastically different icons of Turkish womanhood walking and talking together. The universities typically stand staunchly behind Atatürk's ideas about head-scarves, creating in the spring of 2000 a vociferous protest from women who were banned from taking their medical exams because they wore headscarves to school.

When Merve Kavakçı, a member of Parliament, appeared for the first time in a head-scarf, she fomented a debate that ended with the demand for her resignation. Ironically, people on the far right and on the left have joined forces over this issue, declaring that in a democracy people should be allowed to wear what they want. In principle this sounds like a good idea, but it is not so simple in Turkey, because the Islamists are using the rhetoric of democracy for undemocratic aims. They would not be so permissive toward the mini-skirted women if they were to achieve power. Far more important, in my mind, is that none of them has explored the meaning of hair in Turkish and Muslim society and why women's hair must be covered.[13]

The covering of women's hair has a long history and did not begin with the Muslims. Orthodox Jewish women are also not allowed to show their hair, and many shave their heads and wear wigs. For centuries Christian women, too, covered their heads in keeping with biblical injunctions: "Every man praying or prophesying, having his head covered, dishonoureth his head. But every woman that prayeth or prophesieth with her

Figure 8.4 (a and b) Village women's headgear. Photos by author.

head uncovered dishonoureth her head" (1 Corinthians 11:4–5) because "the head of every man is Christ; and the head of the woman is the man" (1 Corinthians 11:3). Thus began the custom of nuns both shaving their heads and wearing their distinctive habits. Lay Catholic women adopted veils, while Protestant women wore hats. Both customs continue to this day even though they are in decline.

State rules

States have always had rules about attire, even if not as explicit as in the Ottoman Empire. In the 1950s in the United States, girls were not allowed to wear pants to school – not even in the freezing cold winters in upstate New York or Connecticut. And in 1962 I was nearly thrown out of college for wearing pants one day. Things changed dramatically in the mid-1960s and today, it seems, students can wear almost anything they want to school. But this, too, causes problems. Girls are accused of being too sexy and seductive when they wear short-shorts and halter tops, while boys are accused of being slovenly and disrespectful when they belt their pants to their thighs instead of their waists: to me, both are unseemly attire for school. Brand-name consciousness increases the competition that can spark violent antagonisms. It is no wonder that the subject of school uniforms has come up again in public discussion.

In the meantime, some state legislatures and school boards have attempted to restrict school attire. In 2001, New York state responded to the complaints of teachers and school administrators by requiring schools to adopt dress codes. Their principal concern was the sexualizing of girls, who were now forbidden to wear extremely short skirts, see-through blouses, low-cut tight tops with spaghetti straps, and bare midriffs, although they also banned boys' low-slung and baggy pants ("School Dress Codes vs. a Sea of Bare Flesh," *New York Times*, September 11, 2001). Palo Alto, California, banned similar clothing in school.

Uniforms

We generally take it for granted that our clothes express our personality, that our choice of clothes, so far as our means allow, says something about us. Thus many Americans reject uniforms as a matter of principle. But a profound experience challenged and changed my view on this subject.

When I was a Fulbright fellow in Belgium, I decided to go down into a working coal mine. Do not ask me why. I think, in part, it was because nonminers, especially women (who are thought to bring bad luck), are not permitted in mines, hence it was a rare privilege when a friend arranged my visit into the Beringen mine. It was one of the most extraordinary experiences in my life and one I would not want to repeat.

Before getting into the tiny cage that took us deep underground, I had to remove my own clothes, watch, jewelry – anything that could create static and cause a spark – and don the miners' uniform including the cap with lamp. At the bottom we got onto a small train that took us several miles underground, travelling mostly horizontally but also gradually downward. At the end of the train line we walked and then finally crawled between short stubby pillars supporting the weight of the world, literally, just above our heads. The noise was deafening both from the mining equipment and from the huge fans circulating air. It was very frightening and I grew anxious, not only because I could be crushed, but also because I was the only woman among all these men. I could not leave until work ended that evening. Even if I had wanted to I could never have found my way back through the labyrinthine paths. I was trapped.

Dressed in identical uniforms, everyone seemed to look the same. What became very apparent very quickly was that the individuality and personalities of the men stood out more precisely *because* they were wearing identical uniforms. I was thunderstruck. When we came up out of the mine and changed into our ordinary clothes, I became confused. I could hardly recognize the men with whom I had been in such close contact all day, and it was much more difficult to get a sense of their unique personalities even while we talked over drinks at their local pub. So impressive was this experience that it has stayed with me over the past 25 years and made me question the whole issue of uniforms and individual expression. Do we display our identity through clothes, or are clothes a disguise?

Personally, I think uniforms would simplify our lives a great deal. We wouldn't have to think every morning, "What am I going to wear today?" Hating this daily agonizing ritual, my daughter and I came up with an idea of a clothing line suitable for all people at school or at work, young or old, male or female. We liked the style of the Mao suits once worn in China and wanted to elaborate that basic plan, with jackets, pants, skirts, and jumpers in a variety of colors – magenta, aqua, yellow, green, and not just dark blue. Our motto was "A billion people can't be wrong." I still think it is a great idea. Fashion designers beware!

Many people, of course, have to wear uniforms as symbols of their occupations: the police, firefighters, the military, construction workers, doctors and lab technicians in hospitals, and often waiters, waitresses, and maids all wear uniforms to reveal their professions to each other and to the wider public. Uniforms have also long been required in many private schools, both religious and secular. Recently, public schools have begun to reconsider uniforms as a strategy for fostering a focus on learning, school identity, and belonging, rather than on clothing: after all, students' minds are what matter, not their appearance. Still, even uniformed students make tiny adjustments to their outfits both to express their individuality and to resist its diminution. Some people, including some educators, think that uniforms reduce the criminal behavior of some students, particularly those who cannot afford the latest fashion, and diminish the sexualized atmosphere in the classroom. Others, however, say they curtail students' freedom of expression and, therefore, are not appropriate in a democracy.

In Turkey, all children must wear school uniforms from first grade through high school. There the purpose *is* democratic – poor children should be dressed exactly as rich children. The uniform expresses the idea that each child is equal before the law. That, at least, is the rationale. In practice, however, it doesn't always work out that way. First, there is from the outset the distinction of gender – girls wear dresses, while boys wear shirts and pants. Second, gender distinctions intensify as the children get older. Thus at the end of the sixth grade, girls in the village don the headscarf, the primary symbol of sexual difference and, simultaneously, the end of their schooling, since the headscarf is not permitted in the secular public school system. (See figure 8.5.) I do not know how the village is complying with the new law that requires all children to complete the eighth grade.

Figure 8.5   Turkish schoolgirls in uniform. Photo by author.

Figure 8.6   Uniforms required of Turkish men going on *hajj*. Photo by author.

Figure 8.7   Medieval armor. Photograph by Rama, Wikimedia Commons, Cc-by-sa-2.0-fr.

In addition to gender are, of course, the differentials of income and class. Poor children, as in the village where I lived, wore hand-me-down uniforms, sometimes patched, faded, and rarely ironed. The white collars were often made of plastic so they could be kept clean. In the village it didn't really matter because most of them were in the same boat; but in the city where poor and richer kids attend the same schools, it could become more of a problem. (See also figure 8.6 for the clothing worn by Turkish men on *hajj*.)

Cultural constraint

Uniforms connote both cultural constraint (being "forced" to conform to the cultural norm or ideal) and social control (ease of surveillance) to which many people have strong objections. If fashion, in general, can be viewed as imposing constraints on the body, particular kinds of clothing enforce this even more. The most spectacular examples are combat uniforms designed to protect the soldier from lethal violence, while allowing him to inflict lethal violence on his enemies. These fashions are always compromises between immobility and athleticism, as figures 8.7 and 8.8 reveal. Medieval armor no doubt protected the wearer from swords, knives and lances, but cost him agility, flexibility and, for lack of a better word, comfort (see figure 8.7). The modern bomb suit, a key image in the 2009 film *The Hurt Locker*, achieves much the same purpose at much the same cost (see figure 8.8).

Figure 8.8   A modern bomb suit and helmet as advertised by the Allen-Vanguard Corp. 2010 Allen-Vanguard Corporation.

Perhaps the most peculiar forms of clothing constraint are those engineered for aesthetic ideals only, as illustrated by a wide variety of women's fashions. I am thinking of corsets and girdles, foot binding and high heels, and Japanese kimono and Turkish *şalvar* – all of which also impede women's movement. No doubt you can think of many more examples. A major question is why do various societies wish to restrict the free movement of women? I will let you ponder this while I discuss some of the ways this has been done and what they imply about the society in question.

Linda Martin, a fashion historian, claims that "startling correlations appear between the design of female underwear and the exploration, expansion and acquisition of countries and continents by various civilizations" (quoted in Hatfield, *Boston Globe*, October 16, 1986). (If today's underwear is any indication, there is nothing left to explore and conquer.) The sixteenth century was also the time when early modern scientists were trying to bring the natural world under control. Since the natural world, or Nature, has been symbolically female, it is not so surprising that attempts were made to bring women's supposedly unruly nature under control.

> In the sixteenth century, European women bound themselves into corsets of whalebone and hardened canvas. A piece of metal or wood ran down the front to flatten the breasts and abdomen. This garment made it impossible to bend at the waist and difficult to breathe. A farthingale, which was typically worn over the corset, held women's skirts out from their bodies … and made such simple activities as sitting nearly impossible. Queen Catherine of France introduced waist binding with a tortuous invention consisting of iron bands that minimized the size of the waist to the ideal measurement of thirteen inches. (Saltzberg and Chrisler [1995] 1997: 136)

These extraordinary measures and measurements compressed the rib cage, leading to pulmonary problems and damage to internal organs. While Chinese women suffered from bound feet, European women suffered from bound torsos. In the nineteenth century, *hysteria*, a psychological disease felt to be caused by a wandering womb, may instead have been caused by the very corsets made to hold it in check. But that was never considered in the theories, such as Freud's, used to explain the condition.

Steel stays, as well as whalebone, were also used in corsets when the metal was no longer needed for armor, and they remained mainstays of women's fashion until 1914 when the steel was "needed for wartime production. By this time, [American] women were using 28,000 tons of steel per year for corset stays, enough to build two battleships" (Linda Martin, quoted in Hatfield 1986). Discarding the corset as part of the war effort made room for the freer, straighter, more boyish look of the "roaring twenties," a move that also coincided with the women's suffrage movement.

Bound feet   In China, the traditional ideal of feminine beauty was tiny feet. In order to achieve this, the feet of small girls were "bound."

> Beginning at about age six to eight, the female child's four smaller toes were bent under the foot, the sole was forced to the heel, and then the foot was wrapped in a tight bandage day and night in order to mold a bowed and pointed four-inch-long appendage. Footbinding was extremely painful in the first 6 to 10 years of formative treatment. Complications included ulceration, paralysis, gangrene, and mortification of the lower limbs. (Mackie 1996: 1000)

Yet even this sounds too clinical for it does not indicate the broken bones, the blood- and pus-soaked bandages, and the odor. There was no way these women could escape an abusive husband or mother-in-law on such tiny "lotus" feet, which were apparently deeply erotic to men. Not only were the women hobbled for life, unable even to walk, but also they were taught early to endure tremendous pain for the pleasure and stature of men. (See figure 8.9.)

Figure 8.9   An X-ray of a Chinese woman's bound feet. Library of Congress, Prints & Photographs Division, [cph.3c04036].

But it is too easy to dismiss this as a perversion of the Chinese or as an ancient practice, and to overlook the women in today's post-industrial societies who are tottering around in stiletto-heeled, toe-crunching shoes and boots. One writer, in China for the celebration of the fiftieth anniversary of its revolution, captured an image that is unforgettable and worth quoting at length.

> In a single glance, I suddenly saw two women – separated by three generations, but standing less than 10 feet apart. A young man slowly wheeled a frail, elderly woman, curled up in a bicycle basket, through the treacherous traffic. Her five-inch long, bound feet dangled uselessly from under her skirt. Born before the revolution she could hardly walk.
>
> At the very same moment, a young woman, perhaps 20 years old, scantily dressed in a tight, short skirt and perched on four-inch high strapless platform shoes, tried to descend the steps that led to the subway station. She tottered precariously, her shoes slapping against her feet with every step. Born three decades after the revolution, she could hardly walk. (Rosen, *San Francisco Chronicle*, May 13, 2001)

Has anything changed, Rosen wondered. A friend of hers said that women today have a choice – they don't have to wear such shoes. Rosen retorted, "But isn't the young woman still a slave to fashion?" "Yes, but at least her feet won't be mutilated for life." "Oh really?" Women fall and injure themselves when they wear these shoes, and suffer bone, ligament, and nerve deformities later in life. One man writing in response to the article suggested that high-heeled shoes make a woman taller and therefore more imposing, giving her an aura of power and authority much as a buttoned collar and tightly knotted tie confer authority to a man. What he failed to realize is that all of these images of authority are culturally produced.

Kimono   The Japanese kimono is a less obvious means to impede the movement of women, but it does so nonetheless. This garment, worn in various forms for more than a thousand years, is an extremely intricate ensemble. Originally worn by both men and women (with variations), the kimono was abandoned by men "a century ago in the name of modernity and efficiency" (Dalby 1993: 3), but it became *the* symbol of Japanese womanhood.

Proper kimono attire consists of 18 different items, according to Yamanaka (1982), including split-toe socks (*tabi*), undershirts or half-slips, body pads, under-kimono, collars, undersash, obi, obi stays and cords, and a special kind of sandal (*zori*). Not only does it take quite some time to put on a kimono properly, but also many women today must go to a special school to learn how, for the geisha are the only women who wear them as a matter of course every day.

Liza Dalby, an anthropologist who became a geisha for her research, describes how donning the kimono changed not only the way she moved but also her very self.

> A garment as demanding as the kimono, for example, requires a whole new personality, and, like learning a foreign language, it takes a while before we are no longer self-conscious. … Eventually the proper movements became natural, but in absorbing them I discovered that I had developed another self in kimono … [so that] after a while, I actually felt awkward speaking English when dressed as a geisha" (Dalby [1983] 1999: 105)

Because the kimono constricts the body, one has to learn to walk with tiny mincing steps, "with turned-in feet, which makes a kimono rustle delicately." It affects one's movement in other ways too: "Driving a car or just sitting in a soft armchair are among the most awkward things a woman in kimono can do" (p. 327). When Dalby changed her mode of dress, she also changed where and how she sat, how she walked, and innumerable other aspects of body gesture and language.

Şalvar   Wearing Turkish village *şalvar*, I, too, felt differently and apparently spoke differently. *Şalvar* are baggy trousers or bloomers cut from several yards of printed cloth, generally cotton or synthetic. Girls and women rarely had a choice of fabric, design, or color since the cloth was generally bought in town by men in the family. No attempt was made to harmonize them with the blouses and knitted vests that completed the outfit, and the variations in color, pattern, and print often made me dizzy (see figure 8.10). Clearly a very different aesthetic was at work, one in which each item was valued on its own, and not as an element in an ensemble. Some people told me that the women's colorful outfits make them look like flowers, especially when they are out working in the fields. Although I dressed as village women did in *şalvar*, blouse, *yelek* (knitted vest), and headscarf, people began to comment on my color-coordinated outfits – something I could not relinquish easily since color harmony is an important part of my fashion aesthetic.

Şalvar are made from three pieces – two for the legs and one for the center-panel that joins them – with an elastic band threaded at the waist. The piece that joins the two leg sections together is attached near the ankle, making the *şalvar* almost like a long skirt, stitched closed along the bottom with holes for feet. When I asked if that piece on my *şalvar*

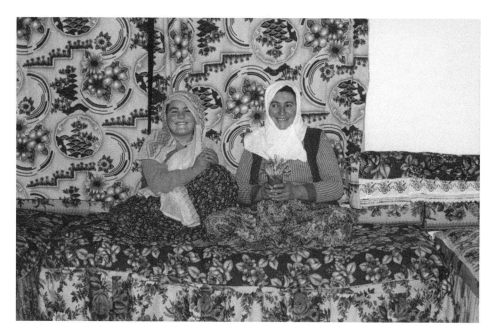

Figure 8.10 Two Turkish women against tapestry. Photo by author.

could be joined higher up so that I could walk at my usual pace, the answer was no. That would be unseemly, for it would be more like men's pants. I also asked if I could have pockets to carry my house key, my pad, pencil, and dictionary around with me less noticeably. "No! Certainly not." Pockets are for men only, for women's hands must remain visible and busy knitting, sewing, working in the field, preparing food, or caring for babies and children. To carry my paraphernalia, I had to make a small cloth pouch which dangled from my wrist.

Şalvar symbolize other values as well, for they make all women look plump and pregnant. Turkish men, traditionally at least, gain prestige by having a plump wife – it shows he could afford to feed her well – and a plump and pregnant wife is even better.

Functionally, şalvar are very satisfactory. Villagers do not normally sit on chairs, but either squat or sit on divans cross-legged or with their legs tucked under them. To squat in jeans or other tight pants cuts off the circulation, and sitting cross-legged is too revealing. Şalvar were roomy, modest, and comfortable. But, once again, women's free movement was very much restricted, not just socially but also by the very clothes they wore.

No doubt practical, functional reasons can be found for any number of items of clothing, but whether those reasons are primary causes or secondary rationalizations is very difficult to tell. What is important is that one learns little about their cultural significance purely from pragmatic practice. If culture is really formed from practical interest, clothing could be interpreted from a functional point of view, but that hardly explains the variety of (often not very functional) designs; such an approach also ignores that practical interests and desires are shaped within a system of values about what life is and how it should be lived.

Political Economy of Clothing

Marshall Sahlins asserts that the clothing system is a system of production, one that produces social distinctions as well as the material items we call clothes. As he did with food (see chapter 7), he undermines our commonsense notions that we produce material goods *because* they directly reflect our needs and desires. Instead, he argues that our system of production is the realization of a symbolic scheme.

> For notice what is produced in the clothing system. By various objective features an item of apparel becomes appropriate for men or women, for night or for day, for "around the house" or "in public," for adult or adolescent. What is produced is, first, classes of time and place which index situations or activities; and second, classes of status to which all persons are ascribed. … Hence what is reproduced in clothing is this classificatory scheme. Yet not simply that. Not simply the boundaries, the divisions, and the subdivisions of, say, age-grades or social classes; by a specific symbolism of clothing differences, what is produced are the meaningful differences between these categories. In manufacturing apparel of distinct cut, outline, or color for women as opposed to men, we reproduce the distinction between femininity and masculinity as *known* to this society. That is what is going on in the pragmatic-material process of production. (1976: 181)

Because of the discriminations in the code, "the set of manufactured objects comprehends the entire cultural order of a society that it both *dresses* and *addresses*" (Sahlins 1976: 180). I like this phrase because it points out the double aspect of clothes: that they both conceal the body and reveal our identity – not the naked animal but the socialized, enculturated person.

In chapter 4 on language, we noted how much we could tell about a person as soon as he or she opened his or her mouth. Clothing provides nonverbal cues and is, perhaps, more unconscious. Let us think for a moment about some of the classifications encoded in clothes. First, they encode time. There are clothes for nighttime and daytime wear, summer and winter and fall and spring, weekday and weekend, and holidays. Second, they encode space. Thus space is divided "between town and country, and within the town between downtown and neighborhood" (Sahlins 1976: 181), and the clothes we wear change accordingly. Third, they encode activity. In the modern (post-)industrialized world, an important distinction is made between work and leisure, and our clothes reflect this distinction. Fourth, they encode life stage and status, not just adults and children, but also infants, toddlers, preschoolers, school-aged children, preteens, subteens, teens, juniors, adults, and the latest, over-60 group, with each category inflected by gender.

Occupations are also encoded in attire, not only through uniforms that designate police, firefighters, surgeons and lab technicians, but also through "white-collar" and "blue-collar" distinctions that differentiate job types. We grow up thinking these categories are natural, but according to Sahlins they are culturally produced. Young people reading this book probably imagine that blue jeans have been around forever, and that they are the natural choice for all kinds of leisure activities. They will be surprised to learn that they became that only in the 1960s during the Vietnam War and the conflict between youth and authority. In this conflict, which was also seen in terms of class conflict, the youth identified with unionized workers (who did wear blue jeans) and appropriated their clothing. According to Sahlins, "nothing could better prove the absence of practical utility in clothing, since work is one of the last things youth has in mind" (1976: 184).

Cargo pants are, perhaps, another example. Just what is a person going to put in all those pockets? Are they designed for particular items? Is storage for gear even the point? Bob Morris of the *New York Times* (October 11, 1998) compared cargo pants to the cargo cults of New Guinea where natives made images of things (cargo), such as guns, telephones, and refrigerators, in hope of obtaining them. By wearing cargo pants, today's youth are trying to obtain the aura of an "extreme athlete, alternative rocker … (or) bushwhacker" (see figure 8.11). If fashion is truly a form of "magic materialism," as Morris claims, what symbolic identifications are made with the latest fashion item or accessory?

Figure 8.11   Cargo pants. © Rubberball/Alamy.

Globalization of the Clothing Industry

As we make increasingly subtle social and symbolic distinctions, we simultaneously open up new domains or niches for the production of objects. For example, there used to be a type of shoe called a *sneaker*, with a canvas upper and a rubber sole, that was used for all kinds of sport activities – tennis, basketball, volleyball, bike riding, walking, and boating. Today, the all-purpose sneaker has been replaced by numerous specialized athletic and casual shoes, each designed for a particular sport, along with different kinds of outfits for each sport or pastime.

For every new distinction made in clothing, a new niche is opened for production. But how are these clothes made, and where? In today's world, much of the clothing worn in the United States is made elsewhere. Look at the labels in your clothing and see what percentage of your wardrobe was made in your own country. "If the US is to remain competitive," said one executive quoted in the 1986 PBS film *The Global Assembly Line*, we must reduce costs, and this profit motive "compels companies to take labor offshore," meaning to Third World countries and "export processing zones" where they can pay workers shockingly low wages. For example, Sweatshop Watch, a California organization that monitors sweatshop abuses, published the following hourly wages for garment workers in 1995: 12 cents in China, 38 cents in Thailand, 48 cents in the Philippines, and $9.95 in the United States. At least 50 countries now host "export processing zones" where the companies are not required to pay duty and thus do not contribute to that nation's income. Although the payment of duties could help to alleviate poverty, this would be counterproductive, because it is the poverty that keeps the wages low. While the work does bring income to individuals, they derive few benefits, work long hours, are often exposed to toxic chemicals, are not permitted to unionize, and are forced to meet quotas. If they do not, the company can threaten to take its work elsewhere. Is this not corporate blackmail?

In addition, an entire garment may not be made at one site, but farmed out in sections to different sites and assembled in still another. This fragmentation of work illustrates Marx's idea of workers' alienation from the products of their labor. In these factories, workers – usually women who "can do the delicate jobs better" (see the film *The Global Assembly Line*, 1986) – may only be tasked with one seam, repeated again and again. Such fragmentation of work also contributes to the deskilling of the workforce, rendering them automatons rather than skilled seamstresses like those who work in *haute couture*.

But "sweatshops" are not just elsewhere, for they are also found in the United States and other industrial countries. The term *sweatshop* was coined because the workers were "sweating" from pressure to produce high quotas and from working in places with little ventilation. Every now and then, an exposé in the press describes the execrable conditions under which people, often immigrants (legal and illegal), are working. One of the most shocking was exposed in 1995 in El Monte, California, not far from downtown Los Angeles.

> The workers were immigrants from Thailand. They were living and working in an apartment complex surrounded by barbed-wire fences. They worked over eighty hours a week for less than $2 an hour and were detained by the company owners until they had supposedly paid

off the debt of their transportation. Some had labored in the factory for years, unsuccessfully pleading for their freedom. They were forced to shop at a store maintained on the premises by the factory owners, and often charging vastly inflated prices, which virtually assured that they would never get out of debt peonage and be able to buy their freedom. (Bonacich and Appelbaum, 2000: 165)[14]

The clothes they sewed were sold at some of the nation's largest retail stores, although the retailers denied knowledge of the conditions under which these women worked. The workers' lawyer, Julie Su, claimed they were making less than 60 cents an hour. Eventually, the 72 women won a lawsuit, were released from their virtual slavery, and were awarded back pay. This aroused the ire of garment manufacturers, who then vociferously opposed the Smithsonian exhibit, "Between a Rock and a Hard Place: A History of American Sweatshops 1820–Present," which opened in the summer of 1998.[15]

In addition to sweatshop production, there has been a proliferation of piecework done at home, mostly but not always by women and children. While this type of work has been going on for a long time, it has become more widespread, even necessary in the economic restructuring that occurred with the developing "niche" market. The "emergence of new systems of production has focused mainly on forms of *flexibility* that enable producers to adapt to volatile conditions in globalized markets. The use of subcontracting is one of the principal characteristics of these new systems" (Eraydin and Erendil 1999: 260; emphasis mine). Turkey has had an important textile industry for some time, but in the last part of the twentieth century textiles and clothing became its "most important export product" (p. 261). And Turkey has a large reservoir of cheap, flexible labor. In order for large companies to meet ever-changing demands, they subcontract work out either to small sweatshops or to groups of workers at home. This type of work can be integrated into the daily schedule when time is available and, thus, is often not seen as work. Such work is temporary and subject to the whims of the market; furthermore, it is unsupervised and offers only occasional income with no benefits (see White 1994). Children learn to do the work, making it resemble apprenticeship. In this way, however, they are interpellated into the capitalist system.

The system of production is no longer rooted in a particular culture, for increasingly global capitalism (primarily from the United States and Western Europe) holds the rest of the world in its grip.

Notes

1. Taken from the title of a book by Emma Tarlo (1996).
2. Jenna Weissman Joselit, author of *A Perfect Fit: Clothes, Character, and the Promise of America* (2001), has also given a freshman seminar at Princeton titled "Getting Dressed," about the social and historical significance of clothes.
3. The title was a reference to the elder Bush's statement, "Read My Lips."
4. I am reminded of the following lines from "The Love Song of J. Alfred Prufrock" by T.S. Eliot (1915):

   I grow old … I grow old …
   I shall wear the bottoms of my trousers rolled.
   Shall I part my hair behind? Do I dare to eat a peach?
   I shall wear white flannel trousers, and walk upon the
       beach.

5. Parastatals are companies partially owned by government and partially by private interests. They are often created to coordinate and facilitate development projects.

6. See, for example, the films *Priscilla, Queen of the Desert*; *Paris is Burning*; and *Ma Vie en Rose*.

7. This was written before 9/11.

8. See also Gremaux (1994).

9. Middlebrook's (1998) psychological portrait may help to unravel this skein of tangled motives, both private and public.

10. For the issue of berdache and also "third gender," see Roscoe (1991, 1994), Callender and Kochems (1983), Trexler (1999); Gutierrez (1989); and also Serena Nanda on *hijras* (1990).

11. I think he meant "straight" men and women (2); "passive" homosexual men and women (2); and "active" homosexual men and women (2).

12. A "be-in" was an informal gathering, for no particular purpose except to be together, held in a public place like a park. Anyone could and did go to "hang out," although that phrase had not yet been coined.

13. See my article "Untangling the Meanings of Hair in Turkish Society" (Delaney, 1994).

14. I acknowledge Andrea Christensen, one of my student research assistants, for garnering this information.

15. There was a massive demonstration in New York on August 17, 2001, by a new anti-sweatshop coalition organized by UNITE (Union of Needletrades, Industrial and Textile Employees) that included unions from many of the other countries (Mexico, Guatemala, Honduras, Hong Kong, Thailand, Nicaragua, Dominican Republic, and Canada) where garment workers for firms such as Ann Taylor, Eddie Bauer, and Banana Republic are working in sweatshop-type operations.

E X E R C I S E S

8.1. Clothes Shopping

Visit a department store such as Target, Macy's, Marks & Spencer, Harrods, Gap, or Nordstrom's. List all the clothing departments in the store, such as baby–infant, girls, teens, and so on. Then visit these departments and describe how the items are organized in each one, such as by age, size, gender, lifestyle, occasion, and so on. What kind of marketing niches have been created? Do you see any openings for new marketing niches?

8.2. Clothes Manufacturing

Examine the labels of your own clothes and see if you can determine how many different locations, industries, and workshops were involved in their production. This means figuring out where the raw materials were obtained, where the fabric and other elements were produced, where the garment was cut and assembled, and where it was sent for sale. Locate all of these points on a map of the world, and connect them to show the production of a garment from its absolute point of origin as a raw material to its final arrival as a finished product in your closet.

8.3. A Special Occasion

Being in harmony with fashion gives a person a sense of security rarely derived from religion.

Oscar Wilde

Choose a particular event or outing. It could be anything from a date for dinner or a movie, to a night out at a pub, a party, a wedding, or a holiday celebration. What would you wear for this occasion? Describe both the event and the outfit in detail and why this is the appropriate attire for the event.

Bibliography

Appadurai, Arjun, ed. (1986) *The Social Life of Things: Commodities in Cultural Perspective.* Cambridge: Cambridge University Press.

Arnaud, Jean-Louis (2001). [Article of July 19]. *France Diplomatie* (23): www.france.diplomatie.fr.

Ash, Juliet, and Wilson, Elizabeth (1993) *Chic Thrills: A Fashion Reader.* Berkeley: University of California Press.

Barthes, Roland ([1967] 1983) *The Fashion System.* New York: Hill & Wang.

Bastian, Misty L. (1996) "Female 'Alhajis' and Entrepreneurial Fashions: Flexible Identities in Southeastern Nigerian Clothing Practice." In *Clothing and Difference: Embodied Identities in Colonial and Postcolonial Africa*, ed. Hildi Hendrickson. Durham, NC: Duke University Press.

Benaim, Laurence (2001). [Article of July 19]. *France Diplomatie* (23): www.france.diplomatie.fr.

Blanch, Lesley (1954) *The Wilder Shores of Love.* New York: Simon & Schuster.

Bonacich, Edna, and Appelbaum, Richard P. (2000) *Behind the Label: Inequality in the Los Angeles Apparel Industry.* Berkeley: University of California Press.

Bourdieu, Pierre (1984) *Distinction: A Social Critique of the Judgement of Taste.* Cambridge, MA: Harvard University Press.

Callender, Charles, and Kochems, Lee M. (1983) "The North American Berdache." *Current Anthropology* 24(4): 443–56.

Craik, Jennifer (1994) *The Face of Fashion: Cultural Studies in Fashion.* London: Routledge.

Dalby, Liza Crihfield ([1983] 1999) "Kimono Schools." In *The Meanings of Dress*, ed. Mary Lynn Damhorst, Kimberly A. Miller, and Susan O. Michelman. New York: Fairchild.

Dalby, Liza Crihfield (1993) *Kimono: Fashioning Culture.* New Haven: Yale University Press.

Damhorst, Mary Lynn, Miller, Kimberly A., and Michelman, Susan O., eds. (1999) *The Meanings of Dress.* New York: Fairchild.

Davis, Fred (1992) *Fashion, Culture, and Identity.* Chicago: University of Chicago Press.

de la Haye, Amy, and Wilson, Elizabeth (1999) *Defining Dress: Dress as Object, Meaning and Identity.* Manchester: Manchester University Press.

Delaney, Carol (1994) "Untangling the Meaning of Hair in Turkish Society." *Anthropological Quarterly* 64(4): 159–72.

Eliot, T. S. (1915) "The Love Song of J. Alfred Prufrock." In *Prufrock and Other Observations.* London: Egoist.

Eraydin, Ayda, and Erendil, Asuman (1999) "The Role of Female Labor in Industrial Restructuring: New Production Processes and Labor Market Relations in the Istanbul Clothing Industry." *Gender, Place and Culture* 6: 259–72.

Fausto-Sterling, Anne (1993) "The Five Sexes: Why Male and Female Are Not Enough." *The Sciences* (March/ April): 20–4.

Finkelstein, Joanne (1996) *Fashion: An Introduction.* New York: New York University Press.

Gaines, Jane, and Herzog, Charlotte, eds. (1990) *Fabrications: Costume and the Female Body.* New York: Routledge.

Garber, Marjorie (1992) *Vested Interests: Cross-Dressing and Cultural Anxiety.* London: Routledge.

Gilroy, Paul (1987) *There Ain't No Black in the Union Jack: The Cultural Politics of Race and Nation.* London: Hutchinson.

Goldman, Albert Harry (1974) *Ladies and Gentlemen – Lenny Bruce!!* New York: Random House.

Gremaux, René (1994) "Woman Becomes Man in the Balkans." In *Third Sex, Third Gender: Beyond Sexual Dimorphism in Culture and History*, ed. Gilbert Herdt. New York: Zone.

Gutierrez, Ramón (1989) "Must We Deracinate Indians to Find Gay Roots?" *Out/Look* (Winter): 61–7.

Hebdige, Dick (1979) *Subculture: The Meaning of Style.* London: Methuen.

Herdt, Gilbert, ed. (1994) *Third Sex, Third Gender: Beyond Sexual Dimorphism in Culture and History.* New York: Zone.

Hollander, Anne ([1975] 1978) *Seeing through Clothes*. New York: Viking.

Hotchkiss, Valerie R. (1996) *Clothes Make the Man: Female Cross-Dressing in Medieval Europe*. New York: Garland.

Jicai, Feng (1994) *The Three-Inch Golden Lotus: A Novel on Footbinding*, trans. David Wakefield. Honolulu: University of Hawaii Press.

Joselit, Jenna Weissman (2001) *A Perfect Fit: Clothes, Character, and the Promise of America*. New York: Metropolitan.

Mackie, Gerry (1996) "Ending Footbinding and Infibulation: A Convention Account." *American Sociological Review* 61: 999–1017.

MansLife.com (2001) [Home page], July 26. www.manslife.com.

McVeigh, Brian J. (2000) *Wearing Ideology: State, Schooling and Self-Presentation in Japan*. Oxford: Berg.

Middlebrook, Diane Wood (1998) *Suits Me: The Double Life of Billy Tipton*. Boston: Houghton Mifflin.

Nanda, Serena (1990) "Hijras: An Alternative Sex and Gender Role." In *Neither Man nor Woman: The Hijras of India*. Belmont, CA: Wadsworth.

Norton, John (1997) "Faith and Fashion in Turkey." In *Languages of Dress in the Middle East*, ed. Nancy Lindisfarne-Tapper and Bruce Ingham. Richmond, UK: Curzon Press with SOAS.

Polhemus, Ted (1994) *Streetstyle: From Sidewalk to Catwalk*. New York: Thames & Hudson (originally published to coincide with an exhibition at the Victoria and Albert Museum, London, Nov. 1994–Feb. 1995).

Ribeyro, Julio Ramón (1986) "Alienation." In *On Being Foreign: Culture Shock in Short Fiction*, ed. Tom J. Lewis and Robert E. Jungman. Yarmouth, ME: Intercultural Press.

Roscoe, Will (1991) *The Zuni Man-Woman*. Albuquerque: University of New Mexico Press.

Roscoe, Will (1994) "How to Become a Berdache: Toward a Unified Analysis of Gender Diversity." In *Third Sex, Third Gender: Beyond Sexual Dimorphism in Culture and History*, ed. Gilbert Herdt. New York: Zone.

Ross, Andrew, ed. (1997) *No Sweat: Fashion, Free Trade, and the Rights of Garment Workers*. New York: Verso.

Rubenstein, Ruth P. (1995) *Dress Codes: Meanings and Messages in American Culture*. Boulder, CO: Westview Press.

Sahlins, Marshall (1976) *Culture and Practical Reason*. Chicago: University of Chicago Press.

Saltzberg, Elayne A., and Chrisler, Joan C. ([1995] 1997) "Beauty Is the Beast: Psychological Effects of the Pursuit of the Perfect Female Body." In *Reconstructing Gender: A Multicultural Anthology*, ed. Estelle Disch. Mountain View, CA: Mayfield.

Seal, Jeremy (1995) *A Fez of the Heart: Travels around Turkey in Search of a Hat*. New York: Harcourt Brace.

Tarlo, Emma (1996) *Clothing Matters: Dress and Identity in India*. Chicago: University of Chicago Press.

Traweek, Sharon (1988) *Beamtimes and Lifetimes: The World of High-Energy Physicists*. Cambridge, MA: Harvard University Press.

Trexler, R. (1999) *Sex and Conquest: Gendered Violence, Political Order, and the European Conquest of the Americas*. Cambridge: Polity Press.

Turner, Terence (1980) "The Social Skin." In *Not Work Alone*, ed. J. Cherfas. London: Unwin.

White, Jenny (1994) *Money Makes Us Relatives: Women's Labor in Urban Turkey*. Austin: University of Texas Press.

Wikan, Unni (1977) "Man Becomes Woman: Transsexualism in Oman." *Man* 12: 304–19.

Woolf, Virginia ([1928] 1960) *Orlando: A Biography*. New York: New American Library.

Yamanaka, Norio (1982) *The Book of Kimono*. Tokyo: Kodansha International.

Young, Antonia (2000) *Women Who Become Men: Albanian Sworn Virgins*. New York: Berg.

R E A D I N G

Alienation (An Instructive Story with a Footnote)
Julio Ramón Ribeyro

Despite the fact that he was a mulatto named López, he longed to resemble less and less a defensive back on the Alianza Lima Soccer Team and increasingly to take on the look of a blond from Philadelphia. Life had taught him that if he wanted to prosper in a colonial city it was better to skip the intermediate stages and transform himself into a gringo from the United States rather than into just a fair-skinned nobody from Lima. During the years that I knew him, he devoted all of his attention to eliminating every tract of the López and zambo[1] within him and Americanizing himself before the bottom fell out and he would turn into, say, a bank guard or a taxi driver. He had to begin by killing the Peruvian in himself and extracting something from every gringo he met. From all this plundering a new person would emerge, a fragmented being who was neither mulatto nor gringo, but rather the result of an unnatural commingling, something that the force of destiny would eventually change, unfortunately for him, from a rosy dream into a hellish nightmare.

But let's not get ahead of ourselves. We should establish the fact that his name was Roberto, that years later he was known as Bobby, but that the most recent official documents refer to him as Bob. At each stage in his frantic ascent toward nothingness his name would lose one syllable.

Everything began the afternoon when a group of us fair-haired kids were playing ball on Bolognesi Plaza. We were out of school on vacation and some of us who lived in nearby chalets, both girls and boys, would meet at the plaza during those endless summer afternoons. Roberto used to go there too, even though he attended a public school and lived on one of the last backstreets left in the district rather than in a chalet. He would go there to watch the girls play and to be greeted by some fair-faced kid who had seen him growing up on those streets and knew he was the laundry woman's son.

In reality, he would go there like the rest of us, to see Queca. We were all infatuated with Queca, who, during the past couple of years, had the distinction of being chosen class queen, an honor bestowed upon her during festivities at the end of the school year. Queca didn't study with the German sisters of Saint Ursula, nor with the North Americans of Villa María, but rather with the Spanish nuns of Reparation. That was no big deal, nor the fact that her father was a blue-collar worker who drove a bus, nor that her house had only one story garnished with geraniums instead of roses. What was important then were her rosy skin, her green eyes, her long, brown hair, the way she ran, laughed, jumped, and her incomparable legs, always bare and golden and which, in time, would become legendary.

Roberto used to come only to watch her play; none of the boys who came from the other Miraflores neighborhoods, or even those who later came from San Isidro and Barranco, for that matter, could attract her attention. One time Peluca Rodríguez flung himself from the highest branch of a pine tree; Lucas de Tramontana drove up on a shiny motorcycle that had eight headlights; Fats Gómez broke the nose of the ice cream vendor who had the gall to whistle at us; and Armando Wolff donned several fine, new flannel suits with a bow tie. But not one of them caught Queca's eye. Queca favored no one; she preferred to talk with everybody, to run, skip, laugh, and play volleyball, leaving behind at nightfall a gang of teenage boys overwhelmed by intense sexual frustration that only a charitable hand underneath white sheets was able to console.

It was a fatal ball that someone tossed that afternoon, that Queca was unable to catch, and that rolled toward the bench where Roberto sat alone and observant. He had always waited for this moment. With a jump he landed on the grass, crawled between the flower beds, leaped over the hedge covered with passionflowers, stepped into a drainage ditch, and rescued the ball, which was just about to roll under the wheels of a car. But as he returned with it, Queca, who was now facing him with outstretched hands, seemed to be adjusting her focus, observing something that only now she was really seeing for the first time: a short, dark, thick-lipped being with kinky hair, something very ordinary that she probably saw daily, just as one sees park benches or pine trees. Abruptly, she turned away, terrified.

Roberto never forgot Queca's words as she fled: "I don't play with *zambos*." These five words decided his destiny.

Every human being who suffers becomes an observer, so Roberto continued going to the plaza for several years, but his look had lost all innocence. It was no longer a simple reflection of the world, but rather an organ of vigilance – penetrating, selecting, and examining.

Queca was growing up; her run was more moderate now, her skirts longer, her leaps weren't quite so bold, and her conduct around the gang had become more distant and selective. We were all aware of these changes, but Roberto observed something more: that Queca tended to turn away from her more swarthy admirers until, through successive comparisons, she focused her attention only on Chalo Sander, the one boy in the group with the fairest hair, the lightest skin, and the only one who studied in a school run by North American priests. By the time her legs were the most triumphant and well-turned, she was speaking exclusively to him. The first time she strolled to the levee holding hands with him we understood that she wasn't part of our turf anymore; there was nothing we could do but play the role of the chorus in a Greek tragedy, always present and visible, but irrecoverably separated from the gods.

Rejected and forlorn, we would gather on the street corner after one of our games, where we would smoke our first cigarettes, arrogantly fondle the newly discovered down of our mustaches, and comment on the hopeless state of things. Sometimes we would go into a bar owned by a Chinese named Manuel and have a beer. Roberto followed us around like a shadow, always scrutinizing us from the doorway, never missing a word of our conversation. Sometimes we would say, "Hi, *zambo*, have a drink with us," and he always said, "No thanks, another time," and although he smiled and kept his distance, we knew that he shared in his own way our sense of loss.

And it was Chalo Sander, of course, who took Queca to the graduation party when we finished high school. We decided to meet in our favorite bar early that evening. We drank more than usual, plotted bizarre schemes, and spoke of kidnapping, of planning some kind of group attack. But it was all just talk. By eight o'clock we were in front of the modest little house with geraniums, resigned to being witnesses of our own privation. Chalo arrived in his father's car, sporting an elegant white tuxedo; a few minutes later he left the house accompanied by Queca, who, with her long evening grown and upswept hairdo, hardly resembled our once playful classmate. Queca, smiling and clutching a satin evening purse, didn't even see us. An elusive vision, the last, because never again would things be the same. All of our hopes died instantly, at that very moment that would never let us forget the indelible image that brought to a close a part of our youth.

Almost no one hung around the plaza anymore, some because they were getting ready to enroll at the university, others because they were moving to other neighborhoods in search of an impossible replica of Queca. Only Roberto, who was now a delivery boy for a bakery, returned to the plaza at nightfall, where other young boys and girls now became the new gang and played our games so naturally that it seemed as if they had invented them. Sitting on his solitary bench, Roberto appeared to pay little attention to the goings on around him, but in reality his eyes were always fixed upon Queca's house. That way he was able to confirm before anyone else that Chalo had been only one episode in Queca's life, a kind of rehearsal preparing her for the arrival of the original, of which Chalo had been a mere copy: Billy Mulligan, the son of a United States consulate official.

Billy was freckled, redheaded, wore flowered shirts, had enormous feet, a boisterous laugh, and the sun, instead of toasting him, made him peel; but he always came to see Queca in his own car and not in his father's car. Nobody knew where Queca first met him nor how he came to be there, but she began to see him often, until she saw only him – his tennis rackets, his sunglasses, his camera – while the outline of Chalo gradually grew more and more opaque, smaller, and more distant until it finally disappeared altogether. Moving from the group to the type, the type to the individual, Queca had shown her hand. Only Mulligan would take her to the altar and, when they were lawfully married, he would have every right to caress those things we had dreamed about in vain for so long.

Disillusionment generally is something that no one can tolerate; it's either soon forgotten, its causes evaded, or it becomes the object of ridicule and even a theme in literature. It turned out that Fats Gómez went off to study in London, Peluca Rodríguez wrote a really ballsy sonnet, Armando Wolff came to the conclusion that Queca was nothing but a social climber, and Lucas de Tramontana deceitfully boasted that he had laid her several times out on the levee. Roberto was the only one who learned a true, valuable lesson from all this; it had to be Mulligan or no one. What good was it to be blond if there were so many light-skinned braggarts who were desperate, lazy, and failures? There had to be a superior state, inhabited by those who could plan their lives with confidence in this gray city and who could effortlessly reap all the best fruits the land had to offer. The problem was how to become another Mulligan, since he was a *zambo*. But suffering, when it doesn't kill, sharpens ingenuity; so Roberto subjected himself to a long, thorough analysis and outlined a plan of action.

First of all he had to dezambofy himself. His hair wasn't a major problem; he dyed it with peroxide and had it straightened. As for his skin, he tried mixed starch, rice powder, and talcum from the drugstore until he found the ideal combination; but a dyed and powdered zambo is still a zambo. He needed to know how the North American gringos dressed, talked, moved, and thought; in short, exactly who they were.

Back then we saw Roberto marauding about during his free time in various locales that seemingly had nothing in common, except for one thing: they were usually frequented by gringos. Some saw him standing in front of the Country Club, others at the Santa Maria school gates; and Lucas de Tramontana swore that he caught a glimpse of him behind a fence at the golf course, and someone else spotted him at the airport trying to carry some tourist's luggage; and then there were several who found him roaming about the halls of the US Embassy.

This phase of his plan was for him absolutely perfect. For the moment, he was able to see that the gringos were set apart from others by the special way they dressed, which he described as sporty, comfortable, and unconventional. Hence, Roberto was one of the first to discover the advantages of blue jeans, the virile cowboy look of the wide leather belt fastened by an enormous buckle, the soft comfort of white canvas shoes with rubber soles, the collegiate charm of a canvas cap with a visor, the coolness of a flowered or striped short-sleeved shirt, the variety of nylon jackets zipped up in front, or the sporty shirts displaying provocative, carefree slogans along with the logo of an American university.

None of these articles of clothing were sold in any department store but had to be brought from the United States, impossible for him to do. But, checking around, he discovered garage sales. Prior to returning to the United States, gringo families would announce in the newspaper their intention to sell everything they had. Roberto showed up on their doorstep before anyone else, acquiring in this way a wardrobe in which he invested himself and his life's savings.

With hair that was now straightened and bleached, a pair of blue jeans and a loud shirt, Roberto was on the brink of becoming Bobby.

All of this created problems. His mother said that no one would speak to him on the street, thinking he was pretentious. What was even worse, they would make jokes or whistle at him as if he were a queer. He never contributed a cent for food, he would stand for hours in front of the mirror, and he spent all his money on old clothing. His father, according to Roberto's black mother, may have been a worthless scoundrel who, like the magical Fu Man Chu, vanished only a year after they met, but at least he was never embarrassed to be seen with her, nor was he ashamed of being a pilot's mate on a boat.

In our group the first one to notice the change in Roberto was Peluca Rodríguez, who had ordered a pair of blue jeans through a Braniff purser. When the jeans came, he put them on and headed for the plaza to show them off, only to run into Roberto, who was wearing a pair identical to his. For days he did nothing but curse the *zambo*, saying he had ruined his act, that he had probably been spying on him to copy him. He even noticed that he bought Lucky Strike cigarettes and that he combed his hair with a lock falling over his forehead.

But the worst thing concerned his job. Cahuide Morales, the owner of the bakery, was a gruff, big-bellied, provincial mestizo who loved cracklings and native waltzes; and one who had broken his back for the last twenty years to make the business go. Nothing annoyed him more than for someone to pretend to be what he wasn't. Whether one was a mixed-breed or white didn't matter: what was important was *mosca, agua, molido*: He knew a thousand different words for money. When he saw that his employee had bleached his hair, he endured another wrinkle on his forehead; when he realized that Roberto had actually covered himself with powder, he swallowed a damn word that just about gave him indigestion; but when he came to work dressed like a gringo, the mixture of father, police, bully, and boss broke loose in him and he took Roberto by the scruff of the neck to the back of the store; Morales Brothers' Bakery was a serious business, and one would have to obey the rules; he had overlooked the makeup, but if he didn't come to work in uniform like the other delivery boys, he was going to boot him out the door with a swift kick in the ass.

Roberto was already on a roll and he couldn't go back now; he preferred the kick in the rear.

Those gloomy days were interminable as he looked for another job. His ambition was to go to work in a gringo's home as a butler, gardener, chauffeur, or whatever, but the doors were always shut in his face. His strategy lacked something, and that was a knowledge of English. Since he didn't have funds to enroll in a language academy; be bought himself a dictionary and began copying the words into a notebook. When he reached the letter C he threw in the towel; this purely visual knowledge of English wasn't getting him anywhere; but, then, there were always the movies, a school that would not only teach but also entertain.

In the balconies of the premier theaters he spent entire afternoons watching westerns and detective films in the target language. The plots were irrelevant; what mattered was the way the characters spoke. He wrote down all of the words he could understand and then repeated them until they were permanently recorded in his memory. By forcing himself to watch the films over and over again, he learned complete sentences and even entire speeches. In his room in front of the mirror he was suddenly the romantic cowboy making an irresistible declaration of love to the dance-hall girl, or the ruthless gangster uttering a death sentence while riddling his adversary with bullets. Besides, the movies nourished in him certain illusions that filled him with hope, leading him to believe he had discovered in himself a slight resemblance to Alan Ladd, who had appeared in one of the westerns dressed in blue jeans and a red and black plaid jacket. In reality, the only thing he had in common with him was his height and the yellow lock of hair he let dangle over his forehead. Dressed the same as the actor, he saw the film ten times in a row, always standing at the movie entrance after each showing, waiting for people to leave and hoping to overhear them say, but look, how strange, that guy looks like Alan Ladd. No one said it, of course; and the first time we saw him striking that pose, we laughed in his face.

His mother told us one day that finally Roberto had found a job, not in the home of a gringo as he had hoped, but possibly something better: the Miraflores Bowling Club. He waited tables in the bar from five o'clock in the afternoon until midnight. The few times that we went there we saw him excelling diligently. He waited on the natives in an unbiased, frankly impeccable manner, but with the gringos he was ingratiating and servile. As soon as one came in he was at his side, taking his order, and seconds later the customer had received his hot dog and Coca-Cola. He was encouraged to use words in English and, as he was answered in the same language, his vocabulary grew. Soon he possessed a good repertoire of expressions with which he won over the gringos who were delighted to see a native who understood them. Since Roberto was difficult to pronounce, the gringos were the ones who decided to call him Bobby.

And with the name Bobby López he was finally able to enroll in the Peruvian–North American Institute. Those who saw him during that period say that he was the classic bookworm, the kind who never missed a class, or forgot his homework, or hesitated to question the teacher about some obscure grammatical concept. Apart from the white students who for professional reasons were taking courses there, he met others like himself who, although total strangers from different backgrounds and other neighborhoods, nourished the same dreams and led a life similar to his. He especially became a good friend of José María Cabanillas, a tailor's son from Surquillo. Cabanillas shared the same blind admiration for the gringos that he did, and years ago he too had begun to smother the *zambo* in himself with really enviable results. Besides having the advantage of being taller and lighter-skinned than Bobby, he resembled not Alan Ladd, who after all was a second-rate actor admired by a small group of snobbish girls, but rather the indestructible John Wayne. The two of them made an inseparable pair. They finished out the year with the best grades, and Mr. Brown held them up as examples to the rest of the students, speaking of "their sincere desire to excel."

As buddies they must have had long, pleasant conversations together. They were always going here and there, their rear ends stuffed into faded blue jeans, and always speaking in English to one another. But it's also true that no one could stomach them; they muddled things so badly that neither relatives nor friends could put up with them. That's why they rented a room in a building on Mogollón Avenue, where they lived together. It was there they created a sacred haven that allowed them to mix foreign culture with their own and to feel that in the middle of this dismal city they were living in a California neighborhood. Each one contributed what he could: Bobby, his posters, and José María, who was a music fan, his Frank Sinatra, Dean Martin, and Tommy Dorsey records. What a fine pair of gringos they made, stretched out on the sofa-bed, smoking their Lucky Strikes while listening to "Strangers in the Night" and staring at the bridge over the Hudson River stuck to the wall. With one big try, hop, they would be walking across that bridge.

Even for us it was difficult to travel to the United States. One had to have a scholarship, or relatives already there, or lots of money. For López and Cabanillas, none of these were possible. They saw no other way out but to cut loose like other near-whites, thanks to jobs as airline pursers. Every year when openings were announced, they both applied. They knew more English than anyone else, liked serving others, were self-sacrificing and enthusiastic; but nobody knew them, nobody recommended them, and it was obvious to the interviewers that they were dealing with powdered zambos. They were turned down.

They say that Bobby wept and pulled out his hair and that Cabanillas attempted suicide by jumping from a modest second-floor window. Within their refuge on Mogollón Avenue they spent the darkest days of their lives; the city, which had always sheltered them, had turned into a dirty rag they covered with insults and scorn. But eventually their spirits lifted and new plans surfaced. Since no one wanted anything to do with them here, they would have to get out any way they could. They had no choice but to immigrate disguised as tourists.

For an entire year they worked hard and deprived themselves of everything in order to save enough for their fare and set up a common fund that would allow them to survive abroad. As a result, the two of them were finally able to pack their bags and abandon forever that detested city in which they had suffered so much and to which they never wanted to return as long as they lived.

It's easy to predict the events that followed, and it doesn't take much imagination to complete this parable. In the neighborhood we had direct sources of information: letters from Bobby to his mother, news from travelers abroad, and finally the whole story from a witness.

Soon Bobby and José María spent in one month what they had thought would last them six months. They soon realized that all the Lópezes and Cabanillases in the entire world had congregated in New York – Asians, Arabs, Aztecs, Africans, Iberians, Mayans, Chibchas, Sicilians, Caribbeans, Mussulmans, Quecbuas, Polynesians, Eskimos, representatives of every origin, language, race, and pigmentation – all of whom had one common goal: the desire to live as a Yankee, for which they had surrendered their souls and altered their appearances. The city tolerated them for several months, complacently, while it absorbed the dollars they had saved. Then, as if through a tube, it led them toward the mechanism of expulsion.

With great difficulty, they got an extension on their visas, while looking for steady jobs that would let them keep up with all the Quecas of the place; and there were many, although the girls just paraded in front of them, paying less attention to them than a cockroach would deserve. They wore out their clothes, Frank Sinatra's music became intolerable, and the mere thought of having to eat another hot dog, which was a luxury in Lima, turned their stomachs. From their cheap hotel they moved first to the Catholic shelter and then to a bench in a public park. Soon they discovered that white substance that fell from the sky, lightened their skin, and made them skate like idiots on the icy sidewalks, a substance which, by its very color, was nature's deceptive racist.

There was only one solution. Thousands of miles away, in a country called Korea, blond North Americans were fighting against some horrible Asians. According to the newspapers, the freedom of Western nations was in jeopardy and statesmen confirmed it on television. But it was so painful to send "the boys" to that place!

They were dying like rats, leaving behind pale, grief-stricken mothers in tiny farmhouses with an attic full of old toys. Whoever went over there to fight for one year would be on easy street when he came home; naturalization, work, social security, integration, medals. Everywhere there were recruitment centers. To each volunteer the country opened its heart.

Bobby and José María enlisted so they wouldn't be deported. And after three months of training at an army base they left in an enormous airplane. Life was a marvelous adventure; the trip was unforgettable. Having been born in a poor, miserable, sad country, and having known the busiest city in the world, with thousands of deprivations, it's true; but all this was behind them because now they were wearing a green uniform, flying over plains, seas, and snow-capped mountains, clutching powerful weapons and were becoming young men still filled with promise, exploring the realm of the unknown.

The laundress María has plenty of postcards of temples, markets, and exotic streets, all written in a small fastidious hand. Where could Seoul be? There are lots of ads and cabarets. Then came letters from the front lines that described to us the first attack, which forced him to take a few days off. Thanks to these documents, we were able to piece together fairly well the things that happened to him. Gradually, step by step, Bobby came closer to his rendezvous with destiny. It was necessary to reach a certain parallel and to confront a wave of yellow-skinned soldiers who descended from the northern hills like kernels of corn. For this, the volunteers, the unconquerable watchmen of the West, were there to lend a hand.

José María was saved by a miracle and proudly showed off the stump of his right arm when he returned to Lima months later. His squad had been sent to scout a rice field, where supposedly the Korean advance guard was waiting to ambush them. Bobby didn't suffer, José María said; the first blast blew his helmet off and his head rolled into a trench, all of its dyed, tangled hair hanging down. Now he had only lost an arm, but he was there, alive, telling his story, drinking cold beer, powder gone now and more zambo than ever, living comfortably off what he received as compensation for having been mutilated.

By then Roberto's mother had suffered her second attack, one which erased her from the world. She never read the official letter informing her that Bob López had died in action and was entitled to an honorable citation and remuneration for his family. No one could collect it.

Footnote

And Queca? Perhaps if Bob had known her story maybe his life would have been different or maybe it wouldn't have; no one will ever know. Billy Mulligan took her to his country, as agreed, to a town in Kentucky where his father owned a pork-canning business. They spent several months in ecstasy in that pretty house with wide sidewalks, a fence, a garden, and all the electric appliances invented by technology: in short, it was a house like hundred thousand others in that country-continent. Gradually the Irish in him, which his Puritan upbringing had suppressed for so long, began to reveal itself; at the same time, Queca's eyes grew larger and acquired that sadness typical of the Limeños. Billy was coming home later each night; he became addicted to slot machines and car racing; his feet grew bigger and developed calluses; he discovered a malignant mole on his neck; on Saturdays he filled up on bourbon at the Kentucky Friends' Club; he had an affair with a woman employee at the firm; he wrecked the car twice; his look turned into a fixed, watery stare; and he ended up beating his wife, the pretty, unforgettable Queca, in the early hours of dawn on Sundays, while he smiled stupidly and called her a shitty half-breed.

Note

1. Ribeyro uses the term zambo to refer to a person who is a blend of Indian and Negro.

CHAPTER 9

VIPs: Very Important People, Places, and Performances

Certain people, places, events, and cultural practices become iconic; they embody cultural myths or epitomize cultural values. Jesse Owens. Princess Diana. Why are certain people described as "larger than life"? The Statue of Liberty. The Beatles. The global circulation of such icons.

VIPs: Very Important People, Places, and Performances

When you visit a different country or a different region in your own country, there are certain sites you are told you simply must see, people you need to know about, and activities you must participate in if you are to get a feel for that culture. This is because the people who live in that country or region or village feel they represent something important about their area. For example, when I was first in Turkey I was told I simply had to see Atatürk's Mausoleum, a huge structure that dominates Ankara's skyline; in so doing, of course, I also had to learn something about Atatürk, the founder of the Republic. Often these very important places are spectacular – highly visible and well known – such as the Houses of Parliament in Britain, the Eiffel Tower in France, the Taj Mahal in India (figure 9.1), the Pyramids in Egypt, or the Statue of Liberty in the United States.

Additionally, there are certain people, including folk heroes and heroines, one must know about if one is to understand a given society. These are figures who have become cultural icons because they epitomize personal attributes and qualities that are culturally valued. In the United States these could be traditional American folk heroes like Horatio Alger and Paul Bunyan, and today might include figures from films such as *The Matrix*, *Star Trek*, or the *James Bond* series.[1] But they can also be important political figures like George Washington, Abraham Lincoln, John F. Kennedy, or Martin Luther King Jr. (figure 9.2). These would be typical choices for Americans, but so too, might Madonna or Oprah. The British might single out Queen Elizabeth (I and II), Winston Churchill, the Beatles, or the late Princess Diana.

Very important performances might include the celebration of the Fourth of July in the United States, Bastille Day in France, the Changing of the Guard at Buckingham Palace, or the celebration of Mardi Gras in Rio de Janeiro. But another type of important cultural

Investigating Culture: An Experiential Introduction to Anthropology, Second Edition.
Carol Delaney with Deborah Kaspin.
© 2011 Carol Delaney. Published by Blackwell Publishing Ltd.

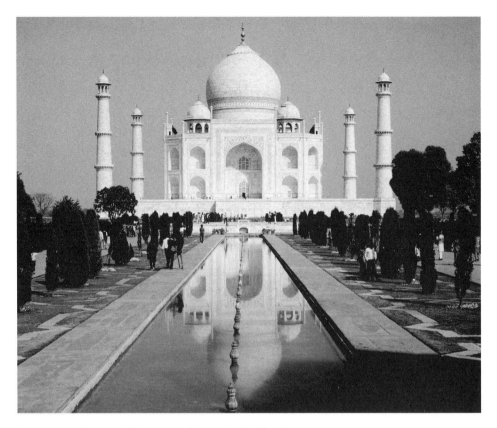

Figure 9.1   The Taj Mahal, Agra, India. © Nigel Hicks/Alamy.

performance could be a baseball game in the United States or the very mundane ritual of making and taking tea in England or Japan or Turkey.

To begin to understand what it is to be British, for example, it might help to know something about the traditional daily ritual of "tea." It might also help you get the rhythm of an English day and a sense of their culinary predilections. It would certainly help you to begin to understand aspects of British history: their relationship to India, perhaps, or the symbolism of the American Tea Party in Boston Harbor. What is it about baseball, for instance, that made it the "national pastime" of the Americans? Does cricket say something important about being British, and does soccer or tango say something equally important about being Brazilian (Archetti 1994, 1999)? Life cycle events, like births or weddings or the rituals surrounding death, are also very important cultural performances; the very different ways that such events are marked incorporate cultural meanings and values.[2]

In this chapter I have chosen to discuss the Grand Canyon, the British (and Turkish) tea ceremony, Princess Diana, the Beatles, the Statue of Liberty, American football, and the Olympics. These are my choices; they would probably not be yours. As I discuss at greater length later in this section of this chapter, to a large extent these choices reflect not only my individual preferences but also my ethnicity, socioeconomic class, age, gender – a wide

Figure 9.2   Martin Luther King Jr. Photo Rex Features.

range of factors. It would be foolish to claim that they are the only – or even the most important – VIPs. I offer them so that you might consider what makes these people, places, and practices cultural icons or archetypal practices. I also hope that you will look anew at those VIPs that you and your fellow students admire. Whom might you choose? What about Mahatma Gandhi? Rosa Parks? Amelia Earhart? Malcolm X? Albert Einstein? Cesar Chavez? Bob Marley?

I found this chapter was a particularly difficult one to write for several reasons. First, it demanded research into a range of topics that, perhaps because they are familiar and popular, are also difficult to get into perspective. Second, because this chapter does not have a single theme like space or language – which could run like a thread throughout the whole and provide coherence – there was no easy way for me to gracefully string my examples together. What's more, as you will see, cultural icons that appear to represent a particular culture cannot be confined within national boundaries; the very things that I found most representative of a certain culture were, I recognized, also global phenomena. That realization might seem to undermine the whole project. And in important ways it does, but I think you will find that this understanding makes us more aware of how porous the boundaries are, how much the so-called individual cultures of various people and countries overlap, and – perhaps most importantly – how the very idea of culture as a static contained object or condition is artificial and misleading. Culture is not and cannot be isomorphic with the nation conceived as a territory with specific boundaries; rather, it is a system of symbols, meanings, and myths that can spread as far and as wide as the people who are its avatars. It might be worth referring back to my earlier discussion on the use of the word *culture* and the concepts of culture in chapter 1.

The spread of culture, or specific aspects of specific cultures, is enabled both by the media and by personal contact. Those of us who have access to a wide range of media learn more about people in other parts of the world more quickly than ever before. Songs sung in one part are carried over airwaves around the globe. The death of an important figure becomes known almost immediately, and through television one can be present, virtually, at the funeral. Travel and immigration also bring us into contact with people whose cultural backgrounds are very different from our own. Films bring us visual images of spectacular cultural sites. Satellites allow millions of spectators around the world to watch sporting events as they occur. Such technological innovations that permit the spread of culture are symbolic of the changing social world we inhabit. It is becoming more and more difficult to say that *this* epitomizes British culture or *that* says something important about what it means to be an American. The people, places, and performances that I have chosen to discuss in this chapter both are and are not representative of their specific cultures. At the same time, I do not believe that we are moving toward a world culture, since each person, place, or performance that we look at is meaningfully incorporated in different ways in different cultural and national contexts. They represent different things not only to people living in different societies but also to people differently located within the same society. Nevertheless, there is overlap. Attending to the "conjuncture," as Marshall Sahlins calls it – where these overlaps occur and how they are variously incorporated – provides yet another way to investigate the things that matter to people and why.

If VIPs generally seem larger than life, it is because they are symbolically significant. In other words, they are more than just individual people, places, or performances. They embody, or are able to tap into, cultural myths that express qualities, beliefs, and values that, even if not consciously understood, nevertheless touch our emotions and make us feel that we, too, belong. We are enlarged because of their presence. The choice of who or what is a VIP will undoubtedly vary depending on one's race, class, gender, religion, and region: my choices in this chapter certainly reflect my own. At the same time, some things

tend to override distinctions of "region, class, formal religious affiliation, political sentiments, gender, ethnic group, and place of residence" (Kottak 1982: 74), even though they
may be experienced slightly differently depending on those variables. There are plenty of
studies that focus on differences but rather few that attend to the things that help to unify
and bind a diverse people into a social whole. It is the broad mythic frameworks that help
to accomplish this task.

Rather than assuming that we know what the important underlying cultural myths are,
it is more instructive to begin with the people, places, and performances that simply attract
our attention. Anthropologists should always begin with what is obvious and tangible –
with what is right in front of them – and only after intensive analysis dig to the deeper
symbolic and systemic levels. If, as I noted at the beginning, everything is interrelated, you
can begin the investigation of culture anywhere.

A Place

As I was thinking about the structure of this chapter, I was sitting at the rim of the Grand
Canyon (figure 9.3). Not only is this my favorite place, but also it is the place that I tell
everyone – friends, relatives, colleagues, and visitors – that they simply must see, at least
once in a lifetime. It is awesome in the true meaning of the word. Being in the presence of
the Grand Canyon is a humbling experience – your life and your problems are measured
against the depth of its temporal perspective – and even the loudest and most rowdy of
souls are subdued.

After driving through woods and meadows, you come upon it so suddenly it takes your
breath away. As one brochure says, "There is no warning … no time to prepare for the
visual impact of the Grand Canyon." Even though I have been there several times, including
a two-week rafting trip through it, I cry when I first catch a glimpse; I cannot help it,
because the impact is overwhelming.[3] Although the Grand Canyon is not normally considered to be a pilgrimage destination, the fact that 5 million people every year make the
journey indicates otherwise. Most people who visit feel it is a sacred place.

But what can such a *natural* wonder say about American *culture*? It is only by accident
that it exists in the United States. Its vastness, majesty, and indomitability perhaps express
something Americans would like to believe about their country. On a more mundane level,
the protection, maintenance, and presentation of the Grand Canyon do say something
about American beliefs and character. The dedication of it as a National Park in 1919, as
a treasure to be preserved for future generations, reveals a foresight that many people would
argue is in contrast to the generally shortsighted, short-term interests of American politics.
More important, although it is probably my love for the place that makes me view things
this way, I believe that many Americans display a less frequently celebrated aspect of the
national character when they are at the Grand Canyon – a quieter, more contemplative,
and less acquisitive side, a side that reveres nature rather than sees it as an exploitable
commodity. Perhaps the grandeur of this site taps into an undercurrent in the so-called
American psyche. This is what Catherine Albanese calls "nature religion" (1990) – a belief
that nature can be a means to the divine or something through which we are healed – and

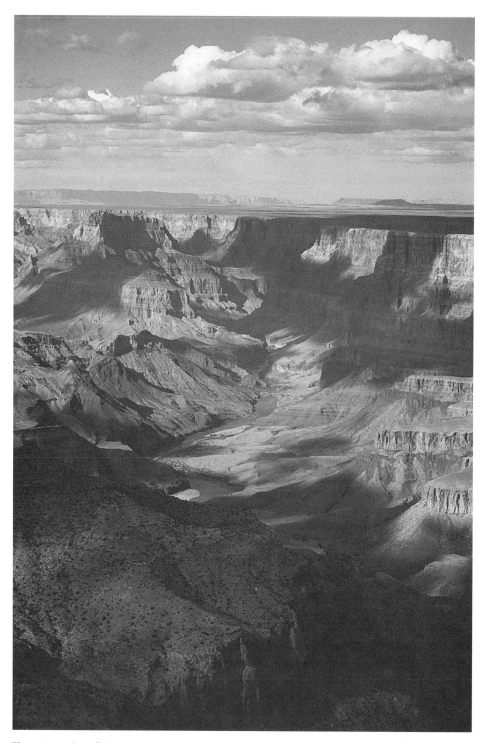

Figure 9.3   Grand Canyon, Arizona. © CORBIS.

which unites the early Puritans, the Transcendentalists such as Emerson and Thoreau, and a variety of New Age thinkers.

In 1979 UNESCO named the Grand Canyon a World Heritage Site, thereby transforming it – at least in name – from an American national treasure to an international site. Today, many of the visitors as well as service personnel at the Grand Canyon are not American. Not only do such individuals have an opportunity to view this extraordinary physical site, they also have an interesting opportunity to observe Americans: to view Americans in a distinct cultural setting and to consider why Americans value this place.

A Ritual Performance

Turning now to a performance that depends on a specific commodity – tea – let us attend to the ways it is ritualized in different cultural contexts. "Taking tea" can be an elaborate ceremony, as in Japan, or a very ordinary, daily ritual, as in Britain and Turkey (although each has its own more formal tea ritual). Since much has been written about Japanese tea ceremony, I will not reiterate that literature here;[4] instead, I will briefly discuss British and Turkish tea rituals.

British tea

Teatime, from my outsider's point of view, seems to represent something quintessential about being British – tea is the national beverage, as, I suppose, beer is the national beverage in Germany or wine in France. The British drink about 185 million cups a day according to one report (Beck, *Wall Street Journal*, October 30, 1998), and tea drinkers down an average of three a day.[5] Ironically, I came to appreciate the custom when I was outside Britain – at the British Institute of Archaeology in Ankara, Turkey. Perhaps it is in such outposts that certain customs are observed most strictly, because it is often when we are "strangers in a strange land"[6] that we cling most firmly to patterns that remind us of our home(land).

In any case, it was in Ankara that I became much more aware of teatime as significant not just to British well-being and as a means of marking time (cf. Hazan 1987), but also as a means of performing their identity. The course of the day's meals followed a very strict pattern. The day commenced with breakfast (which began with tea) and was followed by elevenses, lunch, tea, and, finally, supper. *Elevenses* was midmorning tea and was not as significant or elaborate as afternoon tea. Afternoon tea was and is *de rigueur*; the people at the British Institute were adamant about preserving the ritual of afternoon tea as a cultural institution in an "alien" land. It was, clearly, a way to maintain their distinct identity in Turkey.

"Tea," as one American in London commented,

> is a word used not only to describe the leaves of some Oriental plant that yield an almost-tasteless brownish infusion when you pour water on them, but also to designate the entire feast of scones and biscuits and cakes, jams and honey and clotted cream, even those silly little

cucumber-and-butter sandwiches, for which the sipping of the liquid is an excuse. (Wallberg, *Wall Street Journal*, March 13, 1990)

Words, obviously, of a confirmed coffee drinker. Nevertheless, as a good traveler and nascent anthropologist, he admitted, "I couldn't really experience English culture unless I began to enjoy their national drink." A proper tea, however, is not just the tea itself or even the food but also the service. Proper tea is made in a china teapot (or – in elite circles – in a silver teapot), warmed by swirling boiling water around its interior. Then one places the tea leaves in the pot and pours boiling water over them. The tea should steep for 5–10 minutes before being poured into fine, thin, china cups. Teacups and tea sets are prized possessions, heirlooms handed down over the generations; even people with little material wealth would manage to procure a proper tea cup.[7]

So what, you might ask, does all this have to do with being British? Although the Dutch East India Company first imported tea into Europe in 1610, it took another 50 years or so before English people began to develop a taste for it. "It is the years around 1700 which mark its establishment as a major force in British social life. 20,000 pounds weight of tea a year was being imported by 1700, but in 1721 the figure exceeded a million pounds weight" (Emmerson 1992: 5).

Tea was first enjoyed by the upper class as an expression of hospitality and became a sign of civility and refinement that eventually "trickled down" to the working class and bound all the people into one seemingly unified, seemingly genteel nation. By drinking tea you demonstrate that you are British. Teatime is longer than a "coffee break"; taking time for tea conveys a message that time with friends and family is important, that leisure is, or should be, an integral component of daily life, and that work time has to accommodate teatime.

Curiously, this stereotype of tea's cultural significance is just the opposite of tea's perceived meanings and uses during the industrial revolution in Britain. Then its stimulant qualities, in conjunction with the energy supplied by the sugar that was customarily used to sweeten it, were valued and deployed as a means of keeping workers productive over the long workday. As the workers of that era became habituated to increased consumption of tea and sugar, their eating and spending patterns shifted. In order to afford the quantities of tea and sugar to which they were accustomed, workers started to spend less money on nutritious food and thus, in the long run, their health suffered. People found that tea, especially when consumed with just a bit of food, was quite filling and could replace a meal – especially if followed, later in the evening, by a light supper. Although the typically starchy or sugary food served to accompany tea was less expensive than the protein and vegetables that might comprise a typical dinner, it was also less nutritious. In a cynical mood, one might characterize teatime as an institution whereby Britain managed to power the industrial revolution at lower cost by feeding its population less nutritious food. In *Sweetness and Power: The Place of Sugar in Modern History* (1985), anthropologist Sidney Mintz claims that while "[t]here was no conspiracy at work to wreck the nutrition of the British working class, to turn them into addicts, or to ruin their teeth" (p. 186), there were clearly very different class interests at work.

Although tea, as well as coffee and chocolate, was introduced into England in the seventeenth century, Mintz suggests that tea was pushed harder primarily because of capitalist interests in the production of sugar in the West Indies and the East India Company's interest in tea in China and India. At the end of the eighteenth century, a rural English minister lamented how odd it was "that the common people of any European nation should be obliged to use, as part of their daily diet, two articles imported from the opposite sides of the earth" (cited in Mintz 1985: 116). Indeed, "[s]o vital had sugar and tea become in the daily lives of the people that the maintenance of their supply had by then become a political, as well as economic, matter" (p. 116). Thus the greater the demand for these products among the British populace, the greater the potential for profit for the capitalists and, in turn, the greater the enslavement of native populations who produced these commodities.

One might also understand the institution of teatime to represent England's (former) world dominance, since the tea itself is imported from the countries that were its colonies, especially India, and, thus, the very act of drinking tea is a symbolic reminder of that domination – each sip consuming (the product of) its subordinates. So too, it is not surprising that Americans, in general, have eschewed tea – after all, it was over tea that Americans first staged a demonstration of their independence from Britain. When Americans did resume the consumption of tea, it was in a wholly new form as iced tea with lemon, mint, and honey. Thus transformed, Americans could drink the beverage and still commemorate the Boston Tea Party as a revolutionary icon.

Today in the United States, hot tea is being promoted again, as one can see in the proliferation of upscale teashops and the popularity of so-called exotic blends such as *chai*. Chai, however, is not exotic, except in the Orientalist imagination which associates the term with the traditional Indian brew of tea, milk, and spices. But *chai* is simply another word for tea and is cognate with *çay* in Turkish, *chá* in Portuguese, *chai* in Swahili, and *chá* in Chinese. Perhaps the name change is a way to reclaim a British cultural habit while denying British political domination.

Turkish tea

While many people associate *coffee* with the Turks, tea drinking is actually more widespread and more representative. Coffee must be imported, is more expensive, and, until recently, was a relative luxury, so the majority of the population consumed coffee infrequently. Excellent tea, however, has been grown in Turkey along the Black Sea coast for some time.

Turkish tea was traditionally made in a samovar but is rarely made that way anymore except, perhaps, in specialty teahouses for tourists. Most everywhere – in teahouses, in restaurants, and at home in both the city and the village – tea is made by putting one teapot on top of another. Tea is placed in the smaller pot on top; it is warmed as the water boils in the lower pot. When the water has boiled some of it is poured into the pot containing the tea leaves. More water is added to the lower pot and the whole apparatus then simmers for about half an hour or more – or until all of the tea leaves have settled to the bottom of the top pot. One would think that brewing the leaves for so long would produce a tea that was bitter and very strong but, instead, it produces a silky, soft tea that seems to have less caffeine than the typical British tea. A small amount of the concentrated tea is poured into tiny tulip-shaped glasses, boiling water is added to dilute it to the appropriate strength, and sugar is passed, with Turks typically putting 2–3 cubes of sugar in each tiny glass. It is considered rude if one does not drink at least three glasses. During my fieldwork I would often consume at least 10 glasses of tea a day, yet never had any adverse reaction and was able to sleep well. When I drink any kind of tea made in the normal Anglo-American fashion, I get very jittery – much more so than from coffee.

When villagers noticed I drank my tea without sugar they wondered if I was trying to save money, because skimping on sugar is a sign of stinginess. Sugar, as a former luxury commodity, acquired social significance; it became a symbol of generosity and hospitality.

As is obvious from the above, the making of tea is a lengthy procedure; one does not just "drop in" for a cup of tea expecting to leave soon afterward to get on with one's work. Once tea has been put on to brew, you are expected to settle in for a social visit that will last at least an hour and typically more. Even when villagers went to the fields to work, they brought along all of the tea-making paraphernalia and took leisurely tea breaks. (See figure 9.4.)

British anthropologist Chris Hann argues that the development of the tea industry and the habit of drinking tea in Turkey parallels "the domestication of the Turkish state" (Hann 1990), that is, as it was transformed from the Ottoman Empire into a modern democracy. He claims that the impact of tea – both its indigenous production and the adoption of it

Figure 9.4 A Turkish tea set. Photo by author.

by the population – has had an egalitarian effect. "It has helped foster among Turks everywhere (including migrant workers in West Germany and Saudi Arabia as well as all the regional cultures of Anatolia, including the Laz) the sense of belonging to a democratic national society" (p. 79). What he did not say, however, is that the democratic society is not *yet* egalitarian: tea drinking is still an activity that is often segregated by gender. Men gather in the *çayhane* (literally tea house) from which women are excluded. In villages there is usually only a *çayodası*– a room set aside where men gather for tea. Middle- and upper-class women in the cities can drink tea in *pastahane*s – establishments that basically serve pastry such as baklava, cakes, and tea. Today, upper- and middle-class young men and women can be seen having tea and cakes together in fancy, and expensive, pastry shops in Istanbul or Ankara, but this is not yet an option for people of lower income or women in rural areas; furthermore, such activity (i.e., unmarried men and women meeting together) is frowned upon by conservative Muslims. As we saw in chapter 7, the rituals surrounding the preparation of even the simplest foods or drinks have symbolic import and convey powerful nonverbal messages.

Sports

Soccer is probably the most widely played sport around the world; baseball and basketball are catching on elsewhere, but American "football is an almost uniquely American pastime,"[8] one that "unites Americans regardless of ethnic group, region, state, urban, suburban, or rural residence, religion, political party, job, status, wealth, gender, or sexual preference" (Kottak 1982: 46). Americans travel on weekends to high school or college football games or watch college or major league games on television and "more than half of the adult population of the United States regularly watches the annual Super Bowl" (Kottak 1982: 46). Such impressive cultural facts ought to make anthropologists take note. Yet for a long time sports were not considered a worthy focus of anthropological attention. Serious scholars exhibited "a contempt from which those of us who were having our most important experiences in sport felt ourselves daily to suffer." So confessed John MacAloon, a collegiate runner and Olympic hopeful turned anthropologist (MacAloon 1981: xi). Although studies of popular culture and the media have altered this somewhat, the serious anthropological study of sport remains in the minor league.[9]

If football, especially the Super Bowl, has, as many argue, displaced baseball as the "All-American" sport, perhaps we can read something about American cultural values in this shift. But what? Today, baseball seems nostalgic, harking back to a more innocent age; it was, and generally still is, played in the summer and culminates at summer's end in what is called "the World Series," even though the only teams playing are American. In comparison with football, baseball is a slower and more desultory sport, though nowhere near as slow and desultory as cricket.[10] Football is a contact sport and generally more violent, its players are more anonymous than in baseball, where home-run hitters and strike-out pitchers are eulogized and enshrined in the "Baseball Hall of Fame."[11] Baseball is played throughout the summer, a season that most Americans associate with a more relaxed pace of life, outdoor pleasures, and vacation time.

According to Kottak, football expresses the "technical side" of American society that characterizes industrial organizations and business values. In contrast, popular music like rock expresses the "creative side" of American society (1982: 47–8). He then explores these opposite sides of American cultural life: the value of teamwork versus individual accomplishment (as in the iconoclastic achievement of a rock musician), and the emphasis on traditional notions of gender (e.g., hypermasculinity among football players) versus the blurring of traditional gender roles (e.g., the celebrated androgyny of many rock stars). Football is quintessentially a team sport, and "the values associated with football: discipline, teamwork, coordination, dedication, and submission to authority" are those, according to Kottak, traditionally appreciated in the business world (1982: 52).

The qualities traditionally valued in football players are also valued in the military. It is therefore not surprising that sports, especially football, became an integral part of American military training at the end of the nineteenth century under the motto "The better the athlete, the better the soldier." Military personnel believed that sports would help build stronger bodies and prepare men psychologically for warfare. In military training, as in much sports training, instructors emphasize the importance of *team* spirit, and individual acts of courage are evaluated in light of how they reinforce or undermine the group's sense of solidarity: all for one and one for all. These qualities were so integral to the traditional American sense of manhood that even school curricula were adjusted to reflect them. Male students were expected to participate in sports as a patriotic duty, for the training they received was expected to prepare them for service to the country if they should be called upon to serve (Pope 1997: 147).[12] It is therefore culturally consistent that one of the more important football games in the United States each year is the Army–Navy game, instituted in 1890 – inspiring perhaps a bit of competition between two branches of the armed forces – a rivalry that continues today. Returning to my earlier discussion about what constitutes the most "American" of sports, perhaps the shift in emphasis from the more bucolic baseball to the more aggressive football reflects a similar shift in the way warfare is now conducted: in under a century warfare has grown more destructive, more violent, and much more anonymous. In a humorous paper modeled on the famous "Body Ritual among the Nacirema," one of my students, a former football player and aficionado of the game, made this point:

> The Super Bowl is the culmination of all the football ritual battles that are enacted in the months of autumn and winter. Mock-warriors are divided into thirty-two separate warrior-clans at the beginning of the ritual season. These clans are assigned to battle groups based on geographical location and traditional rivalries. The clans then combat one another on a rotating schedule. The most successful clans are then allowed to battle for the right to participate in the Super Bowl. Only the two best clans make it this far. The Super Bowl is the final battle of the ritual season, and determines which clan will be celebrated as the most dominant and ultimately triumphant.[13]

He also noted that the leaders of each clan (coaches) "who command the attack, defense, and specific actions of the warriors … are much like the leaders of the real armies of the Nacirema." In battle, the warrior is in a genuinely life-threatening position, whereas the football player's risks are minor by comparison and his potential rewards enormous: superstar status and multimillion dollar contracts. Despite these very real differences, there is another, very striking similarity: football players, like the rank-and-file soldiers in the military, are disproportionately black, while the individuals with the authority to give them orders – the coaches and commanders – are disproportionately white. Is this merely a coincidence?

Just as men have traditionally fought to protect the nation, they have also been traditionally been the combatants in ritual battles of sport.[14] Susan Brownmiller, who has written extensively on the gendered nature of war, points out that the age-old idea, "to the victor belong the spoils,"[15] often included access to women. "Down through the ages," Brownmiller writes, "triumph over women by rape became a way to measure victory, part of a soldier's proof of masculinity and success, a tangible reward for services rendered" (1975: 35). In one of the more sinister enactments of this principle, rape of the enemies' women is often committed to humiliate defeated soldiers. It was not until recently that such behavior was criminalized as a war crime.[16] So, let's apply these ideas to our examination of sports culture in the United States. What can we learn? If women were imagined as the spoils of battle in actual wars, and if we recognize that sports competitions are constructed as mock battles, is it then possible that male athletes might consider sex their due after winning a competition?

While we all know that women can make formidable athletes and competitors, regrettably they were traditionally confined to the role of spectators and cheerleaders. As we have seen, in many competitive displays of male prowess, women represented – and in many cases still represent – the prize won. More than that, however, the field on which the game is played is, I believe, symbolically female. The earth is symbolically feminine (as in the phrase "mother earth"), and women are identified, throughout Western literature, as fertile or barren ground, as land, and as soil of the nation. This analogy is encapsulated in the theory of procreation discussed earlier in which men plant their "seed" in women. In war, men fight to protect the land of the nation, to keep it from being violated or penetrated by the enemy. This was clearly appreciated by Mustafa Kemal (later to become Atatürk, founder of the Turkish Republic), who used gendered rhetoric to rally men to come to the defense of the *motherland* that had been prostituted under "capitulations" to foreign powers and was about to be dismembered by partition. His appeal was made to the sense of male honor to rise up against the intruders and eject them from their soil (see Delaney 1995: 186).

Such sentiments, I believe, also provoked the ire of many Muslims during the United States' Gulf War in 1991, where the use of gendered language and imagery was prevalent.[17] While the government of Saudi Arabia, somewhat reluctantly (see Clark 1992), permitted American soldiers (symbolically and overwhelmingly male) on their soil, many Muslims saw the presence of the infidels as defiling the land and as potentially defiling the purity of "their" women. The anger of Osama bin Laden against the United States has deep roots in the Gulf War: "The deployment of US troops to Saudi Arabia – land considered sacred by Muslims – not only has infuriated groups like bin Laden's but has also inflamed popular opinion" (*Boston Globe*, September 13, 2003; see also CNN.com posting, January 2001). The Americans, meanwhile, talked of *penetrating* the enemy and kept score of the bombs dropped and targets hit in a way that many felt was profanely and uncomfortably close to a football scoreboard.

Sports, even the Super Bowl, are *intra*national, that is, different teams, perhaps originally symbolizing different regional affiliations, are like rival clans *within* the nation. They enact a ritual – not a real – battle, although real battles are also ritualized. In any case, the ritual battle is taken to an entirely different level at the Olympics. There the competition is *inter*-national where the contest is among (representatives of) nations. While the Olympics does not symbolize any particular nation, participation in the Games has become an issue of national pride and honor for individual nations.

The Olympics

The Olympic Games, first organized in 776 BC in ancient Greece, were revived at the end of the nineteenth century after a hiatus of more than 1,500 years. The inspiration for the Games came from Baron Pierre de Coubertin (1863–1937), a French educator commis-sioned by the French government to form a universal sports association. His interest in the original Olympics was spurred, in part, by the archeological discoveries of ancient Olympia that were being displayed in the capitals of Europe at that time. The first modern Olympics were held, appropriately, in Athens in 1896 not far from the ancient site. Although the idea was to bring nations together in unity and friendship, the Games promoted competition.[18] The modern Olympics continue to be an arena in which each nation competes against others: to win the privilege of hosting the Games, to best others through the size of the national team and the number of sports in which it competes, to have the most impressive uniforms or the most fantastic stories of achievement by individual athletes, and, above all else, to win the most (gold) medals. The athletes who are selected to participate are intended as representatives of their nation; they are theoretically the best each nation has to offer inasmuch as their success or failure reflects on the honor of their nation as a whole. Interestingly, while each team as a whole represents one nation, the teams are actually composed of several subteams that compete on behalf of the national team in the various events. The language of "national teams" belies the heterogeneous composition of those teams, just as the rhetoric of a homogeneous social body belies the heterogeneity of each nation.

The Games recognize three kinds or levels of identity – the individual, the nation-state, and humankind (MacAloon 1984: 252) – but the nation-state seems to be the most salient. When a team or individual receives the gold medal, their national anthem is played and their own pride and honor appear to merge with that of the nation. But the symbolism stops there. While the individuals represent the nation at the Olympics, the Games are not like the Miss World Pageant in which the winner is said to represent the world.[19]

The winners in games at the Olympics represent their own nation, not a generic human-kind. That seems to reflect the beliefs of Pierre de Coubertin. For him, according to Olympic scholar John MacAloon, humankind

> exists … not in spite of, but because of social and cultural diversity … true internationalism
> understands cultural differences as an enduring and marvelous feature of the human land-

scape and … world peace depends upon the celebration of human diversity and not the eradication of it. (MacAloon 1984: 252)

To be human is not to be "everyman."

The human body – its techniques and capabilities – is, not surprisingly, the primary focus of the Games. And yet it is not the generic human body but these athletic bodies that come to symbolize the nation. This was made clear during the Olympics that were hosted by Germany in Berlin in the summer of 1936. The basic story is familiar to us all. Since coming to power Adolf Hitler had been promoting sport and "physical culture" among German youth (see Mosse 1985) and proclaiming the superiority of the Aryan body. He believed that history was the record of struggles among races and he prophesied that the Aryan race, centered in Germany, would be the final victor of these struggles because of its superiority. Because of Hitler's policies, several countries considered boycotting the 1936 Games. Although the proposal was, in the end, rejected, the Nazis tried to deflect international criticism during the Olympics by putting a humane face on their regime, minimizing the racist and militaristic character of their government, and courting foreign spectators and journalists. But all did not go as planned. Enter Jesse Owens, an African American who was born in Alabama, educated at Ohio State, and a member of the US Olympic track team (see figure 9.5). In a single week in Berlin he won four gold medals, tying one Olympic record, setting three new Olympic records, and breaking a world record. Despite Owens's outstanding performance, Hitler refused to congratulate him because of his race. As sportswriter Larry Schwartz recalled with gleeful journalistic bravado, "When Owens finished competing, the African-American son of a sharecropper and the grandson of slaves had single-handedly crushed Hitler's myth of Aryan supremacy" (n.d.). In an interesting postscript to this dramatic cultural tableau, it is moving to see how gracefully Owens deflected the inclination by Americans and others to vilify Hitler's racism without recognizing the cultures from whence they came. As Schwartz wrote,

> Owens never rubbed it in. Just as sure as he knew fascism was evil, he also knew his country had a ways to go too in improving life for African-Americans. "When I came back to my native country, after all the stories about Hitler, I [still] couldn't ride in the front of the bus," Owens said. "I had to go to the back door. I couldn't live where I wanted. I wasn't invited to shake hands with Hitler, but I wasn't invited to the White House to shake hands with the President, either."

As a comprehensive cultural account of the Olympics, John MacAloon's work is essential reading. This athlete-turned-scholar studied anthropology with Victor Turner at the University of Chicago in the 1970s and made the Olympics the special focus of his research. He looked at the Games from various angles. He considered their frequency, observing that because the Olympics occur every four years, "for many people the routines of daily life grind to a halt for two weeks every four years. Weddings are postponed, crops go untended, work is interrupted, and the Olympics crowd most other topics out of conversation" (MacAloon 1984: 242). He considered the sites chosen for the Games, noting that the "faces of entire cities have been permanently altered by the Games, and their impact on regional

Figure 9.5   Jesse Owens at the Olympic Games, Berlin, 1936. Library of Congress, LC-USZ62-27663.

and national economies is considerable" (p. 241). If we thought the number of spectators at Super Bowl was enormous, it pales in comparison to the Olympics. As MacAloon wrote of the 1976 Games, "According to reasonable estimates, 1.5 billion people – approximately one out of every three persons then alive on the earth – watched or listened to at least a part of the proceedings" (p. 241). Since that time, the number of spectators both attending the Games and watching them on television has increased. The Games bring together athletes from around the world, as well as a diverse group of spectators. People of different nationalities, from a wide range of cultures, and speaking a plurality of languages attend – jostling together, dining together, and getting to know each other in a way different from other interactions because there is no other venue quite like the Olympics. Not only are those who journey to the host country on display, but also the nation that sponsors the Olympics has a rare opportunity to present an image of itself through various cultural performances, food, native dress, and important cultural sites and icons. Indeed, MacAloon uses most of the strategies that we have discussed in each chapter of this book to investigate the phenomenon of the Olympics: space, time, language, social relations, body, food, and clothes.

But what is it about the Olympics – about moments such as Jesse Owens's victories – that has so captivated the imaginations of so many people? What does it represent about our contemporary world? MacAloon finds the answer by distinguishing four kinds of performance genres: spectacle, festival, ritual, and game. While the Olympics incorporates and displays all of them, it is primarily a spectacle, and it is this aspect, he believes, that expresses changes in the world situation, namely, the movement toward globalization and interconnection expressed by such metaphors as the "Global Village" or "Spaceship Earth," and the growth of multinational institutions like the UN (1984: 267). MacAloon notes that while more nations are represented at the UN, the world audience of the Games is much larger. This he attributes to

the felt need for living, dramatic images of the "others" with whom we are increasingly conscious of sharing a biosphere and sets of political economies and ways of living. … From a subjective standpoint, the world has not shrunk, as we like to say, it has immeasurably expanded. Spectacle may be the genre which most reflects and refracts this social expansion. … If in our daily lives, we must increasingly take account of the "size" of the earth, then our performances must surely take account of it too. Spectacle may be society in action, groping on the level of expressive culture, toward a new order in a changing world. (pp. 267–8)

Durkheim wrote long ago that new social forms are created during periods of "collective effervescence" when groups of people are gathered in celebration. At the Olympic Games there surely are such moments, and there is always the possibility that they might create more widespread feelings of what Victor Turner called *communitas* – where we might get a glimpse of what it would be like to break down the barriers dividing rich and poor, white and black, male and female, nation and nation.

That, I believe, was the hope of Coubertin. The Games, for him, were meant to be just such a peaceful and joyful celebration.[20] The *communitas* achieved during the Games was not meant to gloss over social and political inequities and injustices, but to make attendees more compassionately aware of them and committed to doing something about them. Regardless of their celebratory nature, the Games have never been insulated from political eruptions; one need only recall the slight of Owens at the Berlin Games (1936), the killing of Israeli athletes at the Munich Games (1972), the American boycott of the Moscow Games (1980), the bomb at the Atlanta Games (1996), and Canadian and European protests against human rights violations by the Chinese government prior to the Beijing Games (2008). Rather than insulating the public from the political, the Games have become a vehicle for broadcasting political messages to an international audience.

There is yet another way that the Games are political. According to Nigerian scholar and cultural critic Chinweizu, it is questionable whether the Games are really even international or global. He contends "that the Olympic Games are neither in fact nor name the World Games they pretend to be – that is, they are not games organized by all nations, governed by all nations, and free from political domination by a parochial minority of nations" (1987: 201). African nations have, of course, sent teams to the Olympics but the Games have never been held in an African nation. Nor are representatives from African nations included on the governing board. Chinweizu writes,

> When shall we [Africans] stop tolerating our being treated as guests in international institutions? … We have integrated the U.N. and the Olympics: we have even collected some Nobel Prizes. But the owners and managers of these institutions repeatedly make it clear that we are barely tolerated guests. (pp. 206–7)

"The point," he says, "is not to put black nations on the map as it exists, but rather to remake the map." This sounds like Mazrui's views about the map of the world discussed in chapter 2. Chinweizu suggests several options for resisting the current state of Olympic administration: (1) hold the Games in a city in a predominantly black nation; (2) boycott or withdraw from the Games; or (3) withdraw and then initiate a World Games Organization, and "invite all the world to join on non-racist, non-hegemonist terms" (p. 208).

Chinweizu is a compelling spokesperson, and his cultural critique is part of a much larger intellectual and political tradition. I turn now to a discussion of a group of musicians that emerged from another country and other traditions, but also came to be associated with ideas of transglobal, pan-human resistance and celebration.

The Beatles

George Bernard Shaw said that the United States and England were two nations divided by a common language. What language could not do, the music of the Beatles accomplished, for they captured the minds and hearts of the better part of a generation on both sides of the Atlantic. (See figure 9.6.) According to one analyst, they were "the Pied Pipers who led the Western world absent-mindedly from a moribund Modern Age into the Age to come. … [T]hey composed the main musical soundtrack accompanying this transition" (Sullivan 1995: xi). Those of us who lived through the 1960s – both those coming of age and their parents – can all agree that a major social transformation was taking place. And

Figure 9.6   The Beatles in 1964. Photo David Magnus/Rex Features.

it happened very fast – from the parietals of my college days to the removal of them, from formal dates to the "be-ins" of the "flower children," from alcohol to mind-altering drugs, from a fear of sex to the sexual revolution, from a relative lack of political consciousness among the young to the civil rights movement, the free speech movement, and the antiwar movement. Not only did the social transformation happen fast, but also all these different changes were happening simultaneously.

By commemorating the Beatles as the embodiment or icon of the 1960s, I necessarily obscure other enormously significant figures of that time, like Martin Luther King Jr., who came to symbolize the civil rights movement and whose eloquence continues to inspire. Despite the vivid memory of such individuals, for many of us, the Beatles and their music came to symbolize the era, for they both reflected and contributed to its distinct cultural character. Like them, many of us really believed we could change the world – "All You Need is Love." Listening to their music as I write this, it all comes back. There was a brief window through which we glimpsed the possibility of a different kind of world. Regrettably, in retrospect, the hope that many felt, and the vision we tried to advance, provoked a virulent conservative backlash. Indeed, many of the leaders of that era – Martin Luther King Jr., Medgar Evers, John F. Kennedy, and Robert Kennedy – were assassinated.

How to explain the meteoric success of the Beatles? Was there some astral conjunction between their music and the times? The "mass reaction to the Beatles is without social precedent. No religious leader, politician, general or any other public figure has ever been lionized to such an extent or for so long a period" (Davies 1969: 273). If the Beatles were the most significant musical phenomenon of the twentieth century, as so many claim, what do they signify?

Like most Americans, I first saw them on the *Ed Sullivan Show* on February 9, 1964 – generally a stodgy program with a stodgy host. It was my sister's twenty-first birthday, I was two years older and, as a young married person, I was initially not as taken with them as were all the screaming teenagers from whom I wanted to distance myself. But despite my early resistance, I was soon a convert, and by the next year I had a poster of them prominently displayed in my living room. Their music seemed to beat to the pulse of our lives, and because they became cultural icons, their lives, both public and private – including their beliefs, problems, marriages, children, and divorces – became a means of gauging our own lives and the crises we were undergoing in tandem with theirs. Those of us who grew with them can remember exactly where we were when we heard of John Lennon's death in 1980, just as we can remember where we were when we heard of President Kennedy's death in 1963. So too, the subsequent deaths of Paul McCartney's wife Linda in 1998 and George Harrison in 2001 were painful reminders of our own mortality, especially for those of us who are their agemates. Now, accustomed as I am to having their music as a part of my life, I cannot help but wish they had left a song that would help guide us through the end of life.

Several commentators have attributed the success of the Beatles to "their magnificent, original music" (Sullivan 1995: 34). For Davies, the Beatles were modern-day bards, not unlike the ancient Celtic order of singing poets whose instruments were traditionally the guitar, lute, and harp.

> The most striking aspect of their music is the archaic aspect. … The melodic simplicity, limited range, simplicity of rhythmic content, modal tonality, elements of fourteenth-century style, clarity of diction, are all elements of bardic style. (Davies 1969: 275)

Although born in Liverpool, several of the Beatles claimed Irish ancestry, and Paul and John each had a musical parent, so it is not unlikely that they were familiar with Celtic poetic and musical styles.

> The most misleading part of their myth is the idea that Liverpool is 'nowhere,' for nowhere else in Britain – and probably the world – was beat music as alive as it was in the Merseyside scene when the Beatles cut their chops. Over three hundred bands worked the area … [making for] a competitive edge between groups that challenged them all to greater heights. (Sullivan 1995: 39)

Although the seaport was declining, there was a different kind of transatlantic traffic, as American sailors and the Liverpudlians exchanged music in the seamy city clubs. The Beatles "quickly outdid their peers with a talent and ambition that left all the others behind"

(Riley 1987, cited in Sullivan 1995: 39). They never remained in one musical mode but continued to transform it as they transformed their clothes and hairstyles – from the styles of the rough Teddy Boys to psychedelics to the styles of Eastern mysticism.

From Sullivan's perspective, the 1950s in England and the United States were drab. "The clothes people wore were dull: black, gray, dark blue or brown. Automobiles were basic black. Most movies were still shown in black and white. TV was still a black and white medium" (Sullivan 1995: 37). The Beatles brought a range of color into this milieu and in so doing broke apart the class-based social styles in both Britain and the United States.

In Britain in the 1950s, class was still a very important social indicator and was signified primarily by three things: accent, schooling, and pedigree. Sullivan asserts that a person in the UK "situates himself socially for others the minute he opens his mouth" and instantly places him or herself by region and by class (Sullivan 1995: 32). It is amazing, then, how these lower-middle- and working-class lads with nasal Liverpudlian accents and little education beyond what Americans would call "public school" rose so far as to be invited to Buckingham Palace in 1965 for an audience with the queen, when she bestowed on them the MBE – the medal of Member of the British Empire. Years later in 1997, Paul McCartney was knighted and became Sir Paul McCartney. Given their humble origins, Sullivan wonders how "all classes of British society – including royalty and aristocracy … embraced the Beatles with a frenzy of acceptance and bedazzlement little different from the intoxication felt by their teenybopper fans" (p. 32).

In the United States in the 1950s, the salient markers of social identity were race, religion, and money, although class status was also marked through such indicators as inheritance, accent, schooling, and a listing in the *Social Register*. Still, it is somewhat easier to understand the Beatles' success in the United States, since they embodied the American myth of Horatio Alger – that anyone with drive, fortitude, and a little talent can rise from "rags to riches." Of course, this myth, like all myths, promotes a partial truth by obscuring others, namely, the socially ascribed impediments of race and gender: the new bards were white and male. Yet even this reveals an aspect of the Beatles popularity: most of their fans, who were also white and nominally Protestant, were led by the Beatles to black musical styles, on the one hand, and to Hindu mysticism, on the other.[21]

We may never be able to explain the success of the Beatles, but part of the answer has to do with the extraordinarily fortuitous conjunction of talent, personality, and timing. Many people, especially young people, were ready to slough off the shackles in which they felt enchained and explore new possibilities. The Beatles provided the sounds, the words, and the sentiments that ushered in a new age for those individuals. It was a heady period well characterized by Durkheim's notion of "effervescence" that Sullivan also uses to describe the early period of their achievement. During periods of "collective effervescence," when people come together and merge their individual wills for the collective good, new creative elements are released which, in turn, help bring about social change. The Beatles embodied "collective effervescence" and communicated it to others. That time has passed, but their music has been passed down from parents and grandparents and continues to resonate today. While it certainly dates to and characterizes a particular period, it does not seem out of date. For many of us, their music lives on even though the band dissolved decades ago and two of its members have died.

Princess Diana: She Did Not Live Happily Ever After

For many, news of the death of Princess Diana in a car crash in Paris on August 31, 1997, was shocking. Somehow one tends to think royalty is immune from such all-too-ordinary but gruesome events. The announcement went around the world in a flash. But the terrible descriptions of her death along with that of her companion Dodi Al-Fayed cannot explain the extraordinary international outpouring of grief.[22] Such a reaction cannot be attributed simply to the fact that she was a princess, although that had something to do with it; nor was it entirely because of her good deeds or her lovely smile, even though they, too, had something to do with it. Why and how are we to understand that phenomenon? Many have tried, but perhaps it is never possible to completely comprehend such events. Carol Gilligan, a psychologist at New York University, wrote in the *New York Times*,

> I was surprised by my response to the death of Diana, Princess of Wales. I had not expected to feel such a raw edge of grief for this woman I did not know and whose life I had not particularly followed. (September 9, 1997, p. C4)

I confess I felt the same way, and I, too, had not paid too much attention to her life. Many people – especially many women – seem to have responded in similar ways. Why did she affect us like this? Famous people die all the time; why did her death, in particular, strike so many people so hard?

I think one could say that the death of Diana had greater cultural implications. In other words, a princess was killed, but a myth was shattered. She was the archetype of a very powerful myth that resides, subliminally perhaps, in the imaginations of many women. The myth, in essence, is of the young woman who, because of her sweet nature, will one day marry the handsome prince and live happily ever after. In the United States, United Kingdom, and Europe, children read, or are read, such stories from an early age and fantasize about them. They insert themselves into the myth so that "each individual story draws on a common culture" (Samuel and Thompson 1990: 2). By assimilating our own private myth to larger cultural patterns, or even by placing our own in opposition to them, we find meaning in our lives. Despite the reality that ought to dissuade them and that diminishes their own sense of agency, millions of girls still grow up dreaming that they, too, will one day marry the charming prince and live happily ever after. In their imagination, any man can be transformed into a prince.

Diana's wedding at St. Paul's Cathedral on July 29, 1981, had millions of people around the world glued to the television. She symbolized that dream come true: it was real, it did happen. People were entranced by her looks, her demeanor, her clothes, her hair, and sought to emulate her. When she gave birth to William and then Harry, she not only fulfilled her duty as a princess by providing an heir to the throne, but also became, in the eyes of her public, a loving and attentive mother. She was admired because she fulfilled the role of the "good mother" seemingly to perfection. Many lauded her as a role model. The fact that she had begun her career as a kindergarten teacher enlarged her mystique: she was enhanced in the eyes of many because her career took a back seat to her role as wife and mother, and her virtue as wife and mother was simultaneously enhanced by her affiliation with a career that underscored the image of the nurturing "good woman." Her later work only solidified such perceptions, for she championed causes (e.g., ending the use of land-mines and helping people with AIDS) that expanded her persona as the nurturing woman.

Then cracks began to appear in the image. "What drew women to Diana," continued Gilligan, "was that she failed publicly and, in doing that, shattered an *icon* that imprisons all women" (Gilligan 1997; emphasis mine).

> Things that happen to ordinary women happened to her. Her husband rejected her for another woman; she developed an eating disorder; she felt that she was all alone; she tried to kill herself. And then she broke the spell. She aired in the full public eye of the media humiliations that, for centuries, have silenced women because women feel that they reflect failures on their part and because speaking out carried the risk of further rejection and shame. … Like Eve she had come to know both good and evil and shared that knowledge. Unlike Eve she resisted shame and refused to hide. (Gilligan 1997)

When so public a figure does this, it opens a window and brings light to other women who suffer similar problems; it empowers them. Yet until the cracks began to appear, Diana was a conventional woman trying to play a conventional role; she had little interest in feminism. Only after her revelations did she attract feminist attention and become an icon.

> In Diana, the fairy-tale princess who was cruelly awakened to the world of hurt, betrayal, and humiliation, women of all ages found a mirror image of themselves, however magnified and glamorized. (Joyce Carol Oates, *Time*, September 15, 1997, p. 58)

Diana fulfilled, challenged, and ultimately succumbed to the myths about women we all share. For there is another, more sinister myth that collided with the one about the princess who marries the prince and lives happily ever after. That is the myth of what happens to independent women who seek their own happiness outside of conventional boundaries. Quite often they are killed, die a tragic death, or are left to die alone. Go to almost any opera (except for the comedies that end with a wedding), and you will see this theme played out over and over.

Diana's death fulfilled *exactly* that mythological scheme. Thus the reaction to her death is, I think, quite complicated. It is not only that women identified with the flawed "people's princess," as prime minister Tony Blair labeled her, but also because her tragic death per-sonified the specter created by the double standard that many women fear. Her pleasure was obvious and was displayed across the media; she was, at the time of her death, an unmarried mother and was enjoying the company of a man without her children in tow. It is not difficult to see how the conflation of the image of the good and devoted mother and of the sexually active woman created problems for the royal family (and no doubt for others). According to the mythology, she would, or should, be punished. For this reason, suspicions surfaced immediately – and repeatedly – that Diana's death was not an accident. Several investigations have concluded that her death was, indeed, an accident that resulted from the driver's state of intoxication and from the passengers' failure to wear seatbelts.

But many people still cannot accept that a death of such mythic proportions was a random event arising from commonplace causes.

After a long discussion about the nature of royalty, its meaning for Britain, and its importance "in order to warrant the degree of national sentiment her death elicited," British anthropologist C. W. Watson concluded that "Diana is for British society the royal sacrificial victim" (1997: 6). Her death allowed the nation to undergo "a cathartic rite of communal purification: the dross of their lives, the mistakes, the false starts, the failings, are sublimated in the dead person of Diana" (p. 7). It was not just a metamorphosis of Diana into sacrificial victim but her apotheosis into a saint that was the most popular image. This was evidenced by the most publicized reference that accompanied "one of the floral tributes laid by the roadside which … read: 'Born a Lady, Became a Princess, Died a Saint'" (p. 7). Even Diana's final resting place evokes the many myths she embodied and debunked. She is buried on a tiny island in the middle of a pond on the family estate at Althorp – in a setting that many would willingly characterize as fairy-tale-like. (See figure 9.7.)

Since her death, new tribute sites have popped up in London that express aspects of her mythological persona. In 1998, Mohammed Al-Fayed, father of Dodi Al-Fayed and owner of Harrods Department Store in London, established a memorial at Harrods that celebrated Diana and Dodi's fairy-tale romance with photos, a lipstick-smudged wine glass from their last dinner together, and an engagement ring bought the day before they died. In 2000, he

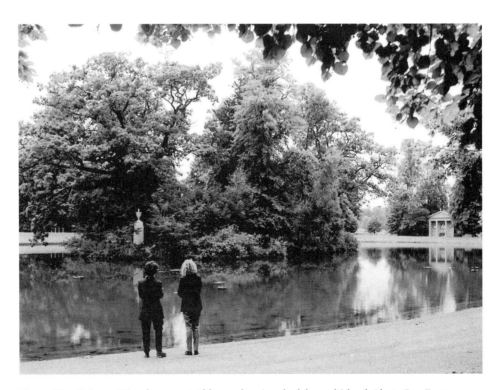

Figure 9.7   Princess Diana's grave at Althorp, showing the lake and island. Photo Rex Features.

added a statue called "Innocent Victims" to revitalize the suspicion that their death was deliberate. Also in 2000, the "Diana, Princess of Wales Memorial Playground" was opened in Kensington Gardens in recognition of her concern for children. In addition, there is a seven-mile Diana and Dodi Walkway that meanders through several royal parks in London, including Kensington Gardens, Green Park, and St. James's Park.

Blood and Nation

According to Watson, the blood of martyrs serves to regenerate the nation. Whether Diana can really be considered a "social martyr," as he calls her, is debatable, but it is important to consider how the blood of innocent victims often elicits the unification of a nation. While happy events such as a royal wedding or coronation are also unifying social forces wherein "the values of the community are celebrated and affirmed" (Watson 1997: 4), it is more often the dead who perform this function. I am thinking here especially of those who die in war, eulogized as those who *sacrificed* their lives for the nation.[23]

A classic anthropological article, "An American Sacred Ceremony" (1953) by Lloyd Warner, describes Memorial Day and the commemoration of the dead from World Wars I and II in a New England town. It was an early attempt to analyze how sacrifice for the nation performs a unifying function. What is it, asked Benedict Anderson in *Imagined Communities* (1983), about the nation – an imaginary construct– that millions of people have been willing to die for it? While the sacrificial rhetoric used to legitimate war continues, it has been less compelling since Vietnam divided rather than unified the American nation.

However, the deaths of all the people at the World Trade Center, at the Pentagon, and on Flight 93 that crashed in Pennsylvania on September 11, 2001, have, in many ways, served this unifying function. The wealth of analysis and interpretation of this extraordinary event is well beyond the scope of this chapter (I am still unable to look at the stack of news clippings and articles piled on a chair in my living room), yet a few words are in order. President Bush immediately labeled the September 11 event as "an attack on America," thus rendering the dead victims of war. Images of the destruction, which did look like a war zone, dominated the media for weeks and months after the event, and the victims were publicly mourned and eulogized; the *New York Times*, for example, printed short biographies of each of the dead and was still running the series almost a year later. Meanwhile, the terrible space left by the destruction of the Trade Center became hallowed ground. Ground Zero, as it is called, became a sacred place to which millions have made pilgrimage (see *New York Times*, January 17, 2002; *San Francisco Chronicle* June 23, 2002). Discussion immediately unfolded over the creation of an appropriate memorial. The two beams of light that reached to the heavens for a month in April–May 2002 were a spectacular and moving memorial, but alas they were impermanent. Some people wanted the World Trade Center to be built again exactly as before, while others thought that would be sacrilege and wanted to see a public park there. Still others thought it should be left as is – a devastating reminder of the event. But almost everyone seems to feel that the ground is sacred; it is, after all, a burial ground, and burial grounds are, by their very nature, sacred.

Still, the unifying effect of the 9/11 attacks gradually disintegrated, as rifts in the "imagined community" appeared. Some of the earliest rifts were created by the September 11 Victim Compensation Fund, which allocated restitutions to the victims' families by assessing each victim's financial potential at the time of his or her death: according to the fund manager, some victims were worth a lot more money than others, and their families were compensated accordingly. Next, disputes and dissension erupted among city planners, site developers, and the public over the ultimate fate of Ground Zero. Despite claims that a development plan was in place by 2007, and the breaking of ground for several new buildings in 2008, as of 2010, Ground Zero is still an empty pit, a function of irresolvable conflicts within the site development team. But perhaps the most consequential divisions in national cohesion emerged as a result of the Iraq war. Initiated by the Bush administration as an appropriate and necessary response to the 9/11 attacks, the Iraq war was undertaken amid widespread public and congressional support. As the length and cost of the war expanded, and the rationale for the war came into doubt, the public and their elected representatives divided into increasingly vitriolic camps. The legacy today is the breakdown of all civility among political leaders, political activists, and the public at large.

The Statue of Liberty

Out of the ashes, like a phoenix, the Statue of Liberty rose to new life, to become, once again, the quintessential symbol of the nation. Of course, the Statue of Liberty has long been a symbol representing America and a very popular destination for visitors and natives alike, but she was mostly taken for granted. I use the feminine pronoun since she is often referred to as "Lady Liberty." During the bicentennial celebrations of 1976 she had a brief period of prominence before receding into the background. At that time, she was seen in the company of the tall ships as they sailed into New York Harbor, and her distinctive, goddess-like headdress was copied (in aqua foam) and donned by millions throughout the nation during the celebrations.

The events of 9/11 catapulted her back into the forefront of everyone's mind. There were photographs and drawings of her in the news and on television. The *New York Times* made reproductions of their Statue of Liberty photo collection available for purchase. One photograph, "Liberty Framed by World Trade Center," became a poignant reminder of what had been and was no more (see figure 9.8). Although the flag also symbolizes the nation, only the Statue of Liberty personifies it. Not surprisingly, after 9/11 media images depicted her expressing the sentiments of America: in one she was weeping, and in another she was defiant with both arms raised. Also not surprisingly, she became sacred. As rumors spread that she was a target, she was cordoned off for months and closed to visitors. For additional protection, the president ordered planes to circle around her to keep watch.

Compared to Britain with its long history and its real crowned queen, the United States is a young country. Still it has its own crowned figure standing as a benevolent, protective deity at the entrance to our land. Why and how did she become this potent symbol?

A symbol doesn't just happen, for there is a process of construction and an accumulation of meaning. Many Americans are unaware that the Statue of Liberty was a gift from

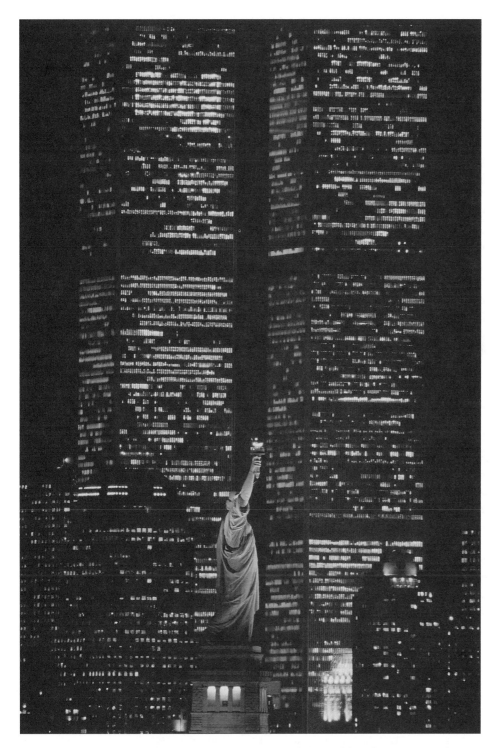

Figure 9.8 The Statue of Liberty and the Twin Towers of the World Trade Center. © Bob Krist/ CORBIS.

France. Not only was she not made in the United States, but also the very *idea* for her construction was French. Story has it that at a dinner party in Paris in 1865, a discussion of American democracy arose. The host, Edouard René Lefebvre de Laboulaye, commented to his guests,

> Wouldn't it be wonderful if people in France gave the United States a great monument as a lasting memorial to independence and thereby showed that the French government was also dedicated to the idea of human liberty? (OhRanger.com n.d.)

Frédéric-Auguste Bartholdi, a sculptor, was a guest at the dinner; the idea took hold, and he began to design the statue. Later he sailed to the United States at the suggestion of Laboulaye to discuss the possibility with the US government. He also determined that the statue would be placed at Bedloe's Island – his first sight of the New World. The steel skeleton to support Bartholdi's design was made by none other than Alexandre-Gustave Eiffel, the same man who designed Paris's famous tower.

Americans were not initially enthusiastic: it was too expensive (they were to pay for the pedestal while France paid for the statue), and many thought it was a New York thing that the rest of the country should not be forced to subsidize.[24] Finally, when it looked as if the project might languish in an *atelier* in France, Joseph Pulitzer used his newspaper, *The World*, to appeal to the people by promising that the names of all donors, regardless of the amount of their contribution, would be published. And so the money was raised. The statue was then dismantled, packed in 214 crates, shipped across the Atlantic, and reassembled on its pedestal on Bedloe's Island. Lady Liberty was finally unveiled on October 28, 1886, to a crowd of more than a million.

The words that have come to symbolize the statue – and which give the meaning that most Americans attribute to her – were not inscribed until much later. The last five lines were taken from a poem written by Emma Lazarus for the campaign to raise money and were engraved on a plaque that was attached to the statue in 1903, 17 years after the statue was unveiled. Lazarus never knew the role her poem was to play, since it was found among her belongings after her death in 1887. Later the lines were included in the Broadway musical *Miss Liberty*, by Irving Berlin, and in 1945 the entire poem was placed over the main entrance to the statue.

The New Colossus

Not like the brazen giant of Greek fame
With conquering limbs astride from land to land;
Here at our sea-washed, sunset gates shall stand
A mighty woman with a torch, whose flame
Is the imprisoned lightning, and her name
Mother of Exiles. From her beacon-hand
Glows world-wide welcome; her mild eyes command
The air-bridged harbor that twin cities frame,
"Keep, ancient lands, your storied pomp!" cries she
With silent lips. "**Give me your tired, your poor,
Your huddled masses yearning to breathe free,**

> The wretched refuse of your teeming shore,
> Send these, the homeless, tempest-tost to me,
> I lift my lamp beside the golden door!"

These words have helped create the myth that many of the downtrodden and oppressed around the world respond to as they set forth for America hoping to start a new and better life. The reality, when they arrive, is often quite different.

Although a woman symbolizes both liberty and America, and female figures, like Britannia, are often symbols of the nation, men traditionally represent it. Ironically, when these lines were written and the statue installed, neither American nor French women could vote, a point made by suffragettes who protested at the installation. And yet, the Statue of Liberty *has* been a beacon to all people, not just Americans, a major symbol of freedom, and a magnet for immigrants.[25] For many, it is undoubtedly a pilgrimage site.

Concluding Section: Pilgrimage, Myth, and Religion

In the discussions of some of the VIPs above, a few of the same words have surfaced repeatedly and in quite different contexts – words like myth, pilgrimage, and sacrifice. I would like to explore these further, for they help us understand why some things, but not others, become cultural icons. As noted in the opening section in this chapter, I believe that cultural icons tap into widespread beliefs or cultural myths. A relatively simple example is tea, which is not just a commodity but also a potent symbol: it represents the British way of life and their former world dominance, as well as American rebellion.

Some of the most powerful VIPs, however, cannot be confined to national boundaries, even though they symbolize a particular nation. VIPs like the Statue of Liberty and Princess Diana are globally recognized symbols, saturated with meaning, and larger than life and location. People in different places feel connected to them in some way and view them as beacons or lodestars providing light and guidance, or a point of reference by which to chart their own lives. Some people want contact and feel compelled to make pilgrimages to the sites connected to them, as if their magic will rub off on them.

Pilgrimage

Pilgrimage is most often associated with religion, and since religion is felt to be transnational, it is not tied to any specific nation. For example, Christians from many different countries make pilgrimages to Lourdes to be cured, or walk El Camino to Santiago de Compostela (Hoinacki 1996), or go to the house of the Virgin Mary near Ephesus in Turkey. Victor Turner, whose work we discussed in chapter 1, was very interested in pilgrimage because of its "liminal" character – one is neither here nor there but "betwixt and between" – which can have transformative effects. The studies he and his wife made of pilgrimages, primarily to shrines of the Virgin in Ireland and Mexico, are classic readings on the topic (see also Turner 1972–3).

These pilgrimages are not generically Christian, but specifically Catholic. Protestants have, in general, not made a practice of pilgrimage. In the English-speaking world, at least, Protestants tend to view life itself as a pilgrimage – an idea influenced, perhaps, by Bunyan's *Pilgrim's Progress* (1678). One is always "on the road," a phrase immortalized by Jack Kerouac and secularized by the beats of the 1950s.

A very different meaning is conveyed by the Muslim pilgrimage, or *hajj*, to Mecca. For most Muslims, unlike Catholics, there is one "canonical" or predominant destination – Mecca. (Shiite Muslims also make pilgrimages to the holy cities of Najaf and Kerbala, both in Iraq.) Muslims from all over the world make the pilgrimage to Mecca, which is considered the one, true, original home – the first place dry earth appeared upon the waters and the place closest to heaven. In some Muslim traditions, it is the place where Abraham was asked to sacrifice his son.[26] It is also where Muhammad cleansed worship of its idols and recalled the people back to the one true religion given in the beginning to Abraham. It is auspicious to die there.

While there are superficial resemblances between Christian and Muslim pilgrimages, they are quite distinct. And while Buddhists and Hindus (e.g. Gold 1988) also have sites of pilgrimage, they are not all undertaken for the same purposes or to accomplish the same goals. As anthropologist Clifford Geertz noted some time ago, "we need to look for systematic relationships among diverse phenomena, not for substantive identities among similar ones" (1973: 44).

This statement inspired me to compare the annual journeys that Turkish migrant workers make to their home villages and the *hajj* that Turkish villagers make to Mecca (Delaney 1990; and see figure 9.9). The migrants' homecoming, like the *hajj*, is conducted at great expense, in physical discomfort, and at risk of life, far exceeding any rational calculation of cost and reward. The explanation for both journeys is to be found not in an economic calculus, but in their similarities as pilgrimages to a "center out there" (Turner 1972–3) which offers spiritual benefits to its visitors. More precisely, the sacred *hajj* provides a structure of meaning for the migrants' homecoming. Thus Mecca is theologically the original and the ultimate home for Muslims, just as the natal village is birthplace and burial site for Turkish migrants. So too, while Mecca offers a glimpse of heaven, the home village offers a point of departure to heaven. The spiritual blessings of both pilgrimage sites are contained in the water – in the sacred well water of Mecca and the local well water of the home village – and imparted to those who drink it. All of these parallels are summarized in the word, *gurbet*, or exile. As a theological notion, *gurbet* refers to the experience of life on earth as exile from one's heavenly home. Turkish migrants use the same word to describe their feelings of being in exile from their natal homes.

By loosening the rigid classifications whereby pilgrimage can only be thought of in conventional religious terms, I was able to see more clearly the secular aspects of religious pilgrimage and the spiritual aspects of secular journeys. In a similar fashion, one might think not only of visits to Princess Diana's grave, Ground Zero, the Statue of Liberty, and the Grand Canyon as pilgrimages, but also of visits to Graceland (Elvis Presley's home) in Memphis, Bob Marley's mausoleum in Jamaica, Jim Morrison's grave in Paris, and even Disneyland which so many dying children long to see. As Kottak (1982) notes, "[T]here is a quasi-religious aspect to our relationship to Disney and his works; this emerges most

Figure 9.9   Circumambulation of the Kaa'ba – an important ritual during the *hajj* to Mecca. Photo Rex Features.

clearly in Americans' behavior at the two Disney amusement parks," which is not unlike that during pilgrimages made to more obvious religious sites. Such a study might seem frivolous to some readers, but the analyses uncover compelling aspects of national mythology.

Myth

Earlier I noted that cultural icons and archetypal practices partake of and express cultural myths, whether personal, family, national, or religious, or some combination of them. When I use the word *myth*, I do not mean an ancient or false story, but "a real or fictional story, recurring theme, or character type that appeals to the consciousness of a people by embodying its cultural ideals or by giving expression to deep, commonly felt emotions" (*American Heritage Dictionary*, 1991).

This is what Malinowski meant when he said, "Myth is not merely a story told, but a reality lived" (1954: 100). So, by mythic framework I mean the underlying stories we tell ourselves about who we are, where we came from, and where we are going – how we make sense of the world and our place in it. This has not been the traditional approach; instead, numerous theorists have tried to plumb them for what they might reveal about human psychology.

Perhaps the most famous example is Freud's interpretation of the Oedipus myth. He felt it reflected universal psychological dynamics as they developed within the family. The story moves us, he said, because it is ours: "it is the fate of all of us, perhaps, to direct our first sexual impulse towards our mother and our first hatred and our first murderous wish against our father" (Freud 1900: 4:262). While he may have captured something about Western, especially Victorian, family forms and values, he was unaware of very different kinds of kinship structures, gender meanings, and their implications (see Delaney 1998 and the discussion in chapter 5 about kinship).

In a similar way, French anthropologist Claude Lévi-Strauss believed that myths expressed something universal about the human condition – "myths get thought in man unbeknownst to him" (1979: 3). He believed they represented the unacceptable contradictions that all humans confront, as well as the underlying structure of the human mind, and not the generative beliefs of any particular culture. Despite the extraordinary detail he documented, the cultural specificity in myth was less important to him than the logical relations between the different elements or "mythemes."[27] While his method has been productive and cannot be dispensed with, I would argue strongly that cultural specificity is important, for people's psychology and identity are affected by the myths they listen to and pass on. As Mary Douglas noted, "Psychological explanations cannot of their nature account for what is culturally distinctive" (1966: 121).

A number of students of Franz Boas, such as Paul Radin and Zora Neale Hurston, were interested in psychology and myth, but unlike Freud and Lévi-Strauss, were not trying to uncover universal psychological structures and themes. In his now classic study, *The Trickster: A Study in American Indian Mythology* (1955), Paul Radin focused on the "trickster" – a prominent figure in Native American myths – to explore its *particular* psychological and cultural significance. He also gave space in his work for informants to speak, a move that foreshadowed some contemporary work. Zora Neale Hurston did so as well, as she traveled throughout the American South, recording folktales of African Americans. She captured some of the mythic structures, values, and worldview in a very intimate way, in part because she inserted her own voice and responses alongside those of her contributors. "Departing from standard ethnographic conventions that demand the use of a distant voice, Hurston readily admits she is part of the cultural scene she observes" (Hernandez 1995: 156). Her insistence on such positionality was extremely unusual for the time, which may be why her work languished until relatively recently; now it is fairly well accepted as standard practice. The specificity in her ethnography, short stories, and novels brings readers closer to the meanings and motivations of the people she studied, much as Elenore Smith Bowen did in *Return to Laughter* (1954 [1964]), which we discussed in chapter 1.[28]

We live by myths, and we cannot live without them; they are active forces in society. Even history – what we normally take to be a factual description of past events – is, according to famous historian William McNeill, constructed within a narrative framework that is, at base, mythic. This is the import of his short but incisive book, *Mythistory* (1986). The title, as one word, shows that he thinks myth and history are two aspects of the same thing. This is summarized in the following passage.

Myth and history are close kin inasmuch as both explain how things got to be the way they are by telling some sort of story. But our common parlance reckons myth to be false while history is, or aspires to be true. Accordingly, a historian who rejects someone else's conclusions calls them mythical, while claiming that his own views are true.

A century or more ago, when history was first established as an academic discipline [so too were comparative religion and anthropology], our predecessors recognized this dilemma, and believed they had a remedy. Scientific source criticism would get the facts straight. Whereupon a conscientious and careful historian needed only to arrange the facts into a readable narrative to produce genuinely scientific history. And science of course … was true and eternal.

Yet in practice something quite different occurred. Early in this century, thoughtful historians began to realize that the arrangement of facts to make a history involved subjective judgments and intellectual choices that had little to do with source criticism, scientific or otherwise. …

Facts that could be established beyond all reasonable doubt remained trivial in the sense that they did not, in and of themselves, give meaning or intelligibility to the record of the past. A catalogue of undoubted and indubitable information, even if arranged chronologically, remains a catalogue.

To become history, facts have to be put together into a pattern that is understandable and credible; and when that has been achieved, the resulting portrait of the past may become useful as well – a font of practical wisdom upon which people may draw when making decisions and taking action. (1986: 3–5)

The patterns that organize facts are the myths we live by. There are different kinds, and perhaps different levels, of myths which, in any one culture, are often interrelated. I mention only three: (1) personal/family myths, (2) national or ethnic myths, and (3) myths of origin (of the world, humans etc.).

1. Stories you cherish about your personal life give it meaning and seem to explain how you came to be the way you are. Family myths are those stories told by parents and relatives about you, your relatives and your ancestors. They give you a sense of your place and belonging but they often tap into myths of national or ethnic origin, that is, how your group came to be as a people.

2. There are two popular myths of national origin told by and to Americans; they are the stories about Columbus and his "discovery" of America in 1492, and the landing of the Pilgrims at Plymouth Rock in 1620 in search of freedom to practice their beliefs. Until fairly recently, we heard little about the betrayal of the native populations, the signing of treaties that were not kept, the raping of women, the spread of disease, and the massacres. If we did, they were rationalized in terms of the bravery of the conquerors and the perfidy of the Indians.

    All myths of national origin gloss over other stories. For example, generations of Turkish children have been taught that they are descended from the Ur Turks who migrated from Central Asia. This origin myth erases the numerous peoples and cultures that occupied the land since ancient times and with whom ethnic Turks intermarried over the centuries. It also sows dissension in Turkey's multicultural society, since only some of its members are, according to the origin myth, authentic nationals. National myths can also be intertwined with origin myths that have wider significance.

3. Genesis, the first book of the Hebrew Bible, is the predominant origin myth of the West. It purports to be about the origins of the universe, of humans, of plants and animals, of language and agriculture, and so on. But it is also the origin story of a particular people – the people of Abraham. Europeans who first came to America often interpreted the country as the new Israel, thus placing it within biblical myth. This was woven into the myth of "Manifest Destiny" that had significant implications for the way the native people were treated and their land appropriated. Myths of origin are extremely important; people fight over them and have been willing to die for them. After all, Navajos might not accept Genesis instead of their own origin story, nor would Christians easily accept an Australian aboriginal myth as equivalent to their own. Clearly, some of the most powerful myths are religious myths.

Religion

Although the study of religion was prominent among early anthropologists, many in the late twentieth century shied away from it, perhaps under the influence of modernization theory which assumed that the growth of science and rationality would lessen the hold of religion on society. For those who belittled the influence of religion, nothing could have been more shocking than the way religion flourished at the end of the twentieth century and the beginning of the twenty-first. Intellectuals heralded the collapse of "master-narratives" (explanatory frameworks such as Marxism, the Enlightenment, modernization theory, evolution, or progress and secularism), but the one thing they forgot to consider was religion, which encompasses peoples' notions of origin, destiny, and identity. I think it is extremely important not just for anthropologists but also for all people to have some knowledge and understanding of the world's religious beliefs and practices.[29]

For those who believe their religion is the whole truth and nothing but the truth, this section will be difficult.[30] From my own experience at Harvard Divinity School and among religious leaders, however, I came to realize that many of those most involved with religion and theology have a far more nuanced view of religion than do laypeople. Part of the problem is that in the United States, religion is not taught in public schools, and thus students do not learn appropriate ways to think about religious differences.

My interest in this section, and in general, is not on liturgy, ritual practices, prayers, or clergy but on religious myths or stories that are told to us and that we internalize. For many people, they form the most basic and pervasive notions of the way the world simply is. Since they are generally told in childhood, children are enveloped by the religious worldview long before they have the ability to see it differently. Parents who may not even be particularly religious often find themselves unwittingly transmitting religious myths precisely because they have become so much a part of the culture. On the other hand, fundamentalists understand very well why it is important to begin religious instruction early. Because religious myths are so pervasive, they are the most difficult to dislodge. They are part of what the person takes for granted, part of what the person is. Threats to his or her worldview can be felt as threats to his or her being. Thus, it should not be surprising that people will defend them with all their strength and unfortunately too often with violence.

Because I feel that religious concepts and worldview are an integral part of culture that both reflect and contribute to its construction, my own work has focused on the religious traditions that have had the greatest effect on Western culture, namely the monotheistic traditions – Judaism, Christianity, and Islam (see figure 9.10). Although many Westerners would not include Islam, it is a branch of the same tree. Despite the revelations given to Moses, Jesus, and Muhammad, all three trace their origins to the story of Abraham, which is why they are called the Abrahamic religions. Although they share a common "father"[31] and many of the same stories, practices, and beliefs, they are construed in three mutually exclusive worldviews – you cannot be both a Muslim and a Jew, or a Jew and a Christian, or a Christian and a Muslim – which is also why, I believe, the fighting is interminable. I see them as three sibling faiths fighting over the patrimony – the promises given in the beginning to Abraham – promises, primarily, to be *the* proper interpreter of God's word, although land, the afterlife, and the number of adherents are also important.

Let's Send All Our Missiles to the Sun

Since I have written a separate book on this topic (Delaney 1998), I will give only a very brief summary of it. The story of Abraham has troubled me ever since I was a child and led to my study of religion at Harvard Divinity School and my study of anthropology at the University of Chicago. According to Genesis 22 of the Bible and Sura 37 of the Qur'an, God asked Abraham to sacrifice his son, and rewarded him and all his descendents with a special covenant because he was willing to obey. There have been innumerable commentaries attempting to explain this story, but none of them has raised the question that motivated my research and my book: Why is the willingness to sacrifice, rather than protect, the child *the* model of faith at the foundation of these religions? Furthermore, what has been the social legacy of this model? The act God required of Abraham was not self-sacrifice or the offering of some*thing* valuable, meanings that are too often conflated, and that distort and diminish what was and is at stake. While the story, its interpretations, and the traditions surrounding it are complex, at the core of these religions is a moral vision that celebrates the patriarchal family, demands blind obedience, and vests in the few the power to interpret the sacred. More profoundly, they produce cultures in which sacrifice and death, rather than celebration and life, are the major unifying themes of society. But, as with the nation, they are unifying only for those who belong. We are witnessing the boundaries between nations being broken down and new, more inclusive, entities coming into being. Is it possible that something similar might happen with religious boundaries, beliefs, and the hatreds that keep people at each other's throats? It would be a wondrous world if *celebration* in recognition of our common *human* life were the worldwide unifying theme at the center of our spiritual values.

Figure 9.10 Fils d'Abraham, published by Brepols, Turnhout, Belgium.

To the Editor:

"Nuclear Designers From East and West Plan Bomb Disposal" (*Science Times*, Dec. 17), on a meeting of scientists to discuss disposal of nuclear weapons, prompts me to offer a suggestion I've been thinking about for some time. Let us mark the year 2000 with a worldwide celebration as we send all nuclear weapons to the sun, itself a nuclear entity.

I call it a potlatch – a feast traditionally practiced by Indian groups of the Northwest Coast and Alaska, in which the chiefs of warring groups tried to outdo one another in disposing of their wealth. Let them guide the leaders of the superpowers in planning the ceremony.

Ridding the planet of these weapons would be a priceless gift and a brilliant message to ourselves – "the human race has overcome the arms race and has chosen life instead of destruction."

Everyone could get involved, from governments to schoolchildren. Scientists could handle the technical side, and the rest of us could plan a party on a scale never seen before. Something of this magnitude would capture the imagination and just possibly might help to unite us to a peaceful world community.

It's just a thought, but we have eight years to try and make it a reality.

Carol Delaney

Stanford, Calif., Dec. 17, 1991 (*New York Times*, December 30, 1991)

Celebration rather than sacrifice can be a unifying theme as occurred in the 1960s and might have occurred with the turn of the millennium. I still believe it is possible but it will take a lot of work. My hope is that young people today can transform the stories, the metaphors, and the symbols as well as the economics and politics to bring this about. To do so, however, demands that you challenge taken-for-granted ideas and structures, look behind cultural myths, and imagine that things might be otherwise. The task ahead demands a very intensive investigation of culture, for which I hope this book is just the beginning.

Notes

1. See "The Story of Bond," where anthropologist Lee Drummond analyzes the deeper cultural significance of the films (Drummond 1988).
2. See chapter 3 for a discussion of weddings.
3. It was also the response of my daughter when she saw it for the first time in the summer of 2003.
4. For those interested, a classic is Kakuzo Okakura's *The Book of Tea* (1956). See also anthropologist Dorine Kondo's "The Way of Tea: A Symbolic Analysis" (1985), and Jennifer Anderson's "Japanese Tea Ritual: Religion in Practice" (1987).
5. It is interesting to compare coffee consumption by Americans, which, according to CoffeeResearch. com (n.d.), is 1.9 cups per day for American men and 1.4 for women. Clearly, I am over the top with four cups a day; however, I drink all my coffee half-decaf.
6. This expression is borrowed from Robert A. Heinlein's classic 1961 novel, *Stranger in a Strange Land*, a social satire and a meditation on cultural investigation. Heinlein tells the story of Valentine Michael Smith, an orphan of the first manned expedition to Mars, who was raised by Martians and then brought back to Earth by a second human expedition to Mars. Upon returning to Earth, Smith ironically finds himself a stranger in a strange land, because everything he encounters is foreign to him and he must now learn how to be human.

7. For a brief history of tea drinking in Britain and an interesting look at tea "equipage" – the equipment deemed necessary for a proper tea ceremony – see Robin Emmerson's illustrated *British Teapots and Tea Drinking: 1700–1850* (1992).

8. The problem is that football for Americans is not soccer but a totally different game.

9. See MacClancy (1996), who claims that although sport is now a major industry, it has received very little serious attention from anthropologists (perhaps more from sociologists).

10. Cricket might be considered a very English game, though it is also played in other countries and even in the Trobriand Islands. A classic anthropological film, *Trobriand Cricket*, shows what happened when the game was transferred to and translated into a different culture. The Trobrianders changed not only the size and material of the ball, but also the wicket and the bat. More important, the goal of the game was not to win but to tie in order to foster a friendly relationship with a potentially warring neighbor! Their cheers, costumes, and commentary, and the game itself, can be seen as a parody of the way it is played in the West.

11. A character in Richard Greenberg's play *Take Me Out* thinks "that baseball is a perfect metaphor for hope in a democratic society. … Equality, that is, of opportunity. Everyone is given exactly the same chance. And the opportunity to exercise that chance at his own pace" (*New York Times*, April 5, 2003).

12. Susan Brownell (1995) provides a parallel analysis of the Chinese government, which uses athletic training to cultivate a Chinese national persona and identity. See also Cynthia Enloe's *Bananas, Beaches, and Bases: Making Feminist Sense of International Politics* (1990).

13. "Ritual Battle among the Nacirema" by Brian Goodman. In this section I have also drawn on a paper by Becky Meldrum, another student of mine.

14. Two films that play with these stereotypes are *A League of Their Own*, about a very popular all-women's baseball league created during World War II, and *Private Benjamin*, about a pampered "dumb blonde" who joins the army when her husband dies and then gets tough; outsmarts all the men, including a general; and becomes part of an elite corps and eventually a top military advisor at NATO.

15. This phrase is attributed to William Learned Marcy, American politician and former US secretary of war from 1845 to 1849.

16. See Susan Brownmiller's *Against Our Will* (1975) and Cynthia Enloe's *The Morning After: Sexual Politics at the End of the Cold War* (1993).

17. The language and imagery of war should not be surprising since war has always been a gendered affair. For important analyses of this, see Brownmiller (1975) and Enloe (1993).

18. The five interlocking rings on the Olympic flag are meant to symbolize the five regions of the world joined together in the Olympic movement: Africa, the Americas, Europe, Asia, and Oceania (from EnchantedLearning.com n.d.). Two students (Jessica Mendoza and Chad Fore) in two different courses during the fall of 2002 wrote papers on the Olympics. I hereby wish to acknowledge their insights, which added to and helped confirm my own research.

19. Such claims to universality can, however, generate conflict. For example, before the 2002 Miss World Pageant began in Nigeria, thousands of Muslims protested that this public display of near-naked women was sinful. Any claim to representing the world that the pageant might have made was pushed aside, for devout Muslims certainly did not see their values represented by it. As a result of violent protests that caused the death of over 100 people in the northern part of the country, organizers announced that they would move the pageant from the Nigerian capital of Abuja to London.

20. The view of Pierre de Coubertin, a French aristocrat who was the primary instigator of the modern Games, was as follows: "If anyone were to ask me the formula for 'Olympizing' oneself, I should say to him, 'the first condition is to be joyful'" (quoted in MacAloon 1984: 248).

21. The same period of time witnessed the proliferation and popularizing of black musicians and musical styles in the United States and the Caribbean, which were important influences on the Beatles. This echoes Hebdige's observations (see chapter 8) about white British youth who defined themselves through their music and clothes, and modeled their countercultural styles on elements of immigrant black culture.

22. According to one reporter, Diana's death "drew an emotional response from the British that contradicted all stereotypes of the English as cold and unemotional" (Lennon 1998: 38), though this judgment depends, of course, on that stereotype.

23. When I was a Fulbright scholar in Belgium, my hosts thought it was very important to take me to all the World War I and II cemeteries where many Americans are buried. Clearly for them, the war dead signified a sacrifice not only for the nation, but also for the historical friendship between nations. This friendship continued through the Fulbright program and allowed me, an American, to spend a year as an honored guest in their country.

24. I have heard from a New Jersey resident that it is actually within the boundaries of that state, but most people associate it with New York. In my opinion, as most would agree, she is bigger than any state, even bigger than the nation, so the debate seems puerile. Costs for her upkeep ought to be part of a national budget; however, retired auto executive Lee Iacocca took on the job of raising the money as chair of the Statue of Liberty–Ellis Island Foundation (*Parade Magazine*, *San Francisco Chronicle*, December 15, 2002). Ellis Island is, of course, the place through which new immigrants passed and were registered. At the new immigration museum displaying its history, descendants of immigrants can trace their ancestry.

25. The symbol has endured despite the difficulties many immigrants face as they struggle to survive in the United States. It will be interesting to see how it fares as America squanders its moral standing among nations in the aftermath of the war against Iraq.

26. Other Muslim traditions have the spot in Jerusalem, as Jews and Christians also believe (see Firestone 1990). The Dome of the Rock, also called the Temple Mount, is now the site of a Muslim mosque. It is perhaps the most volatile place in the world, fought over by the sibling faiths. There have been plots by radical fundamentalist Jews to blow it up, an action that could very easily be the spark for World War III (see Gorenberg 2000).

27. See the bibliography at the end of the chapter for references to Lévi-Strauss's approach to myth (1963, 1969, 1973, 1978, 1979, 1981). Note the wealth of detail in the 4-volume set of *Mythologiques*, where each volume is over 500 pages! Another mythologist, perhaps more familiar to some of you, is Joseph Campbell ([1949] 1968), whose *Hero of a Thousand Faces* became very popular during the 1980s and 1990s. It is a delightful read, but it, too, is reductive, that is, he believes that all stories of heroes are at base one and the same. On the other hand, Marshall Sahlins's *Historical Metaphors, Mythical Realities* (1981) uses a structural approach to a very different end.

28. See the reference list at the end of the chapter for references to Hurston's work ([1935] 1978, [1937] 1991), and to the excellent review of it by Hernandez (1995).

29. One of the best courses I ever took as an undergraduate was a year-long course on the world's religious traditions. It made me aware of different worldviews, different ways of approaching the world, and some of the motivations behind historical events in a way that history courses never did. For interested students, there are at least three different kinds of texts to begin such a study. The first category includes books that discuss each different religious tradition noting the important beliefs, sacred texts, practices, and institutional structure (e.g., Oxtoby 2002; Smith [1958] 1991); the second category are often "readers" in the anthropology of religion that focus on particular themes such as sacrifice, or include classical articles by theorists of religion (e.g., Bowen 1998; Lambek 2002); the third, and arguably the most important, are the sacred texts themselves. Such study should always, however, be complemented by a study of the history and culture of the societies influenced by the religious traditions, and where possible speaking with those who believe and practice it.

30. I highly recommend the now classic *The True Believer* by Eric Hoffer (1951).

31. In the 1970s, many feminists began to question the patriarchal nature, language, and structure of institutionalized religions and the impact of these on social life and definitions of gender. (As noted in chapter 4 under the "Pronouns" subsection, these issues had been raised also by nineteenth-century feminists.) Mary Daly's *Beyond God the Father* (1973) was the first arrow launched in this new endeavor; now they are myriad. My own work has been part of this intellectual trend.

E X E R C I S E S

9.1. Your Own VIPs

A. If you had written this chapter, what VIPs (people, places, and/or performances) would you have chosen? For each one, write a bit about why these choices are meaningful to you personally.

B. Choose one of your VIPs, and explain how it is related to the social groups with which you identify, and how it reflects important cultural values of those groups.

9.2. The Biography of a VIP

A. Identify a VIP that was important to you five or 10 years ago, but is no longer important to you today. What did it signify to you at the time? Why is it no longer important to you now?

B. Identify a VIP that was important to you five or 10 years ago and is still important to you today. Why does this VIP remain important to you, when the other one does not?

Bibliography

Albanese, Catherine (1990) *Nature Religion in America: From the Algonkian Indians to the New Age*. Chicago: University of Chicago Press.

American Heritage Dictionary, 2nd ed. (1991) Boston: Houghton Mifflin.

Anderson, Benedict (1983) *Imagined Communities*. London: Verso.

Anderson, Jennifer L. (1987) "Japanese Tea Ritual: Religion in Practice." *American Ethnologist* 22: 475–98.

Anderson, Jennifer L. (1991) *An Introduction to Japanese Tea Ritual*. Albany: State University of New York Press.

Archetti, Eduardo (1994) "Masculinity and Football: The Formation of National Identity in Argentina." In *Game Without Frontier: Football, Identity and Modernity*, ed. Richard Giulianotti and John Williams. Aldershot, UK: Gower House, pp. 225–44.

Archetti, Eduardo (1999) *Masculinities: Football, Polo and the Tango in Argentina*. Oxford: Berg.

Bowen, Elenore Smith ([1954] 1964) *Return to Laughter: An Anthropological Novel*. New York: Doubleday.

Bowen, John R. (1998) *Religions in Practice: An Approach to the Anthropology of Religion*. Boston: Allyn & Bacon.

Bromell, Nick (2000) *Tomorrow Never Knows: Rock and Psychedelics in the 1960s*. Chicago: University of Chicago Press.

Brownell, Susan (1995) *Training the Body for China: Sports in the People's Republic of China*. Chicago: University of Chicago Press.

Brownmiller, Susan (1975) *Against Our Will: Men, Women, and Rape*. New York: Simon & Schuster.

Bunyan, John (1678) *Pilgrim's Progress*. London: Ponder.

Campbell, Joseph ([1949] 1968) *The Hero with a Thousand Faces*. Princeton, NJ: Princeton University Press.

Caplow, Theodore, and Williamson, Margaret Holmes (1980) "Decoding Middletown's Easter Bunny: A Study in American Iconography." *Semiotica* 32(3–4): 221–32.

Chinweizu (1987) *Decolonizing the African Mind*. Lagos, Nigeria: Pero Press.

Clark, Ramsey (1992) *The Fire Next Time: U.S. War Crimes in the Gulf*. New York: Thunder's Mouth Press.

CoffeeResearch.com (n.d.) [Home page]. www.coffeeresearch.com.

Daly, Mary (1973) *Beyond God the Father: Toward a Philosophy of Women's Liberation*. Boston: Beacon Press.

Davies, Evan (1969) "Psychological Characteristics of Beatle Mania." *Journal of the History of Ideas* 30(2): 273–80.

Delaney, Carol (1990) "The *Hajj*: Sacred and Secular." *American Ethnologist* 17(3): 513–30.

Delaney, Carol (1995) "Father-State, Motherland, and the Birth of Modern Turkey." In *Naturalizing Power: Essays in Feminist Cultural Analysis*, ed. Sylvia Yanagisako and Carol Delaney. New York: Routledge.

Delaney, Carol (1998) *Abraham on Trial: The Social Legacy of Biblical Myth*. Princeton, NJ: Princeton University Press.

Douglas, Mary (1966) *Purity and Danger: An Analysis of the Concepts of Pollution and Taboo*. London: Routledge & Kegan Paul.

Drummond, Lee (1988) "The Story of Bond." In *Symbolizing America*, ed. Hervé Varenne. Lincoln: University of Nebraska Press.

Emmerson, Robin (1992) *British Teapots and Tea Drinking: 1700–1850*. London: HMSO.

EnchantedLearning.com (n.d.) "Olympic Flag." www.enchantedlearning.com/olympics/printouts/Flag.shtm.

Enloe, Cynthia (1990) *Bananas, Beaches, and Bases: Making Feminist Sense of International Politics*. Berkeley: University of California Press.

Enloe, Cynthia (1993) *The Morning After: Sexual Politics at the End of the Cold War*. Berkeley: University of California Press.

Firestone, Reuven (1990) *Journeys in Holy Lands: The Evolution of the Abraham-Ishmael Legends in Islamic Exegesis*. Albany: State University of New York Press.

Freud, Sigmund (1900). *The Standard Edition of the Complete Psychological Works of Sigmund Freud, Vol. 4: Interpretation of Dreams*, ed. James Strachey. London: Hogarth Press.

Geertz, Clifford (1973) *Interpretation of Cultures*. New York: Basic.

Gold, Ann (1988) *Fruitful Journeys: The Ways of Rajasthani Pilgrims*. Berkeley: University of California Press.

Gorenberg, Gershom (2000) *The End of Days: Fundamentalism and the Struggle for the Temple Mount*. Oxford: Oxford University Press.

Hann, Chris (1990) *Tea and the Domestication of the Turkish State* (SOAS, Modern Turkish Studies Programme, Occasional Papers No. 1). Huntingdon, UK: Eothen Press.

Hazan, Haim (1987) "Holding Time Still with Cups of Tea." In *Constructive Drinking: Perspectives on Drink from Anthropology*, ed. Mary Douglas. Cambridge: Cambridge University Press.

Heinlein, Robert A. (1961) *Stranger in a Strange Land*. New York: Putnam.

Hernandez, Graciela (1995) "Multiple Subjectivities and Strategic Positionality: Zora Neale Hurston's Experimental Ethnographies." In *Women Writing Culture*, ed. Ruth Behar and Deborah A. Gordon. Berkeley: University of California Press.

Hoffer, Eric (1951) *The True Believer*. New York: Harper & Row.

Hoinacki, Lee (1996) *El Camino: Walking to Santiago de Compostela*. University Park: Pennsylvania State University Press.

Hurston, Zora Neale ([1935] 1978) *Mules and Men*, pref. Franz Boas. Bloomington: Indiana University Press.

Hurston, Zora Neale ([1937] 1991) *Their Eyes Were Watching God*. Urbana: University of Illinois Press.

Kondo, Dorine (1985) "The Way of Tea: A Symbolic Analysis." *Man* 20: 287–306.

Kottak, Conrad, ed. (1982) *Researching American Culture*. Ann Arbor: University of Michigan Press.

Lambek, Michael, ed. (2002) *A Reader in the Anthropology of Religion*. Malden, MA: Blackwell.

Lennon, David (1998) "London: Diana – One Year After." *Europe* 380 (October): 38–40.

Lévi-Strauss, Claude (1963) "The Structural Study of Myth." In *Structural Anthropology*. New York: Basic.

Lévi-Strauss, Claude (1969) *Mythologiques, vol. 1: The Raw and the Cooked*. New York: Harper & Row.

Lévi-Strauss, Claude (1973) *Mythologiques, vol. 2: From Honey to Ashes*. London: Cape.

Lévi-Strauss, Claude (1978) *Mythologiques, vol. 3: The Origin of Table Manners*, trans. J. and D. Weightman. New York: Harper & Row.

Lévi-Strauss, Claude (1979) *Myth and Meaning*. New York: Schocken.

Lévi-Strauss, Claude (1981) *Mythologiques, vol. 4: The Naked Man*. New York: Harper & Row.

MacAloon, John (1981) *This Great Symbol: Pierre de Coubertin and the Origins of the Modern Olympic Games*. Chicago: University of Chicago Press.

MacAloon, John (1984) "Olympic Games and the Theory of Spectacle in Modern Societies." In *Rite, Drama, Festival, Spectacle: Rehearsals toward a Theory of Cultural Performance*, ed. John MacAloon. Philadelphia: Institute for the Study of Human Issues.

MacClancy, Jeremy, ed. (1996) *Sport, Identity, and Ethnicity*. Oxford: Oxford University Press.

Malinowski, Bronislaw (1954) *Magic, Science, and Religion, and Other Essays*, intro. Robert Redfield. Garden City, NY: Doubleday.

Marty, Martin, and Appleby, Scott (1992) *The Glory and the Power: The Fundamentalist Challenge to the Modern World*. Boston: Beacon Press.

McGuigan, Jim (2000) "British Identity and the 'People's Princess.'" *Sociological Review* 48(1): 1–18.

McNeill, William (1986) *Mythistory and Other Essays*. Chicago: University of Chicago Press.

Merck, Mandy, ed. (1998) *After Diana: Irreverent Elegies*. London: Verso.

Mosse, George (1985) *Nationalism and Sexuality*. New York: Howard Fertig.

Mintz, Sidney (1985) *Sweetness and Power: The Place of Sugar in Modern History*. New York: Viking Press.

OhRanger.com (n.d.) "History of Statue of Liberty." www.americanparknetwork.com/parkinfo/sl/history/liberty.html.

Okakura, Kakuzo (1956) *The Book of Tea*. Rutland, VT: Charles E. Tuttle.

Oxtoby, Willard (2002) *World Religions: Eastern Traditions*. Don Mills, ON: Oxford University Press.

Pope, S. W. (1997) *Patriotic Games: Sporting Tradition in the American Imagination, 1876–1926*. New York: Oxford University Press.

Radin, Paul (1955) *The Trickster: A Study in American Indian Mythology*. London: Routledge and Kegan Paul.

Riley, Tim (1987) "For the Beatles: Notes on Their Achievement." *Popular Music* 6(3): 257–71.

Sahlins, Marshall (1981) *Historical Metaphors, Mythical Realities: Structure in the Early History of the Sandwich Islands Kingdom*. Ann Arbor: University of Michigan Press.

Samuel, Raphael, and Thompson, Paul, eds. (1990) *Myths We Live By*. London: Routledge.

Schwartz, L. (n.d.) "1936 in Sports." http://wn.com/1936_in_sports.

Smart, Ninian (1983) *Worldviews: Crosscultural Explorations of Human Beliefs*. New York: Scribner.

Smith, Huston ([1958] 1991) *The World's Religions*. San Francisco: Harper.

Stokes, Geoffrey (1980) *The Beatles*. New York: Times.

Sullivan, Henry W. (1995) *The Beatles with Lacan: Rock & Roll as Requiem for the Modern Age*. New York: Peter Lang.

Turner, Victor (1972–3) "The Center Out There: Pilgrim's Goal." *History of Religions* 12: 191–230.

Turner, Victor, and Turner, Edith (1978) *Image and Pilgrimage in Christian Culture: Anthropological Perspectives*. New York: Columbia University Press.

Turnock, Robert (2000) *Interpreting Diana: Television Audiences and the Death of a Princess*. London: British Film Institute.

Warner, Lloyd (1953) "An American Sacred Ceremony." In *American Life*. Chicago: University of Chicago Press, pp. 1–26.

Watson, C. W. (1997) "Born a Lady, Became a Princess, Died a Saint." *Anthropology Today* 13: 3–7.

R E A D I N G

The Impact of the Concept of Culture on the Concept of Man
Clifford Geertz

I

Toward the end of his recent study of the ideas used by tribal peoples, *La Pensée Sauvage*, the French anthropologist Lévi-Strauss remarks that scientific explanation does not consist, as we have been led to imagine, in the reduction of the complex to the simple. Rather, it consists, he says, in a substitution of a complexity more intelligible for one which is less. So far as the study of man is concerned, one may go even further, I think, and argue that explanation often consists of substituting complex pictures for simple ones while striving somehow to retain the persuasive clarity that went with the simple ones.

Elegance remains, I suppose, a general scientific ideal; but in the social sciences, it is very often in departures from that ideal that truly creative developments occur. Scientific advancement commonly consists in a progressive complication of what once seemed a beautifully simple set of notions but now seems an unbearably simplistic one. It is after this sort of disenchantment occurs that intelligibility, and thus explanatory power, comes to rest on the possibility of substituting the involved but comprehensible for the involved but incomprehensible to which Lévi-Strauss refers. Whitehead once offered to the natural sciences the maxim "Seek simplicity and distrust it"; to the social sciences he might well have offered "Seek complexity and order it."

Certainly the study of culture has developed as though this maxim were being followed. The rise of a scientific concept of culture amounted to, or at least was connected with, the overthrow of the view of human nature dominant in the Enlightenment – a view that, whatever else may be said for or against it, was both clear and simple – and its replacement by a view not only more complicated but enormously less clear. The attempt to clarify it, to reconstruct an intelligible account of what man is, has underlain scientific thinking about culture ever since. Having sought complexity and, on a scale grander than they ever imagined, found it, anthropologists became entangled in a tortuous effort to order it. And the end is not yet in sight.

The Enlightenment view of man was, of course, that he was wholly of a piece with nature and shared in the general uniformity of composition which natural science, under Bacon's urging and Newton's guidance, had discovered there. There is, in brief, a human nature as regularly organized, as thoroughly invariant, and as marvelously simple as Newton's universe. Perhaps some of its laws are different, but there *are* laws; perhaps some of its immutability is obscured by the trappings of local fashion, but it *is* immutable.

A quotation that Lovejoy (whose magisterial analysis I am following here) gives from an Enlightenment historian, Mascou, presents the position with the useful bluntness one often finds in a minor writer:

> The stage setting [in different times and places] is, indeed, altered, the actors change their garb and their appearance; but their inward motions arise from the same desires and passions of men, and produce their effects in the vicissitudes of kingdoms and peoples.[1]

Now, this view is hardly one to be despised; nor, despite my easy references a moment ago to "over-throw," can it be said to have disappeared from contemporary anthropological thought. The notion that men are men under whatever guise and against whatever backdrop has not been replaced by "other mores, other beasts."

Yet, cast as it was, the Enlightenment concept of the nature of human nature had some much less acceptable implications, the main one being that, to quote Lovejoy himself this time, "anything of which the intelligibility, verifiability, or actual affirmation is limited to men of a special age, race, temperament, tradition or condition is [in and of itself] without truth or value, or at all events without importance to a reasonable man."[2] The great, vast variety of differences among men, in beliefs and values, in customs and institutions, both over time and from place to place, is essentially without significance in defining his nature. It consists of mere accretions, distortions even, overlaying and obscuring what is truly human – the constant, the general, the universal – in man.

Thus, in a passage now notorious, Dr. Johnson saw Shakespeare's genius to lie in the fact that "his characters are not modified by the customs of particular places, unpractised by the rest of the world; by the peculiarities of studies or professions, which can operate upon but small numbers; or by the accidents of transient fashions or temporary opinions."[3] And Racine regarded the success of his plays on classical themes as proof that "the taste of Paris … conforms to that of Athens; my spectators have been moved by the same things which, in other times, brought tears to the eyes of the most cultivated classes of Greece."[4]

The trouble with this kind of view, aside from the fact that it sounds comic coming from someone as profoundly English as Johnson or as French as Racine, is that the image of a constant human nature independent of time, place, and circumstance, of studies and professions, transient fashions and temporary opinions, may be an illusion, that what man is may be so entangled with where he is, who he is, and what he believes that it is inseparable from them. It is precisely the consideration of such a possibility that led to the rise of the concept of culture and the decline of the uniformitarian view of man. Whatever else modern anthropology asserts – and it seems to have asserted almost everything at one time or another – it is firm in the conviction that men unmodified by the customs of particular places do not in fact exist, have never existed, and most important, could not in the very nature of the case exist. There is, there can be, no backstage where we can go to catch a glimpse of Mascou's actors as "real persons" lounging about in street clothes, disengaged from their profession, displaying with artless candor their spontaneous desires and unprompted passions. They may change their roles, their styles of acting, even the dramas in which they play; but – as Shakespeare himself of course remarked – they are always performing.

This circumstance makes the drawing of a line between what is natural, universal, and constant in man and what is conventional, local, and variable extraordinarily difficult. In fact, it suggests that to draw such a line is to falsify the human situation, or at least to misrender it seriously.

Consider Balinese trance. The Balinese fall into extreme dissociated states in which they perform all sorts of spectacular activities – biting off the heads of living chickens, stabbing themselves with daggers, throwing themselves wildly about, speaking with tongues, performing miraculous feats of equilibration, mimicking sexual intercourse, eating feces, and so on – rather more easily and much more suddenly than most of us fall asleep. Trance states are a crucial part of every ceremony. In some, fifty or sixty people may fall, one after the other ("like a string of firecrackers going off," as one observer puts it), emerging anywhere from five minutes to several hours later, totally unaware of what they have been doing and convinced, despite the amnesia, that they have had the most extraordinary and deeply satisfying experience a man can have. What does one learn about human nature from this sort of thing and from the thousand similarly peculiar things anthropologists discover, investigate, and describe? That the Balinese are peculiar sorts of beings, South Sea Martians? That they are just the same as we at base, but with some peculiar, but really incidental, customs we do not happen to have gone in for? That they are innately gifted or even instinctively driven in certain directions rather than others? Or that human nature does not exist and men are pure and simply what their culture makes them?

It is among such interpretations as these, all unsatisfactory, that anthropology has attempted to find its

way to a more viable concept of man, one in which culture, and the variability of culture, would be taken into account rather than written off as caprice and prejudice, and yet, at the same time, one in which the governing principle of the field, "the basic unity of mankind," would not be turned into an empty phrase. To take the giant step away from the uniformitarian view of human nature is, so far as the study of man is concerned, to leave the Garden. To entertain the idea that the diversity of custom across time and over space is not a mere matter of garb and appearance, of stage settings and comedic masques, is to entertain also the idea that humanity is as various in its essence as it is in its expression. And with that reflection some well-fastened philosophical moorings are loosed and an uneasy drifting into perilous waters begins.

Perilous, because if one discards the notion that Man with a capital "M," is to be looked for "behind," "under," or "beyond" his customs and replaces it with the notion that man, uncapitalized, is to be looked for "in" them, one is in some danger of losing sight of him altogether. Either he dissolves, without residue, into his time and place, a child and a perfect captive of his age, or he becomes a conscripted soldier in a vast Tolstoian army, engulfed in one or another of the terrible historical determinisms with which we have been plagued from Hegel forward. We have had, and to some extent still have, both of these aberrations in the social sciences – one marching under the banner of cultural relativism, the other under that of cultural evolution. But we also have had, and more commonly, attempts to avoid them by seeking in culture patterns themselves the defining elements of a human existence which, although not constant in expression, are yet distinctive in character.

II

Attempts to locate man amid the body of his customs have taken several directions, adopted diverse tactics; but they have all, or virtually all, proceeded in terms of a single overall intellectual strategy: what I will call, so as to have a stick to beat it with, the "stratigraphic" conception of the relations between biological, psychological, social, and cultural factors in human life. In this conception, man is a composite of "levels," each super-imposed upon those beneath it and underpinning those above it. As one analyzes man, one peels off layer after layer, each such layer being complete and irreducible in itself, revealing another, quite different sort of layer underneath. Strip off the motley forms of culture and one finds the structural and functional regularities of social organization. Peel off these in turn and one finds the underlying psychological factors – "basic needs" or what-have-you – that support and make them possible. Peel off psychological factors and one is left with the biological foundations – anatomical, physiological, neurological – of the whole edifice of human life.

The attraction of this sort of conceptualization, aside from the fact that it guaranteed the established academic disciplines their independence and sovereignty, was that it seemed to make it possible to have one's cake and eat it. One did not have to assert that man's culture was all there was to him in order to claim that it was, nonetheless, an essential and irreducible, even a paramount ingredient in his nature. Cultural facts could be interpreted against the background of noncultural facts without dissolving them into that background or dissolving that background into them. Man was a hierarchically stratified animal, a sort of evolutionary deposit, in whose definition each level – organic, psychological, social, and cultural – had an assigned and incontestable place. To see what he really was, we had to superimpose findings from the various relevant sciences – anthropology, sociology, psychology, biology – upon one another like so many patterns in a *moiré*; and when that was done, the cardinal importance of the cultural level, the only one distinctive to man, would naturally appear, as would what it had to tell us, in its own right, about what he really was. For the eighteenth century image of man as the naked reasoner that appeared when he took his cultural costumes off, the anthropology of the late nineteenth and early twentieth centuries substituted the image of man as the transfigured animal that appeared when he put them on.

At the level of concrete research and specific analysis, this grand strategy came down, first, to a hunt for universals in culture, for empirical uniformities that, in the face of the diversity of customs around the world and over time, could be found everywhere in about the same form, and, second, to an effort to relate such universals,

once found, to the established constants of human biology, psychology, and social organization. If some customs could be ferreted out of the cluttered catalogue of world culture as common to all local variants of it, and if these could then be connected in a determinate manner with certain invariant points of reference on the subcultural levels, then at least some progress might be made toward specifying which cultural traits are essential to human existence and which merely adventitious, peripheral, or ornamental. In such a way, anthropology could determine cultural dimensions of a concept of man commensurate with the dimensions provided, in a similar way, by biology, psychology, or sociology.

In essence, this is not altogether a new idea. The notion of a *consensus gentium* (a consensus of all mankind) – the notion that there are some things that all men will be found to agree upon as right, real, just, or attractive and that these things are, therefore, in fact right, real, just, or attractive – was present in the Enlightenment and probably has been present in some form or another in all ages and climes. It is one of those ideas that occur to almost anyone sooner or later. Its development in modern anthropology, however – beginning with Clark Wissler's elaboration in the 1920s of what he called "the universal cultural pattern," through Bronislaw Malinowski's presentation of a list of "universal institutional types" in the early forties, up to G. P. Murdock's elaboration of a set of "common-denominators of culture" during and since World War II – added something new. It added the notion that, to quote Clyde Kluckhohn, perhaps the most persuasive of the *consensus gentium* theorists, "some aspects of culture take their specific forms solely as a result of historical accidents; others are tailored by forces which can properly be designated as universal."[5] With this, man's cultural life is split in two: part of it is, like Mascou's actors' garb, independent of men's Newtonian "inward motions"; part is an emanation of those motions themselves. The question that then arises is: Can this halfway house between the eighteenth and twentieth centuries really stand?

Whether it can or not depends on whether the dualism between empirically universal aspects of culture rooted in subcultural realities and empirically variable aspects not so rooted can be established and sustained. And this, in turn, demands (1) that the universals proposed be substantial ones and not empty categories; (2) that they be specifically grounded in particular biological, psychological, or sociological processes, not just vaguely associated with "underlying realities"; and (3) that they can convincingly be defended as core elements in a definition of humanity in comparison with which the much more numerous cultural particularities are of clearly secondary importance. On all three of these counts it seems to me that the *consensus gentium* approach fails; rather than moving toward the essentials of the human situation it moves away from them.

The reason the first of these requirements – that the proposed universals be substantial ones and not empty or near-empty categories – has not been met is that it cannot be. There is a logical conflict between asserting that, say, "religion," "marriage," or "property" are empirical universals and giving them very much in the way of specific content, for to say that they are empirical universals is to say that they have the same content, and to say they have the same content is to fly in the face of the undeniable fact that they do not. If one defines religion generally and indeterminately – as man's most fundamental orientation to reality, for example – then one cannot at the same time assign to that orientation a highly circumstantial content; for clearly what composes the most fundamental orientation to reality among the transported Aztecs, lifting pulsing hearts torn live from the chests of human sacrifices toward the heavens, is not what comprises it among the stolid Zuñi, dancing their great mass supplications to the benevolent gods of rain. The obsessive ritualism and unbuttoned polytheism of the Hindus express a rather different view of what the "really real" is really like from the uncompromising monotheism and austere legalism of Sunni Islam. Even if one does try to get down to less abstract levels and assert, as Kluckhohn did, that a concept of the afterlife is universal, or as Malinowski did, that a sense of Providence is universal, the same contradiction haunts one. To make the generalization about an afterlife stand up alike for the Confucians and the Calvinists, the Zen Buddhists and the Tibetan Buddhists, one has to define it in most general terms, indeed – so general, in fact, that whatever force it seems to have virtually evaporates. So, too, with any notion of a sense of Providence, which can include under its wing both Navajo notions about the relations of gods to men and Trobriand ones. And as with religion, so with "marriage," "trade," and all the rest of what A. L. Kroeber aptly called "fake universals," down to so seemingly tangible a matter as "shelter." That everywhere people mate and produce children, have some sense of mine and thine, and protect themselves in one fashion or another from rain and sun are neither false nor, from some points of view, unimportant; but they are hardly very much help in drawing a portrait of man that will be a true and honest likeness and not an unteneted "John Q. Public" sort of cartoon.

My point, which should be clear and I hope will become even clearer in a moment, is not that there are no generalizations that can be made about man as man, save that he is a most various animal, or that the study of culture has nothing to contribute toward the uncovering of such generalizations. My point is that such generalizations are not to be discovered through a Baconian search for cultural universals, a kind of public-opinion polling of the world's peoples in search of a *consensus gentium* that does not in fact exist, and, further, that the attempt to do so leads to precisely the sort of relativism the whole approach was expressly designed to avoid. "Zuñi culture prizes restraint," Kluckhohn writes; "Kwakiutl culture encourages exhibitionism on the part of the individual. These are contrasting values, but in adhering to them the Zuñi and Kwakiutl show their allegiance to a universal value; the prizing of the distinctive norms of one's culture."[6] This is sheer evasion, but it is only more apparent, not more evasive, than discussions of cultural universals in general. What, after all, does it avail us to say, with Herskovits, that "morality is a universal, and so is enjoyment of beauty, and some standard for truth," if we are forced in the very next sentence, as he is, to add that "the many forms these concepts take are but products of the particular historical experience of the societies that manifest them"?[7] Once one abandons uniformitarianism, even if, like the *consensus gentium* theorists, only partially and uncertainly, relativism is a genuine danger; but it can be warded off only by facing directly and fully the diversities of human culture, the Zuñi's restraint and the Kwakiutl's exhibitionism, and embracing them within the body of one's concept of man, not by gliding past them with vague tautologies and forceless banalities.

Of course, the difficulty of stating cultural universals which are at the same time substantial also hinders fulfillment of the second requirement facing the *consensus gentium* approach, that of grounding such universals in particular biological, psychological, or sociological processes. But there is more to it than that: the "stratigraphic" conceptualization of the relationships between cultural and noncultural factors hinders such a grounding even more effectively. Once culture, psyche, society, and organism have been converted into separate scientific "levels," complete and autonomous in themselves, it is very hard to bring them back together again.

The most common way of trying to do so is through the utilization of what are called "invariant points of reference." These points are to be found, to quote one of the most famous statements of this strategy – the "Toward a Common Language for the Areas of the Social Sciences" memorandum produced by Talcott Parsons, Kluckhohn, O. H. Taylor, and others in the early forties –

> in the nature of social systems, in the biological and psychological nature of the component individuals, in the external situations in which they live and act, in the necessity of coordination in social systems. In [culture] … these "foci" of structure are never ignored. They must in some way be "adapted to" or "taken account of."

Cultural universals are conceived to be crystallized responses to these unevadable realities, institutionalized ways of coming to terms with them.

Analysis consists, then, of matching assumed universals to postulated underlying necessities, attempting to show there is some goodness of fit between the two. On the social level, reference is made to such irrefragable facts as that all societies, in order to persist, must reproduce their membership or allocate goods and services, hence the universality of some form of family or some form of trade. On the psychological level, recourse is had to basic needs like personal growth – hence the ubiquity of educational institutions – or to panhuman problems, like the Oedipal predicament – hence the ubiquity of punishing gods and nurturant goddesses. Biologically, there is metabolism and health; culturally, dining customs and curing procedures. And so on.

The tack is to look at underlying human requirements of some sort or other and then to try to show that those aspects of culture that are universal are, to use Kluckhohn's figure again, "tailored" by these requirements.

The problem here is, again, not so much whether in a general way this sort of congruence exists, but whether it is more than a loose and indeterminate one. It is not difficult to relate some human institutions to what science (or common sense) tells us are requirements for human existence, but it is very much more difficult to state this relationship in an unequivocal form. Not only does almost any institution serve a multiplicity of social, psychological, and organic needs (so that to say marriage is a mere reflex of the social need to reproduce, or that dining customs are a reflex of metabolic necessities, is to court parody), but there is no way to state in any precise and testable way the interlevel relationships that are conceived to hold. Despite first appearances, there is no serious attempt here to apply the concepts and theories of biology, psychology, or even sociology to the analysis of culture (and, or course, not even a suggestion of the reverse exchange) but merely a placing of supposed facts from the cultural and subcultural levels side by side so as to induce a vague sense that some kind of relationship between them – an obscure sort of "tailoring" – obtains. There is no theoretical integration here at all but a mere correlation, and that intuitive, of separate findings. With the levels approach, we can never, even by invoking invariant points of reference," construct genuine functional interconnections between cultural and noncultural factors, only more or less persuasive analogies, parallelisms, suggestions, and affinities.

However, even if I am wrong (as, admittedly, many anthropologists would hold) in claiming that *consensus gentium* approach can produce neither substantial universals nor specific connections between cultural and noncultural phenomena to explain them, the question still remains whether such universals should be taken as the central elements in the definition of man, whether a lowest-common-denominator view of humanity is what we want anyway. This is, of course, now a philosophical question, not as such a scientific one; but the notion that the essence of what it means to be human is most clearly revealed in those features of human culture that are universal rather than in those that are distinctive to this people or that is a prejudice we are not necessarily obliged to share. Is it in grasping such general facts – that man has everywhere some sort of "religion" – or in grasping the richness of this religious phenomenon or that – Balinese trance or Indian ritualism, Aztec human sacrifice or Zuñi rain-dancing – that we grasp him? Is the fact that "marriage" is universal (if it is) as penetrating a comment on what we are as the facts concerning Himalayan polyandry, or those fantastic Australian marriage rules, or the elaborate bride-price systems of Bantu Africa? The comment that Cromwell was the most typical Englishman of his time precisely in that he was the oddest may be relevant in this connection, too: it may be in the cultural particularities of people – in their oddities – that some of the most instructive revelations of what it is to be generically human are to be found; and the main contribution of the science of anthropology to the construction – or reconstruction – of a concept of man may then lie in showing us how to find them.

III

The major reason why anthropologists have shied away from cultural particularities when it came to a question of defining man and have taken refuge instead in bloodless universals is that, faced as they are with the enormous variation in human behavior, they are haunted by a fear of historicism, of becoming lost in a whirl of cultural relativism so convulsive as to deprive them of any fixed bearings at all. Nor has there not been some occasion for such a fear: Ruth Benedict's *Patterns of Culture*, probably the most popular book in anthropology ever published in this country, with its strange conclusion that anything one group of people is inclined toward doing is worthy of respect by another, is perhaps only the most outstanding example of the awkward positions one can get into by giving oneself over rather too completely to what Marc Bloch called "the thrill of learning singular things." Yet the fear is a bogey. The notion that unless a cultural phenomenon is empirically universal it cannot reflect anything about the nature of man is about as logical as the notion that because sickle-cell anemia is, fortunately, not universal, it cannot tell

us anything about human genetic processes. It is not whether phenomena are empirically common that is critical in science – else why should Becquerel have been so interested in the peculiar behavior of uranium? – but whether they can be made to reveal the enduring natural processes that underlie them. Seeing heaven in a grain of sand is not a trick only poets can accomplish.

In short, we need to look for systematic relationships among diverse phenomena, not for substantive identities among similar ones. And to do that with any effectiveness, we need to replace the "stratigraphic" conception of the relations between the various aspects of human existence with a synthetic one; that is, one in which biological, psychological, sociological, and cultural factors can be treated as variables within unitary systems of analysis. The establishment of a common language in the social sciences is not a matter of mere coordination of terminologies or, worse yet, of coining artificial new ones; nor is it a matter of imposing a single set of categories upon the area as a whole. It is a matter of integrating different types of theories and concepts in such a way that one can formulate meaningful propositions embodying findings now sequestered in separate fields of study.

In attempting to launch such an integration from the anthropological side and to reach, thereby, a more exact image of man, I want to propose two ideas. The first of these is that culture is best seen not as complexes of concrete behavior patterns – customs, usages, traditions, habit clusters – as has, by and large, been the case up to now, but as a set of control mechanisms – plans, recipes, rules, instructions (what computer engineers call "programs") – for the governing of behavior. The second idea is that man is precisely the animal most desperately dependent upon such extragenetic, outside-the-skin control mechanisms, such cultural programs, for ordering his behavior.

Neither of these ideas is entirely new, but a number of recent developments, both within anthropology and in other sciences (cybernetics, information theory, neurology, molecular genetics) have made them susceptible of more precise statement as well as lending them a degree of empirical support they did not previously have. And out of such reformulations of the concept of culture and of the role of culture in human life comes, in turn, a definition of man stressing not so much the empirical commonalities in his behavior, from place to place and time to time, but rather the mechanisms by whose agency the breadth and indeterminateness of his inherent capacities are reduced to the narrowness and specificity of his actual accomplishments. One of the most significant facts about us may finally be that we all begin with the natural equipment to live a thousand kinds of life but end in the end having lived only one.

The "control mechanism" view of culture begins with the assumption that human thought is basically both social and public – that its natural habitat is the house yard, the marketplace, and the town square. Thinking consists not of "happenings in the head" (though happenings there and elsewhere are necessary for it to occur) but of a traffic in what have been called, by G. H. Mead and others, significant symbols – words for the most part but also gestures, drawings, musical sounds, mechanical devices like clocks, or natural objects like jewels – anything, in fact, that is disengaged from its mere actuality and used to impose meaning upon experience. From the point of view of any particular individual, such symbols are largely given. He finds them already current in the community when he is born, and they remain, with some additions, subtractions, and partial alterations he may or may not have had a hand in, in circulation after he dies. While he lives he uses them, or some of them, sometimes deliberately and with care, most often spontaneously and with ease, but always with the same end in view: to put a construction upon the events through which he lives, to orient himself within "the ongoing course of experienced things," to adopt a vivid phrase of John Dewey's.

Man is so in need of such symbolic sources of illumination to find his bearings in the world because the nonsymbolic sort that are constitutionally ingrained in his body cast so diffused a light. The behavior patterns of lower animals are, at least to a much greater extent, given to them with their physical structure; genetic sources of information order their actions within much narrower ranges of variation, the narrower and more thoroughgoing the lower the animal. For man, what are innately given are extremely general response capacities, which, although they make possible far greater plasticity, complexity, and, on the scattered occasions when everything works as it should, effectiveness of behavior, leave it much less precisely regulated. This, then, is the second face of our argument: Undirected by culture patterns – organized systems of significant symbols – man's behavior would be virtually ungovernable, a mere chaos of pointless acts and exploding emotions, his experience virtually shapeless. Culture, the accumulated totality of such patterns, is not just an ornament of human existence but – the principal basis of its specificity – an essential condition for it.

Within anthropology some of the most telling evidence in support of such a position comes from recent advances in our understanding of what used to be called the descent of man: the emergence of *Homo sapiens* out of his general primate background. Of these advances three are of critical importance: (1) the discarding of a sequential view of the relations between the physical evolution and the cultural development of man in favor of an overlap or interactive view; (2) the discovery that the bulk of the biological changes that produced modern man out of his most immediate progenitors took place in the central nervous system and most especially in the brain; (3) the realization that man is, in physical terms, an incomplete, an unfinished, animal; that what sets him off most graphically from nonmen is less his sheer ability to learn (great as that is) than how much and what particular sorts of things he *has* to learn before he is able to function at all. Let me take each of these points in turn.

The traditional view of the relations between the biological and the cultural advance of man was that the former, the biological, was for all intents and purposes completed before the latter, the cultural, began. That is to say, it was again stratigraphic: Man's physical being evolved, through the usual mechanisms of genetic variation and natural selection, up to the point where his anatomical structure had arrived at more or less the status at which we find it today; then cultural development got under way. At some particular stage in his phylogenetic history, a marginal genetic change of some sort rendered him capable of producing and carrying culture, and thenceforth his form of adaptive response to environmental pressures was almost exclusively cultural rather than genetic. As he spread over the globe, he wore furs in cold climates and loin cloths (or nothing at all) in warm ones; he didn't alter his innate mode of response to environmental temperature. He made weapons to extend his inherited predatory powers and cooked foods to render a wider range of them digestible. Man became man, the story continues, when, having crossed some mental Rubicon, he became able to transmit "knowledge, belief, law, morals, custom" (to quote the items of Sir Edward Tylor's classical definition of culture) to his descendants and his neighbors through teaching and to acquire them from his ancestors and his neighbors through learning. After that magical moment, the advance of the hominids depended almost entirely on cultural accumulation, on the slow growth of conventional practices, rather than, as it had for ages past, on physical organic change.

The only trouble is that such a moment does not seem to have existed. By the most recent estimates the transition to the cultural mode of life took the genus *Homo* several million years to accomplish; and stretched out in such a manner, it involved not one or a handful of marginal genetic changes but a long, complex, and closely ordered sequence of them.

In the current view, the evolution of *Homo sapiens* – modern man – out of his immediate pre*sapiens* background got definitely under way nearly four million years ago with the appearance of the now famous Australopithecines – the so-called ape men of southern and eastern Africa – and culminated with the emergence of *sapiens* himself only some one to two or three hundred thousand years ago. Thus, as at least elemental forms of cultural, or if you wish protocultural, activity (simple toolmaking, hunting, and so on) seem to have been present among some of the Australopithecines, there was an overlap of, as I say, well over a million years between the beginning of culture and the appearance of man as we know him today. The precise dates – which are tentative and which further research may later alter in one direction or another – are not critical; what is critical is that there was an overlap and that it was a very extended one. The final phases (final to date, at any rate) of the phylogenetic history of man took place in the same grand geological era – the so-called Ice Age – as the initial phases of his cultural history. Men have birthdays, but man does not.

What this means is that culture, rather than being added on, so to speak, to a finished or virtually finished animal, was ingredient, and centrally ingredient, in the production of that animal itself. The slow, steady, almost glacial growth of culture through the Ice Age altered the balance of selection pressures for the evolving *Homo* in such a way as to play a major directive role in his evolution. The perfection of tools, the adoption of organized hunting and gathering practices, the beginnings of true family organization, the discovery of fire, and, most critically, though it is as yet extremely difficult to trace it out in any detail, the increasing reliance upon systems of significant symbols (language, art, myth, ritual) for orientation, communication, and self-control all created for man a new environment to which he was then obliged to adapt. As culture, step by infinitesimal step, accumulated and developed, a selective advantage was given to those individuals in the population most able to take advantage of it – the effective hunter, the persistent gatherer, the adept toolmaker, the resourceful leader – until what had been a small-brained, protohuman *Australopithecus* became the large-brained fully human *Homo sapiens*. Between the cultural pattern, the body, and the brain, a positive feedback system was created in which each shaped the progress of the other, a system in which the interaction among increasing tool use, the changing anatomy of the hand, and the expanding representation of the thumb on the cortex is only one of the more graphic examples. By submitting himself to governance by symbolically mediated programs for producing artifacts, organizing social life, or expressing emotions, man determined, if unwittingly, the culminating stages of his own biological destiny. Quite literally, though quite inadvertently, he created himself.

Though, as I mentioned, there were a number of important changes in the gross anatomy of genus *Homo* during this period of his crystallization – in skull shape, dentition, thumb size, and so on – by far the most important and dramatic were those that evidently took place in the central nervous system; for this was the period when the human brain, and most particularly the forebrain, ballooned into its present top-heavy proportions. The technical problems are complicated and controversial here; but the main point is that though the Australopithecines had a torso and arm configuration not drastically different from our own, and a pelvis and leg formation at least well-launched toward our own, they had cranial capacities hardly larger than those of the living apes – that is to say, about a third to a half of our own. What sets true men off most distinctly from protomen is apparently not overall bodily form but complexity of nervous organization. The overlap period of cultural and biological change seems to have consisted in an intense concentration on neural development and perhaps associated refinements of various behaviors – of the hands, bipedal locomotion, and so on – for which the basic anatomical foundations – mobile shoulders and wrists, a broadened ilium, and so on – had already been securely laid. In itself, this is perhaps not altogether startling; but, combined with what I have already said, it suggests some conclusions about what sort of animal man is that are, I think, rather far not only from those of the eighteenth century but from those of the anthropology of only ten or fifteen years ago.

Most bluntly, it suggests that there is no such thing as a human nature independent of culture. Men without culture would not be the clever savages of Golding's *Lord of the Flies* thrown back upon the cruel wisdom of their animal instincts; nor would they be the nature's noblemen of Enlightenment primitivism or even, as classical anthropological theory would imply, intrinsically talented apes who had somehow failed to find themselves. They would be unworkable monstrosities with very few useful instincts, fewer recognizable sentiments, and no intellect: mental basket cases. As our central nervous system – and most particularly its crowning curse and glory, the neocortex – grew up in great part in interaction with culture, it is incapable of directing our behavior or organizing our experience without the guidance provided by systems of significant symbols. What happened to us in the Ice Age is that we were obliged to abandon the regularity and precision of detailed genetic control over our conduct for the flexibility and adaptability of a more generalized, though of course no less real, genetic control over it. To supply the additional information necessary to be able to act, we were forced, in turn, to rely more and more heavily on cultural sources – the accumulated fund of significant symbols. Such symbols are thus not mere expressions, instrumentalities, or correlates of our biological, psychological, and social existence; they are prerequisites of it. Without men, no culture, certainly; but equally, and more significantly, without culture, no men.

We are, in sum, incomplete or unfinished animals who complete or finish ourselves through culture – and not through culture in general but through highly particular forms of it: Dobuan and Javanese, Hopi and Italian, upper-class and lower-class, academic and commercial. Man's great capacity for learning, his plasticity, has often been remarked, but what is even more critical is his extreme dependence upon a certain sort of learning: the attainment of concepts, the apprehension and application of specific systems of symbolic meaning. Beavers build dams, birds build nests, bees locate food, baboons organize social groups, and mice mate on the basis of forms of learning that rest predominantly on the instructions encoded in their genes and evoked by appropriate patterns of external stimuli: physical keys inserted into organic locks. But men build dams or shelters, locate food, organize their social groups, or find sexual partners under the guidance of instructions encoded in flow charts and blueprints, hunting lore, moral systems and aesthetic judgments: conceptual structures molding formless talents.

We live, as one writer has neatly put it, in an "information gap." Between what our body tells us and what we have to know in order to function, there is a vacuum we must fill ourselves, and we fill it with information (or misinformation) provided by our culture. The boundary between what is innately controlled and what is culturally controlled in human behavior is an ill-defined and wavering one. Some things are, for all intents and purposes, entirely controlled intrinsically: we need no more cultural guidance to learn how to breathe than a fish needs to learn how to swim. Others are almost certainly largely cultural; we do not attempt to explain on a genetic basis why some men put their trust in centralized planning and others in the free market, though it might be an amusing exercise. Almost all complex human behavior is, of course, the interactive, nonadditive outcome of the two. Our capacity to speak is surely innate; our capacity to speak English is surely cultural. Smiling at pleasing stimuli and frowning at unpleasing ones are surely in some degree genetically determined (even apes screw up their faces at noxious odors); but sardonic smiling and burlesque frowning are equally surely predominantly cultural, as is perhaps demonstrated by the Balinese definition of a madman as someone who, like an American, smiles when there is nothing to laugh at. Between the basic ground plans for our life that our genes lay down – the capacity to speak or to smile – and the precise behavior we in fact execute – speaking English in a certain tone of voice, smiling enigmatically in a delicate social situation – lies a complex set of significant symbols under whose direction we transform the first into the second, the ground plans into the activity.

Our ideas, our values, our acts, even our emotions, are, like our nervous system itself, cultural products – products manufactured, indeed, out of tendencies, capacities, and dispositions with which we were born, but manufactured nonetheless. Chartres is made of stone and glass. But it is not just stone and glass; it is a cathedral, and not only a cathedral, but a particular cathedral built at a particular time by certain members of a particular society. To understand what it means, to perceive it for what it is, you need to know rather more than the generic properties of stone and glass and rather more than what is common to all cathedrals. You need to understand also – and, in my opinion, most critically – the specific concepts of the relations among God, man, and architecture that, since they have governed its creation, it consequently embodies. It is no different with men: they, too, every last one of them, are cultural artifacts.

IV

Whatever differences they may show, the approaches to the definition of human nature adopted by the Enlightenment and by classical anthropology have one thing in common: they are both basically typological. They endeavor to construct an image of man as a model, an archetype, a Platonic idea or an Aristotelian form, with respect to which actual men – you, me, Churchill, Hitler, and the Bornean headhunter – are but reflections, distortions, approximations. In the Enlightenment case, the elements of this essential type were to be uncovered by stripping the trappings of culture away from actual men and seeing what then was left – natural man. In classical anthropology, it was to be uncovered by factoring out the commonalities in culture and seeing what then appeared – consensual man. In either case, the result is the same as that which tends to emerge in all typological approaches to scientific problems generally: the differences among individuals and among

groups of individuals are rendered secondary. Individuality comes to be seen as eccentricity, distinctiveness as accidental deviation from the only legitimate object of study for the true scientist: the underlying, unchanging, normative type. In such an approach, however elaborately formulated and resourcefully defended, living detail is drowned in dead stereotype: we are in quest of a metaphysical entity, Man with a capital "M," in the interests of which we sacrifice the empirical entity we in fact encounter, man with a small "m."

The sacrifice is, however, as unnecessary as it is unavailing. There is no opposition between general theoretical understanding and circumstantial understanding, between synoptic vision and a fine eye for detail. It is, in fact, by its power to draw general propositions out of particular phenomena that a scientific theory – indeed, science itself – is to be judged. If we want to discover what man amounts to, we can only find it in what men are: and what men are, above all other things, is various. It is in understanding that variousness – its range, its nature, its basis, and its implications – that we shall come to construct a concept of human nature that, more than a statistical shadow and less than a primitivist dream, has both substance and truth.

It is here, to come round finally to my title, that the concept of culture has its impact on the concept of man. When seen as a set of symbolic devices for controlling behavior, extrasomatic sources of information, culture provides the link between what men are intrinsically capable of becoming and what they actually, one by one, in fact become. Becoming human is becoming individual, and we become individual under the guidance of cultural patterns, historically created systems of meaning in terms of which we give form, order, point, and direction to our lives. And the cultural patterns involved are not general but specific – not just "marriage" but a particular set of notions about what men and women are like, how spouses should treat one another, or who should properly marry whom; not just "religion" but belief in the wheel of karma, the observance of a month of fasting, or the practice of cattle sacrifice. Man is to be defined neither by his innate capacities alone, as the Enlightenment sought to do, nor by his actual behaviors alone, as much of contemporary social science seeks to do, but rather by the link between them, by the way in which the first is transformed into the second, his generic potentialities focused into his specific performances. It is in man's *career*, in its characteristic course, that we can discern, however dimly, his nature, and though culture is but one element in determining that course, it is hardly the least important. As culture shaped us as a single species – and is no doubt still shaping us – so too it shapes us as separate individuals. This, neither an unchanging subcultural self nor an established cross-cultural consensus, is what we really have in common.

Oddly enough – though on second thought, perhaps not so oddly – many of our subjects seem to realize this more clearly than we anthropologists ourselves. In Java, for example, where I have done much of my work, the people quite flatly say, "To be human is to be Javanese." Small children, boors, simpletons, the insane, the flagrantly immoral, are said to be *ndurung djawa*, "not yet Javanese." A "normal" adult capable of acting in terms of the highly elaborate system of etiquette, possessed of the delicate aesthetic perceptions associated with music, dance, drama, and textile design, responsive to the subtle promptings of the divine residing in the stillnesses of each individual's inward-turning consciousness, is *sampun djawa*, "already Javanese," that is, already human. To be human is not just to breathe; it is to control one's breathing, by yogalike techniques, so as to hear in inhalation and exhalation the literal voice of God pronouncing His own name – "hu Allah." It is not just to talk, it is to utter the appropriate words and phrases in the appropriate social situations in the appropriate tone of voice and with the appropriate evasive indirection. It is not just to eat; it is to prefer certain foods cooked in certain ways and to follow a rigid table etiquette in consuming them. It is not even just to feel but to feel certain quite distinctively Javanese (and essentially untranslatable) emotions – "patience," "detachment," "resignation," "respect."

To be human here is thus not to be Everyman; it is to be a particular kind of man, and of course men differ: "Other fields," the Javanese say, "other grasshoppers." Within the society, differences are recognized, too – the way a rice peasant becomes human and Javanese differs from the way a civil servant does. This is not a matter of tolerance and ethical relativism, for not all ways of being human are regarded as equally admirable by far; the way the local Chinese go about it is, for example, intensely dispraised. The point is that there are different ways; and to shift to the anthropologist's perspective now, it is in a systematic review and analysis of these – of the Plains Indian's bravura, the Hindu's obsessiveness, the Frenchman's rationalism, the Berber's anarchism, the American's optimism (to list a series of tags I should not like to have to defend as such) – that we shall find out what it is, or can be, to be a man.

We must, in short, descend into detail, past the misleading tags, past the metaphysical types, past the empty similarities to grasp firmly the essential character of not only the various cultures but the various sorts of individuals within each culture, if we wish to encounter humanity face to face. In this area, the road to the general, to the revelatory simplicities of science, lies through a concern with the particular, the circumstantial, the concrete, but a concern organized and directed in terms of the sort of theoretical analyses that I have touched upon – analyses of physical evolution, of the functioning of the nervous system, of social organization, of psychological process, of cultural patterning, and so on – and, most especially, in terms of the interplay among them. That is to say, the road lies, like any genuine Quest, through a terrifying complexity.

"Leave him alone for a moment or two," Robert Lowell writes, not as one might suspect of the anthropologist but of that other eccentric inquirer into the nature of man, Nathaniel Hawthorne.

> Leave him alone for a moment or two,
> and you'll see him with his head
> bent down, brooding, brooding,
> eyes fixed on some chip,
> some stone, some common plant,
> the commonest thing,
> as if it were the clue.
> The disturbed eyes rise,
> furtive, foiled, dissatisfied
> from meditation on the true
> and insignificant.[8]

Bent over his own chips, stones, and common plants, the anthropologist broods, too, upon the true and insignificant, glimpsing in it, or so he thinks, fleetingly and insecurely, the disturbing, changeful image of himself.

Notes

1. A. O. Lovejoy, *Essays in the History of Ideas* (New York, 1960), p. 173.
2. Ibid., p. 80.
3. "Preface to Shakespeare," *Johnson on Shakespeare* (London, 1931), pp. 11–12.
4. From the Preface to *Iphigénie*.
5. A. L. Kroeber, ed., *Anthropology Today* (Chicago, 1953), p. 516.
6. C. Kluckhohn, *Culture and Behavior* (New York, 1962), p. 280.
7. M. J. Herskovits, *Cultural Anthropology* (New York, 1955), p. 364.
8. Reprinted with permission of Farrar, Straus & Giroux, Inc., and Faber & Faber, Ltd., from "Hawthorne," in *For the Union Dead*, p. 39. Copyright © 1964 by Robert Lowell.

Index

Note: page numbers in *italics* refer to figures.

Investigating Culture: An Experiential Introduction to Anthropology, Second Edition.
Carol Delaney with Deborah Kaspin.
© 2011 Carol Delaney. Published by Blackwell Publishing Ltd.